OUT OF THIS EARTH

'"Development" can be invasive, destructive and ill-informed. This book is a compelling and vital examination of this encounter. The survival and health of tribal society has come to be inseparable from the survival and health of the world. Here is a case-study in the struggle for health, and for survival.'

Hugh Brody, Anthropologist and Filmmaker

'Unmistakably, capitalism is the enemy this book unmasks, and its pages deepen one's concern for those marginalised by global capital.'

**Birendra Nayak, Utkal University, Bhubaneswar
(Editor, *Odia O' Odisha: Sameekhya* 1994–2003)**

Out of This Earth
East India Adivasis and the Aluminium Cartel

FELIX PADEL
SAMARENDRA DAS

Orient BlackSwan

ORIENT BLACKSWAN PRIVATE LIMITED

Registered Office
3-6-752 Himayatnagar, Hyderabad 500 029 (A.P.), India
e-mail: centraloffice@orientblackswan.com

Other Offices
Bangalore, Bhopal, Bhubaneshwar, Chennai,
Ernakulam, Guwahati, Hyderabad, Jaipur, Kolkata,
Lucknow, Mumbai, New Delhi, Patna

© Felix Padel and Samarendra Das 2010
First published 2010
This paperback edition 2010

ISBN: 978 81 250 4164 1

Typeset in Adobe Garamond 10.75/13 by
InoSoft Systems, Noida

Printed in India at
Aegean Offset Printers, Noida

Published by
Orient Blackswan Private Limited
1/24 Asaf Ali Road, New Delhi 110 002
e-mail: delhi@orientblackswan.com

For the people of Odisha, India and other countries, now and in future generations, in the hope that we can find joy in learning to live more equally, consuming less lavishly, before it is too late.

In memory of some outstanding human beings who passed on too soon, whose belief in this book kept us going:

Kishen Pattnayak
Kumuda Chandra Mullick
Rayadhar Lohar
Rajendra Sarangi
John Speirs
Una Padel
Erasmus and Biddy Barlow

Contents

Foreword by Arundhati Roy / xi
Preface / xv
Authors' Note / xxvi
Acknowledgements / xxvii

PART I
SUSTAINABLE LIFESTYLES IN AN AGE OF ALUMINIUM

1. 'It all starts with dirt' / 3
2. Aluminium's Secret History / 29
3. Konds and Khondalite / 54
4. Bauxite Business in Odisha / 72
5. Kashipur's 'Development' / 101
6. Lanjigarh: Vedanta's Assault on the Mountain of Law / 139

PART II
NIYAM RAJA MEETS THE WORLD-WIDE WEB: ALUMINIUM'S SOCIAL STRUCTURE

7. Under Mining Law / 179
8. Aluminium India / 207
9. The World-Wide Web / 226

PART III
'ALUMINUM FOR DEFENCE AND PROSPERITY'

10. Aluminium Wars / 267
11. 'Prosperity' and Price Fixing / 293
12. The Real Costs of Production / 322
13. Cultural Genocide: The Real Impacts of 'Development-Induced Displacement' / 348
14. Cost Benefit Analysis / 373

PART IV
COMPANY RULE AND THE SYSTEM OF ENDEMIC EXPLOITATION

15. Corporate Takeover / 399
16. Starvation Deaths and Foreign Aid / 419
17. Moneylender Colonialism and Bad Economics: The World Bank Cartel / 455
18. NGOs and the Culture of Appropriation / 496
19. *Homo Hierarchicus*: Company Man / 525

PART V
MOVEMENTS FOR LIFE

20. Andolan / 557
21. Sense of Sacredness / 578

Notes / 601

Glossary: Dramatis Personae / 667

Appendices / 679

Bibliography / 693

Index / 721

MAPS

1. Odisha and Neighbouring States / xxii
2. Mountains, Rivers, Dams, Railways and Factories / 9
3. The Aluminium Industry in North America / 37
4. Britain's Aluminium Industry / 40
5. Odisha Districts / 56
6. Malis and rivers of Odisha and Andhra / 61
7. Kashipur and Lanjigarh / 104
8. India's Aluminium Industry / 212
9. Brazil's Aluminium Industry / 254

DIAGRAM

Bauxite to aluminium / 44

Tables

1. Bauxite *mali*s / 62
2. Changes in Utkal Alumina ownership / 130
3. Bauxite mountains and company designs / 136–37
4. The top bauxite countries / 227
5. The top aluminium-producing countries / 229
6. Brazil's refineries and smelters / 255
7. Nalco's profits and the royalty/tax it pays to the GoO / 303
8. Increases in mining finance, 2000–2007 / 309
9. Consumption by sector / 324
10. Displacement by some of Odisha's biggest dams, mines and factories / 354
11. Average cost of production per ton of aluminium / 379
12. Included and Externalised costs / 380
13. Estimated value of bauxite reserves in Odisha and Andhra Pradesh / 381
14. Presidents of the World Bank / 462
15. Comparing the Gandhamardan and Kashipur movements / 561
16. Polarisation into project and movement supporters / 568

Foreword

This book is being published at a time when it could not have been needed more. Felix Padel and Samarendra Das lay bare the complicated and bloody history of the Aluminium Industry which lies at the heart of the world of modern warfare.

The low, flat-topped mountains of Orissa contain some of the largest deposits of the best quality bauxite in the world. The authors of this book calculate its value as being more than two trillion dollars, nearly twice India's GDP (estimated at $1.243 trillion in 2009).

But these bauxite mountains have been home to the Dongria Kond tribe long before there was a country called India or a state called Orissa. The hills watched over the Kond. The Kond watched over the hills and worshipped them as living deities. Now these hills have been sold for the bauxite they contain. For the Kond it's as though god has been sold. They ask how much god would go for if the god were Ram or Allah or Jesus Christ?

Perhaps the Kond are supposed to be grateful that their Niyamgiri hill, home to their Niyam Raja, God of Universal Law, has been sold to a company with a name like Vedanta (the branch of Hindu philosophy that teaches the Ultimate Nature of Knowledge). It's one of the biggest mining corporations in the world and is owned by Anil Agarwal, the Indian billionaire who lives in London in a mansion that once belonged to the Shah of Iran. Vedanta is only one of the many multinational corporations closing in on Orissa.

If the flat-topped hills are destroyed, the forests that clothe them will be destroyed too. So will the rivers and streams that flow out of them and irrigate the plains below. So will the Dongria Kond. So will the hundreds of thousands of tribal people who live in the forested heart of India, and whose homeland is similarly under attack.

In our smoky, crowded cities, some people say, "So what? Someone has to pay the price of progress." Some even say, "Let's face it, these are people whose time has come. Look at any developed country, Europe, the US, Australia—they all have a 'past'." Indeed they do. So why shouldn't "we"?

In keeping with this line of thought, the government has announced Operation Green Hunt, a war purportedly against the 'Maoist' rebels headquartered in the jungles of central India. But 'Operation Green Hunt' is really only a euphemism for 'Operation Adivasi Hunt', the Indian Government's brutal ground-clearing operation designed to open up India's forested heartland for mining corporations.

It is no coincidence that the Union Home Minister P. Chidambaram, the moving force behind Operation Green Hunt was a non-executive Director of the Board of Directors of Vedanta and only resigned from that position the day he became Finance Minister. As Finance Minister he said that his vision for a new India was that 85 per cent of the population should live in cities. To realise this vision would mean persuading or forcing 500 million people to move off their lands. Social engineering on that scale would require India to turn into a police state. In the name of Operation Green Hunt about 70,000 paramilitary forces are closing in on India's tribal homelands. Hundreds of thousands of people have begun to flee their homes. Not unlike US strategy in Vietnam, the Indian Government is pursuing a strategy of 'strategic hamleting', using random police terror to force people to move off their lands into roadside police camps.

But behind this police and military offensive is an elaborate financial structure which links the mining corporations, international banks, NGOs, aid agencies, and the media, all of whom collude to rip bauxite out of the mountains.

The process of refining bauxite into Alumina and then Alumina into Aluminium, is one of the most toxic processes in the world.

What this means of course is, that it is not just the mountains that hold the bauxite that will be destroyed, it's not just the tribes who have lived in those mountains that will be destroyed, not just that others will have to live with the dangerous effects of the toxic 'red mud' that is a waste product of the refining process, it also means that rivers will be dammed, forests will be submerged and of course hundreds of thousands of people will be displaced in order to provide water and electricity for the aluminium refineries.

All of this is exposed in this seminal, absolutely essential book. It makes urgent and wonderful reading.

Arundhati Roy
New Delhi, February 2010

PREFACE

The aluminium companies and how they affect us

Out of earth we are made and to earth we shall return. But how well do we know our earth? How well do we understand how it feeds us? Or what we are doing to it through mining? Our modern lifestyle depends on extracting and processing huge quantities of minerals and oil. But what is the real cost we are making our earth pay?

Adivasis are India's indigenous or tribal people. They developed a lifestyle and social structure close to the earth many centuries ago. Most still live by cultivating the soil and gathering food from the forest. They experience the costs of mining most acutely, and understand its consequences better than most.

Mountains are the foundation of their religion, rooted in an awareness that all life depends on water, sourced from the mountains in countless perennial streams.

The mountains in East India are particularly rich in minerals, which nourish the region's magnificent forests and fertile fields.

But these minerals are also objects of desire for the world's mining companies and financial investors. Coal, iron, manganese, chromite and other minerals to feed power stations and the steel industry are abundant in the area.

Some of the world's best bauxite —the ore for aluminium—is also found here. Its deposits form the summits of the biggest mountains in south Orissa and north Andhra. The trouble is, Adivasis live all around, especially the Kond tribe. Khondalite, the basic rock of these mountains, is named after them. Adivasis facing the invasion of aluminium companies have evolved some of India's strongest people's movements, attempting to stall projects in Kashipur, Lanjigarh and other places.

Entrance to Konark, temple of the Sun, built from Khondalite by king Narsimha in c. 1250

The areas where mineral wealth is concentrated in East India are nearly all in mountain ranges that form the core of tribal areas. And at the core of the government's plan for development are projects meant to vastly expand mining throughout this region, multiplying the factories processing ores into metal, and building more hydro-dams and power stations to supply these factories with water and electricity. The aim of this new wave of rapid industrialisation is to enable India to pay off its debts and become a rich country. Masterminding this are companies and financial institutions that in many ways look like reincarnations of the East India Company, looting India's resources on a scale and at a speed that could never be done before. The dangers are mass displacement, social upheaval and an environmental catastrophe.

Simultaneously, a great awakening has begun, as we open our minds to the extent of danger we face collectively, as a consequence of our rapid consumption of non-renewable resources and emission of Greenhouse Gases (GHGs). A 'denial industry' has been exposed. Large oil companies and their associates have been paying out millions of dollars each year to cast doubt on the scientific consensus on global warming (Monbiot 2006). This consensus is not in question any longer, after the 2007 Report of the IPCC (Inter-governmental Panel on Climate Change). GHGs from rapid industrialisation are warming the earth's atmosphere, and we are nearing a *tipping point* of no return, unless we radically change our lifestyles and reduce emissions soon enough.

Scientists warn that present targets to stabilise emissions go nowhere near far enough. Massive cuts are needed right now. To save our grandchildren from catastrophic global warming, an estimated 90 per cent cut in GHG emissions is required (Wasdell 2006–08, Monbiot 2006). Otherwise an irreversibly accelerating heating process will take place that will devastate life on earth. Yet the political will to achieve this is barely even on the horizon. In India the denial industry is blooming (Bidwai 2008), and the new mines and metal factories going up in forest areas need to be seen to be believed.

Mining and metal consumption have not yet assumed the key place they deserve in climate change debates. In fact, one result of the new environmental awareness is that richer nations are *outsourcing* their most polluting industries to India and other Third World countries, where the environment is lower on the political agenda, and legislation to protect it is enforced weakly, if at all. Metal production is one of the biggest GHG emitters, and tops the list of industries being outsourced to India.

During the seven years we have been writing this book (2002–09), India has experienced phenomenal 'growth', propelled by internal demand as well as pressure to earn foreign currency through exports. The car industry was growing at about 20 per cent per year before the recession hit in 2008. But while some people grew much richer, others, many times that number, got a lot poorer. Industrialisation compounds this poverty. Its ideology promises jobs and food for all, but its reality spells communities torn apart, families thrown into squalor, grinding menial jobs and chronic food shortage.

A lot of the metal manufactured in India's factories is for export, so business interests and consumption patterns in the rich countries are responsible not only for the GHGs these metal factories spout into the earth's atmosphere, but also for encouraging India and other 'developing countries' to increase their emissions and not submit to restrictions. Among the first to suffer from catastrophic climate change are India's poorer citizens.

In fact, the suffering is already upon us. *'Dukho Asuchi'* (Grief is coming, and you too will suffer!), a song from the Kashipur movement, expresses the lines of causality connecting people everywhere with the slow horrors unfolding in this beautiful region of middle India.

We all use aluminium in our daily lives. It is a conductor in our mobile phones and kettles. It is also central to the arms industry. Controlling its trade is an international cartel.

Foil wraps and cartons, drink cans, saucepans, laptops ... Aluminium is in hundreds of the objects we use everyday, in every room of our houses and offices. Even where you least expect it. Health-food shops are full of it. Fruit juice is usually packaged in a compound fusion of aluminium and plastic—an unrecycleable high-tech mix that has made a fortune for Tetra Pak. Generous donations from this fortune flow to the most deserving liberal and green causes.

We are told that aluminium is a 'green metal' because it is easily recycled and reduces the fuel consumption of cars by making them lighter. But actually, only a tiny proportion gets recycled, and recycling has no discernible effect in diminishing demand for new primary metal, which continues to grow steadily at an average of about 10 per cent per year.

Aluminium companies constantly try to increase their production, which means increasing people's *consumption* of aluminium in a wide variety of applications. In India particularly, they are now trying to increase consumption from less than one kilo per person per year (the average till recently) to something approaching the 15–30 kg per year that is the norm in the 'developed world'. Lobbyists are paid huge sums for promoting its use.

But what hidden effects does this aluminium consumption have on our health? What are the actual physical effects of its 'purifying' role in water supplies? Tiny yet significant quantities leach from packaging and pots to our food. The link between aluminium and Alzheimer's disease is frequently denied and hard to prove, yet most scientists are certain it is there. There is no question that aluminium gets into our food chain from these various sources, building up a high, unexcretable concentration of aluminium in our bodies' cell tissues, bones and brains (Exley 2001).

In every sector, the use of aluminium is deliberately promoted. In cars, its image as a green metal, reducing weight and therefore oil consumption, ignores the huge fossil fuel consumption and carbon emissions involved in making it. There is great focus today on promoting aluminium-rich cars in the West, and the fashion for private cars is rocketing in India. Vast quantities of aluminium also go into modern city-centre buildings, and countless military bases far from our gaze.

'*No war can be brought to a successful conclusion,*' declared a US expert in 1951, '*without using and destroying vast quantities of aluminum*' (Anderson 1951). This rings true even today. The cartel promotes aluminium for our domestic consumption because it is also classed as a key *strategic metal*, vital for manufacturing military hardware. A close hidden bond, therefore, exists between aluminium in our daily use and its use in war. We are often asked to calculate our carbon footprint, but not in terms of metal consumption, let alone this bond between our lifestyle and the wars we wage.

Our wars are polluting enough in themselves, even leaving aside their human costs. But the manufacture of arms, and of metal for use in arms, produces colossal amounts of GHGs—virtually absent from present debates on climate change. Reducing our individual consumption is small compared to how vital it is, for the environment alone, to reduce our wars and the armaments industry.

This book can be read as an anthropology of the aluminium industry. Traditionally, anthropologists studied tribal societies. What we present here is a *reverse anthropology*. If anthropologists only study tribal societies, or people who are marginal and have the least power, they reinforce existing power structures. So, instead of analysing tribal societies from an alien point of view associated with the very power structures imposed on them, what we attempt here is an 'objective' view that encompasses an Adivasi perspective. If anthropology is to reach its full potential, the analytical focus needs to be reversed, so that we can understand ourselves and our society afresh through Adivasi eyes.

Felix Padel is an anthropologist trained in Oxford and Delhi universities. His first book (1995, 2nd edition 2000) analysed the colonial invasion of Kond territory from 1835. The present book follows on from this analysis, since the invasion by aluminium companies since the 1980s has many parallels with the British invasion.

Samarendra Das is an Oriya writer and filmmaker, associated with people's movements over many years as a political activist with the Samajvadi Jan Parishad (Socialist People's Council). He studied Maths and Computer Science at Brahmapur and Indore Universities. Following Kashipur events since 1997, he began documenting them on film with his brother Amarendra in 2001.

We met in December 2001, after Samarendra had been filming at an important event in Kashipur. One year earlier, on 16 December 2000, police fired on a large crowd of Adivasi activists meeting in Maikanch village to oppose the Utkal Alumina consortium. These police killings made world headlines, and the Kashipur movement gained a reputation as one of the most important people's movements in India.

At our first meeting, knowing Felix's first book, Samarendra invited him to write together about aluminium and its new invasion of the Konds. This book is the fruit of that invitation. The film Samarendra made, *Matiro Poko, Company Loko* (Earth Worm, Company Man), gives the views of Orissa's Adivasis and Dalits about the mining industry, in songs, interviews and demonstrations that we shall in these pages quote extensively from (Amarendra Das and S. Das 2005).

Analysing the aluminium companies involves mapping a complex and dispersed social structure. The cartel which controls this industry is highly secretive (Stiglitz 2002). Aluminium companies' profits do not reflect their actual cost of production. By outsourcing to the Third World, they get labour and materials extremely cheap, along with outrageous subsidies and tax cuts. Since the 1890s, the industry has lobbied to get and keep steep subsidies on electricity, water, transport, and, above all, an extremely low price for their primary substance, bauxite.

Mining companies act as if they were discrete entities but, in fact, work hand-in-glove with political, financial and legal entities. On the surface, all-out competition flourishes between the aluminium companies. Yet individual executives move comfortably from one company to another, as well as between companies and governments. Beneath the rivalry, aluminium companies work closely together. This is especially clear in East India, where intertwining interests link private corporations with members of the government and the administration. One company makes a deal or statement, while others lie low. They use complex strategies of promises, threats and rewards, working together as a team, like a pack of wolves or dogs. Together and separately, through contacts and deals, they are experts at exploiting people, even as they promise them the earth.

In stark denial to these promises, Adivasis' quality of life drops drastically when their land is taken away. Their rights are eroded by actual changes in legislation—changes instigated by pressure from abroad, orchestrated through the World Bank, to dismantle India's laws protecting land rights, workers' rights, and the environment.

The danger for East India is at many levels. Its natural and cultural wealth is being sold off to companies and banks, pursuing the sole aim of maximising profit, institutionally blind and heedless of destruction to nature as well as human beings.

East India Adivasis also evokes the history of an institution that gave rise to today's corporate power structure (Robins 2006)—the East India Company—which had imposed British rule over India

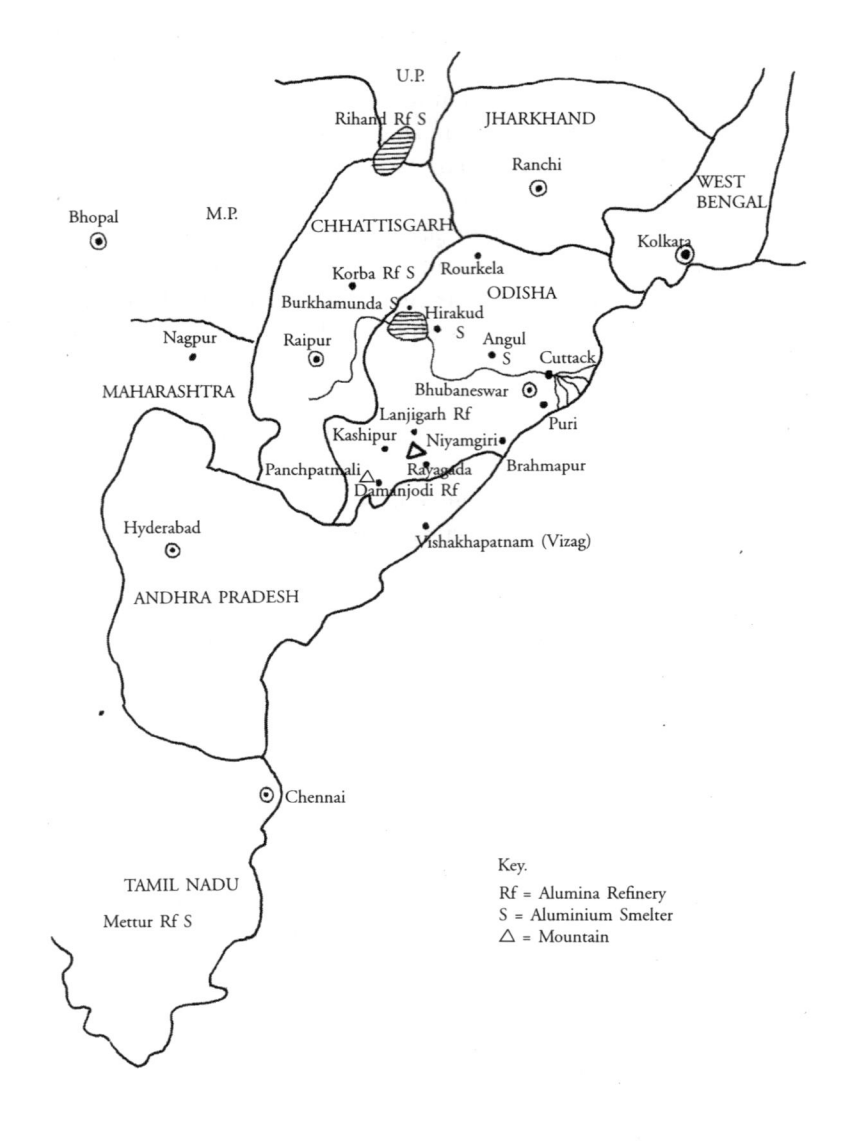

Map 1: Odisha and Neighbouring States

with techniques of financial manipulation and tampering with the law, very similar to those that are evident in present attempts by the mining companies to take over land and resources.

So aluminium is at the frontline of an often unconscious war between two different lifestyles. The mainstream style guzzles unsustainable quantities of metals and oil, while Adivasi life is based on cultivating the earth and nurturing a long-term coexistence with the forest.

When a region like Orissa starts to be rapidly exploited, it plunges into the *resource curse*. For many African countries and regions of India, being rich in minerals has spelt devastation of nature and spiralling poverty, instead of the wealth that is always promised. 'Wealth' turns out to be what is creamed off by company executives and the banks behind them. The resource curse also applies to resource-rich regions in rich countries, such as Quebec in Canada and Queensland in Australia.

Our aim in this book is to bring to light the hidden history of aluminium from many parts of the earth, showing an overall pattern mind-blowing in its implications.

Aluminium plays an unseen hand in the recession, through the insanity of commodity-trading future options, inflating the bubble of unreal money. Particularly so in countries such as Iceland that made aluminium central to their economy and built up massive debts to pay for its infrastructure. The mask that hides the industry's influence began to slip when revelations in mid-2008 revealed sinister links between the Russian aluminium magnate Oleg Deripaska and top politicians of both main parties in Britain and the United States.

In India, perhaps, the industry reaches its apotheosis. Adivasis are not lying down and letting their age-old cultures just die anymore. Their movements against Orissa's mining projects are the cutting edge of anti-capitalist movements worldwide—an *Environmentalism of the Poor* that follows basic Gandhian principles of non-violence (Martinez-Alier 2002). The trouble is, they face huge repression by security forces and company mafias, and their movements get confused in the popular imagination with the Maoist insurgency, which is growing in the region because of people's outrage at the increasing repression and exploitation. India's Prime Minister recently identified

Naxalites or Maoists as India's biggest security threat, and on 12 April 2009 over a hundred Maoist guerrillas staged a major attack on India's biggest bauxite mine—run by Nalco on Panchpat Mali in Koraput district of Orissa—and took away arms and explosives to use in their ongoing war against the government's armed forces. Over a dozen members of the government's paramilitary force for industrial security were killed in the attack.

Guerrilla fighters often show little concern for the preservation of many aspects of tribal culture, even as the forces they fight against seek to plunder the very basis of Adivasi lives and livelihoods, and therefore cause great destruction and misery as part of counterinsurgency operations. This spiral of escalating brutality creates civil-war-like conditions in which the ordinary course of community life gets profoundly disturbed.

We therefore argue for a proper recognition of the importance for all of us of India's essentially non-violent Adivasi movements, which aim to maintain the sustainable lifestyle of Adivasis by resisting the invasion of mines and metal factories. Driving the insane over-exploitation of East India's resources is a ruthless capitalism, brilliant at making profits and demonic in its heedlessness of costs. If anything can save our earth for all of us, it's the uncompromising struggle of these Adivasi activists.

Out of this earth we take such huge quantities of metals and fossil fuels, that we risk destroying it. The Third World's heavy indebtedness to the rich countries is more than offset by the *Ecological Debt* owed by the rich countries to the poor (Simms 2005).

But instead of demanding reparation, India's business and political leaders join the rush to exploit nature and dispossess their own poorer citizens. While Utkal Alumina was stalled by an inquiry into the Maikanch killings, another company called Sterlite or Vedanta swiftly built a refinery at Lanjigarh, and is poised to start mining bauxite from one of Orissa's best-forested mountains, Niyam Dongar, on which Dongria and Majhi Konds have preserved an outstanding biodiversity.

In this book we tend to use the terms 'the West' and 'Third World' in preference to 'North'–'South' or 'developed' and 'developing countries', because Western Europe is the origin of the world's prevalent power structures, along with Europe's most powerful colony to the west, which has become the USA. Focusing on a North–South divide obscures this. As for calling India a developing country, it could be said that it developed a 'civilisation' before Europe. In our view, India's high state of spiritual and social development is being jettisoned terrifyingly fast in a mad rush to follow the Western path of material development through industrialisation. Calling Western countries 'developed' and India a 'developing' country is an ideological statement of the belief that grew up in Europe, that industrialisation equals progress. The term 'Third World' is imperfect, but it evokes the existing gap between the living standards and the power of citizens in different sets of countries.

'Globalisation' and 'anti-globalisation' are also terms that obscure more than they reveal. We are globalising by writing this book, and calling for proper, peaceful support to India's Adivasis. The enemy is capitalism: the insane system of perpetual growth that values money and profits above people or nature.

From Orissa's Adivasis, who live close to the earth and put the earth at the centre of their spiritual values, come glimpses of how we could turn around the suicidal course our species is taking towards extinction. For the companies, banks and politicians used to getting their own way, this is a resistance that rises out of the earth to confront them, and to confront us all with questions about the real meaning and cost of mining and metal consumption.

Out of this earth we rip a ceaseless supply of minerals. Out of this earth rise tribal movements against this mindless mining. And out of this earth is where our own grandchildren will be, if we do not limit our metal and oil consumption very soon.

Authors' Note

On 30 November 2009, Orissa's Assembly took a historic decision to change the name of the state to Odisha, and the language to Odia, so these are the forms we shall use henceforth. Odia is a hard language to transliterate into English, with several distinct 'o' and 'a' sounds. For the staple vowel we prefer 'o' to the more conventional Sanskritic 'a', since this 'o' sound conveys better the speaking voice of people in Odisha.

Simultaneously, the Assembly was rocked by revelations of multiple mining scams. The social structure surrounding these scams is the subject of this book, laid bare through a tapestry of voices from Odisha and other lands bound into this structure.

Acknowledgements

This book should be read as a collective work, from and for the people. As it is a non-funded work, we take responsibility for any shortcomings and request readers' indulgence over any possible errors—please let us know!

Our thanks extend to many whom we cannot name here, not least people who welcomed us into their homes in numerous villages, towns and cities, especially in Odisha, but in many other places including Trinidad, Iceland, Germany, Brussels and the US. In particular we would like to thank for outstanding insights, bits of the jigsaw and sundry nourishments the following people: Achyut and Vidhya Das, Aflatoon, Akash, Ajay, Akhil Nayak, Alai Majhi, Alex, Alibha, Alok, Amarendra, Amarendra Konhar, Amrit Wilson, Anchal, Anke, Ariane Anger, Arman, Arnar, Arundhati Patra, Arundhati Roy, Ashok Pradhan, Ashok Seksaria, Ashwini, Attilah, Baba Mayaram, Baba Thakur, Bala, Banu, Batu, Bhagaban Majhi, Professor Bhagwat Prasad Rath, Bhalachandra, Bhalabhai, Bighneswar Sahu, Bijayabhai, Bijoy, Biju Toppo, Bikram, Professor Birendra Nayak, Biswajit Mohanty, Biswamoy Pati, Biswapriya Kanungo, Biswanath Bagi, Bleslindurapakisi, Braja, Bratindi, Brigitta Jonsdottir, Buluka Miniaka, Bhupen, Cathal, Chanda Asani, Chandrabhushan, Chandana Mathur, Chandramuli Pattnaik, Chandu, Clare Barlow, Claire Shanks and James Brander, Dai Singh Majhi, Daitari Pradhan, Dan the mouldy melon, Debaranjan, Dharman, Domburu, Elfyn

Lloyd, Estella, Eugine, Faith, Gananath Patra, Gargi, Gem and Tina, Gugura, Guomundur Beck, Guliabai, Guman Singh, Gunjan, Gurbirbhai, Gutti Majhi, Hamish and Scott Paterson, Hara, Hari Mohan Mathur, Heffa, Hemanta Dalapati, Hilda Padel, Hugh Brody, Ina Thomson, Indranee, Jaap, Jabir, Jali, Jambubati, Jape, Jason, Jenny, Jeremy Naydler, Jeroen, Jo, Joan Carlisle, Joan Martinez-Alier, Jogin Sengupta, Jonas, Judith Seelig, Professor J.P.S.Uberoi, Professor Kamal Nayan Kabra, Professor Kamal Mitra Chenoy, Kaushik and Sangeeta, Kavaljit, Kumud Ranjan, Kumar, Kumuti Majhi, Lalu Behera, Lenin, Liam, Lila, Lindsay, Borogorh Lingaraj, Lingaraj Azad, Lotty, Louane, Marcus Colchester, Maere, Maguni, Makari, Mamata Dash, Mana, Manjit, Manohar Jhodia, Meghnath, Mihir and Padmini, Miriam Rose, Mridula, Mukta maa, Mukunda Saunta, Murali, Nagaraj Adve, Naiad, Nanda, Narayan Reddy, Nick Hildyard, Nigam, Nigel and Natasha Thomas, Niranjan Bidrohi, Norman Girvan, Ola, Olga, Oliver, Omkar, Pappu, Patrik Oskarsson, Paul Sambrook, Peter Robbins, Piyush Manush, Pradip, Praffulabhaina, Pramila, Promodini, Pratima, Prem Lal, Pyoli, Rabi Majhi, Rabi Pradhan, Rabi Ray, Radha Kanta Sethi, Radhika, Rajkishore, Ramesh, Ramesh Pati, Ramesh Mohapatra, Ranjana Padhy, Ratnalu, Ravi Rebbapragada, Rhea Mungal, Richard Mahapatra, Richard Solly, Rida and Peter, Ritwik Sanyal, Robin Horsley, Roger Moody, Rohit, Romy, Rumi, Ruth, Sabbulal, Saif, Sabine Pabst, Sadhu Majhi, Sally and Chung Fu, Samar Das, Sanatanbhai, Sankar and Susan, Sarah Pank, Saroj, Saroj Suna, Satish, Satya, Satyabadi Nayak, Shambhunath Nayak, Shreedhar, Sibaram Nayak, Sidharth Nayak, Siggi Ponk, Simon Thomas and others in Plaid Cymru, Simone, Sophie Johnson, Srinivas, Subrat Sahu, Sudhir Mohanty, Sudhir Pattnayak, Sumani maa, Sunilbhai, Sunil Minz, Suresh Agarwal, Suresh Khandelwal, Suresh Tripathy, Surya Shankar Dash, Susan Ann Jones, Svala, Tara, Vicky, Vidya Majhi, Yogendra Yadav, Zuky Serper and Naomi Salomon. Thanks to Simon Williams for the five photos on pages 4,150,152,183 and 351, and to Jason Taylor for the one on page 394.

At OBS we would like to thank Hemlata, Satyadeep, Tahira, Rinita and others for helping to birth this book.

We'd like to give special thanks to our wives Anu and Rebecca, who went on believing in this work through the toughest times, even when we were most unforgivably absorbed by aluminium antics. Also to Rebecca for the artwork in the frontpiece, chapter headings, the diagram on page 44, and maps.

As a product of seven years' labour by a pair of writers from different cultures and backgrounds, we see our writing as part of a new level of globalisation—globalising an awareness across national and cultural borders that questions neoliberal invasion.

So above all we'd like to thank each other, for persevering in this work and opening a multitude of doors along the way. Often this transcultural dialogue has been extremely hard work, involving bitter arguments, yet through stage after stage, our perspectives have opened and its fruit, we hope, offers a model of holistic analysis much needed in today's world.

We trust this book will inspire many more holistic studies, helping open many minds to the complexities of the military-industrial complex and global finance, as well as the simplicity of the patterns which underlie this complex web. The unsustainability of present rates of extraction is visible to more and more people. Equally or even more visible should be the long-term sustainability of thousands of communities in East India, and so many other parts of the world (some referred to in this book, others not), who are resisting dispossession and struggling to survive in the face of multiple corporate takeovers. We believe that these people's example is vital to understand and follow if human beings are to truly develop and to survive, with dignity and integrity. We thank the people in these communities from the bottom of our heart for all they have shown us.

PART I

Sustainable Lifestyles in an Age of Aluminium

What is the shape of aluminium's history?
Has modern society become too dependent on aluminium, too quickly for us to comprehend the industry's full impact?
'Wonder metal' of the twentieth century ...
Conductor of electricity through elements and cables ...
Revolutionising transport and packaging ...
Duralumin and other alloys used in making aircraft, taking humans to the skies ...
Explosive properties of aluminium in the thermite process enable mass bombing of civilians ...
Mega-consumer of electricity, prime purpose of big dams ...
Major polluter of water, earth, air and outer space ...
Destroying mountain ecosystems through strip-mining bauxite ...
Underminer of countries' economic independence ...
Invading Adivasi territories and evicting them from their land ...

Part I introduces an outline of juxtaposing histories, and narrates the basic stories of aluminium in East India today.

CHAPTER ONE

'It all starts with dirt'

Deep red, yellow ochre, cream and black—Adivasi houses are painted in earth colours found in clay. Adivasi identity is closely bound to the earth, evoked in a dance-song of women from Kucheipadar, a village that has led the people's movement against mining in Kashipur:

Matiro poko, mati bina aame bonchiba kanhee?
Earthworms we are—without earth how to survive? (Das 2005)

All of us depend on earth. Minerals in the soil nourish the plants we live on. Aluminium, which makes up 8 per cent of the earth's crust, is the commonest mineral in the soil, more common than iron (4–5 per cent). In nature, aluminium's metallic form is always hidden through bonding with oxygen and other elements. Its frequent fusion with H_2O plays a vital role in retaining moisture in the soil, thus helping in maintaining fertility. While we may be conscious of our modern lifestyle's dependence on aluminium for air and road travel, packaging and modern buildings, few of us are aware of our dependence on aluminium's life-giving qualities as part of the soil, transmitting minerals and moisture into plants (Pelikan 1973). The plant-life that nourishes us thus depends on the presence of aluminium in the soil. These life-giving qualities in earth contrast with its qualities once it has been removed from the soil, refined into alumina (Al_2O_3), and smelted in large and polluting factories, or when it returns to the ground in acid rain. Bauxite, the rock with the highest concentration of aluminium, is found in areas with the most abundant plant growth on earth: the tropical and sub-tropical forests of South America, West Africa, North Australia, and East India.

Kond women dancing in Turiguda village, Lanjigarh

Aluminium was discovered in stages in the early nineteenth century, but the 'aluminium age' really began in 1886 with the invention of the means of splitting molecules of aluminium oxide on a large, commercial scale. Aluminium quickly became the wonder-metal of the twentieth century and began to be used in a multitude of applications we now take for granted.

'*It all starts with dirt*' is how Alcoa starts its history on its website, referring to the element's hidden abundance in the soil, and defining our modern era as *the Age of Aluminum*.[1] Alcoa (Aluminum Corporation of America) is the king of the aluminium companies: one of the oldest, and arguably the biggest and most powerful. American English calls earth in the sense of soil 'dirt', and uses the spelling 'aluminum', which was the first name given by its discoverer, Humphrey Davy. (The other spelling was in general use, until, it is said, the head of Alcoa, Arthur Davis, had 'Aluminum Corporation of America' printed on his letterhead by mistake, and, rather than change his stationery, he changed the language.)

The dirt from bauxite dust and the wheels of hundreds of lorries, from red mud and factory fumes, has been the foremost feature of Vedanta's refinery in Lanjigarh, where we have witnessed a tribal area transformed by every kind of pollution, leaving terrible sores on people's bodies and choking their breath. The corruption of values which the aluminium industry has introduced to many parts of the world will be evident in the pages that follow—an ethical dirt or *sleaze* that complements the industry's massive pollution of water, earth and air. In fact, indigenous, tribal societies often experience the impact of mining and manufacturing aluminium as nothing short of a form of genocide.

The Aluminium Age

Stone Age, Bronze Age, Iron Age ... we live in an 'Aluminium Age' now, whether we are aware of it or not. Not many people understand aluminium's true form or see the aluminium industry as a whole. Hidden from general awareness are several features that make it pretty much the defining metal of our age.

Manufacturing aluminium is an intrinsic part of our industrial and financial system as a whole. The gold standard may no longer exist, but currencies are still tied to metals, and top financial institutions are among those presently trying to invest in Odisha's mineral deposits. Metals still form the basis of our currency, but indirectly, through this investment and a complex manipulation of commodity prices.

Most of us have been taught about the benefits of aluminium and its many uses. What is often not taught is that mining and manufacturing this familiar metal are among the dirtiest and most ruthlessly exploitative interactions of the developed West with the Third World. We are not taught that aluminium, moreover, has some extremely destructive effects—environmental, economic, social and military—on human life itself.

Political and financial dirt has characterised the setting up of aluminium industries in one country after another, just as it surrounds the arms deals where record sums of money change hands. The exploitation of aluminium involves financial manipulation so complex and outrageous that economies of whole countries were swiftly enslaved to the purpose of supplying this metal at a cheap, competitive price to those who want it (see, for example, Graham 1982). Even the basic refining and smelting processes are extraordinarily complex and expensive. Smelting demands such a vast amount of electricity that aluminium production has been a major reason for building many of the world's biggest dams, and the histories of aluminium and big dams are inextricably linked. Always, the aluminium industry promises prosperity. And, truly, it does help those at the top prosper, as it often makes outstanding profits, and to a work force prepared to face harsh and insecure working conditions and industrial diseases, it provides jobs. But, for the general population of an area affected by bauxite mining and aluminium plants, this profit comes at a terrible price to health and overall well-being.

Many projects are labelled 'sustainable' when, in the eyes of local inhabitants, they are the exact opposite—displacing, for short-term gain, the very people who had actually been living sustainably!

At the other end of the production line, aluminium's highest-priced forms consist of complex alloys essential to the arms industry, and arms manufacturers are among the aluminium companies' highest-paying customers. Modern warfare came of age using aluminium for planes and incendiary bombs. Ever since the First and Second World Wars, various aerospace and defence applications of aluminium alloys give the metal a unique *strategic importance*. The richest countries make some of their biggest profits by controlling the supply of aluminium and its manufacture into arms, along with the other extractive industries of metals and oil. Controlling the manufacture and sale of arms forms a major part of controlling the world.

East India's environment under threat

Odisha is famous for its wildlife and ancient cultures. Nourished by fertile rivers, important strands of Hindu, Buddhist and Jain *dharma*s developed here in medieval times, through a constant interaction of Vedic forms with indigenous, 'tribal' cultures. Various Adivasi societies, however, continued to nurture religious traditions rich with a different idiom, focused more directly on nature, and with their own shamans and priests, instead of Brahmins.

The mountains of south-west Odisha reach 3,000–5,000 feet above sea level. Their massive bulk is all of a piece, with flat summits—high altitude plains that stretch for miles. Some mountains, such as Niyamgiri and Khandual Mali, are well-forested on the top. Others have fewer trees, except around their rim and flanks. Walking on these expansive summits, one's footsteps resound with an extraordinary hollow ring.

Out of This Earth: Test pit with piles of bauxite on Khandual Mali

Bauxite formed millions of years ago through an annual cycle, alternating monsoon rains with intense summer heat. Below the hollow crust on the summits, the layer of bauxite is like clay, holding moisture, letting it seep out gently throughout the year through streams which form all around the mountain's flank. Nowhere is this fertility more apparent than in and around the Niyamgiri mountain range.

Odisha is defined in economic terms as one of India's poorest states, yet it is one of the richest in 'mineral resources'. The same also applies to Odisha's neighbours. Several massive bauxite-capped mountains in Chhattisgarh and Jharkhand are being mined right beside Adivasi villages. A huge refinery-smelter complex at Korba in Chhattisgarh turns this ore into metal. Andhra's bauxite-capped mountains, just south of Odisha, are beset by similar plans for mines and factories.

Plans to turn Odisha's poverty into wealth by mining and industrialisation can be traced back to the colonial era, when geologists first surveyed Odisha's bauxite deposits, and the British geologist Cyril Fox spelt out the blueprint for exploiting them:

> The analyses of bauxite from Korlapat are so good that, if large quantities exist, the tract must prove important when the railway is constructed ... This importance is heightened by the existence of possible hydro-electric sites in the adjacent Madras (Jaipur State) area to the south-west, and to the fact that a harbour is to be built at Vizagapatanam. (Fox 1932, p.136)

It was thus the British who conceived the present projects, surveying the bauxite cappings during the nineteenth century. Fox mentions most of the Khondalite mountains whose fate now hangs in the balance, highlighting Karlapat, one of the remotest, which has been sought after recently by the world's biggest mining company, BHP Billiton. The rail link from Raipur to Vizag was built in the 1930s, and has since been expanded with aluminium interests in mind. The 'possible hydro-electric sites' near Jeypore, mentioned by Fox, have become at least four major dams.

What do we mean by 'development'?

Bhagaban Majhi is a young man of the Kond tribe, with piercing eyes and a wide smile. His village of Kucheipadar has been at the forefront of resistance to the Utkal alumina project (UAIL), and Bhagaban is a leader and spokesman for this movement. Addressing the SP (Superintendent of Police) of Rayagada district some years ago, he asked:

It all starts with dirt | 9

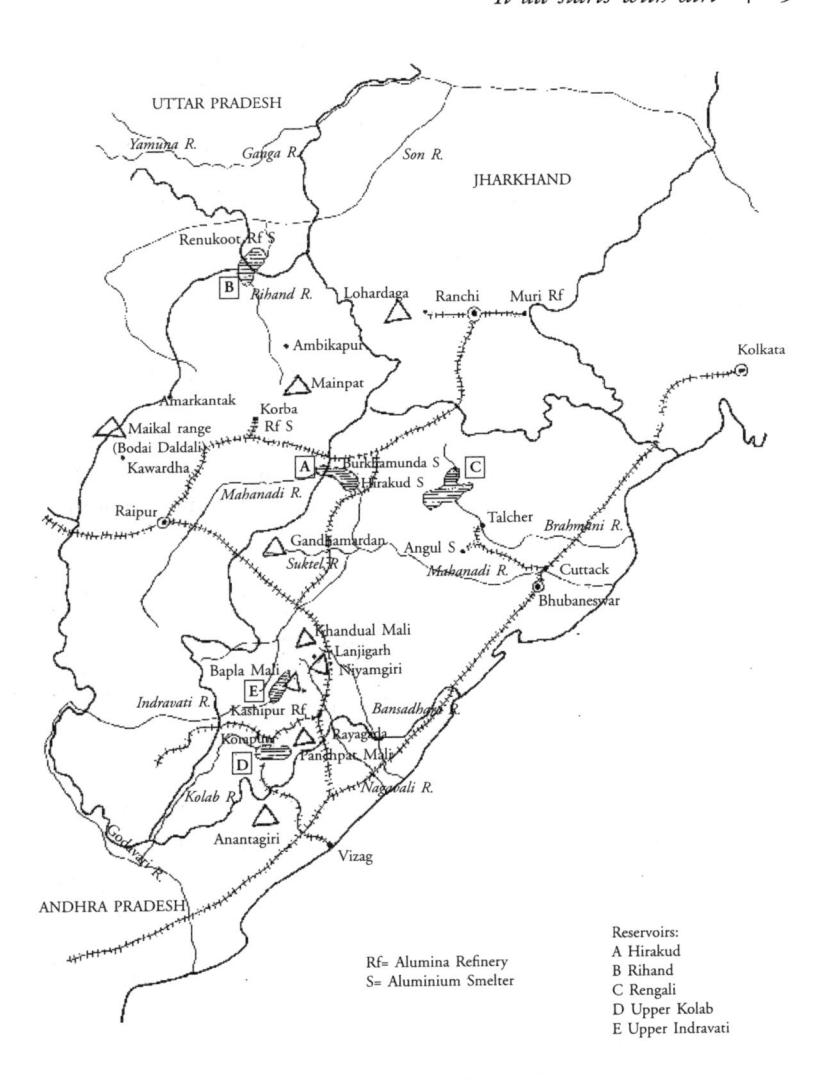

Map 2: Mountains, Rivers, Dams, Railways and Factories

Sir, what do you mean by 'development'? Is it development to destroy these billions of years old mountains for the profit of a few officials? Is it development to displace us from our land? (Das 2005)

People in Odisha, especially around Kashipur and Lanjigarh and near the other mountains, are currently split between those for and those against the projects. This itself is a key aspect of aluminium's social structure in Odisha. One of the commonest effects when mining companies enter any new area is to divide the population like this.

How to heal this split, except by opening up the issues involved to public debate? The aim of this book is to list the key facts about aluminium and encourage peaceful and creative discussion, bearing in mind the asymmetry of power and social distances involved between Adivasis, government officials, company directors, manual workers and consumers.

What are the different beliefs and priorities on each side?

Those who support the aluminium industry's expansion in Odisha describe it as an opportunity to maximise the potential of Odisha's 'mineral wealth' to transform India's 'poorest state' into one of the richest. Odisha has some of the world's best quality bauxite, which could be mined relatively cheaply and sold for a good profit abroad, earning important foreign exchange and attracting large sums of FDI (foreign direct investment). The Government of Odisha would get a share in these profits as royalties, etc., enabling it to pay back its large foreign debts. Thousands of people would get well-paid jobs, and the aluminium industry would stimulate other industries and the economy as a whole. Many Odias see this as an opportunity for themselves, as well as for Odisha, to get rich. Large sections of Odisha's non-tribal, town-dwelling population see in it a chance for the generation of wealth, and dismiss those who are against the projects as 'anti-development' or 'anti-government'. As a female MLA of the ruling BJD party put it at a meeting about Vedanta in Bhubaneswar on 17 June 2006, 'What's wrong with selling off Niyamgiri if this gets rid of poverty?'

Those against this expansion argue that the costs are far too high, in the form of permanent damage to Odisha's environment and a disastrous drop in the living standards of those displaced. They see the prime cause of Odisha's poverty as exploitation and corruption, and point out how mining companies' lavish use of money has already compounded the poverty. Jobs in these projects are always much fewer, and working conditions much harsher, than promised. Such projects bring in large numbers of people from outside the area, corrupting community values. The idea that FDI will enrich Odias as a whole, in fact, ignores the nature and history of the companies and banks involved, which place profits for shareholders far above other priorities (Bakan 2004, Woodward 2001). In effect, mining companies make their profits by dispossessing the land's indigenous population, pushing the people into worse poverty than anything they faced before.

Those opposing the projects insist they are not anti-development or anti-government, but actively seek real development. What they oppose are policies that sacrifice the well-being of village people and are thus 'anti-people'. Most cultivators see the factories that take away or dirty and ruin their lands as 'anti-development', because the factories disrupt their own progress towards well-being.

At issue then are opposing ideas about development and the process of industrialisation:

Is industrialisation the main factor in development?

Or is the main aim of development people's well-being as a whole?

Is people's quality of life often lowered by industrialisation?

Or does industrialisation advance people's quality of life?

Development for whom? Does everyone benefit or just some people?

Does industrialisation effectively 'sacrifice' some people to benefit others?

Does the wealth created by an elite really 'trickle down' to the poor?

Or does it make the majority of the people poorer?

What are its costs? Do these outweigh the benefits?

Are there Indian alternatives to the Western model of industrial development?

How long will a 'development project' last?

Is it for the long-term benefit of future generations?

And, above all, who has the right to impose market values over all other values?

We are convinced that the dangers in imposing a rapid process of further industrialisation have not been adequately assessed, and also that there are many alternatives to such a course.

First, the dangers for the long-term future of Odisha's environment. Mining more mountains will deplete non-renewable mineral resources, which are a major factor in Odisha's fertility and a source of future wealth in later centuries. Metal factories take too big a share of Odisha's water in a context where the groundwater level is depleting all over India, while the big dams supplying electricity and water to these factories also interrupt the natural flow of rivers. Metal factories pump carbon and fluoride into the atmosphere, and toxic waste into the water and land, apart from causing occasional, yet inevitable, major accidents.

Such projects are also a danger to society because the displacement they cause worsens poverty, even as the conflicts of interest they generate polarise society and provide the context for brutal abuses of human rights such as those which the authorities have already perpetrated in trying to force through the aluminium projects. No wonder a common slogan chanted by Adivasis who oppose these projects is:

Aamoro rokto podibo, kintu aamoro jami aame chadibu nai!
Our blood may flow, but we'll not leave our land!

Police shooting into crowds of Adivasi protestors at Maikanch in Kashipur in December 2000, and at Kalinganagar in January 2006 killed several people. These people's deaths are symbolic of a much wider death. Adivasis feel they are being sacrificed collectively, for the benefit of a corrupt and degenerate elite.

The present Odisha government headed by Naveen Patnaik has staked much on a series of deals with mining companies, in the belief that exploiting the state's rich mineral resources will transform a 'poor' Odisha into a 'rich' Odisha, and enable the government to pay off its debts. On 4 December 2004, addressing the Orissa Assembly he stated:

No one—I repeat no one—will be allowed to stand in the way of Orissa's industrial development and the people's progress.

But who defines the people's progress?

Basically, 'development' has become a mask for extremely gross forms of exploitation and corruption in Adivasi areas of India. This is how most of Odisha's Adivasis now see it, and any objective sociological analysis would probably conclude that they are right. As the eminent journalist P. Sainath observes in his book *Everybody Loves a Good Drought* (1996), huge amounts of money are allocated for 'tribal development', very little of which benefits or even reaches the Adivasis.

So movements against these projects must be understood as a vital expression of civil society against forced dispossession. In the words of Kishen Pattnayak:

> The politicians, social workers and pro-people intellectuals should start thinking in this direction: Are mines a bane or a boon to the indigenous people? They must take a clear stand. Have they any evidence for the idea being propagated that leasing out mines to the companies will benefit and make the people and the state prosperous? Why will not the people resist such projects when there is no evidence supporting this propaganda?[2]

Analysing corporate power

In a situation where opinions have become so polarised, we need an eagle's eye perspective, surveying the situation as a whole, as well as the telltale details. We need to lay bare the sets of beliefs and values that motivate different people, and the wider contours of power. Corporations are assuming an influence in all our lives which surpasses anything they had before. This book is an attempt to go further into understanding the nature of this power, uncovering its basic form beneath the complexity.

The first great sociologists sowed the seeds for this exercise. *Collective representations* was Emile Durkheim's term for the conventionally held views of various social groups—significant *social facts*, which we elucidate in quotations from a wide range of people. Max Weber's study of bureaucracy and bureaucratised power provides a reference point for understanding the complexity of aluminium companies, and the way corporate and financial hierarchies merge with the hierarchies of the administration and political parties (an intermeshing of multiple bureaucracies). His *Protestant Ethic and the Spirit of Capitalism* (1930) showed how religious beliefs and values are intrinsic to the energy that motivates capitalism.

Several recent critiques of corporate power offer ways into understanding the overall nature of modern power and the companies' present position of dominance (Sampson 1975–2004, Korten 1995, Monbiot 2000, Klein 2002 and 2007, Bakan 2004). *The Environmentalism of the Poor: A Study of Ecological Conflicts and Valuation* (Martinez-Alier 2002) looks at a large number of movements worldwide, where social and ecological awareness have combined to oppose destructive 'development'.

Extractive industries are at the heart of corporate power. Their impacts on society are being increasingly studied now. Negative impacts of mining on indigenous people are a principal theme in the works of Roger Moody (1988, 1992, 2005, 2007), who has been a helpful guide for this book (see also Evans 2002). There is an impressive critical literature on the World Bank (Rich 1994, Caufield 1998, Stiglitz 2002, Colchester 2003), and on the impact of dams on indigenous communities (Morse Report 1992, McCully 1998, Roy 1999). *Reverse Anthropology* (Kirsch 2006) is a case study in New Guinea, and this title summarises our methodology in this book. Several anthropologists have produced critical studies of traditional peoples zapped by mining (Godoy 1985, Ballard and Banks 2003). But analysis needs to go much further, back to the *social construction of knowledge* (Berger and Luckmann 1966) and the institutions we take for granted at the heart of our own culture, in order to deconstruct the nexus of values that promotes an invasion of mining companies on other people's land.

The oil industry offers important parallels to aluminium, especially in countries where its extraction has devastated the lives and environment of indigenous peoples. Recent studies of the oil conflict in Nigeria (Okonta and Douglas 2003, Rowell, Marriott and Stockman 2005) present numerous similarities to the situation emerging in Odisha, with a similar juxtaposition of politicians and businessmen in the world's top capitals affecting remote villagers in the Third World. Odisha, like Nigeria, is one of today's *commodity frontiers*, and Nigeria shows all too clearly how violence escalates into a *resource war*. In Ecuador too, oil companies have had a genocidal impact on several indigenous tribes in the Amazon rainforest, and a movement has emerged to *keep the oil in the ground*, since extracting it contributes to global warming even as it obliterates local culture and natural species (Pastor and Donati 2008).

In comparison with oil, mining and metal factories are kept far from most people's consciousness. Yet, in terms of momentous issues impinging on the lives of ordinary people—climate change, global financial crisis and the 'War on Terror'—mining is actually of central importance. Making it seem peripheral to our lives is part of a process of *Manufacturing Consent* (Chomsky and Herman 1988). Since Mrs Thatcher broke the miners' strike in Britain, most mining and metal production has been *outsourced* to developing countries, where it is far easier to hide events from the world's view.

East India's tryst with steel and coal repeats a sordid history in the UK, the US and other 'developed' countries, which conventional thought either forgets or classifies as 'unfortunate but a necessary part of our evolution.' This includes communities dispossessed and obliterated, from native Americans to Welsh farmers, and inhuman labour-exploitation of men, women and children, with uncounted deaths and injuries. *The Robber Barons* (Josephson 1934) describes the model of corporate wealth and power set in the US, which is still being copied and carried to new lengths by leading Indian businessmen such as Anil Agarwal, Laxmi Mittal and Sir Ratan Tata, whose impact spans London, New York and the remotest Adivasi villages of Odisha, Jharkhand, Chhattisgarh, Andhra and West Bengal. India's 'robber barons', like those in the US, are projected as national heroes. Perhaps their ruthlessness is part of their appeal, like the love-hate relationship of Americans with the self-made tycoons who 'made America great'. These men claim to be leading India's development, and benefiting the lives of thousands of the poor.

The dire working and living conditions of people swept into the mining-metals vortex in nineteenth-century Wales is captured brilliantly by Alexander Cordell in *Rape of the Fair Country* (1959) and other novels. The reality of what is happening now in remote parts of East India represents a new *Song of the Earth*, that yearns to be told afresh by a new generation of novelists, just as Dickens captured the web of rich and poor in nineteenth-century London, which Marx and Engels analysed so brilliantly at another level.

If our book makes a start at comprehending the enormity of what's going on, it needs filling out with thousands of people's stories, to bring home to the world's reading classes the reality of how corporate power is steering India and other countries into waging war on the fabric of their own natural environment and the sustainable communities that have lived and worked there for thousands of years.

Aluminium is usually defined through 'hard science' and economics (Dietrich 1998). Several aluminium companies have commissioned their own corporate histories, which minimise the shadow side to absurdity, but provide useful facts and reveal the motivating values and ideology (for example, Smith 1988, Heiner 1991). Political and economic studies of the industry have tended to focus on relatively limited aspects (Holloway 1988). Important recent studies have been put together by Barham, Bunker and their associates, bringing experts within the industry into dialogue with critics, focusing especially on connections between megadams and aluminium factories, and the financial exploitation involved (Barham et al. 1995, Bunker et al. 2005).

The pioneering study is Ronald Graham's *Aluminium Industry and the Third World* (1982), which uses a Marxist framework to examine how Guyana, Guinea and Ghana were exposed to an unprecedented level of exploitation through the aluminium industry. In each country, companies created political turmoil to get what they wanted.

An early study focusing on north Australia (Roberts and MacLean 1976) spells out the impact of bauxite mining on the aborigines, supplying what Graham's book lacks: the viewpoint of indigenous people. The tussle for profits between mining companies and Third World governments—the governments are always seduced by promises, and the companies always take away the main profits—distracts from the more human level of village people whose sustainable lifestyle is suddenly ripped apart when they are dispossessed of their land. Like Nwoke's book *Third World Minerals and Global Pricing* (1987),

Graham's arguments for how Third World governments should try and negotiate a fair deal barely mention the interests of the people faced with the catastrophe of displacement. The policy of ousting villages to make way for 'industrial development' has been imposed by Third World governments as heartlessly and cynically as by former colonial rulers and foreign companies. Whatever their tussle of interests over mining profits, Third World governments and mining companies collude in displacing people, who hardly ever get any significant financial profit from the mineral wealth that is taken out of their land.

Graham's book also dwells little on environmental damage. Indigenous people and the environment are conspicuous in a text from the Institute of Policy Studies, Washington, *Behind the Shining: Aluminium's Dark Side* (Wysham 2001). Studies by Gitlitz and Switkes (1993 and 2005) for the International Rivers Network focus on the vital link between aluminium factories and large dams, showing a pattern of heavy subsidies and externalities. These works, however, do not deal with the end-product uses of aluminium. Graham stresses the arms industry's demand as the reason for excessive manipulation by the US and British governments; but does not go into details. Nor does he question conventional ideas about the necessity of aluminium for development, although he points out repeatedly that the industry has never been geared to the needs of Third World inhabitants, but always to the mining companies' profits. He barely mentions the banks and metal traders who probably gain an even larger share of the profits, and are completely removed from any awareness of the people whose lives are destroyed by the industry.

An anthropology of aluminium

Anthropology starts from interpreting tribal societies, and the different social structures humans have created in different times and places. During its own primitive years in the nineteenth century, it depicted tribal society as 'primitive' and industrialised society as 'civilised'. But as experience grew, and colonial prejudices were undermined, anthropologists gradually woke up to the sophistication of tribal societies, realising that while they are much 'less developed' in material terms and division of labour, they may be much more developed in other ways—in their subtleties of human interaction and social structure, and in a relationship with nature based less on domination and exploitation, and more on a living, equal relationship. Adivasi culture does not treat nature as just matter: it is always also spirit.

Anthropologists' knowledge about tribal societies—and however limited this may be, it exists as a counterpoise to the prevailing ignorance—puts them in a position to speak with some authority about the extraordinary level of damage that takes place when Adivasis are moved from their land or swept up in a swift process of industrialisation. Often, anthropologists seem to shy away from speaking out from fear of 'standing in the way of development'. But it is time now to 'bear witness', and make a proper analysis of these situations.

Adivasi culture sees the earth's metals as sacred substances, in line with the ancient Indian concept of *dhatu*—'metal' in Sanskrit (also in Hindi and Odia). Ancient or tantric connotations of *dhatu* include 'consciousness' and also 'semen' or 'seed'. In this view, it is a misuse of *dhatu*—a sign of *abhav*—to mine and fabricate metals from out of the earth, in a way that ignores immediate and highly visible effects on the earth, mountains, forests and streams. *Abhav* (in Sanskrit, Hindi and Odia) connotes 'lack of feeling', 'without consciousness', 'poverty mentality' or 'unnatural'. The extraction of *dhatu* by gouging the tops or sides of sacred mountains for profit is seen as the act of a highly degenerate society. And using the latent power in metals to manufacture sophisticated weapons for war is the act of *asura*s (demons)—a demonic misuse of the powers in nature.

In the bad old days, many anthropologists studied tribal societies in isolation from the power structures imposed on them, and often produced extremely biased accounts in the process. Questioning the status of anthropological knowledge is part of a recent trend to reverse the gaze of enquiry: to study our own mainstream society from a more objective viewpoint that takes none of our own society's assumptions for granted. When we examine what mainstream society has imposed on more sustainable tribal societies, we have a chance to understand our own society's shadow side, by perceiving what it does to 'others', and how. Traditionally, anthropologists studied those with less power than themselves. But it is these very relationships of power that call out most urgently for clear analysis.

An anthropology of the aluminium industry means studying the social structure as a whole: the social relationships and connections that link people digging the bauxite in Odisha or Brazil, or opposing its mining, with people operating metal factories, and with people on other continents who trade the metal or design and manufacture items out of aluminium. This brings together a number of intersecting histories: of Odisha, Adivasis, mining and aluminium, armaments, companies, and of the World Bank (WB) and its loans, which have tempted newly independent countries into a debt trap since the 1950s (Caufield 1998).

An industry's social structure emerges by analysing the interdependent key roles set by the modern division of labour, and collusion (often unconscious) among separate groups of actors. Certain roles established during British colonial rule are perpetuated in the present power structure imposed over the Adivasis: administrators, with their departmental categorisation of forest, revenue and police; missionaries, who were once forbidden by the government, and then encouraged in a role of 'civilising' tribal people by introducing schools and hospitals; anthropologists themselves, 'merchants of knowledge', who dealt in a form of understanding about Adivasis that was often superficial, distorted, and geared towards controlling them; and the role of merchant proper—the original role of the East India Company, which survives, for instance, in the title of 'Collector' as the chief official of a district, who was, originally, a collector of tribute, land rent, or tax (Padel 2000 [1995]).

These roles have multiplied since British times. The administration retains its colonial mould, complemented by the political hierarchy, and the power tussles of the political parties and elections, in Delhi and at the state level, where the Chief Minister sits at the top, running the state government with his chosen ministers. NGOs (Non-Governmental Organisations) have largely taken over the missionary role of organising education, health and 'social development': 'doing good' while working with and/or questioning government policy and practice. Journalist and consultant are two of the 'merchant of knowledge' roles that exercise power and make money with influential writings. Documentary filmmakers are another. The role of merchant has multiplied exponentially. Many kinds of traders and businessmen operate in tribal areas, led by powerful contractors, companies and banks. Less visible hierarchies of officials in foreign-based organisations and governments make major decisions behind the scenes that affect villagers' lives profoundly. Power exercised by the WB and UN agencies is relatively well-known. The influence of the DFID (Department for International Development, Government of UK) is more opaque, and recreates East India Company-era lines of power from London. All these agencies operate by making loans or grants that build up a huge foreign debt for Third World countries.

Analysing the aluminium industry holistically means seeing how all its separate actors and factors relate together as a whole, even though many groups may be completely unconscious of the others. Scientists and traders in aluminium may know nothing about people displaced by bauxite mines, or those who work there. A primary purpose of this book is to give out information about this industry, some of which is surprisingly little-known or hard to find, so that people can see the whole picture more clearly. Usually, when anthropologists or consultants take up a project, they tend to become an unconscious part of the power structure, analysing the situation with a false objectivity, as if they were separate from it. We hope to enable you, the reader, to become more conscious of mining and metals, by looking at all the roles we and our families have played, as company official, scientist, politician, minister, anthropologist, journalist, activist, student, consumer.... In the words of Goethe, one of the world's great thinkers, a scientist as well as a poet:

> The manifestation of a phenomenon is not independent of the observer ... Thus when making observations it is best to be fully conscious of objects, and when thinking to be fully aware of ourselves. (Naydler 1996, pp. 72–73)

This may not always be comfortable, as the tendency of modern power is to hide itself under a false objectivity, which often involves remaining unaware of the real effects of one's own actions. We all play certain roles—sometimes unconscious, manipulated roles—in a larger power game we are often barely aware of.

Many things in the modern power structure are the opposite of what they seem and claim to be—a form of contrast which should excite any anthropologist's interest. For instance, the WB often claims its main aim is to eradicate world poverty. Yet, in the eyes of people affected by the dam and industry projects it has funded, it has vastly increased poverty, displacing huge numbers of people, shattering their previous standard of living, and reducing them to a desperate level of existence.

'Good governance' is promoted by the WB and foreign governments, with 'transparency' and 'accountability' as key criteria. Yet the governments, banks and companies promoting this still operate at a very primitive level of transparency and accountability, hiding their own important information and decisions behind a mask of bland assertions about 'commercial confidentiality' or 'national security', and a complete denial of responsibility for the disastrous effects of their projects and decisions. As we shall see, most Corporate Social Responsibility (CSR) is mere greenwash intended to fend off the claims of campaigners and hoodwink the public (Fauset 2006).

How much aluminium do we really need? Looked at as a whole, what benefits has it really brought? What does it mean to be living in this aluminium age, dependent on a multitude of aluminium objects?

Our aim is a balanced understanding, examining as many facets as possible—social, environmental, historical, economic, political, legal and scientific. Every aspect of environmental impact deserves more research. As non-scientists, all we can do here is present an overview of the main issues. Proper studies of the social impacts barely exist. We mention studies of aluminium projects around the world and elsewhere in India. But other areas and industries, especially steel and coal, merit similar analysis. We hope that this work will stimulate fruitful debate and research in many other areas, wherever companies are taking over land and power, and inside the companies themselves.

There are also various essential roles in the industry's social structure which would benefit from future research. These include the freight companies that transport alumina and aluminium by rail, road and sea, and the construction of new ports for export, of minerals in particular.

This book is a paper construction, written on a laptop. Much of the power we write about is exercised through the medium of writing—from land deeds to mining leases, and the whole world of bureaucracy created by lawyers, legislators and police, to figures on the computer screens of bankers and metal traders in London or New York. This world of *paper power* is oriented against Adivasis, as writing is not part of their traditional culture. They see how it is manipulated against them, and distrust it profoundly. As Gopinath Mohanty puts it in his novel *Paraja*,

> *Porojaro kagazoku bhari doro.*
> Parajas have great fear of paper (Mohanty 1945/1987).

Or as the American Indian activist Russell Means puts this:

> I detest writing. The process itself epitomises the European concept of "legitimate" thinking. What is written has an importance that is denied the spoken. My culture, the Lakota culture, has an oral tradition, so ordinarily I reject writing. It is one of the white world's ways of destroying the cultures of non-European peoples—the imposing of an abstraction over the spoken relationship of a people. (Means 1980/1982)

The pricing of aluminium is something that takes us to the heart of the modern power structure. 'Power' is often used as a synonym for electricity—'power supply', 'power sector'—and also for military might: 'firepower', 'superpower'. In society, power often means 'power over' other people. We tend to forget its original, core meaning, 'to be able' (from French *pouvoir*). With this, we forget our own power. Each of us exercises power through every choice and action we make.

Each of these forms of power is relevant here. Power over others, and power 'behind the scenes', is evident in the amount of resources the aluminium companies get hold of: huge tracts of land for mines and factories, power stations and coal, as well as hydropower and the clout to get more big dams built despite the prevailing consensus that the cost of dams far outweighs their benefits. Nothing demonstrates power like the channelling of vast electrical power, and aluminium plants need a lot of this.

Another aspect in the recent worldwide increase in corporate power is privatisation. Odisha was the first state in India to privatise its electricity supply.[3] Water in the form of dams has already been privatised, and is in danger of being further privatised right now, as are other sectors of India's former semi-nationalised economy. Odisha's biggest aluminium company, Nalco, fought off a privatisation attempt in 2003.[4] We shall see how this privatisation process is pushed by the WB, whose loans to a state such as Odisha carry secret *conditionalities* that accentuate this trend towards *deregulating* and *restructuring* the economy so as to *liberalise* it, in a process overseen by the DFID.

But aluminium takes us to the heart of modern power in another sense too, because of its central place in the arms industry. The bodies and wings of modern aircraft and missiles are based on aluminium alloys. The technology of certain bombs depends on the high temperature reached when aluminium reacts with the oxides of other metals, and it is used in a wide range of bombs, from the 'daisy cutter'—today's most powerful 'conventional' bomb that destroys everything in a three-square-mile radius—to nuclear missiles.

American planes 'bombed Vietnam into the stone age'. Hearing this comment from a US general, the Vietcong responded that on the contrary, they had been 'bombed into the age of aluminium', as the people who were being bombed found creative ways to re-use aluminium from downed aircraft. 'Bombed into the age of aluminium' also evokes the aluminium technology used in daisy-cutter carpet-bombing, as well as napalm. A high percentage of aluminium output has always gone directly into the arms industry; Graham's estimate is 30 per cent (1982, p. 250).

Thus the pressure behind the move to set up more aluminium plants in Odisha comes not just from the companies themselves but from the aluminium cartel, which includes elements within the world's top governments.

India today witnesses a recreation of past power structures, just as the East India Company and the Victorians had consciously replicated the Roman empire, a 2,000-year-old power structure. There are also similarities to the 'pastoral power' or 'power that sacrifices itself', set up under the influence of the Church in Europe's Middle Ages, when the Church held the power of life or death over individuals according to their conformity to current orthodoxy or their penetration by 'heresy' (Foucault 1982, Padel 2000 [1995]). The Christian 'crusades' of the Middle Ages are now being replicated in the so-called 'War on Terror', which is also a war for the control of oil and other resources. Leading this ongoing 'war without end' on people the world over is the US, a powerful country with a shadow history that should not be forgotten: its genocide of indigenous peoples. Indian history, by contrast, shows a pattern of coexistence between Adivasi and mainstream cultures. Is this coexistence under threat now, with India part of a worldwide system tailored to the needs of its predominant military and economic power, the US—a country whose genocidal past lives on in its present attitudes towards other peoples and cultures? A local manifestation of the global 'War on Terror'—the war against Naxalites or Maoists in south Chhattisgarh—is causing mass displacement of Adivasis, and its underlying cause is almost certainly the mining companies' insatiable hunger for land.

Terrorists often use suicide as their main weapon. But does our industrial lifestyle follow a suicidal impulse on a much bigger, collective scale? The latest armaments are always the highest-priced commodities, and when we link the pollution and aggression of mining companies with the money and research going into arms, as well as the bribes notorious in the arms trade, we come face to face with a culture that promotes death (Padel and Das 2005, Burrows 2002).

The *Terminator* films express this in stories of a near-indestructable 'aluminium man' hunting human victims as a humanoid programmed to kill. Another symbol of the aluminium-age ideal of machine-like strength and purity is a woman in a 2006 TV advert for deodorant who turns up her nose at a group of dancing, sweating men. She suddenly turns and squirts deodorant at them, never mind that the aluminium content of deodorants and sun-block creams are a probable cause of cancer. Putting aluminium repeatedly on one's skin seems as perverse and unnatural as putting silicon in one's breasts. In packaging, cars, construction … has the shiny cleanness and lightness of aluminium seduced us all?

Freedom movements

Ongoing movements against excessive industrialisation in Odisha have tended to follow Gandhian principles of *ahimsa* (non-violence), and an alternative view of industry and development, in which the dignity of labour and village life are valued above profit.

In many ways, as Gandhi realised, India's Independence was an illusion. Financial independence has been eroded, with key control exercised from London once again. Would the 'Father of the Nation' have approved an image of his own head on India's paper currency? Or would he have found this an ironic symbol of how his *swadeshi*, anti-capitalist message has been subverted?

Mining project supporters are deeply mistaken when they label protestors 'anti-national', 'anti-social', 'anti-government', 'anti-industry' or 'anti-development'. The movements against aluminium and steel projects are a response to basic injustice and prick the nation's conscience. But how open are government officials when it comes to listening to this conscience?

All over the world, Gandhi is still an inspiring model of resistance to the multiple injustices of government repression and financial manipulation. Movements like those in Odisha may yet show the way to the rest of the world, helping all of us to resist the *ungroundedness* of modern life and its power structures, which threaten the quality, if not the very existence, of human life on earth. These movements represent the interests of the poorer, more exploited sections of society. They are no more 'anti-social' or 'anti-national' than India's freedom struggle was anti-social and anti-national!

Gandhi's ideals were subverted much too soon. Shortly before his death, he had an exchange of letters with Nehru concerning a fundamental difference in their outlooks. For Gandhi, village life and 'industry', in the sense of self-sufficiency in producing one's own food, clothes and other needs, formed the core of civilised living. He thought that the rush towards machine-based industrialisation and city life was making the human race rush headlong on a path to collective suicide. Nehru's view was the opposite, though he did not deny the suicidal tendency in the industrial mode:

A village, normally speaking, is backward intellectually and culturally.... I do not think it is possible for India to be really independent unless she is a technically advanced country.... There is today a tremendous acquisitive tendency both in individuals and groups and nations, which leads to conflicts and wars. Our entire society is based on this more or less.... You are right in saying that the world, or a large part of it, appears to be bent on committing suicide. That may be an inevitable development of an evil seed in civilisation that has grown. I think it is so.[5]

In contrast, Gandhi saw village life as healthier than city life and more sustainable. He saw the whole system of heavy industrialisation as antithetical to freedom and to India's real independence, which he identified with village *swaraj*. As we shall see with the aluminium industry, *industrialisation*—which has little to do with the 'industries' necessary for fulfilling people's needs and ensuring the self-sufficiency of communities that Gandhi's vision incorporates—enslaves a country to foreign-based companies and governments, on the one hand, and replicates this slavery within the country, on the other.

Gandhi's last years were overshadowed by the betrayal of his vision of India's future, as Nehru pursued a policy of rapid industrialisation, through deals with the Birlas and the Tatas. He laid the foundation stone for the Hirakud dam in 1948, which was to power Odisha's first aluminium smelter. In later years he lived to regret his infamous proclamation that 'Dams are the temples of modern India.' Today, the Tatas and the Birlas exert more control than ever over policy decisions. Hindalco (the leading company in Utkal Alumina) is controlled by Aditya Birla, the grandson of G. D. Birla, founder of the Birla dynasty, who was also Gandhi's friend and supporter. Sir Ratan Tata has exercised considerable influence over British politics and world finance.

One of the first recorded instances of industrial pollution and protest in Odisha is a letter written to Gandhi in 1946 about pollution of the Ib River, near Sambalpur, by Birla's Orient Paper Mill (started in 1940). Gandhi passed on the letter to Birla, who did nothing about it. Arjun Panda, of Sapalohora village, filed a court case in 1950 on behalf of 50,000 people. Sraddhakar Supkar, with three others, wrote to the Advocate-General in Cuttack (13 March

1950), for permission to file a case that was probably (according to Sraddhakar's son, Karunakar) Odisha's first Public Interest Litigation (PIL). The case against Birla's mill was for public nuisance, and although the judgment went against Birla, the Orissa Assembly passed a River Pollution Act in 1953, which took away the courts' authority to decide on matters of river pollution. This power was instead delegated to an eight-member board (to be constituted of four government officials and four non-government representatives). Fakir Charan Das resigned from this board in protest against its anti-people tolerance of pollution, and Sraddhakar Supkar led a protest against the Act in the Assembly. But the Act was passed and the Orissa High Court used it to dismiss the case against Birla (20 November 1956). So the factory continued to pollute the Ib, while other sources document its spectacular evasion of tax (Burman 1950). Later, the Hirakud dam submerged this area, where the Ib joined the Mahanadi, while the River Pollution Act continued to serve the Birlas and other industrial houses by facilitating the pollution of hundreds of Odisha's rivers and streams.[6]

Since the US dropped aluminium-detonated atom bombs on Japan in 1945, we live perpetually on the edge of an abyss of self-destruction. The military-industrial complex has aluminium at its core. As Chomsky says (2003, p. 58):

> The reality is that under capitalist conditions—meaning maximisation of short-term gain—you're ultimately going to destroy the environment: the only question is when.

Writing this book, we have come to see the mass use of aluminium as a symptom of the ungroundedness and speediness of modern life, in which business, economics and politics, and all the systems that make up the modern power structure, are alienated from an awareness of where things, including ourselves, come from. Our whole civilisation is spinning out of control, driven by a financial system that recognises only short-term profit. Cleverness of mind tends to be channelled into the profit motive, split off from consciousness of the results of one's actions. This cleverness manifests in repeated promises to share the profit with people whose labour and resources are exploited—promises that are invariably broken. Nowhere is this clearer than in the modern mining industry and its impact on indigenous people.

Odisha played an important part in inspiring Gandhi, thanks to Madhusudhan Das and others (Choudhury 1989). People's movements against various forms of oppression and displacement that have taken place in Odisha since Independence have kept Gandhi's message alive, in a non-violent and persistent spirit of struggle against seemingly impossible odds. This spirit is one of Odisha's most precious gifts to the world.

A major reason for writing this book is our conviction that if humanity is to survive the huge social and environmental problems apparent today, the people who live closest to the earth will have to become a vital model for the rest of us. They have survived enormous exploitation and marginalisation, with a sense of community and knowledge that should inspire us all to strive for a better way of living together in this world. As the then President of India, K. R. Narayanan, said in his Republic Day speech on 25 January 2001, alluding to the Maikanch police killings just five weeks earlier:

> The mining that is taking place in the forest areas is threatening the livelihood and survival of many tribes ... Let it not be said by future generations that the Indian Republic has been built on the destruction of the green earth and the innocent tribals who have been living there for centuries.

CHAPTER TWO

Aluminium's Secret History

A Life-giving Role in Earth and Bauxite

All life depends on the soil. Healthy soil is alive with bacteria and worms, which constantly create new life out of decaying matter and minerals. Charles Darwin's last book (1881) focuses on worms' vital role in creating *humus*—the 'vegetative mould' which keeps the soil alive and fertile. Hence the Kucheipadar women's earthworm song, mentioned in Chapter One.

From this worm-processed life in the soil come the nutrients for plants, on which humans and other life-forms depend. Adivasis recognise this life process and identify with Darwin's heroes, the worms. Yet our modern lifestyle tends to make us unmindful of the soil and its worms, and to forget what it means to grow our own food.

The magic of earth's fertility depends on an alchemy of minerals, combined with proper measures of sun and water. In this alchemy the element of aluminium plays a vital role transforming inorganic into organic matter, through its ability to combine equally with acids and alkalines, and its bonding with H$_2$O, which makes the soil able to retain moisture.

'*Without aluminium there would be no fertile earth.*'[1] Its primary role, in the balance of minerals lying hidden in the earth, is ensuring the nourishment of plants, through this readiness to bond with H$_2$O and other elements. Areas such as Odisha, where aluminium is particularly abundant in the mountains and soil, are therefore regions of outstanding fertility.

As the commonest mineral in the earth's crust, aluminium is a major constituent of rocks, especially feldspar, which makes up as much as 60 per cent of the earth's rock mass.[2] The weathering of rocks forms the mineral content of the soil. This combines with dying plant and animal matter for worms to make into *humus*, on which plants and higher life-forms depend. The worms' digestive tracts give out a constant stream of the finest and richest earth. Aluminium is an essential element in this soil-rooted chain of life, holding moisture and channelling it, along with mineral trace elements, into the root-stems of plants:

> It conveys to the soil the properties of plasticity and water-absorbtion; the ability to unite with the living substance that is water.

This is why as a metal, aluminium alloys easily with other metals.

> It is a gateway through which polarities are equalised in every way, be it those of heat and cold, of electricity, or of the metallic condition, standing as it does between the polarities of calcium and silica in the mineral world, or as an amphoteric element (in hydroxide) between acid and alkali in the chemical world.[3]

In its earth-bound state, aluminium binds minerals together, collects nutrients, and feeds these into the roots of plants. Clay is earth that is high in aluminium-content. Clay's plasticity exemplifies aluminium's natural, earthbound form, moving slowly, combining with other substances to give form to the material world.

Plants grown in 'scientifically-manipulated soils' with fertilisers, grow up deficient in life-force, due to a poverty of mineral trace elements. Fertilisers fix nitrogen in the soil, but as Adivasis say, they 'addict' the soil, and dry it out. The fertiliser industry is based on an extremely narrow understanding of earth processes, boosting the soil artificially, but quickly exhausting it, geared towards swift growth and profits for chemical companies. Earthworms die within four hours of chemical fertilisers being applied to a field. The cost is not just to the soil and its life-forms, but also in the spread of new kinds of disease, and a lowering of resistance. Chemical manipulation of mineral nutrients interferes with the natural life-processes in the *humus,* and neglects the role of aluminium, which ensures the soil's water-holding power. This is one reason why areas that plant cash crops and use chemical fertilisers need more and more water, because the natural process is being interfered with, and the aluminium content is less.[4]

Mainstream soil science has a long-standing, uncomfortable link with the arms industry. Research on the use of ammonia, nitrogen and other substances for bombs and fertilisers developed simultaneously, and unused munitions were channelled into fertilisers and pesticides after the two World Wars.[5] Soil science has systematically neglected the role of *humus* in the soil, as well as the life-giving role of aluminium. A similar bias applies to the mainstream scientific study of bauxite, which is entirely oriented towards the mining industry, and the extraction of aluminium.

Bauxite was first identified as the rock richest in aluminium at Les Baux in 1821, by the French scientist P. Berthier, and named in the 1840s. So bauxite is named after a *baou*—an extraordinary rocky spur, 250 metres high, on which a medieval citadel stands. Les Baux is where bauxite was first commercially mined, and it remained a principal source for European aluminium till the Second World War. Bauxite's role in promoting fertility and abundant plant-life is well-recognised, but only within specialised circles of geo-science. Cape York, an extensively forested peninsula in north-east Australia, is one of the biggest known deposits, and the world's biggest bauxite mine is on Aboriginal land there (Weipa). The whole peninsula is thought by botanists to be an area where earth's plant life may have first evolved.[6] The best forests of Australia, West Africa and the Amazon basin northwards to Guyana–Suriname are areas where bauxite deposits have played this essential role in promoting some of the world's most outstanding fertility.

Several of Odisha's biggest mountains were identified by the Geological Survey of India in the 1970s as another major world bauxite reserve of comparable quality and size (Rao and Raman 1979). Primary forest still standing on top of some of these mountains shows the fertility of their high-altitude, bauxite-nourished soil.

Bauxite has a particularly complex geology, as a mixture of igneous, sedimentary and metamorphic formations, which involves a weathering process called *laterisation*: basically a monsoon-type alternation every year of torrential rain and baking sun. Odisha's bauxite cappings were formed through the alternating rhythm of rain and sun continuing every year for about 40 million years, eroding layers of feldspar and other rocks. Because bauxite is porous, it holds the rain-water and releases it slowly. It contains at least fifty other mineral elements, and because these mountains still have forest on top or round their sides, the water that forms on their flanks is exceptionally rich in nutrients for plants.

Bauxite, therefore, exists in a cycle of flux each year between being soaked and dried out. Water's presence even in dried-out bauxite gives it a particular ability to support plant life so long as it has not been over-exposed to the sun. When bauxite deposits are mined-out after being denuded of vegetation, these life-giving powers go into reverse, and cause a widespread drying-out. The same happens to the forest areas in the aluminium-rich soils when the forest is cut: the soil quickly loses all its main nutrients and vitality.

Aluminium oxide (Al_2O_3) is a major constituent of igneous rocks such as granite and basalt (average 17 per cent), metamorphic rocks such as gneiss, slate and mica schist (18–24 per cent), and sedimentary rocks such as shales and clays (30–40 per cent) (Fox 1932, p. 150). Cryolite is a naturally occurring fluoride of aluminium, whose only commercial mine is at a site in Greenland. It plays a crucial role in the smelting process of aluminium invented in 1886, and is now manufactured synthetically.

The 'highest' form of aluminium oxide is its 'noble rust': rubies, sapphires, and other corundums are pure aluminium oxide plus small amounts of other minerals, which give these their colour. Emerald, topaz, tourmaline and zircon are also based on aluminium compounds, and turquoise is a phosphate of aluminium. Aluminium is intrinsic to the world of colour.

Another form that occurs in nature is Alum, a clay used as a mordant for fixing dyes since ancient Egyptian and Greek times, to which Pliny gave the name *alumen*.[7] Vital for fixing colours in carpets and other cloth, alum remained an important trade item till recent times, and a cause for war between Venice and Turkey.

Bauxite contains 40–56 per cent of aluminium oxide. It consists of the rocks diaspore or boehmite ($Al_2O_3.H_2O$) and gibbsite ($Al_2O_3.3H_2O$)—the monohydrate and trihydrate minerals of aluminium oxide. European bauxite is mostly of the monohydrate type, while most bauxite from Asia (including India), Africa and the Americas is more gibbsitic (trihydrate). In most areas, the two forms are mixed, with monohydrate forms generally more ancient (Patterson 1967, pp. 20, 26).

India's bauxite nearly all takes the form of blanket deposits capping mountains. In Odisha, these mountains are basically basalt and gneiss in their lower mass, dating from the pre-Cambrian era—around 300 million years ago. The upper part is basically khondalite (paragneiss) or charnockite (granitoid gneiss) with 'cappings' of bauxite or aluminous laterite, whose age is ascribed to the Upper Cretaceous or Upper Tertiary (Archaean) epoch—about 40 million years old. Gibbsite is the basic metallic ore associated with this bauxite (Fox 1932, Bardossy 1979).

Nearly all aluminium is made from bauxite, though a few other rocks have been used, such as nepheline, which supplies the Pikavelo refinery in Russia. Many other metals are present in bauxite, including uranium. Vanadium, titanium and gallium are sometimes extracted alongside aluminium. About 90 per cent of the world's bauxite goes to produce metal. The rest (for example, Guyana's bauxite) is classed as chemical grade. This is low in iron oxide, and is used in the refining of petroleum, and in abrasives, refractories and cement (Patterson 1967, pp. 2, 69).

Essentially, bauxite is concentrated clay, nourishing lush foliage in a soil that always retains moisture and therefore supports an intense level of plant life. Where there is erosion at the top of a mountain, the exposed bauxite hardens into a brick-like dryness, through laterisation. Bauxite cliffs and stream-formed rocks are bare, smooth, reddish laterite: clay hardened into sculpture.

Thus aluminium in rock and soil is common everywhere, but good quality bauxite is a rare substance, precious for the plant life it promotes. Its value to aluminium companies is therefore a direct threat to the earth's most fertile regions.

Split from oxygen: A brief history of the industry

To produce aluminium in its metallic form, the element has to be split from its natural form, especially its bond with oxygen. This is what makes the industry so complex.

> One must apply enormous energy, all the splitting forces inherent in electricity, in order to rob the natural aluminium ore (alumina or bauxite) of the oxygen with which it is so strongly connected and thus create the metallic condition. (Pelikan 1973, p. 151)

It was Sir Humphrey Davy who proved the existence of aluminium as an element in 1807–08, though without being able to produce any of the metal.[8] Before him, the French scientists Morveau (1761) and Lavoisier (1787) had deduced the existence of an element they called 'alumine', whose oxide forms the base of alum.

As a metal, aluminium was first produced, in tiny droplets, by the Danish scientist Hans Christian Oersted (1825). Two years later the German scientist Friedrich Wöhler succeeded in making the white powder known as alumina—pure aluminium oxide. Both got their results by reacting potassium with anhydrous aluminium chloride, a process refined by the Frenchman Henri Sainte-Claire Deville, using sodium instead of potassium. He exhibited a 15-pound ingot in the Paris exhibition of 1855, and initiated the first commercial production, when aluminium was still costlier than gold. He also wrote the first book on aluminium, and got financial backing to set up the world's first refinery and smelter at Salindres, which started production in 1860 under Henri Merle, and averaged one or two tons a year. This was the world's first aluminium company: the PCAC (Produits Chimiques d'Alais et de la Camargue). Merle's successor was Alfred Rangod, who gave his father-in-law's name, Pechiney, to the company.[9]

In 1885 the estimated annual production worldwide was 15 tons.

Aluminium was still a luxury item. Products from the Salindres factory included a Danish royal crown, a dinner set and a breastplate for Napoleon III. Other famous early products included the capstone of the Washington monument, and Eros in London's Piccadilly Circus (1893, also known as Anteros and Angel of Charity).

1886 marks the start of the aluminium era. In this year two inventors discovered, independently, a better way of making aluminium, which became known as the Hall-Héroult process, after Paul Louis Toussaint Héroult in France and Charles Martin Hall in the US. Their smelting process involved dissolving alumina in a bath of molten cryolite (a double fluoride of sodium and aluminium) and passing a strong electric current through it. This fuses the alumina into a deposit of the metal, splitting the oxygen from aluminium and isolating the metal. Very quickly, companies in France, Switzerland, Britain and the US started making aluminium on a big scale.

Hall's first backers were the Cowles Brothers in 1886, who were making 'aluminum-bronze' (a copper-aluminium alloy) in Cleveland, but their support was minimal. Six industrialists in Pittsburgh founded the Pittsburgh Reduction Co. in 1888 to invest in his research. From 1889 the head of this company was Arthur Vining Davis, whose family continued in the management of Alcoa (Aluminium Company of America) as well as Alcan (Aluminium Canada). The banker-director who financed the company was Andrew Mellon, who was also a founder-director of Gulf Oil. From 1891 to 1903 there was a patent dispute between the Cowles Brothers and the Pittsburgh Co. The Cowles' were using Hall's patent method of dissolving alumina in a bath, while Pittsburgh was using the Cowles' system of 'internal heating' of the bath or pot, to keep the fusion process continuous. They eventually settled out of court to avoid the ruination of both: the Pittsburgh firm paid the Cowles' a large sum, in effect to establish a monopoly on production.[10]

In 1888 the Austrian Karl Josef Bayer received a German patent for an easier method of refining alumina out of bauxite, setting the stage for a huge expansion. Alcoa bought rights to the Bayer process in 1905 and, with modifications, this is still the main process used in the world's alumina refineries. It involves 'digesting' bauxite under pressure with caustic soda to form sodium aluminate

(Na_2AlO_2). Filtering this solution produces aluminium trihydroxide, and separates it from the waste product, red mud. This trihydroxide is then washed and calcined to produce alumina powder. Bayer's process was soon bought by Hall and others. It made production cheaper, so that the cost of aluminium fell from over $4 per pound to just over 70 cents.[11]

In 1907 the Pittsburgh firm changed its name to Alcoa (Aluminum Company of America). Hall's patent expired in 1909, ending this company's guaranteed monopoly. But by this time Alcoa was 'vertically integrated' from bauxite mining to fabricating wire and sheet. Its first smelter was at Niagara Falls in 1893, where it was the first and biggest customer of the Niagara River Power Company, creating hydropower from the waterfall. In 1899 it acquired its own first hydropower site at the Shawinigan Falls in Quebec (Canada), to build a second smelter. Smelter number 3 formed a new township named Alcoa in Tennessee, for which a series of dams on the Little Tennessee River were built (1914). Number 4 was at Badin, North Carolina, for which it built a dam on the Yadkin River (1915–16). Its first refinery was near St. Louis (Illinois) near a plentiful coal supply. It also began to acquire bauxite mines, in Georgia, Arkansas, Alabama and Montana, at a place named Bauxite, where mining has left a wasteland. From 1909 Alcoa was basically a mining company ('upstream integration'), as well as a fabricater and manufacturer ('downstream integration'). It was also starting to acquire its own railways and boats to transport materials and output.

In the 1890s Alcoa's main output was cooking pots. Between 1891 and 1895 its potential for sea-craft was exploited in several light-weight pleasure boats. One was commissioned by Alfred Nobel. Another won a key boat race in America. Military uses followed soon after: in the early 1900s Britain's Yarrow shipyard was building torpedo boats for the French and British navies.[12] Aluminium wire and cable began to become widespread and displace copper from 1908, when an electrical engineer at Alcoa called William Hooper patented a process of winding six strands of aluminium wire around a galvanised steel core to produce strong cables of the type still in use today.

Aluminium's Secret History | 37

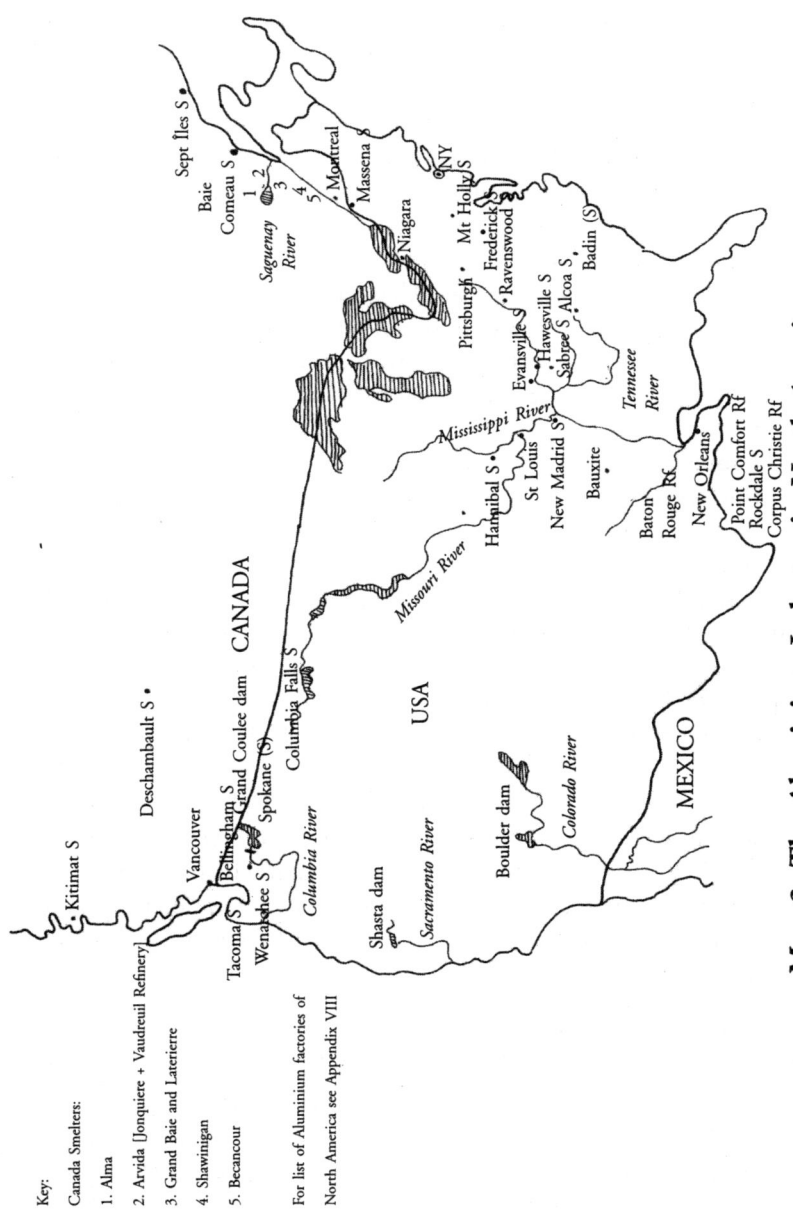

Map 3: The Aluminium Industry in North America

Key:

Canada Smelters:
1. Alma
2. Arvida [Jonquiere + Vaudreuil Refinery]
3. Grand Baie and Laterierre
4. Shawinigan
5. Becancour

For list of Aluminium factories of
North America see Appendix VIII

In engine components aluminium swiftly assumed a key importance. The Kitty Hawk had aluminium in its engine in 1903 and, from then till now, aluminium has remained vital for engine components in cars as well as aircraft.

Several aluminium-bodied cars were made from 1904. Car bodies soon returned to steel, retaining a small mix of aluminium. This rose little till the 2000s. During 2002–09 the aluminium content of cars has increased dramatically.

It was another scientist at Alcoa in 1901 who discovered ammonal—a mix of ammonium nitrate with aluminium powder—an invention also known as thermite, with profound consequences for bomb technology, seeing application in all the wars of the twentieth century and since.[13]

Héroult's process was initially rejected by Pechiney, and purchased by the Swiss company AIAG (Aluminium Industrie Aktien Gesellschaft), which built a number of aluminium smelters powered by dams on rivers descending from the Alps, and eventually became Alusuisse. Héroult also sold the licence for his process to British entrepreneurs who set up the British Aluminium Corporation (BAC) in 1895. In the next ten years the BAC built several refineries and smelters in Scotland as well as dams to power them. A second French firm in which Héroult was involved, called SEMF (Société Electro-Metallurgique Française), set up a factory at Froges, which finally merged with its rival, Pechiney's PCAC, in 1921.[14]

The aluminium alloy which sent humans up into the sky was duralumin, a mix with copper and magnesium, which was patented for use in aircraft by Alfred Wilm in 1908. It was soon being used in Germany's Zeppelin. During the First World War, when the Germans made extensive use of it, Alcoa researched to produce an equivalent alloy ('17S'), seeing that *Duralumin was to plain aluminium what steel was to iron* (Smith 1988, p. 129).

Early aluminium factories harnessed hydropower from waterfalls: Europe's first Héroult refinery at Neuhausen (Switzerland) used the Rhine Falls, Pechiney's Calypso plant at Maurienne used another waterfall from the Alps, Alcoa's first smelter used Niagara (1893) and the British used the Falls of Foyers near Loch Ness (1894–96).

From the 1900s, many of the biggest dams being built in Europe and America were designed to power aluminium smelters. BAC smelters 2 and 3 were a short way west of Foyers, at Kinlochleven and Lochaber, for which the Blackwater, Laggan and several other dams were built. When they started up in the 1900s–1920s, these were the world's biggest smelters, supplied with water by huge pipes that dropped down mountainsides to drive turbines—one of the first prototypes of the design used 70 years later in Odisha's Upper Indravati project. Kinlochleven was eclipsed by the Lochaber (1924–43), which involved digging a 15-mile tunnel through Ben Nevis (Britain's highest mountain)—another model used in Indravati.[15]

This connection between big dams and aluminium smelters has remained extraordinarily close from early days till now. Megadams and other hydro-projects gave an essential stimulus to the aluminium industry, whose refining and smelting processes needed electricity on a massive scale, while the aluminium companies helped finance the dams. The building of dams and metal factories in the 1920s–1940s was part of what pulled America out of its Depression and helped win the Second World War. The second half of the twentieth century saw aluminium production exported to other countries, along with dam construction on a massive scale to power it. Some of the most controversial and destructive megadams in India/Asia, and the continents of America, Australasia and Africa have been built specifically to give cheap electricity to smelters. The Three Gorges dams in China and a series of dams being built now in Iceland for new monster-size smelters continue this connection.

The manufacture of aluminium involves four basic processes: mining the bauxite, refining it into alumina, smelting this into metal, and 'fabricating' it to create alloys and shape the metal into sheets, extrusions and other forms. At this point it's important to introduce a basic understanding of how the aluminium industry works, in terms of its basic science and impacts on the environment.

Mining the ore, nearly always bauxite, is the first stage. The purest grade, such as that in Odisha, combines aluminium oxide with iron silicate, which gives this rock a deep red colour (Al_2O_3 + Fe_2O_3 + SiO_2). The bauxite is nearly always strip-mined—dug out, open-cast. One exception is underground bauxite mines in Mounts

Out of this Earth

Key:
(S) (Rf) Smelters or refineries now closed
S Smelters still in use
M= Mills (fabrication plants)

- Invergordon (S)
- Loch Ness
- Inverness
- Foyers (S)
- Laggan dam
- Lochaber S (Fort William)
- Ben Nevis
- Blackwater dam
- Kinlochleven (S)
- Burntisland (Rf)
- Glasgow
- Edinburgh
- Falkirk M
- SCOTLAND
- Lynemouth S
- Larne (Rf)
- IRELAND
- Leeds
- Manchester
- Warrington M
- Latchwood Locks M
- Anglesey (S)
- Dolgarrog M (S)
- Milton M
- Birmingham
- Wednesbury M
- WALES
- ENGLAND
- Newport (Rf)
- Cardiff
- London
- Cornwall

Map 4: Britain's Aluminium Industry

Quarrying bauxite at Bodai Daldali, Kawardha, Chhattisgarh

Parnassus and Helikon in Greece. In India, mountain summits are blasted out and dug to a depth of 30–100 feet. Covering forest is stripped. Springs diminish or dry up. Because bauxite exists in thin but extensive layers, when it is strip-mined a larger surface area of ground is destroyed than in the mining of any other mineral.[16]

The second stage starts by calcining the bauxite (baking it to reduce its water content, which is usually 10–30 per cent), and crushing it in a rod mill. It is then mixed with caustic soda and 'digested' in the Bayer process, producing sodium aluminate. This is filtered and decanted to separate the alumina from the red mud. The alumina is then precipitated into crystal form over about three days. Alumina refineries, like Nalco's at Damanjodi ('the largest in Asia'), Vedanta's at Korba and Lanjigarh, and Utkal's being built in Kashipur, are huge. Apart from copious emissions of carbon and other gases, their worst pollutant is toxic red mud, which is dumped in 'ponds' or 'lakes' near the plant. Early refineries, on the coast, often dumped it in the sea. Red mud tends to contaminate the groundwater over a large area, with dangerous, dessicating effects, despite recent attempts at 'dry-packing'. Photos we took of a red mud lake in Korba (p. 340 below) show the substance leaching down into an area where there are streams and grazing animals. Iron, silica, titanium, gallium and uranium are among over 40 elements present in bauxite, which exist as highly toxic, destabilised 'heavy metals' in red mud, making it radioactive.

Roughly speaking, a refinery uses 2.3 tons of bauxite to make one ton of alumina powder, leaving over a ton of toxic red mud. This proportion varies with the chemical composition of different bauxite deposits, and every refinery is adapted to local conditions. The low silica content of Odisha bauxite allows Nalco to save costs by using lower temperatures to treat it than most other refineries. This is one of Odisha's attractions for aluminium companies.

In the smelter or *reduction* stage, two tons of alumina yield one ton of aluminium. The element is separated from its molecular bonding with oxygen by passing a huge electric current through the alumina—between 13,500 and 17,000 kilowatt hours to produce one ton of aluminium (compared to 250 kWh per ton of alumina at a refinery). This fuses or smelts it into the metallic form. Essentially, '*aluminium is clay plus electricity*' (Pelikan 1973, p. 151), and that is why the building of megadams evolved side by side with the aluminium industry.

Smelting is done in a vast building called a potroom, often about a kilometre in length. This houses lines of 50–250 rectangular steel vats, lined with refractory (non-burnable) material, covered at the bottom of each cell by a carbon cathode. Above this is a layer of molten aluminium, and a 'bath' of cryolite (Na_3AlF_6) at a temperature of 960–70 °C, into which the alumina is dropped by overhead hoppers, and stirred. The alumina dissolves in the cryolite, and when a huge electric current is passed through it from a carbon anode suspended by steel bars into each cell, this splits off the oxygen, which reacts with the carbon to form CO_2, which is vented into the atmosphere, while the pure aluminium collects at the bottom.

Modern 'pre-bake' technology places 15–20 anodes baked with petroleum coke and pitch into each cell. As an anode is consumed at the bottom, it is lowered further in, maintaining a distance of one and a half inches between anode and cathode. The older Söderburg technology used one large anode coated with carbon paste which was baked in the cell while new paste was added above. The molten aluminium is continually siphoned off and formed into ingots. The process has to run continuously. If it is interrupted for more than three hours, the mixture in the cells *freezes,* and is very hard and expensive to clean up.

Anodes must be replaced every few weeks, which can be done without disrupting production. Pot linings are replaced about every five years. Their removal necessitates a stop in production. Spent pot lining (SPL) is laced with cyanide, and thus a major pollutant needing careful disposal. At Korba, SPL is visible lying around outside the factory.

Smelters emit large amounts of greenhouse gases, including fluorine, carbon monoxide and dioxide, and CFCs including tetrafluoromethane. Modern smelters have hoods over the chimney stack that capture most of the fluoride gases, to recycle them back into the cryolite, for these emissions put fluoride into the groundwater for several kilometres around the factory, which causes serious wasting diseases in crops and trees, animals and humans. This 'skeletal fluoridosis' is well documented, not least from the vicinity of Odisha's two smelters (and the smelter in Anglesey in Wales), but aluminium companies tend to cover up and deny its prevalence (often with government collusion). While asserting that bauxite mining in Odisha has a brilliant future, with 1,400 million tons in 13 deposits, a senior director of the Geological Survey of India, B. K. Mohanty, admitted that fluoride pollution from smelters affects certain areas.[17]

Other toxic chemicals, including PCBs, are released directly into water sources. Two of the fluorocarbons released by smelters, CF_4 and C_2F_6 (fluoromethane and hexafluoroethane), are among the worst greenhouse gases.[18] The aluminium industry is thus notorious as one of the world's most electricity-consuming and polluting industries.

The fourth stage is the production of alloys, and fabrication of pure or mixed aluminium into sheets, protrusions, extrusions and other such forms. This stage has generally been less examined for effects on the environment, but the most sophisticated aluminium alloys, especially the lithium range used in the arms and aerospace industries, are known to be particularly polluting to manufacture.

They also make the highest profits—an exponential increase in value that starts with getting bauxite cheap.

Splitting molecules of aluminium oxide was an invention with extraordinary consequences. Aluminium as a metal is doubly split from its natural, earth-bound state: first by separating alumina from its bonding with H_2O, iron, silicon, etc. (in refineries), second by the electrolytic splitting of alumina molecules to separate aluminium from oxygen (in smelters).

The falling price of aluminium was controlled by setting up a series of four international cartels between 1901 and 1912, which raised prices, but kept failing due to competition between companies. America's legislation forbids monopolies and cartels. The outstanding success of US Anti-Trust laws was to break up Rockefeller's Standard Oil Company in 1911, and in 1912 the Justice Department made a ruling against Alcoa's monopoly—its 'unfair trade practices' against competitors, as well as its participation in a Europe-based cartel.[19] Yet the cartel never really ceased, and evidence suggests that American interests exercise a decisive influence.

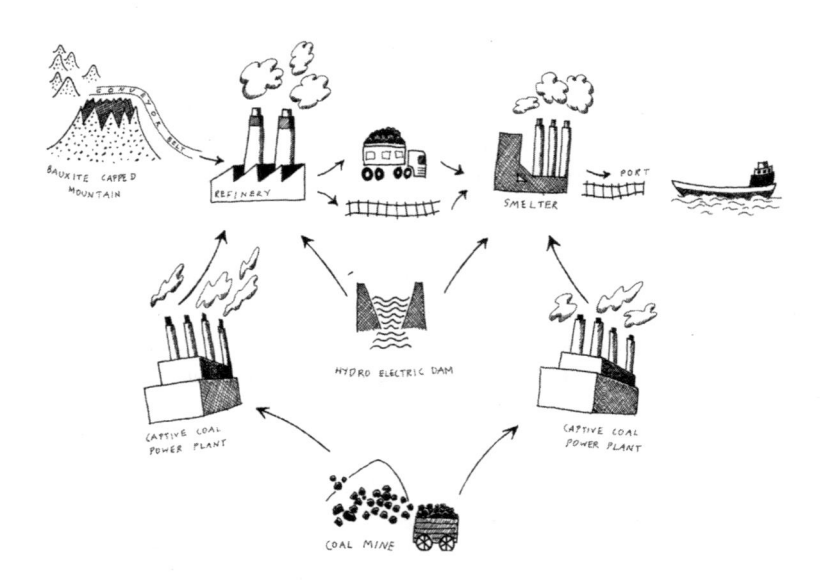

Bauxite to aluminium

Alcoa's financier-director, Andrew Mellon, was appointed US Treasury Secretary in 1921 for eleven years under three Republican Presidents: Harding, Coolidge and Hoover. When he left office in 1933, Mellon was widely blamed along with Hoover for policies that subsidised big business and brought about the Depression, and though he had ceased to be a director of Alcoa and Gulf Oil on taking office, his involvement with both companies continued through meetings and phone contacts.

The connection between aluminium and painting is of interest here. Stalin ordered the best paintings from Moscow's Hermitage Museum to be sold off in 'the sale of the century', to pay for his first five-year plan, and it was Mellon who bought them, as one of America's richest citizens, bequeathing them to Washington DC's National Gallery of Art as his main memorial. With this money, Stalin employed US engineers to build Soviet steel plants, and also the first Soviet aluminium smelter, overseen by experts from Alcoa.[20]

Aluminium production roughly doubled in each decade of the twentieth century, as the use of aluminium was promoted more and more widely, first for utensils, then for wires and cables, partly substituting copper, and for essential parts of car, ship and aircraft engines, and soon after, as the main metal for aircraft bodies, and a key 'strategic' metal, essential for war.[21]

World War profits

'War was good to Alcoa'—the company's official biography records. By 1916, 90 per cent of its output was for the war industry (Smith 1988, pp. 125–27).

World production rose by two and a half times between 1914 and 1918, and the German government created VAW (Vereinigte Aluminium Werke—United Aluminium) in 1915. The same year saw the invention in Britain of the 'Mills bomb' hand grenade, using the explosive properties of aluminium in the mixture known as thermite, in which powdered aluminium reacts with iron oxide—a reversal of the smelting process. This reaction generates huge heat through aluminium re-bonding with oxygen. Britain made 75,000 Mills Bombs during the Great War.

It was during the First World War that the aluminium companies came to realise that their fortunes were very closely linked to the production of military materials. (Graham 1982, p. 20)

The sudden jump in production led to scarcity of bauxite and a search for new sources. Britain had almost no bauxite of its own and had been dependent on French bauxite which was cut off by the war. Deposits in the US were also depleting fast. British colonials discovered bauxite in the Gold Coast (Ghana) in 1915, but did not start to mine it till the Second World War. In 1916, huge deposits were discovered (or rather, as was often the case, an earlier discovery was consolidated) in British Guiana, and pressure from the US government persuaded the British to lease these to Alcan, which thus became vital for supplying Britain's arms industry. Soon after, Alcoa established its main source in neighbouring Dutch Guiana (Suriname).

The First World War was thus a turning point for humans' relationship with aluminium. In the inter-war years, *'every leading industrial nation without a domestic aluminium industry established state-run concerns to ensure sufficient aluminium for the arms industry'* (Graham, p. 23). Within Europe, bauxite was mined in Hungary, Yugoslavia, Italy and France. Germany supplied its first refineries from Italy's mines in Istria. Alcoa was also swiftly buying up European bauxite mines at this time.

The world's first aluminium-skinned monoplane was tested in 1930, and large-scale production followed soon after. Unlike First World War biplanes, the bodies of monoplanes were mainly aluminium.

When Hitler came to power and planned for war, getting the raw materials for aluminium and other metals played a major part in his planning. From 1933, he ordered his designers, Messerschmidt, Junkers and others, to begin mass production of aluminium-based warplanes, taking the use of alloys such as duralumin much further, and building the world's strongest airforce. By 1937, Germany had overtaken America as top producer, and VAW was Europe's biggest aluminium company, followed by AIAG in Switzerland. Both got most of their bauxite from mines in Hungary, which started in 1927. Against them was an alliance between Britain's BAC and France's

Pechiney, who jointly owned Norsk Hydro's smelter in Norway. The main source for these companies was Les Baux.

World production of aluminium-based warplanes was estimated at 4,000 in 1933, rising to 40,000 in 1940. The aluminium industry and arms manufacturers were replacing the armaments depleted by the First World War, and played a major role in pulling America out of the Depression. Yet the build-up in arms before both World Wars is reckoned as a major cause of each.

In the US, Alcoa determined the price of aluminium, lowering it dramatically each time a competitor from Europe tried to enter the US market, and raising it again after the competition was killed off. The drive to create an aluminium cartel between the wars was more effective than before, and it was instigated by Alcoa, despite the Anti-Trust Laws. In 1928 Alcoa changed the name of its subsidiary from Northern Aluminium Company to Alcan (Aluminium Canada) and made it nominally independent, free to play a key role in an international cartel (though both continued to be controlled by the Mellon and Davis families who had started Alcoa in the 1880s). This cartel was institutionalised in 1931 as the 'Alliance Aluminium'. It fixed quotas and a minimum price. Germany left in 1934 as it increased production beyond the set limit. Yet the cartel continued to operate during the war, as the US Attorney-General revealed in 1945. Alcoa was termed *'the world's most perfect monopoly'* (1940).[22]

The Second World War saw a massive increase in demand. Alcoa could not cope alone. Under fire for its monopolistic tendencies, it helped the US government build and operate extra refineries and smelters. A prime purpose of America's new megadams was to power these aluminium smelters. *'Electricity from the big Western dams helped to win the Second World War,'* by producing aluminium for arms and aircraft, and later plutonium for nuclear bombs (McCully 1998, p. 18). The US Administration also subsidised a new aluminium company, Reynolds Metals, which struggled to compete with Alcoa during the war.

This is when bauxite mining and aluminium production took off in India, through Alcan, to aid the war effort. In 1943 new bauxite deposits were also discovered in another British colony, Jamaica. These immediately became the subject of a bitter dispute between the British and US governments. Both had taken aluminium under central planning. The British were loth to lose control of another colonial asset, and even wanted to take over Alcan—which though nominally Canadian and therefore based in the British empire, was owned mainly from the US. Britain was importing about 150,000 tons of aluminium per year from Alcan, which was about half the total required for its war effort. So the main Jamaican deposits were leased to Alcan. Reynolds was excluded, despite strong US government pressure, but discovered bauxite on neighbouring Haiti at the end of 1943, and immediately acquired the lease.

Post-colonial colonialism

Eventually Reynolds got a share of Jamaica's deposits (1950), thanks to its donations to the Democrat Party. Alcoa and Alcan were Republican supporters. After the war the US government sold off its extra aluminium plants to Reynolds as well as to a new company, started up in an impressive gamble by the entrepreneur Henry Kaiser. Kaiser made a deal with Arthur Vining Davis for Alcoa to sell him bauxite from Suriname. From 1950, Jamaica became the main source for Kaiser as well as Reynolds (Graham, pp. 24–40). Within a few years, Kaiser was branching out to Ghana, Australia and India, where his son formed Hindalco in a joint venture with the Birla family empire.

There are many ways of writing aluminium's history. One is to use statistics showing increasing world outputs of bauxite, alumina and primary aluminium from the 1890s to now, and shifts in percentage between countries (appendices II–IV). Refineries and smelters were huge to start with, and have increased steadily in size. Refineries tend to be made specific to the quality of their local bauxite supply, and trade in bauxite itself has decreased. In 1962, 72 per cent of aluminium content was traded as bauxite, 10 per cent as alumina and 18 per cent as ingot. By 1988 only 32 per cent was traded as bauxite, and this figure has continued to fall.[23]

Complementing this, other statistics show consumption by country, and by sector within each country, and shifts between the main sectors of auto, construction, packaging and electric cables. Average per capita consumption in various countries show marked differences: 26 kg per year in the US, surpassed by 29 kg in West Germany, and 30.9 kg in Japan, with the West Europe average between 20 and 26 kg (1989). In India, per capita consumption was just 0.65 kg in 1998, which the aluminium companies and lobby groups have been working hard to increase since, in all sectors, especially packaging, auto, and construction. India passed regulation early on to reserve 52 per cent of its aluminium output for electric wiring to promote programmes of village electrification. After the industry was liberalised and decontrolled, this percentage came down to 34 per cent (1996), against a world average of 9 per cent, and the project of giving electricity to villages proceeds very slowly now.

Another history would focus on prices and metals trading (appendix V), and how this relates to the history of finance through the big merchant banks, and promotion by the WB and IMF. While we cover these aspects, our work remains focused on the actual power relationships in the industry as a whole, especially in how it is being set up in India.

After the Second World War, aluminium companies moved ever further into exploiting Third World sources of bauxite, as well as their sources of hydropower for refining and smelting it into aluminium. This process started just before, during and after several countries' Independence, especially Guyana, Suriname, Jamaica, Haiti, Ghana and Guinea. The aluminium industry therefore dictated the process of these countries' Independence, placing them under highly exploitative financial dependence from the start, while bringing about a vicious dynamic of *internal colonialism* within these countries. In most of them, as well as in Australia and many parts of north and south America, aluminium projects have caused a fundamental dispossession or exploitation of the 'fourth world' of First Peoples, the indigenous or tribal people (see Chapter Nine).

In India, several aluminium companies were set up with foreign collaboration in the 1960s. Hindalco, the fruit of Kaiser's deal with Birla, made its central factories at Renukoot in Uttar Pradesh. To provide these with cheap electricity and water, the massive Rihand dam was constructed, which displaced and dispossessed over 200,000 people.

An interesting connection emerges in George Clooney's film about the McCarthy era, *Goodnight and Good Luck* (2005), which juxtaposes 1950s Alcoa adverts with US news shows, for Alcoa was a patron of the very show on which the journalist Edward Murrow confronted Senator McCarthy, and suddenly withdrew funding from this show in order to support McCarthy.

One sign of a shift in aluminium power politics was the so-called Aluminium War in London between 1957 and 1958, when the BAC suffered a hostile takeover. BAC's share price had dropped from 80 shillings to 37, and in 8 days in November 1958, Reynolds bought up 80 per cent of BAC's stock, with designs on the British company's concessions in Ghana.[24] Soon Reynolds sold these assets in Britain on to Alcan, which has controlled Britain's refineries and smelters in Scotland ever since.

During these 'middle age' years of aluminium, six aluminium companies dominated the industry in a fairly stable pattern: Alcoa, Alcan, Reynolds and Kaiser in north America, Pechiney in France, and Alusuisse in Switzerland. With the exploitation of Australian and Brazilian bauxite, Rio Tinto, Comalco and then Billiton entered the picture as major aluminium producers.

From the 1980s, this stable picture began to fall apart, as more companies entered the fray, with huge mergers: an old pattern with a new intensity of 'raiding' and takeovers. It was at this time that Russia privatised its aluminium industry, forming the companies Sual and Rusal. With the Cold War coming to an end, aluminium consumption by Soviet arms manufacturers declined, and cheap Russian aluminium on the world market depressed prices. This was when Stiglitz, serving on Clinton's Council of Economic Advisers in 1994, witnessed from the inside the setting up of an aluminium cartel, proposed by Paul O'Neill, the head of Alcoa, and implemented by the Treasury Department. The law firm Vinson and Elkins acted as Alcoa's lobbyist, working 'a loophole into Texas environmental regulations that allowed Alcoa to emit 60,000 tons of sulphour dioxide each year.' This firm was the third largest contributor to George W. Bush's election campaign, and when Bush was elected (or rather persuaded the US to make him President, since many believe Al Gore really won more votes), O'Neill left Alcoa to become Treasury

Secretary under Bush, selling his Alcoa shares only after they had risen 30 per cent during his first weeks in office. The cartel was thus consolidated from the apex of the US Treasury Department, just as it was when Mellon was Treasury Secretary in 1921–33.

Alcoa took over Alusuisse and Reynolds in 2000, with a few of Reynolds' assets going to Billiton. Norsk Hydro took over VAW (2002), Kaiser went bankrupt (2004), not long after a terrible fire destroyed its Baton Rouge alumina refinery in Louisiana. Alcan staged a merger with Pechiney (2002–04)—relevant for Odisha, since Nalco started in effect as a subsidiary to Pechiney.

By 2009, the pattern has changed even more, as Indian and Chinese companies grow in power and wealth, including Vedanta, based in London since 2003, with rising outputs in copper, zinc and iron as well as aluminium. Hindalco bought up Novelis, a US-based aluminium company specialising in rolled products and cans, created in 2005 as a spin-off from the Alcan-Pechiney merger. In July 2007, Rio Tinto started the process of buying up Alcan (which had just withdrawn from the Utkal project in Odisha), and in October 2007, Rusal with Sual staged a merger with Glencore, to become the world's largest aluminium company, producing 11 million tons of alumina per year and 4 million tons of aluminium. As for Nalco, it is contemplating its own foreign acquisitions through greenfield joint-ventures in Indonesia, Iran or South Africa.

The story of recent deals is very complex, and brings a shift in the balance of power. We are entering a new phase of monopoly control in the markets of every commodity. The boost in scale and importance of speculation involves electronic trading of trillions of dollars daily. What effects do hedge funds and futures trading have on the demand for aluminium?

Several big companies have established important places within the industry focused on *trading* and *speculating* more than on production, a trend Marc Rich ('Aluminium Finger') pioneered in Russia/Switzerland, with offshoots in Glencore and Xtrata. The emphasis on speculation and futures trading has shifted aluminium's profits, as in most other sectors of the economy, away from manufacture. In this process, access to the world's relatively unexploited bauxite deposits, such as Odisha's, assumes even more significance, making company-government deals a key factor at the London Metal Exchange and Stock Market. Profits from this speculation are made far away in London and other capitals, not in Odisha, and have played a hidden role in the derivatives bubble at the heart of the Recession.

Vedanta, as well as Hindalco, Tata and Mittal, all represent a new level of Indian corporate power. Indian companies' purchase of foreign mines and metal factories in Africa, Brazil, Armenia or Indonesia follow the pattern of colonial exploitation carved out by European firms.

In every deal there is a multitude of factors and power games. Aluminium company mergers and takeovers worldwide represent a new kind of monopoly or cartel. Changes also involve advances in technology, leading to an extraordinary new range of applications, as well as claims that environmental impacts are much less. Metals matrix composites (MMCs) fuse aluminium with alumina or silicon carbide (carborundum) for key components of lightweight aircraft and racing cars. Tetra Pak combines aluminium with oil/plastic derivatives for cartons and packaging. Car manufacturers increasing the aluminium percentage in vehicles argue that aluminium is greener than steel on the basis that lighter cars consume less oil and that their aluminium content has a smaller embodied energy (partly because a high percentage is recycled). As aluminium-rich satellites patrol the skies, nano-aluminium-particles of spent rocket fuel pollute the stratosphere.

Along with these changes, there has been an increasing shift of mining and metal manufacture away from Europe and the US to Third World countries and the Middle East.[25] The UK had 720,000 mineworkers in 1961, and now has less than 10,000. While Britain has closed down most of its coal and other mines since the 1980s—though it has opened several new, secretive and highly mechanised open-cast coal mines—it has been actively promoting the huge expansion of coal mines in India. Britain closed its last alumina refinery at Burntisland in 2002, and all over Europe refineries and smelters are closing. India is one of the few countries building new refineries. Several countries are building monster-size new smelters however, including Saudi Arabia and other countries in the Middle East, and Iceland, with more planned in Greenland and Trinidad.

While the UK under Thatcher started to close down many traditional manufacturing industries, it retained several smelters. Britain's most profitable industry—arms/aerospace—continues to consume huge quantities of the metal. It is significant here that India's former President, Abdul Kalam, who was a leading scientist in developing India's arms industry, envisages a key role for the aluminium industry, especially 'strategic' alloys of use in the arms industry, in India's transition from 'developing' to 'developed' nation status (Kalam and Rajan 1998).

So, whatever industries are being *outsourced* to 'developing countries', mining and metal production should head the list. This outsourcing consumes India's minerals and water at a ferocious pace, and lays heavy costs on people and environment. In Europe, the US and Japan, the tendency has been growing to shift the industry out. For Japan this trend started with smelters built in the 1970s–80s in Brazil, Venezuela and Indonesia, along with megadams, to save costs and avoid environmental criticism at home.[26]

But bauxite is the real wonder-mineral the aluminium industry depends on, and one thing that has not changed is that the price of bauxite is kept as low as possible. When Jamaica led the way to remedy this by setting up the International Bauxite Association (IBA) to get a better price for bauxite, the WB immediately withdrew loans, and the CIA orchestrated a campaign of destabilisation (Blum 2003). So what are Odisha's chances to insist on a high price for its bauxite? Meanwhile, doesn't the 'War on Terror' guarantee an aluminium demand for arms for years to come?

CHAPTER THREE

Konds and Khondalite

The Kalinga legacy

The threat to India's mountains, rivers, forests, fields and climate, and the threat to Adivasis, are basically one and the same. The mountains are threatened with a slow disembowelling. Bauxite mining is the biggest threat in south Odisha, but iron-ore and coal mining have a longer history and, along with chromite and manganese mines and steel plants, have already made a wasteland of large areas in north and central Odisha. An estimated 80 per cent of India's iron-ore is exported to China, much of it from Paradip port on Odisha's coast.[1]

Among more than thirty new steel plants in various stages of construction, two have attracted high-profile opposition. Resistance to Posco (Pohang Steel Company of South Korea) is led by betulvine farmers, who refuse to leave their fertile fields on the proposed factory site near Paradip; and by Pauri Bhuiya Adivasis, who live around the magnificent Khandadhara mountain in Sundargarh district, where a spectacular waterfall falls several hundred feet down a rock face striped bright red and black from copper and iron. As for the other, Tata's attempt to force-start construction of its steel plant on tribal land at Kalinganagar led to the killing of a policeman and thirteen tribal protestors on 2 January 2006.[2] These deaths became symbolic of Adivasi resistance to displacement.

Kalinganagar is named after the Kalinga people of ancient Odisha, who put up a determined resistance to conquest by Ashoka in the third century BC. India's recorded history virtually begins with this episode. In Ashoka's own words:

> 150,000 people were deported [enslaved], 100,000 were killed and many times that number perished.
> The beloved of the gods conciliates the forest tribes of his empire, but he warns them that he has power even in his remorse, and he asks them to repent, lest they be killed.
> All men are my children, and just as I desire for my children that they should obtain welfare and happiness both in this world and the next, the same do I desire for all men.[3]

Ashoka's edicts are inscribed on various rock faces throughout his empire and are India's first major inscriptions. Two are in Odisha: at Dhauli near Bhubaneswar, and on a remote rock formation at Jaugada on the Rushikulya river in Ganjam district. Ashoka's honesty and regret for the suffering he caused makes his inscriptions an exceptional record. Yet his threat to the forest tribes is unmistakable.

So naming a steel complex on tribal land 'Kalinganagar' is deeply ironic—an echo of the Mauryan invasion and genocide of the indigenous Kalinga people over 2,000 years ago. An estimated 3 million people have been displaced since 1951, about half of them Adivasis, and a quarter Dalits. Nearly all have suffered a massive drop in their quality of life.[4] Large-scale mining of mountains, depletion of rivers and forests, emissions from metal factories—the impact of all this on Adivasi society as well as on local climate is impossible to quantify, but exceedingly destructive.

Tribal and Hindu traditions in Odisha meet in a rich and complex web, blending Dravidian, Aryan and Munda languages and cultures. Jagannath 'Lord of the Universe', and patron deity of Odisha, encapsulates this blending of diverse traditions. His myth says he was stolen from the Sabara tribe, 'tribal priests' still serve him, and

Map 5: Odisha Districts

his unique wooden image links to the sacred post in the centre of every Kond village. Buddhist influence shows in the title *Jagannath*—a standard title of Buddha in Odisha before the Puri temple tradition crystallised in 1300–1450 AD. *Ekopado Bhairav*, a form of Shiva shown on Odisha temples (1000–1300 AD), is another source, along with Krishna—the human prince and charioteer transformed into an intimate and playful manifestation of God.[5]

The Kond language, Kui or Kubi, is of the Dravidian (South Indian) language family, related to Tamil and Telugu.[6] It is the original, indigenous language over a large area of central and south-west Odisha, where all the mountains and other natural features have Kui names. The fact that Khondalite is the geological term for the base rock of these mountains expresses the two-way connection between Konds and their mountains: the quality of this Khondalite-bauxite rock partakes in the nature and identity of Konds.

Konds' name for themselves is *Kuinga*. They were still living over large parts of south-east Odisha during the nineteenth century, where British gazetteers recorded their gradual displacement by Odia rajahs intent on expanding their territories and revenue.[7] Many factors suggest that the *Kuinga* are essentially the same people as the *Kalinga*, who were almost certainly Dravidian-speaking. In other words, Konds hold a special place in Odisha's cultural heritage, and Odia culture owes them a lot. Every *sahi* ('quarter' or street) in a west Odisha town has its own 'tribal' sense of community and kinship. A traditional Odia *sahi* consists of houses joined together in two opposite rows, and celebrates festivals as a close-knit community. This is a pattern taken directly from the Konds, whose village layout is almost always two rows of joined houses facing each other across a wide street.

Sacred mountains of Khondistan

The Konds' indigenous identity shows in the supreme importance of local mountains in their religion and mythology, compared with the mountains' minor significance to most Odias. Gopinath Mohanty—one of Odisha's most famous writers who wrote extensively on Odisha's tribal peoples and the exploitation they face—recorded an exchange he had with a Census official in 1941. Asking the standard question: 'What is your religion?' Konds answered: 'Mountains'. The official found this reply hilarious. His categories allowed for 'Animist', 'Hindu' or 'Christian'. 'Mountains' was not a religious category.[8]

The significance of the bauxite deposits capping Odisha's highest mountains was realised by a succession of British geologists. T. L. Walker made a survey in the first months of 1900, and named these mountains' base rock Khondalite after the Konds around Khandual Mali in Kalahandi. *'The tract from which certain graphite–garnet–sillimanite–quartz schists were named Khondalites by T. L. Walker'* (Fox 1932, p. 135). Walker (1902) introduced the Konds as

> hill men of the 3,000 foot plateau who are aborigines only very slightly influenced by the doctrines of the Hindoos who inhabit the low country. Though the Khonds are still regarded as wild tribes, they devote themselves to agriculture and to the collection of forest products, and ... seem to be little behind their Hindoo neighbours in civilisation ... The great moral virtue of the Khond is his truthfulness. ... The lightheartedness of childhood is characteristic of Khonds of all ages. (1902, p. 2)

As for the ancient mountains, with their special geology:

> Their distribution in Peninsular India so far as at present known is almost subject to the same boundaries as Khondistan or the country of the Khonds. Instead of the awkward descriptive name garnet-sillimanite-graphite schist, I propose to call these rocks Khondalite, in honour of those fine hill men the Khonds in whose mountain jungles Khondalite is better developed than in any region hitherto described. (p. 11)

He attested the exceptional abundance of fresh water coming down from these mountains, and the use which Konds made of it.

> The frequent occurrence of perennial springs of clear cool water from beneath these laterite caps has been mentioned by both Ball and Smith. A very good example occurs south of Korlapat, where in March, in the dry season, I noticed a tiny rill which dashed down the precipitous face of one of these hills, to be utilised to irrigate a second rice crop in the fields of the valley below.

This is a vital detail. Kond villagers in Kapsiput, who live below the mining area on Panchpat Mali mine have shown us the streams that have dried up, that used to be plentiful for growing several crops a year. One gave testimony (Das 2005):

> Our water sources are drying, because of mining. We cannot rotate our crops. I, Sri Lasu Jani, speaking on behalf of my community, say we are struggling to survive.

Geologists' (re-)discovery of these cappings started in 1966 (in the case of Panchpat Mali), and culminated in the East Coast Bauxite Project survey by the Geological Survey of India (GSI) in 1976–78.

The deposits surveyed in south Odisha and north Andhra are actually quite far from the coast—the name is an allurement to mining companies, conjuring plans for easy export. They were estimated at 1,600 million tons, and increased India's total classified deposits from 350 to over 3,000 millions tons (2008), placing India as the world's fourth richest country in bauxite, after Guinea, Australia and Brazil.[9] The Khondalite mountains in north Andhra Pradesh are even higher than those in Odisha (several over 5,000 feet), but their bauxite deposits are slightly smaller and more broken up, making them harder to mine than Odisha's *Malis*, which are more massive and regular.

The survey was carried out over eighteen months by 'a team of 52 Geologists, 28 Surveyors and 29 Drillers.' Open shafts and other signs of their drilling are visible on several mountain tops. The maps they made of the bauxite deposits on these summits form the basis of mining leases. Certain important mountains were excluded from the survey however, such as Gandhamardan and the mountains in Kandhamal district.

The East Coast Bauxite Survey (Rao and Raman 1979) was timed for a UNDP conference on bauxite ('laterisation processes') at Trivandrum (Kerala) in December 1979 (Venkatesh and Raman 1979). The survey results became essentially the property of the Orissa Mining Corporation (OMC), to sell to mining companies, and Nalco was set up in 1981 to exploit one of the largest deposits, on Panchpat Mali. The three districts where Odisha's bauxite was concentrated were Kalahandi, Bolangir and Koraput (i.e. south-west Odisha), which were soon termed the KBK districts, and have been earmarked for 'rapid development' and foreign aid since the

10-year plan inaugurated in 1986[10]—supposedly to eradicate their poverty, though the corporate agenda of exploiting the bauxite is clear. Certainly, the huge amounts of aid and loans 'invested' in the region since this time have been basically aimed at creating an infrastructure for aluminium.

Suffice it to say that the supposed aim of 'alleviating poverty' has not been achieved. On the contrary, people in this region face an acute level of poverty, especially around Nalco's operations at Panchpat Mali and Damanjodi.

The deposits cap the summits of a number of mountain ranges outstanding for their forest and wildlife, and form the source of at least four major river systems: Indravati has its source between Khandual and Bapla Malis, flowing south-west to join Godavari in Andhra, as do Kolab and other rivers from the Koraput mountains, including Deo Mali, Odisha's highest. Hati/Tel and Suktel rivers start from Krishun Mali and Gandhamardan, finally joining Mahanadi, Odisha's Great River.

Bansadhara forms directly out of Niyamgiri's threatened northwest ridge, and is soon joined by streams from the Kandhamal *Malis*. Nagavali has sources in Niyamgiri and Khandual, Siji and Kuturu Mali, and like Bansadhara flows south-east, entering the sea in Andhra.

Plans to mine all these mountains are moving fast in both states. All these bauxite cappings are outstanding for their purity.[11] Their mountain-top formation contrasts with the Weipa (Australia) and Jamaica deposits, which occur near sea level. The bauxite forms a layer averaging 30–100 feet thick, under topsoil and overburden of 3–15 feet. The low silicon content of Odisha's bauxite has allowed Nalco to refine it at a lower temperature, and therefore more cheaply, than bauxite from other parts of India—one of the main reasons why these mountains are such a magnet for the aluminium companies.

Soon after starting this book, we started a series of *padayatra* (foot-journeys) over Odisha's bauxite mountains, crossing over them and staying in villages, listening to people's stories to try to understand what it will mean if the aluminium industry takes over here. The first *padayatra* took us up Sasu-Bohu Mali (Mother-in-law Daughter-in-law Mountain) on the east side of the Kashipur plain, which had

Konds and Khondalite | 61

Mountains:
1. Anamini Parbat/ Kandhamal mountains
2. Niyamgiri
3. Khandual Mali
4. Krishun Mali
5. Siji Mali
6. Kuturu Mali
7. Sasu-Bohu Mali
8. Bapla Mali
9. Ghusuri Mali
10. Kodinga Mali
11. Panchpat Mali
12. Mali Parbat
13. Deo Mali
14. Chittamgondi
15. Galikonda & Raktakonda
16. Sapparla
17. Jerrela
18. Gudem.
19. Katamrajkonda

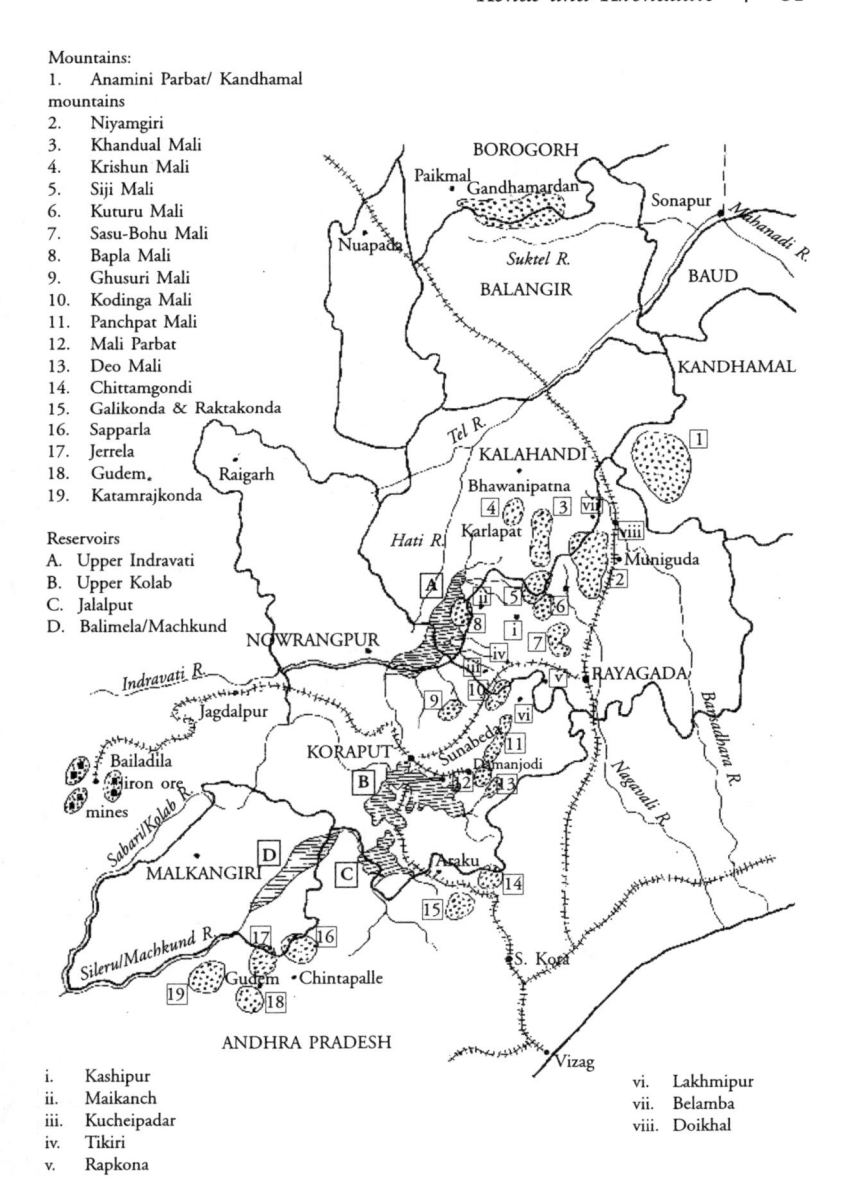

Reservoirs
A. Upper Indravati
B. Upper Kolab
C. Jalalput
D. Balimela/Machkund

i. Kashipur
ii. Maikanch
iii. Kucheipadar
iv. Tikiri
v. Rapkona
vi. Lakhmipur
vii. Belamba
viii. Doikhal

Map 6: Malis and Rivers of Odisha and Andhra

Mountain	District	Height (metres)	Bauxite deposit (million tons)
Gandhamardan	Borogorh–Bolangir		213
1. Anamini Parbat	Kandhamal	1,543	
2. Niyam Dongar	Rayagada	1,306 [1,515]	72
Passanga Mali			81
3. Khandual Mali	Kalahandi	1,060 [1,213]	165
4. Krishun Mali	Kalahandi	1,040	
5. Siji/Putuli Mali	Kalahandi–Rayagada	1,217	250
6. Kuturu Mali	Rayagada	1,228	
7. Sasu-Bohu Mali	Rayagada	1,150–1,205	119
8. Bapla Mali	Kalahandi–Rayagada	1,094	197
9. Kodinga Mali	Koraput–Rayagada	1,274	91
10. Ghusuri Mali	Koraput	1,161	
11. Panchpat Mali	Koraput	1,337	377
12. Mali Parbat	Koraput	1,500 [1,329]	
13. Deo Mali	Koraput	1,673	
Sirimanda Parbat	Koraput	1,415	69
'Pottangi'	Koraput	1,264	
14. Chittamgondi	Vishakhapatnam		
15. Galikonda & Raktakonda (Anantagiri)	Vishakhapatnam	1,543	240 with Sapparla
16. Sapparla group	Vishakhapatnam	1,246	
17. Jerrela group	Vishakhapatnam		
18. Gudem group	Vishakhapatnam	1,441	
19. Katamrajkonda	East Godavari / Khammam	1,360	

Table 1. Bauxite *malis*

been leased to Sterlite for bauxite mining.[12] Sumuni Jhoria, a woman leader in Siriguda village nearby, played a part in stopping this mine. Like the other bauxite *Mali*s, Sasu-Bohu has an extraordinarily flat and expansive summit, which stretches for about 5 km in a wide, horseshoe-shaped ridge. There are few trees on top, but the slopes on every side are well-wooded, with *sal* and other trees. Everywhere the rich reddish rock, overgrown with miniature date palms and *amla* bushes, gives the distinctive hollow ringing underfoot.[13] One or two households of Gauros (cowherds) live up here with their cattle. They make and sell the most delicious creamy *dohi* (yoghurt), and the dung of their cattle is said to fertilise not only the top of the mountain (which is cultivated in patches), but all the fields around it as well.

The top of all these *Mali*s is a wide expanse, with a characteristic landscape over the flattish hollow-sounding reddish rock. Woodland, shrubs and grasses stretch far and wide in every direction. All the summits are surrounded by small cliffs, and trees grow on the edges of these cliffs and the slopes below them.

Our next *padayatra*, with four English walkers in the winter of 2002–03, took us to Bapla Mali, whose bauxite deposit, estimated at 197 million tons, is the basis of the Utkal project. Here too, a number of Gauros keep their cattle and make *dohi*, on the top as well as the slopes, where there are several Pengo villages. The summit is a vast expanse, about 15 square kilometres, criss-crossed by many paths. There are several uncovered shafts left by geologists, next to piles of reddish bauxite, and ruined huts with *gendu phulo* (marigolds), where geologists lived during their survey.

Since then we have been up several of the other bauxite *Mali*s. Siji Mali, north of Kashipur, has two Kond villages on its summit, which grow rice, mustard, lentils and other crops. The slopes, and parts of the 3 km summit of this mountain, are well-forested. To the south-east is Kuturu Mali (or Tangiri Dongar), which also has a tribal village on top. These two mountains are assigned to a joint venture between Dubal (Dubai Aluminium) and the construction/arms company Larsen & Toubro. This company set up an office at Sunger, north of Kashipur, during the 1990s. Dramatic confrontations between people for and against the mining put those plans on hold, until L&T joined Dubal in November 2006 in talks with Orissa's

Chief Minister, where they drew up plans to build another refinery near Kalyan Singpur, just where several major tributaries join the Nagavali.

Further north, near Karlapat, is the long mountain range of Khandual Mali/Kelua Mali. Its summit is a rolling alternation of excellent *sal* forest and clearings, with occasional fields of mustard, millet and *olosi* (oilseed). Some years ago, surveyors from the Mining Exploration Corporation Limited (MECL) were driven away from this mountain by Kond villagers with guns. Khandual Mali is presently leased to Sulakshani Mines and Minerals, which represents leading local interests, who have been negotiating to sell the lease to a large foreign company. BHP Billiton expressed an interest back in September 2004. Since then it has made donations to the NGO Gram Vikas for constructing a mini-hydel project on a stream coming down from the mountain, to supply electricity to Karlapat and a few other villages.

Khandual Mali's fate is linked to that of Niyamgiri to the east, whose north-west ridge, Niyam Dongar, is under imminent threat as we write. We have been up this many times. It is one of the best-forested, with *sal* forests of great beauty on its long top and thick forests on its sides, where many springs gush forth—sources of the Bansadhara. Sterlite's literature and lawyers have misrepresented this summit as bare, or with only 'stunted forest' (2002), but leopards, tigers and elephants are known to come up here, though the hunting mafia has already taken a toll on these creatures. The reason Niyamgiri is the best-forested of Odisha's bauxite *Malis* is that it is the only mountain with its own special tribe, the Dongria Kond, who live only in the Niyamgiri range, and have preserved the forest on the mountain summits as sacred to Niyam Raja, Lord of the Law.

South of Kashipur, Kodinga Mali is assigned to Hindalco, which plans a refinery below at Kansariguda. Nearby, Deo Mali and Mali Parbat are at risk from Hindalco, Ashapura, Jindal and Nalco. In Andhra, the companies most advanced in their plans are Jindal, and Ras Aluminium-Khaimah (RAK), from the United Arab Emirates like Dubal. Jindal plans to mine Galikonda and Raktakonda, above the dramatic Borra Caves complex, while RAK has got clearance to mine the remote, well-forested Jerrela mountains.

Invading a highly-evolved ecology

Tribal society is still usually denigrated as 'primitive', when its reality is extremely sophisticated. When the East India Company extended colonial rule over India, Britons saw even mainstream Indian culture as primitive, because their own value system was a crude materialism geared to exploiting nature, and the technology of war. But India was not primitive. It was considerably more sophisticated than Europe in many areas of life, from manufacturing skills to a social diversity of very different cultures and religions that had coexisted for centuries. The trouble is that India today is in the grip of the same corporate materialism that drove Europeans to denigrate and devastate their own and other cultures.

Between the seventeenth and nineteenth centuries, Western Europe had killed off most of its indigenous tribes, and was already starting to commit one genocide after another in the New World of America and the Pacific. In India the conquest of tribal cultures was at least much slower, and the remoter tribes led an independent existence under the nominal rule of Hindu rajahs, who legitimised their rule by patronising the cult of tribal deities. Kautilya's *Arthashastra*—a treatise on 'wealth' that is actually a text on power and diplomacy—outlined a pattern of kings using the forest tribes in the mountains as buffer allies between kingdoms.[14]

So side by side with India's ancient policy of coexistence with the tribes is the colonial legacy of negative stereotypes—the tendency to denigrate them as 'primitive' or inferior. Colonial anthropologists defined them as primitive in every sphere of life. Unfortunately, this colonial attitude has persisted in modern India, partly through the writings of Western-trained sociologists, such as Ghurye, who saw the Scheduled Tribes as 'backward Hindus', quoting the most reactionary and closed-minded British colonials as authorities for the basic idea that tribal society is primitive on every front: religion as superstition, shifting cultivation as unsophisticated and destructive, sexual mores as backward and promiscuous. Ghurye's *Scheduled Tribes* (1943) is a classic statement of social evolutionism—the idea that society progresses in set stages, from 'primitive' to 'civilised/industrialised'. His prescription was 'assimilation', the US policy of that period towards native Americans. 'Backward Hindus' is a concept that empties tribal traditions of any intrinsic value, and justifies erasing them. Throughout America and Australia, assimilationist campaigns to 'detribalise' the natives regularly involved taking children away from their families.[15]

This takes us back to the concept of 'development'. One main input was the application of Darwin's 'evolution' to society, by Herbert Spencer and others—the paradigm of 'social evolutionism' which became dominant from the nineteenth century. The concept was poorly applied. In Darwin's paradigm, hundreds of species interact, each evolving in its own unique path in relation to other species. Applied to society, a single path, represented by industrialised Europe and America, was seen as right and inevitable, characterised by stages from 'primitive' to 'developed', and the forcible imposition of this path onto other societies through colonialism. Marx and Engels were among the nineteenth-century thinkers who propagated this paradigm of set stages.

As anthropologists became less primitive and colonial in outlook, they started to realise that tribal societies are highly developed and well-adapted to their environment, with profound knowledge of nature. Through anthropology's influence, the most open-minded thinkers today are waking up to the extraordinary wisdom and ecological awareness which the world's surviving tribal peoples embody. This is still a minority view, because on many fronts, tribal values are the direct opposite of mainstream values, and challenge everything we think we know (Mander 1991).

However, from the time when Columbus first met the Taino people in Haiti/Dominica, mainstream Western society's predominant attitude to tribal people was a contempt and prejudice that has often veered towards genocide. *'Their manners are decorous and gentle'*, Columbus wrote—and quickly captured 12,000 to sell as slaves back in Europe. Massacre and enslavement, aided by new diseases to which native Americans had no immunity, led to total genocide. Within 80 years a population of about 3 million who had developed a sophisticated indigenous civilisation on this island, had ceased to exist (Brown 1975).

Modern anthropologists and psychologists see forest peoples in the Amazon as extremely highly-developed in terms of their sense of community and respect for children. The *continuum concept* describes how children in a tribal village relate to the world around them as a continuum, with no books or TV to distract them from a continuity of awareness about everything in their environment: almost everything around them is part of nature, or something they learn to make from nature with their own hands and skills (Liedloff 1986).

Russell Means, as a modern leader of the Lakota or Sioux, who fought white settlers and soldiers invading their land during the 1850s-70s, rejects European paradigms of development and knowledge as based on greed and illusion, in stark contrast to the harmony with nature characteristic of indigenous cultures:

> There is another way. There is the traditional Lakota way, and the ways of the other American Indian peoples. It's the way that knows that humans do not have the right to degrade Mother Earth—that there are forces beyond anything the European Mind has conceived, that humans must be in harmony with all Relations, or the Relations will eventually eliminate the dis-harmony. A lopsided emphasis on humans by humans, the European arrogance of acting as though they were beyond the nature of all Related Things, can only result in a total dis-harmony, and a re-adjustment, which cuts arrogant humans down to size—gives them a taste of that reality beyond their grasp or control, and restores the harmony. There's no need for a revolutionary theory to bring this about. It's beyond human control. The Nature Peoples of this planet know this, and so they do not theorise about it. Theory is an abstract. Our knowledge is real. (1980/1982)

Indigenous people are *rooted* to the places where they live, and keep as true as they can to a traditional close relationship with their natural environment. This is often strained to breaking-point by mining companies. What is the ingrained prejudice and profit-oriented mindset that manipulates tribal people to get their land and resources, then devastates them in the name of development, blind to the sources of life?

A revealing glimpse into this mindset emerges in the first colonial writings on the Konds from the 1830s. A senior civil servant of the East India Company, the Honourable G. E. Russell, sent from

Madras to oversee the Ghumsur war and impose British rule over the Konds, advocated markets on the grounds that

> giving them new tastes and new wants will, in time, afford us the best hold we can have on their fidelity as subjects, by rendering them dependent upon us for what will, in time, become necessities of life.

As his superior, Lord Elphinstone, Lieutenant-Governor of the Madras government put it, *'with the extension of this commerce their wants will increase.'*[16] Belief in markets was as strong in 1830s as it is in the 2000s.

For Adivasis, as for Hindus, time and place are sacred, and the year is punctuated by a succession of festivals. Hindu festivals celebrate different deities and myths. As Adivasis relate more directly to nature, their festivals emphasise the seasons, the first fruits of various crops, the sacred hunt, the sowing of seeds, etc. Adivasi religion revolves around the spirits of nature, especially earth, streams and mountains, and does not depend on Brahmin priests as intermediaries. Many local Hindu deities in Odisha derive from Kond *penu*. The patron deity of Bissamcuttack is Ma Markoma, whose temple stands in a patch of forest just outside the town— basically a Kond goddess, to whom Konds and Hindus still sacrifice goats and cockerels. On the west side of town, facing Niyamgiri, is a temple dedicated to Niyam Raja.

Environmentalists largely support indigenous peoples' struggles to retain their land, recognising that they lead the most 'sustainable' of lifestyles. Environmentalist critiques of industry through scientific analysis have an essential counterpart in tribal cultures' systems of knowledge about the earth and nature—knowledge which is simultaneously practical and mystical. The mainstream, desacralised, view of nature is the antithesis of this, reducing everything to economic value, seeing the *sources* of life in terms of *resources*—water, forest, agricultural land and crops, as well as the minerals lying under the earth's surface. Not taking too much from nature, and wasting virtually nothing are at the heart of Adivasi culture (Padel 1998, Ramnath 2004).

The word 'sustainable' sustains extraordinary abuse nowadays. The tribal way of life is almost the only lifestyle that could be defined as really sustainable, and it has sustained ever since Ashoka's time. In business discourse, 'sustainable' has been narrowed to mean basically 'profitable', over a short time span, often just 20 years. What about the next 2,000?

The phrase 'sustainable mining' began to be used from 1999, when the world's biggest mining companies met to launch a project called Mining, Minerals and Sustainable Development (MMSD, part of their Global Mining Initiative), to see how the mining industry could 'contribute to the global transition to sustainable development'.[17] The long-term vision—how to plan to live sustainably in the long term—is completely absent from this corporate perspective. There is a pervasive blindness to the fact that our limited resources are being permanently destroyed for the sake of short-term gain—that 'current forms of extraction, and the trend for ever-increasing extraction and consumption of mineral products is totally unsustainable.'[18]

A Kond elder once asked us, '*Where are the saints in your society? In a village like this, we're all saints.*' His point is that making do with very little materially is the Adivasi norm, without excess or wastage. Most people still do not seek great wealth or power that would set them apart from the rest of their village, and still support themselves by their own labour, growing and making most of their own food and possessions—close to the self-sufficient village that Gandhi held up as an ideal. Odisha's tribes have a very strong egalitarian tradition of sharing, cooperative labour, and decisions reached through consensus—which frustrated colonial Britons who expected them to 'follow orders' through their appointed 'chiefs', just as corporate and political leaders today try to buy off or browbeat certain leaders to make them sign documents to let the companies in.

In terms of moral values, Adivasis see our non-tribal society as corrupt and degenerate. Projects for 'tribal development' are especially notorious for the creaming-off of 'PC'—local jargon for the Per-Centage regularly pocketed by most traders and officials involved (Sainath 1996).

It is still fashionable in India, as in the West, to dismiss respect for tribal peoples' culture and lifestyle as 'primitive romanticism'. This dismissal comes as much from the Left as the Right. A recent influential text on this theme is Archana Prasad's *Against Ecological*

Romanticism: Verrier Elwin and the Making of Anti-Modern Tribal Identity (2003), which engages barely at all with actual tribal people and their point of view. Yet the briefest scrutiny of the history of attitudes to tribal people in India, as well as worldwide, shows that the dominant attitude has never been to regard them as 'noble savages'. The romantic, idealised image was always only a fringe view that coexisted as an unreal inversion of the main attitude, which was to view tribal people as 'ignoble savages', 'primitive' in all aspects of their life (Meek 1976). Tribal knowledge is dismissed as 'ignorance', and those who denigrate them cultivate a missionary zeal to 'civilise' or 'develop' them, inherited from colonial times. Dismissing a positive view of tribal culture as 'ecological romanticism' serves to justify the ongoing dispossession of Adivasis, which is taking place throughout tribal areas of India on a vast scale. This dispossession is turning people whose cultural norms of sharing and equality are very close to the ideals of communism into an industrial labour-pool of near-slavery.

The Adivasi way of life contrasts with the more parasitic mainstream lifestyle in the towns, which culminates in conspicuous displays of wealth at marriages and festivals aimed at raising prestige. Few of the higher castes are willing to soil their hands with physical work. For Adivasis, hard physical labour is a fact of life, and a basis of self-respect. Making their own fields by clearing patches of earth, and sowing, weeding, harvesting them is the central activity of their lives.

Taboos in tribal culture often play a vital role in preventing over-exploitation of forest plants, guaranteeing the constant renewal of the forest. For example, a taboo on eating mangoes before the First Fruits Ritual helps some of the fruits to seed, and a taboo on cutting bamboo at certain times allows it to regenerate. Most of India's forests were protected in this way by traditional taboos far more effectively than by any Forest Department Regulations. The Dongrias' taboo on cutting trees on top of Niyamgiri is a classic example of restraint.

What are the taboos in our own society? Do we think we are free of taboos? In many circles, such as those of WB officials and their associates, exposing uncomfortable truths is taboo—'just not done'. For instance, when Dr Michael Irwin resigned from the WB in 1990 and wrote an article in the *Wall Street Journal*, in which he criticised the WB's 'bloated and overpaid bureaucracy, wasteful practices, poor management and unjustified arrogance', his colleagues were shocked, because 'never going public ... is like a blood oath here.' They wondered why he had, when he came from such a 'respectable background' (Caufield 1998, p. 188).

In other words, institutional life is full of taboos and norms of self-censorship that many people take for granted and are more or less unconscious of. But this unconsciousness extends to the nature and cost of things we use every day—and here we come back to aluminium and the lifestyle it feeds. A really sustainable lifestyle leaves a minimal ecological footprint. Most modern lifestyles have a heavy impact on the environment, and aluminium's footprint is particularly heavy.

Bauxite mining on top of the *Mali*s threatens the most basic of Adivasi values. All these mountains have their stories and myths, and are sacred entities for the people who live on and around them. One of Bapla Mali's songs goes

Nanaki Ichi Nana le	Sister O Little Sister
Nanaki Kaja Nana le	Sister O Elder Sister
Tirilo Miri Bandata	Shining Dew-drop Pool
Tumbaya Guri Manunde [19]	The fickle sisters became mountains

In a myth of Bapla Mali, from a village now separated from the mountain by the expanse of Indravati's reservoir:

> A younger sister and an elder sister go to bathe at night in the moonlight. Their father warns them not to get enchanted by the silver reflection of the moonshine. They stay ages there, playing in the beautiful moonlit water, not heeding the shrill warning cries of the bats (*bapla* in Kubi). Until finally they turned into the mountains we call Baplamali, Elder Sister, and Palangamali, Younger Sister. Oh beloved Baplamali, we worship you, for the mini date palms and the wild grass you grow.

CHAPTER FOUR

Bauxite Business in Odisha

Aluminium dams

The histories of aluminium and dam construction go hand in glove; linked from birth. Supplying electricity and water to aluminium factories has been a principal reason for big dams, from the first wave of those built in Europe and north America in the early twentieth century to a massive, controversial Bechtel dam project built recently in Iceland to power a new Alcoa smelter.[1] Plans to mine Odisha's mountain tops and refine their bauxite into alumina and 'reduce' or smelt this into aluminium, are formed alongside plans to provide electrical power and water to these refineries and smelters.

In this chapter we introduce four stories about the early days of aluminium companies and dam-builders in different parts of Odisha, highlighting the effects on Adivasis. They show an undeclared, perhaps unconscious, policy of driving tribal people off their land. A 'Highland Clearance' is going on, removing tribal people from their land, using the same justificiation given in Scotland 200 years ago: the idea that these peoples' lifestyle is 'backward' and that their land should be made more profitable.[2]

Smelters, we have seen, require exceptionally large amounts of electricity to split aluminium from its strong bonding with oxygen. Smelting one ton of aluminium consumes 13,500 kilowatt hours of electricity and emits an average 13.1 tons of carbon dioxide, while refining a ton of alumina demands 250 kWh. A smelter's carbon emissions go down to 5.6 tons of CO_2 if it is hydropowered from dams; and up to 20.6 tons if it is all powered by coal.[3] It would be hard to calculate how much electricity Odisha's aluminium plants get from hydropower, since each has its own 'captive' coal-fired power plant (ccpp), to supplement hydropower from Odisha's grid. A smelter cannot afford any variation or stops in supply of electric current to its precious pots, while each dam's output varies with the seasons. At least 60 per cent of the electricity generated in Odisha goes into metal factories. Worldwide, at least 55 per cent of smelters' electricity comes from dams.[4]

Dams supply not just electricity, but also water. According to the Wuppertal Institute, one of the world's most reputable resource study centres in Germany, producing a ton of steel demands 44 tons of water, while a ton of aluminium consumes a staggering 1,378 tons of water.[5]

Gitlitz's report for the International Rivers Network, *The Relationship between Primary Aluminium Production and the Damming of the World's Rivers* (1993) makes the dam–smelter connection clear, and spells out some of the enormous subsidies in the price of electricity which aluminium plants invariably receive from dams. Electricity is the highest cost in producing aluminium, generally 21–30 per cent of the total.[6] Energy supply is the great variable for aluminium companies, which is why they aggressively pursue the cheapest possible costs through subsidies and hydropower. Getting a country to build a dam and supply low-cost hydropower for aluminium plants is an old strategy now.

With some of the world's biggest dams, it was never in question that their primary aim was to power aluminium smelters. This is true of Ghana's Akosombo, which displaced about 80,000 people, and Brazil's Tucurui, which supplies two smelters, and displaced about

30,000—all seven of Brazil's smelters use hydro. A similar situation exists in Venezuela where a number of vast dams on the Caroni River supply several smelters.[7] Among numerous other examples are Suriname's Afobaka, Indonesia's Asahan dam and smelter project, New Zealand's Mannapouri Lake dam for its Bluff smelter, several of the biggest dams in Canada and the US, recent dams in Iceland, and plans (so far defeated) to dam several of Chile's 'wild rivers' in the south.

In other cases, the connection is clear, but not spelt out. The Aswan dam turned the Egyptian Nile into a series of canals, creating Lake Nasser, which displaced over 100,000 indigenous Nubian people. Its hydropower supplies the whole country, but a steady 15 per cent of its output goes to the Nag Hammady smelter. The Three Gorges dams in China were almost certainly driven partly by plans for several aluminium smelters. Dams supply thirteen out of sixteen smelters in the former Soviet Union (2006). Similar dam-smelter complexes have been set up in recent decades in several other countries.

Some of India's biggest dams were built for aluminium: Koyna was planned in the 1920s for the hydropower it would give a refinery-smelter complex that was never built. In Tamil Nadu, Malco's refinery-smelter complex draws from the older Mettur dam. Rihand dam was built for Hindalco's refinery-smelter complex at Renukoot (UP), by a US-led consortium, and the big subsidy this company received on its electricity price was a scandal exposed in Parliament by the socialist MP Lohia, during Nehru's time.

The aluminium motive is clear in Odisha's dams but not spelt out (except in Fox 1923, 1932). Was Hirakud dam constructed primarily to supply the smelter Indal built beside it soon after? Was Rengali built to supply Nalco's smelter nearby at Angul? Was Upper Kolab built for Nalco's Damanjodi refinery? And were the Upper Indravati dams funded by WB loans with aluminium plants in mind? Pipes laid while we wrote this book, from the Tel river to Lanjigarh, take Upper Indravati water to Vedanta's refinery.

The mining and metals industry is obviously a key driver for big dams, and a lion's share of hydropower goes to metal factories and other heavy industries in India and worldwide.[8] Approximately 25 per cent of India's electrical power comes from dams.[9] The Central

Electrical Authority calculates India's total hydro-potential at 84,000 MW, of which 70 per cent is not being utilised, which is why the Planning Commission in August 1998 decided that 92 per cent of the total potential must be in use by 2025, setting a faster pace for 'hydro-development' (i.e. dam building), since non-renewable fossil fuels are being used up fast, and hydropower is, amazingly, still seen as *clean energy*, while dams 'help in opening up avenues for the development of remote and backward areas'.

This cleanness, and the wisdom of 'opening up' these areas, are highly questionable, as we shall see. The India Report for the World Commission on Dams (WCD) spells out numerous problems. India had built over 3,000 big dams by 1996, with another 695 under construction. Problems include costs multiplying and many technical problems of rapid siltation, etc., that lead to under-performance. But a basic fault in methodology is that Cost Benefit Analysis invariably minimises social and environmental costs. Evidently these figure small in the minds of those bureaucrats and engineers who make the calculations and take the decisions.

The dams' heaviest cost falls on the thousands of people they displace. These are never consulted or given any choice about moving. Displacement invariably causes great trauma and a massive drop in people's standard of living. Only since the 1990s have Public Hearings been required, and these are rarely free and fair.

As for effects on nature, even Environment Impact Assessments (EIAs) have only been required since 1978, and many of these are of a very poor standard. Flooded forest decomposes, creating methane, one of the main greenhouse gases. What survives around a reservoir is invariably depleted fast, first by those constructing the dams, then by people displaced and struggling to survive, and by loggers using the new access roads. Water quality drops dramatically from lying stagnant instead of getting oxygenated by constant movement in complex currents. This deadness in the water kills off large populations of fish and other life-forms which lived in the river. Siltation is frequently twice as fast as estimated, and large areas get overgrown with algae and weeds. Mosquitos breed, spreading malaria and other diseases. The difference between 'living water' and stagnant, 'dead water' is an aspect too little studied.[10] What does it mean for the health of a region's water, to dam the circulation of rivers over the land?

Despite the dangers in big dams, the ideology promoting them is still extremely strong. ICOLD (International Commission On Large Dams) is the international lobby group for dam constructing companies. It has ensured that the momentum for constructing new dams remains strong, and counters the steadily growing opposition to dams worldwide effectively, through PR, painting a gloss of respectability over the deals being made for new dam contracts. It estimates that the world's 45,000 big dams have improved living standards—ignoring or denying large chunks of evidence to the contrary. The International Aluminium Institute (IAI) in London also lobbies on behalf of dams. For instance, in 2006,

> The IAI Board ... agreed on continuing lobbying efforts aimed at both governments and international organisations to make sure that the option of future hydropower projects was not prejudiced.[11]

So knowledge about dams' destructive impacts on eco-systems and traditional communities worldwide has not stopped the flow of new projects, even though strong campaigns have managed to prevent certain dams: Silent Valley was saved in Kerala in the 1960s, while a worldwide campaign to stop the Ilisu dam on the Tigris in Turkey, which threatens Kurds with cultural genocide, has been successful so far.

The campaign against the Sardar Sarovar dam on the Narmada showed how easily a belief in a dam's benefits can be made a popular issue. The Morse Report (1992), an independent review for the WB, showed very clearly the disastrous impacts that the Narmada dams would have on tribal people and the environment. Alongside this, it showed that the authorities in charge of the project had avoided making any accurate assessment on social, environmental and many technical impacts. Yet the courts gave clearance to the projects, despite failure to provide legally required studies. Dams are symbols of progress, modernity, and humans' technological power, and the movement to build this dam was unstoppable.

Present plans for rapid further industrialisation in Odisha and neighbouring states involve a number of huge new dams, even though Odisha's rivers have already been dammed more than enough. There were 131 big dams in Odisha in 2000, with another 18 under construction. Present plans are part of a massive 'Interlinking of Rivers' project. The Indravati dams are an example of one river being diverted into another. A Lower Suktel dam which the authorities are pushing to construct in Bolangir district is likely to be geared to supplying a refinery near Gandhamardan, and a likely purpose of the massive Polavaram dam planned on the Godavari is to supply the refinery-smelter complex which Jindal plans near Vizag.

In India, the relevant authorities have avoided even looking at the evidence against big dams, refusing to engage with the World Commission on Dams (WCD).[12] The WCD was funded by the WB and UN, and it takes the central ground, in the sense that it goes into the negative impact of dams, juxtaposed with the arguments for dams. The vice-chair was Lakshmi Chand Jain of India's Industry Development Services. So it is a conservative report, though in the India case study, it does include critical material.[13] Arundhati Roy's critique goes much further (1999), though neither highlight dams' connections with metal factories.

Those for and against dams are divided by different mindsets. For one group, economics is all-important, for the other the environment and people are what matter. But why won't the government engage with the overwhelming evidence of dams' dangers? The answer lies in vested interests, and the thirst for aluminium.

The Hirakud dam and Indal

Bauxite business started in Odisha with a huge aluminium smelter built at Hirakud in 1950–56 by Indal in collaboration with Alcan, its parent company. Its supply is from bauxite mined and refined at Lohardaga and Muri, north of Odisha in what is now Jharkhand. It was built next to the Hirakud dam on the Mahanadi ('Great River').

The history of this dam begins a dark chapter of Odisha's history, of forced displacement, repressing resistance, and environmental degradation on a massive scale. It was planned before Independence, and after Odisha's last British Governor laid a foundation stone, Nehru himself laid another on 12 April 1948, while the State's 'Gandhian' Chief Minister, Nobokrishna Choudhury, promoted the Hirakud project in a speech in the Orissa Assembly on 13 March 1950, promising the dam would inaugurate an era when every person in the state would reap the benefits of development (Viegas 1992).

But the dam faced resistance, and in the mid-1950s, two Tehsildars were murdered by villagers outraged at facing the loss of their homes and land with no proper compensation. Between April and May 1955 the police staged flag marches in disaffected villages—a British-era exercise in intimidation still in use. The next year, when the dam was completed and the water submerged an estimated 285 villages, anger over the massive scale of displacement became the cause of Nobokrishna's resignation.[14]

Estimates on how many people this dam displaced have ranged from 110,000 to 180,000. Over half these people were Adivasis.[15] The reservoir flooded about 180,000 acres of good agricultural and forest land. Its water is said to irrigate an area of up to 400,000 acres through canals, out of 800,000 planned. These irrigated areas, in Borogorh and Sambalpur districts, are mainly non-tribal lands where rice is intensively cultivated as a cash crop. The dam was built to generate 270 MW of electricity (its 'installed capacity'), but generates only 120.

Apart from irrigation and electricity, its other stated benefit, flood control, has failed conspicuously several times during heavy rains, when huge amounts of water have been released suddenly, causing widespread destruction and many deaths. In 1980 a sudden release of water drowned at least 200 people and caused a million to flee their homes. The cyclone of October 1999 caused another disaster, and floods from excessive rain in 2008 displaced over 100,000 people.

Indal's smelter became one of the biggest customers for the dam's hydropower. The consensus is that electricity supply for the Alcan-Indal smelter was a prime reason for constructing this dam in the first place. The smelter supplemented this hydropower by building its own captive coal-fired power station (ccpp), presumably to ensure a steady supply and cheap cost; also perhaps because of a decrease in the dam's generating capacity due to rapid siltation. The smelter also doubled its production from 195 to 400 pot-furnaces while we wrote this book, against strong local opposition.

So Hirakud was Odisha's first and clearest dam-smelter complex. As McCully comments, a major reason for the building of megadams—though often a relatively hidden one—has been to supply power to aluminium smelters, fuelled by 'the belief that a dam–smelter complex will spark off the rapid industrialisation of a region' (1998, p. 282).

Alcan set up Indal (then the Aluminium Company of India) as its Indian subsidiary during the Second World War, when demand for aluminium increased enormously to supply Britain's arms industry. Alcan–Indal started the Muri refinery on the Subarnarekha River in the early 1940s, which processed bauxite mined to the west, beyond Ranchi, at Lohardaga. Muri is India's oldest refinery. We visited it in 2002, and saw how, despite an ISO 14001 (International Standards Organisation) classification, its toxic red mud lake seeps down onto grazing land. A rail link carries Muri's alumina to Hirakud, where Indal also built an aluminium coil factory, and has captive coal fields nearby at Talabira to supply its power station.

Like all smelters, Hirakud emits huge quantities of toxic waste into the air and water. Locally one of the worst impacts is in fluoride contamination of surrounding villages, where crops, cattle and people suffer from wasting diseases. Although a medical survey has been made, Indal has not allowed its publication. At present a local movement based near Sambalpur and Hirakud is campaigning to stop the smelter's further expansion, on the grounds that it is already causing a lot of contamination and ill health locally. In the words of Santosh Telenga, a farmer near Hirakud:

> All the vegetation around this smelter is sick, because of the fluoride emission during the south-west monsoon. Even the leaves of date palm and drum-stick plants can't withstand it. I have been living in this area for the last 40 years and can assure you of this even if the experts say otherwise. The health and agriculture department know all this. Sometimes the scientists visit us and don't do anything about it. They provide medicine but our suffering escalates. The company is also smelting aluminium with open pot door to cut costs. We think because of this we are exposed to the fluoride pollution more than the permissible level.

This is nothing compared to the way they truck in and dump fly ash in our area. Go and see how they carry it in trucks and you can see dust flying everywhere, destroying the few ponds and wells we have left, where we bathe and drink. (Das 2005, Pani 2008)

The reservoir's capacity has diminished from siltation, and water levels along the reservoir's two main canals have declined dramatically. A recent refurbishment, financed through the DFID since 2005, is geared to supplying water not for farmers, but to a series of new factories, including the Bhushan steel plant, and two huge new aluminium smelters, for Vedanta and Hindalco. This has led to major protests by west Odisha farmers, already affected by water scarcity in the canals. On 20 October 2006, 18,000 people linked hands in a line 22 kilometres long around the reservoir, demonstrating their opposition to these factories. A government report by the Jayasaleem Committee submitted on 21 September 2007 alleged that the diversion of Hirakud water to industries will not affect agriculture and irrigation—in a context where it is increasingly clear that even the few factories taking Hirakud water are causing the canals to run dry. Farmers in Sambalpur district passed a resolution during a protest on 26 September, which said

> while the storage capacity of the dam has declined due to siltation, diversion of water to Bhusan Limited will deprive 20,000 acres of irrigation. Under the circumstances, the government should consider the report of earlier committees which clearly said that diversion of water would affect irrigation and power generation.[16]

At another huge rally in November 2007, farmers demanded the cancelling of plans to give Hirakud water to the two new smelters and Bhushan. Police lathicharged this protest—a political embarrassment, after which Naveen Patnaik invited the movement's leaders for a meeting, where he admitted he had been misadvised. He promised publicly that Hirakud's water would go to farmers, though experts say if all the deals signed for supplying metal factories go through, the water reaching farmland through the canals will diminish hugely. Odisha is classed as a water-rich state, but the dams and metal factories threaten to reduce this water-wealth rapidly.[17]

Nalco and the Kolab dam

When Nalco's aluminium complex was being set up in Odisha during the early 1980s, an article in a leading intellectual weekly journal commented that to understand its effects, one must comprehend 'the past, not very pleasant, history of the Indian aluminium industry'. Another gave a range of economic arguments against setting up Nalco—in particular the low price for bauxite enforced by external pressures (i.e. the aluminium cartel), plus excessive consumption of electricity and water, and excessive pollution.[18]

As we saw in the previous chapter, Panchpat Mali (Five-shrine Mountain) was the biggest bauxite deposit found in the 1970s survey of Odisha and Andhra mountains (Rao and Raman 1979). It was given as 300 million tons, covering 16 sq km on a 21 km ridge. To mine and process this ore, a new state-sector company was formed: the National aluminium company, or Nalco.

So Panchpat Mali, about 35 km east of Koraput town, was Odisha's first bauxite mine—the only major one so far (2009), on the central section of the mountain. It is by far India's biggest bauxite mine—a heavily mechanised operation on a huge scale. About 164,000 tons a day is mined. In the 1980s the yearly average was 2.4 million tons per year. This has increased to 6 million tons per year, nearly half India's annual output. About 400 people work the mine. The main extraction is done by about 70 'dozer-rippers' and trucks. The work-force is divided into unskilled, semi-skilled and skilled. A notice at the mine entrance lists the daily wage for each—between 55 and 117 rupees. Like most bauxite mines, it is open-cast. The mined-out area on top of the mountain stretches far already. It is 're-landscaped', which means putting the overburden and topsoil back and planting trees, but most of these are eucalyptus, and large areas are sterile pits. The building where the bauxite is placed onto the conveyor belt is tall and vast.

At the foot of the mountain, several Kond villages including Kapsiput and Gortili receive the full impact of noise and waste. In the words of a villager from Kapsiput, who walks up the mountain most days to labour in the mine:

There's no grazing land for our cattle, and the dust after the blasting settles everywhere near our villages. Vehicles have fallen off the side of the mountain onto our villages. We have written applications to the authorities three or four times. Still they don't care.

The collector invited a few elders of our community and then abused them by calling them goats, sheep, bloody fools and they were beaten by the security forces. We had to run away from there.

The police told us before not to come with arms, otherwise it would have turned violent. Still they charged and fired gas on us. 70 of us had false cases made against us. 15 of us still have court cases pending against us for the last five years. They don't listen or give us any job.

Our water sources are drying, because of mining. We are unable to rotate our crops. I, Sri Lasu Jani, speaking on behalf of my community, say that we are struggling to survive. Not only us, many villages around the mine are struggling too. Nalco promised us to give us all facilities around a radius of 10 km, but nothing has happened. They promised us medical help, and this also has not happened. Nalco is doing us a grave injustice. (Das 2005)

A conveyor belt 14.6 km long carries the bauxite from mine to Damanjodi refinery, which started in 1985—'the largest alumina refinery in Asia'.

This refinery displaced at least 3,000 people from nineteen villages, who lost the land they supported themselves from.[19] Amlabadi is the 'model resettlement village', near the factory. It is painted in bright colours, but the people there live under the stress of considerable work insecurity, and many attest that they have to beg and give bribes to get even the toughest labouring job in mine or factory. In Chapter Thirteen, we shall hear from a young woman who was a schoolgirl when her village was among those destroyed. She remembers her childhood there as a time of hard work growing vegetables and herding cattle, but also beauty and joy, gone forever. Nobody starved then. Now, in Amlabadi, they do—testimony supported by studies showing extreme levels of poverty around Damanjodi.[20]

Many people failed to receive any compensation for land they lost, or land that has since been polluted. That around Damanjodi and Panchpat Mali is now seriously polluted over large areas, due to the bauxite dust and toxic red mud as well as factory smoke.

Vijay Muduli, a local leader in the town, describes the pollution and drying up of water sources in the area:

> It is acidic water falling here. Cattle drink it, our tribal and Dalit people also use it. They see their cattle dying. Those who fall in it get their skins peeled off. We have been telling Nalco about it, only to get the reply, "Why did you take the cattle there? It is acid water." Not a single frog or fish is living in it. On that mountain the villagers of Runjangi, Champapadar and Khariguda live on these water sources.

The road up to the mine caused a landslide over land in the village of Bhitara Bhejaput. Yet the blasted surfaces of rock on one side of it are inscribed with inspiring words:

ONE EARTH—PROTECT IT … GREEN MINES …
SAFETY FIRST—PRODUCTION MUST …

The old owners of Panchpat Mali were the Bahinipati family (now settled at Amlabadi), who show a copper plate granting them 3,900 acres on it by the Maharaja of Jeypore in the eighteenth or nineteenth century. They say they received no compensation from Nalco, and for the last twenty years have taken on the task to try and get the compensation that was promised to other villagers as well as themselves, without success.

In Damanjodi and Amlabadi, noise pollution affects everyone when the machinery is overhauled for several hours each day and night. The refinery employs a workforce of about 3,000. There have been at least 200 deaths from work-related accidents since its construction began in 1982, as well as many unacknowledged and poorly treated cases of industrial disease.

Construction of the Upper Kolab dam started in 1976, and continued till 1992, when it started to generate electricity. It was built by the Central Water and Power Commission (CWPC), which had also built Hirakud. Lobbying from the electricity sector and industrialists played a decisive role in the decision to build it, and Damanjodi refinery is among its main customers.

The dam formed a vast, irregular-shaped reservoir, flooding valleys between hills now bare and badly eroded. It displaced at least 14,000 people from sixty or more villages, between 1984 and

1990, as the water level rose. Estimates vary wildly. As with most dams, the administration has not kept a proper count. Most 'oustees' now live in poverty-stricken rehabilitation villages, or had to resettle themselves. Of 3,171 families officially recognised as displaced, 528 resettled in new colonies, while 2,643 accepted cash and resettled by themselves.[21]

> The neglect of social and environmental costs, projecting the interests of powerful groups as the national interest and the belief of planners that it is obvious that some people will have to make the sacrifices for the nation, do not provide an integrated strategy to redress the problems of affected people....
>
> The displaced people ... sacrifice their home, land and sources of livelihood, but do not benefit from the project either in terms of irrigation, electricity or employment....
>
> The objective of the Upper Kolab Project was fast economic growth.... It was planned that the dams would be multi-purpose projects aimed at providing irrigation and low-cost power. The latter, it was expected, would help in the establishment and expansion of electrometallurgical industries in the state and provide irrigation in the Koraput district. (Jojo 2002, pp. 83–84, 90, 92)

This dam formed part of a plan to increase Odisha's electricity generation by 15 per cent per year, for internal use (over 50 per cent of which has gone to industry), as well as 'inter-state transfer of power' (Odisha's power stations selling electricity to neighbouring states).

Of Odisha's megadams, Machkund (on a tributary of the Kolab) and Hirakud were built first in the 1940s–50s, Balimela (which displaced at least 60,000 people) in the 1960s, and Rengali in the 1970s. Protracted protests made the government offer slightly better resettlement terms at Rengali. But 'universally, the implementation of R&R is always poor', and the improved terms were not applied in the Kolab project. Upper Kolab, like Rengali and the other dams, showed *'an over-estimation of benefits and an under-estimation of the project cost'* (Jojo 2002, pp. 83, 96 and 104). By 1994, only 30 per cent of the planned electricity was being generated, and irrigation had not started, while the cost was six times more than the original estimate.

In other words, almost the only benefits went to industry, especially the Damanjodi plant, and to the various construction companies employed, including Bharat Heavy Electricals, which made the turbines. The money to build it was loaned by the Overseas Economic Cooperation Fund of Japan (3,769 million yen), and one may assume that foreign engineering and construction companies won some of the best-paid contracts, as has happened with India's other big dams.

Also during these years, a new railway line was built from Koraput to Damanjodi (1986), then on to Rayagada, in order to carry Damanjodi's alumina to the smelter which Nalco was building at Angul in central Odisha, as well as for export via the port of Vishakhapatnam (Vizag, see maps). This railway snakes high through the bauxite mountains, with stations at convenient places for future mines and factories. Several long Nalco trains of sealed wagons transport alumina along this line from Damanjodi to Angul and Vizag every day.

Building the smelter at Angul involved a history of intimidation and displacement that has barely been told, including a desperate act of resistance, when one Bholeswar Sethi stabbed to death the ADM Gopabandhu Pattnaik (Additional District Magistrate), as he was addressing a crowd on 23 December 1987.[22] Officially, 4,000 families were displaced from 40 villages. The smelter started producing aluminium in 1987. Like Damanjodi refinery, it has its own coal-fired power station, but also draws power and water from a dam, in this case Rengali, one of Odisha's biggest, which, again, may well have been built to supply the smelter. Agitation against this dam between 1972 and 1978 was ruthlessly suppressed. Were people displaced by Rengali really given 'better R&R'? By the time the reservoir was finished in 1985, it had displaced between 225 and 287 villages.[23]

Just days after the Maikanch firing, on 31 December 2000, there was a huge spill of toxic chemical waste from Angul smelter power station's second ashpond. Part of the dam wall containing the slurry cracked, and the waste spread over thousands of acres, causing a toxic flash flood in the Nandira and Brahmani rivers, damaging land and buildings in 10–20 villages. Several people died of gastro-entiritis or from immersion in the toxic water, a number of homes were destroyed, and at least 300 animals were swept away.[24] Nalco paid government-agreed compensation, as it had when the ashponds flooded during the cyclone in October 1999. On that occasion it paid 4 crore rupees to 11 villages, and installed piped water for them.

Like the Hirakud smelter, Angul causes regular pollution to nearby rivers and surrounding villages, apart from these serious spills. National TV news on 13 September 2004 reported fluoride contamination over 500 acres of fields, making the crop unfit for consumption, and interviewed villagers, who spoke furiously of not getting medication for their bone disease because Nalco officially denies this exists, and because people hate the indignity of begging for compensation like slaves. As an old woman said,

> We've been suffering so much for ten years. Why can't they close this factory and leave? We can't go on begging them for compensation!

Nalco officials were shown refusing to be interviewed, speeding away in their air-conditioned cars. The same programme announced Nalco's huge increase in production to 6 million tons of bauxite, and expansion of the Angul smelter.

Inhabitants of nearby villages, as well as their few remaining cattle, show severe signs of skeletal fluoridosis—a wasting disease from fluoride poisoning. Basically, acid rain from the smelter pollutes their water. A medical survey was conducted of the 41 affected villages in 1992, but the results of this have never been made public. It is well-documented that aluminium smelters cause serious fluoride pollution through smoke emissions. The smelter at Anglesey in Wales has a similar history of fluoride poisoning on people and livestock in the vicinity, and a medical study carried out around 1980 was withheld from publication. A study by Nalco showed that fluoride is 'endemic' in the Angul area, but was slanted to make it seem as if the fluoride is naturally endemic, while studies that have been suppressed show it has become endemic only since the smelter started up.

Visiting Gadarkhari village, just beside the smelter in October 2002, and seeing the wasted bodies of people and cattle, the symptoms of skeletal fluoridosis were clearly visible. Its cattle population declined from 3,000 to just 100 in the smelter's first ten years. Those that remain look like skeletons. The Nandira and Brahmani rivers near the smelter, into which its effluents run, are seriously polluted. All fish have died in them for a stretch of at least 30 km.[25]

From 1992–95 the smelter's pollution of the rivers was exposed by the Norwegian government aid organisation, Norad, until a Norwegian firm supplied new, 'green' technology for treating the effluent. This improved the pollution only marginally, but Norad funds ceased, which left local activists suspicious of its motives. A team from the Supreme Court Monitoring Committee on Hazardous Wastes visited Nalco's smelter on 6–9 June 2006. Its report lists numerous violations of pollution levels and confirms that fluoride and other emissions into air and water remain unacceptably high, while Spent Pot Lining (SPL) is not being properly disposed of.[26]

In mid-2002 there was an outcry in Odisha at the proposed privatisation of Nalco, which is considered one of Odisha's key achievements in industry, as well as its most profitable PSU (Public Sector Undertaking). Reportedly, Nalco was about to be sold at far too low a price, as had happened with Balco's privatisation in March 2001. On 28 October 2002, Nalco workers at the Angul smelter prevented Hindalco representatives from visiting the plant. Most of the world's leading aluminium companies were among the 15 bidders in 2002, with Hindalco the frontrunner. Under pressure from workers and trade unionists, as well as popular pressure to save '*the pride of Orissa*', Chief Minister Naveen Patnaik eventually opposed the privatisation plan at the end of 2003—though when he was the Union Mining Minister back in the late 1990s, in a BJP-led alliance, Naveen was instrumental in privatising an initial 12.85 per cent stake in Nalco, and had proposed privatising 20 per cent.[27]

The company has sold an increasing amount of its aluminium abroad. In 1998–99 export sales amounted to 37.69 per cent of its earnings. In 2000–01 this rose to 51.25 per cent. The company wrote a cheque to the Government of India for Rs 224,60,00,000 as its dividend for 2001–02 ('62.75 per cent of its after-tax profit').[28] Critics ask why the government should sell off such a profitable concern, and see the influence of foreign pressure, orchestrated by the WB and DFID, to privatise and open the door to 'foreign direct investment'. A committee of Nalco employees wrote a revealing letter to the CM in July 2003 that helped persuade Naveen to back away from privatisation. Nalco's township for employees at Angul ensures considerable loyalty from workers, who know their job security would vanish with privatisation. So these plans have been shelved for the moment, though Nalco staff live in fear of its sudden re-emergence.

Recent expansion of Nalco's bauxite mine was done in partnership with an American firm, Alumina Technology Associates. Nalco alumina production was boosted from 800,000 to 1,575,000 tons per year; and the aluminium from 230,000 to 350,000 tons per year, making Nalco the largest alumina producer in Asia.

Nalco was started as a joint venture with a foreign company, Pechiney (recently merged with Alcan), and the Damanjodi and Angul plants used Pechiney technology, in 'a flag project of Indo-French cooperation'. How much of Nalco's actual profit disappeared abroad?[29]

A number of other projects and factories are connected with Damanjodi, apart from the dam and railway. At Sunabeda, Hindustan Aeronautics Ltd. (HAL) set up a factory for MiG fighter planes in the 1960s, which presumably uses some of Damanjodi's alumina, or alloys from IMFA's (Indian Metal Ferro-Alloys) ferro-manganese factory at Therubali (near Rayagada). The HAL factory displaced many tribal villagers, starting in 1968, when over 400 Gadaba and Paraja families in Chikapur village, suffered a sudden, forcible evacuation one rainy night. They were told they'd all be given a house and a job. No one got a house, and only a dozen got jobs, at the lowest-paid, most menial level of the 4,500 people employed at HAL. Re-establishing themselves on another piece of land they owned, the Chikapur people were displaced again by the Upper Kolab dam in 1987. When journalist P. Sainath visited a few years later they had been told they would have to move a third time, to make way for the Military Engineering Services, or a chicken farm! As one resident put it:

> Basically, they don't want us to be around like an eyesore, sticking out here. That way we would be telling our tales of woe to others—especially the minister, if he ever comes. They have got their

development and their land. We have got no development, not even a proper school, and have lost our land.

These displaced villagers are even labelled 'encroachers on government land' simply because their land was never registered by the survey commissioners. So instead of getting proper compensation they have been fined for this 'encroachment'! In many ways, those displaced by all these projects have become the *Nowhere People*.[30] HAL is essentially an arms factory, manufacturing parts for military and civil aircraft with orders from Boeing and Airbus, and specialising in advanced composite materials, in which aluminium composites play a significant part.[31]

Profits from Nalco's refinery and smelter are huge, and stem partly from the superior quality of Odisha's bauxite. This is why other aluminium companies are viewing this commodity, as well as Nalco itself, with such interest.

Even though Nalco's deposits on Panchpat Mali are so extensive, the company has applied for prospecting and mining leases on several other mountains, in Koraput, including Deo Mali, and in Andhra, as well as bidding for a magnificent mountain in west Odisha, saved from bauxite mining by a successful movement twenty years ago: Gandhamardan.

Balco and the movement to save Gandhamardan

As Nalco was starting up, another bauxite mine was proposed on a mountain straddling Bolangir and Borogorh districts. Gandhamardan is an exceptionally well-forested range, and the success of the movement which saved it during the 1980s has never been forgotten.

The particular richness of Gandhamardan's forest links to its mythical status as the place where Hanuman got the herbs for healing Lakshman in the Ramayana. Two prominent medieval temples stand by waterfalls on either side of the main ridge, so the movement here received a lot of support from Hindu devotees.

Balco (Bharat Aluminium Company), like Nalco, was a public-sector company, started in 1965 in collaboration with Russian and Hungarian firms, who helped construct a refinery-smelter complex at Korba, west of Odisha (now in Chhattisgarh). Water and electricity for Korba come from Hasdeo Bango dam, completed in 1977, which displaced tribal people from 58 villages. Balco's bauxite mines at Amarkantak and Phutkapahar in Madhya Pradesh were of inferior quality and size.[32]

The Gandhamardan deposit was surveyed in 1972–78, and estimated at over 200 million tons, stretching 10 km along the mountain ridge. Orissa's Chief Minister J. B. Patnaik came to lay the foundation stone on 2 May 1983 at Paikmal, against a scene of angry local protest. Opposition was intense. 104 villages of the Kond, Binjar and Majhi tribes stood to be directly affected.[33]

Balco built a 9-km road up the mountain, and set up mining operations and an ore crusher at the top by December 1984. Hindu devotees joined opposition to the project after blasting on the mountain in August 1985 toppled the Garuda pillar at Narasingh Nath, the medieval temple of Narsimha, the Lion Avatar of Vishnu. A visit by the veteran Gandhian campaigner Sunder Lal Bahuguna in February 1986 also helped to galvanise resistance (Bahuguna 1986).

Dalits took a leading role, and with Adivasis and other activists, set up a blockade on the mining road. Hundreds were beaten up and arrested by police. Women played a crucial role at this point, and placed their babies on the road, right in front of police and mining vehicles, saying 'Drive over them if you're going to mine. What future will they have?' Among Dalit women leaders, Jambubati Bijira from Dungripalli village was prominent, encouraged by her husband, who worked for Balco, and got fired.

> My husband was working as dozer operator. He told me, *"Many women are resisting Balco, why don't you join them? They are going to dig the mountain. Let my job go to hell, if we save this mountain, we all will be saved. The Gandhamardan mountain has minerals, medicinal herbs and so many things to offer. Everything will be destroyed if they mine. Our streams will dry. There will be drought everywhere. This also is abode of Lord Narsingh Nath. People from faraway places will stop visiting our area."*
>
> But I replied, *"I have kids to look after. If I join the other women how will I run my family? If they put me behind bars who will take care of them?"* But actually I was convinced, and one morning before the

rooster crowed we all went to blockade the road. We had mobilised many people through the night. Many youth and women prevented the vehicles from moving.

The police asked us, "*Why are you stopping the vehicles?*" We replied, "*To save our lives, to protect our mountains. We the Dalits and tribals all depend upon it. Won't we all die if you mine it? We don't care about our own lives, we are doing it for our children. We live on this land.*"

Then the district magistrate came. We lay with our children in front of the vehicles and told them, "*Move on, start, we are old, but they are our future.*" (Das 2005)

Another leader was the blacksmith Rayadhar Lohar. We met him in 2002, and as he lay on his death-bed in December 2004, he gave another interview to Samarendra:

> It started in 1982, under a Congress party government. They jailed so many people. In the meetings we called we expected 7,000 people. Out of fear seven would appear. The history is very difficult to explain. The company thought "*old Lohar is trying to use kids and lambs to plough his land*" because most of the activists were very young. These demons ... they have made everybody a coward. The world can't go on like this. Everything is collapsing. All of us have become powerless.
>
> It was not so difficult in my time. There were other ways. Now whoever promises liquor, people vote for them. I don't have energy to speak....
>
> The gate which I was guarding, ten strong young men would even be scared to guard. Which gate? Balco gate. Thousands of policemen watch you every day. But this did not succeed in scaring us. You have to participate with your heart and mind.
>
> Your Kashipur resistance should emulate ours. Do you fear death? Look at the girls here and their mothers. Once the chief of police asked one of them, "*Mother, why did you lay your child in front of the wheel?*" She replied, "*I am doing it for my baby. If you kill me you are killing her anyway.*"
>
> Do you have such brave girls in Kashipur? The day you find them, you will be successful in saving your mountain. Andolan is not an easy thing.

By June 1986 the blockade had completely stopped work at the mine. Balco had built a large colony of flats for workers, investing

A waterfall on Gandhamardan

23 crore rupees. The MoEF (Ministry of Environment and Forests) released a report of the project at this time that was strongly critical, especially of Balco's claim that it would only affect 0.32 per cent of Gandhamardan's environment, leaving 99.68 per cent untouched. The Ministry report stressed four major areas of impact: biological diversity, water, Adivasis, and sacred sites.

In response to this, the central government's Department of Mines commissioned a High Level Committee on the project's environmental aspects, headed by B. D. Nagchaudhuri (former Vice Chancellor of Jawaharlal Nehru University in Delhi). Nagchaudhuri's enquiry lasted from October 1986 to January 1987. Along with M. G. Upadhyaya (a senior bureaucrat) and scientist V. K. Gour, he visited the area just twice (27 October 1986 and 16 January 1987). His report lists the main arguments on both sides, and their widely differing estimates of impact on Gandhamardan's forests (which covered a total of

350 sq km), its 150 springs and 22 perennial streams, and on the tribal population who would be directly affected—less than 10,000 or 50,000 (according to company and protestors respectively); as well as the impact of a conveyor belt to take the bauxite down the mountain, and a 25 km railway extension to Paikmal, which would take it to Balco's refinery at Korba. Nagchaudhuri's view was that the impact had been much exaggerated by the protestors, though Balco's Environment Management Plan (EMP) came two years too late, and was highly inadequate—'at best a statement of intentions.' Twelve families already displaced were living in squalor. He concluded that there 'should be no concern for irreversible adverse impact on Gandhamardan's environment.' But by this time the Department of the Environment in Delhi had taken a stand against the project and refused Environmental Clearance.

Even though the Nagchaudhuri report (1987) favoured Balco and was considered a whitewash (GSYP May 1987), it was the beginning of the end, focusing public opinion against the Gandhamardan project, which was cancelled later in the year. The movement had succeeded. Balco's derelict colony near Paikmal at the mountain's base stands as a silent testament to the success of a people's movement in the face of corporate arrogance and severe intimidation. Beautiful trees stand amidst the ruins.

After this failure, Balco started mining on Mainpat (north Chhattisgarh), disrupting the lives of thousands of Adivasis there. Activists on both sides of Gandhamardan remain vigilant, with periodic reports that the mining lease was about to be reactivated. Around 1996 it was apparently sold to a US company, Continental Resources, and surveyors have been seen making clandestine approaches. Continental Resources has an office in Bhubaneswar, next door to DFID, and a visit there (2008) revealed a clip-board with maps of Gandhamardan.

In 2006, a Nalco plan to mine the mountain was reported in the media, and in 2008, Vedanta announced an interest. Plans for a Lower Suktel dam in Bolangir district are almost certainly linked to these plans for mining Gandhamardan, and for another refinery below it. Though the dam's ostensible purpose is irrigation, its real aim seems to be supplying water and hydropower to refine Gandhamardan's bauxite. Inhabitants of villages due for submergence have been virtually forced into signing agreements to accept compensation. This dam threatens to flood at least 26 villages, where many peole have organised a movement to stop it, the Lower Suktel Budianchal Sangram Parishad. Between 11 and 14 January 2005, police staged flag marches in three villages, and took inhabitants of each in turn to Bolangir to receive compensation—by force, in the name of 'protecting them', ignoring a High Court Order for the authorities to show affected people a Detailed Project Report.[34] Intimidation has often been ferocious. In the words of Ghunu Sahu, a leader of the Save the Lower Suktel campaign:

> On 11 May 2005, Narasingh Mishra, a state politician, came to the inauguration ceremony of the dam construction. We held a demonstration. Women and men were severely beaten by the police for taking part. They took 55 of us to the Bolangir jail. We said "Release our people". Instead they beat us, forcing their way into our homes and harassing our women. (Das 2005)

In a woman's words:

> I did not know why they beat me. I am old and was just a bystander. All of a sudden they hit me. I have a broken hand, and it is swollen. I can't eat. My grandchildren have to look after me. I asked why they beat me. I cannot understand why.

Another woman was threatened by police who came to her house while her husband and father-in-law were away campaigning:

> Four policemen entered without asking permission. There were no men at that time. They started destroying my home and even hit my child. Look at his chin. It's swollen.

Between sobs as he showed his wounds, a village elder named Ram Pradhan, told us he had heard of such things happening when the British ruled India, but never thought he would live to experience such a thing.

> Listen with an open ear, oh my Government,
> Stop building Lower Suktel dam.
> We won't cow down. (Graffiti on a village wall, Das 2005)

Some of the Gandhamardan activists published important tracts in Odia. Madan Mohan Sahu (1987) criticised Nagchoudhuri's report, citing a study of Gandhamardan's rare flora and fauna by G. Panigrahi (1963), and making a pioneering economic evaluation of Gandhamardan's primary forest far higher than conventional evaluations that have become standard practice since then, funded among others by Deutsche Bank (Gundimeda et al. 2005 and 2006). Madan pointed to the impact of mining on climate, long before this topic was widely recognised:

> *Parivesha artha jangala jala o jami, silpo sabhyatare ei teeni jiniso nasht heuchhi, o taha sangore bayu mandala dushito hebare lagichhi ... Rutu anujayee paga thik rahu nahee ...*
> (Environment means forest, water and land. Industrialisation destroys all three. Due to pollution of our atmosphere, the weather is not behaving according to season ...)

Among articles written during the protest, 'Adivasis resist Balco mining operations' in the *Telegraph* (13 November 1986) sums up the situation:

> Will the Prime Minister save the bounties of nature of the Gandhamardan range and the Adivasis depending on it, or go to the succour of Balco and bring about an ecological disaster? The Adivasi agitation has taken an organised form and acquired new militancy.

In March 2007 several of us walked over Gandhamardan from Narsingh Nath temple on the Paikmal side to Hari Shankar in Bolangir district. On each side a *mining rasta* winds up to the summit, overgrown and derelict. On the Paikmal side a tiny path winds through rock beside and beneath a magnificent waterfall that cascades over a series of rocks for several hundred feet.

Damming the Indravati

The Indravati reservoir is among the saddest places in Odisha. Financed by WB loans in the 1980s–90s, its impact on tribal people and forest is as destructive as any dam project's, but because of the area's remoteness, it got much less publicity than the Sardar Sarovar on the Narmada, which the WB was funding at the same time.

Like the Kolab dam, the cost of Upper Indravati escalated wildly, by at least six times the original estimate (from Rs 208.15 crore in 1978–79 to Rs 1,200 crore in 1993). This money came in loans which the Odisha government has to repay. Much of it went to foreign construction and engineering firms—a scandal applying to many dams.[35] An article in the Odia daily *Pragativadi* on 24 December 2004, announced a case against the state government for *Indravati durniti* (corruption).

The first villages were displaced in 1989, when a local movement started up to try and stop the dams. In 1990 this became the Indravati Gana Sangharsh Parishad (Indravati People Protection Committee), with support from advocate N. Ahmed. Workers constructing the dam also showed support, especially after many died in a big accident in July 1991. Early in 1992, a *padayatra* around the reservoir focused more support, but the movement was effectively suppressed in April when police lathicharged a crowd, injuring 180 people, including 30 women, and arresting 28 or more protesters, who were taken to Nowrangpur jail.[36]

There are seven dams, four on the Indravati and three on its tributaries (Padagada, Kapur and Muran). Near one of these, on Muran river, a female consultant for the WB visited a village in April 1993, where she was surrounded by tribal women who spoke of the hardship of resettlement, and appealed to her:

> We have nothing in our houses. Nothing to give you. You are a woman and we are women. You can see our situation and our children and you must understand. We can tell you things. Many things. You are a literate person from a big country. You understand these things that are happening to us. So please, as a woman, help us.

The fee a WB consultant is paid for a short visit to India is probably more than everyone together in a Kalahandi village would earn over several years. A man standing nearby put this more starkly: '*If I starve, you also bear a responsibility.*'[37]

A main purpose of the Indravati dams was almost certainly to supply electricity and water to proposed aluminium plants, though the rapid siltation occuring at this reservoir means the hydropower is much less than planned. None of the remote villages in the reservoir's vicinity have received the electricity they were promised.[38]

The project's most unusual and costly feature is a water tunnel 4 km long, which in effect redirects the Indravati River, channelling water from the dam area in the south to Mukhiguda (north-west), from where it is redirected into the Hati River and through canals north into Kalahandi. This tunnel was designed by the Japanese construction company Mitsubishi, and funded by loans from the Japanese International Aid Agency—another link with the Kolab Dam. The Indravati turbines were built jointly by Mitsubishi and Bharat Heavy Electricals. The design evidently did not take account of the rich red bauxite soil, excellent for forest and agriculture, but terrible for holding water. An exposure in *Samaj* newspaper on 6 September 2003, during a visit by three Japanese technocrats from Mitsubishi, reveals that two of the four turbines had stopped working: the rapid silting process had put them out of action. This power failure cost the authorities a large sum. The installed capacity is 600 MW, the actual output not more than 300 MW. De-silting the tunnels and repairing the turbines is difficult and expensive, and Mitsubishi does not take responsibility or pay for this. That it has silted up and gone wrong so quickly implies that the design was completely inappropriate to the region, and cannot cope with normal monsoon flood.

A large number of people died during the tunnel's construction, in a terrible accident on 28 July 1991, when the temporary earthen dam holding back the water gave way after heavy rain, flooding the tunnel and drowning the workers inside it. Official accounts of this accident give the number of dead as 16 killed at the tunnel mouth. In an interview conducted by Subrat Sahu among displaced villagers living in extreme poverty near Mukhiguda (19 December 2007), an old man told his story as the sole survivor of a work gang of 20 caught at the mouth of the tunnel by this flood. He and other locals say that 400-500 people were killed, mostly workers caught inside the tunnel. If it had not been a Sunday, thousands would have died (Sahu: *DAMaged!* 2009).

Other villagers described the paltry compensation that left them without land, the unkept promises of electricity and pressure cookers, the exploitation by banks and moneylenders, and the survival tactics of cutting down the forest for firewood. The Hirakud dam has a memorial to about 200 named workers who died during its construction. No such memorial commemorates Indravati's victims, let alone the thousands who lost their homes.

The reservoir started to fill in 1997, and the turbines started generating power in 1998–99. Since the water rose, soil erosion on the reservoir banks has already become a serious problem, which the authorities have barely begun to tackle, and acre after acre of dead trees surround the reservoir. A huge area of forest was drowned along with the villages and fields, and the forest that remains is dwindling daily. Most of the more than 40,000 people displaced by the dam received either no compensation at all (for those who had no legal document proving ownership of their land) or a ludicrously small amount of cash, and moved to places around the reservoir edge, where cutting the forest to sell as firewood is one of the few activities that keeps them from starvation. In other words, thousands of people's lives, and a huge area of forest have been ruined. What was this sacrifice in aid of?

One of the reservoir's main purposes was to supply irrigation to a large tract of Kalahandi district, whose drought had been much highlighted in the media. But it obliterated a huge area of even poorer villages' agricultural land, and virtually stopped the Indravati's flow through areas of Nowrangpur and Koraput—districts as dry and poor as Kalahandi. The Indravati only starts again after more tributaries have joined it after more than 50 km, and its flow over the next 200 km is far less than it used to be. If one were to calculate the number of villagers who live on the edge of starvation as a result of the Indravati dams (i.e. most of the 40,000 directly displaced plus an even greater number, perhaps, who have lost their river), compared to the number of villagers who are better-off, it is clear that the reservoir has increased rather than diminished the threat of starvation.

When we visited the Mukhiguda works in May 2004, and passed through the area of south Kalahandi that has got irrigation, we saw the canals being extended, and heard how rich immigrants purchased much of this irrigated land in advance, and are growing two crops a year there using fertilisers. So irrigation from the dam has 'solved Kalahandi's drought problem' by deflecting the Indravati's water, and introducing drought to the area where it used to run, to the south.

The reservoir is about 30 km long. At its north end is the water intake, manned by three or four officials: a tall concrete structure overlooking the reservoir, with its shores of dead trees: a desolate view, haunted by strange sounds at night. Below the viewing platform starts the tunnel, which carries water 4 km, underneath the village of Mohulpatna, to the pump house high on a hillside, where it drops down through four giant pipes and the turbines to the power station below.

The NGO Agragamee started work on behalf of people displaced by the reservoir in 1993, funded by the British NGO Action Aid for a period of ten years (ending in December 2002). Its survey estimates that 80 per cent of those displaced are Adivasis. They were offered only token compensation for their displacement, or none at all:

> during the socio-economic survey of the displaced it was found out that the rates of compensation paid for the land, house and trees are so low that they do not permit a family to reconstruct their life styles at even half the level they were used to.[39]

From its local centre at Padepadar, Agragamee works with forty villages, 36 of them displaced. These lie west of the reservoir. The fact that none has electricity, and only five have road access, indicates the remoteness of the area. The villages to the east are a lot worse-off still, cut off by the reservoir and neglected. An Agragamee official described their involvement with this resettlement as 'a bitter lesson', since the displacement brought these tribal people no benefits, only disaster and resentment. Agragamee was perceived as colluding with the dam-builders, and no one was doing anything to soften the blow for the cut-off villagers on the reservoir's east side.

We crossed the reservoir in a series of boats in December 2002. These boats are in poor repair. Their danger was shown in an accident shortly before our visit to Mukhiguda in May 2004, when one capsized and about twenty people drowned. They are the main transport for many villages that are now cut off from road access. We visited a house marooned on an island with a few fields, where a single family lives alone, cultivating land that used to be a hill-top. They were threshing rice, bitter about the complete neglect they have received from the government. That evening we were welcomed in the village of Konasukli, which still exists, but has lost over half its land to the reservoir. The people there are cut off and extremely poor, furious at the neglect. The 'Resettlement Advisory Committee' consisted of government administrators, elected politicians, and NGO officials, but none of the villagers themselves—an extraordinary omission.

During the winter of 2004–05 it became clear that one of the purposes of the Indravati scheme was to supply water to the Lanjigarh refinery. Pipes were laid from the Tel river (swollen with Indravati's water via the Hati) near Kesinga, to the site at Lanjigarh, though demonstrations at Kesinga in the first half of 2006 protested against this diversion of their water.

An item in the Odia newspaper *Sambad* (14 January 2007, frontpage) summarises the effects of these dams:

> *Nowrangpur keu nadi pani paibo?*
> **Nowrangpur: Where's river water to be found?**
> The Indravati and Kolab Rivers have dried up. The villages located beside the beds of these Rivers have lost their once mighty water supply. Now they have to take water from the Upper Indravati and Upper Kolab Reservoirs, which is stale and does not promote their health.

Odisha was classified by the WB as one of India's most water-rich states. But damming this water wealth has in effect privatised it, channelling a large amount to industrial projects, while enormously diminishing the flow for villages and fields.

CHAPTER FIVE

Kashipur's 'Development'

Once upon a time there was a beautiful land, of mountains and rivers, forests and fields. This was the land of the frogs—a rich and fertile land, because of the special rock on the mountains. Then one day the companies of snakes arrived ... (Buluka Miniaka's story, Barigaun village, Kashipur)

Often now, the world seems divided into those who can hear what India's village people are saying, and those who cannot, and will not listen, because it contradicts what they want or what they believe. *'Listen with an open ear, oh my Government ...'* There are many officials who do listen, and do want to know. But they often seem a small minority, and for them too, there's a limit. The suffering and outrage is everywhere, and it's easier to close one's ears and mind than take it in. Words are inadequate to convey what thousands of us have witnessed in Kashipur and Lanjigarh. Words are misused systematically, truth turned upside down.

Kashipur and Lanjigarh are household words in India now for the alumina refineries being built on their bauxite mountains, and for the people's movements against these projects. In the next two

Buluka Miniaka

chapters we attempt a balanced account of what has happened in these two areas of south Odisha, introducing an outline of events and network of 'stakeholders', which we analyse more deeply in the rest of this book.

People in Kashipur often speak of themselves as frogs and fishes. When the construction and mining companies move in and start levelling their fields and forest, how many frogs and other life forms are ground into dust?

There are many ways to tell a story, especially when two sides are polarised. On one side in Kashipur are those who want the Utkal project and feel furious that a few Adivasis managed to stall it for so long. On the other, villagers on the front line have lived many years now in a state of constant fear and insecurity. They experience aluminium company tactics at first hand, and witness collusion by politicians and police, and a corruption of values and deterioration in community relations unimaginable to outsiders who lost any roots in land or village generations ago. Losing all they value—fields, family and friends—is a daily reality unfolding in slow motion before their eyes: cultural genocide—a slow death, and a soul death.

What has happened is complicated though. The story of Utkal, its refinery, and its designs on Bapla Mali is one strand among many. Salu Majhi, an elderly, blind musician in Kucheipadar, lives close to the Utkal refinery that his village resisted over many years. It is going up now, changing the familiar landscape for miles around. But Utkal consists of a consortium of companies, and the companies involved have completely changed. At first it was Indal, Tata and Norsk Hydro. Then Alcan came in, and helped Hindalco buy up Indal, while the other two left. Now Hindalco is alone in the project—the company started by Gandhi's friend, Birla—alongside numerous other construction and engineering companies it works with. Buluka Miniaka's village is affected by Hindalco in a separate project, focused on the mountain of Kodinga Mali, while villagers in the north of Kashipur face another entity, Larsen & Toubro (L&T), focused on Siji Mali and other mountains.

Kashipur is a strange and hauntingly beautiful region, ringed by several of the greatest bauxite *Malis*; a high-altitude plain of rolling hills, largely deforested. Yet the soil is fertile from its high alumina content, and the main approach from the south at Rapkona emerges through thick forest and granite rock formations. Kashipur's streams, till recently, ran clear and free, drunk and bathed in by all the villages. Until 1960, Kashipur was part of Kalahandi district. Now it is in Rayagada, yet geographically separated from the rest of the district by its ring of high mountains.

Over half of Kashipur's population is Adivasi, belonging to three different tribes: Kond, Jhoria (who speak Odia), and Pengo, a smaller and shyer group, concentrated in villages on the slopes of Bapla Mali and other mountains, who have their own, distinct language and culture.

Kashipur's woes have hit the headlines many times. During the 1960s and 1980s, starvation deaths there were highlighted by activists and then the media, and in 2007, after years of aluminium-instigated 'development', a cholera epidemic swept the region. Eradicating poverty is the prime promise the aluminium companies use.

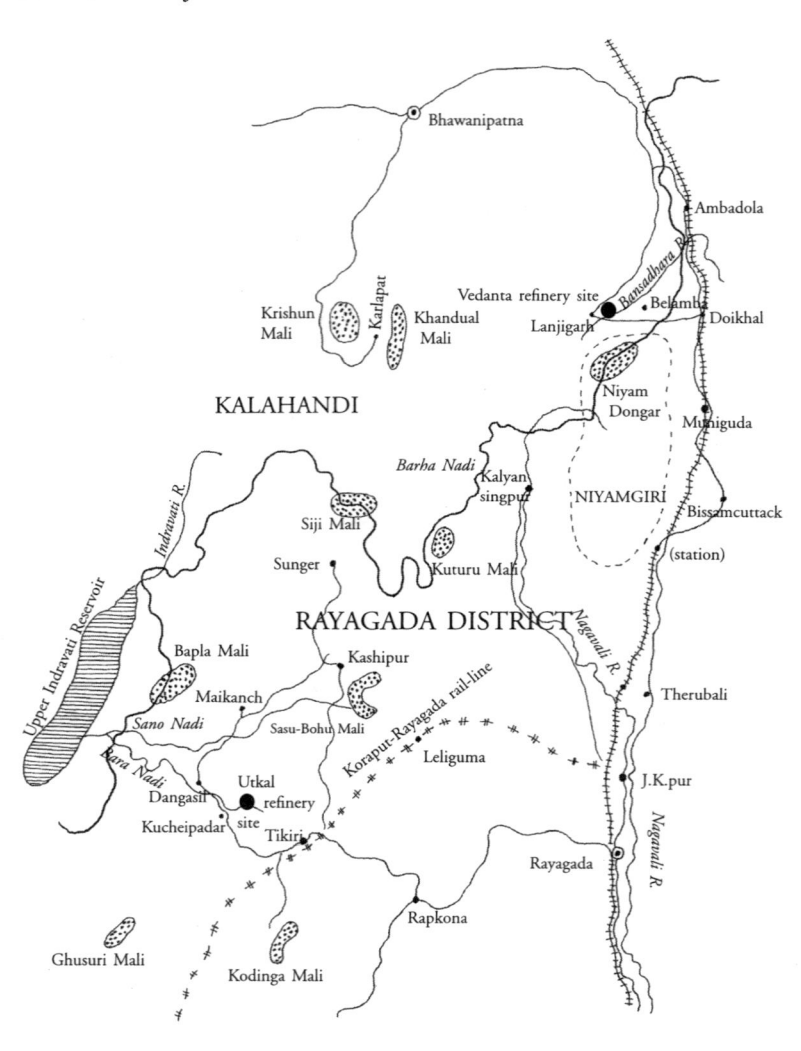

Map 7: Kashipur and Lanjigarh

So maybe it's not surprising that starvation deaths were the issue that drew Prime Minister Rajiv Gandhi to Kashipur, Maikanch and Bissamcuttack on 24–25 September 1987. The newspaper *Samaj* printed a special English supplement to coincide with this visit, devoted entirely to the starvation deaths taking place in the 'Distressed Districts of Orissa', in which the PM is said to have taken great interest. This broadsheet highlighted corruption by local officials, as well as the area's 'backwardness'.[1]

Chief Minister Biju Patnaik vehemently denied that anyone had died of starvation, but a number of law suits eventually established at least some of these cases. Biju belonged to the Congress like Rajiv, but split and formed his own party shortly after this—the Biju Janata Dal (BJD), which has ruled Odisha since 2000. It seems that Rajiv's interest during this visit was steered towards the plan of reducing the region's poverty by developing its 'infrastructure' with a view to setting up the mining and refinery plans now materialising. Initial development work focused on irrigation, which the newspaper had suggested would alleviate the drought problem, as well as roads and bridges. So the Indian government applied to IFAD—the International Fund for Agricultural Development of the UN.

IFAD had recently gone through a major shift. Set up in 1977, it gave out soft loans for agriculture to 135 countries in its first six years, and then went into a slump till it received a new lease of life in January 1986, geared to a more corporate agenda. IFAD's executive board agreed a loan for the Kashipur Project in December 1987, and the first funds started in May 1988, for an entity named Orissa Tribal Development Project (OTDP). This involved channeling state funds through a branch of the Integrated Tribal Development Agency (ITDA) at Rayagada.[2] The project was designed around cooperation with Agragamee, which was 'in close contact with some 30 per cent of villages' in Kashipur Block.

Agragamee left the IFAD project after a series of disputes in February 1993, claiming that the OTDP was not listening to its advice or villagers' feedback. There was a marked lack of communication between project staff and the villagers they were supposed to be helping—a major fault highlighted in IFAD's end-appraisal report.[3] It was also widely understood that funds were misappropriated by many involved, and work done was often poor in quality. Villagers believe that the project's infrastructure of roads and waterworks was basically done to prepare the ground for the mining companies. Although IFAD is supposed to fund 'agricutural development', it has been noticed that many regions get IFAD projects just before industrialisation, to prepare the ground. It is also a criticism levelled against other IFAD projects in India, that they tend to show a gross disregard for local opinion, and often work with highly corrupt NGOs—that IFAD has a tendency to 'throw huge amounts of money around', fulfilling its own bureaucratic spending pressures, even though this money is in the form of loans that the host government will have to repay.

The project was closed in December 1997, after a 21-month extension. Its total cost was calculated at $24,400,000, of which IFAD loaned half, and the World Food Programme loaned $1,400,000. By the original end-date (March 1996) only 51 per cent of IFAD's loan had been disbursed. This became 81 per cent by the end of the extension in December 1997. The rest was disbursed by June 1998—hence the charge that misappropriation was especially marked during the project's last days.[4]

IFAD's end appraisal is relatively frank, admitting that the project was flawed by a complete lack of knowledge about the tribal people and their own system of knowledge. *'Their know-how has been developed and refined over centuries,'* so they were unlikely to take kindly to new, superficial schemes that they could see were being introduced with arrogance and no real understanding of local conditions.[5] What the report does not mention is that the whole IFAD–OTDP scheme was locally perceived as an exercise in domination and interference, and as paving the way for the mining companies, which is why villagers defaced many of the IFAD/OTDP signboards recording statistics about construction works.

For simultaneously—as if by chance!—Kashipur was being 'developed' by IFAD and prospected by the aluminium companies. Villagers claim that they found mining company surveys being carried out by people who said they were officials of the OTDP. According to a DFID-funded report,

> Workers from Kucheipadar provided labour to help in the study, unaware of the purpose of the work. Rumours began to circulate

that a forest project was planned. The secrecy and misinformation surrounding the project's inception created suspicion and mistrust amongst local people.[6]

The starting up of Utkal, deceptively fused with IFAD-funded 'tribal development', made villagers question the whole purpose of IFAD's loan. That people carrying out surveys supposedly for OTDP/IFAD were actually surveying for Utkal Alumina implies a far-reaching collusion between IFAD and the aluminium companies, and a joint purpose. The main anti-Utkal activists have remained suspicious of Agragamee ever since, despite this NGO's support for their cause. Before they left IFAD and criticised it, what kind of deal had Agragamee made? What is certain is that IFAD's groundwork in Kashipur from 1987 to 1997 'opened the area up', leaving behind a legacy of division and distrust.

An insider who worked as a clerk in IFAD's office in Kashipur, with a supervisory role in many of its projects, confirmed to us that corruption was rampant. Adivasis doing labouring work were paid half what they should have been. The other half was embezzled by IFAD officials. Good quality quarters built for 130 OTDP officials in Kashipur town were stripped by staff when they left, taking even the doors and windows and leaving them as empty shells. Everywhere their work was sub-standard. Costs were cut, and project officials pocketed the difference. Seeds and fertilisers meant for the Adivasis were hoarded and sold off.

At the same time, the new Koraput-Rayagada line was being built for Utkal as well as Nalco, snaking up and through the high mountains around Kashipur, which got a station at Tikiri, close to Utkal's planned refinery. This railway is 164 km long, and has 36 tunnels, several over a kilometre long, in which a number of construction workers died in accidents. The line cost an estimated Rs 442 crore, of which 80 crore came as a loan from the Saudi Fund for Development—sign of a long-term Saudi interest in Odisha's bauxite.

The line links Odisha's south-west with the rest of the state, connecting the Bailadila-Koraput-Vizag line, constructed in 1968 to take iron-ore to the coast at Vizag from the mines of Bailadila— another mountain range of outstanding biodiversity devastated by mining. When this railway was inaugurated by PM Narsimha Rao in December 1995, it was described as 'conquering the eastern ghats', a 'Lifeline of South Orissa', promising 'plenty and prosperity in the backwaters of Orissa.' Topping its list of benefits is the rapid industrialisation of the region:

> This hinterland of Orissa i.e. Koraput and Rayagada districts is rich in mineral resources such as limestone, manganese ore, bauxite, graphite and quartzite, apart from its immense forest wealth. The rapid expansion in industrial and other fields would be the logical outcome.
>
> This rail link passing through ravines, ghats, lush green forests presents a breathtaking view of nature's beauty to the viewers on a platter. There are several tribal and ethnic communities in this region who provide the anthropologists an ideal opportunity to study and document their customs and rituals. Not surprisingly the Government of Orissa are developing potential tourist spots … in the vicinity of Koraput. Now more and more tourists would be lured by the hitherto unsullied landscape of this region.[7]

Every day, Nalco trains ply this line, bringing alumina from Damanjodi to Angul. The mountains around Koraput and Damanjodi have been severely deforested—'unsullied' the area is not. Constructing the railway involved big gangs of coolies living for months at a time near little-contacted tribal villages. Some of these have ceased to exist, and so has much of the forest. As with similar railways built in other remote regions of the world, constructing this railway contributed greatly to the area's deforestation.[8]

Thus by 1993, when the Utkal consortium was making its clandestine bauxite surveys on Bapla Mali, the rail-project was nearing completion, and so were IFAD's roads and bridges in Kashipur. There is little doubt that a master plan was coordinating these activities in preparation for the aluminium companies. Suspicions that the real purpose of IFAD's loan was to open the area for penetration by industry are confirmed by the story of Indravati dams going up just to the west, and the brutal suppression of the protest movement there in April 1991.

Company *Hawa*

And then came the Companies. In Bhagaban Majhi's words:

> We had no idea of what a company was before the movement started. When the company people came and did their survey we were having a discussion in the village to open a market. At that time we did not oppose the company.... Someone was constructing a pillar for the company. We went to him. We told him that we would carry the pillar for him for some money.
>
> We had asked for some money from the company and from the contractors of the company for our work, but we were not sure about doing this. So we held a village meeting which was attended by Anantaram Majhi, an ex-cabinet minister, Akhil Saunta, the MLA of Lakhmipur constituency, and Biju Patnaik, the chief minister of Orissa.
>
> The decision took place in the meeting. Anantaram Majhi said, "*Brothers! Think how happy we all are without the company, living our lives simply in the traditional way. If the company is set up, we'll lose our land and also our happiness for ever. We won't be able to live without our lands. As we all are like earthworms, we should never part with our lands. So together let's all oppose the company from tomorrow.*"
>
> We all became very happy to hear him speak like this. Next morning, all the villagers, men, women, young and old alike, opposed the company with our sticks in hand. The way we protested against the company, the company people were very scared. Some of them fled leaving their tools behind. Even Anantaram Majhi was afraid to visit the village again. (Das 2005)

This is because Anantaram did a 'flip-flop' (about-turn) soon after, supporting the project.

Utkal was the ancient name for a part of Odisha—actually the coastal area of north-east Odisha, while the Utkal project is active in Kashipur in south-west Odisha. When Utkal Alumina International Ltd. (UAIL) emerged in 1993, Indal and Tata were in Joint Venture with Norsk Hydro, Norway's biggest firm.

The bauxite deposit to be mined, estimated at 198 million tons, covers 10 or more square kilometers on top of Bapla Mali. A 20-km conveyor belt is planned for carrying the ore to an alumina refinery on the site of Ramibera and other villages, removed in 2006, while a 12-km railway spur is being built from Tikiri station.

Several other companies or consortia signed deals (MoUs: Memoranda of understanding) for other mountains in Kashipur during the 1990s. L&T (Larsen and Toubro, a Danish-origin cement, construction, engineering and arms company) made its base near Sunger just below Siji Mali, signing MoUs for this and Kuturu Mali. Balco had an MoU for Sasu-Bohu Mali, as well as Niyamgiri—leases which Sterlite inherited when it took over Balco in 2001. Since becoming active in Niyamgiri–Lanjigarh, Sterlite's lease for Sasu-Bohu Mali has been cancelled—one of the bauxite mountains at least won a reprieve. Hindalco signed a separate MoU for Kodinga Mali, and was drawing up plans for a refinery beside it—plans reactivated in 2005, as confrontation escalated again. Several of these projects were Joint Ventures with foreign mining companies.[9] But Utkal was the front-runner, and the other companies waited to watch its progress.

Kashipur villagers became aware relatively early of what was planned for them, and resisted, understanding that if the mines and factories came up, they would displace far more people than was officially claimed, and have a huge impact on their existence as communities. They went and saw the effects of 'development' in the Damanjodi and Indravati regions, as well as learning from Gandhamardan activists. The Prakrutika Sampad Surakshya Parishad (PSSP or Natural Resources Defence Council) was set up in Kucheipadar in 1993, and a similar organisation was set up in Sunger against L&T, the Anchalik Surakshya Parishad (which later joined PSSP).[10]

The first confrontation took place that year, when PSSP activists discovered that survey work was being done under false pretences by surveyors claiming to be *gram sevakas* (village-level workers), vets or schoolteachers, after some Kucheipadar people got work on the survey without being told its purpose. Village activists started to disrupt the survey. Kucheipadar villagers enact an annual drama with humourous portrayals of how the surveyors came under false pretences and were sent packing.

On 11 November 1993, representatives from five villages met the CM, Biju Patnaik, who promised to try and find an alternative site for the project. On 27 November the PSSP organised a boycott of a meeting with the Tehsildar and other local officials.

Utkal has claimed that its 'R&R package' (Resettlement and Rehabilitation) is exceptionally generous. This is far from true. Compensation was offered to twelve villages that were to be 'Project-Affected' (i.e. to lose some or all of their land), though only 147 families in three of these villages were listed as completely displaced, while members of another twelve villages would lose land to the conveyor belt. Kucheipadar was the only village to refuse compensation *en masse*. Compensation was offered only in cash (i.e. not land for land), and only to restricted categories of people (e.g. not to those without written land-deeds, or whose land is classified as government land), and the rate was extremely low. A job was also offered to each displaced family, but such jobs (the lowest available unskilled labour in mine or factory) do not begin to make up for losing their own land, and when Kashipur villagers met people displaced by the refinery at Damanjodi they saw that in practice such promises have rarely been kept.[11]

Land for the project was demanded on the basis of the notorious Land Act of 1894, though even the basic requirement of this act to inform people in advance was not followed. Nor was the Fifth Schedule of the Indian Constitution, that protects tribal lands, and stipulates that in the event of their land being demanded by a project 'in the national interest', local government (i.e. village authorities) must be consulted first. Cash compensation for tribal land has always been notorious for the corruption and disintegration it causes—in Kashipur, Hirakud, Upper Indravati, and countless other places. Traders immediately approach those compensated, with offers that enmesh them in debt, and the money is rarely invested with any lasting benefit. Many stories emerged from Kashipur about misuse of cash compensation (Barney et al. 2000, pp. 46–48), such as buying vehicles that couldn't be maintained, manipulation by the banks, and villagers who died of a heart attack after being given his money.

Confrontation escalated in 1994, with approach roads built and more surveying done using police protection, while protestors destroyed surveyors' equipment and drove them away, kidnapping some briefly in December. On 23 April 1995, Tikiri police arrested a dozen PSSP activists, including Gurunath Majhi. Maharaj Majhi, a Kucheipadar leader, was arrested twice, in April and August. Each time popular pressure forced his early release, in the form of hundreds *gherao*-ing Tikiri police station.

In the Sunger area, L&T men and the police carried out surveys of Siji and Kuturu Malis, with similar intimidation of hundreds of village protestors of the Anchalik Surakshya Parishad (for example on 25 February 1995 and 21 January 1996), and there were many fights with pro-project *goondas*.

Goondas destroyed Agragamee buildings early in 1995, while villagers set fire to an L&T survey camp. Goondas usually dress in shirts and pants, with a liking for baseball caps and smart trainers. The majority of Adivasi and Dalit activists dress more traditionally, in a *gamcha* (loincloth) and *pagri* (a *gamcha* wrapped round the head like a turban) or a *sari*, and often no sandals. Bare feet are the main means of transport, and women demonstrate alongside men.

J. B. Patnaik was elected as Orissa's Chief Minister in 1995, promising to speed up industrialisation and push the Utkal project through fast, 'bulldozing opposition'. The Ministry of Environment and Forests granted environmental clearance for mining Bapla Mali and for Utkal's refinery (25 and 27 September)—even though the required Environmetal Impact Assessment (EIA) and Management Plan had not been submitted.

But opposition grew. The Bapla Mali Surakhya Samiti (Bapla Mali Protection Society) was formed towards the end of 1995, and on 26 January 1996 nearly 6,000 people collected at the mango grove in Kucheipadar, when the Collector of Rayagada and the local MLA came to try and persuade them about the project. Instead, the people presented them with a memorandum listing reasons why they would not leave their land. Soon after this (on 14 February 1996), another meeting hosted Medha Patkar, one of India's most famous female activists, a leader of the Narmada Bachao Andolan (Save the Narmada Movement), and Manmohan Choudhuri, an eminent Gandhian who passed away in 2003 (Choudhuri 1989).

The movement also found an ally in the Chairman of the Orissa State Pollution Control Board (OSPCB), R. C. Das, who wrote a paper in March 1996 opposing any more bauxite mining or aluminium plants in Odisha, purely on environmental grounds:

> Further addition of alumina plants in this belt (Rayagada and Kashipur) will add to environmental problems, besides resource constraints.

For this comment he was apparently sacked by the CM, while the OSPCB gave the required environmental clearance (Mahapatra 1999). On 5 January 1997 police attacked Kucheipadar—one of a succession of violent attacks in these years, in which many people were beaten and/or arrested on false charges.

Kucheipadar has been at the centre of resistance to the project, and the PSSP office is here. It is (or was) one of the most dignified and self-confident Kond villages, and the people relate on equal terms with outsiders, without the usual subservience, standing up for themselves and speaking directly, even to a Collector or Tehsildar, proud of their reputation of refusing to be bullied by officials.

Villagers' self-respect shows in well-kept streets and vegetable gardens, and in their songs and dances. For several years, political education was offered in evening classes. A proud notice stood at the village entrance—'NO ENTRY WITHOUT PARMITION'—which applied to government officials and police as well as to NGOs. The bathing places in the stream near Kucheipadar are particularly fine, separate for men and women. The men's place is a pool below a small waterfall, a truly wonderful place to bathe. What will happen to this if the refinery starts up?

Bhagaban Majhi is recognised as a leader and spokesman of the movement. In public gatherings he often sings a song that became a symbol of the movement, composed by a fellow-villager named Rato Majhi, a wonderful player on the flute, who was one of the first to warn people about Utkal, and died early in 2007.

Hawa, Hawa, Company Hawa
Wind, Wind, Company Wind
Blowing all over Orissa.

Let us all stand together for Justice.
We will save our mother Earth
And redeem ourselves.

We will not hand over our land to these companies.
Let us all stand together,
Don't just watch us and wait,
Don't you see the danger?
What we are facing today,
You will face tomorrow.
You are not immune.
Look ahead!
Grief is coming [*Dukho asuchi*]
Hey Company and Government!
We are Aware!
Don't try to cheat us anymore!
Listen! In our own village, we are the Government.
In our village we'll be the Judge.
Our Land, our Water cannot be sold.
This Earth is ours.

To try and fill the credibility gap, the Utkal Rural Development Society (URDS) was set up in 1997, with a Manager for 'Community Social Responsibility' (CSR—an acronym soon standardised as Corporate Social Responsibility). Glossy pamphlets in English advertised 'good works', in stark contrast to events on the ground. URDS was modelled on Tata's Rural Development Society (TRDS). To begin with, it had nine directors, six staff, 'village animators' working in six villages, and an aim of promoting 'socio-economic development and welfare or uplift the people'. But most people saw it as a mask—a 'Bingo' (Business NGO), set up to sugarcoat the company's real intentions. The fact that it had so many directors (five from UAIL) implied that its intention to become a 'world class' NGO meant glossy self-promotion, not listening to villagers, or relating with them as equals. No one believed its claim to be independent. A DFID study concluded: 'It is clear that URDS has a legitimacy problem … perceived as an agent of the "project".' At the same time, Norsk Hydro sent an anthropologist, Rolf Lunheim, to study the situation.[12]

Bhabagan describes how the movement learnt to get proper permission for meetings, yet faced endless harassment from *goondas* and police, as well as company officials who visited the villages in disguise.

> They even came to us as ANM (Auxiliary Nurses and Midwives) and enquired about the statistics of village population. Like: How many women are there? How many girls and boys? Their ages, etc. They would make a list of them on the pretext of doing a survey.
>
> We got suspicious of their intentions after many such surveys, and wouldn't let them hold any more…. When they couldn't do any more surveys, they formed an organisation called URDS. The idea was that people would not oppose this organisation as they did the company. They held free health check-up camps, free seed donation camps, and they started free adult education in the area.
>
> We saw that these were in fact company people. Their real intention was to first win the confidence of our people and then divide us. That was the conspiracy. So we had to oppose them, and protested against this organisation too. Some of our people understood their plan, others did not.
>
> So URDS failed. Then came another organisation called BPD [Business Partners for Development]. We opposed this too. The company now understood that we were not afraid of jails, false cases and lathicharge. Maybe murder would scare us away'.

The WB was taking a keen interest in Utkal at this time, and listed it as a model project in its Business Partners for Development scheme (BPD), a worldwide scheme promoting 'tri-sectoral partnerships' between government, companies and civil society. The UK was the only government that became officially involved, through its Department for International Development (DFID).[13]

Alcan, which officially entered the Utkal consortium in 1995, was Indal's parent company, and a prime mover. It had remained closely connected with Indal since setting it up in the 1940s. Utkal's management shifted to Hindalco after Alcan bought a controlling stake in Indal, and then sold this on to Hindalco (Indal's former rival), in March 1998. Tata left the consortium—it was meeting more than enough opposition elsewhere in Orissa: a prawn-monopoly project (from 1991) and a steel plant at Gopalpur (1996–9), both defeated by people's movements during these years.[14]

Meanwhile, in Andhra Pradesh in 1997, an NGO called Samatha won a landmark court case against corporate takeovers of tribal land. Samatha first filed the case in the AP High Court in 1993, when a stay order was granted on mining activities. After the High Court threw out the case in 1995, Samatha went to India's Supreme Court, winning its case against the AP government and curtailing the activities of several companies mining calcite, graphite and other minerals (yellow ochre, phosphates etc) on the bauxite mountains just south of Odisha, around Borra Caves, India's largest cave complex. The Samatha Judgment stopped all mining in the area, which had been led by Birla Periclase (in the same group as Hindalco), whose 120-acre lease to mine calcite for its magnesia plant on the Andhra coast was now redundant. Behind Birla Periclase, there were undoubtedly aluminium interests at work, which the Samatha Judgment stalled. Since then, these Andhra bauxite interests have been pushing for mining and refinery projects, just as in Odisha, trying to bypass this ruling.[15]

The Samatha Judgment was based on the Fifth Schedule of India's Constitution, which protects the land rights of Scheduled Tribes, and forbids the transfer of their land, imposing 'a total prohibition of transfer of immovable property to any person other than a tribal.' The tribal areas of Andhra and Odisha, in which all the bauxite mountains are located, are Scheduled Areas, in which this prohibition is supposed to apply. So the Samatha Judgment gave support to everyone trying to prevent tribal land being forcibly expropriated by mining companies all over India. The long text which details the Judgment quotes anthropologists and activists on the history and extent of non-tribals' exploitation of tribal people, and the threat to tribal people's standard of living posed by mining projects.

The Samatha Judgment is complemented by PESA—the Panchayat (Extension to Scheduled Areas) Act—passed in December 1996, which is based on the findings of the Bhuria Committee from 1993 (when the 73rd amendment to the Constitution was passed) to 1996, which extended Panchayat rights in the Fifth Schedule (i.e. tribal) areas of India (excluding North-East India where the Sixth Schedule applies). A key provision is that tribal land can only be acquired after proper consultation with local Panchayats. This consultation process has been conspicuous by its absence in Kashipur and other areas.

The Government of Orissa (like other state governments) has tried to deny the implications of the Samatha Judgment and PESA as an 'unnecessary check on development plans', 'not in the tribal people's real interests.' Yet this legislation remains in force, underused but still potent, a clear statement of the Scheduled Tribes' fundamental rights, guaranteed in India's Constitution.

In 1998 the confrontation in Kashipur reached a new level. On 5 January police lathicharged and tear-gassed a roadblock at Kucheipadar, beating and badly injuring about 50 protesters. The Tehsildar of Kashipur and a Sub-Inspector of police from Rayagada commanded about a hundred policemen, who were shouting 'Why do you join this agitation against the project? We'll teach you!' One villager was taken to jail and 35 were booked on false charges. The activist Prafulla Samantara visited Kashipur and wrote a series of letters to the higher authorities at this time, accusing the district administration of Rayagada of 'unleashing a reign of terror':

> Thousands of people of the said tribal area have been agitating peacefully to protest against the arbitrary decision of the State government to acquire their land.... The affected tribal people are never consulted nor have their rights to life been secured.... During the past decade the development work done in the name of the tribal people [i.e. roads and bridges built by OTDP/IFAD] will be enjoyed by the companies once the tribals will be evicted from their original land and natural resources.... To counter the peaceful protest, the Government of Orissa has been using brutal police force to suppress the villagers and terrorise them to vacate their native places without their consent, though the enacted law of self-rule of tribal through the Gram Sabha has been incorporated in the Constitution since 24 December 1996, and the Government of Orissa has accepted it in its special Panchayat Raj Act passed in Orissa Assembly in the month of December 1997.[16]

On 29 March a rally was planned, and officially announced to police in the correct form, on Martyrs Day, which commemorates the death by hanging of Laxman Nayak, a tribal leader who resisted

British rule in this part of Odisha during the 1940s. This rally was disrupted by *goondas*, who beat people up while police stood by and laughed. Rabi Misra and Sanatan Pradhan, were taken into Indal's office at Tikiri and beaten up there. Prafulla Samantara and Lingaraj were in a vehicle that was chased and stopped by *goondas* in an Indal jeep. After being beaten, they went straight to the Collector's house in Rayagada and lodged a complaint with him and the Odisha police authorities, as well as a warning that the *goondas* had said they were going to attack Agragamee's offices near Kashipur next.[17]

Meanwhile, the senior engineer at the Upper Indravati project, Dasarath Nanda, added his voice to the case against Utkal on environmental grounds, writing an open letter dated 24 March 1998, questioning: (1) Utkal's figures on effluent from their planned refinery, and their ability to dispose of it safely, pointing out that 2 million tons of red mud would be created every year; (2) the refinery's use of river water from the Bara Nadi, which is the main water source for at least 70 villages; and (3) the project's dangerous impact on the Indravati reservoir. Mining Bapla Mali would inevitably damage the flow of water into the reservoir, since an estimated 350 streams starting from its slopes are its main source.

A memo at this time from one of Odisha's most powerful bureaucrats, Pyari Mohan Mohapatra, to Tapan Mitra (a senior Utkal executive) was frank about the ill reputation of URDS: 'You will appreciate that when a running battle is being fought between the company and the oustees, the society whose managing committee (the implementing agency) is dominated by the company's men, is not likely to inspire confidence in the eyes of the beneficiaries. I am afraid it will no longer be possible for me to associate with the society under these circumstances.'[18]

In July, the Rayagada Collector and SP (Superintendent of Police) again went to Kucheipadar to try and persuade the people to accept the project. In the confrontation that took place with a crowd of several thousand, the police arrested another leading activist, Krushna Saonta, on false charges.

On 17 November 1998, villagers detained three Norsk Hydro officials. Ivar Oellingrath, Dag Syltevik and Bernt A. Malme and an Indian official were stopped on the road near Kucheipadar by a crowd armed with bows and arrows and axes, and held for a day in Kucheipadar, where they had to write a brief memorandum saying that they recognised the local people throughout the area were against the project and wished to continue cultivating the land. The three were released after a day's detention. But police intimidation grew even worse after this. There had been altogether about 500 arrests by this time.[19]

This detention by villagers caused the local administration to ban four NGOs, blaming them for instigating the tribal people, and labelling them 'anti-development'. These four NGOs were deregistered for about a year in 1998–99: Agragamee, Ankuran, Laxman Nayak Society and WIDA (Weaker sections Integrated Development Agency). Some of these played an important part spreading awareness about the mining threat among villagers, alerting pressure groups outside the area, and facilitating visits to the area by Norwatch, the Stromme Foundation (Norway) and other campaigners, but they were certainly not leading the protest. Many in the movement resented the NGOs' style of functioning and refused to have anything to do with them.[20]

An elder of Ramibeda, Mangta Majhi, died at this time. This incident, told to us by his son and other villagers, is one of the darkest and least reported incidents in the history of the Kashipur movement. His family, like most families in Kucheipadar, had managed to keep their land deeds, making him one of the biggest landowners in Ramibeda, right in the middle of the site of the planned refinery. His refusal to part with his land or accept compensation made him a marked man. Shortly before police arrested him at night, company people (and perhaps an anthropologist?) took a photo of him by the ancient tamarind tree, surrounded by the ancestor stones that stood at one end of the village. They asked him to take his shirt off for this photo (tribal men normally wear a shirt when meeting visitors, but not when working), and stand in just a loincloth.

Villagers say the police came at night in Utkal vehicles. They found Mangta guarding his crops on a *machan* (covered platform), and asked him for water. When he came down, they beat him mercilessly with rifle butts and took him away, tied together with two Dalit men from Kendukhunti, the next village. When he was released, his face was a mess from the beating and he died a few days later—the first to die, apparently, for standing up to Utkal. Ramibeda and Kendukhunti were bulldozed in 2006, along with the beautiful tamarind tree, to level the ground.

During 1998 Hindalco became active in the area south of Tikiri, with plans to mine Kodinga Mali and build another refinery next to it at Kansariguda village.[21] When Hindalco surveyors came to the village of Barigau nearby, Buluka Miniaka and Alai Majhi (a male and female elder) were among the many villagers who confronted them and prevented their work. A big meeting was held at Kansariguda on 25 December 1998, despite the bureaucracy's attempt to stop it.

In January 1999, a four-person team from the Council for Social Development (CSD) in Delhi visited Kashipur, Rayagada and Bhubaneswar to assess the situation. They met people in five affected tribal villages, members of three of the deregulated NGOs, and senior administrators and politicians of Rayagada district, as well as the Chief Secretary of Orissa. Their report makes clear the extent of feeling against the project by the villagers: they had not been properly consulted, and the cash they had been pressured to accept was no recompense for losing their land; nor was the offer of one job per displaced family, since they knew these jobs were the lowest paid and could not guarantee the quality of life they were used to. Everywhere people said they would rather die than leave their land. The team found the administrators and politicians completely identified with the companies' ideology, believing that the alumina industry would bring 'development for all', and completely misrepresenting the resistance as the work of only a handful of hardcore villages, instigated by NGOs or 'outsider' activists—which was why the Orissa government had deregulated the NGOs, preventing them from receiving foreign funds in order 'to teach them a lesson'. By contrast, the team found that 'Education is not incitement': the NGOs had behaved honourably and courageously in the face of repeated harassment (CSD 1999).

The protesters were winning, in the sense that they had managed to prevent any real work on any of the aluminium projects—Utkal/Indal in the Bapla Mali–Kucheipadar area, L&T around Sunger, Balco on Sasu-Bohu Mali, and Hindalco south of Tikiri.

Against this background of people's protest, 46 local politicians of the three main political parties came together early in 2000 to support these projects (Barney et al. 2000, p. 42). In Bhagaban's words:

> So politicians made an All-Party Committee of political parties—BJP, BJD and Congress. Their aim was to mediate between the pro-company and anti-company groups. All of them were financially supported by the company. They were only carrying out the company's agenda. The all-party committee is never neutral. It is ineffectual too.

The purpose of this Committee formed a stark contrast to promises made by Naveen Patnaik, in an election advert placed in *Samaj* newspaper (15 February 2000), when he was running for Chief Minister, representing a BJD-BJP alliance:

> Leasing Jungle and Mountains to the Companies,
> Adivasis today are getting destroyed
> The people dwelling in the forest do not have rights over their forest, it's all state property. From the jungle they collect resin, honey, kendu leaves, brooms, etc., but for all these items they never get a proper price, as dishonest traders cheat them. The precious minerals they dig out from underneath their land are appropriated by big, big companies. When the people who live in the lap of nature are forcibly evicted in the name of protecting wildlife and national parks, there's nobody to speak for them.
> During its prolonged reign at the centre and state level, the Congress has deceived the Adivasis. But the BJD–BJP alliance, with a splitting roar, declares that Adivasis are our brothers—our forest-dwelling brothers.
> The BJD–BJP alliance has taken an oath to restore to Adivasis a fair share of their land, forest, animals and wealth beneath the land. We've little time at hand. Decide for the future. For making a new Orissa the BJD–BJP is the only choice.

The police killings at Maikanch

If Mangta's death was kept very quiet, another incident made headline news. In December 2000 the movement planned a *chokka jam* ('wheel jam' i.e. blockade) at Rapkona, to block Kashipur's main approach road, on the 20th of that month. On 15 December, politicians from the All-Party Committee went in four cars (reportedly against police advice) to attend a meeting at Nuagan, a pro-company village just beyond Maikanch. They were halted at the long-term blockade near Maikanch, manning the approach to Bapla Mali. As the politicians knew, Maikanch that day was the scene of a gathering of people from many villages, coordinating plans for the *chokka jam*. Bhagaban describes what happened:

> We organised a road blockade on the national highway for 20 December 2000 … so that people far and wide will come to know about our plight. Once we had decided to hold it, our preparations were under way…. Such meetings were being held at four or five different places. At Maikanch it was held on 15 December.
>
> The All-Party Committee also had a meeting the same day at Nuagan. They were pro-company people, so they had to pass on the same road. We opposed any meeting that would welcome the company, and did not allow them to pass through the road. The clash began between them and us. They were renowned leaders of the area who had never met with such ill-treatment.
>
> As they had always been revered by the common folk, they felt severely slighted when they were attacked by the same people. Being offended, they lodged false complaints against us in the police station that the mob had actually tried to kill them, but they managed to escape. Then they returned to Maikanch with magisterial power, shooting orders and two platoons of police.
>
> As the meeting was held on the 15th evening, people were still there expecting the police to arrive following the clash. The police came. They asked for our leaders so that they could talk to them. They asked our women about our leaders. Our womenfolk told them, "*The leaders are not here anymore. There are no men here. You can tell us what you have to tell them. They are off to the fields for work; we will tell them when they return.*"
>
> The police got angry. They began to scold them, "*Rascals! Tribals! We have come here with orders today. You get them soon or we'll get them finished.*" The OIC of Kashipur police station knocked a woman down. All the womenfolk got scared. They began to run in different directions. The police hit out. Events followed on from this. They opened fire at us and left soon after.
>
> They fired at us just to clear the road blockade at Rapkona. For it would get in the way of setting up the company. All their hopes

would be futile then. So they scared us with fire-power at Maikanch ... We nursed the wounded with herbal and root medicines. The dead were dead. We burned them together in a heap in the night of the 17th.

The government did not provide the injured with any treatment in the next 24 hours. We got them admitted in a hospital at Kashipur. This is how the firing took place at Maikanch. Seven people were injured. Three were killed. Three cows got killed too. Firing, firing, firing.

The politicians, outraged by the exchange of blows on 15 December, filed a report at Kashipur police station alleging that the tribals were led by Achyut Das of Agragamee (certainly not true), had tried to kill the leading politician in the BJD car-party, N. Bhaskar Rao (unlikely), which is also what the *Statesman* reported the next day, adding that journalists travelling with the politicians had also been beaten.

It seems that the politicians then phoned Bhubaneswar, and a Minister sent in the armed police, with the intention of 'teaching the tribals a lesson'. The men were up the nearby hill, to avoid a fight, and only came near when they heard their women screaming. As they came close, the police opened fire. The two sides recount the story very differently. Nobody disputes the deaths and injuries. The police took a seriously injured man away and admitted him to hospital. Those who died were two men and a youth of the Jhoria community: Damodar, Abhilash and Ragunath. Their memorial stands above the entrance to Maikanch village where they were shot. Another marks the hill where they were cremated, by their home village of Bhagrijhola. As a popular song remembers them:

Our beloved Damodar is reminding us
It is in our resistance that we retain our dignity

The next day the town of Rayagada (about 80 km away) was closed down by its business community—not in protest at the killings, but at the tribals laying hands on the politicians and journalists. On the protestors' side, at least 5,000 turned up for the *chokka jam* on 20 December, to show their solidarity with the movement and their outrage at the police killings.

They thought that the agitation would automatically die down with the firing. We decided about our future plan of action. We would rather die than leave our land. Whether or not to hold road blockade at Rapkona? No we must.

We held the road blockade at Rapkona on 20 December. About five thousand people arrived there armed with weapons. A petition was written there which was meant for the Chief Minister. No one, not even the collector, came to see us. The blockade went on till five o'clock in the evening. The officers of the company were frustrated by our success. We were not bothered if some SP or Chief Minister had come, as we had obtained due permission. Election was coming. They had to beg for our votes. This is the democratic and peaceful way we have carried on the movement.

On 29–30 December, 22 of the 24 affected villages passed resolutions opposing Utkal, as did a meeting convened by the Collector of Rayagada of the five local *gram sabhas*, which was sent to the CM and PM (IPTEHR 2006, p. 14).

In January 2001, the Chairman for Scheduled Castes and Tribes, Dileep Singh Bhuria, visited Maikanch and issued a statement that the forced acquisition of tribal land in this area was illegal, that the tribal people recognised correctly that the project would ruin their lives and bring them no lasting benefit, and that Rayagada district's BJD President, Bhaskar Rao, should not have visited the village on 15 December, nor should the police have done so on 16 December.[22] Five weeks after the attack, the President of India, K. R. Narayanan, alluded to Maikanch in his Independence Day speech (*'Let it not be said by future generations ...'* quoted above, p. 28).

The police firing made international news. Norsk Hydro was already under pressure in Norway over the human rights situation in Kashipur, and withdrew gradually from Utkal over the following months. Strong criticism by foreign activists was a factor, focused through Norwatch, Future in Our Hands and other NGOs, though sourcing bauxite elsewhere may have been a more important factor. Norsk's insistence on human rights had been *'frustrating'* for Indal and the administration, which were not used to taking these considerations seriously, and considered them a sign of *'weakness'*, according to the report *Engaging Stakeholders* (Barney et al. 2000), commissioned by the DFID from the Centre for Social Development at Swansea in Wales, which looks at the Utkal project as one of three business ventures in Odisha. The places Barney visited, just two months before the firing took place, included Kucheipadar and Maikanch. On leaving Maikanch, armed *goondas* threatened his vehicle with violence if they returned. In Kashipur town he held a tense meeting with local politicians who called those supporting the project '*patriots*', and those against it '*traitors*', furious at disruption by 'a few ignorant tribals'. These were evidently the same politicians who called in armed police to 'teach the tribals a lesson'. Barney's report is one of the few relatively neutral appraisals of Utkal, giving balance to the views of those for and against the project, and it deserves to be better known.

At the same time as this DFID study was under way, the WB was moving on with its sponsorship of Utkal Alumina as a key BPD scheme. Just days before the Maikanch firing, there had been talks in Rayagada between a BPD team, Utkal Alumina and government officials, who had called Bhagaban Majhi, Professor B. P. Rath (retired head of Rayagada College), and other activists, to hear their views.

Pressure from the WB to get the project started may even have been a factor leading up to the firing. All the projects considered under the BPD scheme turned out to be seriously flawed. Utkal was taken off the list soon after the firing, and the WB has never publicly explained why.[23]

A Commission of Enquiry into the police shooting was ordered on 20 January 2001. Justice P. K. Mishra, an Orissa High Court Judge, was chosen to preside. At a session on 29 June 2002 we witnessed B. K. Otta, Utkal's Chief Executive Officer, in the witness box. He claimed, among other things, that he could not get the balance sheet to explain where an unaccounted-for Rs 70 crore had gone—listed under 'miscellaneous' in Utkal's accounts, and allegedly set aside for bribes. Otta could not account for these missing funds, and passed on responsibility to Ola Lie, the head of Norsk (resident in London), indicating that Mr Lie was in effect his superior in the Utkal hierarchy. The judge made a joke about the appropriateness of Mr Lie's name given Utkal's reputation for tampering with the truth.

Otta had presented a written affidavit to the enquiry on 20 April 2001, where he refers to opposition to Utkal as 'some groups who are in microscopic minority and working against the establishment of project for no ideal intention [sic],' and reveals that Indal's decision to make a greenfield Alumina Project in Kashipur was made in 1991, followed by an agreement with the OMC for a prospecting licence in 1992, and that the Government of Orissa gave the go-ahead

> since the project would aid in harnessing Orissa's vast natural resources and potential, accelerate economic and industrial growth, generate employment in large scale in this backward area, provide education, increase skills of local people, provide health facilities, and also stimulate and strengthen the local farmers and entrepreneurs

... as well as generating tax and royalty income for the GoO. '*The bauxite deposits of Baphlimali were lying idle.*' He also states that the Ministry of Environment and Forests gave environmental clearance for Utkal's mine and refinery in September 1995, on the basis of its Environmental Plan, which involved taking water from Bara and Sano Nadi—the two biggest rivers in the area.[24]

After Otta, two women came to the witness box, an Adivasi and a Dalit, who had witnessed the shooting in Maikanch, and whose relatives were shot. The whole time each woman stood in the box she kept her palms joined in *Namaste* or *Johar*—a plea for justice and truth in that alien environment of the courtroom, where the judge kept an impartial aloofness, while the company lawyers pretended friendliness, but tried to trip them up with complicated lines of questioning about who had paid for them to come to Rayagada that day, and where they were during the shooting, implying that they couldn't have seen it, or to cow them with scorn. For example, in answer to the question 'Occupation?' when one of the women answered '*Chaso*' (cultivation) the lawyers led a round of titters, as if to dismiss her as an illiterate peasant. Before the end of the session, when the witnesses had left, the judge made the whole courtroom stand while he said that lawyers can be more violent than guns, and that treating villagers with such little respect will erode their faith in our courts.

A summary of Mishra's report was finally released to the media on 10 October 2003, when *Dharitri* published an account under the title 'Maikanch firing was justified'. Basically, according to the extracts released, Mishra's report reaches the contradictory conclusions that grossly excessive force was used, but the firing was justified. It singles out the OIC of Kashipur police station 'for continuing with firing beyond requirement', after the Magistrate had given the order to fire, but also admonishes this Magistrate, Golak Badajena, for giving an open-ended order. The excerpts released call the nineteen rounds fired excessive, and question the prior intent of the police visit to 'investigate' and 'maintain law and order', but do not highlight the height at which bullets were fired, nor the live ammunition in the guns, which imply a prior intention to cause harm. The report accepted villagers' account that the incident was provoked when police laid their hands on two of the women.

Most controversially, the report went beyond its brief to justify the alumina project, stating that 'the state cannot afford to remain backward for the sake of so-called environmental protection', and 'the extraction of bauxite need not have any adverse impact on the environment, particularly relating to protection of water, as is evident from the mining operations undertaken by Nalco at Damanjodi.' Reportedly, Mishra was given a quick VIP ('very important person') tour of Damanjodi, which made the red mud and other environmental effects appear harmless. Mishra's Commission refused to meet tribal people from the Damanjodi area who wanted to tell him the real situation there.

A number of eminent people with experience in Kashipur were also not called to give evidence, even though they submitted affidavits. These included: Banka Bihari Das, a noted environmentalist and former Minister in the Government of Orissa, Kishen Pattnayak, who had led a citizen's Commission to study Kashipur's deteriorating human rights before the firing, Vivekananda Dash, a journalist who had studied the Kashipur events in detail; and Swami Agnivesh, who had led a fact-finding human rights enquiry with Justice Tewatia immediately after the firing. Their report concluded that there was solid evidence of collusion between politicians, administrators and police behind the firing, and that the firing was premeditated murder, aimed at suppressing the tribal people's protest.

So Mishra's report, like Nagchoudhury's Gandhamardan report 15 years before, went out of its way to advocate the company line of economic necessity, denying any adverse impact on the environment. The *Lonely Planet* guide to India (August 2003 edition, p. 506) carried a box titled 'State Repression in Kashipur', describing the Kashipur movement. This was omitted from subsequent editions—censored, presumably, by pressure behind the scenes.

Critics of Utkal had hoped Mishra's enquiry would reveal the collusion between politicians and ministers, police, and company officials. The fact that the report did not apparently touch on the question of who called out the armed police, or how this decision was reached, makes the whole exercise look like a whitewash. Although the report blames the OIC for excessive use of force, it justifies the firing and says no one should be penalised for it.[25]

In Maikanch, one of the widows of the men killed, pregnant at the time of his death, refused an offer of 2 lakh rupees in compensation, asking 'will you give me the head of the man who killed my husband?' In later chapters we shall look more closely into the background of 'unholy alliances' behind the firing, between police, mining companies, politicians and journalists. The history of police firings goes back to Colonel Dyer ordering Gurkha troops to open fire at Jallianwalla Bagh in 1919, and several large-scale firings in Odisha during the Quit India Movement in 1942, as well as a pattern of more recent firings on Adivasi protestors, including eleven killed at Mandrabaju (Gajapati district) in December 1999.

Legal harassment is another story. As we have seen, over 500 arrests were made against anti-mining villagers in Kashipur up to 1999 alone. A division was exploited between Jhorias and Konds. The three martyrs of Maikanch were Jhorias, though several Konds also got bullet injuries. Jhorias were officially de-registered as a Scheduled Tribe, possibly to undermine their resistance to this project, and a move to re-register them as a Tribe got help from of one of the pro-mining politicians, K. C. Mahapatra.

With the firing, the Utkal project effectively shot itself in the foot. The enquiry gave three years' breathing space to Kashipur, free from company intimidation. But mining companies rarely give up in an area once they start investing. They are adept at waiting and manoevering for a comeback, and when they face an *impasse* in one area, they come up in another. While Utkal was stalled, Sterlite Industries started up in Lanjigarh, 100 km to the north-east, moving fast to avoid the momentum of opposition which had stalled Utkal. When Sterlite's refinery had started construction, Utkal moved again, with a second reign of terror, this time moving with an unstoppable pace, following Sterlite's example.

A new wave of repression

On 11 September 2004, *Dainik Bhaskar* reported that 'all obstacles to the much awaited Utkal project have been removed,' and that villagers had agreed unanimously to a new, generous R&R package.

This was far from true, and repression took off again in November, as police constructed a barracks at Dom Karal, 2 km from Kucheipadar. There were big rallies for and against Utkal at Tikiri and Kucheipadar, and the police started arresting residents of anti-mining villages. On 1 December, 300 people, mainly women, were sitting in protest near the barrack site at Dom Karal, when they were ordered to disperse and then tear-gassed and lathicharged by about 500 police. On the 16th (the fourth anniversary of the police killings), a convoy of several vehicles going to show solidarity with Kucheipadar was held for several hours at Tikiri police station. Among those detained for some hours were two MLAs and five foreigners, which made headline news in Odisha.

On the same day, a group called 'Alcan't in India' held a demonstration outside Alcan's HQ in Montreal, in solidarity with Kashipur villagers, putting pressure on Alcan to take responsibility for the reign of terror there, and withdraw from Utkal. In particular they focused on the fact that Utkal's 1995 Environmental Impact Assessment (EIA) had never been made public nor Environmental Clearance renewed. On 22 April 2004, Alcan's Chief Executive for bauxite and alumina, Michael Hanley, had promised 'Alcan't' and two journalists to let them have a copy of the EIA in two days, but this never happened, even though keeping an EIA secret is against Indian law and company practice. It seems that Hindalco would not allow this, knowing that its contents would not have stood up to international scrutiny.[26]

Utkal in 2004 consisted of two companies: Hindalco (55 per cent) and Alcan (45 per cent). Alcan had overseen the establishment of Utkal in 1992, along with Indal, Tata and Norsk. It reduced its majority share in Indal in 1987, raised this to a majority share again in 1998, and then sold this to Hindalco, which by this manoeuvre effectively bought up its biggest rival. Indal officially merged with Hindalco in 2005,[27] and Alcan finally left the consortium shortly before being bought up by Rio Tinto in 2007:

1994	Norsk 60%,	Indal 20%,	TATA 20%	
1995	Norsk 40%,	Indal 20%,	TATA 20%,	Alcan 20%
1999	Norsk 45%,	Indal–Hindalco 20%,		Alcan 35%
2004		Hindalco 55%,		Alcan 45%
2008		Hindalco alone		

Table 2. Changes in Utkal Alumina ownership

The situation in Kashipur remained very tense. According to a report by the People's Union for Civil Liberties (3 May 2005):

> The area is teeming with armed policemen for ... today again terror is in the air. Another Maikanch is just waiting to happen. In an area that desperately needs more schools and healthcare facilities, money is being spent to set up a new police outpost against the expressed wish of the villagers and their panchayat. For all practical purposes, the police are acting like a private army for the company. They are operating out of UAIL premises.

On 8 June 2005, Adivasi protestors in Guguput village blockaded the road and turned back company vehicles. A week later, on 15 June, police lathicharged a meeting inside this village, using tear-gas again, a significant escalation of the conflict, putting tribal villages on par with big urban confrontations. Harrassment by police flag marches and arrests continued. In October, 26 local activists were in jail.[28] The Orissa government with Utkal were promising jobs with attractively boosted salaries to a member of every displaced family, as an incentive to leave the movement and join the project. Finally, in mid-2006, Ramibeda, Kendukhunti and Tolo Karol were removed and construction on Utkal's refinery began. Under pressure from Alcan't and a new report (Goodland 2007), Alcan finally with drew from Utkal in April 2007, shortly before being taken over by Rio Tinto.

On 17 October 2006 the Orissa State Pollution Control Board held a public hearing at Tikiri for expansion of Utkal's refinery from 1 to 3 million tons per year. Villagers and activists boycotted the meeting, pointing out that construction was illegal, since Utkal had not got a renewal on its five-year environmental clearance, which expired in 2000, and an expansion cannot be applied for without clearance for the initial plan. Also, land acquisition had proceeded through force and intimidation; against the guarantee of Adivasi rights under the Fifth Schedule and Samatha Judgment; and numerous *gram sabha* resolutions had already rejected the project.[29] There was a strong police presence at the hearing anyway, so villagers held their own meeting with over 1,000 people, and declared the OSPCB hearing illegal.

As Utkal's construction proceeds, the area between Tikiri and Kucheipadar, and for miles around, has been transformed into a vast construction site by an army of bulldozers and dump-trucks. Meanwhile, other projects are in the air. South of the Kashipur plain, just south of Tikiri, Hindalco's sister company Aditya Aluminium has a construction site below Kodinga Mali, and is also active further south, near Mali Parbat. Aditya Aluminium is part of the same group as Hindalco, run by Aditya Birla, grandson of G. D. Birla. These bauxite and refinery projects are linked to Aditya Aluminium's smelter planned in Sambalpur district near Hirakud.

A Public Hearing was held on Mali Parbat in August 2005, and in December a fact-finding committee led by a sympathetic MP, Jayram of Pottangi, highlighted the opposition of 22 villages dependent on this mountain and its streams.[30] The Koraput District Zilla Parishad (ZP—a district-level council, under non-tribal control) gave its consent to this project at a meeting on 28 April 2006. In May, several hundred armed Adivasis demonstrated in Similiguda, declaring that the consent given by the ZP and Palli Sabha was under false pretences. However in September the convenors of the *Maliparbat Surakhya Samiti* sent a letter to the Orissa Governor and

PM apologising for their opposition and retracting it.[31] This letter clearly contradicted the will of the majority of villagers, who have continued to hold meetings against mining on Mali Parbat. On 20 August 2008 pro-company *goondas* attacked protestors in their village of Maliguda, injuring ten severely and mistreating women (*The Hindu*, 15 June 2008).

L&T's plans to mine Siji Mali and/or Kuturu Mali were re-activated in September 2005, along with plans to build a refinery near Kalyan Singpur, just where the Nagavali is joined by major tributaries. This project was now a Joint Venture with Dubal (Dubai Aluminium—74 per cent to L&T's 26 per cent).[32]

In October 2007, Indian Metal Ferro-Alloys (IMFA) announced plans to mine Sasu-Bohu Mali, building a million-ton refinery near its ferro-manganese factory at Therubali (already a major polluter of the Nagavali river), and a 250,000-ton smelter at Choudwar near Cuttack 'mainly for export'. IMFA's ferro-manganese plant started production in 1967:

> Therubali in the erstwhile Koraput district was as remote a location as can be imagined. Other than a collection of mud huts there was little else on offer for the local population which consisted almost exclusively of Adivasis (indigenous tribals)… It all changed in 1962 when Bansidhar Panda, an American educated research scientist, chose this remote area to be the cornerstone of his dream of an industrialised Orissa.[33]

IMFA already has three major chromite mines in north Odisha, and has been planning a move into aluminium since the 1990s. Bansidhar's son Jai Panda is the owner of one of the two Odia news channels, OTV, and therefore exerts considerable control over Odisha's media.

Nalco has been exploring plans for more mines in Andhra, Koraput, or on Gandhamardan, as well as holding talks with the Governments of Indonesia, Iran and South Africa for further mines or factories in those countries.[34]

BHP Billiton announced plans to mine a mountain in Kalahandi in November 2005, maybe Khandual Mali, an exceptionally well-forested mountain like Gandhamardan and Niyamgiri.[35] Several companies have designs on Krishun Mali nearby. Both these mountains are elephant territory. The Karlapat Wildlife Sanctuary was declared in

1992, leaving the bauxite summits outside (though no mining is allowed within 10 km of a Sanctuary).

Another bauxite-capped mountain was publicly identified in mid-2008 in the midst of the Kuttia Kond territory in south-west Kandhamal district—Anamani Parbat or Ushabali.[36] This was surveyed by a company called Gimpex at least five years before. Prospecting Licences were secretly signed by BHP Billiton and other companies for several mountains in this area, at the height of the brutal 'ethnic cleansing' that drove at least 50,000 Christians from their homes in the district in 2008.

Alcoa is also contemplating projects based on Odisha's bauxite, and has twice sent a team from the US according to highly-placed officials in the Odisha government. Alcoa's Vice-President Helmut Wieser confirmed this, adding that 'controversial environmental issues' have caused delay, implying that Alcoa would only come if it was offered big subsidies in electricity, transport, etc.[37]

To complete the invasion of aluminium companies, in October 2008, Rio Tinto (just after buying up Alcan) announced plans for setting up an integrated aluminium industry in Odisha or Andhra, in joint venture with Jindal.[38] The timing of this announcement came only days after the recent financial crisis hit the world's banks and companies. Rio Tinto was known to be vulnerable to a hostile bid by BHP Billiton, while Chinalco and Alcoa had bought a 12 per cent stake in RT, through Lehmann Brothers, whose fall thereby threatened China with massive losses.

Sterlite/Vedanta announced plans for a mine on Sasu-Bohu Mali early in 2008, reactivating Balco's dormant lease there (first established in 1995), and for a second refinery below. In June it announced designs on Gandhamardan,[39] following Nalco—plans linked to a Lower Suktel dam.

All these projects were facilitated by a highly flawed document hastily put together by the MoEF for the Supreme Court between September and October 2007, which listed south Odisha's main bauxite deposits, and declared that mining them would have little or no negative impacts on forests or the wider environment. On 5 October 2007, India's Attorney-General presented this during the hearing on Vedanta. The text argues that bauxite mining would stimulate development and proposes that the companies involved should set aside a proportion of their profits for reforestation, wildlife management and tribal development. It presents a list of ten mountains in south Odisha, and a highly tendentious set of arguments for turning them all into bauxite mines. To date (December 2009) Panchpat Mali remains south Odisha's only major bauxite mine. The MoEF document says that clearance has been granted or is in process for three of the mountains, and indicates that the other six deposits in its list have a staggering 27 Prospecting Lease applications and 53 Mining Lease applications pending on them.[40]

Meanwhile, similar manoeuvres are afoot over the border in Vishakhapatnam district of Andhra Pradesh, where several companies are in the process of getting clearance to mine bauxite in Joint Venture with the AP Mining Development Corporation Limited (APMDC). Jindal is the front-runner, planning mines on Gali Konda and Rakta Konda—the mountains near Borra Caves saved from mining by the Samatha Judgment. Local opposition remains strong there, and also at Sruangavarapu Kota, where Jindal plans a refinery, linked to the mountains by a 30-km conveyor belt (like Nalco's from Panchpat Mali).

The status of APMDC as a Public Sector corporation (like OMC in Odisha) is being used to circumvent the proscription in the Samatha Judgment and Fifth Schedule against private companies taking over tribal land. APMDC has filed no less than 25 mining lease applications, since the Andhra bauxite cappings are more numerous and broken-up than those in Odisha. The AP government has also overriden the Forest Department's initial refusal to grant clearance due to the mountains' exceptionally rich flora and fauna and local people's opposition.[41]

Jindal has seen enormous expansion recently (2008), with a notorious new steel plant near Raigarh (Chhattisgarh), another at Kalinganagar on Adivasi land, plans for 'India's biggest steel plant' near Angul, whose finance is supported by an Export Credit Guarantee from the UK government, a contentious chromite mine application in Jajpur district, and recently acquired iron-ore mines in Bolivia.[42]

Its plans in Andhra have been opposed by politicians of several parties, as well as social workers active on Adivasis' behalf, especially

Samatha. Among many other issues, the question of where the refinery at Sruangavarapu Kota would source its water has not been settled. At a Public Hearing in November 2006, Jindal said it would build a canal, while its Environmental Impact Assessment (EIA) names Tatikonda reservoir as the source. On 4 June 2007, when flaws were pointed out in this plan, Jindal said it would draw water from the Godavari river, although studies of flow volume make it clear this would exceed the Godavari's limit.[43]

Another company is moving ahead with plans to mine bauxite further west, on remote mountains of the Jerrela group. This is Ras Aluminium-Khaimah (RAK, also called Anrak), from the United Arab Emirates (UAE), like Dubai. The AP government signed a MoU for Jindal's project on 1 July 2005, and with RAK on 14 February 2007.

In October and December 2007, the MoEF granted environment clearance to Jindal, RAK and Nalco to mine these mountains, even while noting that the Jerrela group supports outstanding biodiversity. When a helicopter was making a survey on Pittapunuku mountain there in March 2008, police made tribal people from three villages vacate their homes. A CPI-M politician led a protest, meeting these villagers but reaching Pittapunuku after the helicopter had left.[44]

On 8 June 2008, a Public Hearing was held by the AP Pollution Control Board (APPCB) at Rachapalli for RAK's planned refinery-smelter complex at Makavalapalem. Despite huge police presence, local people all opposed the project.[45]

On 3 October, the APPCB held a hearing at Chintapalle near Jerrela, boycotted by local people and political parties. Opposition politicians (who rocked the AP Assembly by a walkout on the issue on 6 September), E. A. S. Sharma, a senior civil servant, and Samatha had already drawn authorities' attention to numerous procedural illegalities: the APMDC was being used 'in a benami manner' on behalf of a private company to circumvent the Samatha Judgment; large areas of pristine forest would be lost and no team from the CEC had visited the site; deployment of the much-feared Greyhounds (anti-naxal squads) meant intimidation that made any fair Public Hearing impossible; the Tribal Advisory Committee (TAC) had not approved the current plan; no *gram sabhas* had been held by the APMDC as required under PESA; the EIA was based on faulty information, with no proper survey and a 'cut and paste job' importing information from another EIA, a report by the Salim Ali Institute (for birds) in Coimbatore that had spelt out the dangers to rare species; and the plan would hit 66 villages of Vishakhapatnam district as well as eight villages of Malkangiri district (Odisha). Despite these violations, and a boycott by affected villages 40 km away, the authorities held the meeting and sent its flawed minutes to the MoEF.[46]

Reviewing our list of bauxite mountains in south Odisha and north Andhra, in the light of the MoEF document (October 2007) and Andhra plans, the following tie-ups are in place:

	Mountain	District	Status and Company Interest
1.	Niyam Dongar	Kalahandi–Rayagada	OMC/Sterlite
2.	Khandual Mali	Kalahandi	BHP Billiton application
3.	Krishun Mali	Kalahandi	
4.	Siji/Putuli Mali	Kalahandi–Rayagada	L&T/Dubal (UAE)
5.	Kuturu Mali	Rayagada	L&T/Dubal
6.	Kodinga Mali	Koraput–Rayagada	Aditya Birla clearance
7.	Panchpat Mali	Koraput	Nalco mining since 1986
8.	Mali Parbat	Koraput	OMC/Aditya and Jindal applications
9.	Pottangi	Koraput	
10.	Balada	Koraput	
11.	Sasu-Bohu Mali	Rayagada	Sterlite and IMFA interest
12.	Bapla Mali	Kalahandi–Rayagada	Utkal (Hindalco) application
13.	Ghusuri Mali	Koraput	
14.	Deo Mali	Koraput	Ashapura & Bhushan applications

15.	Gandhamardan	Borogorh–Bolangir	Continental Resources lease, Nalco and Sterlite applications
16.	Anamani Parbat/ Ushabali	Kandhamal	Gimpex with BHP and others
17.	Raktakonda (Chittamgondi)	Vishakhapatnam	APMDC/Jindal
18.	Galikonda (Anantagiri)	Vishakhapatnam	APMDC/Jindal
19.	Sapparla group	Vishakhapatnam	APMDC/Jindal
20.	Jerrela group	Vishakhapatnam	APMDC/RAK (UAE) and Nalco
21.	Gudem group	Vishakhapatnam	
22.	Katamrajkonda	East Godavari/ Khammam	

Table 3. Bauxite mountains and company designs

Clearly, these plans envisage a massive industrialisation programme sweeping Odisha and neighbouring states, and involve mass dispossession of the land's original inhabitants. Aluminium's take-off moves alongside iron, steel, coal and power projects, including the gigantic Polavaram dam project on the Godavari, and Posco's mega-investment in Odisha, opposed in Jagatsingpur district throughout 2005–09.

After highly publicised killings at Kalinganagar, and at Nandigram and Singur in West Bengal, tension and polarisation over industrial projects increases by the month. Memorial meetings for the Maikanch martyrs each 16 December have passed off peacefully, attracting hundreds of campaigners from other movements. Utkal construction is under way on a vast scale, right next to Kucheipadar, though work has often been stopped by protests of the displaced villagers (e.g. from February 2008), and half the land needed still has not been acquired. Bulldozers are flattening small hills to make a level site for the refinery, which plans to use over 30,000 cubic metres of water a day from Bara and Sano Nadi (literally, Big and Small Rivers)—the two 'wild rivers' that run from Kashipur through gorges south of Bapla Mali to join Indravati. Many villages depend on these rivers, which are likely to be sucked dry.

CHAPTER SIX

Lanjigarh: Vedanta's Assault on the Mountain of Law

While Utkal was stalled in Kashipur, a different company moved into the lull, using craftier tactics. A notice from Sterlite in *Samaj* newspaper on 8 June 2002 advertised its application to acquire the land of 12 tribal villages in Lanjigarh block of Kalahandi district, to build a refinery there. On 22 June, several hundred villagers went to the Revenue Office in Bhawanipatna, where they lodged a memorandum opposing this project, filing 200 individual petitions against it. But the Kalahandi Collector wrote an official letter to these villages on 26 June, serving notice that sixty families would be displaced and 302 would have their land acquired.[1] The Collector, Saswat Mishra, visited these villages several times in person, to persuade people to accept compensation in the form of cash, new houses and jobs. Basically, four agreed. The rest refused, and were left outside the refinery's wall. People from these villages founded the Niyamgiri Surakhya Samiti (Niyamgiri Protection Society) soon after his visit.

In January 2004, a group of us watched from the forested summit of Niyam Dongar, as police trucks carried people from their villages, which were then swiftly bulldozed. These were the ones that had accepted a compensation package, though they never expected this sudden forced removal. A few days later, we visited them in their brand-new colony of concrete shells, where their grief was palpable. This colony, Vedantanagar, was built in 2002–3 by a firm called Metro Builders on Revenue waste land, taken from 64 families from Jagannathpur village who had cultivated it.[2]

Niyam means Rule or Law in Hindi and Odia, in a sense similar to *Dharma*, indicating the divine or natural Law or truth which permeates existence. Niyam Raja or Neba Raja is the God of Universal Law to which human law aspires.

Niyam Dongar, which stands at the north-west of the Niyamgiri range, is one of Odisha's best-forested mountains, possessing the most extensive and wildest forest in the entire range, contiguous with an area of dense forest that stretches away to the west towards Karlapat—one of Odisha's last remaining areas of relatively untouched forest. The presence of elephants, tigers, leopards, bears, king cobras, pythons and monitor lizards is recorded here, to mention only a few of the apex species.

The long, wide summit that forms the lease area is 4,000 feet above sea level (1,306 metres). Over 80 per cent is covered in forest, contrary to Sterlite's claim in its Environmental Impact Assessment (2002). The reason that forest still covers this summit, unique among Odisha's mountains, is the Dongrias' taboo on cutting trees on the summit, seeing it as Niyam Raja's abode, and aware of a 'magnetic force' which the forest exerts on the whole region's fertility from up there.

Dongrias are among the few peoples in India still classed as a Primitive Tribe. Their society is far from primitive. One area where it is highly developed is in terms of rules (*niyam*) that protect the environment, which many other tribes now no longer observe. Their identity is bound up with Niyamgiri, and all of them live within the range. Their religion is not separate from Hinduism. Dongrias attend town festivals of Jagannath, Shiva and the Goddess in large numbers. Yet they do not look to the authority of Brahmins or texts, but deal with the spirit world around them directly, through

Niyam Dongar, near Lanjigarh

female and male shamans (*bejuni* and *beju*), dreams and signs in nature. The image of triangles which they paint on their temples in clay colours expresses the balance in nature of mountain and valley, water and sun.

As for the company threatening Niyamgiri, its name is taken, with cruel irony, from the profoundest roots of Indian civilisation. *Vedanta* is the name given to the body of knowledge formulated in the *Vedas*, over 3,000 years ago, and for the tradition of philosophy and religion formulated in medieval times based on the *Upanishads*, which took the essence of the Vedas to a higher level. *Advaita Vedanta* is the non-dualistic, non-materialist philosophy expounded most famously by Shankara in the ninth century. A basic concept is that there is no real separation between *Atman* and *Brahman*—the individual and universal soul, which become one when we open to a higher purpose than our individual desires. All polarities of religion, caste, and race are based on illusion.

While *Vedanta* developed as a purely abstract or religious tradition, it also inspired some of India's greatest thinkers to follow a path of social action, attempting to sweep away the unjust manifestations of polarity in society, such as colonial rule or untouchability. *Advaita Vedanta* is the philosophy which inspired Gandhi and made *ahimsa* his guiding force: harm to another being is actually harm to oneself, because at the level of what is most real, all separation and conflict between self and other is an illusion and falls away when one opens to the force of the higher self. Mining mountains and forging metals inevitably cause great harm to nature and people, for the sake of profit and power. So when a mining company takes the name 'Vedanta', how is the original tradition, that challenged material values, subverted?[3]

Vedanta the company has broken many records, both for its rapid rise in size and capital, and (as we shall see) for its cavilier attitude to the law, in India as well as other countries.[4] In December 2003, it became the first Indian company to register on London's Stock Exchange, backed by J. P. Morgan, who sponsored a long report on the company. Before this, the foreign acquisitions by Sterlite/Vedanta in Australia, Armenia, Zambia and other countries predated those of other Indian metal companies such as Tata, Hindalco and Jindal. Shortly before the company was listed in London, its head, Anil Agarwal, bought a £10 million home in Mayfair that had belonged to the Shah of Iran.

Malco—Balco—Sterlite—Vedanta

So how did Sterlite become Vedanta?

When Sterlite signed the MoU for Niyamgiri with the Orissa government in 1997, the mountain was due to be declared a National Park, and 77 per cent of the mining lease area is Reserved Forest. How could such a sensitive area be leased for mining?

Sterlite became an aluminium company by buying up Malco and Balco. Malco (Madras aluminium company) started as a public sector company in joint venture with an Italian firm, Montecatini (1964), and its refinery and smelter at Mettur (Tamil Nadu) get water and power from the Mettur dam on the Kaveri river (1934).

Malco's bauxite mines are on the Shevaroyan, Kolli and Yercaud mountains (all in Tamil Nadu). Mining has taken 200 feet off several mountains, causing many streams to dry up. Malco was originally under government control (73 per cent + 27 per cent Montedissan, the technology supplier). It was shut down in 1991 because of intermittent disruptions to its power supply. Sterlite restarted it after buying it up in 1995. A People's Tribunal in May 2005 recorded numerous accounts of malpractice at Malco since it came under Vedanta: industrial diseases of lungs, stomach, skin and eyes for people working in the plants and living nearby, and pollution and serious spills from fly ash, bauxite dust and red mud.[5]

Balco was a public sector company too, starting in 1965 as a joint venture with Soviet and Hungarian companies (Vami, AluTRV, Rusal). Its central refinery and smelter complex at Korba (now in Chhattisgarh) started production in 1973–75, with a 270 MW coal-fired power plant. This complex is named after the Korva tribe, who were effectively driven out of this area. Korba displaced Adivasis from 1,650 acres of land, both at Korba and mining sites. Balco had bauxite mines on a number of mountains, including Amarkantak (near the Narmada's source) and Phutkapahar (both closed now). After its defeat at Gandhamardan, Balco started mining Mainpat (Surguja district) in 1993, subverting tribal opposition by buying out the bigger landowners.

In March 2001, Arun Shourie's Ministry of Disinvestment organised the sale of a controlling 51 per cent stake in Balco to Sterlite. Balco's assets at this time consisted of the smelter and refinery as well as a captive power plant and flats for 4,000 employees at Korba, three mines, a factory in Bengal, and offices in Delhi. These were sold for Rs 551.5 crores, a price set by the hurried valuation of consultants for the Hong Kong-based firm, Jardine Fleming. Most analysts put the real value of these assets at about ten times this amount. The Balco Union leader A. M. Ansari, who led opposition to this deal, estimated them at even more. When he led the 7,000-strong workforce out on a 67-day strike, Balco sacked him on a false pretext (Bidwai 2001). During the strike, aluminium in the smelter's 408 pots solidified—the ultimate danger at a smelter, and the reason that it needs a constant power supply. Most pots had to be relined, at considerable cost.

Questions were also asked in Parliament about whether selling off a nationalised company like this without Parliament's approval contravened existing legislation? It is significant that Chhattisgarh only came into existence the previous year. There had been no widespread movement for its separation from MP, and the evidence suggests that mining interests were a major reason behind its formation.

After Balco was privatised, work conditions became a lot harsher. Workers in the Korba plants told us they had to work unpaid overtime, and many were made redundant. Asked about health problems, they said the company does six-monthly health checks, but these are a sham, and they would lose their jobs if they talked about what really happens (March 2005). In July 2005, after at least a dozen deaths during the construction of a new, London-financed smelter at Korba, police lathicharged a crowd of strikers there.

In 2004–05, under Sterlite-Vedanta's regime, new mines were started in Kawardha district, at Bodai Daldali in the Maikal range, on the edge of Kanha National Park (MP), the area of central India made famous by Kipling's *Jungle Books*. The Balco mines at Mainpat and Bodai Daldali, like Hindalco's mines at Samirpat in north Chhattisgarh, are mostly run by the contractors R. K. Jain, whose managers at Bodai Daldali testified to us (June 2006) that they were running at a loss because of delayed payments from Vedanta. This harshness is passed on with interest to workers, who lack the most basic amenities—no school for their children, no medical centre for miles, and no compensation for accidents. The report commissioned by J. P. Morgan and released to investors in December 2003 confirms the low safety standards at the Balco and Malco mines, and mentions highly dangerous road conditions in the Malco area that pre-figures the large number of road and factory deaths since, in and around Lanjigarh. In September 2009 a tall chimney at a new Balco power station at Korba collapsed, killing at least 40 workers.[6]

Odisha's bauxite mountains are massive, and some have one or two tribal villages on their summits (Siji and Kuturu Mali). Chhattisgarh's bauxite mountains have similar steep ascents through winding forest roads. But their summits are even vaster, extending for miles, with forty or more tribal villages. At Bodai Daldali, on the Maikal range, these are of the Gond and Baiga tribes, and company tactics for land acquisition have accentuated tension between these groups. Bigger landowners are bought out, while smaller ones' claims are largely ignored, and rarely compensated. At both places, mines are right next to the villages, encroaching on their land and drying it out. As their fields and the land's fertility disappear, many of the villagers near the mine become dependent on labouring work hacking out the bauxite. The dispossession of Adivasis started when Balco was a public sector company, and has intensified under Sterlite, even though its right to take tribal land as a private company contravened the Samatha Judgment, on which Anil Agarwal, as company chairman, commented: '*I'm not a legal person. I have no idea about the judgment. All metal industries are in tribal areas.*'[7]

Before Sterlite entered the aluminium scene, five companies controlled the market in India: Malco (at first), Balco and Nalco were PSUs (Public Sector Undertakings), Hindalco and Indal private companies. Sterlite's buy-up of Malco and Balco, and Hindalco's merger with Indal left three: Hindalco/Indal with 51 per cent of the market, Nalco 23 per cent, and Sterlite 15 per cent, while the other 11 per cent was made up by imports of speciality alloys.

Sterlite bought up another PSU in 2002, Hindustan Zinc Ltd. (HZL: 64.9 per cent holding) which operates three zinc and lead mines (two underground) and two smelters in Rajasthan, and another zinc smelter at Vizag. It is currently building new zinc and lead smelters and a captive coal-fired power plant at Chanderiya (Rajasthan). Sterlite's great expansion in India was thus boosted by the Ministry of Disinvestment (i.e. privatisation) of the BJP government. HZL constructed a controversial dam in Rajasthan which displaced Adivasis, and Vedanta got police to remove protesters in order to finish it.[8]

Copper wire was Sterlite's original business, and becoming India's biggest copper producer was its path to fame. In 1975 it was based in Patna and making copper wires for telephone cables, etc. Anil Agarwal bought up Samsher Sterlite in 1976, a cable producer based in Bombay. This company became Sterlite Industries (India) Ltd. (SIIL), and in 1982 became the first in India to deal in jelly-filled cables (used for computers, etc.), where it made high profits, and bought heavily into India's copper business, acquiring a copper refinery and two rod factories at Silvassa in Gujarat.

In 1993 Sterlite met stiff opposition to its plans to build a copper smelter in Maharashtra, and the next year started reconditioning an existing plant—bought on the cheap from Australia—and set it up at Tuticorin in Tamil Nadu. Sterlite's smelter on India's southern tip has contravened basic safety standards and caused serious pollution, from sulphur dioxide fumes to uncontrolled toxic waste effluents of heavy metals, which have contaminated drinking water in at least ten wells with arsenic. Copper poisoning has also been diagnosed in local residents. The company made a pipeline to discharge its waste into a sensitive marine National Park 16 km away, against regulations, and despite protests by fishermen. The smelter continued operation despite legal judgments against it, without meeting environmental controls. Between 1997 and 1998 there were at least four blasts and other serious accidents, killing and maiming numerous workers and residents. The smelter has been vastly expanded in recent years, without dealing with the pollution properly, and without the proper permit being issued by Tamil Nadu's Pollution Control Board.[9]

So before it became Vedanta, Sterlite was already a company with a dubious environmental record. It was indicted in 1998 and 2001 for illegal insider trading on the Bombay Stock Exchange, by SEBI (the Securities Exchange Board of India). A promoter called Harshad Mehta (convicted of filching 5 billion rupees from the State Bank of India in 1992) had set up a number of front companies known as the Damayanti group, to which Sterlite lent 30,000 of its Malco shares. Sterlite's scrip price went up 41 per cent between April and June 1998. When Damayanti went bust, and SEBI managed to lift the corporate veil, it found a scam of front companies and an artificial boom that pre-figured the Enron scam. Sterlite was one of three companies found guilty of involvement and banned from trading on the Bombay Stock Exchange for 3 years. On appeal this order was lifted for Sterlite, though Mehta died in jail. Sterlite was also declared by the Enforcement Directorate to be violating the rules requiring companies to repatriate assets back to India.[10]

In 2002 Agarwal set up a subsidiary, Sterlite Opportunities

and Ventures Ltd., to facilitate foreign acquisitions and monetary transfers. Technically Sterlite was at this time a subsidiary of Twinstar Holdings, registered in Mauritius, and therefore a foreign company. Mauritius is a tax haven, and thus an easy conduit for channelling money out of India. The owner of Twinstar was a certain Vinod Shah, a non-resident Indian based in London, who owned it through another private company called Volcan Investments, registered in the Bahamas, another tax haven. Volcan had a 100 per cent stake in Twinstar, while Twinstar had a 55 per cent stake in Sterlite, and an 80 per cent stake in Malco.

It was through Twinstar that Sterlite made a huge deal to buy two Australian copper mines in 1999, Mt. Lyell (Tasmania) and Thalanga (Queensland), through Monte Cello Corporation (Netherlands), apparently a front company, set up to avoid tax. Around the same time, Sterlite bought the Zod gold mines in Armenia. The Australian and Armenian acquisitions were bought from Bob Friedland's First Dynasty Mines (Canada). Agarwal fired Rajat Bhatia, his Vice-President for Mergers and Acquisitions, in July 2000 when Bhatia warned against 'illegal and unethical' aspects of this acquisition in Australia. Agarwal reportedly 'threw his digital diary at him', saying 'I will make sure that you do not have a place on this planet'. For this indignity a London employment tribunal awarded Bhatia record compensation of over £800,000 for wrongful dismissal in December 2003.[11]

In 2002 Sterlite bought the Kongola Copper Mines (KCM), Zambia's biggest industry, from Anglo-American UK—a problematic, though huge and lucrative venture. In this purchase, Sterlite made it a condition that it would not have to take responsibility for existing environmental and human rights violations. Sterlite's Zod Gold Mine and processing plant near Mt Ararat in Armenia have also faced strong opposition from environmentalists and involved complicated financial intrigues.[12]

It is this dubious history which Sterlite wiped away with the adoption of a brand new—and very ancient—name: Vedanta.

Lanjigarh to London

It was Sterlite Industries (SIIL) that signed an MoU with the GoO to mine Niyamgiri on 7 June 2003, and during the forced removal of Kinari and other villages near Lanjigarh, the company was still known locally as Sterlite. When Saswat Mishra came to the Majhi Kond villages in 2002 to persuade them to accept compensation and give up their land, he told them they would get real development—jobs, tractors, education, money and bank accounts, and homes in a nice new colony.

'They are flooding us out with money' was Dai Singh Majhi's terse analysis.

> Sterlite-Vedanta was insisting to pay us money, for our land, for our house, but we are saying to them that money will not last. The district administration told me, *"Dear friend, I will pay you money for your land, which is owned by the government. Only one foot of soil is yours, the rest is owned by the government."*
>
> But we insisted that we won't decide everything in this village meeting. They had brought in too many outsiders and bribed people with free food and drink. They had slaughtered a few goats on that day for the people trucked in. It was a stage-managed village meeting. We the people of 12–13 villages wrote an application to the district administration, saying *"We are not going to give up our Water and Forest. We won't part with our Niyamgiri Mountain"*. But the District Magistrate said: *"Who has written this? A pig or a goat? Does he have a name or an address?"* [13]

Dai Singh stood up to the Collector when he visited Belamba, saying 'We cannot eat your money.' He was at the forefront of this village's refusal to accept compensation, telling Saswat that this land and village belonged to their forefathers for generations and represents their whole life. They could not leave it. After several visits the Collector got angry, and finally told them, 'Your village will be destroyed anyway. I'll never come here again', before getting into his jeep and going away.

Bhim Majhi is an elder of Turiguda village and another founding member of Niyamgiri Surakhya Samiti. Some of Turiguda's lands were

Chandra and Dai Singh Majhi, Belamba

to be taken for the refinery's red mud pond. Bhim also stood up to the Collector, showing a clear grasp of climate change.

> They asked, "*Why are you opposing Sterlite company? Is it taking your village?*" I replied, "*We are resisting for our motherland, for our mountain. So we oppose Sterlite. We oppose the government. The summer is very hot already, it will get worse if Sterlite comes. You won't get rain then. The summer is so hard for us already, so we want them to stop.*"
> Then they say, "*You are opposing us, can you compete?*" We reply, "*It is not about winning or losing. We will resist, for our mountain.*" Then they ridicule us and say, "*What are you Konds up to? What do you know about these things?*"

Kotduar was one of the villages which accepted compensation. Gurbari Majhi's house and land stood apart, on land just enclosed by the refinery wall. When we met her, the pressure she and her husband faced was unbearable. As she told us later:

> We had to leave. What to do *agya*? They encircled our house by the boundary wall. We were alone. How long could we last? There was no way out.... We had to leave.

Khetra Parabhoi and his wife Tula Dei in Sindhabahili hamlet had title-deeds and refused compensation. Their neighbours had accepted, and when they were suddenly removed and the bulldozers

Tula Dei at her house just inside the wall, Sindhabahili

came to demolish this hamlet she guarded her house and kept the demolishers off with a long pole. Her house stands just inside the boundary wall, where a gap has been left for her family's use.

> We have managed so far, why would we die now—just because the company has come and told us to live on money? Can we eat money? These children who live on mangoes and dates and millet and pulses, who are not educated enough, what will they do with money? They are not going to get any job in the company. We have been living on these lands a long time. We have sustained our children like this. We don't want your money.

Under pressure from the company, the tribal community was split into accepters and refusers. Many families (such as Gurbari's) could not prove title to their land, so had no legal grounds to stay put. After positions hardened, Sterlite announced it would take the land of only six villages, leaving the others just outside the boundary wall. Kopaguda (just 50 yards away), Belamba, and Bandhoguda were soon overshadowed as the refinery went up, with work proceeding under strong lights 24 hours, day and night. The landscape around these villages has completely changed, and after a while, villagers accepted labouring work quarrying nearby rock formations to make stone chips for construction.

On 7 February 2003, a very un-public Public Hearing about mining Niyamgiri and building the refinery and power station, was held in the Lanjigarh office of the Kuttia Kandha Development Agency, presided over by the Kalahandi Collector, Saswat Mishra. This was supposedly to satisfy requirements in MoEF guidelines, though since no Dongrias were present from communities which would be impacted by mining, its validity is questionable. Similarly with a Public Hearing held at Muniguda by the Orissa State Pollution Control Board (OSPCB) on 17 March 2003, where a number of villagers made their case against the Lanjigarh project. Dongrias went there to demonstrate their opposition, but were not allowed in. So much for consultation.

In the following months, tribal activists were often intimidated or beaten. On 1 April 2003, an activist named Lingaraj Azad of the SJP was arrested and taken to Lanjigarh police station. Villagers who went there to demand his release the next day were attacked by members of a Sterlite-funded youth club. This began close to the police station, and Lingaraj overheard an officer giving instructions to beat people over the phone. According to victims, their attackers left a game of cricket and used bats and stumps to beat people. Seventeen people were severely injured, including women, and the attack continued as far as Basantpadar village. An old man named Maya Nayak died two months later from injuries.

The incident was reported in *Samaj* on 9 April, and on the 15th a four-person team from the People's Union for Civil Liberties (PUCL) visited the area and interviewed people, including police. They concluded that the Lanjigarh police had colluded in the attack.[14]

It was following these events, in December 2003, that Sterlite became Vedanta—though local people did not hear of this for a while. The new holding company came into being when Vedanta Resources plc was registered as a British public company on the London Stock Exchange in December 2003. This came about with the help of various foreign connections, including J. P. Morgan, which offered a record IPO (Initial Public Offering) on the New York Stock Exchange of $879 million, after first commissioning an extensive report on the company, promoting it as a promising investment.[15]

Vedanta's first AGM, London, 2004

Among the personalities involved was the world's highest-paid CEO for 2002–03, Brian Gilbertson, who became Vedanta's first Non-Executive Chairman. Gilbertson's approval was hugely influential. He had engineered a merger between BHP and Billiton, to produce the world's biggest mining company in June 2001. BHP was an Australian company, whose initials stand (appropriately) for Broken Hill Proprietaries. Billiton was a Dutch company which started out mining tin in Indonesia. Gilbertson led the merged company in the direction of further investments in South African mining ventures, which others in the company did not want. Hence his record 'golden handshake'—a $16 million redundancy payment on top of his $9 million fee.

Gilbertson's presence in Vedanta got the investments rolling in, and Vedanta immediately attracted nearly $1 billion for a new smelter at Korba plus the Lanjigarh project. J. P. Morgan and Barclays were instrumental in sponsoring this float. Their representatives, with Gilbertson and several other foreign executives, flew to Lanjigarh by helicopter for the laying of the refinery's foundation stone by Orissa's Chief Minister, Naveen Patnaik, in June 2003.

The London registration was also effected with the help of a DFID official named Piers-Harrison, and one of Vedanta's first directors was Sir David Gore-Booth, ex-High Commissioner to India. Britain's Department of Trade and Industry advertised the refinery on its website for its 'investment and employment opportunities', until this was questioned by an activist from Action Village India.

Another highly influential director was P. Chidambaram, a senior advocate at India's Supreme Court, who had been India's Finance Minister (1996–98), and resigned from Vedanta to be so again from mid-2004, when a new Congress government won the election. As the present Union Home Minister, he leads the central government's most intense and single-minded military and propaganda campaign ever against the Maoist insurgency.

Not many in Lanjigarh realise that there are at least two Vedantas. One is the British company Vedanta Resources plc, owning a majority share of Sterlite (55.1 per cent in 2003–04), with Lanjigarh a 'key growth project'. However, the refinery is actually operated by an Indian subsidiary company, Vedanta Alumina Ltd. (VAL). In the British press, the names Sterlite and Balco have hardly been mentioned, while at Lanjigarh or Korba few knew the name Vedanta until its deal with Naveen's government became a major issue in Orissa's Assembly between November and December 2004.[16] Morgan Stanley warned in January 2004 that the balance of Vedanta's risks and rewards was not favourable: 'We think there is a considerable risk that its key growth project, the greenfield Orissa alumina refinery, could go over time and budget, or indeed not go ahead at all.'[17]

The foundation stone for the Lanjigarh refinery was destroyed by outraged villagers, but work started soon after, constructing a boundary wall for the site several kilometres in circumference.

Then within two weeks, starting on 23 January 2004, police went to each of the villages that had accepted in turn, and gave them a couple of days to leave their homes, fields and animals—everything they had existed for—before taking them away in trucks to the new colony, now named Vedantanagar, built for them between the mountain and the refinery site. Bulldozers immediately reduced their villages to bare red earth. In just a few days, by early February, four Kond villages had ceased to exist: Kinari, Borabhata, and most of

Sindhabahili and Kotduar. Other villages lost land. The process of acquisition and pressure to sell has continued ever since.

Villagers had not expected this sudden removal and destruction, and bitterly regretted saying yes. This is when a woman in the colony said to us, 'They even destroyed our gods,' for the main Kond deities, *Darni Penu* and *Jakeri Penu*, exist in the stones and posts embedded in the centre of each village. These had been bulldozed into oblivion. They had cash for the moment, in new bank accounts, and they had the food grain they grew the previous season, knowing this was the last they would ever grow. Otherwise, they had nothing—just alien concrete shells to live in, no land, no gods, and little self-respect or community. The houses and fields they and their parents made and worked at for so many years—all gone. Even their connection with their relatives in other villages was fractured: by accepting the company's money, they had made way for the refinery to be built.

The colony's location at the bottom slopes of Niyam Dongar places them as a captive labour pool between mine and the factory. Working for the company is the only viable way to earn a living, though some said they had not been paid yet for jobs they had done. Houses in the colony stand separate, unlike those in any normal Kond village. The people were watched over by security guards, as if this was a concentration camp, and when we entered (in February 2004) and talked with the people, these guards sidled close to our conversation and radioed their masters, who sent police to record our names.

The refinery was built on a plan drawn up with a specialist Australian engineering firm, Worley MMC (Minerals Metals and Chemicals), which services Worsley and other refineries in Australia.[18] The main engineering firm on the ground was a Chinese company, Guiyang Aluminium and Magnesium (Research and Development) Institute (GAMI), who also built Vedanta's new smelter at Korba.

Protests continued as tensions rose in Lanjigarh. Already there were reports of over 100 deaths by accident at the work site, where harsh conditions and much secrecy prevailed. Most jobs went to outsiders, and people held demonstrations at the lack of jobs for locals, especially in Rayagada district. The Niyamgiri mine lease area is divided between Rayagada and Kalahandi, but the refinery and displaced villages lie just within Kalahanadi. There are even persistent rumours of children from poor families who have been kidnapped locally and actually sacrificed at the mine site on the mountain or at the refinery site. Industrial anthropologists say that no large-scale industrial project starts in Odisha without at least one human sacrifice—a degenerate tantric rite by no means restricted to superstitious villagers, though other anthropologists see these stories as a persistent 'myth' (Parry 2007).

On 7 April 2004 about 2,000 people took part in an Oath March from Belamba village to Lanjigarh town, to strengthen resistance to the Vedanta project. Kishen Pattnayak gave one of his last speeches there (Chapter Eighteen).

The next day, police arrested 15 people for setting fire to Sterlite machines. Lanjigarh was now divided, like Kashipur, between those for and against the project.

Soon after, Vedanta Resources held its first AGM, in London. Michael Fowle was the spokesman for Anil Agarwal, seated next to him. Brian Gilbertson and Sir David Gore-Booth were absent (Gilbertson resigned soon after this, and Gore-Booth died), while Chidambaram had resigned to become India's Finance Minister. The other directors included Peter Sydney-Smith (Finance), and Jean Pierre Rodier (from Pechiney). As owners of a share each, we have joined other shareholder-activists to attend every AGM (2004–09), to witness and speak out. The venue has got grander over the years, and in 2008 took place under chandeliers at the Royal Institute of Engineers, round the corner from Downing Street and the Houses of Parliament.

One of the worst deaths occurred on 27 March 2005, when Sukru Majhi of Kansari village was run over while walking back alone from a meeting at Panimunda. He was a prominent activist, and other local people were convinced he had been run over on purpose, especially since it seemed that the vehicle had reversed over him to make sure of his death. This happened close to his village, on the newly metalled road from Doikhal to Lanjigarh.[19] The road is smooth and beautiful, unlike most local roads—an example of project benefits. It was night and there were no witnesses.

The fear level and pressure on other tribal villagers was huge after this. It was clear that whatever the company people and their local supporters did had the full support of police. Yet police have also suffered, for instance, in the large number of road accidents caused by Vedanta vehicles. On 23 January 2008, the Assistant Sub-Inspector at Lanjigarh, Rabi Naraya Das, was killed by an alumina lorry on the same road to Lanjigarh, where a witness saw his motorbike under the lorry (reported also in *Sambad*, 24 January 2008, frontpage).

The other aluminium companies had been watching Sterlite's progress at Lanjigarh, waiting for the barrier of local resistance to break there. In March and September 2004, BHP Billiton (now, thanks to Brian Gilbertson, the world's biggest mining company) announced plans to set up a bauxite mine and alumina refinery in Kalahandi, as well as iron-ore mines and a steel plant in Odisha. BHP had just conducted a training programme for NGOs in Odisha, and donated a large sum to Gram Vikas to install a mini-hydel scheme on a stream near Karlapat, bringing electricity in a clear attempt to woo the area's villager communities.

Karlapat is remoter than Lanjigarh, and the Konds are determined not to part with their land and mountains. The prospecting lease for Khandual Mali was held by Sulakhani Mines and Minerals, which was set up by local businessmen in 2002–03, including a contractor named Subhash Ponda, and Pramod Singh, the Karlapat Raja.

BHP's announcement in September 2004 prompted Sterlite/Vedanta to announce its own plans for a steel plant. In the same month, Anil Agarwal met Raman Singh, Chief Minister of Chhattisgarh, in London, and announced a deal with the Chhattisgarh State Industrial Development Corporation (CSIDC) to set up an 'Aluminium park' at Korba, 450 km from Lanjigarh, where the new, London-funded smelter was expanding production from 100,000 tons of aluminium per year to 345,000.[20] Given that roughly a ton of toxic red mud is produced for every ton of alumina refined, it is not surprising that Balco has produced large quantities. In 2003 there were six red mud lakes at Korba, three in use and three already full, with a seventh under construction.

The new smelter was built during 2004–6, 'with pre-baked technology' provided by GAMI (from China). It was built next to the old smelter, providing a striking contrast, the new one white and blue, the old one of rusting metal, requiring a larger workforce. Each building is based around the pot-room, nearly a kilometre long. The pots, in which the high-temperature electrolysis occurs, smelting molten alumina into metal by separating off the oxygen, are fiery furnaces in the old smelter; more enclosed in the new. Men open the doors of the old pots, removing Spent Pot Lining (SPL), the highly toxic used-up anodes, which are heaped at the sides of the smelters. The project involved making a new 540 MW ccpp, supplementing the existing 270 MW one. Construction started before the GoI Secretariat of Industrial Assistance had approved engineering and design fees for GAMI, and before permits for expanding Korba's capacity were obtained—a pattern of forcing projects through without waiting for legal formalities that Vedanta has pioneered, and other companies are now following.

This expansion involved felling 20,000 trees on 1,000 acres of government land. Chhattisgarh's Revenue Minister, Mr Kanwar, brought this to light in July 2005—and was promptly transferred to the Agriculture ministry, where he again demanded that 'Balco free the land. I want to take the battle with Balco to a logical end', while the new State Agriculture and Law Minister Brijmohan Agrawal stated that

> The Chhattisgarh government will not allow Balco to continue with its illegal possession of the land. The company has to surrender all the encroached land with massive penalty.

But nothing could dent Agarwal's deal with the Chhattisgarh CM.[21]

Vedanta was already planning a new smelter in Odisha, at Burkhamunda in Jharsaguda district, where a Public Hearing was held at the end of 2005. In May 2006 it was approved by a high level Committee of the GoO chaired by Naveen Patnaik, as an investment of 3,000 crore rupees, and work started soon after—illegally, since environmental clearance had not been given. This was granted *post facto* in March 2007. On 9th May 2007, the project was granted Special Economic Zone (SEZ) status, which gives heavy subsidies on water, land, electricity, transport, etc. Here too, villages have been displaced with inadequate compensation. Vedanta's Burkhamunda smelter is one of several huge new factories supplied by the DFID-funded refurbishment of Hirakud reservoir (Chapter Four). At Brundamal nearby, Vedanta is building a huge coal-fired power plant for the smelter and to sell surplus electricity.

Prafulla Samantara brought a case highlighting illegal aspects of this smelter at the Court of the National Environment Appellate Authority in Delhi, arguing that construction was illegal without prior environmental clearance, and that the smelter depended on Niyamgiri bauxite in a case *sub judice*. Moreover the EIA was full of misleading errors: contrary to its claim, there was forest on and around the site, part of a vital elephant corridor, with numerous other rare species; and it was just 200 metres from the flood-prone Berren river (less than the permitted distance). An evaluation of the smelter's EIA by Mark Chernaik of Environmental Law Alliance Worldwide (ELAW, US) shows that it also falls far short of international standards on control of PFC and sulphur dioxide emissions; on disposal of SPL in landfills (prohibited in the US where SPL is classified as hazardous waste); and on particulate emissions from the power plant and fluoride emissions from the smelter.[22]

Bauxite mining in Chhattisgarh shows the level of exploitation in store for Odisha, if Vedanta starts mining Niyam Dongar. On Mainpat and Kawardha the work is done by hand, blasting down 30 or more feet below the surface, and then breaking up the rocks with mattocks and loading them onto trucks which take the bauxite, without covers, to Korba, located 150 and 260 km from these two mining areas, causing immense dust pollution on the way. Niyam Dongar's bauxite is much deeper than the Chhattisgarh deposits. Bauxite brought from Rayagada is covered by tarps, but bauxite transported the few kilometres from Doikhal station is in open trucks, so the dust pollution between there and Lanjigarh is already prodigious.

Law of the land

Vedanta's rise is one of the most rapid of any mining company, ever. Its lofty aims of benefits for people in Odisha contrast sharply, as we have seen, with ground realities of obliterating landscapes, pollution, corruption and death. The stories of this company are both unique and symptomatic of what is happening in many parts of the earth. Examining them in some detail gives an inside view into challenges facing all of us, since Vedanta takes the pattern to a certain extreme, which has a wide influence. Since its Sterlite days, it has played near the edge of the law. Examples are its use of Mauritius and the Bahamas as tax havens for transferring profits out of India, evidence of insider trading, a tendency to ignore or override regulations which safeguard the environment, while using the power of influential contacts to get its way. Anil Agarwal is quoted as saying:

> I understand the Indian psychology. That's my biggest advantage in India. You must have patience. Everything will come through.[23]

These words evoke his company's tactic of starting to construct factories before getting the required clearance.

Vedanta's 'dance with the law' follows in the footsteps of America's Robber Barons, who showed a smug disregard for the law, manipulating it and paying large sums at the courts to get the land and metals they wanted, and made conspicuous donations to 'good causes' that prefigure Agarwal and Mittal topping Forbes' list as 'heroes of philanthropy'.[24] The company's pursuit of mining clearance for Niyamgiri at the Supreme Court from 2004–08 is a legal case study. Witnessing three of the last sessions (September–October 2007) was a revelation for us. Niyamgiri is the mountain of Law/*Dharma*/truth, and this case has a profound significance for India and far beyond.

Vedanta first came into the forefront of Odisha news in November–December 2004, with allegations of bribes to politicians in the GoO, and irregularities surrounding the company's recent deal with the OMC in October. A High Court ruling went against the Orissa Government in December over another mining lease it had signed with Jindal Strips for chromite mining at Tangaparha in Dhenkanal district. Several cases on Vedanta raised in Orissa's High Court (Cuttack) were now transferred to India's Supreme Court in Delhi, which in turn called for reports from its advisory body, the Central Empowered Committee (CEC).[25]

On 18–23 December 2004, a CEC Fact Finding Team of S. C. Sharma and S. K. Chadha came from Delhi to Lanjigarh, and took statements about infringements of Forest Laws. Senior Forestry officials spoke frankly about these violations, and the team saw for themselves where large areas of village forests had been felled. They asked: why was the resettlement colony sited right at the edge of the Niyamgiri Reserved Forest? Why was the refinery's red mud pond placed right beside the Bansadhara river, where it first forms below the mountain? Above all, why had application for the refinery been *delinked* from the bauxite mining application, which had not been submitted yet? The team also commented that Sulakhani's lease on Khandual Mali was too close to the Karlapat sanctuary, encroaching on its Elephant Reserve.[26]

They asked a number of questions about the behaviour of the MoEF (Ministry of Environment and Forests), and several letters were exchanged during March 2005 between the CEC, MoEF, Vedanta and the GoO, and a succession of hearings began at the Supreme Court. Like the Robber Barons, Vedanta was clearly using political contacts to help 'adjust' the law to suit corporate demands. This was Agarwal's 'patience'—a conviction that his contacts would get him Niyamgiri.

A second CEC team visited Lanjigarh-Niyamgiri on 14–16 June 2005, holding public meetings of enquiry. Their report was submitted in September 2005, and stands as a strong statement of Vedanta's infringements of the law. This CEC report starts by outlining the Sterlite/Vedanta project and the applications of Biswajit Mohanty (Wildlife Society of Orissa), Prafulla Samantara and R. Sreedhar (Academy of Mountain Environics) against it.

Basically, the project involved the bauxite mine as well as alumina refinery. Yet Sterlite applied for Environmental Clearance for the refinery in March 2003, requesting the MoEF in March 2004 to *delink* the two projects, on the grounds that the refinery would take three years to construct, while the bauxite mine would take only a year, and the legal side of mining operations would be handled separately by the OMC (Orissa Mining Corp.).

It is one of the CEC's main conclusions that environmental clearance was 'granted on the wrong premise that no forest land is involved' due to 'inappropriately delinking the mining component' from the refinery.[27] The project's two components were:

1. To mine 3 million tons of bauxite per year on 721 hectares of land (672 of which is forest) in a Joint Venture Company with the OMC. The OMC would have a 26 per cent share and two directors and would handle legal matters. Vedanta would have a 74 per cent share and four directors and *de facto* control, paying the OMC the cost of mining the bauxite plus 50 per cent royalty. The lease area, on top of Niyamgiri, was divided between Kalahandi and Rayagada, and the bauxite lay to an average depth of 12.4 metres below the surface.[28]

2. To build an alumina refinery for producing 1 million tons of alumina per year on 723 hectares of land in the plains below the mountain, plus a 75 MW captive coal-fired power station, and a water requirement of 30,000 cubic metres of water per day, at a total cost of Rs 4,000 crore over. Over 58 hectares of this land was forest, though the first application for clearance (in March 2003) stated there was no forest land.

To get environmental clearance for the refinery first, Vedanta changed its stance with contradictory statements. When challenged by the fact-finding team, the company, as Respondent, stated that

the concept of the mining project being integral to the alumina refinery project is inaccurate and [the Respondent] would also like to clarify that it has not been this Respondent's stand, before this Committee, that the mining from the proposed forest area is an integral part of the refinery project without which the refinery project cannot be viable ... this Respondent therefore seeks to make clear that even without such mining activities, the alumina refinery would still be functional and this Respondent would, in such an event, obtain bauxite from other sources. (28 March 2005).

The CEC then pointed out that if mining Niyamgiri was not absolutely necessary, the guidelines of the MoEF indicated permission was unlikely to be given, on account of the forest land which would have to be cleared. In response, Vedanta again changed its stance, stating that '*the mining project [is] necessary for the successful functioning of the refinery project*', and had dictated the location of the refinery below the mountain (affidavit dated 28 April 2005).[29]

Sterlite's Rapid Revised Environmental Impact Assessment (2002, p. 11) states that 'About 77 per cent of the mining lease area falls within reserved forest.... However, the actual bauxite deposit sites characteristically have little vegetation.' Not till the Wildlife Institute of India issued its report (WII, July 2006) was this properly contradicted. The WII concluded that at least 80 per cent of the lease site was covered in prime forest, and that mining would have a huge negative impact on wildlife, surrounding forest, and streams.

The applicants against the mine made the case that 'the mining of bauxite is bound to destroy the water recharging capacity of the hill and will also cause the desertification of the streams; there is an intimate relationship between the bauxite-topped mountains in Orissa and the perennial flow of water.... This is because the bauxite is oolitic and pisolitic with high level of porosity giving it a high water retention capacity'. Summarising the applicants' case, the CEC states that 'Niyamgiri forms the source of the Vamsadhara river and a major tributary of the Nagavali. 36 streams originate from within the mining lease site.'[30] As for the area's wildlife, the lease area formed part of a wildlife sanctuary approved by the MoEF in December 1998, with numerous species of animal and six plant species listed in the IUCN's Red Book of endangered species.[31]

It was first planned to take water for the refinery from the Bansadhara (Sterlite 2002, p. 3), building a dam close to its starting point. When this was judged unfeasible, the GoO gave approval for taking water to the extent of 30,000 cubic metres per day from the Tel River near Kesinga (October 2003). People in Kesinga held demonstrations against this, but underground pipes now take Tel water (which had increased because of water diverted into it from Indravati Reservoir) 65 km to the Lanjigarh refinery.[32]

The whole project therefore impacts local water in several ways: by using this river water, and through the refinery's effluent contaminating the Bansadhara (already a serious problem in 2007–08); as well as by drying out Niyamgiri's perennial streams if mining starts.[33]

As for use of forest land for the refinery, the Collector's first n* of land acquisition dated 6 June 2002 observed that 108 acr* village forest land would be needed for the refinery. However, S* application for environmental clearance of March 2003 sta* no forest land was involved and there was no Reserved Forest within a radius of 10 km. Later (August 2004) it applied to use more than 58 hectares of forest land without modifying the original application for environmental clearance. This land consisted of 30 hectares of Reserved Forest for the conveyor belt up the side of the mountain, and mote than 28 hectares of village forest, mostly within the boundary wall, 10 hectares of which had already been *encroached* and cut, for which Vedanta was fined slightly over 11,000 rupees.[34]

This issue was raised during a session at the SC on 28 February 2005, and the CEC wrote about this violation of the law to the MoEF (2 March 2005), which issued a 'stop work' order to Vedanta on 23 March. The next day Vedanta wrote back saying it did not need this forest land after all, and the GoO applied to withdraw the contentious proposal for forestry clearance (27 March). The MoEF granted this the next day without checking the details. So work was carried on. The line of pillars for the conveyor belt stop at the bottom of the mountain. Marching them up the slope would involve cutting Reserved Forest (RF), and will not be done now until and unless clearance is granted.

As the CEC observes, 'the Alumina Refinery construction work has been started and continued in blatant violation' of MoEF guidelines which forbid construction work to start on a project which will require forest land until clearance for use of this forest land has been granted. Vedanta's project clearly requires use of 30 hectares of RF going up the mountain, and 672 hectares on top. So it circumvented the order to stop work (23 March 2005) on false pretences.[35] The CEC report draws its conclusions and recommendations as follows (21 September 2005):

> The allegations about the improper rehabilitation and the forceful eviction [of displaced villagers] needs to be looked into carefully through an impartial and unbiased agency. The alumina refinery project should have been allowed to be constructed only after carrying out in-depth study about the effect of proposed mining from Niyamgiri Hills on water regime, flora and fauna, soil erosion and on the Dongaria Kandha tribes ... and after careful assessment of the economic gains vis-à-vis environmental considerations. By delinking the alumina refinery project from the mining component an undesirable and embarrassing situation has been allowed to happen

(by the MoEF) where in the event of Niyamgiri Hills forest not being approved under F[orest] C[onservation] Act for mining lease, the entire expenditure of about Rs 4000 crore on the alumina refinery project may become infractious as the project is unviable in the absence of Niyamgiri Hills mines.

RECOMMENDATIONS

The CEC is of the considered view that the use of the forest land in an ecologically sensitive area like the Niyamgiri Hills should not be permitted. The casual approach, the lackadaisical manner and the haste with which the entire issue of forests and environmental clearance has been dealt smacks of undue favour/leniency and does not inspire confidence with regard to the willingness and resolve of both the State government and the MoEF to deal with such matters keeping in view the ultimate goal of national and public interest. In the instant case, had a proper study been conducted before embarking on a project of this nature and magnitude involving massive investment, the objections to the project from environmental/ecological/forest angles would have become known in the beginning itself and in all probability the project would have been abandoned at this site.

Keeping in view all the facts and circumstances brought out in the preceding paragraphs it is recommended that this Hon'ble Court may consider revoking the environmental clearance dated 22 September 2004 granted by the MoEF for setting up of the Alumina Refinery Plant by M/s Vedanta and directing them to stop further work on the project. This project may only be considered after an alternative bauxite mine is identified.

This Hon'ble Court may please consider the above report and may please pass appropriate orders in this matter.

Yet the SC passed no such orders. The case was repeatedly deferred, giving Vedanta time to complete construction of its refinery on schedule, avoiding penalties from the Worley engineering company.

Rather than implement the CEC's recommendations, the SC requested further reports from the MoEF, via the Forest Advisory Committee (FAC). One of these was from the Wildlife Institute of India (Dehra Dun), who sent a team to the area in May 2006 and submitted a report in July, which delineated in scientific detail exactly why the forests on and around the Niyamgiri mining lease area are of such importance: they have an exceptional density of plant life as well as animals, including apex species such as tiger and elephant, and the bauxite plays a vital role on the mountain and for surrounding areas in conserving and channeling water. It lies in a layer approximately 13 metres thick below a laterite cap about 2 metres thick. These 'plateau beds' retain 'huge quantities of rainwater and allow water discharges to continue at a slow rate through the emanating streams' lower down the mountain. 'Mining on this mineralised plateau will impact these aquifers in their discharges.' It is likely that water reaching the Nagavali and Bansadhara rivers will be severely reduced. 'This will eventually make the habitat drier and reduce its potential for productivity and biodiversity' over the whole area watered by these rivers, bringing about 'irreversible changes in the ecological characteristics of the area.'[36]

The WII Report confirmed the CEC Report's conclusions that bauxite mining should not be allowed. However, the other report submitted to the SC was by the Central Mining Planning and Design Institute, at Ranchi (CMPDI), a subsidiary of Coal India—hardly an independent body—that exists to facilitate mining companies, not to give an objective analysis. So when the CMPDI report (2006, pp. 18–20) says that during mining micro-cracks will develop in the side of the mountain which will 'facilitate run-off' and help 'recharge ground water', this involves a monstrous distortion of science. When micro-cracks develop and water runs fast off a mountain, this may seem OK, and could be said to recharge the groundwater, during the monsoon period. But in the hot summer months, when there is no rain, this means that streams will run dry, and groundwater will drop overall.

Evidently under pressure, the WII added comments that examining the water and soil was not in its remit of study (this task had been assigned to the CMPDI). Without changing its earlier stance, additional comments recorded from the WII were used at the Supreme Court to reverse the CEC/WII consensus that mining would cause irreversible damage to Niyamgiri's forest, wildlife and water regime. On 16 May 2007, K. K. Venugopal, as head advocate for Vedanta, quoted these comments to give an impression that the forest was sparse and nothing special. Forest cover would increase, since a maximum of 50,000 trees would be cut and the company planned to plant 1,600,000; elephants, if they really came to the area, would be able to pass safely under the conveyor belt; Dongria would benefit by being 'raised above the mere survival level'; and Kalahandi would benefit through direct and contract employment for 7,000 persons.

Many of the arguments in the SC case have been bizarre. The tree statistics mentioned above are highly questionable, and take no account of the basic difference in biodiversity between primary natural forest and plantations. Much pressure was applied to the CEC as well as the WII, and the power of money to override a strict application of law was illustrated many times, not least in Vedanta's claim that it was losing an estimated 1.73 crore rupees per day from the delay in mining Niyamgiri. Throughout 2006–08, bauxite from Bodai Daldali (nearly 700 km away) was being transported in lorries and trains to Lanjigarh, and stored in the refinery. It was coming from Korba via three stations (Doikhal, Rayagada and Kesinga), and these roads (for example, the 80 km road from Rayagada) were soon in a terrible condition. More bauxite was reportedly brought from Australia.

Violations of regulations have been equally evident in Sterlite/Vedanta's behaviour at the Tuticorin Copper smelter in South India.[37] The Niyamgiri case showed a more fundamental subversion of legal process. On 6 September 2007, the SC Judges called for a comprehensive report from the MoEF on bauxite leases in Kalahandi and Koraput and their forest cover, applications pending, and impacts on water, forest and tribal life and ecology if these applications are granted, as well as safeguards which would mitigate negative impacts.

On 5 October, India's Attorney-General read out a hastily written report, full of errors and misrepresentations, which summarised ten of the bauxite mountains, and argued that there would be no negative impacts, and that large sums offered by the company for tribal development, re-forestation and wildlife management would compensate for any detrimental effects. The case was reserved for judgment on 26 October. It was apparent that the project would be granted clearance, on certain conditions, involving large sums the company would have to pay for the compensatory measures.

When senior advocate Sanjay Parikh, counsel for Kalahandi advocate, Siddharth Nayak, petitioning on behalf of the Dongria Konds, rose to speak, one of the Judges, Arijit Pasayat, shouted him down, saying 'This case has nothing to do with the tribals'.

The Judges admitted that Vedanta had been blacklisted by the Council on Ethics of the Norway Government Pension Fund (May 2007), but on 26 November 2007 they called on Sterlite—which had been equally blasted in that report!—to create a Special Purpose Vehicle (SPV) with the Orissa government and OMC for the purpose of mining Niyamgiri. After this SPV had been constituted, an order from the same panel of judges on 8 August 2008 granted clearance conditional on MoEF approval.

In principle, MoEF approval came through on 11 December, and again on 28 April 2009, three days after a deeply flawed Public Hearing held by the OSPCB at Belamba village. Ostensibly, this was not held about mining at all, but for a sixfold expansion of the refinery from a capacity of 1 million tons per year to a colossal 6 million, making it one of the biggest refineries in the world. Dai Singh and other residents of Belamba and several other villages now—after a soul-wrenching struggle lasting several years—agreed to lose their land and be resettled. Dai Singh mentioned the pressure he and others were under from false cases. Almost everyone spoke of the refinery's unbearable pollution, and many spoke strongly against mining Niyamgiri. This issue was not in the remit of the Belamba PH—the only public hearing on the mining issue has been the small one at Lanjigarh in February 2003, where no Dongria were recorded as present. Yet the overall opinion at the meeting was reported as 'favourable' by the administration, even though 26 out of 27 speakers spoke strongly against the project! In November 2009 Environment Minister Jairam Ramesh highlighted some if these violations, cancelling 'in principle' approval.[38]

'Our Vedanta'

At Vedanta Resources plc, we believe in sustainable development and are committed to raising the quality of life and social well-being of communities where we operate. (Vedanta Resources Annual Report 2006, p. 48)

All the villages near the refinery were given signboards, naming their village with an 'our vedanta' logo. Nearly all were swiftly defaced by furious villagers. The discrepancy between the company's lavish CSR claims and the bitter reality of mind-numbing pollution, uncounted deaths on roads and work-sites, impoverishment and repression could not be greater.

The company's efforts to subvert this reality, through PR offensives on a multitude of fronts, has been exceptional (examined more fully in Chapter Nineteen). As the stakes for mining Niyam Dongar grow higher (mid-2009), local people blocking the track up the mountain to prevent mining vehicles reaching the top have been beaten up, and on 18 March 2009, Dongria attacked company people on the summit, and burnt their vehicles. So Vedanta's PR offensive is aimed at winning Dongria over, dividing local opposition, and implying to the outside world that everything is well in Lanjigarh, and that Dongria are ready to welcome the mine, recording statements to this effect after taking a group of Dongria to see 'no ill effects of bauxite mining' at Panchpat Mali.[39] This offensive is carried out in the media, through articles on the net and video clips on 'youtube', and even a 2008 diary with beautiful photos of Dongria, called *Kalahandi: A Way of Life*.

One may assume, of course, that the directors' intention really is to benefit people around Lanjigarh, and that they do believe that they have raised people's quality of life. If so, the core of this is a naïve belief that raising people's quality of life is effected simply by spending large amounts of money. When we questioned Vedanta's 'development' at Lanjigarh in front of other shareholders at the AGM in 2006, Kuldip Kaura read out the list of large sums and achievements given in the Annual Report—no proof at all, when one understands the inequality and dissension which Vedanta 'investment' has introduced to Lanjigarh communities. The vision is irredeemably top-down, in line with 'there was nothing here before we came'. What is involved, in other words, is an ignorance about Adivasi culture that leads inevitably to flooding it out with money.

Vedanta's 2007 Annual Report includes a 20-page 'Sustainable Development Report', with colour photographs. This speaks of:

- 'More clarity and transparency of our reported performance', 'Stakeholder inclusion and dialogue' (p. 32)
- Setting targets for improvement on safety, water management, energy conservation, employing 328 HSE ... and community development experts and 126 village extension workers, with 'a healthy 5 per cent' of the workforce represented in joint management-worker health and safety committees as per the Global Reporting Initiative G3 guidelines
- 'As a standard operating philosophy, before commencing any project and/or any process modifications, we carry out detailed investigations like environmental impact assessments, risk assessment studies, HAZOPs, social mapping and needs assessments which form the basis of our planning'
- 'Linking safety performance to annual performance review for all executives' (p. 32)
- Certification of all Indian operations by the international system of certification (ISO140001 and OHSAS18001), except for Bodai Daldali mines (in process) (p. 33)
- 93.6 per cent peak current efficiency of the new pre-bake technology Korba smelter, and continuous monitoring of pots at the old Sodenberg technology Korba smelter to reduce PFC emissions (pp. 33, 35)
- Recycling Korba's water discharge and phasing out wet disposal of red mud. 'Water being a precious commodity, we have maintained a zero effluent discharge status at all our Indian operations' (p. 34)
- Reducing fluoride emissions from pot rooms at Korba and Mettur smelters by introducing dry scrubbing technology, improving efficiency from 70 per cent to 98.5 per cent, reducing SO_2 and other GHG emissions [but no mention of CO_2] (p. 37)
- Waste utilisation: red mud used for making cement (Malco), and fly ash for making bricks, employing 80 youths in 20 units (Balco) (pp. 36, 38, 40)
- 'We continue to develop green-belt and green-cover in and around our operations. With expert botanists and horticulturalists engaged across our operations ... we have increased the green-belt coverage by planting over 270,000 trees and over 1 million Jatropha saplings' (p. 37)
- Experts employed at all mines for regular occupational health examinations monitoring exposure to bauxite dust, etc. (p. 39)
- 'At Vedanta, we lay particular emphasis on enhancing the quality

of life for the communities in which we work' by running 10 schools for 7,500 children, 53 pre-schools centre for 2,500 children, a post-graduate girls' college in Rajasthan, 14 adult education centres teaching literacy to women, 66 youths in three batches at VAL taught literacy and trained and the first batch given jobs, and scholarships for 350 children and teachers,

- Running eight hospitals which provide healthcare for 750,000 people, with mobile health units for a million people, building 1,000 low cost toilets at 13 villages near Korba, providing drinking water for 78 villages, malaria programme for 78,000 households (p. 40), 60 biogass plants near Korba
- Setting up 550 Self-Help Groups (SHGs) to improve income generation for 8,000 women
- 84 Vision Entrepreneurs selling cheap glasses
- Internal assessment of these facts corroborated by three external auditors, in addition to PriceWaterhouseCoopers monitoring the Sustainable Development Report by review of select data (pp. 40, 49)
- For HZL plants, a four-star rating on health and safety performance by the British Safety Council, and gold award for accident prevention by the Royal Society for Prevention of Accidents, UK (p. 41), TERI CSR award of the year and 'Best SHG Award' for a Lanjigarh SHG awarded by Naveen Patnaik
- Donating 11.3 million rupees for Habitat for Housing houses for the poor
- Agricultural improvements in Korba and Lanjigarh villages, including improved seeds and multicropping. 'Across Vedanta's operations we motivated 1,300 farmers to till 1,100 acres of land with vegetable and cash crops' generating Rs 3,000 (pp. 40, 46)

What is the reality behind these claims? Is there any real accountability? We shall examine them more fully later (Chapter Nineteen). Violations of CSR standards at Lanjigarh are examined in a case study published by the London School of Economics and Political Science (Macdonald, May 2009).

For now, let us note a few points: the transparency claimed is at variance with what villagers say, and the claim to do proper EIAs before starting projects is not borne out by the Odisha operations. The reality of workers' safety and health presents an extreme contrast to company claims, according to reports from Malco and spontaneous interviews with workers at Korba, Mainpat, Bodai Daldali and especially Lanjigarh, where several hundred workers are reported to have died during construction. Just one death is mentioned in this Vedanta report (p. 51)—a discrepancy mainly explained by the system of extensive sub-contracting, by which Vedanta can disclaim responsibility for deaths in operations run by sub-contractors.

Repeated demonstrations by workers as well as people denied jobs at Lanjigarh and other sites tell a different story. Workers in Korba told us that regular medical checks were mainly for show, and that they would lose their jobs if they told us the actual situation of health and safety. They were doing overtime without extra pay, in constant fear of 'voluntary redundancy', that had been forced on the majority of Balco staff since Vedanta's takeover.[40] Workers at Mainpat said they had no medical facilities or help with injuries and no schools. We have heard many instances of labourers at Lanjigarh not being paid for their work. The hospital there is reported to function only for company employees (July 2007), and similarly with other claims.

On the issue of Self-Help Groups (SHGs), for example, it is questionable how much they raise women's position in the long term at all. One of their main functions is to lend money, and the interest rate is much higher than bank rates, so—contrary to popular ideas—SHGs tend to get families into debt, and undermine people's ability to organise collectively to assert their basic rights, especially since the industrialisation process tends to bring women even more under male control by taking away their independent role as growers and sellers of food.[41] Tree-planting mostly consists of eucalyptus and other foreign species, which, like jatropha (for biofuel), are grown in monoculture plantations and involve outrageous scams, and a drying-out of the soil that causes severe damage to a region's biodiversity.[42] Using red mud to make bricks is banned in many countries as a health hazard, since red mud is radioactive.

'Quality of life' indicators reflect villagers' experience very poorly. The egalitarian spirit intrinsic to community relations before Vedanta came has been replaced by relationships of dependency and hierarchy. Villagers in the Lanjigarh, Burkhamunda, and Chhattisgarh bauxite areas were largely in charge of their own lives and the land around their villages, and largely self-sufficient, growing most of their own food, before the aluminium company invasion. Vedanta programmes follow a standard model that is colonial and missionary in conception, geared towards control and exploitation. The 'welfare' aspects of health and education were, until recently, the government's responsibility. Now advancement depends basically, for each family or individual, on pleasing company officials.

So in what sense is the Lanjigarh project 'our vedanta' for local villagers?

The 'our' on the village sign-boards never included Adivasi 'stakeholders' in decisions, let alone profits. It is the company directors, shareholders and investors who can speak of 'our vedanta'. Likewise certain influential elements in the British and Indian governments. A brief prosopography of Vedanta's directors is called for.

Anil Agarwal and his brother Navin are the Executive and Deputy Executive Chairmen of Vedanta Resources. All the original Europeans on the Board of directors have disappeared: Brian Gilbertson was succeeded as Non-Executive Chairman by Michael Fowle (from KPMG, ICICI UK and other companies). Sir David Gore-Booth (UK's Ambassador to Saudi Arabia 1993–96, High Commissioner to India 1996–98, and Chairman of HSBC Middle East, etc.) died without appearing at an AGM, but his presence on the Board of directors shows the interest in the company by a section of the British establishment. Fowle, Sydney-Smith, and Rodier (who was Chairman and Chief Executive of Pechiney, 1994–2003) all resigned for unexplained reasons within the first three years, leaving Euan MacDonald, who came from twenty years in Warburg (including Warburg India, 1995–99) and ten years with Lazard Brothers, and was Executive Vice-Chairman of HSBC (1999–2001).

Among the remaining directors are: Naresh Chandra (India's Home Secretary in 1990, Cabinet Secretary 1990–92, Senior Adviser to the PM 1992–95, and India's Ambassador to the US 1996–2001); S. K. Tamotia, who joined in November 2004, having served at Nalco (1986–96), and as CEO of Indal (2000–04); Kuldip Kaura, Chief Executive, who worked in ABB bank before joining Sterlite in 2002; and Aman Mehta (a banker from HSBC); T. L. Palani Kumar, managing director of Balco; and Tarun Jain, Sterlite's director of finance.

As for the shareholders and main creditors who have loaned Vedanta the capital for its projects, these include some of the world's

Lanjigarh: Vedanta's Assault on the Mountain of Law | 173

top banks. In the following chapters we shall look more closely at some, including Deutsche Bank. Certainly these banks could say 'our vedanta'. So could certain politicians. In August 2006, questions were asked about Vedanta's donations to political parties, referred to in the 2006 Annual Report, though without mentioning which parties.[43]

Plans for a Vedanta University in Odisha surfaced in May–July 2006, to be based on a $1 billion donation from Anil Agarwal himself—a 'personal donation from his private funds to the people of Orissa' as the *Financial Times* put this. The university plans an initial intake of 100,000 students. Its projected site is on prime agricultural and forest land between Puri and Konarak. It is planned as a 'world class university like Oxford or Harvard.' For a state with high unemployment and a movement for more higher education this seems an irresistible offer. But for most of the villagers living for generations in over forty villages, who number around 100,000 and stand to lose their land, this is a project they are determined to resist. Relatively few are landowners: the majority are sharecroppers. Most of the land belongs to the Jagannath temple or the king of Puri. Two other sites were rejected first. The idea of building this university right next to Puri, centre of Odia culture and one of India's most-visited pilgrim sites, is typical of the company. According to an advertisement in *Sambad* (2 February 2007), placed by the Anil Agarwal Foundation:

EVERY TOWN NEEDS A UNIVERSITY. THIS UNIVERSITY NEEDS A TOWN. VEDANTA UNIVERSITY WILL BE ONE OF THE BIGGEST UNIVERSITIES IN THE WORLD. BUT OUR VISION IS EVEN BIGGER ...

Demonstrations against the project in Puri started in January 2007, bringing about 10,000 people to the streets, and have continued since. A 'medical camp' sent to the villages to soften them up for the university idea in March 2008 was sent packing, with a Vedanta medical vehicle shown smashed in the papers.

The university plan is linked to plans for a business centre, and a new port, Astranga, officially announced in the press on 23 December 2008, and mineral sands mining on the beach. This complex would completely change Puri's environment, destroying the nesting beaches of Olive Ridley turtles, and the forest cover for deer and hyenas—let alone the city's character. Division among villagers have already begun (December 2008), with *Dharitri* reporting arguments between villagers as some accept sums as large as Rs 65 lakh (nearly £1 million) for land that had been communally owned.[44] The very offer of a university has the appearance of a kind of bribe to Odisha to facilitate getting clearance to mine Niyamgiri's bauxite. From these examples, it is important to consider what kind of knowledge would be taught in the university? What are the implicit concepts of knowledge, law and truth?

To name a company trying to mine a mountain sacred to the principle of law 'Vedanta' is an extraordinary insult to India's spiritual tradition. The name is used in a very primitive way, as a talisman of power, forgetting or perverting the content of the *Advaita Vedanta* philosophy, to set up a system of hierarchy and control antithetical to the original teachings. Far from the ancient ideals encapsulated by sages teaching non-attachment, the company promotes materialism in its crudest form. The usage implies a strong element of *Hindutva*—a world of separation, starting with separate standards for the directors, with their exorbitant salaries, and for bauxite miners and displaced villagers, condemned to a new level of poverty.

In January 2007, at a meeting of the World Environment Forum in Kolkata, the ex-Prime Minister of Sweden, Ola Yulstein, presented a Golden Peacock award to Naveen Patnaik and Anil Agarwal for their 'outstanding business leadership', and 'service in a short time to promote industrial development in Orissa', 'enhancing stakeholder value' and for 'outstanding work in the field of Sustainable Development'.[45] These two gentlemen's main contribution to 'sustainable development' has been more in the realm of subverting the term's original meaning.

In December 2007, the MoEF refused a Vedanta/Balco application to increase bauxite mining at the Balco sites in Chhattisgarh, calling the company's attitude towards concerns the Ministry had raised 'deplorably callous and casual'.[46] Malco/Vedanta's bauxite mining in the Kolli Hills (Tamil Nadu) was halted by the Chennai High Court in November 2008, after campaigners showed that mines had operated without proper clearance for ten years.[47]

Between November 2007 and January 2009, Orissa's Pollution Control Board (OSPCB) reported repeated violations by Vedanta of the environmental safeguards it had signed up to or promised to correct. The Bansadhara is already heavily polluted. The red mud lake was not sealed properly and has been seeping into the ground water and river. Livestock and people have been poisoned, bathing in this river and drinking it, near its source, where they have always sourced their water. In this context, expanding the refinery's capacity to 6 million tons per year spells death to tribal communities as well as Niyamgiri's wildlife.[48] Amazingly, given these violations, whose effects are obvious to everyone in the Lanjigarh area, the British Standards Institution awarded the Vedanta's refinery ISO awards for 'zero discharge, zero accident and zero fatality', after a five-day audit in December 2008.[49] In May 2009, another worker died in an accident, and a major strike followed officials' attempts at a cover-up

During these years, the Sterlite-Vedanta group of companies also bought up Sesa Goa (April 2007), becoming India's biggest exporter of iron-ore, mainly to China). The environmental impact of Sesa Goa's mines is atrocious, and has got worse since Vedanta took over.[50] Expansion is on many other fronts, including long-drawn negotiations to buy up bankrupt US copper giant Asarco. On the aluminium front, it announced plans in March 2008 to build another smelter at Asansol in West Bengal, on the site of India's first smelter, and seeks another bauxite mine on Gandhamardan.[51]

UK Parliamentarians have been briefed about some of Vedanta's iniquities, especially at Lanjigarh/Niyamgiri (May 2008), and several high profile NGOs have taken a strong stand on the issue, including Survival International, who have brought a complaint against Vedanta at the OECD, Amnesty International, War on Want, and Action Aid, who invited Kumti Majhi to speak at Vedanta's AGMs in London in 2007 and 2008.[52] Rahul Gandhi visited a Dongria village, and supported their stand against mining their mountain in March 2008.[53]

Opposition to mining has sometimes been represented as 'NGOs misleading the poor tribal people' or even as a 'Maoist threat' (March–April 2009), and there has been a media war for and against the company's designs.[54] Congress politician Bhakta Das started the organisation Green Kalahandi in 2006 in opposition to mining Niyamgiri, and was re-elected as MP in May 2009 on this ticket.[55]

Tamotia resigned from Vedanta in February 2009, and faced three years in jail, after being convicted in a special court of the Central Bureau of Investigation, Bhubaneswar.[56] Among many other scandals, nothing, perhaps, shows better the dangers in store for Niyamgiri and the Dongria than the fact that the first people to make major use of the large roads built in 2006–09 into the heart of Niyamgiri with funds from the PM's road fund, were the timber mafia. Dongria friends stopped them taking felled trees out at night in July 2008, but locals estimate that irreplaceable timber, with a high monetary value, is being extracted from Niyamgiri on a daily basis. Neither the Dongria Kond Develeopment Agency (who coordinated the road-building), nor Forest officials have been proactive in preventing this. These roads are suspiciously wide, and have involved a lot of tree felling in their own right. An article in the *Financial Times* in November 2003, about Vedanta's imminent listing on the London Stock Exchange, mentioned an option on a 'second' bauxite deposit of about 70 million tons. One of the new roads penetrates the heart of Niyamgiri, to the village of Dhamanapanga, just below Niyamgiri's highest peak, in the centre of the range—one of the highest and most sacred peaks in Odisha. Is this peak in danger too?

The Jharsaguda smelter started up in late 2008, and by August 2009, it was reported that the Bheden rive was heavily contaminated with fluoride, killing all fish in the vicinity of five villages: Katikela, Brundamal, Srirupa, Khelual and Malda. Thousands of people have drunk and bathed in this water for centuries. Will they ever be able to do so again?[57]

On the issue of mining Niyam Dongar, the Environment Minister Jairam Ramesh questioned the process that had granted 'provisional clearance', and sent a team to investigate illegal felling of 3,000 trees, which forest officials confirmed had been cleared to start building the mining road up the mountain: 'Vedanta flouts rules, Ramesh asks why?' (*Statesman*, 28 November 2009)[58]

PART II

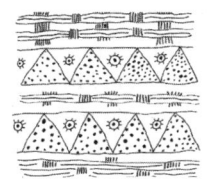

Niyam Raja meets the World-Wide Web: Aluminium's Social Structure

Having surveyed the basic stories and history behind aluminium's entry into East India, we now start to analyse what anthropologists call the *deep structures* that underlie the industry, in India and worldwide. How do people in the aluminium companies relate with different groups? What beliefs and values motivate them? What are their links abroad?

In Part II we look more closely at the patterns of violations outlined in Part I, and at the world-wide web of companies, institutions and operations. Aluminium projects that appear as Indian concerns are often controlled from abroad, on closer inspection, and 'expatriate' their main profits.

As a senior Pechiney/Alcan executive confided to us, more than economics, aluminium is about diplomacy. Making the complex series of (mostly secret) deals behind any project—for cheap bauxite, electricity, water, transport, for land, political support, and loans to finance infrastructure—is top priority.

What will happen if the planned projects go through in Odisha and Andhra Pradesh can only be understood if one comprehends what has happened in a series of countries where bauxite/aluminium was made a key industry, whose citizens have faced a complex pattern of effects, and whose leaders find themselves enmeshed in a web of secret financial agreements made by their predecessors. Samarendra's visit to Iceland at the invitation of political leaders in July 2008 revealed a hidden world of aluminium impacts, shortly before the country's financial bubble burst in October. This bubble was blown from loans financing an infrastructure for dams and smelters. Like East India, Iceland has been a key field for aluminium expansion....

CHAPTER SEVEN

Under Mining Law

Subverting the Rule of Law

Niyam Raja embodies the ancient Indian concept of *dharma*: universal law implicit in nature and human action. The Vedanta case highlights a contrast of great irony. Adivasi values are rooted in a strong belief in the principle of law. Yet the legal safeguards for Scheduled Tribes built into India's Constitution are flouted wherever industrial projects invade tribal lands. As we have seen, mining companies are often cavalier with the law, infringing regulations almost at will, while the law comes down heavily on anti-mining campaigners, even when these are Adivasis trying to protect their land and basic rights. Often, as Dai Singh said, false cases enmesh them. With such double standards—'Please, everyone stand' as Justice P.K. Mishra said at the hearing about the Kashipur firing (above, p. 126)—is it surprising when poor people's faith in India's justice system gets eroded?

If advocates are arrogant, this is only a reflection of the arrogance of those who pay them. Not only are mining companies subverting

India's laws, they are also changing them, through Acts such as the SEZ Act (2005), and the new National Mineral Policy (NMP drafts 2006–08), which is heavily influenced by foreign companies' interest in getting hold of key mineral deposits in India. We saw how Orissa's Rivers Pollution Act (1953) gave Birla's paper mill licence to pollute (Chapter One). The Bansadhara getting polluted by Vedanta's refinery is a continuation of this licence.

During Vedanta's 2009 AGM in London, Naresh Chandra, as a key company director who was one of India's most senior and influential civil servants and diplomats, made a strong reply to critics who questioned Vedanta's legal integrity, saying that India is the world's largest democracy and its courts give impartial justice.

Would that they did! In some ways, the judiciary is the least accountable institution in the country. Infringements of law by Sterlite/Vedanta have been shown in many places.[1] Many violations occurred outside India too, instigating record UK compensation (December 2003) for Rajat Bhatia's unfair dismissal over deals in Australia in 2000. Vedanta was indicted in November 2006 for wilfully using a defective pipeline to dispose of tailings in Zambia, causing massive pollution that turned a major river blue.[2] In Armenia, Sterlite Gold was accused of mining more gold than permitted, deliberately undervaluing its reserves, and failing to dispose of its wastes properly, culminating in

> a scandalous piece of quasi-insider trading which merited not a single adverse comment from the UK financial press. Worse, the deal received the approval of that 'responsible' accountancy firm, Ernst and Young (who also happen to be Vedanta's auditors).

Moreover, Ernst and Young also declared Anil Agarwal its 'Entrepreneur of the Year' in 2008![3] Collusion by accountancy firms was a feature of the Enron scandal, and demonstrates the dance with the law that mining companies often make, keeping near the edge of the law by exploiting loopholes, and subverting regulations with a canny sense of how far to push the limits at any moment. Sterlite's violations of insider trading prohibitions in the Damayanti-SEBI case (1998) were judged 'the greatest indictment by any statutary body yet of corporate malfeasance in the stock market'—an Indian prototype of the Enron scandal (in which collusion by Arthur Anderson accountants was a major factor).[4]

The basic infringement of law at Lanjigarh—building the refinery without first obtaining environment/forest clearance for mining Niyam Dongar—was prefigured by gross violations at Tuticorin: illegal siting of the copper smelter 14 km from the Gulf of Mannar Special Biosphere Reserve (25 km was the legal limit), no prior EIA, huge expansion without permission from the Tamil Nadu State Pollution Control Board (TNSPCB), disregarding orders from the Supreme Court Hazardous Wastes Monitoring Sub-Committee (SCMC), and illegal storage of thousands of tons of arsenic-contaminated slag, contaminating ground water and wells over a large area. The TNSPCB granted the smelter retrospective clearance in April 2004. In May 2005 the SCMC demanded why, and has received no explanation.[5]

The legality of Balco's sale to Sterlite in March 2001—immediately after Chhattisgarh was formed—has been questioned by many. A report released in January 2007 showed that the company broke 'virtually all the terms of an agreement it made with its workforce when it took control'.[6] Balco had already displaced Manjhi–Manjhwar Adivasis on Mainpat for bauxite mining on their land, acquired with false promises in 1992, an injustice compounded by Sterlite's takeover, since the Samatha Judgment (i.e. India's Constitution) forbade the mining of Fifth Schedule tribal lands except by public sector companies (which Balco had been but Sterlite was not). Agarwal's comment at this time that he had 'no idea about the judgment' is sinister in the light of violent intimidation which police and *goondas* have used against tribal people attempting to get basic compensation from Sterlite.[7] When Jagarved Yadav refused to leave his land on Mainpat without compensation, police jailed him and his family, including his wife and daughters, and broke his arm. Attempts to complain to district- and state-level administration brought no punishment of police and no compensation.[8] In other words, it seems that a mining company can infringe the law with impunity, while Adivasis trying to assert their most basic rights get beaten up or have false cases lodged against them, as Kashipur villagers have found often. Without the ability to pay huge fees, justice often seems impossible.

Displaced people soon become desperate for work, and on Mainpat, as at Lanjigarh, contractors frequently abscond without paying weeks of wages.[9] Manoj Pingua, as Collector of Surguja district, noted numerous violations on Mainpat, including illegal felling of 4,000 *sal* trees and infringements of basic Health and Safety regulations, and recommended the mines should be closed. Instead, the Chhattisgarh government in 2007 allowed an expansion of Mainpat and Bodai Daldali from 750,000 to 2,050,000 tons per year, probably to supply Lanjigarh refinery, although this contravened a law that bauxite mined in Chhattisgarh should be refined there.[10] The company's bauxite mines in Tamil Nadu have caused even worse environmental damage.[11]

At Lanjigarh, the CEC (2005) made a long list of violations, but its recomendation that mining and refinery should be prohibited were not allowed to get in the way of the company's tight schedule with Worley MMC, and the distortions of truth before the Supreme Court were extraordinary to witness. At a session on 28 April 2005, the company's lawyer C. A. Sundaram contradicted a statement made a month before that mining Niyamgiri was not integral to the refinery project. The CEC was bypassed through the Forest Advisory Committee (FAC), and when the Wildlife Institute too recommended strongly against mining, it was 'leant on', and forced to write an addendum, while the CMPDI's comment that bauxite mining has no ill effects on water, since micro-cracks caused by mining 'facilitate the run-off', is a ludicrous travesty of proper science. The CEC was fighting this case with their 'hands tied behind [their] back.'

For example, the lawyers for Vedanta argued on 6 September 2007 that modern companies like to develop 'greenfield' rather than brownfield sites, linking this word with the idea that aluminium is called a 'green metal' because it substitutes wood, so saves trees, and is environmentally friendly at every stage of production—a ludicrous distortion. The project was painted as 'pro-people' on the grounds that Kalahandi had many starvation deaths and the project offered its inhabitants 'two square meals a day'. Justice Arijit Pasayat said that it was necessary to strike a balance between environmental and human/economic interests. The judges asked the Amicus Curiae representing the CEC, U. U. Lalit, to suggest alternative sites where

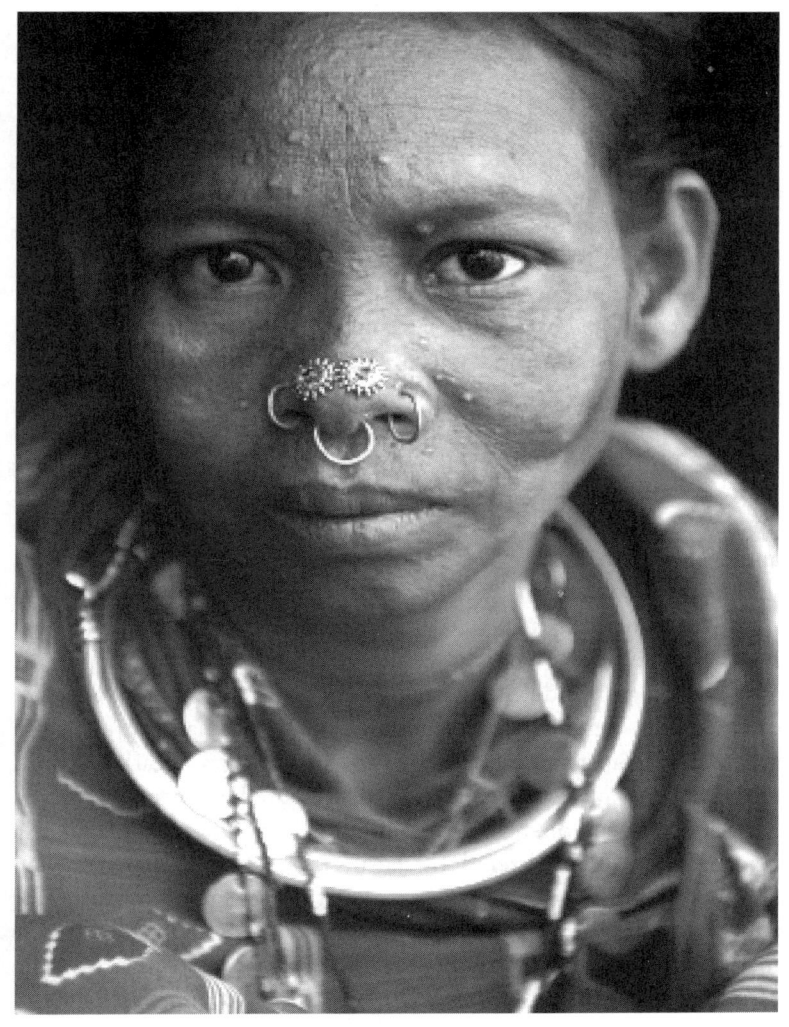

Majhi

the company could mine bauxite. This is how the MoEF came to produce its Note on Bauxite Mining (October 2007). Lalit had stood in stoic silence for most of this session, unable to press the CEC case strongly. The next day, 7 September 2007, Harish Salve appeared in the same courtroom defending the CEC, arguing for its continuation against vested interests from the MoEF wishing to discontinue it—suggesting to uninitiated observers some kind of deal allowing the CEC to continue as advisory body on condition that it let Niyamgiri go.

The CEC's attempts to save a bare minimum of India's forests have often been a heroic and thankless task, and its Niyamgiri report (September 2005) represents one of the strongest stands it has taken. The MoEF's Note on Bauxite Mining by contrast, presented by the Attorney-General on 6 October 2007, was full of flaws and misrepresentations, arguing, for example, that forest on the bauxite deposits in Kalahandi-Koraput formed only 0.4 per cent of the geographical area, or 1.52 per cent of the total forest in these districts, with no indication that these are the districts' apex forests, covering the summits of the state's highest mountains! During this hearing, senior advocate Indira Jaising registered an official objection to this document. She resisted pressure to list this as a mere Suggestion, and registered it as an Intervention in the case.[12]

The hearing on 25 October 2007 focused on 'compensatory measures'. The judges spent a long time going over details of how much money the company would give for tribal development, afforestation and wildlife management, and which company?—Sterlite or Vedanta?—before Lalit made a last stand, summarising the CEC arguments against mining. He was cut short. It was nearly an hour later that Sanjay Parikh stood up to present the objections to the MoEF document on behalf of Siddharth Nayak and the Dongria (the intervention registered by Jaising). He had prepared strong arguments based on over 2,000 pages of documentation, but Arijit Pasayat shouted at him abruptly: 'How many Dongria are there? How many people do you represent? No, I'm not going to allow this. The case is over. Your writ petition is now an interlocutary application. Whatever you want to say, we have heard it from the Amicus Curiae. Tribal people have no place in this case.' Parikh had a copy of Mihir Jena's book on the Dongria Konds (2002) handed to each of the three judges. While Sanjay was still trying to make his points and initiate a proper discussion, judgment was reserved, closing the case up after over three years. The court stood as the judges left, leaving a delayed shock: instead of a proper discussion of key environmental and social issues, the session had revolved around sums of money. Outside, a Kond elder, understanding that Niyamgiri had in effect been sold off, summed up the judge's situation with the words: '*Taro Karma, Amoro Dharma*' (his the *karma*, ours the *dharma*).

On 23 November, the Forest Court issued its judgment, hampered by the release a few days before of the Norway Government Pension Fund's Council on Ethics Report on Vedanta (2007), which spelt out numerous violations of human rights and environmental regulations, worldwide. The judges admitted that Vedanta was now a 'blacklisted company', and forbade it from mining Niyamgiri. Instead, they invited Sterlite to constitute a Special Purpose Vehicle for mining Niyamgiri in joint venture with the Orissa government and OMC—apparently unaware that Sterlite was part of the same group, criticised alongside Vedanta throughout the Norway report.

On the same day, the OSPCB showed its teeth, sending a letter to Vedanta Alumina stating that 25,000 people had been affected by air and water pollution from its Lanjigarh refinery, and demanding immediate actions: closure of boiler no. 3, emptying of alkaline water impounded in the red mud pond, and a stop to 'bauxite filling'. The CEC was reconstituted in February 2008, perhaps to help facilitate CEC compliance in the Niyamgiri and similar cases, with two members dismissed, and four new members—three from Orissa Forest/Government service.[13]

Vedanta's smelter at Burkhamunda has danced a similar jig with the law[14] (above, Chapter Six). It is often said that India has excellent legislation to protect the environment and people's basic rights, but poor implementation, allowing mining companies to get away with atrocious levels of pollution. If the State Pollution Control Boards often fail to control companies, one has to understand the constraints they work under. As mentioned in Chapter Five, R. C. Das, as director of the OSPCB, wrote a report, *Recommendation for Environmentally Sound Growth of Aluminium Industry in Orissa* (5 March 1996), spelling out the dangers of rapid expansion. The Hirakud and Angul smelters were emitting such large amounts of fluorine, even after installing the latest technology, that nearby villages were heavily contaminated. The Hirakud smelter had emitted fluorine at the rate of 14 kg per ton of aluminium for thirty years. Even

Nalco's new plant was emitting 1 kg per ton, totalling 220,000 kg a year. This report rules out any further expansion of these plants, and prohibits the greenfield refineries being planned in Kashipur by Utkal and L&T, on environmental grounds. For this, R.C. Das was apparently dismissed by Odisha's current Chief Minister. Since then, the OSPCB has often acted as a facilitator for industry, showing its teeth at rare intervals. When it reports pollution and orders companies to take immediate steps, these orders appear to carry little weight, and are often, as we shall see, ignored.

On 19 December 2007 the OSPCB held a seminar in Bhubaneswar on environmental law at which Arijit Pasayat was chief guest. He is quoted in this meeting as expressing concern about water pollution.

> "*We certainly cannot head for an Ethiopia-like situation where the green cover has given way to vast tracts of desert today,*" he noted. On the ongoing conflict over industrialisation and protection of environment, he underlined a sustainable development model that takes all concerns into account.
>
> However he noted that in the name of protecting environment no law should be too draconian in nature to deny others their rights.[15]

The UNEP's official forecast for the coming years is of massive deforestation in India and worldwide. Any attempt to prevent this and to make development truly sustainable demands the strictest implementation of India's forest protection laws by the judiciary. Surely draconian implementation of environmental law to keep mining companies on a tight leash is exactly what is needed? At present, it is the people campaigning for companies to observe the law who meet draconian treatment. Hundreds of villagers in Kashipur have had their lives reduced to misery by false cases, which ensnare them in monthly trips to the court in Rayagada.[16]

Any project for mine, dam or factory goes through various stages, and needs various forms of clearance. The New Mineral Policy reduces these stages from the 34 steps required earlier. The deals made at various stages of this process are the main points where corruption creeps in, or is institutionalised: a discrepancy between the formal structure of what is supposed to happen, and the *actual social structure* of what really happens.

The first stage is to survey a deposit; a company applies for a Reconnaissance Permit (valid for three years), followed by a Prospecting Licence. Then a Memorandum of Understanding (MoU) is signed. Negotiations continue after this, often for several years, until a Mining Lease is signed. For this a Mining Plan and EIA (Environment Impact Assessment) must be submitted, before Environmental and Forest Clearance can be granted. This involves clearance by DFOs (Divisional Forest Officers) as well as by the MoEF in Delhi (Ministry of Environment and Forests). There are numerous reports of DFOs being offered huge sums, and threats to their career, or life, to persuade them to give Forest Clearance. In the case of Niyamgiri, the DFO is known to have held out against both, insisting that destruction of prime forest like this was against all regulations. He was transferred—a pattern replicated in many other projects.

Public Hearings (PHs) must also be held, as part of a process of formally consulting and notifying the local people. This has only been necessary since 1997. Yet in one PH after another, as we have seen, pressure and intimidation is either excessive, or villagers refusing their consent are misrepresented in reports forwarded to the MoEF by the administrator in charge. In the Lanjigarh area, four PHs are known to have taken place: on 7 February 2003 under Collector Saswat Mishra at the Kutia Kandha Development Agency in Lanjigarh, attended by ten committee members and a few villagers; at Muniguda under the OSPCB on 17 March 2003, when Dongrias were angry at being excluded; at Batlima village on 27 October 2006, when villagers defied police intimidation and refused consent for the refinery's railway siding to take their land, and at Belamba on 25 April 2009, where the ADM recorded overall opinion for the refinery expansion as 'favourable', a considerable distortion (above, Chapter Six).

In Odisha, Andhra, Chhattisgarh, Jharkhand and other states, Public Hearings for mining projects are often occasions of violent coercion. As a symbol of democracy, a PH is often seen as the people's main chance to register their dissent.[17] The Lanjigarh PHs are mild compared to some. In south Chhattisgarh, PHs for Tata and Essar steel plants at Lohandiguda and Dhurli were held under extreme intimidation between June amd September 2006.[18] Manipulated Public Hearings are a classic case of *manufacturing consent*, through a pretence of 'consultation'.

EIAs and PHs became mandatory in 1994 and 1997 respectively under the Environment Protection Act (EPA) 1986, which has been amended repeatedly since to loosen restrictions, such as for new ports. EIA and PH notifications require a company to submit copies of an EIA and executive project summary to the SPCB, which must notify the public about a hearing in two leading dailies at least thirty days before holding a Public Hearing. EIAs are often hopelessly flawed, as we have seen. They are often plagiarised: for example, Ashapura Minechem's EIA (which the MoEF approved) for its Ratnagiri bauxite mine plan (Maharashtra), cut and pasted passages from a Siberian project, mentioning impact on birch and spruce trees—species which would be extraordinary to find in South India!—while silent about effects on Ratnagiri's famous mango trees.[19]

The National Environment Appellate Authority was constituted by an Act of 1997, and first found its teeth in December 2007, when it overturned MoEF clearance for the Polavaram dam, granted on the basis of a highly flawed PH on 10 October 2005.[20] Opposition to mining Mali Parbat, in Koraput district, has been organised through a Maliparbat Surakhya Samiti (MSS), which demanded cancellation of manipulated Public Hearings. Division among villagers shows in a grovelling letter from the MSS office bearers to the district and state authorities dated 27 September 2006—but dissent did not end here.[21]

A new phase of clearance for iron-ore mines in north Odisha started with a ludicrously flawed PH on 6 November 2008 for a crucial Mittal mine in Keonjhar, when police locked up 250 villagers (including 110 women), to prevent their attendance. The Collector's report on this PH recorded ten villagers as present and 80 per cent of these as in favour![22]

What is at stake in all these cases is the basic independence of Indian law. As we shall see when we meet the WB, the history of its structural adjustment programmes is to demand removal of 'restrictive legislation', as 'conditionalities' for loans to avert financial crisis, when countries face a balance of payment crisis over unpayable debts. What this means is, removal of laws that protect the environment, land rights, workers and human rights. One stage of this took place in 1991–93 when Manmohan Singh as Finance Minister steered India out of its debt crisis by enacting new economic and mineral policies.

Another stage is represented by the SEZ Act (2005), under which several hundred enclaves are being set up as Special Economic Zones, so that normal laws apply only at the discretion of the officials in charge. India's PM was quoted as saying that India stands to lose a vast sum of FDI if SEZ legislation does not go through fast.[23] This legislation reduces EIA requirements, does away with Public Hearings altogether, and offers huge subsidies on electricity, water, tax and land acquisition. There is strong opposition to SEZs throughout India, not least in Goa, where Vedanta's subsidiary Sesa Goa is a most notorious polluter.[24] The SEZ idea is anything but new. It is hailed as the reason for China's economic success, though China had four SEZs, while India plans several hundred, modelled on the kind of industrial enclaves that the aluminium industry, in particular, has used in many countries. Also, the costs of China's 'economic miracle' are often forgotten by Indian emulators. China also had over 50,000 protests in 2007, most of them brutally suppressed (Economy 2007).

During the 1980s–1990s, international standards for safeguarding the environment were brought into India's Constitution, defining the right to a clean and safe environment as part of an individual's right to life. These standards were enshrined in legislation, including the Environment Protection Act (1986), and insisted on by the Supreme Court, especially principles of 'polluter pays', absolute liability and reversal of burden of proof.[25]

However, implementing the 'polluter pays' principle has introduced a new level of threat, by reducing natural resources to an artificial monetary value—often a gross underestimate—in effect subverting the principle into a *licence to pollute*. The concept of Net Present Value (NPV) of forests has been propagated in India by a number of studies from the Green India States Trust and TERI (Gundimeda et al. 2005 and 2006), for which Deutsche Bank was a key funder. While these appear as a 'green initiative', their danger has emerged starkly in the Niyamgiri case, whose final judgment grants mining clearance on the basis of 'compensatory afforestation' computed according to the NPV of forest lost. The SC order of 8 August 2008 aims

> to strike a balance [between development and environmental protection] in order to subserve the principle of sustainable development. Under our Order we suggested [a] Rehabilitation Package, under which, apart from NPV, SIIL is also required to deposit 5 per cent of profits before tax and interest from Lanjigarh project or rupees 10 crore whichever is higher.[26]

In other words, Net Present Value of forest or biodiversity becomes a formula, blurring the elementary distinction between primary forest and plantations. Lado Majhi, a Dongria of Lakhpadar village, put this point most powerfully at the Belamba PH on 25 April 2009, where he was first to speak:

> Niyamgiri is our Mother. Our life depends on the mountain. Can you pay five *lakh*s for each tree? Our *Sarkar* [government] should not sell out to a foreign company. Even if everyone else accepts the project, we won't allow mining on Niyamgiri.

In other words, biodiversity—especially in a forest on top of a mountain, where a tribe has always protected it as inviolate—cannot be costed or compensated in financial terms. The GIST-Deutsche Bank enterprise of working out the NPV of forests becomes a pretext for selling them off. The Niyamgiri case makes this crystal clear—not least because Deutsche Bank is a prominent investor in Vedanta.

What will foreign investors gain from trading aluminium made from Niyamgiri bauxite? Who could weigh this gain against the loss of Niyamgiri's forest and ancient culture?

The Samatha Judgment and India's New Mineral Policy

An impression of balance was given at the Supreme Court by stressing Kalahandi's poverty, while suppressing all mention of impoverishment caused by mining projects, censoring any mention of tribal people's views, and using the concepts of 'polluter pays' and 'net present value of forests', to create an impression that forest, water and land resources being taken or polluted can be compensated by money. The idea of making the company pay also ignores the corruption known to be standard practice in tribal development projects.

These trends in India are in line with international moves, orchestrated through the WB and WTO, to dilute environmental law through 'sustainable development' projects that act as a mask for exploitation. India's new mineral policy, drafted in 2006–08, carries the undermining of protective legislation to a new level.

The Samatha Judgment (1997) affirmed tribal people's fundamental right to the inalienability of their land, enshrined in the Fifth Schedule of India's Constitution, but frequently disregarded. The clause in the Schedule excepting projects deemed 'in the public interest' has provided a massive loophole allowing companies to acquire tribal land. The Samatha Judgment insisted that only tribal-owned or public sector companies could acquire tribal land for projects. This opened the door, as we have seen, for state-owned mining companies to operate mines on behalf of private ones (OMC with Sterlite, APMDC with Jindal), subverting tribal people's constitutional guarantee.

India's Planning Commission is an apex power in India. The second Planning Commission report (1957) was clear on the dangers mining posed for conservation, seeing mineral resources as 'wasting assets: once they are taken out of the ground and utilised they are lost forever.' Fifty years later, the attempt to circumvent the Samatha Judgment has inverted priorities. The *Report of the Working Group on Mineral Exploration and Development* (September 2001) summarised the Samatha Judgment's restriction on mining, and made a first step towards negating its power:

> One of the areas of concern is multiplicity of legislation in respect of environmental aspects i.e. forest, environment, mining and labour, which need to be harmonised.... Another area of concern in the way of mineral development is the implication emanating from the Samatha Judgment of Supreme Court which is applicable in all the ten states ... where scheduled areas have been declared under the 5th schedule of the Constitution. After the Samatha Judgment, the State government of Andhra Pradesh does not have any recourse to granting mining lease in scheduled areas to anybody other than the PSUs or to the cooperatives of tribals.

Implications of the Samatha Judgment
The directive of the Supreme Court that all industries, be they natural or juristic persons to stop forthwith operations within the scheduled areas, has far-reaching consequences. Andhra Pradesh has the second largest deposits of bauxite in the country which lies largely in the Scheduled Areas....
In fact such a provision may have the unintended effect of leaving the mineral resources unexploited, as well as depriving the tribals of developmental spin off of mining industry....
Mining activity being temporary can never be understood to be deprivation of all rights of tribals.[27]

In other words, mining projects should promote the view that they are in tribal people's interests—even when tribal people make their opposition clear through protests. Ever since the Samatha Judgment, the Planning Commission and State governments often appear to have been seeking ways to avoid its implications, drawing attention away from its main point, which is an affirmation of the Constitution's insistence on tribal people's inalienable rights to their land.

An example was demonstrated in a Sub-Cabinet Committee Meeting held on 8 July 2002 at the Orissa CM's conference room, which decided that Andhra Pradesh laws prohibiting transfers of tribal land do not need replicating in Odisha, since 'adequate care has been taken to protect the tribal interests in the existing laws of the State'. In fact Orissa's Scheduled Areas Transfer of Immovable Property Act (OSATIP, 1956) is in line with the AP laws as well as with the Fifth Schedule and the Samatha Judgment. All agree on restricting the transfer of tribal land to non-tribal persons (including companies), in a way that cannot be circumvented by allocating a percentage of profits towards tribal development (which is how this meeting interpreted the Samatha Judgment).

Jindal's plan to mine bauxite near the Borra caves invades the very area where Samatha won its case. The MoU for bauxite mining was signed on 1 July 2005 and, in 2006–07, as the company became active in the area, there were demonstrations by tribal people, supported by Samatha staff, who were threatened by Jindal supporters. With the help of the AP government, Jindal took people from Beespuram village on an 'exposure tour' to Damanjodi (exactly as Vedanta took Dongria there in 2009), before pressing villagers to give a No Objection Certificate (NOC) for mining. To obtain Environmental Clearance, a Public Hearing was arranged in November 2006 in Vizag, far from the area. Fifty villagers who went there to register their objection were arrested.[28] A PH was held at S. Kota for the refinery by the APPCB, where 36 out of 40 people who spoke (out of about 1,000 present), opposed the refinery.[29] In this case, the Collector correctly communicated the people's opposition to higher authorities, but even so, in December 2007, the MoEF gave clearance for the project.

Minutes of a meeting of the AP government in the Revenue Minister's chambers on 2 July 2005 express the larger plan clearly. To facilitate extensive bauxite mining on the mountain-top deposits in north Andhra Pradesh, it is necessary to make use of loopholes in the Fifth Schedule and Samatha Judgment that projects declared 'in the public interest' can go ahead if they make use of PSUs (Public Sector Undertakings)—in this case, the AP Mining and Development Corporation Ltd. (APMDC).

The aim of the new National Mineral Policy is to encourage investment in mining, and speed up clearance procedures for exploration as well as actual mines. The role outlined for the government is as 'facilitator' for mining companies, keeping an 'arm's length' from direct involvement, in line with neoliberal orthodoxy.

The Hoda Committee was set up to write a first draft, submitted to the GoI in July 2006, and released to a wider public in December. Anurwal Hoda was a senior administrator in Bihar and the Ministry of Commerce from the 1960s–90s, becoming India's chief policy coordinator during the Uruguay round of GATT talks (1986–93), and then deputy director general of GATT (1993) and the WTO (1995), after which he joined India's Planning Commission as a senior member in 1999.

The Hoda Committee was commissioned to make a report in the aftermath of a committee under R. K. Dang, whose report (September 2005) recommended captive iron-ore mines for Indian steel companies, a ban on export of certain ores, and allowing foreign mining companies to make joint ventures in India only if they supplied 85 per cent of investment costs and joined with a public sector company. India's private sector industrialists, led by the Federation of Indian Mineral Industry (FIMI) strongly attacked this report. The Hoda Committee was commissioned in the aftermath, with the mandate of 'expeditious clearance from the environmental angle'. A report on India's mineral potential by McKinsey Global Institute, commissioned by the GOI, was submitted at this time, instigating hundreds of new MoUs for mines and metal factories in East India.[30]

But the view promoted by the Planning Commission that ridiculous delays in granting clearance were holding up mining projects and crores worth of FDI was itself ridiculous, when one looks at statistics of Forest Clearance granted by the MoEF since 1980 (when the Forest Conservation Act [FCA] made a lengthy clearance process mandatory):

- 317 mining leases were granted for 34,527 hectares of forest during 1980–97.
- 881 mining leases were granted for 60,476 hectares of forest during 1997–2005.

In other words, after 1997, the rate of forest cleared for mining increased fourfold. So why this pressure to crank up the speed of the process even more? The Hoda Committee and drafts of the NMP from 2006 go much further than the 1993 NMP and the Dang Committee in promoting private sector mining companies and foreign investment.

The new NMP, formulated on the basis of the Hoda Committee, reduces the cutting of India's forests to mere financial cost and the empty formality of submitting an EIA, in complete disregard of their biodiversity value. As a commentary by the CPI-ML puts this:

> diversion of *any* forest, however valuable, and however rich in biodiversity, is allowed for *any* development project as long as the payments for 'compensatory afforestation' are made. The very idea that afforestation can compensate for deforestation is flawed. Once a forest, a biodiverse region, or a wildlife habitat has been destroyed, it means destruction forever of *that particular* ecosystem. Nothing can replace it, or replicate it…. There can never be adequate 'compensation'

for deforestation.... Protecting the environment from adverse impacts of industrialisation has been reduced to a bureaucratic necessity of submitting an EIA report. Whatever analysis the EIA reports come up with, the prevalent practice is to clear any project, as long as there is a proper 'environment management plan' and adequate 'mitigation'. The quality of the EIA reports is itself highly suspect. Companies pay consultants to prepare EIA reports, and the obvious conflict of interest ensures that EIAs rarely do an honest environmental impact assessment. Inaccurate data, 'cut-and-pastes' from other EIA reports, shoddy analysis and sometimes plain untruths, are unfortunately the hallmarks of EIA reports.[31]

Hoda's December 2006 draft of the NMP starts by looking at ways of giving a massive boost to exploration/prospecting by incentives, and removing anything that foreign companies might regard as obstacles. In particular a 'seamless transfer' from exploration to mining lease is advocated, and speedy decision-making.

The document carefully glosses over areas of conflict. In contrast to the 2001 Planning Commission Report, which warned that the Samatha Judgment potentially denies mining companies' right to acquire land in tribal areas, the present document quotes the Samatha Judgment with approval, but fundamentally distorts its import to mean that compensation for tribal people must guarantee them a fuller life. No mention at all of Fifth Schedule areas and the non-transferability of tribal land.

First, a note of political correctness: 'the policy should provide for environmental concerns and the local communities to be fully taken into account in mining operations.' Now the crunch: 'In line with current economic policy, in future the core functions of the State in mining will be facilitation of exploration and mining activities'; nothing here about overseeing the rule of law or the rights of citizens. The purpose of government here is to cede power to mining companies, setting them free from 'restrictive regulations'.

State governments are exhorted to apply a first-come-first-served policy rather than making secret deals with favoured applicants. (Annexure 3 records the only note of dissent: a representation from the governments of Orissa, Chhattisgarh, Jharkhand and Karnataka against transferring jurisdiction to the central government).[32]

Chapters 2–3 review procedures for granting mineral concessions and the reason for delays; applications pass through 77 desks and often take over a year. Forest and Environmental Clearance is examined in detail, looking at ways to fast-track procedure. It is significant that this section quotes the authority of the MMSD report *Breaking New Ground* (Mining, Minerals and Sustainable Development 2002). This was orchestrated by the world's top mining companies with a view to short-circuiting calls for regulation. It starts with frank admission of the harm and conflicts mining causes, but all it recommends is '*voluntary regulation*' to '*best-practice standards*'. By contrast, the Extractive Industries Review (EIR) in 2004 (commissioned by the WB, and then rejected) made strong recommendations, one of which was that projects should not proceed without 'Free Prior Informed Consent' (FPIC) from people threatened with displacement. None of this finds mention in the NMP.

Like the MMSD report, the NMP starts by admitting that mining companies have a legacy of 'abuse and mistrust with local communities', that projects often conflict with the aim of conserving nature, and that 'a democratic decision-making process' is required. 'Land is often used without the consent of the indigenous people', and companies have a responsibility to 'ensure that living standards are not diminished'.[33] In practice, it is well-known that almost every displacement of tribal people involves a massive drop in their quality of life. The WB guideline that people's living standards should not fall has rarely been realised in practice (Padel and Das, December 2008). The NMP recommends involving NGOs in tribal development programmes.

'Sustainable Development Performance' is to be measured in a 'Global Reporting Initiative' (typified in Vedanta annual reports), on a model set by the MMSD and ICMM (International Committee on Mining and Minerals, the organisation run by the world's top mining companies to implement the MMSD report). The Samatha Judgment is cited, as if it merely demanded adequate R&R. Model R&R packages, suggested by the Samatha Judgment, should set aside 20 per cent of company profits to provide Project Affected Persons (PAPs) with roads, houses, schools, medical facilities, water and employment, in an idiom of Corporate Social Responsibility.[34]

The report then outlines methods to overcome 'the enormous difficulties of obtaining forest and environmental clearance' which mining companies have faced, recommending that Public Hearings should be limited to local people and locally registered NGOs: 'outsiders should not be allowed to participate', and should only be allowed to make written suggestions. What this misses out is the massive police intimidation recorded in a host of recent PHs.[35]

Later chapters explore SEZs, financing infrastructure, value addition, royalties, captive mines for steel companies, restrictions on the export of iron-ore, and mineral sands. Recommendations include 'immediate action' to streamline forest and environmental clearance, cutting the whole procedure down to the 'international norm of six months', and transferring the DFOs' duty to make a Cost Benefit Analysis of a project to 'competent private sector consultants', i.e. taking away their power to withhold clearance.[36]

In other words, what the NMP leaves out is even more significant than what it says. No mention of transparency and right to information, or the government's duty to disclose information about mining projects, no mention of externality: how mining companies externalise their costs, or the subsidies for electricity, transport and infrastructure. In particular, no mention of how costs to the environment or communities are to be audited, beyond standard recommendations (promoted by the ICMM) for compensatory afforestation, and using up to 3 per cent of a company's turnover for local development.

Of particular note is the way this document distorts the Samatha Judgment, ignoring the principle that Scheduled Tribes's land cannot be sold to non-tribals in Fifth Schedule areas, where a large proportion of India's minerals lie. The royalty regimes are also a distorted selection, missing out key countries.

The new NMP allows 100 per cent foreign ownership—a huge shift from careful restrictions that existed before. The priority is to fast-track clearance. 'Prioritising critical infrastructure needs of the mining sector' is a euphemism for subsidies in the form of specially built roads, railways, ports and power stations to draw investment— normally funded through loans that enmesh states such as Odisha into ever-higher levels of debt.

One of the chief influences on the NMP document is revealed in a speech by Guy Elliot, Rio Tinto's Director of Finance, at a meeting in London of the India-UK Business Leaders' Forum on 27 June 2006.

> Rio Tinto has been exploring for diamonds in India since late 2000. We have spent more than US$16 million on this search and have discovered several very interesting prospects.... Unfortunately, here the Indian mining code stands in the way of progress, as we have made comprehensive submissions, but have to wait for the right licences and permits to be granted. As you would expect these delays do not encourage foreign direct investment....
>
> With the right business environment and in partnership with experienced global mining companies, India can unlock its mineral wealth and the country could become a major player in world minerals markets. This sets it apart from China ... whose mineral resources are less abundant.
>
> Let me repeat this message: I think India has the potential to be a major source of minerals, but now more than ever, India needs competent mining companies to develop large scale, internationally competitive operations. These would supply local markets efficiently, and act as a catalyst for wide economic growth.
>
> India's present growth rate has little contribution from the mining sector. In order to get to the double digit growth that India aspires to, and to realise its full potential, certain things need to change.
>
> What are they? What should India do to make itself more attractive to foreign direct investment in the minerals sector?
>
> We are all awaiting with interest the publication by the Planning Commission Committee chaired by Mr. Anurwal Hoda, on this subject. This will ... propose changes to mineral law and policy.
>
> First, there is the question of 'security of tenure', meaning full rights from the preliminary exploration stage through to mine development. It is essential that any company investing in high risk exploration is rewarded, after satisfying permitting criteria, by guaranteed progress through the approvals process....
>
> Second, we need a stable fiscal regime. By their nature, mines are very long-term undertakings with high up-front costs ... Unless international investors feel confident that they will not be subjected to random imposts that will radically affect their forecast financial return, they will tend to stay away.

Third, international investors want free access to markets, prices and free market competition for their product....

With regard to my fourth point, India's bureaucracy, it would be impertinent of me to tell India how to manage its affairs. Every country has its own culture and its own way of doing things, and we must always respect this. Nevertheless, it's only fair to point out the consequences of India doing things India's way. Bureaucratic delays and red tape serve as potent disincentives to the overseas companies that want to respond positively to the government's desire for greater foreign direct investment. In my job, a great many investment proposals cross my desk. Attracting mining investment is a competitive business. As a result of its administrative processes, India may be missing out on a potential boom. This is certainly the risk it runs in the minerals sector.[37]

Here is a director of Rio Tinto, one of the world's most powerful mining companies (already involved with the OMC mining iron in north Odisha), essentially telling India's decisions-makers what should go into their new Mineral Policy: fast-track clearance procedure, and allow 'security of tenure', i.e. grant long-term lease rights to foreign mining companies. Consequences for India's environment, or the inhabitants of mineral-rich areas, are not an item on this agenda.

From *Arthashastra* to Global Compact

The new national policy, then, is geared to furthering the interests of mining companies. For village people and the environment, and for the well-being of future generations, the policy's overall effect is to weaken the laws and regulatory bodies that are supposed to ensure their protection.

Odisha is one of the few places in the world where new, 'greenfield' alumina refineries are being built—an indication of the strength of interest in India's bauxite. The Indian companies building them are all linked with and backed by foreign-based companies and banks, as we shall see more fully in the next chapter. 'Greenfield' refers to green vegetation sacrificed over a huge area.

Kautilya wrote his celebrated book on statecraft (Scripture on Wealth) for Ashoka's grandfather Chandragupta. The book highlights mining and metals as a key source of power and wealth, and warns of dangers to the state if private or independent operators are allowed to take charge of mines. It is revealing to look at this advice in the light of today's globalising mining boom.

2,300 years after the *Arthashastra* was written, the policy of a newly independent India was to keep most mining carefully under government control in PSUs (Public Sector Undertakings), and to limit foreign investment to less than 40 per cent of ownership in any project. Yet as we shall see, all India's aluminium companies started up as joint ventures with foreign companies. Half these stories have barely been told.

India's New Economic Policy (1991) and New Mineral Policy (1993) started to change this, extending the right of foreign-based companies to invest in and exploit India's minerals, and to take profits out of the country ('expatriation of assets'). This policy was masterminded by Manmohan Singh as India's Finance Minister, as a solution to India's biggest balance of payments crisis (1989–91), in effect starting the liberalisation process in India, under pressure from the WB and its loans.

Since then, this process has gone much further. The new NMP goes to the farthest possible extreme from Kautilya's advice: government should keep 'an arms length' from any direct involvement in mining, and play the role of 'facilitator' for mining companies, encouraging as much foreign investment as possible, fast-tracking clearance so that projects can start up as quickly as possible with a 'seamless transfer' of prospecting to mining lease, ensuring 'security of tenure', short-circuiting democratic procedures which allow indigenous people to veto projects that would displace them or threaten their environment.

The new *Arthashastra* promoting this vision, cited in the new National Mineral Policy as a benchmark for international best practice, is the MMSD Report, *Breaking New Ground*, and its follow-on, the ICMM. The story of this Mining, Minerals and Sustainable Development process, and the International Council on Mining and Minerals, reveals much about the way that mining company interests are being promoted worldwide, paying lip-service to environmental and activist concerns, while attempting to do away with democratic control over the power of mining companies.

Worldwide frustration at the abuses of big corporations was being assuaged in 1992 by a Code of Corporate Conduct drafted by the UNCTC (Centre for Transnational Corporations). This was side-stepped by a proposal for voluntary corporate self-regulation at the Rio de Janeiro World Summit on Sustainable Development, introduced jointly by the Business Council for Sustainable Development (BCSD) and the International Chamber of Commerce (ICC). The proposal was welcomed by corporate and government interests, who were keen to avoid any formal regulation, and the UNCTC was disbanded in 1993.

When the World Industry Council for the Environment (WICE) merged with the BCSD to form the World Business Council for Sustainable Development (WBCSD, 1997), this was under the firm control of mining company heads. Rio Tinto's Chairman Robert Wilson proposed a Global Mining Initiative (GMI) at the Davos Summit in 1999, at the same time as he also formulated with Kofi Annan a Global Compact to bring together companies, UN agencies, labour and civil society organisations.

The Global Mining Initiative, in which Rio Tinto had been joined by other big mining companies, set up the MMSD to put in place a new order, more effectively under their control. Its Report was finished in time for the second World Summit on Sustainable Development, at Johannesberg in 2002, where the Chairmen of Rio Tinto and other apex mining companies kept close contact with Tony Blair, who announced an Extractive Industries Transparency Initiative (EITI) at this summit.

The MMSD project cost millions of dollars, paid for mainly by a consortium of about 30 leading mining companies. The WBCSD contracted the project to the IIED in London (International Institute for Environment and Development). While the study starts out admitting abuses by the mining industry, and involved numerous consultations and submissions, most of the civil society groups and NGOs whose grievances had brought about the project were conspicuous by their absence. And after completion in 2002, when the MMSD project was closed down, its guidelines were handed over to a group run by mainstream mining interests, the International Council on Mining and Minerals (ICMM). 'Voluntary self-regulation' under the banner of 'sustainable development' had replaced any firm controls over mining company practice. The Global Reporting Initiative (GRI) is a key part of the Global Compact, and allows mining companies in effect to supply their own data, instead of allowing regulation with external verification. In other words, this is a system that is not based on independent verification of data, and is therefore unscientific and undemocratic.[38]

The *Arthashastra* outlined a policy based on a long-term vision. The Global Compact accentuates corporate power and its key values of growth and privatisation based around maximising short-term gain. 'India rising' showed a growth rate of 8-9 per cent (October 2007). In aluminium consumption this is reflected in thousands of new cars, a construction boom of new Western-style aluminium-rich architecture in cities, and a huge increase in aluminium packaging, including large-scale promotion of un-recyclable Tetra Paks and other oil-aluminium fusing 'flexibles' and 'closures'.

Instead of the central government controlling mining projects and keeping them in order, the new mineral policy encourages mining all or most known deposits as quickly as possible, and upping steel and aluminium exports as a priority. As a result, to put this very simply: if most of the leases applied for on forest land in Odisha (and the same applies to other parts of India) are cleared, Odisha will have no forest after a few years.

The events we have witnessed on the frontier of the industry's expansion in Odisha show that powerful corporations are in effect controlling the government and dictating its policies. If this is part of a worldwide trend for corporations to take over governments, examining aluminium companies in Odisha provides a case study of how this happens.

'Money isn't God, but by God, it's no less than God'

The new policy makes no suggestions about how to make mining deals more transparent. As the UN puts this, politely and diplomatically:

Mining deals generally provide governments with much needed fiscal revenue, easy to collect and in considerable amounts, at least within a short time frame.[39]

A deal involves advance payments of various kinds by companies to a range of ministers and other government servants, building up a form of debt that is often based on a hidden corruption. 'Briberisation' (as it is often called in India) has negative effects on society, including a 'conspicuous consumption' more wasteful and tasteless than ever. The corruption involved in mining projects is notorious. As the Odia daily *Sambad* refers to a new scandal surrounding a coal mine near Talcher, in a front-page article on 21 February 2007:

> **Yet another mine corruption: this time coal. KICK-BACK OF 200 CRORES** [about $45 million]. With Tangarapada, Niyamgiri and Khandadhara mining leases still unresolved, another mining scandal has caught fire. This time the corruption involved over a single coal-mining lease is being estimated at more than 200 crore rupees. [our translation]

Corruption exists among lower officials because it is tolerated at higher levels. In November 2003 India's Minister of Environment and Forests was captured on hidden camera receiving a large bribe from a mining company for granting clearance for leases in Odisha and Chhattisgarh, with words that reveal much about modern attitudes to money: '*Paise khuda to nahi, par khuda ki kasam, khuda se kam bhi nahi*' (Money isn't God, but by God, it's no less than God).[40]

The model for this behaviour was set in the contempt which America's Robber Barons often showed for the process of law. Cornelius Vanderbilt, one of the first 'railway kings', once remarked when challenged, 'What do I care about the law? Hain't I got the power?' In 1866–68, during the ferocious 'railway wars', rival companies bribed Supreme Court judges. One party was exposed as paying over $1 million in bribes, describing it in expenses as 'extra and legal services'. There was an established system for purchasing elected politicians and judges. As Collis P. Huntingdon, another of the railway kings, put this in a letter of 1877:

> If you have to pay money to have the right thing done, it is only just and fair to do it.... If a man has the power to do great evil and won't

do right unless he is bribed to do it, I think the time spent will be gained when it is a man's duty to go up and bribe the judge. [41]

The prevalence of this corruption explains why Abraham Lincoln, shortly before he was assassinated in 1865, drew attention to the dangers of company power for America:

> Corporations have been enthroned.... An era of corruption in high places will follow and the money power will endeavour to prolong its reign by working on the prejudices of the people.... until wealth is aggregated in a few hands ... and the Republic is destroyed. [42]

'Breaking rules at opportune moments' was one of the secrets of Carnegie's success, and for the other Robber Barons too, laying down a pattern in which politicians and the judiciary were in effect making and implementing the law at the Robber Barons' bidding—a pattern painfully visible in corporate takeovers today, in Odisha and worldwide.[43]

The use of *goondas* by mining companies is another blatant example of double standards towards the law. As 'outrage against displacement spreads',[44] it is clear to observers in Odisha that the orchestration of mafia elements in support of mining companies is a nexus that involves certain politicians and senior administrators, as well as the mining companies they promote. The murder of gangster Biranchi Das in Bhubaneswar on 13 April 2008 pointed to senior administrators' involvement in campaigns to terrorise displacement protestors.[45]

We have seen the role played by pro-company *goondas* in the aluminium projects in south Odisha. In the iron mining areas in the north, contract killings have a long history. In the Kalinganagar area too, there have been a number of serious attacks by *goondas* on leading activists of the BBJM (People's Platform against Displacement [by Tata and other steel companies])—the movement of tribal communities whose people were killed in the police firing in January 2006. Amin Banara was a tribal activist shot dead by a *goonda* near the Tata factory site in May 2008. The next month Dula Mandal, a villager active in the anti-Posco movement, was killed by pro-Posco *goondas* in his village of Govindpur.[46]

For villagers trying to stand up and hold onto their land, homes and communities, the threats of court cases or violence is often extremely wearing. The irony is that these people are an example to all of us of living sustainably. Protecting the environment is a major motivation in all the movements we highlight in this book. Tribal villagers, even after years of exploitation and struggle, often retain a view of their own well-being as dependent on the well-being of their natural environment. This is a healthy view that all of us in mainstream society could learn from.

American legal expert Cormac Cullinan's book *Wild Law: A Manifesto for Earth Justice* raises the question of whether systems of law now shouldn't make protecting the basic fabric of life a fundamental concern? As he says,

> Most lawyers and legislators do not know enough about natural regulatory systems, and in any case, do not believe they are relevant to humans.

We need to

> recognise that at the moment the governance systems of most countries and of the international 'community' actually facilitate and legitimise the exploitation and destruction of Earth by humans. [47]

Much of what is called 'development' is essentially destructive: the removal of unrenewable mineral resources and irreplaceable forests, and dangerous overuse of water, as well as destruction of communities who have lived for generations in harmony with nature, with minimal consumption. Much of what we have learnt to call 'development' promotes *over-consumption*:

> [w]hile economists look with pride on the fact that the world economy expanded sevenfold between 1950 and 2000, and world trade is expanding more rapidly, ecologists see that these are based on a profligate use of Earth's 'natural capital'. [48]

Cullinan calls for a swift change in countries' legal systems so as to protect the fabric of life in a world which most ecologists see as entering a period of severe environmental crisis caused by economic growth out of control.

Courts and the judiciary have often played a key role in facilitating corporate takeovers of natural resources. Sometimes they give impartial verdicts, going against the trend of political and corporate interests, as in the Samatha Judgment. Perhaps as the recession bites, and awareness deepens about the dangers of global heating, Courts will start to take more decisive action against corporate misdeeds. India's Chief Justice, K. G. Balakrishnan (one of the three judges in the Niyamgiri case) took a stand against mining in the Aravali range in May 2009, and in the same month, spoke of the strong role judges should play in protecting India's environment and shelving harmful projects.[49] As Arijit Pasayat also said, it is often difficult to strike a balance between economic imperatives and environmental protection. But time is running out, and all of us, judges included, need to stay awake to patterns of irreversible destruction promoted in the guise of development, and put a stop to this trend.

Niyam Raja stands for the principle of law implicit in human society and our proper balance with nature. *Niyamgiri,* the *Mountain of Law,* stands as a witness to whether we can achieve this balance, or not.[50]

CHAPTER EIGHT

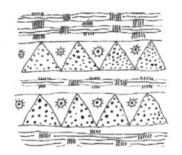

Aluminium India

Jaa! [Go!] ... *Alco Balco Nalco Malco Chalco jaa!*
Utkal company Indal company Alcan company Nalco company Sterlite company America company ... Jaa!

Alai Majhi, an old woman in Barigaon, Kashipur, squats on the floor and sings an exorcism of the aluminium companies from her land, during our visit in 2004.

If, as our narrative suggests, aluminium companies' invasion of Odisha's tribal areas involves long-term damage to the environment and serious human rights abuses, who should take responsibility for this? Why are the laws being circumvented and subverted?

We would like to believe it is basically out of an ignorance about basic patterns of cause and effects, and our main purpose in this book is to try and rectify this ignorance, by bringing a wide network of such patterns to light. But correcting the situation calls for a basic shift in attitudes. Many modern habits of thought promote a lack of causal thinking, and a sense of individual separation from the whole, or from a sense of the results of one's actions.

Adivasis in Kashipur have spent the last fifteen years encountering the real nature of the aluminium companies, and understand them as well as anyone. Mainstream views often regard tribal people protesting against the aluminium or steel industries as doing so out of 'ignorance', or because they have been 'misled' by outsiders. We believe the opposite is true. Adivasi and Dalit activists have been our main teachers. They know all too well the results of displacement and pollution from experiencing its effects at first hand, or witnessing it in the lives of countless relatives and neighbours.

To Alai, Bhagaban and others, these companies are invading their area and taking their land. The companies have no right to do this, and it is in no one's real (i.e. long-term) interest. The company people are ignorant of the real value of the mountains, rivers and forests they destroy. Devastation of village people and their land form an intrinsic part of mining operations.

Villagers also understand that aluminium companies are not discrete entities. They fuse and merge into each other, and into the police and political structures. This fusion is financial, and in terms of who pulls the strings.

Behind the deals: A dispersed and hidden social structure

In Part I we heard many stories, highlighting Utkal and Vedanta. It is significant that both these key projects have ancient Indian names, evoking an Odia or Indian pride, masking the companies' foreign links and export orientation. Each project is on a massive scale, changing the face of a whole region and the pace of life for thousands of villagers, with the khondalite mountains the crucial targets of corporate desire.

In their corporate, financial, political and legal structures, aluminium companies are extremely complex. Yet part of this complexity is a front, masking a brutal simplicity. Tribal people know how aluminium companies really operate because they are in the firing line, and know better than most of us what is really at stake, in terms of the fabric of life of fields, forests, mountains, rocks, rivers and streams, intrinsic to their material as well as sacred and mythological world, which aluminium companies treat as inanimate resources that can be made to yield huge profits.

Aluminium companies have close links with governments, as well as their wars—a relationship that is often hidden, shifting its form, complex and hard to unravel—and meant to be! Party political links with companies are a theme in numerous mining deals. Vedanta mentions donations of $2.6m to political parties in its annual reports.[1]

In different contexts, towards different groups of people, mining companies have changing faces: respectable towards influential people, thuggish to those standing in their way; full of promises and flamboyant generosity at the start of a project, very different when a project's up and running and its real effects are obvious. Anthropologists draw a distinction between a culture's definition of itself, and interpretation from outside, analysing it from a more objective standpoint. This 'emic'/'etic' distinction can prove especially fruitful for analysing corporate culture, where a company's behaviour often contradicts the self-image it projects.[2]

The official front is the mask of corporate respectability one meets when one tries to find out about companies through their brochures and offices. Clean, shiny images of beautiful nature and smiling employees, and factories working to make this a better, cleaner world. For the officer class this image defines their social reality and aspirations, and what they would like to believe is true. But behind it lies another reality of dirt and corruption: gouging out mountains, disrupting village life, polluting and destroying nature, human rights abuses and shady deals, and extreme hierarchy. At the local level, in Lanjigarh or Kashipur, this hierarchy shows in a coolie work gang. Men and women labour, digging and carrying rocks and earth, under the command of a foreman or *thikedar* (contractor), who stands over their work gangs and talks down to them with *saheb* arrogance. The intimidation and violence we have seen in Kashipur and Lanjigarh is a regular feature of mining company strategy—the other side of the coin to the fine words used in different contexts.

Aluminium companies are not discrete entities. 'Revolving doors' operate between governments and corporations. On the surface, aluminium companies compete with each other, sometimes ferociously, culminating in ruthless takeovers and mergers. But these highlight the fact that companies merge into each other in terms of ownership, and also into the banks and other financial institutions that invest in them. Often top executives in an Indian company are 'promoted' to a foreign company. Aluminium companies' common vested interests also push them to operate together to fix prices, as a cartel.

Another striking thing about the social structure of the aluminium industry is its dispersed—even anti-social—character, in the sense that different parts of it have no direct relationship with other parts, and often no knowledge about them. This was brought home to us when a British executive at the 2004 Vedanta AGM in London exclaimed: 'If you were targeting arms companies I could understand it, but there's no link between the aluminium industry and arms companies!' All, or most, of the arms companies have supply agreements with aluminium companies, and vice versa, but financiers and shareholders do not necessarily know this—or want to know.

Miners and factory workers, company officials, traders, financiers, accountants, commodity analysts, scientific researchers, transporters— each deals with a different aspect, in a different place, without an overview of the industry as a whole—an extreme example of the division of labour characteristic of modern society. This social and spatial separation of the industry's parts is useful to those in control for reasons we shall gradually see more clearly. Any one part of the industry is a little world unto itself. People living in a Nalco township serving Damanjodi or Angul exist in a tidy world of other employees, defined by Nalco's image as 'Pride of Orissa'.

But the schools and clubs there do not exactly encourage knowledge about the village people dispossessed or poisoned by the aluminium plants, even though these may live just down the road—let alone about the use of their aluminium in arms, or the real story of their company's finances and its close relationship with foreign companies. Most people know little more about aluminium than what they are 'supposed' to know: that it has given the world a huge range of products which make life easier—kitchenware, electric wires, cars and planes, foil and packaging to keep food fresh—and that it is a 'green', 'environment-friendly' metal because it is recycled a lot. Few understand its close relationship with big dams; fewer still know of its role in bomb technology and the arms industry. As for understanding the intrinsic patterns of exploitation, these have been made hard to comprehend, and can only be seen through an overview of the industry. This is why our book journeys to such seemingly disparate places and areas of life.

An aluminium company operates through a wide range of carefully cultivated links with influential people and organisations in many different professions, and other companies in a wide variety of sectors. Through foil, an aluminium company supplies packaging companies, working closely with food and medicine companies. Through extrusions, it supplies car manufacturers. For energy needs it works closely with transport, oil and coal companies. Construction companies build its dams, power stations and metal factories.

In all there are presently six operating refineries and six smelters in India (2009). To summarise present operations of India's three main aluminium companies: Nalco's mine, refinery and smelter are all integrated in Odisha and provide nearly half the country's output. Hindalco has a refinery and smelter in UP, as well as Indal's refinery and smelter at Muri and Hirakud, mainly sourcing bauxite from Chhattisgarh and Jharkhand mines; its Utkal refinery being built in Kashipur plus its smelter-plan in north in Odisha are based on plans for mining more mountains in Odisha. Sterlite-Vedanta controls the Malco refinery-smelter complex plus mines in Tamil Nadu, the Balco refinery-smelter complex (with two smelters) plus mines in Chhattisgarh, and the VAL refinery at Lanjigarh (operating since 2007), based on its plans for mining Niyamgiri plus the new smelter going up in north Odisha.

The Indian Bureau of Mines (IBM) in Nagpur has records of 354 bauxite mining leases (2006), 190 of them in Gujarat, where deposits lie on hills where local rivers start in Jamnagar and Kutch districts (accounting for 16 per cent of India's bauxite mined), mostly run by the Gujarat Mineral Development Corporation (GMDC), which plans an alumina refinery in the state.[3] By contrast, Odisha presented only seven bauxite mining leases recorded at the IBM (four in Sundargarh district, presumably for the steel industry, which uses bauxite in the refining process).

The Geological Survey of India (GSI) and IBM are extensions of the Ministry of Mines in Delhi. The GSI, based in Kolkata, was set up in 1851 out of a Coal Committee (1837), to exploit India's coal

Map 8: India's Aluminium Industry

and later iron deposits for East India Company ships, so they would not have to 'carry Newcastle coals to India for the journey from as well as to India.'[4] The IBM is a regulatory as well as consultative body, which leads to an intrinsic conflict of interests.

Another subsidiary of the Mining Ministry, also in Nagpur, is the Jawaharlal Nehru Aluminium Research Development and Design Centre (JNARDDC). The UNDP helped set it up (1987–89) and fund it, and it started work in 1996, as a research institute. Questions were asked in Parliament in 2002 about its 'languishing and pathetic conditions ... due to lack of funds'. The reason seems to be that in practice its members earn most of their salaries as private consultants to foreign as well as Indian mining companies.[5] JNARDDC research mostly services aluminium companies' needs around their basic resource, bauxite.[6]

Also based in Nagpur is the Mining Exploration Corporation Ltd. (MECL), 'the premier exploration agency of the country', started in 1972 as a PSU.[7] Though technically administered by the Ministry of Mines, it is essentially a private enterprise. It carries out surveys for mining companies, and has also done aerial surveys of mineral deposits in various parts of India. Aerial surveys in Odisha during the 1990s were carried out by the World GeoScience Corporation (Australia), later bought up by Fugro (Netherlands), whose survey over central Odisha at times used a pretext of doing a ground water survey. The mineral charts produced for Odisha are now the property of the director of Geology and Mines.[8]

The web of Indian institutions that facilitate aluminium projects, and the linking of government-business interests, often appear daunting. The 2008 website of an organisation called India Brand Equity Foundation gives an insight into the web of interests in Odisha, aiming to promote an attractive *investment climate*, with a 'Single Window Clearance mechanism ... to facilitate speedy implementation of industrial projects'. Apart from the private electricity companies and banks, and emphasis on road building and ports under modernisation, the key *nodal agencies* it introduces are: Industrial Promotion and Investment Corporation of Orissa Ltd. (IPICOL), Industrial Development Corporation of Orissa Ltd. (IDCOL), Orissa Industrial Infrastructure Corporation (IDCO),

Orissa State Financial Corporation (OSFC), Directorate of Export Promotion and Marketing (DEPM). The revolving doors between top-ranking GoO bureaucrats and company directors are a prime example of 'contaminated governance'.[9]

A number of institutions work closely with aluminium companies. Tata AIG, partner of the US insurance firm American International Group, wrote Sterlite's Rapid EIA, which promulgated the false idea that there is no proper forest on the Niyamgiri lease area. Crisil is India's biggest Credit Rating Agency, an associate of Standard & Poor. The rating it assigned to Vedanta Aluminium Ltd. in October 2008 was 'AA+'. Perfect Relations (serving Posco and Tetra Pak) is one of India's leading PR companies. Vedanta's PR is managed by two London-Based firms, Finsbury's and CO3.

The main lobby group is the Aluminium Association of India (AAI), which pushes for high tariffs on secondary products, and has organised five International Conferences on Aluminium (INCAL 1985, 1991, 1998, 2003, 2007), whose papers focus on technical and financial aspects, with barely a mention of the industry's impacts on society or environment, and a deafening silence about opposition to projects.

The industry was regulated in 1970, and an Aluminium Control Order in 1975 required aluminium producers to make at least 50 per cent of their output in the form of wire to supply the Rural Electrification Programme, at a government-set price (compared to a world average of 9 per cent for this sector). The program of bringing electricity to all India's villages slowed down in the 1980s, and then ground to a halt—leaving many villages without, such as around the Indravati reservoir (Chapter Four). Electricity grade fell from 61 per cent in 1977 to 35 per cent in 1988, when the Bureau of Industrial Costs and Prices produced a key report, advocating keeping aluminium consumption low in India, due to the industry's high costs in subsidies and environmental impacts (BICP Dec 1988).

In 1989 the industry was decontrolled, removing import duties on aluminium. This coincided with a new policy of promoting aluminium aggressively in every sector. Papers from INCAL and the Forschungszentrum institute in Germany (Vasudevan 1999) reveal an aim of increasing per capita consumption in India from less than one kilo a year towards the world average of 25 kg, and to double aluminium use to 200 kg per passenger car, just when India was becoming a major manufacturing hub for cars. In the words of Tamotia, when he was Indal's CEO (2004):

> Unfortunately, even after 65 years of existence, per capita aluminium consumption in India is very low at 0.65 kg against 10–12 kg per capita in other developing nations.

This policy trend is also visible in the book co-authored by India's former President, Abdul Kalam (*India 2020*, 1998, pp. 96–98), which advocates a massive increase in India's aluminium production, as part of a drive to make India a 'developed country', 'competitive' against even faster Chinese growth. Kalam's background was in military technology, where he played a key role in India's nuclear missile and satellite programmes. His book mentions a particular need to develop high-tech alloys for defence applications, such as the aluminium–lithium range, and aluminium-based Metals Matrix Composites (MMCs, in which aluminium is alloyed with oil/plastic derivatives). The National Institute of Foundry and Forge Technology in Ranchi is among the highly funded centres carrying out research in aluminium alloys. Aluminium consumption in India saw a huge increase during the first decade of the twenty-first century, in foil, cement, and vehicles. The policy trend is clear: to expand India's output enormously, on the view that to become 'globally competitive' India must open up its bauxite deposits.

Alok Sheel promoted this policy as Secretary of Mines for the GoI, when he advocated a low tariff regime, to turn the country into a major aluminium exporter, and counteract a situation where, as he saw it, 'aluminium product penetration in India is abysmal.' He was

> part of the inner team that worked on the privatisation of the state-owned Bharat Aluminium Company (Balco), effectively the first successful privatisation story out of India. My assignment also involved attracting overseas investment into the mining sector.[10]

This brings in the role of banks, which has been evident in finance for Vedanta's projects, as well as for Iceland's new series of smelters, where the investment bubble crashed in October 2008 (Chapter

Nine). This recalls the role Mellon's bank played financing Alcoa's rise from the 1890s to 1930s, and Kaiser's heavy borrowing to set up his aluminium empire from the 1940s. Papers by executives from the Export-Import Bank of India (EXIM) and HSBC spell out the key role of certain banks as offshore debt financing sources.[11]

The AAI in Bangalore is modelled on the European Aluminium Association (EAA) in Brussels, the International Aluminium Institute (IAI) in London, and the Aluminum Association (Washington), which serve as international lobby groups for the industry, coordinating the discourse on environment and CSR, and building aluminium's 'green and friendly' image.

We visited the EAA and IAI in July 2006. The former had a Kafkaesque approach through an unmarked door in central Brussels. Its neighbour on the floor below is Northrop–Grumman, one of the top US arms companies! One of the director's main worries was the closing down of relatively new refineries and smelters in Europe, due to escalating costs and their 'outsourcing' to the Third World: Alcan closed the UK's last refinery in 2002–03 (at Burntisland in Scotland), just as it was trying to build the Utkal refinery in Kashipur. The emphasis in IAI literature (2004–06) is on the industry's increased energy efficiency, decreasing pollution levels (PFC emissions down 60 per cent since 1990), better health and safety standards, and hundreds of applications essential for modern life.

Alfed (Aluminium Federation), in Birmingham, is the UK's main lobby group. Its influence over Parliament was shown when it got MPs to scupper a Climate Change Levy on aluminium's GHG emissions in 1999, which was 'causing a real furore … behind the scenes and perhaps even in front of the scenes.'[12]

This relates to a scandal that hit both the main parties in the UK (as also in the US) in October 2008, when it was revealed that George Osborne (Tory) and Peter Mandelson (Labour) had visited Oleg Deripaska on his yacht off Cyprus, shortly before Mandelson lowered the tariff for aluminium foil, which favoured Deripaska's company Rusal in 2005.[13]

Foreign threads behind Hindalco and Nalco

The First World War and after was a time of vast expansion for aluminium companies, with fierce competition between governments to get control of the world's known bauxite deposits, because of their importance for arms (Graham 1982). The British Aluminium Company (BAC) helped set up India's first fabrication works from 1922.[14] India's first bauxite mines were in Gujarat, Madhya Pradesh and by Tata, near Belgaum in Karnataka. Bauxite in the 1920s was used for cement and refining petroleum, under Lafarge and Tata, whose plans for a refinery-smelter complex (never built) were a factor in building the huge Koyna dam (1923),[15] which burst in December 1967, killing about 200 people.

The JK Corporation started India's first alumina refinery at Asansol (West Bengal). JK is named after the founders, Juggilal Singhania (1857–1922) and his son Kamlapat (1884–1937), Marwari businessmen who had migrated from Rajasthan to Kanpur (UP), where they set up a cotton mill in 1921, followed by a steel plant and the alumina refinery. The big JK paper mill at JKpur near Rayagada was among south Odisha's first big factories, on the Bansadhara river, cause of considerable pollution and deforestation, not least from extensive eucalyptus planatations.[16]

During the rapid rearmament leading up to the Second World War, BAC joined Alcan (1938) to set up Indal (christened Indian Aluminium Co. in 1944), whose first plants were a sheet rolling mill at Belur in Karnataka (1941), the Muri refinery, and a smelter at Alupuram in Kerala, inaugurated with a conference on aluminium in 1943.

Indal's brochures for 2002 advertise its ownership of mines, plants and offices in 14 places in India, and describe its relationship with Alcan in glowing terms:

> Indal was born out of the international giant, Alcan.... Interaction between us has always been frequent and close.
> So you'll often find an Alcan member overseeing progress at Indal. We, in turn, send some of our very best engineers to Alcan for a period of intensive training.

> We cannot help but marvel at the difference the Alcan experience makes to them. For when they're back, we always feel like we've imported the finest skills in the foil business... Over the years Alcan has steadily acquired the role of our resource base—a matter of much satisfaction to us. [17]

The next three Indian aluminium companies—Malco, Balco and Hindalco—entered the stage in the 1960s, through similar contact with foreign firms.

Hindalco was set up through an association between G. D. Birla and the American company Kaiser Aluminium in 1957–59. Hindalco's refinery and smelter at Renukoot (UP)

> came about as a result of a suggestion of G. D. Birla, one of India's leading industrialists, to Edgar Kaiser, whom Birla knew from Kaiser Engineers' dam-building projects in his country. In August 1959 Kaiser joined with Birla in a partnership to build an integrated primary aluminium facility. At a cost of $30 million it was the largest single US private investment in a venture with an Indian firm.[18]

Edgar's father Henry J. Kaiser entered aluminium in 1945–46, and masterminded a massive expansion in the industry (Chapter Nine). Kaiser took a leading role constructing some of India's first big dams, including Rihand, designed to supply water and power for Renukoot aluminium, using WB loans, through influence on George Woods (about to become WB President). The Rihand dam displaced at least 200,000 people on the UP-Chhattisgarh border, many of them Adivasis. They were given no proper warning or compensation when their lands and homes were flooded in 1961. Questions were asked in Parliament about this dam, notably by Lohia and other socialists, especially about the huge subsidy Hindalco received on its electricity—1.99 *paise* per unit, guaranteed for 25 years, instead of the going rate of about 40 *paise*. Kaiser's empire of companies was a model for the Birla dynasty. Hindalco is now part of the Aditya Birla Group, under control of G.D.'s grandson Aditya. Until 1986, Kaiser held a 26 per cent share in Hindalco, while Birla's was 25 per cent.[19]

There is much in Hindalco's history that remains hidden from public knowledge. The BAC set up subsidiaries in India and Pakistan in 1947:

At the time of the partition of India it was decided to strengthen the organisation for selling semi-fabricated products and Aluminium Hindustan Ltd. and Aluminium Pakistan Ltd. were formed. The Indian company has its headquarters in Calcutta.[20]

Birla laid the foundations of his business empire long before Independence and was a close associate of Gandhi and Nehru. Even though he owned textile mills, Birla gave financial patronage to Gandhi's All-India Handspinners' Association, believing that 'This spinning was of symbolic rather than practical significance.' We have seen how the first Birla factory in Odisha, Orient Paper Mill, got away with polluting the Ib River, despite a complaint to Gandhi, while *Mystery of Birla House* (Burman 1950) is a tax commissioner's exposure of this factory's tax avoidance (Chapter One). The Singhania and Birla families, like the Agarwals, are Marwaris, who have played a major role in India's industrialisation (Kochanek 1974).

Before the end of the war Birla and J. R. D. Tata were among the industrialists who drafted the Bombay Plan for India's post-war industrialisation. When Nehru put this plan into effect through the Planning Commission, set up in 1950,

> The scheme soon depleted the sterling balances in the Bank of England which had accumulated due to India's forced saving during the war—when the British had taken away much of India's production on credit—and by 1956 India had to turn to the Western nations in order to finance the ambitious plans.[21]

In other words, Britain was heavily in debt to India at the time of Independence but, within ten years, the situation had reversed, and India was heavily in debt to foreign banks.

The exploitative nature of Alcan's relationship with Indal, and Kaiser's with Hindalco, is not something obvious and open. Clearly these partnerships were a source of great profit to top executives, but there is little doubt that a large part of the main profits diasappeared abroad.

The same applies to Nalco, set up in 1980 as a joint venture with France's aluminium company, Pechiney, to exploit Odisha's biggest bauxite deposit on Panchpat Mali (Chapter Four). Pechiney was the world's oldest aluminium company (Chapter Two), operating nine smelters in France, with aluminium enclaves in many countries, from Greece to Africa, America and Australia. Pechiney has a murky past of its own, merging with the chemical and nuclear giant Ugine-Kuhlmann in 1971, and building the James Bay hydro-electric scheme in Quebec to power its smelter on the St Lawrence river—a catastrophe for affected Cree and Inuit Canadian Indians. Pechiney was at the centre of France's nuclear power industry, and thus a manufacturer of uranium as well as aluminium for arms companies. Pechiney's aluminium technology, used in Nalco's plants, was controversial for exposing workers to high pollution levels.[22]

American National Can, which Pechiney bought up in 1988 made it the world's largest producer of metal drinks cans—inherited by Novelis after Alcan bought up Pechiney (2004), and thus by Hindalco when it bought up Novelis.[23]

So Indal, Hindalco and Nalco were set up in collaboration with foreign giants: Alcan, Kaiser and Pechiney. Alcan's manoeuvre, buying up Indal and selling it to Hindalco in 1998–2000, shows the decisive importance of the Utkal project, which was geared to 100 per cent foreign export from the start, following the trend set by Nalco's switch to selling the bulk of its output abroad from the year 2000.

Until the Maikanch firing, the lead company of the Utkal consortium, with the biggest share and top management role, was Norsk–Hydro, Norway's biggest company, which has a long history of dams and hydropower for aluminium plants. After leaving Utkal, under fire from Norwegian human rights campaigners, Hydro became even bigger when it bought up the giant German aluminium company VAW in 2002, and made a deal with Rusal. It is at the forefront of new 'clean technology' for aluminium, but has a large stake in Brazil's aluminium industry (Chapter Nine), and a major business selling synthetic fertilisers to Third World markets (with a subsidiary in India called Viking), which release large quantities of nitrous oxygen into the atmosphere—a GHG 270 times more powerful than CO_2.[24]

Larsen & Toubro is another company with bauxite-alumina plans in Kashipur. This construction, engineering and arms company was started by two Danish businessmen in Goa in 1938. Its HQ is in Mumbai, with arms factories (e.g. in Gujarat), and a plethora of construction engineering contracts, including the Delhi metro and major role in Vedanta's Lanjigarh refinery. Its foreign partner in the Kashipur plan, Dubal, is from the United Arab Emirates, which is becoming a centre of aluminium smelting. Alumina from the refinery planned on the Nagavali, where other rivers join it at K-Singpur, is earmarked for the Middle East.[25]

Vedanta-Sterlite's corporate web

Sterlite's notorious purchase of Balco for a fraction of its real worth in March 2001 was accompanied by other purchases of privatised companies that made the Sterlite-Vedanta group India's leading producer of zinc, lead, and other minerals.[26] Before it registered in London, the group had already acquired some foreign assets with shady links. The two copper mines in Australia were bought through Vinod Shah's Twinstar Holdings, registered in the tax haven Mauritius, by buying a share in First Dynasty (a $7.5 million investment, giving a 43 per cent stake in this company), with Agarwal and two others from Sterlite sitting on its Board of directors. First Dynasty was a Canadian company set up by the mining industry's most notorious maverick, Bob Friedland—Toxic Bob as he is called in Canada and the US for the environmental catastrophes he has caused in North and South America.[27]

Another Friedland company, Diamond Fields Reserve, discovered the world's biggest nickel, copper and cobalt deposit, on tribal land in Labrador (1994), and he made a Canadian $4.3 billion deal in 1996 giving him the biggest share in the world's biggest nickel company, INCO. Another of his companies, DiamondWorks, bought the Koidu diamond mine in Sierra Leone, and in 1996 hired Executive Outcomes (a mercenary army of controversial repute in several countries) and Branch Energy to capture this mine back when rebels overran it, resulting in many civilian deaths.

First Dynasty was a company set up by Toxic Bob in Singapore (1995) to buy a share in a Kazakhstan gold mine, and gold and silver mines in Java plus controlling shares in various mines in Vietnam, China, Mongolia, Burma, West Papua, Fiji and Tasmania. In Burma he bought a 50 per cent share with the military government in the

Monywa copper mine and other ventures through another of his companies, Ivanhoe, and became that notorious regime's biggest foreign exchange earner, going against international law. Monywa causes outstanding devastation to the environment and communities in Burma. Sterlite sold its investments in Burma/Myanmar in 2000.

Twinstar (i.e. Sterlite) bought a 43 per cent share in First Dynasty in 1998–99 with a view to Armenia's gold business. The Zod and Meghradzor gold mines plus processing factory at Ararat had been owned by First Dynasty in a joint venture with the Armenian government, and were finally acquired by Anil Agarwal in 2002 through a new Canada-registered subsidiary called Sterlite Gold. Sterlite/Vedanta's management of this business, the Ararat Gold Recovery Company, started to go horribly wrong, with several hundred workers laid off when they demanded safer conditions, and Sterlite trying to move the cyanide processing plant from Ararat to Lake Sevan, where it threatened severe environmental damage. By November 2005 Sterlite faced criminal charges in Armenia on several counts, and in June 2006, Agarwal arranged for Vedanta Resources to buy up Sterlite Gold to profit from high gold prices. Numerous irregularities have caused the Armenian authorities to shut down Zod mine, while news that Vedanta was trying to sell off the business without consulting national interests caused fury in Armenia.

Sterlite's acquisition of the Konkola copper mines in Zambia in 2002, out-bidding Glencore and other rivals, has been plagued by similar environmental and human rights disasters.[28]

When Vedanta was listed on the London Stock Exchange, this was financed by the biggest ever IPO sale, for which the bookrunners were J. P. Morgan, HSBC, Cazenove (UK), Citigroup, ICICI (both US), and Macquarie (Australia). Morgan commissioned a 400-page report on Vedanta, with technical chapters by SRK Consulting (UK). Since then, Agarwal's multimillion Shah-of-Iran house in Mayfair (London) has been the company's key centre. London-negotiated deals with Brian Gilbertson, Raman Singh, and others brought a spectacular rise in fortune, placing Agarwal no. 12 in the list of India's richest, and no. 42 in Britain (October 2007).

The main engineering firms building the Korba and Odisha aluminium plants were Worley MMC (Australia) and GAMI(China), and an influx of Chinese workers was visible at Muniguda-Lanjigarh, as well as building the smelter in Jharsaguda district, where a deal to build a Rs 300 crore township, designed by a leading Chinese architect firm, ECADI, also involved the Hyderabad-based company Maytas Infra Ltd. This deal went wrong in February, and a case was brought against Vedanta.[29]

A financial analysis of investors in Vedanta and its subsidiaries shows the main shareholder in 2004 was Volcan Investments (Bahamas, with a 53.83 per cent shareholding). Other main shareholders included Merrill Lynch (US, 3.01 per cent holding), Barclays (UK, 2.38 per cent), Standard Life (UK), HSBC (UK), Universities Superannuation Scheme (UK), ABN AMRO (Netherlands), ANZ Investment Bank (Australia), Scotiabank (Canada), AXA (Belgium), and banks from Italy, France, US, Singapore, Dubai, Thailand, Japan, Bahrain and Kuwait, and at least thirteen Indian banks.

ABN AMRO led the consortium of eighteen banks giving loans totalling $218m for Balco's new Korba smelter (agreed September 2003). In December 2004 Vedanta made a second issuance of bonds worth $500m in London, arranged by ABN AMRO, Barclays Capital and Deutsche Bank (Germany).[30] Among Vedanta's minor investors, riding on the wave, a number of British Councils and Pension Funds were noted in June 2008.[31]

In early November 2008, after the credit crunch began, Vedanta reported a more than 9 per cent profit drop for April–October due to falling metal prices, and announced it was reducing its planned investment in India for the next four years from $14b to $9.1b.[29] Further announcements, however, promised Rs 42 crore investments in Lanjigarh, and a total investment in India of Rs 70,000 crore, 50,000 of which would be in the aluminium sector. These promises came with a warning that

> We are operating at 50 per cent of capacity at Lanjigarh, producing 60,000 tons of alumina per month, pending operation of captive bauxite mines in Niyamgiri Hills nearby ... [thus] incur[ring] a loss of half a crore of rupees [around half a billion dollars] every day.[33]

During the first half of 2009, a subsidiary of Vedanta named Scala Land Group was offering shareholders in UK opportunities in property investments, clearly taking advantage of the housing crisis. Vedanta was in the midst of long-drawn-out negotiations to buy the debt-riddled US copper giant Asarco. Agarwal announced that the company was to 'rationalise its work-force to cut costs by 30 per cent (March), to counter falling profits (a 70 per cent drop in attributable profit in May).[34]

Each of the UK's 'Big Four' accountancy firms has played a part in legitimising Vedanta's operations: Deloitte and Touche LLP as Chartered Accountants, and Ernst & Young with an Assurance statement for the 2005 Sustainable Development Report, which concluded that according to documents presented and site visits to key factories in Korba, Mettur, Tuticorin and Udaipur (Rajasthan), the company had shown commitment to implementing a HSEC (Health, Safety, Environment and Community initiatives) governance system, though few Key Performance Indicators were shown on HSEC matters (in other words, few facts?). PriceWaterhouseCoopers gave a more elaborate Assurance for the 2006 SD Report.

Vedanta's 60-page Sustainable Development Report for 2008 received an Assurance Opinion from the fourth of the 'big four', KPMG—with a lengthy disclaimer that this review expresses no conclusions about Vedanta's internal controls, and does not constitute an audit in terms of generally accepted auditing standards! Site visits were made to the Mumbai HQ, Korba, Tuticorin, Sesa Goa and Chanderiya (Rajasthan), but not Lanjigarh. As KPMG attests, Vedanta is a keen supporter of the Global Reporting Initiative (GRI), under the Global Compact (Chapter Seven), where data supplied by the company do not have to be independently verified. GRI Index no.46 mentions 'one fatality among our employees and eighteen fatalities among our contract employees' at Lanjigarh—a wild under-estimate according to reports from the area. The system of sub-contracting means that nearly all the deaths that have occurred on the roads and work-sites around Lanjigarh (a fair number of which have been mentioned in the local Odia press) are not counted here. Five of the nine Human Rights Indices in the SD Report are listed as 'not covered', incuding basic human rights guarantees, such as 'Total number of incidents of violations involving indigenous people and actions taken'.

Anthony Sampson analyses the role of London's big four accountancy firms in affirming the established order of power (*Who runs this place? Anatomy of Britain in the 21st century*, 2004). When the Satyam scam was exposed in India (in which Maytas figured significantly), the role of these accountancy firms was briefly questioned in the media (e.g. *Economic Times*, 23 February 2009: 'Ban the big four accountancy firms').

In its foreign investors, political and business links, accountancy assurances, and affiliation to the MMSD process, to mention a few aspects, Vedanta's London centre puts it in a similar structural position to the colonial machinery of the Raj era, geared to exploiting resources from India and other countries. Many in middle-class India may regard Agarwal, Mittal and Sir Ratan Tata as national heroes. But in many ways, certainly in their class interests and techniques of profit, these company directors appear to have merged with the colonial elite to exploit and displace citizens in their own country.

CHAPTER NINE

The World-Wide Web

Whatever the benefits of aluminium, bauxite mining and aluminium factories have had a devastating impact on people's lives and the environment in many regions of the earth. Here we take a brief overview of some of the main countries where the industry has taken hold, to understand its history and underlying patterns.

In terms of bare statistics, India ranks fourth in the size of its bauxite reserves, and roughly fourth, with Guinea and Jamaica, after Australia, Brazil and China in terms of tons of bauxite being mined. What is striking about recent changes is the decline of European countries (France, Hungary, Yugoslavia), and the rapid growth of China and Brazil (fuller figures in Appendix II).

In alumina refining, India came seventh in 2004, producing 2.26 million tons, after Australia (16.7 million tons), China (6.1 million tons), the US (5.3 million tons), Brazil (5.1 million tons), Jamaica (4 million tons) and Russia (3.27 million tons). Here too, Western countries showed a decline, the US being overtaken by China, which along with Brazil, Venezuela, former USSR countries and Iran was increasing fast, while production in several European countries declined or ceased (Appendix III).

Estimates of bauxite deposits (million tons)		Tons mined per year (million tons)				
			1979	2000	2005	2008
1. Guinea	8,600	1. Australia	30.4	53.8	58	64
2. Australia	7,900	2. Brazil		13.8	18	21
3. Brazil	4,900	3. China		9	17	(?)
4. India	3,011	4. Guinea	13.5	15.7	16	14
5. Jamaica	2,500	5. India	7.5	14	14	14
6. China	2,300	6. Jamaica	12.7	11.1	14	17
7. Guyana	900	7. USSR*/ Russia	7.2*	4.2	6	6.6
8. Greece	600	8. Venezuela		4.4	5.5	8.5
9. Suriname	580	9. Kazakhstan		3.7	4.6	4.8
10. Kazakhstan	350	10. Suriname	5.3	3.6	4.0	5.6
11. Venezuela	320	11. Greece	3.2	1.9	2.2	2.4
12. Russia	200	12. Guyana	3.7	2.4	1.5	1.4

Table 4. The top bauxite countries[1]

In aluminium output, India ranked ninth in 2000, and eighth in 2008. The rising output of China and Russia, overtaking the US, is phenomenal. But more than ever now, the siting of smelters is determined by cheap sources of power, and where the US and Europe were keen to build capacity fast during the Second World War, they are now happy, overall, to reduce it, due to the hidden costs. Encouraging other countries to expand production means that the real costs fall in these countries. Meanwhile the highest consumption remains in the West, while the Western pattern of high consumption is promoted everywhere.

In 2007, the world's biggest and newest smelters included ones in Bahrain (872,000 tons per year) and UAE (Dubai) (861,000), as well as a couple of Russian monsters (Bratsk 950,000, Krasnoyarsk 937,000). South Africa has a new one (670,000) and several other mega-smelters have been built as enclaves in relatively poor countries, including Tadjikistan (520,000) and Mozambique (330,000). New Zealand's Tiwai Point is a huge one (352,000). The output of Iceland's biggest smelter has come up to 322,000, part of a massive expansion in that country, with more enormous, controversial smelters planned there, as well as in Greenland and Trinidad. These figures give a scale for comprehending the recent expansion of India's three biggest smelters (Renukoot up to 360,000 tons per year, Angul to 359,000, and Korba to 345,000), and the new smelters being raised by Vedanta and Hindalco in Odisha, which aim for 500,000 tons per year, with plans to double this as soon as possible.

In this chapter we extend an eagle's eye perspective to survey the world-wide web of bauxite mining and aluminium factories. As one researcher expresses the discrepancy between the industry's initial promises and actual effects:

> In all countries, in spite of large-scale foreign investment, the bauxite industry failed to be an *"engine for development"*. (Holloway 1988, p. 52)

To understand why is to enter the realm of externality costs and the resource curse, analysed in the following chapters. Here, we survey a multitude of histories that illustrate the complex forms of corporate control exercised from abroad, 'eating up all the wealth from all the earth', in the apt words of Jamaica's greatest singer.

	Production in millions of tons		
	2000		2007–08
1. US	3.6	1. China	5.9
2. Russia	3.3	2. Russia	4
3. China	2.8	3. US	3.2
4. Canada	2.4	4. Canada	3.1
5. Australia	1.8	5. Australia	1.54
6. Brazil	1.3	6. Norway	1.36
7. Norway	1	7. Brazil	1.27
8. South Africa	0.69	8. India	1.17
9. India	0.649	9. Bahrain	0.872
10. Germany	0.644	10. UAE	0.861
		11. Iceland	0.761

Table 5. The top aluminium-producing countries

Guyana, Jamaica: Freedom undermined

The aluminium industry got its biggest boosts in the First and Second World Wars. With aluminium becoming vital for defence/offence, governments and companies started manoeuvring to secure the world's known bauxite deposits from the first years of the twentieth century. Outside Europe, those known were mainly in South America and Africa.

British Guiana's deposits had first been noticed in 1876. When Alcoa surveyed them in 1915–16, the British government was unwilling to hand them over to an American company, even though the US was an ally, manufacturing aluminium to make military supplies for Britain. So Alcoa lobbied the US President, who threatened to cut off arms supplies to Britain unless it granted a mining concession to Alcoa in Guyana. Fighting in the trenches, 'Britain was in no position to resist this kind of pressure', and Alcoa-Alcan acquired mining leases for most of Guyana's bauxite by the end of the year, through a specially created subsidiary, Demba, the Demerara bauxite company.[2]

Alcan was first created as the Northern Aluminium Company in 1900 to exploit Canada's hydropower for smelters. Demba was made an Alcan subsidiary in 1928, when Anti-Trust legislation made Alcoa separate off from Alcan (which it only did partially). Alcan was used by Alcoa, as we shall see, to partake in, and even orchestrate, a succession of 'European' aluminium cartels, from which Alcoa was formally barred by US legislation. Being technically a Canadian company, the British and others were less suspicious of Alcan's motives. Alcan became a separate company, and acquired its present name, in 1928, though ownership remained mainly in US hands. During the Second World War, bauxite from British and Dutch Guiana was shipped to Canada and turned into aluminium in vast new smelters at Arvida, sited in Quebec to make use of Canada's huge hydro-potential (like most of Canada's smelters) and helped win the war. By 1945, over half the world's bauxite was coming from these two countries.

Demba, with its own township, became a central part of the colonial economy imposed on British Guiana, along with the sugar plantations. Tensions grew between Demba's black mine-workers and white managers. In 1950 Alcan exported 1,500,000 tons of bauxite. It paid no royalties on bauxite from its own land, only 10 cents per ton on bauxite from 'Crown lands', and only $68,000 in taxes—nothing compared to its huge profits (Canadian $29 million in 1951). The price of bauxite was kept artificially low while the price of aluminium was doubling. The British government realised that the high price it was paying Alcan for aluminium was in effect a subsidy for Alcan's new smelters in Canada. Moreover, Alcan was manipulating currencies, keeping Demba poor so as to accumulate the profits in Canada. 'Essentially, neither the Colonial Office nor the colonial government knew how much Alcan was supposed to pay, or how it arranged payment.' (Graham 1982, p. 9)

In 1953, the British arranged elections as a step towards Independence. Cheddi Jagan, who won, was a socialist, and his first tentative steps towards nationalising the bauxite business and redressing other injustices caused the British government to ship over troops and remove him from power after only 133 days in office, suspending the Constitution and justifying this by talk of 'intrigues of communists'. From being elected Prime Minister, Jagan was jailed with hard labour for six months—an action supported without question by the Labour party in opposition.

At this time Britain was engaged in a war in another colony whose Independence was also being delayed by financial interests: Malaya, where the assets Britain was fighting to retain were rubber plantations and tin mines, with bauxite a subsidiary interest, and communism the enemy. British violence in the Malayan war was extreme: tactics of bombing villages and inhuman concentration camps foreshadowed Vietnam. Malaysia was only granted Independence in 1957 after communists had been virtually exterminated, and 70 per cent of the country's commercial interests were still held by British firms.[3] Hence the swift and drastic action removing Jagan and cancelling Guyana's Independence—essentially on behalf of Alcan and a British sugar company, Booker Brothers McConnell.

In 1957 when elections were held again, Jagan was re-elected, and the British again retained power, so that Jagan held office without real authority. The same happened when he was elected a third time in 1961. Meanwhile another big American aluminium company, Reynolds Aluminum, had opened a mine in 1953, while Alcan made an alumina refinery in 1961. Reynolds' agreement exempted it from paying income tax for ten years, and the royalty both companies were paying was tiny—between 1.5 per cent and 4 per cent of the bauxite's estimated value.

Exploitation was leading to social unrest, and from 1961 this was actually being orchestrated by MI6 and the CIA, who provided funds to undermine Jagan's popular appeal. Jagan was critical of the foreign companies' unfair power and high profits, and was making friends with Castro in Cuba. British Prime Minister Macmillan held secret talks with President Kennedy, and Britain suddenly changed the electoral rules in 1963, to make Jagan lose the 1964 election, even though he got the most votes once again. His rival, Forbes Burnham (with 22 seats against Jagan's 24), was invited to form a government in alliance with a third party (which won 7 seats). Only after this, in 1966, did Britain finally allow Guyana its Independence. In return, Burnham dropped his election promises and let Alcan and the other companies (including Union Carbide) stay on without paying more tax.

But unrest grew, and it became increasingly obvious that Guyana was not getting a proper revenue from its bauxite, while neighbouring countries had got a better deal—Jamaica under Michael Manley, and Suriname too. So in 1970, Burnham's government passed the very law that Cheddi Jagan had threatened: all mining projects had to be at least 51 per cent state-owned. Alcan took an uncompromising stand in negotiations, and though Demba was fully nationalised in 1971, becoming Guybau and Guymine, Alcan got its own back by demanding compensation. The US government forced Burnham to pay by getting the WB to threaten to withdraw a vital loan if this compensation was not paid.

Despite Alcan's intransigence and this irresistable pressure from the US, the nationalisation of Alcan's Guyana subsidiary was seen as a radical step and a victory for the poor bauxite-exporting countries. In the compromise eventually reached, Alcan agreed to buy half of Guyana's output. Guyana's nationalisation of Demba was followed by the creation of the International Bauxite Association (IBA) in 1974, under Jamaican leadership, and the same year, Reynolds' mines in Guyana were also nationalised.

Burnham wanted to build a dam to power a smelter, so that Guyana would have a fully integrated aluminium industry. This would have displaced an estimated 4,500 of the Akawaio Indians, Guyana's largest surviving indigenous tribe, flooding their forest area of about 1,000 square miles.[4] Plans for this dam were cancelled in the 1980s, but 'Guyana had become a land of horrors' by then, with vicious state repression to bolster the mines-and-plantations economy. Finally, after Burnham's death, Jagan was elected yet again in 1992 to lead a shattered country, that was as much controlled by foreign finance as it had ever been, this time under dictates from the WB and IMF, who forced Jagan to follow their programme of re-privatisation. Guymine had become inefficient and corrupt, and during the 1990s, as part of the ERP (Economic Recovery Programme) imposed by the WB/IMF, it was divided into two companies, Linmine and Bermine, in which 'a kind of creeping privatisation through new foreign investment' was promoted. In 2000 the IMF was still pressurising the country to privatise its bauxite mining.[5]

Guyana presents a typical example of 'enclave colonialism', with a tussle over profits between aluminium companies and government, and foreign companies and their governments controlling the 'post-Independence' economy, with WB support.[6] When bauxite mines are the basis of a country's economy, whether these are nationalised or directly in the hands of foreign aluminium companies, it is the foreign companies and foreign governments that call the shots. Aluminium companies always pay the least for a country's bauxite that they can get away with.

Guyana's neighbour Suriname (formerly Dutch Guiana) witnessed a similar story. Alcoa got its own supply there in 1917, and Suriname's bauxite mines provided the raw material for 65 per cent of US aluminium produced during the Second World War, and most of the aluminium consumed by the Korean war as well. By 1945 the two Guianas provided over half the world's bauxite.

Alcoa exercised a controlling influence over the country's finances through its subsidiary, Suralco (so named in 1960). Billiton started a seperate bauxite mine in the early 1950s, when Suriname became the world's biggest bauxite exporter. After Independence, the huge Afobaka dam was constructed to power a huge aluminium smelter, which started up in 1963. This dam displaced 6,000 of the Saramaka Maroons, descendants of Africans who were taken to the Guyanas as slaves. After this, the state company Grassalco started a project for new bauxite mines in the Bakhuis Mountains in the west of the country, building railways, roads, and a port city at Apura on the Corantyne River.

But Apura remains a bauxite ghost-town like Gandhamardan, after a horrendous 'aluminium war' gripped the land. In 1980 the army staged a coup, Dutch aid was withdrawn, and army massacres were perpetrated in Maroon villages. Suriname spiralled into a civil war between the army and the Maroons' 'Jungle Commandos', who blew up the pylons supplying hydro-electricity to the aluminium smelter.[7] A ceasefire was signed in 1992.

By 1994 an estimated 87 per cent of the country's national income came from bauxite and aluminium. Bauxite mining has denuded huge areas of Suriname's mountains and forests, in collusion with foreign-owned logging companies. BHP Billiton with Alcoa and Grassalco started mining bauxite in Bakhuis in 2006.[8] Suriname's smelter is owned 55 per cent by Alcoa, 45 per cent by BHP Billiton.

Second World War pressures led to the discovery of Jamaica's bauxite in 1943, while Alcan was setting up its subsidiary Indal in India. Alcan got the mining lease in Jamaica too, despite strong pressure from the US government to give Reynolds a share—the new aluminium company which the Democratic administration was supporting as a counterweight to Alcoa. By 1950, US imperialism was replacing British control, using mining-based industrialisation as the medium. Kaiser and Reynolds were soon allowed in, and made Jamaica their main source.[9] From 1957 to 1971, Jamaica overtook Guyana–Suriname and became the world's leading bauxite producer and exporter, until overtaken in turn by Australia. Alcan built two alumina refineries in Jamaica (1959–60), and Alcoa built a huge one in 1972. In 1998 Jamaica was still the third largest bauxite exporter, after Australia and Guinea. A decline set in after Kaiser's alumina refinery in Louisiana blew up in 1999, denting demand for Jamaican bauxite.

So like Guyana, Jamaica emerged at Independence in a state of economic dependency on the aluminium companies, who were buying the country's bauxite for far too little. In 1971 Norman Girvan published a classic study showing that Jamaica was getting less than half the proper price for its bauxite, and that real profits from the industry were disappearing abroad. A Commission was formed in 1972 that set up the Jamaican Bauxite Institute (JBI), which has carried out studies from 1976 till today that offer an example towards real understanding and change for the entrenched pattern of exploitation.[10]

When Michael Manley, Jamaica's socialist Prime Minister, began campaigning on this issue in 1972, he was bluntly told by America's ambassador (in effect by Kissinger) not to make bauxite an election issue—that trying to nationalise the US aluminium companies operating in Jamaica could lead to war. This was no idle threat, considering CIA support for Pinochet's bloody coup against Allende in Chile a few months later, sparked by Allende nationalising US mining companies.

Despite this threat, Manley imposed a Bauxite Levy in 1974, greeted with jubilation by his country, and nationalised a 51 per cent stake in his country's mines. The same year he formed the IBA (International Bauxite Association of bauxite-producing countries), which for a while negotiated a higher price for bauxite with the aluminium companies, by making the price of the raw material (bauxite) 7.5 per cent of the price of the finished product (aluminium ingots). This increased the price of bauxite by about $10, from $8 to $19.94—a feat the IBA has never repeated. In the first year, Jamaica's revenue increased from $27 million to $185 million. After this, Alcan and other aluminium companies started to leave, and income exports dropped swiftly. So the IBA did not remain effective for long, but did deals and compromised to bring the aluminium companies back. Also, the CIA organised a severe destabilisation of Manley's government to dent his popularity.[11]

Till recently, few in Jamaica questioned the larger picture of bauxite mining and alumina refining, since Jamaica has been dependent on this industry since Independence, and it still brings in about 60 per cent of the country's foreign earnings.

But many are now clear that the impact of all this bauxite mining on Jamaica's environment has been a catastrophe. Since bauxite covers large areas in a crust 20–70 feet thick, mining it devastates a huge surface area, and much of Jamaica's formerly forested interior now consists of mined-out, sterile pits. Over 5,000 hectares of forest have been strip-mined for bauxite, and much more has been stripped by access roads opening it up to illegal loggers.[12] Some mining has also been done underground, but houses above these tunnels have often collapsed.

Red mud pollution and refinery smog are major problems in Jamaica, causing numerous ailments and birth defects. Huge red mud lakes, which were supposed to dry out but never did, have contaminated much of the country's ground water with sodium. Sulphur dioxide and trioxide produce acid rain.[13] Soil has been drying out over much of the country, and the consensus is that the industry has severely affected Jamaica's weather pattern, which has suffered a 20 per cent decrease in rainfall in the last 30 years.

So benefits from Jamaica's bauxite industry are now questioned, and there is a campaign to prevent Alcoa mining new areas, and to close down its monster refinery. In particular, activists are trying to prevent new bauxite mines in the Cockpit Country, one of very few remaining areas of extensive forest wilderness left in the Carribean, a proposed UNESCO World Heritage site due to its karst limestone rock formations and biodiversity, and the homeplace of about 5,000 Maroons, with a long history of independence—descendants of slaves who escaped and fought for their freedom in these Cockpit mountains, signing a peace treaty with the British in 1738.[14]

Foreign aluminium companies chose to go for capital-intensive production methods which have done little to help Jamaica's employment problems. The industry's 'impact on the lives of construction workers is volatile, periodically throwing thousands out of work', introducing a distortion and a 'classic self-contained autonomous sector in Jamaica's economy', which mainly benefits 'a highly paid elite group of workers'.[15] But as Girvan and Manley showed, once a country is gridlocked into supplying the aluminium industry, it's extremely hard to get out of its grip.[16] In 2008 Jamaica's four refineries were as follows:

- Nain, owned by Rusal (65 per cent) and Hydro (35 per cent), producing 1.7 million tons per year
- Clarendon, owned 50–50 by Alcoa and Jamalco, 1.4 million tons per year
- Ewarton, owned by Jamalco and Rusal, 675,000 tons per year
- Kirkvine, owned by Jamalco, Rusal and Rio Tinto Alcan, 625,000 tons per year

Bauxite exploitation was a major factor in the devastation of another country that has suffered a particularly cruel history of violence and impoverishment. Reynolds mined bauxite in Haiti from 1957 till the early 1980s, depleting the island's environment and finances together, and mining an estimated 15 million tons (of total deposits of 25 million tons). Haiti's bauxite was named Lescotite after the country's President Elie Lescot, by grateful geologists, flown over the ore-bearing mountains in the Haitian air force![17]

When Alcan became nominally independent of Alcoa in 1928, it was headed by Edward Davis, younger brother of Alcoa's founder-director, Arthur Vining Davis, while the Mellon family owned 52 per cent of both companies. In 1951, Anti-Trust legislation challenged Alcoa's monopoly, making it relinquish Alcan. Even this was a sham, and in 1969, Alcan's manager, Nathanael Davis (a nephew of Arthur and Edward), admitted that 'the majority of our shares are located in the USA'.

This was the year that Alcan bought up the biggest smelters in apartheid South Africa, setting up a South African subsidiary, Hulamin, which sold aluminium to the country's monstrous arms industry. Recently, South Africa has witnessed intense opposition to plans for a massive new Alcan smelter at Coega, involving a new port and dirt-cheap electricity. Protestors have a song:

> It's Alcan the Aluminium Man,
> The Aluminium Man with the Aluminium Plan
> For making lots of aluminium
> Out of other people's land.
> Will this Man of Aluminium Realise what he has done
> Once he's done what he's about to start?
> He's got Aluminium but he's got no Heart.[18]

Alcan violated the land rights of indigenous peoples in many parts of the world. In the 1990s, Canada's First Nation groups took Alcan to court for damages over the desecration and pollution of indigenous land by the company's Kitimat/Kemano smelter project, in a remote part of British Columbia (see Map 3), where the Kenney dam, then the world's biggest, was built to power and water it. This formed the vast Nechako reservoir in 1954, 450 × 800 km in size, displacing members of the Cheslatta tribe, who were not properly warned or resettled, and lost 80,000 hectares of their hunting territory.[19]

Kitimat smelter represents a key shift in US policy towards outsourcing production, as we shall see in the following chapter. But Quebec, the other side of Canada, is an 'aluminium colony', due to its ruthlessly exploited hydro-wealth. Alcan's first smelter opened at Shawanagee Falls in 1901. James Bay phase I flooded over 11,000 square kilometers. The dam-smelter complexes in north-east Canada have destroyed stocks of fish and other wildlife on a scale hard to comprehend, and impacted badly on Cree, Inuit and Mohawk Indians, who have lived for at least 5,000 years in the region.

Pollution from smelters along the St Lawrence has caused cancer and deaths among rare beluga whales. Subsidies on electricity to Quebec's dozen smelters are huge. Alcan and aluminium have long dominated Quebec's economy.[20]

Canada's indigenous people have faced aluminium colonialism and sustained a resistance that comes from their identity as First Nations—an important parallel to Adivasi movements in Odisha, not least because Alcan was a prime mover behind Utkal's attack on Adivasi land—a link that found expression in a Canadian pressure group, 'Alcan't in India'.[21]

Britain got most of its aluminium from Alcan, from the First and Second World Wars till recently. Alcan ran Britain's refinery at Burntisland in Scotland (closed 2002), and Scotland's smelters remain under Rio Tinto Alcan.[22]

In 2002 Alcan staged a takeover of Pechiney. This came under close scrutiny by the US Monopolies Commission, which insisted on breaking up some parts of the conglomerate. Novelis was formed in January 2003 as a spin-off from this break-up, bought up by Hindalco in May 2007, shortly before Alcan itself was swallowed up by Rio Tinto to form Rio Tinto Alcan in July. This happened after Alcan finally withdrew from Utkal in April 2007, when Alcan was weak and about to succumb to Rio Tinto's $38.1 billion takeover bid. Rio had already been surveying iron and diamonds in Odisha for some years, and we have noticed its influence over India's new mining policy.[23]

Kaiser's regime removal in Ghana and the world's worst dam

Every big dam is the worst in some way, at least for people whose land it obliterates. But Akosombo—the dam on the Volta River in Ghana—has a special claim. Its construction from 1961–66 created the world's biggest reservoir, around 8,500 square kilometres, and displaced a record 740-plus estimated villages, about 80,000 people. The waterlogging and salinisation it has caused are extreme, and so is the disease.

The dam blighted Ghana's economy from the start, since the hydropower is set up in such a way that the greater part has to go to the huge aluminium smelter built alongside the dam by Kaiser Aluminium. The dam was built to service the smelter's needs—also true for another Kaiser project: Rihand dam and Hindalco (Chapter Eight). This prevented Ghana making a real profit from either: it could not even use the hydropower to supply its towns and villages or start up other industries. How this happened is another tale of darkest intrigue, involving the WB and CIA, demonstrating the extraordinary power that aluminium companies can wield.

Henry Kaiser is a mythical hero in America's business history, an archetype of the self-made man. Starting life working in a small hardware store, he went into road-building, befriended by Bechtel in 1921, who was building up one of the world's biggest construction companies. During America's Depression in the 1930s these two joined with others—'scavengers of poverty and war'—to make record size dams in America's wild west, especially Hoover (Boulder) on the Colorado River (Nevada, 1931–34), Bonneville and Grand Coulee on the Lower and Upper Colorado (Oregon and Washington, 1934–38 and 1937–42). These dams destroyed populations of migratory fish and other wildlife, and obliterated Native American sacred sites. By 1942 the Bonnesville and Grand Coulee were powering aluminium smelters to aid America's war effort. Grand Coulee's reservoir was named after President Franklin Roosevelt, a close friend of Kaiser.[24]

From dams and cement, Kaiser branched out into magnesium and steel. During the Second World War he set up a magnesium factory making chemical 'goop bombs' (Chapter Ten), and built aircraft carrier 'Liberty Ships'. By the end of the war Kaiser was a major arms manufacturer. This led him into aluminium.

Alcoa was paid by the US administration to build and operate extra aluminium factories, using electricity from recent dams, to supply the war effort with material for aircraft, etc. These 'surplus plants' were sold off cheap after the war to Kaiser and Reynolds, and Kaiser got Alcoa's help, thanks to a 'special chemistry' between Henry Kaiser and Arthur Vining Davis. Kaiser made a deal for bauxite from Dutch Guiana until Kaiser's own mines started in Jamaica (1950).

Within a few years he had set up a 'carbon copy' of Alcoa's vertically integrated aluminium industry, with a series of refineries, smelters, rolling mills and fabricator-factories across America.

When he entered the aluminium industry in 1946, many thought aluminium would prove unprofitable due to the slump in arms manufacture. Kaiser started out advertising civilian uses. But his 'genius' was to 'bet' on the Korean war of 1950, which was fought using Kaiser aluminium in its warplanes and bombs, bringing him copious praise for his 'extraordinay contribution to the Korean war'. By 1952, his factories were making aluminium parts for B-52 bombers needed in Korea, a supply pattern that continued into the Vietnam war.[25]

Soon America wasn't big enough for Kaiser Aluminum, and there was a dip in aluminium demand after the Korean war ended. Between 1957 and 1967 Kaiser's main expansion was abroad, in India, Spain, Argentina, Australia and Ghana, where some of his ventures proved particularly destructive for local communities. At the same time as he was 'setting up factories in India' with Birla, he was engaged in an even bigger and more blatantly exploitative venture in West Africa.

For most of Ghana's inhabitants, the aluminium industry has been a curse. Its bauxite deposits were first discovered in 1914, and plans for a dam on the Volta were sketched soon after, when it was it was known as the Gold Coast, another British colony. Bauxite extraction began there 'on a war footing' in 1941. The Awaso mine was sold off cheap to BAC in 1949, while negotiations were hotting up for the dam and smelter plan, which Nkrumah supported in his manifesto for elections held in 1951 under British stewardship. He promised his electorate to negotiate the best possible deal with foreign companies. When Independence came in 1957, and Nkrumah became the country's first Prime Minister, negotiations had fallen through with the BAC and Alcan. First Reynolds and then Kaiser seemed to offer better terms. Reynolds staged a takeover of BAC in 1957–59 (Chapter Ten), but immediately sold off the bauxite interests in Ghana and Australia, and later, the BAC refineries and smelters in Scotland too, to which most of Ghana's bauxite was shipped.[26]

Finally, Nkrumah signed a deal with Edgar Kaiser. But it turned out that Kaiser's reduced price for building the smelter was based on reducing any help the dam might give to Ghana's development process. The WB considered lending Ghana the money to construct the dam, but played hard to get, and warned of the dire consequences it might have for the country's future, at the same time as warning that Ghana would have to offer 'very favourable conditions … to attract the aluminium companies'. What this basically meant was: exceedingly cheap electricity—about one twentieth of what other customers paid.

In effect, the WB and, behind the scenes, President Kennedy, would only allow a loan for the Akosombo dam if the smelter was guaranteed to be its main customer. Only when Nkrumah had granted this did the WB sign the loan, even though its own analysis showed it was unlikely that Ghana would ever profit from the dam or smelter. Kaiser essentially passed on the cost of building the smelter to Ghana through the subsidised electricity prices. The sum in this first loan to Ghana was $300 million.

In frustration, Nkrumah also negotiated with Kruschev, visiting the USSR. Kruschev had just helped Egypt complete its Aswan High Dam after US companies made difficulties. This dam created Lake Nasser, effectively turning Egypt's Nile into a lock-controlled canal, displacing between 553 and 740 villages of Nubians, whose 'relocation' was a humanitarian disaster. The Aswan dam spread the disease of schistosomiasis along the Nile at an infection rate estimated at 35 per cent. But Egypt's Nag Hammady aluminium smelter has obtained an unlimited supply of hydropower.[27]

President Kennedy met Nkrumah just before his Soviet visit. The US administration was following the negotiations closely, supporting Kaiser interests, while Kaiser saw himself as 'a useful instrument' of America's foreign policy. A senior Kennedy official described Ghana as a 'decisive battlefield' where 'a major battle in the cold war is being waged in Africa'. The CIA was already destabilising Nkrumah's government, and the WB aided this instability by vetoing loans to Ghana. John McCone, head of the CIA from 1961–65, was a friend of Edgar Kaiser, and Kaiser's personal financial adviser was George Woods, who had played an important part in financing Kaiser through the First Boston Corporation. Woods was about to become President of the WB (1962–68)—and was acting as Ghana's adviser too![28] The Kaiser empire was built on borrowed money, and on close ties of mutual self-interest with the banks making the loans, which included Bank of America and Mellon Bank (also Alcoa's biggest investors). In 1956 the Kaiser debt stood at the same sum Ghana was borrowing—$300 million—while Kaiser profits for that year were $40 million.

In December 1961 Nkrumah signed the Master Agreement with Valco (Volta aluminium company), the subsidiary which Kaiser set up to run the smelter. Dam and smelter were split as separate businesses. Valco was Kaiser-run, while the Volta River Authority was to manage the dam and its hydropower—essentially servicing Valco. Nearly all agreements between aluminium companies and Third World governments have imposed harsh conditions, but the conditions in this one set a record: Valco imports alumina tax-free from Jamaica and Australia, takes 70 per cent of the hydropower, pays a record low rate, fixed for 30 years, and exports aluminium tax-free for over ten years, while the Ghanaian government has to pay for expensive damage caused by blackouts. The rate is fixed at just 11 US cents per kilowatt hour—17 per cent of the cost of generating the electricity!

Valco paid reasonable wages to its Ghanaian workforce, but it was run by Americans—a foreign enclave, feeding off Ghana's economy, and in effect enslaving it. Ghana was unable even to use its own bauxite to make an integrated aluminium industry. Bauxite from the Awaso mine was being exported for processing in Scotland, and a British white paper in 1952 stated that the dam's main purpose was to supply aluminium to Britain. There was no help for building a refinery in Ghana, so the country had to import aluminium, or buy it from Valco using foreign currency. In other words, all the profits from the dams and smelter were creamed off by Kaiser abroad, while Ghana was saddled with crippling costs.

Nkrumah gradually realised the terms were unfavourable but thought he should get the dam and smelter set up as a catalyst for his country's development.[29] But while construction on both went ahead, the CIA was supporting Nkrumah's political enemies, sowing dissension among the country's elite and armed forces. A month after he attended the official opening of the dam in 1966, a US-supported coup removed Nkrumah from power. The smelter opened the next year, but with no effective Ghanaian leader able to question the Valco agreement, the whole project took its pre-planned course, under foreign control. Ghana was kept away from the Soviets, Nkrumah was kept out of power. Ghana was kept poor and dependent, a 'captive state', while Kaiser, owning 90 per cent of Valco, was making a fortune.

Evidence suggests that Kaiser's engineers, who masterminded the Akosombo dam, deliberately designed a dam that could not be used for irrigation, and was exceedingly restricted in other uses. This is also true of the Rihand dam, designed by the same Kaiser engineers to supply Hindalco's dam-smelter complex in Uttar Pradesh. The WB lent the capital for Akosombo partly from fear that Nkrumah would veer towards the Soviet camp, as his enthusiasm had been aroused by seeing megadams in the USSR, and the industrialisation they had fuelled under Stalin.

People displaced by Akosombo got hardly any amenities or compensation. Over 500 villages were resettled into just 42 new colonies, far too fast, as the floods rose. Without land and crops, many faced starvation in 1966, and USAid sent 6,000 tons of food. Imposed fertiliser-based cash crops failed, and over half the people left the new colonies.

The reservoir spread schistosomiasis (bilharzia), river blindness and malaria. Schistosomiasis, the debilitating disease spread by snails, affected 1–5 per cent of the local population before the dam. Now it affects at least 75 per cent of those around the lake. River blindness spreads through black flies, which have become resistant to insecticides. This now affects at least 100,000 people in north-west Ghana, 70 per cent of whom are completely blind. The lack of silt downstream has also caused a grave deterioration of Ghana's estuary and shoreline.

In January 2005, after the smelter had been closed for some years, Alcoa, which had a 10 per cent stake, signed a MoU with the Ghanaian government to re-open it. The price for power was not disclosed, and in June 2008 Alcoa withdrew because it was not low enough. This left the smelter a shell, owned by a government immersed in debt from its beginning. All for aluminium.[30]

Up the coast from Ghana, Guinea has the world's largest bauxite deposits. It became independent in 1958, when its bargaining power was not yet strong.

> At the very time that the aluminium companies were looking to Guinea for supplies, Guinea was looking to the companies for the technology and capital to develop the economy.[31]

The Fria bauxite mines were started in 1958–60 by a consortium of top aluminium companies—Pechiney, Alusuisse, VAW and BAC. Halco (Harvey aluminium company) was a small American company that bought leases for another bauxite reserve in 1963. By the time mining started, ten years later, Halco's 51 per cent share had been divided among more powerful aluminium companies, thanks to WB pressure: Alcoa (27 per cent), Alcan (27 per cent), Halco (20 per cent), Pechiney (10 per cent), VAW (10 per cent) and Montecatini (6 per cent), the Italian aluminium company that set up Malco in South India. And Halco had been taken over by the arms manufacturing company Martin Marietta! Mining was on a large scale, for which the Guinean government had to invest in railway and port facilities—like the railways, roads and ports being built now in Odisha and Andhra, with WB and other loans.

Guinea's President Sekou Touré negotiated more effectively than Nkrumah. The Halco project at Boke was 49 per cent government-owned from the start. Touré managed to nationalise 49 per cent of the Fria enclave too in 1973.

Yet bauxite remains a typical 'enclave-industry' in Guinea, set up in a way that prevents any broader benefits to the country. And a third bauxite mine set up with Russian investment in 1974 had an agreement for 90 per cent of its profit to go to the Russian company. By 1976 Guinea was exporting over 11 million tons of alumina per year, and a similar quantity of bauxite. It has an alumina refinery (in which Alcoa partners the government), but no smelter, just as Ghana has a smelter but no refinery. The aluminium companies have ensured these countries have to compete. Even though they are so close, Ghanaian bauxite is not refined in Guinea, and Guinea's alumina is not smelted in Ghana.

Guinea earned about 80 per cent of its foreign money from bauxite in 1980, though the aluminium companies get at least four times the income which comes to the government. Nevertheless,

> Guinea has remained one of the most militant of the bauxite-producing countries and Sekou Touré's attitude to the foreign mining countries has led to a number of attempts to overthrow his regime. The French, Portuguese and American secret services have all at one time or another been involved in these attempts to destabilise his regime.

Struggles by Third World governments to avoid foreign exploitation do not stop them exploiting their own citizens. Norwatch reported in 1998 that several villages had been removed by Fria without compensation, while toxic red mud has contaminated water over a huge area, filling at least one whole valley. In 1999, an IMF Report on Guinea's 'Enhanced Structural Adjustment Facility' showed the pressure on Guinea's government to relinquish its ownership and privatise. This IMF pressure on Guyana and Guinea to privatise their bauxite business raises questions for India. Was it a similar pressure, applied behind the scenes, which led to Balco's privatisation and Nalco's narrow escape?

Violent protest broke out in Guinea in October 2008 against Rusal, for not providing promised amenities, and security forces shot dead two protestors.[32]

Another West African country with large bauxite deposits is Sierra Leone, whose 'mineral wealth' has made it one of the worst sufferers of the resource curse. Diamonds were at the heart of the country's terrible civil war (1991–2002), but bauxite and rutilite mining (for titanium) were also highly exploitative. In 1990, just before the civil war began, Peter Robbins was asked to examine allegations of transfer pricing against Alusuisse's bauxite business there, the subject of a BBC documentary, *Trade Slaves* (directed by Steve Hewlett, 1991). Bauxite mining started in 1963 on the Mokanji Hills. Alusuisse's transfer pricing basically collected profits in Switzerland, keeping its Sierra Leone subsidiary Sieromco (Sierra Leone Ore and Metal Company) poor, thereby avoiding tax in the country and getting its bauxite cheap. The annual turnover of Alusuisse was about 30 times greater than Sierra Leone's total export earnings. An inequality of information allowed the company to export 1.5 million tons of bauxite per year with almost no returns to the Sierra Leone government.[33]

Rebels overran the mines in January 1995, and Executive Outcomes was hired to clear the area of rebels by January 1996, but they did not reopen. Only recently were the titanium mines nearby restored by their French owners, and Alcoa has shown an interest in re-opening the bauxite mines. In *The Economist's Tale*, a WB consultant portrays with unusual frankness the WB-abetted price manipulation of basic commodities that existed alongside bauxite transfer pricing on the eve of the civil war.[34]

Weipa bauxite and the tragedy on Cape York

Australia has been the world's largest bauxite producer since 1971, extracting over 60 million tons per year from 2006, from five main bauxite mine areas, processed in seven refineries and six smelters. Companies involved include Rio Tinto's subsidiary Comalco at Weipa (Queensland), Alcan at Gove on Arnhem Land (Northern Territory), and Alcoa in the Darling Mountains and Huntly, near Perth (Western Australia).

Cape York, Queensland, is Australia's northernmost peninsula, jutting out towards New Guinea. Like Arhnem Land, it is one of the last areas where Aborigines kept control of their sacred sites and lived a traditional life till recent times. This changed when they guided a mineral prospector named Harry Evans to make a major discovery of bauxite deposits there in 1955. Cape York is the world's biggest and purest bauxite deposit. The area is also extraordinarily rich in plant life, which includes mangrove and eucalyptus forests, and hundreds of unique species of trees, flowering plants, animal, bird and insect life, from crocodiles to butterflies. From the ancient character of its species, botanists see the bauxite-earth of Cape York as a cradle where many of the world's plant-forms evolved.[35]

Evans worked for a company called Conzinc (Consolidated Zinc Corp.), which acted fast to grab this deposit, negotiating in secret with the Queensland government to get exclusive rights over at least 4,000 square miles of Aboriginal reserve land on the east and west coasts of Cape York. Queensland's Parliament passed a Special Act to confirm this in 1957, granting a record low rate of rent and royalty, with no profits or compensation for the Aborigines displaced.

Comalco (Commonwealth Aluminium Corp.) was set up by Conzinc as a subsidiary in 1956 to manage the Weipa deposit. Kaiser, who had been searching for more bauxite, bought a 50 per cent share of Comalco in 1959–60. Conzinc/Comalco bought the Bell Bay refinery and smelter in Tasmania, and negotiated complex deals to build a huge new refinery at Gladstone in Queensland (which, like states in India, made it a condition that bauxite mined in its territory should be refined there), and a huge new hydropowered smelter in New Zealand.

Comalco set up a consortium called the Queensland Alumina Ltd. (QAL), to run the Gladstone refinery on the east coast. Kaiser was the leading partner (with Alcan, Pechiney and others) and had a managerial role over QAL, which started producing alumina in 1961. By 1972 Gladstone had become an 'industrial slum'. The smelter's impact did not bring the hoped-for benefits. Labour dispute led to the sacking of 600 people in 1972—half the workforce. QAL, like Demba and Valco, was kept poor, to avoid tax, etc., allowing its parent companies to make their profits selling alumina far away.

Conzinc's deal with the New Zealand government in 1960 got Manapouri and another lake dammed to generate power for a huge smelter at Tiwai Point in Bluff Harbour. Politicians desperate to attract the smelter to New Zealand did not foresee prohibitive costs their country would have to pay, stemming, once again, from an extremely cheap electricity price fixed for the smelter, and environmental costs of the dam. The Bluff smelter, supplied from Gladstone, started production in 1971.[36]

Gladstone alumina went to the new smelter in New Zealand, to the controversial Bell Bay smelter in Tasmania, to Valco in Ghana, and to the nuclear powered smelter in Anglesey in Wales (owned by Comalco's parent companies, Kaiser and RTZ, now RT Alcan). From 1965, Weipa bauxite, refined at Gladstone and reduced in Kaiser smelters, went into planes and bombs used in the Vietnam war.

The interlocking hierarchy of companies exploiting Weipa's bauxite is not easy to conceptualise—complexity here, especially, has served to hide the lines of power. The complexity deepened when

Conzinc merged with Rio Tinto to become Rio Tinto Zinc (RTZ) in 1962. The Australian subsidiaries of the two merging companies merged to form yet another company, CRA (Consolidated Riotinto of Australia). So Comalco (which owned the Weipa deposit, as well as the two refineries and two smelters to process its ore) was now owned by Kaiser and CRA (45 per cent each), while CRA was 80.6 per cent owned by RTZ. As CRA established itself as Australia's biggest mining company, RTZ's percentage reduced to 49 per cent, but it retained decisive, though hidden, influence.

While Kaiser and CRA (RTZ) each held 45 per cent of Comalco, the other 10 per cent was sold off as shares, in a notorious scam—offered first, at a super cheap price to politicians, judges, businessmen and media people, and only later, at a much higher price, to others, allowing many powerful people to make a huge profit. This pattern was repeated in New Zealand over shares in the Bluff smelter, causing an even nastier scandal, and seen as a rip-off for New Zealanders. By 1990, CRA's share in Comalco (i.e. RTZ's share) had increased to 67 per cent. RTZ's share increased further after Kaiser went bust, and in November 2006 Comalco became Rio Tinto Aluminium.

Evicting Weipa's Aborigines began in 1960. At this time they were living together, around a mission station, making it easy for police to remove them by force. In 1963 they were moved to a 308 acre reserve called Weipa South, 9 miles from the affluent new mining town coming up at Weipa North. The Weipa people lost everything—the huge territory where they had always hunted and gathered, the trees where they left their dead, and their sacred sites. All they had at Weipa South was a few buildings, a primary school, and a few low-grade jobs and amenities; no land—and Comalco was put in charge of their administration. The very company that had stolen and started devastating their land was put in charge of a people who, till then, had lived an independent life as hunter-gatherers, ranging over hundreds of square miles, and whose culture was based on the sacred rocks and rivers of this land and knowledge of its Dream Lines.

Weipa is a classic case of cultural genocide, imposed through wilful ignorance. Comalco/CRA claimed the role of protecting Aboriginal rights and culture, employing one of the world's biggest

PR companies to advertise this notion in 1980. One argument they used—the same model used by mining companies in India—was the jobs reserved for Aborigines, but these formed only the lowest, 'unskilled' 10 per cent of jobs. A journalist and sociologist who visited the South Weipa community in 1976-79 described it as the most alcoholic and crime-ridden town in Australia, and the people's former hunting grounds as 'acres of dead craters unrelieved by a single growing thing'. The film-maker David Bradbury made a documentary called *State of Shock* (1989), which woke up many Australians to the tragedy at Weipa.[37]

Mining began in 1963, and Weipa became the world's biggest bauxite mine. Like others it is open-cast, strip mining the ore to a depth of about 30 feet. Weipa's bauxite lay under forest just above sea level, not on a mountain. By 1974 an estimated 53 million tons of bauxite had been taken, and production was over 9 million tons per year: up to 7,000 tons per acre, with an average of over 3,000 acres of land deforested and strip-mined each year.

To the north of Weipa, the Mapoon Aborigines were also forcibly evicted in November 1963. Police came at night in boats, arresting everyone in the village and setting fire to all the buildings. Till today, the Mapoon territory has not been mined. The eviction was aimed at securing a 'trouble-free' agreement with Alcan, whose mining rights were confirmed in an Alcan Act, passed by the Queensland government soon after. The Mapoon people were allowed to return to their site in 1979, after a failed attempt in 1974, but their life there is overshadowed by the mining leases and township plans.[38]

After Weipa and Mapoon, it was the turn of a third tribe, the Aurukun, to have their land sold off in mining leases. Aurukun, south of Weipa, stood up to Dutch colonisers in 1606, and have stood up to the aluminium companies.[39] The Aurukun had been lucky to have sympathetic missionaries, who hadn't tried to change their lifestyle much. All over Australia and the US, missionaries of various Christian sects were effectively given control of different tribal groups, and set out to detribalise them through rigid boarding schools. Both the Weipa and Mapoon people had been more heavily missionised, and both were abandoned to their fate by their missionaries after the churches had made token demands for Aboriginal compensation.

Comalco's attempts to regenerate mined-out lands have also been pathetic—basically plantations of non-native species, to be harvested and turned into wood chips. In 2005, Chalco (China aluminium company) won the bid to start 'developing' this Aurukun lease.

In 2008, Australia's refineries were as follows:

- Pinjarra, West Australia, owned 100% by Alcoa, producing 4.2 million tons per year
- Wagerup, West Australia, 100% Alcoa, 2.4 million tons per year
- Kwinana, West Australia, 100% Alcoa, 2.15 million tons per year
- Worsely, West Australia, owned 86% by BHP Billiton and 14% by Japanese aluminium companies, 3.5 million tons per year
- Gladstone, Queensland, QAL (majority RT Alcan owned), 3.95 million tons per year
- Yarwun, Queensland, Rio Tinto Alcan, 1.4 million tons per year
- Gove, Northern Territory, Rio Tinto Alcan, 3.6 million tons per year

And the smelters in Australia and New Zealand:

- Boyne Island, RT Alcan 59.4% with Sumitomo, Marubeni and Mitsubishi, 545,000 tons per year
- Tomago, Rio Tinto Alcan 51.5%, 520,000 tons per year
- Bell Bay, Rio Tinto Alcan 100%, 178,000 tons per year
- Portland, Alcoa 55%, 353,000 tons per year
- Point Henry, Alcoa 60%, 185,000 tons per year
- Kurri Kurri, Hydro Aluminium [Norsk], 164,000
- Bluff/Tiwai Point, NZ, owned 79% by RT Alcan and 21 per cent by Sumitomo, 352,000 tons per year

Alcan's mine in Arnhem Land (Northern Territory) is on Australia's other northern peninsula, west of Cape York, originally a joint venture by Alcan and Alusuisse. This has encroached on territory of some of the most traditional Aborigines. The Gove refinery, like Gladstone, has caused extensive pollution to the mangrove forest along the shore-line.

Alcoa has two bauxite mines in the Darling range of Western Australia near Perth, Huntly and Willowdale, which have denuded an estimated 13,500 hectares of *jarrah* forest, supplying its three refineries nearby. Huntly may have overtaken Weipa as the world's biggest producing bauxite mine. Alcoa's claim that it has a high success rate reforesting *jarrah* forest is the best-advertised case of bauxite mine rehabilitation, and was cited by lawyers for Vedanta and the GoO at India's Supreme Court as a model for Niyamgiri.[40]

Wagerup refinery has a long history of serious pollution offences, as well as denial, and in 2007, 160 residents of Yarloop village, nearby, called in a famous US lawyer, Erin Brockovitch, to bring a class action suit for serious respiratory diseases and cancers allegedly caused by Wagerup. Brockovitch became famous for taking on Pacific Gas in California, winning a multi-million dollar settlement for residents whose health was damaged by chromium pollution the company denied—a story made into an award-winning film starring Julia Roberts.[41]

So Australian aluminium comes at a heavy cost, devastating the lives of Aborigines, along with irreplaceable forests where these people had lived for thousands of years. The biggest shock is often the desecration of sacred sites, understood essentially as power points on the earth—places of great beauty, honoured in stories of the Dreamtime. To see them vandalised is painful beyond words. The behaviour of mining companies in the outback shows an intrinsic aspect of mainstream culture—its crude materialism, and ignorance about the value of minerals *in situ* for the health of a living earth.

> up in the bush, the country which once was Riratjingu hunting ground, there are still hills of bauxite left and they will remain for years. Yet the consortium is like a tribe or big family; some problem always pops up, not only to make you miserable, but to bring hard times for your friends as well....
>
> I often wonder why white men are so mad on rocks.... during a lifetime, many of them have destroyed whole mountains. (B. Wongar 1978, pp. 13 and 54)

Genocide in Brazil and other stories

In many ways, Brazil is a model for Odisha, on a vaster scale, with a similar combination, of bauxite, iron and coal, great rivers, excessively dammed, and great forests, under threat. The destruction of Amazonian rain-forest is better known, and displaced tribal communities preserve an exotic traditional image, with body-paint and feathers. They are survivors from a 500-year history of genocide though their present numbers are far fewer than tribal groups in Odisha.[42]

'Alcan's bauxite mine lies on the frontier of extermination' of Brazil's native peoples.[43] Earlier decades exploited deposits and built factories in south Brazil. Discovery of extensive bauxite at Oriximina on the river Trombetas shifted the focus to the north in the 1970s, where mines yield 16 million tons of bauxite a year, stripping large stands of forest, including precious brazil nut trees, and contaminating Batata Lake, where the Quilombola people live —black descendants of escaped slaves, who have won a land-mark court case demanding a clean-up.

Tucurui, on the Tocantins, is one of the world's biggest dams, 10 km wide, with a reservoir over 2,400 square kilometres in size. The reservoir flooded between 24,000 and 35,000 people out of their homes in 1984, dislodging the already-depleted Parakanan and Gaviao tribes, while Tucurui's drowned forest emitted 9,450,000 tons of CO_2 and 140,000 tons of methane when this was tested in 1990. Swarms of flies and mosquitos have made life unbearable nearby, spreading malaria and other diseases.[44]

The dam was built for aluminium. Its water and more than half its electricity supply two refineries and two smelters, Alumar and Alunorte-Albras, financed by loans from Japan's Import-Export Bank, which swiftly tripled Brazil's aluminium production.[45] Among Alcan assets spun off to Novelis are two of Brazil's five bauxite mines, a refinery, and two of its smelters. As many as 80 more large dams are planned in north Brazil, with plans to expand aluminium production still further. Alcoa's offer to invest $1 billion in building a Belo Monte dam on the Xingu (first of six planned for this river), would displace 10,000 people, including more indigenous Indians, and is strongly opposed.

Research by Stephen Bunker and associates has exposed Japanese investment in Brazil's aluminium industry, and the pressures behind it, involving close coordination between Japanese aluminium companies, banks, government agencies, shipping companies, and a programme of 'underdeveloping the Amazon', enmeshing it in an unequal exchange. Seven Japanese aluminium companies led by Nippon made a joint venture with Brazil's mining giant CVRD (Companhia Vale do Rio Doce), which got Eletronorte, the Brazilian government electricity company, into massive debt building Tucurui. The guaranteed price for hydro-electricity paid by the new smelters is far below its cost of production, while interest charged on the construction loans is phenomenal. As a result, Eletronorte could not bring the electricity that had been promised to nearby villages—as with Odisha's Indravati dams, in which Mitsubishi from Japan was a key partner. The programme of dam building with aluminium plants was driven by a sophisticated PR programme, marshalling facts and figures in glossy presentation to build a false prognosis. These plans were developed, secretly, at the same time as similar plans for smelters in Venezuela, Indonesia and Canada. The resulting glut of aluminium depressed world prices, and prevented these countries from making the promised profits.[46]

BHP Billiton's involvement in Brazil dates back to 1963, when Billiton set up a tin mine in Mato Grosso, where ranchers perpetrated sadistic, genocidal massacres on the Cintas Largas (Broad Barkcloth) tribe.[47] Billiton merged with Shell in 1970, when it bought into Australian bauxite in the Kimberly mountains and joined the consortium grabbing Aurukun land on Cape York. It was complicit in huge human rights and environmental abuses in Nigeria.[48] Billiton separated from Shell and merged with the Australian giant BHP (Broken Hill Proprietary) in 2001, which had already trespassed on a lot of Aboriginal land, and was notorious for one of the world's worst pollution disasters at Ok Tedi in New Guinea.[49]

BHP Billiton has majority shares in smelters and refineries in Suriname, Australia, Mozambique and South Africa, as well as Brazil. Its Odisha plans are pending as we write. Brian Gilbertson, who masterminded the merger with BHP, may well have been influential in getting finance for Vedanta's Lanjigarh refinery.[50]

Venezuela has a refinery and two large smelters, powered by the vast Guri dam, on the Caroni River, which was built in two phases in the 1960s–80s, with backing from Japanese aluminium companies. Five of these, led by Showa Denko, formed a consortium to build the Venalum smelter, after Japanese activists had managed to stop a

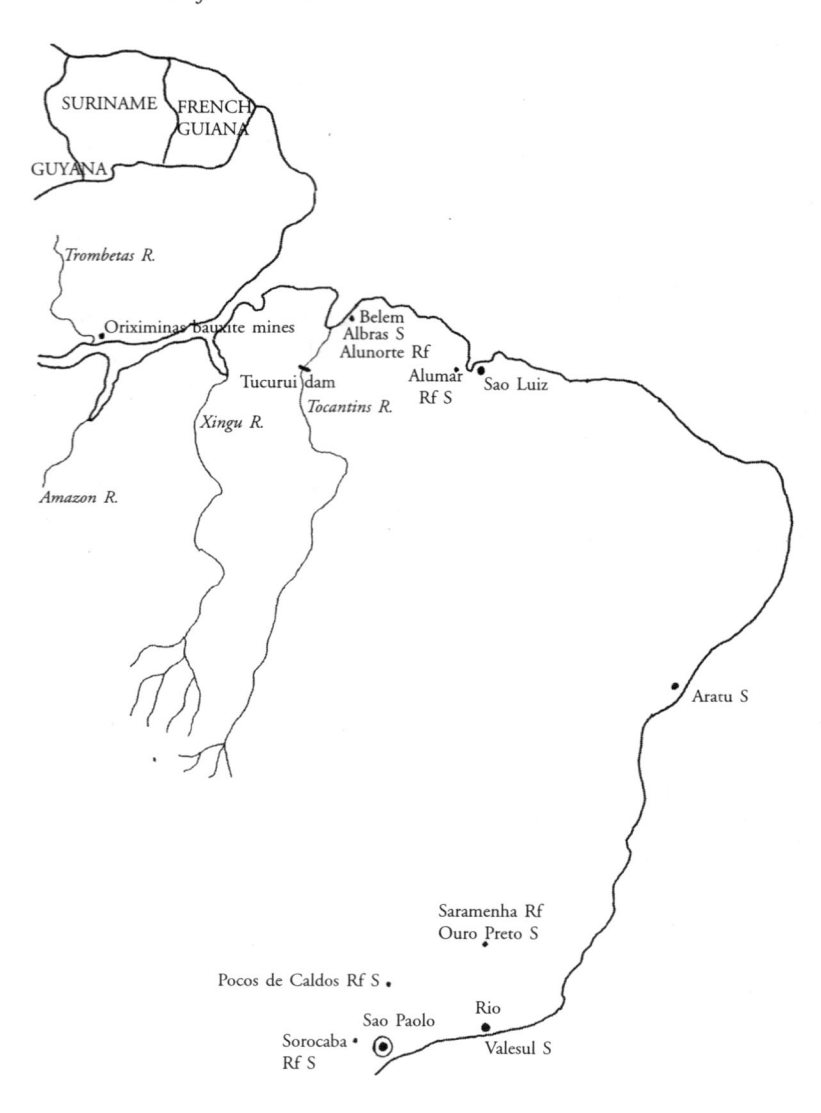

Map 9: Brazil's Aluminium Industry

Refineries	Tons per year	Smelters	Tons per year	Year started	Owners	Province
1. Ouro Preto	150,000	1. Saramen-ha	52,000	1951	Hindalco/ Novelis	Minas Gerais
2. Pocos de Caldas	390,000	2. Poco de Caldas	96,000		Alcoa	Minas Gerais
3. Sorocaba	940,000	3. Sorocaba	475,000	1955	CBA (Brazil)	Sao Paolo
		4. Aratu	57,000	1979	Hindalco/ Novelis	Bahia
		5. Valesul/ S.Cruz	96,000	1982	Nippon 49 per cent	Rio di Janeiro
4. Alumar/ S.Luiz	1.4 million	6. Alumar/ S.Luiz	433,000	1984	Alcoa, BHP, RTA	Maranhao
		7. Albras/ Barcarena/ Belem	460,000	1985	CVRD and Norsk/ Nippon	Para
5. Alunorte/ Belem	412,600			1995	CVRD and Norsk/ Nippon	Para

Table 6. Brazil's refineries and smelters [51]

new smelter in Japan—a classic example of how and why aluminium factories have been steadily transferred to 'developing countries'.[52]

A movement in Chile, based on a broad alliance, has so far saved a wilderness tract in Patagonia from an 'alumysa project' based on an aluminium smelter for Noranda (Canada), preventing six big dams on 'three wild rivers'.[53]

It was Japanese aluminium companies led by Nippon, that financed the Asahan dam-smelter project in north Sumatra during Suharto's regime in the 1980s, one of Japan's largest overseas investments, and a 'deliberate export of environmental damages' from a rich to a poor country.[54]

BHP Billiton is a partner with Mitsubishi in Mozambique's Mozal smelter, which consumes four times more electricity than the rest of Mozambique together, and. was funded through the International Finance Corporation of the WB, which also gave the loans for Sual's plants in Russia, and two ports for exporting aluminium from Venezuela.

In 2007, Rio Tinto Aluminium (Australia) took up construction of a smelter in Sarawak (Malaysia), which was notorious even before being built, because of the infamous Bakun dam already made to supply it, that displaced about 9,000 indigenous people, including at least 15 traditional longhouse communities.[55]

Iceland to Vietnam: The new invasion

New dams and smelter projects have divided Iceland's population since 2003, when campaigners against the Kárahnjúkar dam gathered strong international support. Evidence suggests that these dams and smelters caused the collapse of Iceland's banks in October 2008.

Iceland's first smelter was made by Alusuisse at Straumsvik in 1966. Kárahnjúkar was the third, and three more are being planned.

Kárahnjúkar was built by Bechtel in one of Europe's last unspoilt wilderness areas, remarkable for its bird and animal life, to power a new, super-size Alcoa smelter at Fjardaál/Reydarfjördur in the remote east of the country. Iceland witnessed a historic protest march by 15,000 people on 28 September 2006, when the dam locks were closed to start the slow drowning of an area that included 60 waterfalls and a reindeer breeding area.

The new Alcoa smelter was built by an Italian firm called Impreglio, who employed workers from East Europe. Samarendra met a group of Romanians who were labouring about 12 hour days under hazardous conditions. As in Odisha, a number of poorly recorded deaths of these construction workers have occurred.

Work on these projects started despite Iceland's Supreme Court and National Planning Agency ruling that their EIA was inadequate—a judgment over-ruled by the Environment Minister Siv Fridleifsdottir, with the words 'Just because something is protected it doesn't mean it will be protected forever!' Protesters who camped in the area to try and prevent construction faced strong harassment by police.[56]

Controversy over the issue split Icelandic society as never before, with camps of 200 and more people confronting the construction companies, and police intimidation of protestors. In July 2008, Samarendra visited the country at the invitation of a coalition of Green and Left party MPs, who were highlighting the aluminium industry's dire implications for Iceland's economy.

Iceland's population of 340,000, live around a remote interior containing some of Europe's last undamaged wilderness, whose future hangs in the balance now. Century Aluminium (a US company formed by Glencore in 1995) has started construction of a fourth smelter at Helguvik, in south-west Iceland (near Reykjavik, the capital), where a highly polluting anode rod factory has also received planning permission. Four new megadams are planned, as well as geothermal plants, likely to damage the island's famous hot springs and geysers. Geothermal plants have an unjust reputation for low environmental impact that belies extensive pollution and unknown dangers. Alcoa's plans are for dams, a geo-thermal plant and smelter on Iceland's remote northern shore. All these projects offered the land 'new wealth', in secret plans 'wrapped in deception and exploitation of the land and people, and Icelanders are always the last to know the scale of the backroom deals being done in their ancient Parliament.'[57]

The dramatic crash of Iceland's three main banks in October 2008 illustrates this deception. The credit rating agencies had been promoting investments in these banks until a few days before. Iceland topped the UN's Human Development Index (HDI) in 2007 as 'most developed country in the world', and the OECD declared it, per capita, the fifth richest country on earth. When a large number of British investors, including county councils and NGOs, seemed likely to lose their money, and Iceland's government announced it was unable to offer guarantees, the UK government threatened it with anti-terror laws!

Iceland had been caught up in a bubble typical of aluminium capitalisation, with huge loans (taken by the local government, banks and companies) to pay for the infrastructure needed by the aluminium companies. The money traded in Iceland's banks was more than ten times what the country really had. The view promoting these investments emerges from a passage in a book by one of the world's most influential economists, which contains a particularly revealing passage contrasting Iceland with India:

> As a small north Atlantic island economy, Iceland has leveraged its plentiful fishstocks and geothermal energy into spectacular development, mainly by reinvesting its natural resource earnings into very high levels of education and skills for its small population. Iceland has used its mid-Atlantic proximity to the US and Western Europe to foster an open society in which its leading students, businessmen, artists and entrepreneurs move effortlessly between two vast markets, equally at home and abroad.
>
> India, of course, is at the opposite extreme, with a population that is 5,000 times larger than Iceland's. India's challenge, completely different from Iceland's, is to transform a densely populated sub-continent of subsistence farmers into a modern and largely urban society. (Jeffrey Sachs, *Common Wealth: Economics for a Crowded Planet*, 2008, p. 219)

No mention of the controversial dams! Perhaps Iceland and India have more in common than meets the eye, not least the massive loans to finance an infrastructure for aluminium, promoting debt-bondage and a risky economic future. Plans to transform millions of Indian farmers into industrial labourers (in which Sachs seems to have played an influential role) come out of the same neoliberal mind-set that brought about Iceland's crash, and, from an Indian village perspective, seem insane.

Iceland's economic danger was highlighted in 2001 by evidence that 'the close links between the government and the business community could generate opportunities for corruption,' and a police investigation into price-fixing by three oil companies (2003). After a group of scientists had advised Parliament on considerable dangers posed by plans for the Kárahnjúkar reservoir, the Left-Green MP Kolbrun Halldorsdottir described how 'the minister for industry advised the house that these scientists were politically motivated and not to be listened to.'[58]

These episodes have pushed some of Iceland's leading thinkers and artists into a profound re-think of their culture and path of development. Andri Snaer Magnasson's *Dreamland: A Self-Help Manual for a Frightened Nation* (2008), with a foreword by pop-singer Björk, has opened many minds, and reflects similar divisions in society to those so evident now in Odisha, and wherever the aluminium industry is promoted. Another Alcoa smelter is being planned in Greenland's even more fragile wilderness amidst the melting icecaps. Campaigner Mikkel Myrup, of Avataq summarises the situation:

> In June 2009 Greenland obtained status as a self-governing entity within the Danish Commonwealth. About half of the Greenlandic GDP consists of an annual block grant from the state of Denmark. This has naturally spurred the Greenlandic Government to seek out new possibilities concerning alternative income sources, so that the country can develop a more self-sustaining economy. Greenland, the globe's largest island, is considered to hold great amounts of mineral resources and several foreign mining companies have large extraction projects on the drawing board.
>
> Another resource found in Greenland is energy. Energy in the form of hydropower. But with a highly dispersed population of only about 56,000 individuals, the Government has been led to believe that this relatively large energy potential is suitable only to accommodate the needs of energy-intensive heavy industry, in this case aluminium smelting. In 2006 American transnational Alcoa Inc. had already won over key civil servants and together with company representatives they soon had the key cabinet members convinced. The public was told that aluminium is a 'green' metal, and by using hydropower to produce it, Greenland will take a global responsibility in fighting climate change while creating a more self-sustaining economy. By 'self-sustaining', the pro-aluminium civil servants and convinced politicians mean entering into an ownership model in which the Greenlandic public should own up to fifty percent of an overall project with costs estimated to be around $5 billion. International financing institutions would provide Greenland the loans. Up to fifty percent of $5 billion, a society with a population of less than 56,000 and a GDP just above $1 billion!
>
> Confronted with questions concerning the vast environmental and social destruction caused by the aluminium industry around the world, the civil servants in Greenland simply refer to the websites and different reports published by Alcoa and the aluminium industry's

pressure groups. Alcoa is, in all seriousness, mentioned as one of the world's most ethical corporations and being unaccustomed with the industry's way of propagating half-truths and myths, a majority of the public, including the parliamentarians unfortunately, accept these types of statements.

Alcoa's hydropower scheme requires damming of several large melt-water lakes. One of these lakes is called Tasersiaq, meaning 'the found lake'. By its shores a unique cultural landscape bears witness to human life spanning over 4,000 years. This cultural landscape is considered very important in illustrating the cultural history of the Arctic as a whole, as well important in the understanding of the post-glacial European hunter-gatherer societies. The Greenland National Museum recommends that it be nominated as a UNESCO world heritage site. It will be lost forever if the lake is impounded as a reservoir for the Alcoa hydropower plant. The final parliamentary votes are due in 2010.

More smelters are planned in Trinidad and Tobago, where local campaigners have galvanised momentum, inviting a visit from Samarendra in mid-2009. In the words of environmental engineer Cathal Healy-Singh:

> Trinidad and Tobago (T&T) is a small twin island developing state with an area of just over 5000 square kilometres and a population of 1.3 million—a mature hydrocarbon province producing 123,000 barrels of oil per day and approximately 4 billion cubic feet of natural gas. Of this, about 50 per cent is exported as LNG. The balance services heavy industrial, commercial and domestic needs. Successive governments have pursued a policy of 'heavy gas based industrialisation' which has made Point Lisas Industrial Estate the home to some of the world's largest ammonia, methanol and urea plants. The proximity of bauxite deposits in Guyana, Suriname and Jamaica and the availability of 'cheap' gas in Trinidad provides the logic for the establishment of an aluminium smelter in Trinidad. Alcoa has operated a transhipment facility for bauxite and alumina in Trinidad for over 60 years.
>
> In 1998, a letter of intent was signed by the Government of Trinidad and Tobago for Norsk Hydro, the Norwegian industrial giant, to establish a 474,000 million tons per year aluminium smelter at Point Lisas with an investment of US$2 billion (*Guardian*, 23 July 2009). This development did not materialise. In early 2006, Alcoa

applied to the Environmental Management Authority (EMA) for a Certificate of Environmental Clearance (CEC) to establish a 341,000 million tons per year smelter in Chatham, South-West Trinidad (EMA Public Register). The Chatham community mobilised against Alcoa. Several environmental groups formed in 2006 to support the community. After a long battle of sustained protest by opponents and an extensive publicity campaign by Alcoa which played out in the national media, the Prime Minister announced in December 2006 that Chatham would no longer be the location of Alcoa's smelter. During the same speech he also announced his intention to construct an off-shore island to locate a cluster of heavy gas-based industries including a smelter.

In April 2005, the National Energy Corporation (NEC) applied to the EMA for a CEC to construct 'Alutrint', a State-owned 125,000 million tons per year smelter at Union Industrial Estate (UIE), La Brea, Trinidad. A year earlier, the NEC began clearing close to 1000 acres of secondary forests and agricultural lands to make way for UIE. No notice of the pending industrialisation was given to the approximately 10,000 people living within 4 km of the site (Union Village Council). The land clearing resulted in the destruction of natural and recreational assets valued dearly by the surrounding communities. The CEC process allowed for the lands to be cleared before an assessment of land use was considered. This 'fragmentation' of land clearing and land use gave the impression that irrespective of public opinion the proposed developments were a foregone conclusion.

Alutrint went on to receive environmental clearance in April 2007. Alutrint is being financed and built by the Chinese government. The smelter, port and power plant are expected to cost US$1.5 billion. Construction of Alutrint began in late 2008. Separate applications for environmental clearance were made for the related port and power plant. The Environmental Management Authority's decision to grant approval to Alutrint was challenged in the High Courts by local residents and NGOs through the Judicial Review process. In June 2009, the claimants were successful. The CEC awarded to Alutrint was quashed. The EMA immediately appealed. The case went before local Appeal Courts several months later. The judgement is pending. Should they lose, claimants are determined to take the case to the UK-based Privy Council, the highest court of appeal in the Caribbean.

Alutrint had proposed to ship Spent Pot Liner to Arkansas in the US but no firm commitments were secured to receive the waste and insufficient information was submitted on how the SPL would be handled and transported. Given the hazardous nature of the waste the judge considered this to be "outrageous". Additionally, the judge ruled that the EMA's consideration of "cumulative impacts" of the smelter and associated power plant and port, to be "irrational" and "procedurally irregular".

The attempts to introduce aluminium smelting into Trinidad and Tobago have given birth to a 'green movement'. It has also revealed fundamental flaws in the decision-making process, including a lack of mandatory public awareness, consultation and understanding of hazardous industries and the lack of cost-benefit analysis to inform the decision-making process.[59]

The Iceland saga of busting banks and mega-scale recession, alongside other histories summarised above, should warn prospective countries, including India, that the economic prosperity offered by the aluminium industry is an elaborately fabricated mirage, that invites an unprecedented level of debt and creates a bubble whose bursting can be very painful. Iceland lost millions of dollars, even before the crash—'eaten by the sea', through transfer pricing by Alusuisse at the country's first smelter, which accumulated profits in Switzerland, and kept the smelter's profits in Iceland artificially low. When the credit crunch hit home, in late October 2008, Century announced it was stopping construction of its Helguvik smelter.[60]

Iceland, Greenland and Trinidad may seems a world away from Odisha, with small populations and different climates. But they all possess an attractive energy potential, which makes them magnets for the aluminium industry. In each case, governments have made deals without understanding the real history of aluminium in other countries. Natural wealth can turn around and become a curse when it is misused, and Icelanders' crash in living standards provides a stark warning.

As for bauxite wealth, the dangers hanging over Odisha and Andhra are replicated in Vietnam, where deposits on the mountains in the central and southern highlands have been estimated recently at 3-8 billion tons—even more than India! During 2004–05 BHP Billiton set up an office in Vietnam, planning a bauxite-aluminium project there, at the same time as it was manoevering for some of Odisha's deposits.

In December 2005, Chalco (China) signed an MoU for a $2 billion bauxite-aluminium project with Vietnam National Coal Corporation (Vinacoal) based on a deposit known as Gia-Nghia, in Dak Nong province,[61] and in May 2006, the Russian government offered Vietnam help in building a nuclear power station in exchange for access to its bauxite for Rusal, against Alcoa and Chalco competition. Rusal signed a MoU for this project in October 2008.[62] This was after the country's top war hero made a public statement against bauxite mining in January:

> Vietnam's revered revolutionary military leader has stepped into a debate over bauxite mining to cite its potential to harm the environment, highlighting tensions between conservation and economic development in the fast-growing country. The 97-year-old General Vo Nguyen Giap, the mastermind behind the defeat of the French colonialists and then the Americans, has called on the government to reconsider plans to expand bauxite mining in Vietnam 's Central Highlands.... Previous environmental studies, Giap wrote, have shown that bauxite mining could have a "very serious and long-term harmful impact on the environment that could not be remedied." The Central Highlands are home to many of Vietnam's ethnic minority groups, who farm in the region.[63]

So tribal people in Vietnam and Odisha face a similar threat. Is a country that fought so hard against American capitalists going to capitulate to this new invasion?

PART III

'Aluminum for Defence and Prosperity'

Aluminium's connection with war goes extremely deep. Discoveries of thermite and duralumin in 1901–08 soon commercialised its potential for bombs and aircraft. The First and Second World Wars caused a massive boom in aluminium sales, and every major war since has created a surge in demand.

Military applications and the economics of aluminium involve the murkiest areas, with secret deals and hidden bribes or 'commissions'.

Everywhere the industry is set up people are promised a new age of prosperity. The scale is necessarily so vast that mammoth construction sites fill the landscape with dams, railway systems, factories and townships. But always, the same stories of huge subsidies on electricity, and promised profits not materialising.

Subsidies are the tip of an iceberg. What is revealed in the following chapters is how real costs of production are *externalised* by the companies onto local populations and governments, through debts and hidden costs that 'enslave' national economies to the finances of aluminium. The companies create great prosperity—for those at the top of the hierarchy. For workers in mines and factories, conditions are harsh, compensation for work accidents is meagre, and extensive industrial disease is uncompensated and repeatedly denied.

For people displaced or outside the system, the companies create poverty worse than anything they knew before. As we have seen, environmental controls in India barely function. Pollution Control Boards have no teeth to impose real penalties on mines or factories flouting the rules, let alone shut them down, so the toxic impact on the environment at every level is extreme.

CHAPTER TEN

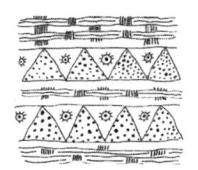

Aluminium Wars

Double death

The world's most lucrative and powerful companies are those producing arms in 'defence' or 'aerospace', and these are the aluminium companies' highest-paying customers. The whole history of mining and metal technology is connected closely with the history of arms. Weapons have driven and funded inventions from Bronze and Iron Age times till now. The Industrial Revolution led to a huge arms build-up during the first half of the twentieth century. Killing in both World Wars was on a new, industrial scale. To what extent is the 'War on Terror' driven by mining companies and the arms industry?

Arms companies are among the key customers for all the metals. Aluminium has pride of place. The collective madness of the arms industry is not just that it wastes our natural resources and national economies, but also that the manufacture of arms, and their build-up in an insane arms race, are a prime cause of war.

So aluminium promotes a *double death*: of eco-systems and indigenous communities, and in escalating wars, through weapons of ever massive destruction. Together these cast a growing threat of collective suicide over all of us.

As one example, when India and Pakistan went to war in 1965, both sides were using arms bought from the US. As America's former ambassador to India, J. K. Galbraith, commented:

> The arms we supplied under this policy caused the war.... If we had not supplied arms, Pakistan would not have sought the one thing we wanted above all to avoid: namely a military solution. (Sampson 1977, p. 179)

The arms industry and aluminium's political economy are really different aspects of the same phenomenon: the war industry's centrality to our financial system.

Looked at as a whole, it's an insane system, where the richest people consume non-renewable resources at suicidal speed, and half our human population live in dire poverty. As one part of this, since the Second World War, some of the richest countries have made manufacturing arms the biggest source of national income. Any suggestion to reduce a country's arms industry meets the arguments that people will lose their jobs, and that 'if we don't make them, someone else will'.

So the arms industry is promoted for its role in boosting employment—just like the Lanjigarh and Kashipur refineries— sweeping aside all sense of the destructiveness of what is being produced and how. But, for example, Britain's arms industry is subsidised to the extent of an estimated £13,000 per job.[1] How many Third World governments have sunk deeper into debt, and deprived poorer people of proper development, through buying arms? And how often are these arms turned on their own or neighbouring populations? The arms race works alongside the destruction of indigenous people's lifestyle in Odisha and all the other places where the necessary industries are located.

As we began to research this book, we became amazed at certain basic facts about aluminium—amazed that we had not known these things before, and amazed at how few people do: the life-giving qualities of aluminium in the earth, and in bauxite on the mountains, the basic link between big dams and aluminium factories, the extent of subsidies, and the link with war.

The first arms magnates included Alfred Nobel, the Swedish inventor of dynamite, who became a millionaire by selling explosives. Somehow, he believed that deadly weapons would bring an end to wars, and styled himself a pacifist—hence the Nobel peace prize! Krupp's steel company in Prussia became the major supplier for Germany's arms industry in the two World Wars. In Britain, Lord Armstrong, Edward Vickers and Sir Hiram Maxim amassed legendary fortunes by their inventions and sales. Vickers in the 1890s was employing the services of

> the most celebrated of all the international arms salesmen ... the archetypal "merchant of death"... a master of salesmanship and bribery ... who understood the connection between arms and diplomacy ... who could serve as both salesman and spy.[2]

Sir Basil Zaharoff (knighted for his contributions to the First World War) was an unrepentant warmonger: *'I sold armaments to anyone who would buy them.' 'I made wars so that I could sell arms to both sides.'*

The Russo-Japanese war of 1899–1905 is one example: Maxim-Vickers workers were congratulated on Russian success using their Maxim machine guns to kill thousands of Japanese soldiers—a weapon used throughout the British empire for *'stopping the mad rush of savages'*. Some weeks later, workers at Armstrong—the rival firm—were given a day's holiday to celebrate Japan's victory over the Russians at Vladivostok in 1905, using Armstrong warships.

Sir Basil justified his arms sales in terms that apply now more than ever: they provide the intelligence and influence over foreign countries that enable the major powers to control them—even when these countries become our enemies. This showed in America's two wars on Iraq, where American and British forces faced weaponry their governments had previously sold to Saddam, during the ten-year long Iran–Iraq war, when Western governments blatantly sold to both sides, using the war as a testing ground for weapons systems.

The military-industrial complex in the First and Second World Wars

The potential of aluminium for war was first grasped by Napoleon III of France, who wanted it for helmets and breastplates. It was too costly then. He was aluminium's first head-of-state patron, but all he got was a nice aluminium dinner set. Kaiser Wilhelm was a different story. It was his scientists who invented the alloy for aircraft.

1901 saw the invention of aluminium bombs by H. Goldschmidt, using ammonal or the thermite process, also used in welding:

> if a mixture of finely granulated aluminium and iron oxide is ignited by a strip of magnesium ribbon, the combustion so started attains a temperature of nearly 3000 degrees…. This enormous liberation of heat caused by the combination of finely divided aluminium and oxygen has been utilised for the production of the high explosive, ammonal. It is a safe explosive, consisting of a mixture of aluminium and ammonium nitrate, which can be fired with a suitable detonator, resulting in a violent smokeless explosion with the production of nitrogen, steam, and alumina as the products of the explosion. It has a shattering, disruptive effect, best utilised in bombs.[3]

These bombs use aluminium's high heat of formation—the high temperature at which it is separated from oxygen—to create a huge explosion that effectively reverses the smelting process. Smelting achieves a split or fission of aluminium from oxygen at the molecular level. Bombs create an instant fusion of aluminium with oxygen as it attempts to return to its natural state of Al_2O_3.

For inventing the British hand grenades used in the First World War, William Mills was knighted in 1922. About 70,000 of these were used, and the British Aluminium Company helped to make them, with metal smelted using Scottish hydropower. This grenade remained the standard model for many years.

'*War was good to Alcoa,*' and the company expanded production phenomenally during 1914–18, when 90 per cent of its output went to military supplies—ships, vehicle and aircraft parts, army kit and much more (Smith 1988, p. 127). Duralumin was the alloy invented by German scientists in 1908, giving their aircraft an edge, till Alcoa scientists produced a similar fusion.

The 1920s saw a lot of research into aluminium alloys, especially for aircraft. Lindberg flew the Atlantic in an aluminium-skinned plane in 1927, and in 1934 aluminium aircraft started to be built in large numbers, as a new arms race took off.

Meanwhile, many people after the First World War opened to a widespread understanding that the arms companies had played a major role in causing the war. The League of Nations organised a Conference on Disarmament at Geneva in 1927, bringing a motion *'that the manufacture by private enterprise of munitions and implements of war is open to grave objection.'* Vested interests proved too strong —an American lobbyist was paid $27,000 for six weeks' propaganda for the arms companies, which scuppered an agreement. The arms industry was already at the centre of the most powerful countries' economies, and the key to their power. As a British commentator noted after the complete failure of this conference: *'War is not only terrible, but is a terribly profitable thing.'*[4]

Andrew Mellon left his job as Alcoa's Chief Executive to became the US Treasury Secretary in 1921, and kept this post for eleven years, while Alcoa expanded into Europe and Canada, buying bauxite mines as well as factories and dam sites—as one of the world's first real multinationals. In 1925 it engineered a merger with James Duke, one of the foremost dam-builders since 1906.[5] By 1928 it was producing half the world's aluminium. In 1929 the Depression caused a set-back, but Alcoa expanded its dam-building drive during these years, to power a new generation of smelters. Overall though, the arms companies, and mining companies suppying them, were laying off record numbers of workers in the 1920s–30s.

In 1934 a bestselling book called *The Merchants of Death* exposed the role of arms makers and sellers, and their influence on public opinion through control over major newspapers. The same year, an enquiry under Gerald Nye in the US into the arms business exposed shady deals and bribes during the First World War and after: *'was ever a more insane racket conceived in depraved minds or tolerated by an enlightened people?'* In Britain, Charles Craven, Vickers' Managing director, facing a Royal Commission of the House of Commons, used the classic arguments that thousands of jobs depending on his industry, and selling arms did not necessarily promote their use. In a public ballot, over 90 per cent said '*Yes*' to banning the manufacture and sale of arms for private profit.

The same year, the British and American governments initiated a programme of re-armament against Hitler, and aluminium production received a massive boost—coming out of the Depression by making weapons.

> An economic boom, spurred by the demands of war, propelled Americans out of the lingering depression they had come almost to take for granted. (Smith 1988, p. 191)

The build-up started with Germany's construction of a massive fleet of aluminium-based warplanes. By 1938 Germany was the world's no.1 aluminium producer. In America, Alcoa could not meet the demand alone. The new Reynolds Company began operations, and the administration used Alcoa's assistance to swiftly double the country's refineries and smelters. In 1940, President Roosevelt called for 50,000 planes to be built, with a public plea from Henry Kaiser for more aluminium—already eying its potential!

The Second World War initiated a new level of man's inhumanity to man. Civilians became prime targets. From early on, bombing cities was a key strategy. Among the most lethal bombs were incendiaries, which used aluminium in various combinations. Some were based on aluminium in the form of thermite, others used a phosphorous or pyrogel mix containing napalm. Aluminium formed a crucial 4–8 per cent of most incendiary bombs. The most powerful, which Kaiser made, used magnesium in combination with 3–13 per cent aluminium. These were known as 'goop bombs', from the sticky mixture, which caused fires that could not be extinguished in the normal way—as also with napalm.

Germany started the bombing of cities, but Britain and America brought it to another level of destruction. Essentially this was chemical warfare. The Allies dropped 41,000 tons of goop bombs by 1944, and America's Chemical Warfare Service used them 'to burn out the heart of Japan'. Kaiser was commended after the war by a captain in this Service:

> The goop bomb and other incendiaries did so well on the industrial strongholds of Japan that nearly 160 square miles of industrial areas

were bombed out. You helped immensely to shorten the war and save thousands of American lives. (Heiner 1991, p. 112)

Before the atom bombs, these incendiary bombs had already created carnage beyond calculation among German and Japanese civilians.

Napalm was invented during the Second World War by a scientist named Louis Fieser at Harvard, using an 'aluminium salt or soap' containing NAphthalene and PALMitate. Half the British bombs dropped on Dresden in 1945 were napalm. These were authorised by Churchill, and killed about 25,000 civilians in what became essentially a giant fire ball. Huge quantities were later dropped in the Korea and Vietnam wars, manufactured by Dow Jones Chemicals. The mixture burns at a ferocious temperature, and when it gets onto the skin, it burns the flesh slowly, and cannot be extinguished by water. The photo of a young Vietnamese girl fleeing her bombed village, on fire with napalm and screaming, played a big part in provoking the revulsion that ended that war. But the story didn't end there—in August 2003, Colonel James Alles at the Pentagon admitted that US forces were using napalm in Iraq: 'The Generals love it. It has a great psychological effect.'[6]

America's permanent war industry: Korea, Vietnam, Afghanistan, Iraq ...

Coming to Britain's aid and winning the Second World War propelled America to superpower status. By 1945, Britain's financial debt to the US was enormous, and the loss of its empire was inevitable, while the US was poised to fill the gap.

After the war ended, Kaiser bid for some of America's surplus war-economy aluminium plants, while Reynolds bid for others. Many considered this an impossible challenge, even though Kaiser was getting them for much less than it had cost to build them—a classic model for Balco's under-priced sell-off! The Justice Department had just delivered a judgment in its Anti-Trust case against Alcoa, to try and break its monopoly.[7] But this monopoly was so extensive, with 'vertical integration' backwards into bauxite mines as well as forwards into fabrication factories and rolling mills, that people doubted if Kaiser could bring this off.

After the war, aircraft-makers and other arms companies faced the same slump that hit them after the First World War. But Kaiser was in the know. More war was to come.

> Then in June 1950 came the Korean War, and with it a sudden new up-swing on the roller-coaster—a swing which this time would never again turn abruptly down.... The Korean war was held to show that [in Walt Rostow's words] "industrial capital could, to an important degree, be successfully substituted for manpower against an Asian land army". (Sampson 1977, p. 99)

For these reasons, a *military–industrial complex* was gradually put on a permanent footing—to sustain America's supremacy, and fend off another economic depression.

The Korean war set a pattern for a succession of later wars, culminating in Afghanistan and Iraq. Maintaining superiority in firepower justified ever-vaster increases in Pentagon spending. Aerospace shot from $2.6 billion in 1950 to $10.6 billion in 1954.

The US government started stock-piling aluminium in large quantities at this time, to make sure they had enough for at least two years in case of any hitch in supply. Aluminium production more than tripled in America between 1948 and 1958, ushering in a 'golden new age' for the aluminium companies. Long before he became infamous for promoting the toxic-debt policies leading to the 2008 credit crunch, Alan Greenspan cut his teeth promoting 'the economics of air power' during the Korean war, remaining proud of his ability to work out the aluminium content of military aircraft (classified information).[8]

Boeing was Kaiser's first customer, and soon his factories were making parts for B-36 bombers for use in Korea. This war pitched Western capital, in the form of military hardware—especially aluminium-rich planes and bombs—against North Korea's superiority in number of soldiers, who were slaughtered in huge numbers. But for US companies this was good business as well as a crusade against communism. The Korean war, followed by Vietnam, kept America's arms industry on top.

This was the context of Dewey Anderson's 1951 text, *Aluminum for Defence and Prosperity*, published by the US Public Affairs Institute.

Its significance is that it is one of the few public documents ever released that reveal the real policies surrounding the aluminium industry, written by an insider. Anderson had been Executive Officer of the Congress-appointed Temporary National Economic Committee, which examined monopolistic tendencies in the aluminium and steel industries under the chairmanship of 'the great trust-busting senator' Joseph O'Connor during the 1930s, when Reynolds was trying to get in on the act and Alcoa was trying to prevent this. After the war, Anderson masterminded the cheap sale of extra aluminium plants to Reynolds and Kaiser.

This pamphlet sold for just 50 cents. So hard is it to consult a copy now that even the Bodleian library in Oxford had to order one from the US! So it is worth quoting key passages from this document, since Anderson spells out many of the issues so clearly, and till now, there is no comparable testament to aluminium's vital importance in war, and negative impact on a country's resources and finances.

Anderson reveals the industry's destructive impact on the environment and society, and an outline of how America was managing the world's aluminium industry, with a view to supplying the military-industrial complex being set up in the 1950s under President Eisenhower, who warned when he left office in 1961: 'We have been compelled to create a permanent arms industry of vast proportions' (Sampson, p. 103). Aluminium was at the heart of this complex:

> It is largely the exceptional qualities of the metal as a material for war that have allowed the companies manufacturing it to command such a high degree of state support and to establish the industry as a whole as one of the most strategic sectors of the Western industrial economies. The imperatives of national defence ... compelled the leading capitalist powers to minimise their regulation of the industry despite its increasing concentration and well-documented monopolistic tendencies. The industry's position at the very core of the military-industrial complex, its almost total reliance on overseas supplies of raw materials and its private ownership of a non-exhaustible form of information—the technology of aluminium production—have all enabled it to dominate its relationship with the state, both at home and abroad. (Graham 1982, p. 79)

Anderson's starting point is America's need for an unfailing supply for arms.

> Aluminum has become the most important single bulk material of modern warfare. No fighting is possible, and no war can be carried to a successful conclusion today, without using and destroying vast quantities of aluminum. (1951, p. 3)

This remains true today. The context then was an imminent threat of 'the most senseless and deadliest war in history' with the Soviet Union.

> Aluminum is strategic in defence. Aluminum makes fighter and transport planes possible. Aluminum is needed in atomic weapons, both in their manufacture and in their delivery....
> Aluminum, and great quantities of it, spell the difference between victory and defeat....
> With the prospect of a recasting of our entire defense plans to modernise our equipment and also to reduce the overall cost of operating the military for the long years of the cold war, aluminum becomes of even greater importance. Brian McMahon's proposals for extending atomic production and putting guided missile and aircraft programs now on the drawing board into mass production at once is gaining ground rapidly in the thinking of Washington. (ibid., p. 5)

This involved nearly doubling America's air force, and threw out all previous estimates. Demand would be huge.

> Yet aluminum is a scarce metal.... There appears to be almost complete unawareness of the absolute necessity of providing now all the aluminum required for War-Day. (ibid., p. 6)

Anderson saw America's aluminium industry as 'bogged down in a labyrinthine obstacle course', and calls for 'a private, hard-hitting, widely inclusive Aluminum Association,' as a lobby group for 17,000 'small fabricators' as well as the 'big three' (Alcoa, Reynolds and Kaiser). The metal's 'ever-widening variety of important uses' is subservient to military applications.

> It is so critical for defense that government steps in for prolonged periods of time, determines how much aluminum there should be, expands production at government expense, and decides what part

of the supply will be available for civilians.... Aluminum making is dependent on vast continuing grants of low-cost electricity ... the sudden great expansion of economically profitable reduction plants became practical only as government developed the TVA [Tennessee Valley Authority] and the north-west hydro-electricity installations which lowered power costs for aluminum reduction purposes. (ibid., p. 10)

Even the entry of Kaiser and Reynolds added little increase in production of metal until *'the government came forward with another round of tremendous subsidies.'* Even the apparent breaking of Alcoa's monopoly did not bring prices down, *'for there is a "managed" price of metal, as witnessed by the follow-the-leader pattern in vogue between the Big Three, with Alcoa leading off on price.'* For American arms companies, getting the metal cheaply is an imperative—*'The strategic importance of aluminum in abundance at lowest possible cost'*. This means that *'More than any other modern industry, aluminum is dependent on government policies and government actions for more production and consumption.'* In other words, its 'strategic importance' for arms is a major factor behind the huge subsidies.

At the end of the Second World War, America disposed of its stockpile—only to create another just after Anderson's text was written, in response to his policies. He mentions a loan from the British government to buy a large percentage of Alcan's output for several years, signed on 22 November 1951, evidently to supply American forces during the Korean war.

Anderson's comments on energy and environment reveal that America was already planning to outsource aluminium smelting to other countries, in order to cut costs and conserve America's natural resources. Congress had just refused 'to approve the rapid development of the hydro-electricity potentiality of the Columbia River System: the only remaining large source of low cost electricity in the US', and he argues that if and when dams were built there, using them for aluminium would be a waste, noting that the TVA dams gave low-cost electricity for aluminium smelters when they were first built, but the cost escalated fast, and that 'Aluminum production from gas-generated power is a wasteful use of an irreplaceable natural resource'. As for the classic arguments for jobs and development:

> *Aluminum reduction is no great maker of employment, uses little skilled labor, and adds little to the independent development of an area.* The Northwest should find much more valuable uses for its great industrial spark, electricity, than allowing aluminum metal manufacture to consume it all with such relatively small return in community advancement.... A calm survey of our natural situation leads one inevitably to the conclusion that we are just about at a point, given no great changes in aluminum making, when *the US cannot any longer afford to make aluminum if it can be obtained in large enough quantities and on favourable price terms from other sources.* (ibid., p. 21, emphasis ours)

In other words, a top US imperative is to get a large and regular supply of aluminium as cheaply as possible from other countries—hence the Akosombo dam and the whole history of the world-wide web.

Anderson ends by advocating a policy of importing metal from Alcan, which is 'primarily a metal-producing organisation' (i.e producing mainly for export), and was presently engaged in 'the vast wilderness project at Kitimat' in west Canada, where a huge new hydropower project was under way to supply the record-size Kemano smelter. Just beside this, the township of Kitimat was named after an obliterated Indian settlement.

One of the most massive weapons of destruction used since Korea is the 'daisycutter', technically the BLU-82. Its principle of adding water to the explosive mix to make an 'aluminised slurry' was invented by a 'creationist' (i.e. a Christian fundamentalist) named Melville Cook in 1956. It was used for 'carpet-bombing' vast areas during the Vietnam war, as well as in the two wars against Iraq, and in Afghanistan.

> The bomb's warhead contains 13,600 lbs (7 tonnes) of GSX [Gelled Slurry Explosives], a slurry of ammonium nitrate (the basis of nitrogen fertiliser), highly inflammable aluminium powder, and polystyrene-based soap as a thickener. ... When it explodes it generates a massive pressure wave.[9]

This pressure is estimated at 1,000 lbs per square inch, over an area of about 3 acres: every human being within this 'carpet' is killed. Basically it is *'the world's largest non-nuclear weapon'*. It has always been used for psychological effect, to instigate terror. Pilger catalogues the grim story of thousands of people it killed in Vietnam, Cambodia and Laos (Pilger 2002, pp. 101–02). During the first war on Iraq, 11 were dropped, preceded by leaflets from US planes with a picture and a warning to *'Flee and live or stay and die'*. The power of its blast harnesses the explosive power of aluminium to maximum extent.

Apart from use in aircraft and bombs, aluminium is used in many other items of military hardware, especially in tanks and other armoured vehicles, howitzer guns, girder bridges, in which aluminium alloys with zinc and magnesium are especially prevalent. These products were highlighted in an Alcan Booth publication entitled *The Military Uses of Aluminium* (1973), a kind of catalogue from Alcan's British subsidiary, specialising in military alloys.

It is hard to get accurate figures for the percentage of aluminium that goes into the arms industry. Coming down from 90 per cent during the First World War, the *Guardian* mentioned 10 per cent in 1981, and Graham mentioned 30 per cent.[10] Lists of aluminium consumption by sector miss out arms manufacture, and when 'defence' or 'aerospace' is given it does not rise above 4 per cent. If this is correct, it is still substantial, since it represents aluminium's most complex and highly-priced alloys. However, we believe the figures have been considerably 'massaged' through listing many defence applications under 'auto', 'construction' (in military bases), etc., and not taking account of stockpiling. The US started its aluminium stockpile in 1950, and the Defence Production Act of 1959 prioritised this and classed aluminium as one of four 'controlled metals' for defence. The stockpile reached nearly 2 million tons in 1963, and was again prioritised in the first year of Reagan's administration in 1980.

So the reason we get aluminium so cheap is because its whole production is heavily subsidised, and this is because it is vital for 'defence', as a prime component of aeroplanes, bombs, missiles and other military hardware. Arms manufacturers want the metal as cheap as possible, and since their main customers are the world's governments, these have a vested interest to keep prices as low as possible through massive subsidies. This is what gives aluminium its key place in the world's power structure, alongside oil and uranium.

And this is the essence of the hidden agenda behind the long campaign to 'sell' aluminium as a benign, attractive wonder-metal, that will transform the lives of workers and consumers in every land.

At one end of the spectrum of military uses are guns: the standard Kalashnikov assault rifle has had an aluminium frame since 1961. At the other end, aluminium's most 'strategic' uses are in nuclear missiles, aerospace, radar, satellites, and related 'star wars' programmes (National Missile Defence Systems—NMD or MDS). In nuclear reactors, aluminium's imperviousness to radiation makes it a key component in insulation. The special-alloy aluminium tube, that was at the centre of the alarm about Iraq developing nuclear missiles, was probably a standard item used in nuclear reactors.

As for nuclear missiles, the bodies of Cruise missiles, Russia's R-27s, and India's Prithvis are made of aluminium alloys, and use aluminium in the explosive mix and as rocket fuel. Solid-fuel aluminium mixtures took the place of liquid propellants in the Polaris model in 1956, and in Soviet models from the 1970s.[11] From the 1990s a revolutionary use of exceedingly fine aluminium powder in rocket fuel extended this use from missile propellant, to a solid fuel in space-craft, including the space shuttle. Honeycomb nano-structures of aluminium oxide were one of the first fruits of nanotechnology, and aluminium in the form of an incredibly fine powder forms about 18 per cent of rocket fuel.

> The key breakthrough was devising a way to manufacture the fine particles in industrial quantities. The technique involves heating aluminium to an eyewatering 9,000 degrees centigrade, so that the metal turns into a gas. When the gas cools it condenses into tiny nano-particles. And the remarkable ability of these particles to rapidly combust illustrates one of the central claims of the nanotech revolution—namely that the properties of even ordinary materials can change dramatically when their scale is shrunk to the nanometre level.' [12]

Yet these aluminium nano-particles have also introduced a whole new level of pollution into the atmosphere and outer space, and are probably pathogenic, like asbestos. They easily enter the pores of the skin, so have to be handled very carefully with special gloves. Another new application is nano-particle coatings applied to aluminium alloys.

To save weight a great deal of aluminium is used in aircraft construction. But although aluminium is light and strong, its surface is difficult to treat. Unlike steel, for example, aluminium cannot be galvanised to protect it against corrosion.[13]

Coatings of chromic salts are highly toxic and banned by the EU from 2008. Replacing them, coatings of aluminium nano-particles are applied to recent models, such as Harrier Jets and Euro-copters. 'Aluminium alloys reinforced with alumina particulates' have expanding uses in defence and aerospace—part of the range of aluminium-based Metals Matrix Composites (MMCs).

Gallium, obtained as a by-product of bauxite, is another key component of nuclear reactors, where it acts as a coolant due to its low melting point and high boiling point. In nuclear war-heads, use of gallium as an alloying agent lacing the bomb pits was only recently de-classified, and is a costly, polluting factor in decommissioning old warheads.[14] As 'defence' spending continues to rise, the main nuclear arsenal in the US is being replaced by Reliable Replacement Warheads (RRW), in the National Nuclear Security Administration (NNSA). Congress cut off funding in 2004 for the 'Robust Nuclear Earth Penetrator' ('bunker-buster'), yet it seems that a new generation of 'mini-nukes' are being developed anyway under the category of RRW, even though they bring the likelihood of nuclear war far closer.[15]

Defence deals

During the 1950s, America supplied 'free arms' to Europe. Under McNamara, Kennedy's Defence Secretary (from 1961), this was turned into arms sales, and organised under a special department in the Pentagon, under a typically obscure name: International Logistics Negotiations (ILN), headed by Henry Kuss, a church-going Lutheran, who

> soon became a legend in Washington and the European capitals with his bulldozing methods ... and his missionary style. Like all the great salesmen ... he saw no difference between weapons and any other goods; but from his authority in government he elevated arms sales into a special crusade, so that not to sell arms was almost a crime.... "From the political point of view international trade is

the 'staff of life' of a peaceful world. With it comes understanding". (Sampson, pp. 114–16)

From 1962 American arms companies, sponsored by the Pentagon, were selling an average $2 billion of arms per year. Members of Congress were angry that the Military Assistance Advisory Groups staff ('MAAGs') attached to US embassies were essentially acting as arms salesmen under Pentagon authority, pressurising Third World governments to buy US arms that they could not afford. Moreover, there was a lot of evidence that the Pentagon was condoning large bribes ('commissions'), paid by the arms companies to contacts in foreign governments.

Aluminium-rich aircraft were the prime items, and sales to Third World governments have involved some of the direst corruption recorded (Burrows 2002). Lockheed's sale of its Starfighter to West Germany in the 1950s involved the services of Prince Bernhard of the Dutch royal family, director of the Dutch airline KLM, who started the shadowy, influential Bildenberg conferences from 1954, as well as the World Wildlife Fund (WWF, 1961). Lockheed and its rival, Northrop, paid bribes to various *'top of the top contacts'* in Germany and Holland—Bernhard worked secretly for both. These and others, including Boeing, were shown to use bribes as a matter of course, channelling them through 'slush funds' (front companies) and Swiss bank accounts, in a scandal that erupted in 1975–6, in a US just reeling from Watergate. 'Commissions' included $106 million to Kashoggi to get Lockheed aircraft bought in Saudi Arabia, and others in Indonesia, Iran and Japan, where revelations caused a 'political earthquake', and the arrest of an ex-PM and others, while a senior French general committed suicide, and several reputations were tarnished, including that of the Dutch royal family, and Britain's PM, Ted Heath, who had lobbied in Japan on behalf of the Lockheed deal, since the aircraft had Rolls Royce engines, and Britain needed the money. Donald Rumsfeld, as Defence Secretary acted to 'save' Lockheed at this time, and the firm's executives justified the payments (including $12 million to Japan, and $1 million to Bernhard, whom it accused of 'extortion') by saying that 15,000 US jobs depended on its export sales.[16]

Northrop's Tiger was one of the main warplanes pushed by the Pentagon in the 1960s–70s. About 1,500 were ordered in total, and it was

> regarded as a key instrument of [US] foreign policy, through the military assistance programme, providing the nations of the Third World with their links with the West. As McNamara's doctrine spread, of selling rather than giving, so the Tiger became one of the most popular of all arms sales. (Sampson, p. 151)

In 1974 General Howard Fish became the Pentagon's new arms salesman, overseeing 95 per cent of US arms sales through a new department called Defence Security Assistance Agency (DSAA). He justified pushing sales to the Third World by saying they were intended 'to deter conflicts', and pointing to the USSR—though US companies' fiercest competitors were actually each other plus British and French firms, likewise supported by government diplomats. Britain's Defence Ministry even had a catalogue of 'Defence Equipment' in several volumes, to promote sales directly. And France's 'Ministry of bribes' secured worldwide sales, including the Mirage fighter-bombers that Israel used to win the Six Day War in 1967. An estimated 65,000 jobs in France depended on arms sales abroad in 1977.

Of course, bribes were only one aspect of these sales, which aided a general trend towards militarising Third World countries, tying their economies into intolerable debt burdens and dependency on the West. They also made the arms industry central to the richest countries' economies, and exerted hidden influence on diplomatic relations. With each sale of aircraft came a whole industrial complex, along with foreign technicians and trainers. The Bofors scandal in India played a major part in bringing down Rajiv Gandhi's government in the early 1980s, after commissions of $17.7 million were shown to have been paid through an Italian businessman on behalf of the Swedish company to push its sale of 410 howitzers. Soon after, Britain was affected by the scandal of Hawker jets sold to Indonesia 'for training', used to bomb villages in East Timor. More recently, the Nepal army used two British Islander aircraft donated by the 'Conflict Prevention Fund' in air attacks with helicopters on 'Maoist' villages.[17]

In Britain, the government agency overseeing arms sales is the Defence Equipment Supply Organisation (DESO). In 2006–7, an inquiry by the Serious Fraud Office (SFO) into allegations of huge bribes paid to the Saudi Royal family by British Aerospace (BAe Systems) was terminated by PM Tony Blair on the grounds that it was 'jeopardising national security'—though even MI6 did not agree, and evidence had also emerged that a £12 million bribe had been paid into a Swiss bank account to push the sale of a military radar system to Tanzania, among the world's poorest countries.[18]

This action by Tony Blair has the appearance of justifying the whole system of arms sale 'commissions', as well as the extravagant, unrepayable debts they impose on some of the poorest of nations. Campaign Against the Arms Trade (CAAT), a London NGO campaigning intensively against Britain's arms companies and DESO, has faced several infiltrations by spies.[19]

The deals made for arms bear an uncanny resemblance to those made over aluminium. Both impose extravagant debt burdens onto governments, mortgaging their peoples' future. The two systems are inextricably linked by the high aluminium content of aircraft.

And what of the BrahMos missiles developed by Indo-Russian collaboration in arms technology? An agreement in January 2007 was aimed at selling 'about 1,000 missiles in the near future to clients in India, Russia and some friendly countries.'[20] The role of arms manufacturer is part of former President Kalam's vision for *India 2020* (Kalam and Rajan 1998).

These cases are the tip of an iceberg. The arms industry promotes death at several levels: through wars and violent repression, by impoverishing citizens in the world's poorest countries through the burden of debt, and through a colossal waste of the earth's resources. All these bribes and wars are fuelled by aluminium smelted at great cost out of bauxite, dug from indigenous land.

It seems that all the major aluminium companies have contracts to supply arms companies, though details of these supply contracts are often only available piecemeal, and in retrospect. Kaiser's first contract was for Boeing bombers, Alcoa was the main supplier to Lockheed, Balco had a contract to supply aluminium to India's nuclear weapons programme (probably inherited by Sterlite/Vedanta).[21]

Alcan had a role as 'a key supplier to both North American and European military markets', recording 16 per cent of sales from its 'Aerospace Unit' as going to military uses in its 2006 *Annual Report*. Alcan's CEO Travis Engen was on Donald Rumsfeld's Defence Business Board. Its subsidiary Alcan-Baltek, is a principal supplier to the three biggest US arms companies: Northrop-Grumman, Lockheed-Martin, and Boeing.[22] Meanwhile, India's mining barons have made a series of recent deals with the arms makers: Mittal with BAe, Tata and HAL with Lockheed to make F-16 warplane components, and Hindalco with Boeing and Airbus to make 'speciality aluminium for the aerospace industry'. The photo of a fiendishly grinning Ratan Tata in the cockpit of an F-16 on the frontpages of Indian newspapers on 8 February 2007, shortly after buying up Corus (British steel), captured the national mood of 'India rising'. Like post-apartheid South Africa, India's expanding arms industry is at the heart of its new status bid as regional superpower. It is interesting therefore that Naresh Chandra, Vedanta director and ex-ambassador to the US, was invited onto BAe Systems' advisory board in September 2009.[23]

Two lesser-known minerals present in bauxite have increasingly important military/nuclear applications, and many, if not most, aluminium companies have developed an extraction process and supply contracts, including Nalco, Malco and Balco. Gallium is used in nuclear technology as well as in light filaments, etc., and Nalco makes around 1,000 kg a year at Damanjodi. Even more secrecy surrounds production of hafnium, which has applications as a rocket fuel, and is reportedly being researched on by hundreds of scientists in the US for a new kind of de-materialising bomb. One ounce of hafnium is said to be worth $28 billion.[24]

Aluminium currently forms around 80 per cent of a Boeing 737's unladen weight. Its alloys with lithium and other metals, and with oil derivatives in MMCs, maintain its place with steel and titanium as one of the key materials for arms.[25] The quest for military supremacy, in other words, is a driving force and key source of profit behind aluminium production, now as much as ever.

Aluminium wars

So the fighting presently engulfing the world is played out in aluminium hardware from satellites to guns, tanks, planes, bombs and missiles. Our war technology is based in an alchemy of combining metals, and aluminium is at the centre of this alchemy, thanks to its combinability with other elements and its properties as a conductor (e.g. in computers and mobile phones).

This puts aluminium right at the centre of the world economy, with oil. The biggest banks are the biggest investors in mining, and aluminium is the most investment-intensive of major metals. Iron and copper deposits come more directly out of their ores. Even compared with steel, aluminium needs vast quantities of electricity and water to take form out of bauxite, and then the most sophisticated blending skills to combine into the right alloys to take a helicopter, plane, satellite or missile into space, using aluminium nano-particle rocket fuel.

If we use this understanding to get more insight into the present 'War on Terror', we find there are arms suppliers to both sides. But the 'terrorists' use their body as the ultimate weapon—the suicide belt—and 'primitive', hand-held weapons: razor-blade, knife, sword for beheadings, plus guns and rocket-launchers. The 'War on Terror', on the other hand, is essentially hi-tech, following Rostow's dictum that superior weaponry can beat superior numbers—even though it is becoming obvious to most observers that air attacks that kill civilians in Afghanistan and other countries create great anger and often fuel support for the 'terrorists'. Bombs and missiles rained on insurgent-affected areas cost millions of dollars. Each item 'costs a bomb'. Military aircraft and everything that comes with them are a monumental drain on our collective economy, as well as a colossal waste of the earth's precious resources. At the same time as they spread terror, they also end up teaching the 'terrorists' to respect superior firepower. However misguided and cruel the terrorists might be, at one level they are simply reacting to the superiority ascribed to this firepower and all that it represents, including the diabolical ingenuity of the weapons scientists—the lethal shards that spin out of a Mills hand grenade or a mine, with 'a piece for everyone like a box of chocolates', the design of modern bullets, gyrating as soon as they enter the soft tissue of a human body, tearing our insides to shreds, the slow-burning death from napalm.... What could convey more horror and terror?

Today's wars, which are tearing so many countries apart, are watched in a highly censored, 'packaged' form on our TV screens—almost as a form of entertainment. In truth, these wars are the arena of our arms business and the product of the military-industrial complex we now take for granted: of aluminium and other mining companies, arms manufacturers and dealers, with their 'top of the top' government contacts. It's a very profitable arena: all the missiles, bombs and bullets dropped on 'insurgents', every plane or helicopter, tank or armoured car destroyed, must be replaced. Each day of conflict brings sales for the aluminium companies, and provides for the good salaries that scientists and the trained, better-off factory workers earn.

How could things be different? How could the arms and mining companies lose their power? The starting point must be in seeing the whole system clearly, grasping an outline of how successive governments in the twentieth and twenty-first centuries have given them this power—each country using all its influence to boost their own country's arms sales, to the point where governments now are not even trying to control the arms producers. In fact, the roles seem to have reversed: if anything, it's the arms and mining companies who control our governments. When a British PM or Foreign or Defence Minister travels to meet ministers of other governments abroad, the visible diplomacy on how to resolve certain military conflicts often takes second place to a wide range of trade deals, and top of the list, frequently, are arms deals. It is sobering to see modern society as frozen into the mould of a Warrior Society: liberal, polite and benevolent on the surface, but actually driven by an addiction to war that is partly financial. For those at the top, war is 'a terribly profitable thing.' Maybe the only thing that can help break out of this vicious cycle is an awareness here and now that our war machine leads inevitably to destruction for all of us, and that there is another way to live together on this earth, with East India's Adivasis setting a prime example.

So much for the external aluminium wars. The industry has also fought its own internal wars, between companies, or between the magnates or power groups who control them. London had its 'great aluminium war' between June 1958 and January 1959: a hostile takeover of the British Aluminium Company by Reynolds. This ended in a defeat for the British establishment that had run the BAC, as well as for rival companies such as Alcoa and Kaiser. But Macmillan's government managed to insist that majority ownership remain British. Reynolds bought BAC in a merger with a British metal manufacturer called Tube Investments, and Macmillan got Tube to hold 51 per cent of BAC to Reynolds' 49 per cent. Reynolds sold its share in 1978, and Alcan (as Britain's main supplier for arms) bought this in 1982–83 with the help of various investors, particularly the Royal Bank of Scotland, to form British Alcan.

Russia's 'aluminium wars' are a much darker episode, essentially a series of mafia killings between rival gangs as their bosses, the 'oligarchs', vied for control of the de-nationalised industry. A number of prominent murders took place, while the bosses became Russia's richest tycoons. As the Cold War drew to an end and the USSR started to break up in 1991, 480,000 tons of Russian aluminium were authorised to be sold on the open market, in a context where alumina supplies from Hungary and Yugoslavia had been drastically reduced (by 1.5 million tons), while refineries in Ukraine, Kazakhstan and Azerbaijan were now on foreign territory, offering new opportunities for trading another 2.5 million tons of alumina. Aluminium was soon being sold far below its cost of production. Marc Rich and others formed the Trans World Group to capitalise on this trade, which involved toll-smelting imported alumina, and exporting the smelted product, in a context where the Soviet military-industrial complex was being dismantled. A glut of Russian aluminium hit the world market as a result, causing dramatic price fluctuations in 1991–98, and instigating cartel activity from the US administration (next chapter).

The start of Russia's aluminium wars is usually blamed on Marc Rich, who earned the nickname 'aluminium finger' forging a new style of commodities trading, after fleeing the US in 1983 (wanted for 'the biggest tax evasion in history' and a major oil scam, involving

deals with Iran during its conflict with the US). He traded US and/
or East European grain to Russia in shady exchanges for aluminium.
'Rich made tens of millions of dollars helping Russia's communist
bosses loot their country.'[26] Russia's former Trade Minister Oleg
Davydov attributed Russia's rising mafia business culture to Marc
Rich and similar traders. When

> legal channels became inconvenient, there appeared a huge mass of
> foreign entrepreneurs, mostly crooks like Marc Rich, who began to
> teach us various ways of taking the money out through offshore
> companies. That is what bred our whole system of corruption and
> criminality. [27]

Marc Rich settled at Zug in Switzerland during the 1980s–90s,
continuing to orchestrate deals using Swiss Bank accounts. His
company (Marc Rich) was renamed Glencore when he sold his
stake in it in 1994. It remains one of the world's largest aluminium
companies, owning the Aughinish refinery in Ireland, and other plants
in Sweden, Italy, Jamaica and the US. Marc Rich was pardoned by
Clinton in January 2001, along with Toxic Bob.

By this time, Russia's aluminium exports were controlled by
a Moscow-based company called Trans-Seas Commodities, run
by brothers Lev and Mikhail Chernoi, which dealt through the
London-based company Trans-World Metals, run by brothers David
and Simon Reuben, after (according to a WB report) Marc Rich
gave it some seed capital. Davydov said that the Chernois were
buying Russian aluminium for about $500 a ton and selling it for
about $2,000, doing deals with the aluminium producers, who had
become immersed in debts, dependent on the traders for credit and
raw materials.

> The tragedy is that if the privatised companies were state enterprises
> today, they would be recording good profits, they would be paying
> taxes, paying workers' wages, investing in their plant and equipment.
> But these so-called owners arrived, and what happened? There are
> no profits. No tax payments. The plant and equipment are getting
> worn out. And the money goes abroad.

It was Yeltsin who masterminded the privatisation of Russia's
aluminium and oil companies, and behind him 'the grey cardinal',

Boris Berezovsky, who was close to both the Chernois and Marc Rich. By 1998, Trans-World controlled over half of Russia's aluminium production, making over $6 billion per year, becoming briefly the world's third biggest aluminium company. But in 1997 officials in Russia were investigating allegations that Trans-World was responsible for defrauding the Central Bank and sponsoring violence, and in June 1999, the company was involved in a struggle to control the world's second biggest smelter, at Krasnoyarsk. By 2001 the Chernois and Reubens had parted ways, and Trans-World was out of Russia. [28]

Most of the killings took place in battles to control the main smelters—for Krasnoyarsk in particular from 1994, an episode styled Russia's 'great patriotic aluminium war'.

> Dozens died in a series of murders, including local bankers, crime bosses and factory officials. The victims included both allies and competitors of Trans-World, though David [Reuben] angrily denies any hint that they or their partners had any role in the violence.[29]

After a raid on Krasnoyarsk's offices in April 1999, Anatoly Bykov was accused of 'laundering money obtained by illegal means', and arrested in Hungary in November, after about 100 aluminium company employees had been bumped off.

But the story continues. In the winter of 1999–2000, Roman Abramovitch bought the controlling share in the world's two largest smelters—Bratsk (870,000 tons) and Krasnoyarsk (835,000)—from Trans-World and the Chernois. On 17 February 2000, Abramovitch did a deal with ex-rivals Oleg Deripaska and Mikhail Chernoi, involving Boris Berezovsky as well, which established Rusal (Russky Aluminium), in a bid to end the aluminium wars. This was part of an extensive restructuring of Russia's aluminium industry. Abramovich is one of Russia's top oligarch-billionaires, a major shareholder in Sibneft (one of Russia's main oil companies), and owner of Chelsea Football Club in London. Deripaska, married to Yeltsin's grand-daughter, had been director of Sayanogorsk smelter since 1994, and of Trans-CIS Commodities, a subsidiary of Trans-World Group (which he split from in 1997), and another company called Basic Elements. The purpose of the merger was to concentrate the ownership of Russia's aluminium and oil industry in a few hands. Berezovsky sold up and fled Russia in 2000. Rusal's present plans include modernising Krasnoyarsk and it has considered buying a mothballed smelter in Nigeria, as well as raising foreign funds for a new $3 billion Siberian smelter at Irkutsk, which Bechtel may construct.

Till 2006, Rusal and Sual divided Russia's industry, with Rusal controlling 75 per cent of Russia's aluminium output, and Sual (Siberian-Urals aluminium company) controlling 90 per cent of Russia's bauxite mines, in the north Urals, etc., with a number of refineries and smelters, plus a new refinery-smelter complex planned at Komi in the Arctic, for which the Russian government guaranteed $200 million to supplement foreign investment. Viktor Vekselberg of Sual raised $90 million from the WB's IFC and the European Bank for Reconstruction and Development (EBRD). But Sual's deal with Alcoa for a Joint Venture in this project collapsed in mid-2004, after the Kremlin blocked Alcoa's attempt to buy two Russian rolling mills, and Sual failed to make a deal for cheap enough electricity. The dirty politics and financial scams behind the scenes in Russia's aluminium wars serve as object lessons in the dangers for society in India and other countries, in the scope for aluminium barons to concentrate their power.[30]

Brian Gilbertson became Sual's Chairman in August 2004, for a fee of $50 million, after leaving Vedanta, apparently to try and launch Sual on London's Stock Market (just as he had launched Vedanta), where it gained the support of Fleming Family and Partners, to invite 'respectable' investment. (Roddy Fleming is nephew of Ian Fleming, creator of 'James Bond'). Soon after this, Viktor Vekselberg was accused of embezzlement in the great merger between BP and TNK (Tyumen Oil Co.), and both Sual and Rusal were named by Russia's Ministry of Taxes for large-scale tax evasion, similar to the case which destroyed the Yukos Oil Co. and landed its main shareholders in jail.[31] In August 2006, Sual was bought up by Rusal in a merger that included Glencore and Xtrata.[32]

Some of the worst scandals in Russia's aluminium wars were revealed by journalist Paul Klebnikov in his book *Godfather of the Kremlin* (2000), which focuses on Berezovsky. Contract killers shot Klebnikov dead on a Moscow street on 9 July 2004—a murder that has never been solved, and links to Klebnikov's exposure of corruption surrounding another 'worst' of modern conflicts—the Chechen wars. Anna Politskaya, who also exposed this corruption, was also assassinated, while Berezovsky had a suspicious agility in dealing with the rebels over high-status hostages.[33]

The Russian connection sheds light on a recent phase in US control over the the world aluminium cartel (next chapter). Russia's aluminium wars can be seen as a mafia microcosm of the wars being waged on the world stage, and a parallel to aluminium scandals erupting in every country where the industry takes hold

And what is the concept of 'defence'? Weapons made with aluminium are essentially for *offence*, even if wars are invariably legitimised as response to attack—'keeping the peace' by waging wars.

CHAPTER ELEVEN

'Prosperity' and Price Fixing

Analysing aluminium economics

The industry's finances are extremely complex, partly because large areas are kept well hidden. Commodity analysts for metal trading are some of the world's highest paid professionals, and their reports published by Roskill and CRU sell for up to $19,000 a piece (the price of CRU's 2007 volumes on bauxite and alumina).[1] The high price of these reports commands basic commercial data, and needs to be understood in relation to prices for bauxite and aluminium. Having examined some, we can safely say that even for this money, the information is extremely one-sided, containing almost nothing about the real environmental costs or the people impacted by and resisting the aluminium projects. The same is true of Thomson's *Financing global mining: the complete picture*, a compilation of financial information about the capitalisation of banks' investments, deals and takeovers.[2]

The complexities are indeed formidable. Our research has led us to understand however that this complexity is basically a front. The main outline of aluminium economics is fairly simple when one perceives the connections between interest groups, and how the system functions as a whole. The subject is made hard to comprehend by the way certain pieces of information are removed from the public domain and hardly ever brought together to be seen as a whole, and by the mystique of the highly priced data and the secretiveness of the crucial deals and policy decisions. The significance of Anderson's 1951 essay is that it lifts a corner off the veil and reveals a few of the basic facts about the industry: that it offers little real boost for employment or regional prosperity, depends on huge subsidies for its existence, and is vital for the arms industry.

In other words, the complexity of aluminium economics is in large part a manipulated product—a mask which conceals a pattern of extreme levels of exploitation and destruction of the environment, as we began to understand in the first half of this book. The essence of this pattern is *externality*—how the industry externalises its real costs. In other words, *aluminium economics does not make economic sense*—it is *uneconomic*.

This is why the Bureau of Industrial Costs and Prices recommended containing the industry in 1988. During the years 1972-84, the general cost of aluminium production increased over five times, while the electrical energy component within this cost increased by more than ten times. As a result, 'resource constraints in respect of ... electrical energy' mean that 'a judicious use of aluminium is therefore a must for conservation of energy'—a policy now completely reversed. This is why R. C. Das (1996), as Chairman of the OSPCB, made a strong recommendation against Utkal, and against plans to expand Nalco and Indal smelter capacity—and was 'transferred' (penalised) for doing so (above, pp. 185-86); and why at the same time, India's Environment Secretary T. N. Seshan said that Panchpat Mali alone should take care of all India's aluminium needs for the next 100 years.

As the world financial crisis deepened in the second half of 2008, the price of aluminium halved ($3,200–$1,586, July–December) and investments in mining projects were drastically scaled back, including a cut in Vedanta's next-four-years India investments from $14b to less than $9b.[3] Many scandals have erupted, revealing certain structural features of aluminium economics with unusual clarity. The collapse of Iceland's banks seems largely due to an aluminium loan-bubble, with over $2b borrowed for Kárahnjúkar dam alone, while revelations about links with Oleg Deripaska—winner of Russia's aluminium wars and Russia's richest man—caused embarrassment for leading US and UK politicians of both main parties. Media coverage of these links illustrates much about aluminium's social structure, including the web of connections between tariff policies, PR firms, media tycoons, political parties and aluminium barons.[4]

The Enron bubble was a sure sign of things to come in India as well as the US. Enron's accountants, Arthur Andersen, were found complicit in the bubble, and went bust too. Moody's, the top credit rating agency (CRA), was also questioned about the high rating they gave the company.[5] Monstrous scams surrounded Enron's Dabhol power plant, built in 1994 as the biggest-ever investment in India, with support from five Export Credit Agencies (ECAs).[6] Enron's emphasis on derivatives/futures trading multiplied real money into a monstrous bubble. But far from being curtailed by Enron's collapse, 1999–2008 saw derivatives trading and unrepayable, toxic debts blossoming throughout the financial world. Credit Rating Agencies were giving Iceland's banks a triple-A rating till a few days before they went bust. Deven Sharma, head of Standard & Poor (another top CRA), called before a US House Committee to explain why his firm had continued validating unsound investments, admitted that many basic assumptions had been wrong.[7]

Derivatives trading has created a vast disparity between 'real money' and traded money, with analysts estimating that the greater part of an estimated $531 trillion being traded is toxic debt.[8] People know a bit more now about mortgage derivatives trading. There is much less focus on futures trading in metals, and the role of accountancy firms in validating aluminium companies deserves far closer scrutiny, as we have seen.

Auditors continue to act as advisers to the companies that they audit. They are hired and remunerated by the very organisations that they are supposed to be auditing. The auditor's dependence for fees on corporate barons makes it impossible for them to be independent.[9]

Warnings about a bubble building in India's Stock Exchanges were made some years ago by economist Kamal Nayan Kabra (1992).

Meanwhile, the pressure to start mining India's bauxite mountains grows, even while many point out that India's ores are being sold off far too cheaply (Lingaraj 1995–97; Sarangi 2002–04; Vidhya Das, January 2003; Padel and Das 2004). Chief Ministers of mineral-rich states have understood something of this. Naveen Patnaik was one of five CMs to meet the PM and Planning Commission in December 2007, pressing for more state-level decision-making, a better royalty rate, and a demand that industries give 5 per cent of their profits towards local development, to offset the notorious impoverishment of mining areas. The trouble is, measuring this 5 per cent and deciding how it is spent are not placed under democratic control, and between the promises of mining companies and the reality of what they actually give, there is a chasm.[10]

Mainstream perspectives remain set in growth-oriented models of neoliberal economics, valuing economic/industrial growth above all other measures of prosperity. Project benefits are promoted in terms of high investment figures. S. K. Tamotia, the director whose path from Nalco to Indal to Vedanta follows the privatising trend, wrote several articles advertising the cost advantages of expanding the industry in India, in terms of vast untapped bauxite deposits and cheap labour.[11]

The low price for bauxite is part of what attracts mining companies so strongly now to Odisha, and appears to be a main reason for Vedanta patronage of numerous organisations and events in the state. The company donated $2.6 million to political parties listed in their 2004–07 Annual Reports, made record donations to Jagannath's chariot festival in Puri, virtually taking the event over, with similar PR patronage of dance and music festivals in Odisha, and of Odia artists, whose paintings Tamotia and other directors have bought for lavish sums. In mid-2007 they even donated funds for a major law conference in Bhubaneswar, with a large notice reading 'Vedanta welcomes India's lawyers', and among the participants was Arijit Pasayat, one of the three judges on the Forest Bench presiding over the Niyamgiri case at the Supreme Court. The billion dollars from Anil Agarwal's personal fortune for a Vedanta University at Puri, which the *Financial Times* described as one of the biggest charitable donations ever, lavish fees for the London PR firms—all to facilitate access to Niyamgiri's bauxite? Sums such as these form an intrinsic part of aluminium economics.

Another way into the subject is Material Flow Analysis, and the new discipline of ecological economics. Inputs into the economy from nature are consumed, accumulated, or traded between nations, and eventually released back into nature in an altered form—e.g. carbon stored in the earth released through combustion into the atmosphere[12]—and we shall see that studies by the Wuppertal Institute for Climate, Environment and Energy show that the material intensity of aluminium is exorbitant in terms of its water consumption and airborne emissions.

As an example, it is significant that Vedanta's new smelter under construction at Jharsaguda does not conform to present environmental standards.[13] So when 'developed' countries import aluminium from India, they are imposing the intrinsic pollution-costs of its production onto the country's poorest regions. India's present rapid industrial growth is part of a huge increase in overall emissions—an outdated and completely unsustainable model of growth.

As we have already seen, the aluminium industry's promises of prosperity have been betrayed in one country after another, basically because the industry is deeply hierarchical and ruthlessly exploitative. Not that the people at the top necessarily see their actions as exploitative. More that their understanding is blinkered by complex theories of economic growth and 'trickle-down' benefits, with no counter-balancing experience of the realities of life 'at the bottom', among the villagers they displace or the workers they exploit. Hence the outlandish discrepancy between Vedanta's Sustainable Development Reports and CSR programmes and the ruthless exploitation evident on the ground.

Dai Singh's comment that 'They are flooding us out with money' evokes an indigenous economics. Anthropologist Marshall Sahlins showed the falsity of conceptions that tribal people are 'uneconomic' in his book *Stone Age Economics* (1972). Adivasis and Dalits understand economic realities, and the value of basic commodities, from the bottom, not the top, judging companies by what they do, not what they say. They see all too clearly the madness of what is being done to their mountains and rivers in the name of 'prosperity'.

The institutionalised conceptual split between economics and ecology spells grave danger for everyone. Many economists are just beginning to realise how deeply the two are linked—a link embedded in language. *Oikonomia* and *oikologia* come from the same Greek root. *Oikos* means 'house', standing for a nation-state, region, industry, or our planet, while *nomos* means 'law' and *logos* means 'word/logic'. *Oikonomia* indicates the laws of housekeeping, while *oikologia* refers to the logic of the system as a whole. How have these two disciplines got so divorced that economists can analyse the financial system in isolation from its effects on ecology?

Tax-breaks and subsidies

Many sources agree that it is impossible for a smelter or refinery to make a profit without massive subsidies. This is attested strongly by Anderson about the industry's history in the US. Electricity subsidies are an area where aluminium companies exercise an extraordinary influence to get favours. For electricity (even subsidised) is usually estimated to account for 21–30 per cent of the cost of making aluminium, as the biggest single expense after the cost of alumina. This is why smelter agreements frequently fix rates paying a lot less than the electricity's cost of production.[14]

We have seen that Valco's electricity price in Ghana was fixed for 30 years at 17 per cent of its cost of production—less than a quarter of the rate US smelters paid, and less than a tenth of what ordinary Ghanaians had to pay for electricity.[15] A similar agreement in India fixed the price Hindalco paid at Renukoot at about a twentieth of the going rate.

Brazil's new Albras and Alumar smelters had agreements to pay about a quarter the going rate—well below the cost of producing the electricity, and the massive debts incurred by building Tucurui dam involve a form of *embedded subsidy* observable in Odisha and many other places.[16]

In Russia and China, information on subsidies and environmental impacts are hard to come by, but Rusal 'enjoys ample low-cost power—less than US$0.1per kilowatt hour—from hydroelectric plants in Siberia.'[17]

Alcan's Kitimat smelter (started 1954) got its electricity, land and water extraordinarily cheap, paying just 5 per cent of the going rate for water.[18] These kind of rates apply to all 13 of Quebec's aluminium plants (1993), though most fought tooth and nail to 'preserve confidentiality' about the electricity rate they paid, and when this information was eventually made public, it had to be officially declared as a subsidy.[19] Given aluminium's vast water-consumption, it seems likely that the dam-smelter (and refinery) link is for water supply as much as electricity. Subsidies in water have been much less scrutinised than electricity subsidies, and beg vital questions, especially in the Indian context of dwindling water supplies.

In Europe now, the huge subsidies on electricity necessary for smelters are hard to maintain, and most refineries and smelters have closed as a result. The aluminium lobby based in Brussels sees this in terms of a 'non-functioning market' of electricity prices rising unfairly, due to concessions for wind power and the Emissions Trading System (ETS). Aluminium companies have lost their bargaining power—or rather, it makes more economic sense, as Anderson spelt out for the US over 50 years earlier, to import most aluminium from poorer countries, where subsidy agreements are much easier to fix.[20] The pro-subsidy argument stresses the constancy of aluminium's demand and glosses over the real costs and how they are externalised. The lobby group presses the European Commission to 'reward the advantages of nuclear power for base load electricity, energy supply and CO_2 emission reductions.' But nuclear energy also receives steep subsidies.

Norway is proud to power its smelters 100 per cent by hydro-electricity, but even here the rate has been held low and static for long contract periods, at about a sixth of the price which residents and other companies pay.[21]

West European countries cannot maintain the large tax-breaks and subsidies which Asian and South American countries can still be persuaded to impose, 'leading to an on-going trend of EU de-industrialisation' at the same time as rapidly imposed further industrialisation in India, China, Brazil and other 'developing countries'. In India, speeches at the INCAL conferences (1998, 2003) call openly (and, it seems, successfully) for huge subsidies.

In Britain, Rio Tinto Zinc approached Harold Wilson's Labour government in the 1960s with a plan for a nuclear-powered smelter. Wilson wanted to make it a public enterprise, but this failed and Anglesey ended up costing far more than planned, for which Wilson was heavily criticised. Another smelter built under Wilson was at Invergordon on Scotland's north-east coast, by Reynolds/BAC, but this ran only from 1971–82, because the necessary electricity subsidies could not be arranged.[22]

In other words, the process of constructing a refinery or smelter is (always?) heavily subsidised, and without heavy subsidies, a factory has to close down. Invergordon running for just eleven years is a lesson in the dangers of building factories that are going to be uneconomic.

Transport is another sector that is often heavily subsidised. The model goes back to fiercely guarded secret rebates which Rockerfeller and other Robber Barons negotiated for transporting oil in rail-road-mad America.[23] Do Nalco and other aluminium companies in India receive similar rebates on rail freight? West Odisha is full of whizzing ore-trains these days. Even the cost of building the bauxite railway from Koraput to Rayagada was through a loan from the Saudi Fund for Development. Whether in Brazil, Ghana, Iceland or Odisha, the heavy debt deals for building dams to supply electricity absurdly cheaply for making aluminium show a pattern of subsidy that needs consistent exposure. Also with subsidised land purchase: alongside the construction deals, we also frequently observe aluminium companies taking on a role of property dealing, acquiring much more land than they need at heavily subsidised rates.

The SEZ Act (2005) institutionalises enormous subsidies for export-oriented industries. About 800 energy-intensive Special Economic Enclaves throughout India had received clearance by 2006, each receiving promises of outrageous tax-breaks on land, electricity, infrastructure, water, transport, exports and imports. The new smelters being built by Vedanta and Hindalco in north Odisha stand to gain enormously from these subsidies. The attempt by the West Bengal government to implement the Nandigram SEZ (for Indonesia's Salim

Industries for a huge chemical factory, probably including cathodes for aluminium smelters) shows the kind of human costs involved. The SEZ scheme has been strongly backed by Manmohan Singh, whose past as a WB official is evident in his enthusiasm for the FDI it will bring to India. But the history of aluminium contracts shows how dangerous promises of subsidies use up resources and bind areas into long-term systems of exploitation that are very difficult to escape from. As Gitlitz says about an essential feature of the aluminium industry,

> In countries with low capita income and high national debt, government officials may be strongly tempted to believe the promise of a hydroelectrically-driven aluminium industry as an incentive for development. (1993, p. 137)

The WB's *Worldwide Investment Analysis* of the aluminium industry (1983) compared different countries' distances from mine and factory to port (including Nalco's in Odisha), with market predictions for the year 2000, setting a bench-mark of cost-effective factors, obviously to stimulate countries to compete in setting up transport systems to 'attract investment'.[24] In Odisha, WB loans for ongoing road and railway building projects form another level of hidden or *embedded subsidy*.

Pricing riddles

Beneath mesmerising fluctuations in aluminium prices, several riddles lurk. What is the relation between the price aluminium is traded for and its cost of production? Between the price for aluminium and the price of bauxite? Between the investment a company offers for a project, and the prosperity it will bring?

Bauxite has no set price. How much different companies get it for and how much royalty and other taxes they pay vary greatly around the world, and there is no free market for bauxite. A particular draw of Odisha is Nalco's low raising cost of bauxite. Bauxite prices in India are among the world's lowest and Greece's the most expensive. India's royalty on bauxite per ton has increased from Rs 41 per ton (1997) to Rs 64 per ton (2007).[25] Nalco's raising cost of bauxite from Panchpat Mali is given as Rs 236 per ton (more than $5), i.e. royalty of Rs 64 plus Rs 172 as average cost of extracting the bauxite. A BJD pamphlet in 2004 argues that the price Vedanta was offering, of Rs 250, 14 rupees more than the Nalco price, represents a great deal for Odisha.[26] But the international average in 2004 was $16–17 per ton of bauxite (about Rs 775), with $160 the price for metallurgical grade bauxite in Guyana. As Shivaji Pattnaik pointed out in 2003, Rs 14 is peanuts compared to this: Odisha and its government stand to lose at least Rs 525 per ton—billions of dollars! When one takes into account the evidence that bauxite mining does great damage to the environment and that the world average is kept far too low through influence of the cartel, one starts to comprehend the enormity of exploitation in store for Odisha and Andhra Pradesh.

The differential between what Vedanta is offering and what it actually delivers is evident in the goings-on around the Lanjigarh refinery and Kawardha bauxite mines where, for example, the drivers of bauxite lorries as well as vehicle owners operate at the edge of what is economic. Everyone faces cut-throat exploitation, and the result in lorry accidents we have witnessed is sometimes horrific. So Vedanta's initial investment of Rs 4,000 crore at Lanjigarh, and Rs 12,000 crores at Jharsaguda gives little joy to people working for the company through subcontractors.

Supply of bauxite to refineries is cheapest when it is close—that is the point of the WB analysis (1983). Hence Nalco's conveyor belt from Panchpat Mali to Damanjodi, and the similar belts planned by Jindal in Andhra and from Niyam Dongar's summit to the Lanjigarh refinery below. While that is stalled, Vedanta has to transport bauxite several hundred kilometres from Chhattisgarh by lorry and train: a fleet of trucks brings it daily from Mainpat and Bodai Daldali to Korba (260 and 150 km), whence trains take it 450 or 370 km to Rayagada or Doikhal stations. Then another fleet of at least 500 trucks carry it on the last leg to Lanjigarh (80 and 5 km respectively). Transport like this raises costs considerably, and has a strong impact on the local environment. These trucks have killed many people on Odisha's small roads, breaking up and badly eroding the road surface. Lorries from Rayagada cover their loads with tarps, but bauxite is transported in open lorries within Chhattisgarh and from Doikhal station, creating a huge problem of dust pollution.

Indal was a company plagued by a lack of ready bauxite, and had to buy part of its quota from other companies, which raised costs in the years before it was taken over by Hindalco. Vedanta in 2008 was buying bauxite for Lanjigarh from Gujarat and abroad, as well as from Chhattisgarh. Bauxite is still sometimes transported large distances by sea. Weipa's bauxite is transported a distance of several hundred kilometres to the Gladstone refinery. Bauxite for the UK's last refinery at Burntisland on the east coast of Scotland (closed in 2002–03) was transported from Australia, Africa or the Carribean.

So a company that integrates bauxite mines, refineries and smelters within a compact area saves considerable costs. This is what Alcoa and the other giant aluminium companies did in the early years of aluminium. This is what Nalco set up in Odisha in the 1980s. Nalco's profits rose steadily till early 2007 when the dollar stabilised. In 2005–06 it earned a record Rs 2,306.20 crore in foreign exchange by selling 862,000 tons of alumina abroad and 95,747 tons of aluminium, as well as 258,094 tons of aluminium within India.[27] All the ingredients are available locally: bauxite, hydropower, coal, limestone, cheap labour, and low silica bauxite, which can be refined at a low temperature, cutting costs significantly. Yet out of Nalco's profits, the Odisha government only got a small percentage, especially when the true costs are understood.

	2000–01	2001–02	2003–04	2004–05	2005–06
Total Turnover	2557	2541	2762	3324	4374
Profits Before Tax	843	525	751	1052	1870
Profits After Tax	655	409	520	737	1234
Royalty and Cess paid to GoO				24.16	35.35

Table 7. Nalco's profits and the royalty/tax it pays to GoO (in crores of rupees)[28]

(Rate of Royalty/taxes per ton of bauxite = Rs. 64.62
Transfers to GoO = of 2.29% of profit before tax)

The economics of Nalco exemplifies the prospect that is drawing the world's aluminium companies to Odisha. Many observers are amazed that Nalco has not yet been privatised. When we passed through Angul in mid-2003, and tried to visit Nalco's smelter, our visit coincided with high drama at the smelter gates. Nalco was being offered for sale (disinvestment). Suspicious of everyone, the management could not allow us in. Just the day after we visited, Nalco employees—mindful of the scandalous sell-off of Balco two years before—threw stones at a Hindalco team and prevented their entry.

The high charge around this issue shows in the discourse during this period. Strong pressure had built up to sell off Nalco, which most Nalco employees and the majority of Odias strongly and successfully resisted. A letter from Nalco officers to the Prime Minister, dated 14 July 2003 is particularly revealing, pointing out Nalco's 'unparalleled track record' of high profits, bringing large sums to the governments of India and Orissa. The main arguments are as follows:

1–3. Nalco is a *'core sector ... mining-based industry with bauxite deposit (5th largest in the world) at its disposal.'* It has *'miniratna'* status, and selling it would lead to an aluminium monopoly in India.
4. It pays an annual dividend to the State of 60 per cent.
5. *'Disinvestment through IPO sale will lead to back door entry of private owners whose sole aim is to take away the bauxite deposit at the earliest possible opportunity. The State and the Nation will lose huge financial profit in the long run.'*
6. Nalco is *'a jewel in the crown with unmatched records'*, far more profitable than Balco was or than its main competitor in the private sector, Hindalco.
7-8. With its current expansion complete in 2004, it would give an even higher profit margin. If privatised the huge amounts of foreign exchange it earns would go to private hands.

Saying that Nalco 'has at its disposal' the world's fifth largest deposit reminds us that all Odisha's deposits may originally have been earmarked for the company. At any rate, the security of Nalco's position vis-a-vis its ore source is highly significant in the context of the strong emphasis on security of tenure in the new National Mineral Policy being promulgated since 2006, and in the influence of mining companies such as Rio Tinto on this policy.[29]

A drop in the value of the dollar since April 2007 brought an unexpected 11 per cent decline in export earnings to Nalco, losing the company 120 crore per month over the following 6 months, and December 2008 saw it enter a worse crisis.[30]

When Nalco started up, many observers advocated that its produce should all be kept within India and not exported. Dependence on exports builds a fragility into the company that is only now showing. Sudden loss, for Nalco and other companies, is built into the system of 'dollarisation'. Tying India's economy to the dollar brought inevitable inequities due to rigged foreign exchange rates and control (Sunil 2004).[31]

London's *Financial Times* gave a pro-privatisation view in November 2003: 'Holding onto Orissa's Jewels: Sale of Nalco, the State company, has been stalled', which describes the disappointment of BHP Billiton, Pechiney, Hindalco, and Chinese, Russian and Brazilian aluminium companies, which had all hoped to buy a stake in Nalco until Naveen finally sided with Nalco employees and opposed the sale.[32] The article reveals that a major share of Nalco's foreign earnings come from selling alumina to the smelters in Bahrain and the United Arab Emirates, powered by cheap natural gas, and that Nalco makes a profit out of paying a toll to have alumina smelted there ('tollsmelting'). This article forecasts a 5 per cent growth in Indian demand for aluminium, and describes the Niyamgiri lease with considerable distortion: 'Sterlite recently acquired from Orissa 73 million tonnes of bauxite deposits, with a promise of an additional 77 million tonnes.' As we have seen, without any guarantee of forest clearance, this 'acquisition' is of dubious validity. Yet this rash statement, strategically placed in the *FT*, probably played an important part in building Vedanta's street-cred to launch it on London's Stock Exchange a month later—alongside the influence of Brian Gilbertson, DFID officials, and British and Indian government contacts. The 'promise of an additional 77 million tons' raises questions. Is this the highest peak of Niyamgiri, in the centre of the range—one of the most sacred spots in tribal Odisha?

The construction of a road to the Dongria village of Dhamanapanga in 2007–09 makes this a distinct possibility.

An article one year later, 'Investor interest grows …', repeats this error, along with an upped forecast of a 7 per cent aluminium growth rate in India:

> On the assurance that it will build a 1 million ton alumina refinery with the 'option to set up an aluminium smelter' of 220,000 tonne annual capacity in the downstream, Vedanta has secured the right to mine bauxite at a 75 million ton deposit at Lanjigarh.[33]

This was false—this right had not been secured and was about to be contested in a court case lasting over 3 years. An article in *Aluminium International Today*, 'Orissa—the newly emerged "Klondike" of India' reinforces a view of great new possibilities opening up for aluminium companies in India.[34]

The Jamaica Bauxite Institute was set up in 1976 to remedy an acute lack of reliable information available to Jamaica's government and citizens about bauxite trading and other aspects of the aluminium industry. The JNARRDC by contrast has played no role in keeping Indian government servants—let alone the general public—informed in a business where 'Facts means money'.[35]

The market in alumina and aluminium goes through extraordinary contortions. Demand goes up and down, often very fast. Demand from China has been one significant factor among many influencing alumina and aluminium prices recently. While the Lanjigarh refinery was being built, China was buying large quantities of alumina from abroad to supply its numerous, relatively small smelters. Several of these have since been ordered to be closed. As a result, China's alumina import has dropped drastically, and within one week around 1 September 2006 the world alumina price fell by 22 per cent as a result.

Since 1977, aluminium prices have been set 5 days a week at the London Metals Exchange (LME). This institution plays a decisive role in the industry. Prices are set in the 'outcry' which happens in the second 5 minute trading period for aluminium soon after midday, Monday to Friday, using obscure hand and finger gestures between traders. Through the viewing gallery, it is hard for a non-initiate to comprehend what is really happening in the bull ring below. Only

12 out of 80 registered member companies are full Ring Dealing Members with an 'exclusive right to trade in the ring'. Among these is Barclays Bank. Other leading banks in the second category of Associate Broker Clearing Members include ABN AMRO, Merrill Lynch, J. P. Morgan, Morgan Stanley, Citigroup, Deutsche Bank, Goldman Sachs, and HSBC. The third category of Associate Trade Clearing Members includes Glencore, Hunter Douglas and Hydro Aluminium. The fourth category, Associate Broker Members includes Alcan, BHP Billiton, Mitsui, Noranda, Pechiney and Rio Tinto.[36] But on the floor who is who? The Punjabi man at the door told us that everyone inside was a millionaire and only traders from certain British families are allowed to partake!

Banks which invest in mining projects thus play a vital role behind the aluminium companies, as we saw in the original set-up of US aluminium companies, such as Alcoa and Kaiser. And behind the banks, hedge funds and other speculators. Barclays, for instance, a leading UK investor, manages hedge funds which are known to have bought up a substantial portion of Vedanta's shares when it started up in London in December 2003. When the hedge funds sold these on, at a profit, Vedanta's share price temporarily fell. This caused Vedanta to issue more shares.

Hedging's original purpose was to hedge bets for security, but this has now led to the surreal game of futures trading, where 3-month, 15-month and 27-month contracts are traded for huge short-term gains. How much mining is actually fuelled by this betting game of speculation? Peter Robbins has drawn attention to this, a commodity analyst who often made $200,000 a day speculating on metal deals at the LME during the 1960s–80s, but points out now that

> Third world governments everywhere find their expectations of a tax bonanza swiftly evaporate as mining companies transfer profits out of the country and mineral prices internationally remain very low. (Peter Robbins 1998)

The LME registers warehouses as delivery points for deals: 7 in Britain and 16 in Europe, plus more outside added in recent years: one in Singapore (registered 1987), 16 in Japan (from 1989), 10 in the US (starting 1991), and one in Dubai (1999). Several recent scandals have occurred when stocks in warehouses did not match deals being done.[37]

The price of aluminium is notorious for its fluctuations, caused sometimes by wars (which push the price up as the arms industry increases its sales), but also by shortages (or fear of them), overproduction (pushing prices down), speculation and stockpiling—not just by governments, but also by companies, which have often promoted a shortage to push the price up. Worldwide prices of the 3 basic commodities in 2007–8 averaged:

Bauxite around $30 per ton [metric ton]

Alumina $300-600 per ton, with large fluctuations

Aluminium's average price averaged $2,450 per ton in 2007 ($3,200–1,586 July–Dec 08)

To summarise fluctuations in the aluminium price, as fixed by daily tradings at the LME (London Metals Exchange) five times a week: between 1978 and 2004, prices ranged between $1,000 and $2,000 per ton, dropping to $978 in 1982 and peaking at $2,582 in 1988. Since 2005 it has mostly stayed above $2,000, peaking at $3,240 in May 2006, and $3,200 in July 2008, but dropping to $1,870 in November.[38]

Demand from China has been a main cause of the rise, as well as a stabilisation or fall when Chinese demand drops. China has the largest number of smelters of any country—53 in 1995, rising to 138 in 2002 with another 47 under construction.[39] But many came under pressure to close when the over-capacity problem became acute. The country imports alumina for these smelters from India and other countries, as well as large quantities of aluminium scrap for recycling. Alumina prices have fluctuated sharply, rising from $140-180 in 2002, and peaking at over $500 in 2004.

LME prices are in three categories—primary aluminium, aluminium alloys and 'NASAAC'—'North American Special Aluminium Alloys Contracts'. The former is pure, while the latter two involve alloys and recycling that concern auto markets, etc., and are around 10 per cent lower than primary prices. The LME trades only copper, nickel, tin, lead, zinc, and these three categories of aluminium, though steel is reportedly due to be added soon. Traders at the LME trade these categories for cash in the present, as well as in futures trading in which aluminium stocks are sold (whether or not they already exist as finished metal ingots or still lie as deposits in the earth) at 3, 15 or 27 months in the future. This is in order to hedge the risk of prices changing—supposedly 'the opposite of speculation' but in practice, an extreme form of it. Prices are thus regularly manipulated by many hidden factors, in a 'game' likened to poker.

When Vedanta was launched on the London Stock Exchange (December 2003), this was done through a record IPO sale (Initial Public Offering) by J. P. Morgan for $879 million.[40] To put Vedanta's launch in London into its proper context, Morgan's issue of Vedanta bonds forms part of a pattern of a massive rise in finance to mining companies, consisting of various forms of loans and speculation. To show the rates of increase in various markets for the seven years from 2000 to 2006 (from Morrison 2007):

	Increase from	to	approx. rate of increase
Loans to projects	$20 billion	$60b	3 X
Issue of bonds	$2b	$10b	5 X
Specific project finance	$0.4b	$3.2b	8 X
Mergers & Acquisitions	$17b	$134b	8 X
The IPO market	$0.82b	$6.7b	82 X

Table 8. Increases in mining finance, 2000–07

Among the pricing riddles that need demasking, we should include: the use of transfer pricing and technology transfer, manipulation of the exchange rate, and use of tax haven holding companies in dealings between India and other countries. The rise in profits is exponential as one progresses further downstream, from bauxite (where profits are minimal or negative), to alumina, to aluminium ingot, to rolled and extruded products, to alloys (especially those used in aerospace/defence). Indian aluminium consumption is expanding extremely fast in four main sectors: *construction* of a new style of aluminium-rich buildings, the *auto* industry, using higher aluminium quotas to save weight, the *arms and aerospace* industry, including missiles and satellites, and *packaging* with foil and flexibles (product mix with plastics).

In June 2007 an IPO sale for Sterlite (SIIL) in the US was underwritten by Merrill Lynch, Morgan Stanley and Citigroup, whose report is explicit about numerous risks, including the danger that mining leases sought for bauxite, copper and zinc might not be forthcoming.[41]

A cartel in all but name

Keeping the price of bauxite far too low is where the cartel comes in. But what is a cartel? *Webster's Dictionary* defines it as 'a combination of independent firms or enterprises formed to control a market, for example by keeping up prices, monopolising production, etc.; a political alliance or bloc.' Among obsolete meanings are 'a written challenge' and 'an agreement for exchange of prisoners', and the original meaning is 'a card with writing on it'—ironic in the light of modern usage, since cartels are illegal (at least under US law), so formal organisation on paper cannot exist.

The combination of economic meaning (price control and monopoly) and political alliance is significant, since the power represented by cartels joins governmental power with economic control. Cartels create monopolies, so can be seen as against the principles of free trade and competition; but by those who promote them, cartels represent the apex of free market competition and 'survival of the fittest'—an ultimate in competition which paradoxically diminishes competition.

The classic examples of cartels include Rockerfellar's Standard Oil, J. P. Morgan's US Steel Corporation, Alcoa's control during crucial periods over a world aluminium cartel, and De Beers' Central Selling Organisation, which controls 80 per cent of the gem diamond trade. These are essentially trader-cartels, whereas OPEC and the IBA are exporting country or producer cartels. The aluminium cartel is well-known, and in what follows, we draw from others' research (e.g. Holloway 1988, Lynch 2002).[42] The existence of a cartel controlled by the US administration is attested by Stiglitz (2002, pp. 171–79). Aluminium was born in the age of the 'great trusts' set up by the Robber Barons. Smelters had to be on a huge scale, because of the vast amount of electricity required to split aluminium from its natural, earth-bound bonding with oxygen (Al_2 from O_3). So the aluminium companies formed cartels from the start, and to trace the history of this process in some detail brings into clear focus recurring patterns—what anthropologists would term the aluminium industry's *deep structure*.

Cartel 1. From the start, the Pittsburgh Reduction Company took steps to ensure a monopoly in the US, first against Hall's original backer, the Cowles Brothers—a dispute that ended when Pittsburgh paid the Cowles' a large sum to depart the scene (1891–1903). At the same time, against European competition, Pittsburgh lobbied the US government to impose an 8 cents duty per pound of imported aluminium (when the going rate was 33 cents per pound) in 1897, and also started buying up the major bauxite reserves in America, along with the mining companies that ran them: Georgia Bauxite and Mining (1894), General Bauxite Co. in Arkansas (1906) and Republic Mining in Alabama (1909). The name 'Aluminum Company of America', officially used from 1907, suggests a national monopoly. Hall's 20-year patent expired in 1909, so the monopoly which Hall's patent had ensured was now guaranteed by an extraordinary 'integration' of ownership that included all major bauxite deposits in America, all refineries and smelters, fabricators and rolling mills, as well as 'downstream' firms like the Aluminum Cooking Utensil Company, and major hydropower projects—ten times more power than it needed for its smelters!—and shipping and rail companies. Meanwhile, in Europe, there were four main aluminium companies:

- PCAC (Produits Chimiques d'Alais et de la Camargue), the first aluminium company started by Deville in the 1850s, which became Pechiney, in France.
- SEMF (Société Electro-Metallurgique Française) in France (at Froges).
- AIAG (Aluminium Industrie Aktien Gesellschaft) in Switzerland, with German interests, which became Alusuisse.
- BAC (British Aluminium Corporation) in Britain.

The first cartel involved monopolies on the Héroult-Hall process, after Héroult sold his process to AIAG, and later to BAC. Alcoa sold its Hall process to PCAC in rivalry with SEMF, and reached an agreement with AIAG not to enter each other's markets.

Cartel 2. On 2 November 1901 a fuller agreement was signed by these first five aluminium companies, assigning them quotas, with an agreement not to sell into each other's markets. Alcoa could not be involved directly according to US Anti-Trust Law, so on 31 October—two days before the cartel was formed!—it formed its Canadian subsidiary Alted or 'Northern' (later Alcan) to sign on its behalf, reserving a 21 per cent share in world production. The cartel enforced a world price of 36 cents, increasing profits, except that Alcoa by prior agreement kept to 33 cents, and shifted to the new price in 1906.

Cartel 3 in 1906 attempted to re-affirm the 1901 system, but failed and wound up in 1908.

Cartel 4 between Alcoa and AIAG also had limited duration and effects, so by 1910 European aluminium companies were selling in the US, where the price dropped to 22 cents.

Cartel 5 was proposed by Alcoa's President Andrew Davis on a trip to Europe in 1911—just when Rockefellar's Standard Trust was being broken up by the US Justice Department, which next turned to investigate Alcoa. The company was doing well, with profits stabilising at around 20 per cent. Alcoa signed a Consent Decree on 7 June 1912, agreeing not to take part in any cartel activity in Europe or the US. Five days later its Canadian subsidiary, Alted or Northern Aluminium, signed the European cartel on Alcoa's behalf!

The First World War broke the cartel apart. VAW formed in Germany, and its first plants were built using hydropower in neutral Norway. Aluminium-production increased exponentially, and after the war, Europe started dumping aluminium in America, undermining Alcoa's monopoly. Alcoa responded by buying into the new European assets—50 per cent of Norsk Aluminium, 50 per cent of Societa del'Alumino Italiano, and large shares in Der Norske Nitrid and Alumino Espanol, along with their factories, hydro-plants, bauxite mines and the companies running them—the Société des Bauxite Françaises, and three Yugoslav companies between 1922 and 1926.

Alcoa's financial head, Andrew Mellon, was US Treasury Secretary at this time—reportedly overseeing this expansion in secret transatlantic phone-calls, and presumably masterminding Alcoa's participation through Alted in *Cartels 6* and *7* (1923 and 1926), which re-established quotas and limited the competition, standardising delivery prices, etc. An ancillary Zurich Agreement in 1930 divided up the Japanese market, and later agreements divided up India and Russia too. Alted had now become Alcan, in charge of Demba in Guyana, while Alcoa kept Suriname.

Cartel 8 was agreed on another Andrew Davis trip to Europe in 1930. All the major aluminium companies signed an Alliance Aluminium Compagnie at Montreal in 1931—a 'super-firm' incorporated in Switzerland. The Alcoa-Alcan combine now controlled 50 per cent of world production, protected against anti-trust laws by Mellon's Treasury post.

Popular opinion blamed Mellon for the Depression and displaced him in 1931. President Hoover protected him by making him ambassador to Britain, but after 11 months, Hoover was out too, and Roosevelt won a Democrat victory to make a New Deal. Mellon was impeached in 1932, facing a gruelling court case. This included charges that he was still controlling Alcoa and Gulf Oil while he was Treasury Secretary in a flagrant conflict of interest. He had given big rebates to industry, promoted use of aluminium in major public construction work, and was thought to have been behind a rise in tariffs on aluminium imports.[43] Proof of this was lacking, and he was cleared, but (like Clive and Hastings in England over a hundred years before) his reputation was severely dented. Donating his art collection as the new National Museum in Washington was, in part, a gesture to regain his lost respectability.

The AAC stabilised prices and divided up the market between five dominant companies.[44] But then VAW started to supply aluminium on a mass scale to build Hitler's airforce, and left the Alliance, becoming for a while the world's biggest aluminium company. Re-armament in America and Europe boosted sales, helping to end the Depression—at the cost of war and imposed industrialisation. Or,

> As John Kenneth Galbraith so aptly expressed it, the Great Depression never ended, it just merged into the war economy. (Neeraj 2001, p. 15)

This war economy gave a tremendous boost to Alcoa. From 1937 the company faced a formal complaint and investigation under Anti-Trust Law, but was cleared—or at least encouraged to appeal—by

Judge Caffey in 1940. During the war, Alcoa helped build and run eight new US smelters. As the war progressed, the US and UK governments blacklisted the cartel, which was still operating, and whose last known meeting was in May 1944. Alcan requested the cartel's dissolution in 1945. The same year, in a continuation of the Caffey case, Judge Learned Hand penalised Alcoa for being a monopoly, ordering the sale of the 8 new surplus smelters, in a judgment severe on the surface, but actually lenient and pro-Alcoa (Smith 1988, pp. 201–14).

The new aluminium plants were sold off at a third of their cost to Reynolds and Kaiser/Permanente. In this division, Alcoa got 51 per cent of production capacity, Reynolds 29 per cent, and Kaiser 20 per cent. Alcoa petitioned in 1947 to be recognised as no longer a monopoly, but in another long and complex case, Judge Knox's verdict in 1950 was that Alcan and Alcoa must disinvest from each other, since nine individuals (particularly from the Davis, Mellon and Hunt families) owned 46.3 per cent of Alcoa and 44.7 per cent of Alcan. These individuals now had to invest in one or another company but not in both. In other words, Knox made the fiction of the two companies' separation into a fact (Smith, pp. 269–76)—though they were still coordinated.

Cartel 9. After this ruling by Knox, North America was divided between four vertically integrated giant aluminium companies, with Alcoa 'leading off on price' (above, p. 277). Competition also came from Europe: Pechiney and Alusuisse invested in new aluminium plants in the US through new subsidiaries. When BAC tried to do the same and built a smelter in the US, it overstretched its finances. This is when Reynolds staged its takeover in the great London aluminium war, by merging with Tube Investment Ltd. (a British aluminium fabricator firm) in May 1957, and buying up 80 per cent of BAC's stock by January 1959.

This was the era of six big aluminium companies: Pechiney, Alusuisse and the four American companies. Relative stability was taken as a sign of cartel management behind the scenes, though now completely secret—*'for there is a "managed" price of metal'*, as Anderson admitted (1951). The cartel was most evident in the great consortia in Ghana, Guinea, Australia, Brazil and other local companies, which joined the big aluminium companies in Joint Ventures in many different combinations. It was also evident in the Aluminum Association (AA, Washington, 1933), the Aluminium Federation (Alfed, Birmingham, UK, 1962), and the International Primary Aluminium Insitute (IPAI, London, 1972), which later became the IAI. In 1975, when the European Economic Commision began a three-year investigation into the cartel, it found evidence of foreign companies 'swapping' to save transport costs, and buying up cheap surplus Russian aluminium to resell at the standard aluminium company rate. European aluminium producers had created a Liechtenstein-registered company in 1963 that appeared to be a front for the cartel, named the International Fair Trade Practice Rules Administration (Holloway 1988, p. 35).

10. The Bauxite Cartel and the Aluminium Cartel. When Michael Manley in Jamaica coordinated with Guyana, Guinea and other countries to form the International Bauxite Association in 1974, they quickly more than doubled the world price of bauxite. But setting this up faced an obstacle course.

In Guinea, Halco (Harvey aluminium company) made an independent bid to enter the market. It had built a small smelter in Oregon, and imported alumina from Japan when the big four US aluminium companies would not sell to it. Newly independent Guinea was trying to assert majority control over its bauxite and alumina business, against pressure from the big countries to let them keep control. So Halco and Guinea formed a joint venture, but needing capital, they turned to the WB, which made a study costing $2 million, whose verdict was: the project was too small and should be made six times bigger! Halco could not finance this, so a consortium was formed where it was joined in its 51 per cent ownership of the Sangaredi bauxite plateau by Pechiney, Alcan, Alcoa, VAW and Montecatini. Halco was soon after swallowed up by Marietta Martin. The aluminium cartel had now joined a newly independent government in a joint venture, but done so by getting rid of an independent rival (Holloway, pp. 33 and 45).

OPEC's formation in 1973 swiftly tripled Jamaica's oil import bill. This created a momentum, and in November 1973, Jamaica, Guyana, Suriname, Guinea, Australia and Yugoslavia met in Belgrade to form the IBA on the OPEC model. In March 1974 it was formally established with a seventh member, Sierra Leone. Manley's government in Jamaica increased bauxite revenue from $27 million in 1972–3 to $200m in 1974, and his government swiftly negotiated 51 per cent ownership of the Kaiser mines. Deals were done with all four of the big American aluminium companies by 1978, leaving one small aluminium company out, Revere Copper & Brass, who had been dependent on the cheap bauxite, and could not pass on the increase in aluminium's price.[45]

As for the big aluminium companies, they used the IBA to increase their prices and stabilise their pricing system. When aluminium started being traded at the LME in 1977, the *Business Week* reported that 'aluminium's bosses are beaming'. Essentially the IBA was sharing increased profits with them. 'IBA staff and company personnel attend each other's parties and seem on wholly friendly terms.' [46] In a 1981 meeting of the IBA to which the aluminium companies were invited, the speeches of executives were followed by brief 'clarifications' by their lawyers, to disclaim any *'collusive overtones'*—implying, in other words, that with lawyers' help, an unacknowledged cartel-style collaboration was standard: all working together, Alcoa still leading off on price, but no public sign of collusion.

So within a few years of its formation, the IBA was apparently coordinating with the aluminium cartel, its challenge swallowed up, never again to push for such high bauxite prices, especially after Australia and Brazil, with fully integrated industries, brought the price down again. The original IBA initiative proposed that mining wealth should be openly assessed, and profits shared with local people, affected or displaced—as the Extractive Industries Review recommended in 2003.[47]

Yet the reality is that this has hardly ever happened. The IBA rebellion has been the only concerted attempt to get a fair price for bauxite, and it lasted only a few years. And when Third World governments try (against the balance of power and all the odds) to negotiate a higher price for their produce, the benefits do not necessary trickle down to local affected people, or challenge corporate control (Girvan 1976).

11. O'Neill's cartel. In 1994 Paul O'Neill, as head of Alcoa, masterminded a cartel under US control. Josef Stiglitz witnessed its formation when he was on Clinton's Council of Economic Advisers. Russia was selling its stocks of aluminium at a price that undercut other companies, due to a 'cutback in Russian aluminium use for military planes'. This contributed to a world lowering of aluminium prices and in early 1994, US aluminium companies accused Russia of dumping—incorrect in Stiglitz's view. US companies wanted to keep control of the trade, and prices high. By claiming Russia was dumping, and getting this claim 'verified' by the Department of Commerce on the basis of America's 'fair trade laws' (relatively easy as the Department acts as judge, jury and prosecutor), the companies were trying to keep Russian aluminium out by making it face 'anti-dumping duties'—a 'tariff wall' against foreign imports.

But Paul O'Neill, as head of Alcoa, proposed something far beyond this: a global aluminium cartel, aiming at restricting output through quotas, to keep prices high and stable. America was supposed to be promoting free trade. This cartel went in the opposite direction. It was blatant protectionism, promoting US interests against those of other countries.

> O'Neill's interest was no surprise to me; what did surprise me was that the US government would not only condone a cartel but actually play a pivotal role in setting one up... Cartels are illegal inside the United States. And they should be illegal globally.... For the United States now to help create a global cartel was a violation of every principle.[48]

Most people in the Council of Economic Advisers and the Justice Department were furious at the idea, Stiglitz says. He and others in the President's Council were allies of the Anti-Trust Division of the Justice Department, and opposed this cartel. But the Head of the Council, Robert Rubin, along with the State Department, supported O'Neill's move, and Alcoa got its way:

> in a heated subcabinet meeting, a decision was made to support an international cartel.... With a cartel, each country would be given certain quotas, amounts of aluminium they could produce or export. The ministries would control who got the quotas. This was the kind of system with which they were familiar, the kind of system that

they loved. I worried that the excess profits generated by the trade restrictions would give rise to a further source of corruption. We did not fully grasp that in the new Mafiaised Russia, it would also give rise to a bloodbath in the struggle for who got what quotas.

O'Neill officially left his position as Alcoa's head and became Treasury Secretary under George W. Bush, a post which also pretty much controls the WB and IMF, and plays a decisive role in deciding US policy at home and abroad. In this transition from head of Alcoa to Treasury Secretary, he followed in Andrew Mellon's footsteps 78 years before.

At the very same time as O'Neill's aluminium cartel was being sanctioned, the US Enrichment Corporation (USEC) made a deal to import Russian de-activated nuclear warheads and bring them to the US for use in nuclear reactors. But the import of Russian uranium, like Russian aluminium, was labelled as 'dumping', and in 1996, Stiglitz came across a secret agreement in which USEC itself refused a double or triple quantity of Russian de-activated uranium from Russia's Ministry of Atomic Energy, and gave them $50 million as 'hush money' to keep this secret. Russians

> were told that trade liberalisation was necessary for a successful market economy, yet when they tried to export aluminium and uranium (and other commodities as well) to the United States, they found the door shut.... They were told that competition is vital ... yet the US government was at the centre of creating a global aluminium cartel, and gave the monopoly rights to import enriched uranium to the US monopoly producer.

In 1998, Clinton's administration privatised USEC—a process involving considerable corruption, using the bogus claim that USEC would help de-activate Russia's nuclear warheads. The real plan was for uranium to travel in the opposite direction—essentially, for American nuclear waste to be dumped in Russia. In 2001, Putin got the Duma to pass a law allowing the import of nuclear material. The US institution overseeing this scheme was the Non-Proliferation Trust (NPT Inc.), presided over by ex-CIA officers and Thomas Cochran of the Natural Resources Defence Council (NRDC), which has played a major role in 'greenwashing' environmentally destructive policies, including the selling of 'pollution credits'—a scheme first implemented by the TVA in 1992 with highly dubious results. By 1997 the US was selling pollution credits to Russia, with support from the NRDC and Environment Defence Fund.

As we saw in the previous chapter, privatising Russia's aluminium involved mafia wars and murders, as rival companies tried to get the quotas now being imposed from the US, with Russian Ministries handing these out for bribes, and the highly suspect role of Marc Rich.

Stiglitz strongly opposed the IMF's treatment of Russia. First, they insisted on 'shock therapy' rapid privatisation. When it was clear this was bringing in gross corruption, they sided with those responsible for it. Anatoly Chubais in particular, who had orchestrated a 'loans-for-share scam', and was seen as particularly corrupt, was treated with a show of hospitality by Larry Summers, Deputy Treasury Secretary, who exercised key control in the WB. (In India Arun Shourie, Minister for Disinvestment during the BJP years when Balco was sold to Sterlite, played a somewhat similar role). The position of Chubais was symptomatic of the foreign pressure on Russia to privatise, and the deals being made for the privatisation of particular assets were corrupt in their essence. In Russia, as in India now, it was the ideology and greed of the businessmen that forced the pace of privatisation. That it was a disaster for most of the population did not seem to matter, compared to the huge profits being made by directors, banks and certain politicians.

How the cartel works is secret by definition. In the public domain there are accounts of the pre-war cartels, and a small number of refences to cartel formations since (e.g. Holloway 1988, Stiglitz 2002).

The essence of the aluminium cartel is that it cuts between government, banks and industry, and that it prevents a 'free market' in bauxite. Its hand is plain in the ruthless undermining of opposition to US aluminium companies in Guyana, Suriname, Ghana, Guinea, Jamaica and elsewhere—control exercised, among other channels, through the WB and CIA, and aptly termed *corporate imperialism* by Norman Girvan (1976).

The cartel witnessed by Stiglitz in the 1990s continues a pattern set by Alcoa under Davis and Mellon in the 1900s–1930s. This concerns the fixing of prices and quotas, and the removal or circumvention of tariffs and monopolies. At a more general level, one could use the term loosely to indicate the exercise of power in the interests of corporations, by close coordination between corporate directors and government experts on aluminium in the top countries. Usually these people don't talk or write about what they do. Anderson (1951) is an exception. Apart from the WB, we glimpse the role of DFID (Chapter Sixteen), the influence of Alfed on MPs,[49] and the influence of Credit Rating Agencies and the financial press in promoting certain companies or projects.

More recently, its hand is visible—coordinating with other top mining companies—in the formation of the MMSD, International Council on Mining & Minerals (ICMM) and their Global Reporting Initiative (GRI). Influence from these organisations, and from particular mining companies such as Rio Tinto, is visible on India's new Mining Policy (Chapter Seven). Influence from top banks, such as Deutsche Bank, HSBC, ABN AMRO, Barclays, J. P. Morgan Cazenove, is also a key factor in the power structure. The IAI, EAA, AAI (in India) and AA (US) act as lobby groups and coordinate the GRI, etc. With aluminium, the influence of the arms industry and Ministries of Defence in the US, UK and other countries is highly significant, to ensure abundant supply of aluminium for arms.

In each country, the international cartel seems to stimulate similar power structures. In India, for example, a similar pattern of influence is visible in the workings of the Planning Commission and Hoda Committee in formulating policy, with an internal *corporate imperialism* exercised by the heads of key business houses, including influence from FIMI (Federation of Indian Mineral Industries, based in Delhi), and from defence interests and arms manufacturers. Tentatively, we could summarise the cartel's key aims as follows:

1. Keeping bauxite prices low, and preventing a 'free market'
2. Boosting production by raising consumption in all sectors, especially in packaging, construction and the auto sector
3. Lobbying for subsidies and against taxes
4. Keeping aluminium prices advantageous

5. Lobbying for particular projects, often in close coordination with the WB and International Commission on Large Dams (ICOLD, the lobby group for big dams)
6. Because of aluminium's status as a 'strategic metal', to ensure an uninterrupted supply for the richest countries and their arms companies

And within particular countries and regions, such as India and Odisha? At least twice since 2006 the state government has had the honour of a visit from Alcoa officials, showing that the king of aluminium companies has its sights on Odisha. But cartel activity also shows in coordination between other aluminium companies, including Alcan, Indal, Hindalco, Vedanta, BHP Billiton, L&T, Nalco, Jindal, Dubal, RAK and others, in attempting to mine the region's bauxite and start up projects, with support for 'infrastructure development' by IFAD, the WB, DFID and other international organisations. A report from London accountancy firm Coopers and Lybrand, *Prospects for Industrial Development of Orissa* (April 1996) played a significant role in stimulating interest in the region's aluminium and steel potential.

CHAPTER TWELVE

The Real Costs of Production

Consuming Al

Shiny. Light. Easy to use. Aluminium is a symbol of prosperity and marketability at the heart of modern capitalism and advertising.

> Aluminium is essential to modern living. We are never far from its help. Fundamental to air travel in the construction of planes, it is increasingly used to conserve irreplaceable energy resources by saving weight in every other mode of transport—ship, bus, car, train and truck. Its durability and insulation characteristics save costly maintenance in modern buildings: its electrical properties help to bring electricity and information to our homes and offices.
> But it is in the realm of packaging that aluminium has become most obviously an essential part of our everyday lifestyle.
> All packaging saves resources by conserving and delivering food and other essentials....
> From the very first moments of the day, freshness comes in aluminium tubes, aerosols and foil-laminated sachets. Impervious aluminium-foil and tubes guard the product's quality until the moment of use. Sometimes we need to 'freshen-up' inside too! [1]

This text from a glossy EAA brochure on packaging spells out a subliminal message we have all grown up with, geared to raising our aluminium consumption, which has increased massively over the years. Be modern! Be efficient! Be safe! Consume!

Increasing aluminium consumption out of a 'dismally low level' to create a more 'developed' lifestyle on the western model is at the heart of 'India shining' imagery, and visions of a 'developed India'.[2] National pride is invoked to increase consumption, even though an environmental consciousness would view India's low consumption as way ahead of 'developed' countries in terms of sustainability.

The packaging message has certainly got through. *Gutka* foils, chips packets and Tetra-Packed fruit juices draw customers on every market road in India. The country's car industry is taking off, though Tata's new, lightweight (aluminium-rich) Nano car, due to hit the roads in 2008, hit the farmers in Singur instead, whose opposition, after numerous gruesome killings, eventually drove Tata's car factory out of West Bengal, to Gujarat, and delayed the project.[3] The new style of lightweight car is advertised as 'fuel-efficient' on the basis of its high aluminium content, replacing steel—the 'green metal' claim, on which more below. India's roads are filling up with cars and motorbikes at breakneck speed—a classic case of *conspicuous consumption* in a country where a motorbike has been a prime 'dowry gift' for many years.[4]

The biggest shift in India was the ending in 1989 of the control order reserving 49 per cent of aluminium for cables to bring electricity to all India's villages (Chapter Eight). Visiting villages on the edge of Indravati reservoir, who were promised electricity by the dam-builders, but never received it and live in extreme neglect, one realises how much was left behind then.

Elsewhere, the construction sector is booming, including alumina-reinforced cement. Forward linkages involve numerous industries that make use of aluminium, from food companies and pharmaceuticals to car, boat, train and plane manufacturers. *Paan* shops offer over a dozen different strips of spicy chewing mixtures, individually wrapped in aluminium-plastic packages. Street sweepers incinerate thousands of aluminium foils every day, oblivious of the toxic compounds released into the atmosphere.

	Worldwide	Recycled	India before 1989	India 1996
Transport	26%	60–95%		22%
Packaging	20%	30%	7%	16%
Construction	20–22%	85%		8%
Electrical	9%		52%	34%
Other	25%			

Table 9. Consumption by sector [5]

The EAA packaging manifesto continues, alongside tempting, glossy photos of shiny packaged chocolates and juices:

> The long-life freshness of fruit juice depends on a hidden layer of aluminium in the carton [the Tetra Pak technology]. Milk and cream portions have a peelable lid of aluminium foil reducing exposure to light which can affect the taste and food value of delicate dairy products. Alufoil butter wraps also shut out the light from the product's surface, so eliminating rancidity and moisture loss, and protecting its flavour.
>
> Ready when you are—coffee comes fresh from high performance foil-laminated vacuum packs.... Only the best barrier is good enough to keep this moisture-sensitive product from rapid deterioration....
> At Christmas, Easter and on special days throughout the year, the glitter of aluminium foil-wrapped chocolate is never far away....
> Aluminium Cans are outstanding in their design potential—a very bright finish, and the right malleability to suit special shapes and embossing.
>
> The toiletry sector is one of the most enthusiastic and effective users of aluminium, whether in the shape of aerosol cans, bottles, tubes, sachets or in the closure and embellishment of high quality perfumery....
>
> People in a hurry know well the convenience of foil-packed take-away meals. Pop them in a hot oven to cook or brown while you prepare the table: there's no melt-down! Every day, thousands of airline passengers enjoy piping hot meals thanks to foil dishes. Also on their meal tray travellers may find a foil-lidded juice, foil-wrapped butter and foil sachets....

The counterpoise to this ideology of a modern lifestyle most of us take for granted, is Gandhi's famous maxim that the world has enough resources for everyone's need, but not for everyone's greed. Aluminium company advertising follows in a direct line from Russell's 1836 comment that new tastes and wants promoted among the Konds will soon become *'necessities of life'*, providing the best means to control them (above, p. 68). Capitalism enslaves us through our desires. To question the logic of expanding wants built into the mainstream doctrine of unlimited growth and market forces, we need an anthropology of consumption.[6]

The discipline of Ecological Economics offers a means to analyse the present system and assess its sustainability, while the 'Story of Stuff' presents a popular way to look at the out-of-control materialism that enslaves us into insane patterns of consumption.[7] A Gandhian activist's reply to a question of what help Indian villagers need from the West: 'Just reduce your consumption.'

The packaging text reminds us that there is also a literal side to aluminium consumption. As people in cities consume more and more aluminium-wrapped eatables, many tribal people have been laying aside their clay or brass pots, using aluminium ones instead. In a remote area on the border between Odisha and Chhattisgarh, a seller of aluminium pots and pans peddles his wares in tribal villages, bicycling from one village to the next, bringing the aluminium age in the form of cheap and light cooking pots to thousands of Adivasis.

The debate on whether use of aluminium utensils has a role in promoting Alzheimer's disease has not gone away, despite an apparent consensus of scientists that a causal link cannot be proved. Was this consensus achieved through aluminium company-funded science and lobbying?[8]

What is not in question is that a residue of aluminium builds up in humans from three main sources: water supply (where aluminium is added for hygiene and appearance), packaging (which leaches tiny yet significant amounts into the airtight food products) and cooking utensils. Parts of this residue cannot be excreted via the kidneys, and collects in neurons inside the brain. The most authoritative collection of scientific studies of aluminium's link with Alzheimer's is by Exley (2001), who introduces the problem as follows:

> The widespread use of products made from or containing Al is ensuring the omnipresence of Al in our bodies. It is unlikely that Al is absent from any organ, tissue, body fluid or even cell in our body. New research continues to document our continuing exposure to Al … and in some cases has linked the observed burden of Al to human health.… However, the emergence of Al as an environmental toxin has not yet received serious recognition in human toxicology. It is intriguing that the advent of the recognition that the most abundant metal in the lithosphere is inimical to life has not been sufficient by itself to arouse the precautionary principle. (Exley 2001, pp. v–vi)

As we have seen in Chapters Two and Three, in its natural state in the soil, where it is bonded with oxygen and other substances, aluminium is actually a basic element of life, essential for moisture in the soil. But in its pure, separated state, the human body cannot excrete the trace elements of aluminium which are introduced through the three sources mentioned, standard in modern life—even though these are tiny compared with amounts ingested of other minerals.

In water supplies aluminium sulphate is used as a flocculating agent to remove contaminants. The WHO permits 0.2 milligrams per litre of water, an application partly dictated by appearance, to deliver water that is completely clear. It is generally admitted that tiny yet significant amounts leach from foil packaging and cans into the food, drink or medicine inside. So the use of aluminium (like fluoride) in mains water without adequate research on side effects is open to question, as is the huge increase we have seen in aluminium packaging of an ever-expanding range of products in the last ten years, especially in Tetra Packs and other high-tech packaging that moulds layers of aluminium with layers of polymers.

> There is no homeostatic control of the concentration of Al in either the intra cellular or the extracellular environment. Al is a silent visitor to our bodies and its transport and fate are governed by a large number of Trojan Horse-like molecules. We are fortunate that some of these molecules facilitate the removal of Al from our bodies via the kidney. However, other molecules actually contribute towards an increase in the body burden of Al by delivering it to more permanent body stores such as bone and the brain.
>
> The brain is an obvious target for Al intoxication. The longevity of neurones identifies them as sinks for systematic Al. The uptake of Al

into the brain is at least an order of magnitude more efficient than its release ... and this ensures an increase in neuronal Al with age. There can be no dispute over the presence, and indeed accumulation, of Aluminium in the human brain....

Certainly Al is not inert in the body. Wherever it is found it will be biologically available. The question is whether the biological reactivity of Al is sufficient to influence vital biochemical processes or physiological functions in any particular environment. In the brain, during an acute exposure to Al, for example ... the concentration of biologically available Al will be both high and persistent and normally robust biochemistry will be irreversibly altered within a very short timeframe. However when the brain is subjected to a chronic exposure to Al (similar, perhaps, to our everyday exposure to the metal) the concentration of biologically available Al in the human brain will be low, though it will increase with age and it will persist thoughout the lifetime of the individual ... Al has been implicated in every stage of [Alzheimer's] disease and it is only a red mist of controversy and not any decision based on sound scientific principles that has blinded some individuals and organisations to its possible role in the aetiology of the disease. (2001, p. vi–vii)

'Per capita aluminium consumption' thus has effects on the human body—effects that have not been properly researched or understood. Whether an individual consumes economically less than 1 kg or 15–30 kg of aluminium per year obviously determines how much aluminium he or she ingests.

The science is complex. Interpreting the results of research on mice suggests aluminium intake has effects on *tau proteins* consistent with Alzheimer's.[9] But experiments are inconclusive. There is agreement that kidney dialysis treatment involving high levels of aluminium intake produced Alzheimer's, so this treatment was discontinued, but no consensus on whether intake from regular modern sources has negative effects or not. This makes it possible for a book essentially promoting the aluminium industry to discount evidence of the link, and shift the burden of proof to scientists whose work suggests it is dangerous:

The controversy surrounding the relationship between elevated aluminium concentration in drinking water and increased risk of

Alzheimer's disease in elderly populations has ignited the debate about setting standards for aluminium in drinking water. At present there is inadequate scientific basis for setting a health-based standard for aluminium in drinking water.[10]

Surely there is a fault in the scientific methodology here? Asbestos was regarded as innocent till proven guilty: proving its health hazards happened tragically slowly and was fiercely resisted by the industry, leaving a trail of thousands of delayed deaths by cancer. If 'funding determines knowledge', to any degree at all, it's relevant to ask: what proportion of the medical science on aluminium is funded by the aluminium industry?

Recycling Al

Official estimates of the amount of aluminium recycled vary from 20–33 per cent, though since most figures come from lobby groups such as the IAI, it is possible that these are too high. For example, it periodically enters the news that huge quantities of British and American household waste collected by local councils for recycling are actually sold to companies at $80 per ton, who ship them to India where they are land-filled in huge quantities (even though it is illegal by UK law to export material for land-filling). 12–14 million tons of recycling waste are estimated to be exported from the UK per year, and no proper check is kept on whether it is really recycled or dumped. Likewise in the US, basic research by concerned citizens finds the same thing: *'No real recycling was taking place. We were being conned.'*[11]

The International Primary Aluminium Institute in London initiated a Life Cycle Analysis (LCA) of aluminium in 1997, to emphasise the benefits of recycling, and soon after, changed its own name to the IAI, cutting out the emphasis on new, primary metal, and putting out the message that about 30 per cent of aluminium is recycled (highly suspect in our eyes), and that 400–500 million tons of aluminium is in circulation. This shift in emphasis was because

> the Industry needed to develop as complete an understanding as possible of the positive contributions that aluminium makes to the

environment and economic well-being of the world's population as well as of any negative economic or environmental impacts that its production might cause.[12]

Recycling takes an estimated 5 per cent of the energy that smelting primary aluminium takes, and produces 5 per cent of the carbon emissions of primary aluminium.

Numerous speciality alloys used in defence applications, including lithium alloys and MMCs (Metals Matrix Composites), are among the most polluting forms to manufacture, and the least recycled. Tetra Pak is another form too energy-intensive to recycle: micro-thin composite layers of oil derivatives with aluminium may be a sign of technological sophistication, but separating the materials for recycling is very difficult and uneconomic. So most of our fruit juice cartons end up in land-fills. Yet in India, Tetra Pak is promoting these cartons right now, for milk as well as juice, even though recycling is not on the agenda, and milk in Russia is known to have been contaminated through Tetra Pak technology from the company's factory in India.[13]

Tetra Paks are one of aluminium's hidden scandals. We take them for granted now as containers for a huge range of products, including many in the health food industry. Yet the green and environmentally sound image which Tetra Pak promotes is misleading in the extreme. The Rausing family that made its fortune through the Tetra Pak firm has become one of Europe's richest, leaving Sweden in a tax-avoidance scandal, and spending generous amounts on excellent human rights, environmental, cultural and political causes, without directly confronting the environmental and health damage their original products are still responsible for.[14]

In packaging, the best recycling rate is said to be of beverage cans. According to 1990s statistics, 41 per cent are recycled in Europe, more than 62 per cent in the US, and 78–79 per cent in Brazil and Japan, though these figures must be considered suspect for the reasons given above, that what happens to waste set aside for recycling is rarely investigated. In 1990, 7.7 million tons of aluminium were reportedly recycled. But this needs to be set against an estimated 5 million tons landfilled in the same year—1.54 million in the US alone in 1988 according to the US Environmental Protection Agency.[15] The aluminium industry's promotion of can recycling seems an obvious step in the right direction. However,

> While it is commendable (if self-serving) for the aluminium industry to encourage the public to recycle beverage cans ... it may not be enough ... These "feel-good" ads ... convey the overall impression that aluminium consumption does not have serious environmental impacts. Even if beverage cans were recycled at rates approaching 90 per cent, there would still be a need for primary aluminium production to replace the amount landfilled, and [for] ... many other end uses.[16]

Even if a third of world demand was really being met by recycled aluminium, the relentless promotion of aluminium for so many applications represents an unacceptable drain on the earth's resources. Aluminium in construction in European cities is a symbol of affluence, as in packaging ('tomorrow's lifestyle today'), and in cars. The auto sector, which uses standard, easily separated alloys, claims the highest recycling rate of 95 per cent. Yet even Alcan, Hydro, and the lobby associations who stress the 'green metal' argument do not claim that recycling has any effect in actually reducing the amount of bauxite being mined or aluminium being smelted.

'Aluminium is a metal so expensive to refine that it should always be re-used and never thrown away,'[17] which is why 'Aluminium for future generations' is a slogan used by the EAA, a European lobby group. Friends of the Earth rightly join the aluminium industry in promoting recycling, but often without questioning how recycling masks expanding production of new metal.[18]

Many critics claim that the aluminium industry's recycling figures are highly inflated. Since drink cans have particularly been sold on the 'recycling therefore green' ticket, it is appropriate to mention that a press release from the Aluminum Association (Washington DC) in May 2006 prompted a joint press release by the Container Recycling Institute (CRI, also in Washington) and the International Rivers Network (IRN, in Berkeley): *The Aluminium Can's Dirty Little Secret: On-going Environmental Harm Outpaces the Metal's 'Green' Benefits.* The AA claimed, an increase of less than one percentage point in the national [US] aluminium can recycling rate from 51.2 to 52.0 per cent ... but they failed to mention that we still are trashing 800,000 tons of aluminium beverage cans a year....

The beverage and aluminium industries tout the can as the "most recyclable" package in America, said Jennifer Gitlitz, CRI Research director. "But recyclable doesn't necessarily mean recycled. More than half of the 99 billion cans sold in the US last year were landfilled or incinerated." Gitlitz said a similar amount wasn't recycled in other countries, for a total of about 1.5 million tons of wasted cans.

"These trashed cans must be replaced by new cans made entirely from virgin materials," Gitlitz said, "and that is where the environmental damage occurs."

She cited bauxite mining and processing as a major source of water pollution. "Each ton of aluminium cans requires 5 tons of bauxite ore to be strip-mined, crushed, washed, and refined into alumina before it is smelted.... We're talking about immense energy consumption.... While aluminium companies often cite big savings from recycling, they fail to mention that at current wasting levels, about 23 billion kilowatt-hours are squandered globally each year through replacement production."[19]

Worldwide, Gitlitz estimates the industry's annual electricity consumption at 300 billion kilowatt hours—about 3 per cent of the world's consumption. On every continent, as we have seen, whole ecosystems and cultures have been destroyed forever by dams whose main purpose is powering aluminium smelters. At the same time these dams have placed immense, unsustainable debt burdens on these countries.

Eleven US States have 'bottle bill' laws that claim 75-95 per cent recycling of cans. The other States do not, and average 35 per cent recycling. But how reliable are these figures? Who is verifying them? Meanwhile, the relentless smelting of primary metal continues unabated. Carbon emissions by refineries and smelters contributed about 95 million tons of greenhouse gases to our atmosphere in 2005 alone, making the industry one of the worst of all causes of climate change.

Hindalco's acquisition of Novelis puts India in the heart of the system. Novelis controls the biggest aluminium can business, conveniently headquartered in Atlanta, right next to Coca Cola:

> Novelis acquisition puts Indian stamp on every Coke, Budweiser can. ... GRABBING BIGGER PIE: after Novelis buy-out, Hindalco will get access to beverage container market that kicks about 200 billion cans across the world ... (*Times of India*, 14 February 2008)

Hidden externality

Externalities are 'costs of production that companies do not pay for by dumping the costs on the larger society.' They also figure in a more hidden form in the 'metal in traded products and semi-products', which can be a major factor in determining a country's import/export dependence, and consumption patterns.[20] Aluminium's externality denotes the cost of destroying forests and mountains, damming and polluting the flow of water, throwing thousands of people off their land and ruining their lives. Most environmental costs are not factored into the price the metal sells for. Aluminium's externality cost is more than twice that of steel. Some studies estimate its externality cost at $2,000 per ton, over and above its cost of production. So the real cost of producing aluminium is far more than the price it is sold for.[21] As we shall see, even this estimate is much too low.

How could the impact on communities be quantified? Who can put a price on the displacement and break-up of long-established communities of people cultivating the earth and living sustainably on it? And despite varied attempts to do so, how can an accurate figure be placed on the cost of destroying primary forest on the summit of sacred mountains, or disrupting Odisha's rivers and pattern of rainfall? Cost Benefit Analysis can only take us so far. Classical economists equate value with price, whearas ecological economists focus on divergent, incommensurable systems of valuation (Martinez-Alier 2002, pp. 269–71).

Pollution is of many kinds, from the physical poisoning of ecological systems, leading to drastic decline in the land's fertility over a wide area, to a pollution of values, referred to in India as a 'culture of briberisation'.

The externality costs of aluminium are not restricted to the bauxite mines and factories, but also involve the dams and coal mines and power plants which supply each factory with its water and electricity; the new roads and rail lines, and the new ports being constructed in Odisha for export. The dams and coal mines displace large numbers of people in their own right, and the coal-fired power stations have major and little-studied effects in drying out the land around them.

Environmental Impact Assessments are required for all major projects in India since 1994, but as we have seen, EIAs are often extremely shoddy, and involve cut-and-paste methods that sometimes introduce Siberian flora into peninsular India! (above, Chapter Seven) This makes clear a depressing truth, similar to the recycling scam: many people are simply writing what corporate interests dictate.

Producing one ton of aluminium consumes an estimated 1,378.6 tons of water. This information is from the Wuppertal Institute for Climate, Environment and Energy in Germany, one of Europe's most respected study centres for environmental impact. It gives the *material intensity* of producing one ton of aluminium as 85.38 tons of abiotic material (overburden, waste matter, etc.), and 9.78 tons of air (i.e. pollution).[22] We visited this institute in July 2006, where a leading scientist gave us a quick introduction to their key concepts and methods, which focus on quantifying the *Material Input Per Service unit (MIPS)* from *cradle to grave*, calculating the *ecological rucksack* of various products, including their *material intensity*.

Consuming water on this scale has staggering implications for Odisha, where farmers are already aware that water from the Hirakud reservoir is drying up in the canals built to supply them, while new smelters are being given priority. '*We use resources as though we have four earths at our disposal.*'[23] Far from supporting present moves towards huge new investment in nuclear power stations, Wuppertal analysts highlight the dangers of this energy in terms of the costs of uranium mining and subsidies, as well as disposal.

Shortcomings of the Wuppertal models are their failure to include impacts on people and cultures among the externalities they study, and avoidance of outright calls for a massive reducuction in material consumption, stressing instead the idea of an 'eco-efficiency' revolution, which reinforces the 'new green image' promoted by industry lobbyists.[24] Because their funding comes through industry, they help promote new, 'eco-efficient' technology, that reduces destructive impacts only marginally, rather than questioning massive increases in output from new 'greenfield' factories.

By contrast, the discipline of Ecological Economics focuses more holistically on consumption patterns and Energy Flow Analysis, calculating for example the Human Appropriation of Net Primary Production (HANPP), the contrast between equations for countries' Total Energy Requirement, Total Energy Consumption and Physical Trade Balance, and the *Ecological Embeddedness of the Economy* as a whole.[25]

Andrew Simms (2005) shows that that the debts which Third World countries have accumulated towards First World banks, etc., are more than offset by the *ecological debt*, and specifically the *carbon debt*, which the 'developed world' has accumulated and owes to less polluting countries. A recent study applies Simms' model to Odisha, focusing on the pollution and human costs emanating from Nalco (Khatua and Stanley 2006).

The externality cost of carbon emissions alone is calculated at $85 per ton by a recent UK government report, giving at least $1,275 per ton as the carbon cost of aluminium.[26] If other emissions and effluents were properly costed into the industry, including those from sulphur dioxide, fluoride, HFCs, Spent Pot Lining, and Toxic Red Mud, the metal's externality cost per ton would be far above conventional estimates of $2,000 per ton—without even counting the consumption and pollution of water, or bauxite mining. When the Lanjigarh refinery polluted the Bansadhara river within two months of starting production in September 2007, how to calculate these costs?

Classing all these damaging by-products as 'externalities' means they are not included in the cost of production, and it is not the companies that pay these costs: they fall on the host country and local people.

Metal factories are rarely mentioned in most climate change debates, which focus on cars, planes, oil and individual footprints, but little on aluminium or arms. Yet aluminium factories consume 3 per cent of the fossil fuels we burn, making them a major factor in global heating. The IPCC reports on climate change have at last brought a consensus on industrial causes of global warming and a need for a massive cut in GHG emissions to prevent global catastrophe. So how come India is building so many new metal factories, with such glaring pollution costs to the country's own environment?

One answer is a complete absence of the political will necessary to translate the need for cuts into practice. India's high growth rate makes it appear a model of neoliberal success—when the human and environmental costs are disregarded!—leaving the free market free to dictate an acceleration of foreign investment and imposed industrialisation.

Another factor is the recommendations of the IPCC itself, which include carbon trading and biofuels. No-one involved seems to really believe that the system of trading carbon credits really helps to cut emissions. It is promoted cynically as a new way to make money out of climate change and pollution. Many of the 300 or so extremely polluting sponge iron factories in East India receive large sums in the Clean Development Mechanism (CDM) scheme, despite blatent disregard for regulations, that has often been highlighted by the State Pollution Control Boards. Many metal factories receive millions of dollars in carbon credits each year for installing new technology that is supposed to limit their emissions, from factories in the 'developed world' that are 'paying to pollute'. The reality of these sponge iron factories involves displacement of communities, huge water consumption, appalling health and safety records for workers, and pollution levels that have grown no less with new technology. One of the worst, Jindal's giant factory near Raigarh (Chhattisgarh), is earning enormous sums through four separate CDM projects. Even the Hirakud Smelter (now officially Hindalco) was approved for a multi-million dollar CDM grant in October 2007.[27]

Clean Development Mechanism projects are approved and validated in India, as in other countries, by an indulgent authority that clears projects almost as soon as they are submitted, without an adequate process of critical evaluation.[28] The system reflects the way neoliberal economists managed to capture the agenda of IPCC Working Group III, charged with drawing up responses to climate change.[29]

As for biofuels—Vedanta boasts it has been planting a million jatropha bushes a year on 'wasteland' in Chhattisgarh—part of a massive promotion of the biofuel industry that is replacing natural forests and indigenous biodiversity with monoculture plantations. All the mining companies have been acquiring land in excess of what they need for their projects, and jatropha grows easily with little water, since it is efficient at sucking moisture out of the soil (like eucalyptus). Biofuels, like carbon trading, have been shown repeatedly to be a false solution to climate change. But they make money for their promoters. As with carbon trading, hedge funds pour in investment, make profits through speculation, and new, un-needed industries spiral out of control. Fidel Castro was among the first to point out the insanity of planting crops to feed cars when there is already an alarming food scarcity. Already the EU and US have fixed 10-20 per cent targets for biofuel to start to replace fossil oil as a fuel, so the industry is hard to stop, even though reports from around the world indicate that biofuel plantations are displacing thousands of indigenous cultivators.[30]

'Green metal' greenwash

In September 2007, Vedanta's lawyers at the Supreme Court stated 'M'lords, aluminium is called a green metal because it is widely substituted for wood, so its use saves trees …' The lawyers actually confused 'greenfield' and 'brownfield' projects, stating that 'greenfield' projects are better for the environment—an error also promoted by the PR team at Lanjigarh! While a brownfield project renovates or adds to an existing plant (as at Korba), 'greenfield' has a more attractive ring to it, but what it means is turning an area of green fields and forest brown as the area is cleared and polluted—a dramatic transformation witnessed by everyone in the Lanjigarh area during 2004-9.

Aluminium is promoted as a 'green metal' for two main reasons: because some of it is recycled, and because its use in cars reduces their oil consumption by making them lighter. The reality is, because of forest destroyed in strip mining bauxite, water and electricity consumption of the factories, and their pollution, aluminium is one of the un-greenest materials we can use.

Aluminium can nearly halve the weight of a car, which allows it to cut fuel consumption by about 10 per cent. In the car industry, thanks to this, aluminium is winning the fight against steel. The 'people's car' or Nano car that Tata planned to manufacture at Singur is an aluminium-intensive vehicle. The Ferrari Modena, one of the first aluminium-intensive cars, reduced weight by 36 per cent. The EAA and IAI give statistics whose upshot is that each kilo of aluminium replacing steel saves 3–7 litres of fuel per 100,000 kilometres. The focus is on saving oil and recycling, masking the pollution from aluminium manufacture.[31] Even if cars use 85 per cent recycled aluminium (highly debatable), the increase of aluminium in cars is a major factor driving extraction of new bauxite mining and aluminium production far more than it promotes recycling! In other words, the car-weight issue is basically a huge distortion, hijacking the climate change issue into an advertising gimmick, getting people to believe that buying a new aluminium-rich car helps the environment.

The car industry is symptomatic of the causes of global warming, showing why it is so hard politically to reduce emissions. People with cars are addicted to driving. People without cars want them. Cars increased from about 70 million in the world in 1950 to 700 million in 2000, and car sales in India are rising particularly sharply, congesting the roads and polluting the air. Raising the proportion of aluminium used in cars in India from 10 to 20 kg may (or may not) save 20 per cent of fuel costs, but the high cost of greenhouse gases emitted in smelting aluminium alone far outweighs any environmental benefit.[32]

So how do lobbyists get away with calling it a 'green metal', in tune with a 'sustainable' lifestyle? The case for greenness involves a basic distortion of facts. It is true, as literature from the lobby groups stress (AA, IAI, EAA) that the aluminium companies they represent have tried to improve aluminium's 'sustainability' in various areas, but the self-regulation scheme (GRI) is unscientific, producing endless unverified statistics that create a distorted impression of environment-friendly processes.

On the rehabilitation of bauxite mines, the 23 companies affiliated to IAI who responded to a survey in 2003 indicated that most had tree planting plans in place on their bauxite mines, allowing the

IAI to claim that 'In 2002, 83 per cent of the total area mined was rehabilitated'[33]—definitely a gross exaggeration.

> Restoring pre-mining biodiversity requires areas to be protected from erosion and for the original topsoil to be managed to retain its value as a seed source and growing medium. Eighteen operations (92.2 per cent of reported bauxite production) reported that they separate the topsoil from the remaining overburden and retain it for use in rehabilitation. [34]

Such statistics mislead: separating the topsoil is very different from restoring biodiversity. Without regulation and monitoring by a neutral authority, companies give themselves glowing reports, and there is no way to check their figures.

The re-forestation programmes we have seen by Nalco in Odisha, Balco on Mainpat, and Hindalco at Amarkantak (MP-Chhattisgarh border) are very meagre and consist predominantly of eucalyptus. The industry's showcase is Alcoa's re-forestation of native species on *jarrah* forest at its Huntly and Willowdale mines in Western Australia, which was mentioned as an example in the SC case as a model to be followed on Niyamgiri, but here too, confirmation by independent researchers appears to be lacking.[35] On the mountains of East India, at an altitude of 4,000 feet, there is no question that the original biodiversity is likely to be obliterated, and the Supreme Court case shows all too clearly how 'green accounting' studies of forests' Net Present Value serve to legitimise this obliteration (above, p. 190).

In practice, most 'rehabilitation' takes the form of monoculture plantations. The laterisation process which dries out the areas of exposed earth has turned huge areas of exceptional fertility into sterile land or plantations in north Australia. There is also no acknowledgement from the industry of bauxite's importance in preserving ground-water, especially on mountains, nor the desertification process that follows from removing it.[36] In Odisha and Andhra, removing the mountains' bauxite cappings will inevitably damage a whole region's network of streams and rivers.

As for red mud, the toxic, iron-rich waste-slurry mixed with caustic soda invariably sited by refineries, evidence is overwhelming that it has contaminated water sources over countless areas of the world. Recent projects claim to 'dry stack' red mud, but it is rarely, if ever, sealed effectively. One ton of red mud is produced for each ton of alumina, so the Lanjigarh refinery's 6 million ton capacity promises 6 million tons of red mud a year, and in its first two years of operation, its red mud lake has already contaminated the Bansadhara river right at its source, causing several deaths and a lot of skin problems, in a population that has always depended on this river for washing and drinking. Repeated violations pointed out by the OSPCB, and orders to prevent leaching into the river have had little or no effect.[37]

Despite propaganda to the contrary, the storing of red mud does not seem to have improved since 1986, when a senior Hindalco official was questioned about the Renukoot red mud lake's annual contamination of water sources, at a conference in the Jamaican Bauxite Institute:

> Chair: I just wanted to probe a little bit more on the difference between the monsoon period in July, August and the dry periods. Is there really not a problem in monsoons?
> Hindalco official: The rain water flows down into the valley and the river over the mud, without mixing, and hence there is not much contamination due to caustic soda.
> Chair: So it's not a completely closed system—you dispose some of it into the river?
> Hindalco official: Yes.
> Chair: Is that just during the monsoon period, or during other periods as well?
> Hindalco official: Just during the monsoon period, two months.[38]

In other words, leaching of these highly toxic tailings is a regular occurrence in red mud lakes in India—impossible to prevent in the monsoon, but actually happening all the time. At Korba and Muri we have seen red mud spilling down onto grassland where streams flow and cattle graze, while kids go up onto the red mud lake to fly their kites there. 'Dead on the ball there' was our IAI guide's comment when we pointed out that red mud is radioactive. Bauxite contains at least 14 rare earths and 22 radioactive elements, all of which are present in red mud.[39]

As an Australian government report describes this substance, 'The extreme alkalinity of the red mud is such as to destroy all plant life

Kids we met flying kites on one of Balco's red mud lakes in Korba

it comes into contact with' making red mud areas 'utterly sterile' (Roberts et al. 1976, p. 92). P. K.Mishra's report on the Maikanch killings went out of its way to say that Nalco's operations prove that refineries need not harm the environment, but residents of Damanjodi say that when Mishra was taken on a tour near their homes, Nalco officials showed him plants they had just transplanted into red mud, to persuade him it was not toxic!

In March 2008, Vedanta joined an international Red Mud Project, whose website reveals that out of 84 refineries worldwide, seven still dispose of red mud at sea, and despite use of red mud in bricks being banned in Australia after tests by the Health Department in 1983 found that radiation levels were unacceptably high, vast quantities are used to make bricks in China, while in India, 2.5 million tons of red mud were used for cement in 1998–9 alone.[40]

At least the OSPCB has continued to point out Vedanta's violations at Lanjigarh, which figured in the Norway government report blacklisting Sterlite/Vedanta (Council on Ethics, 2007). Residents of Chatrapura and other villagers have attested that the refinery regularly discharges highly toxic chemicals into the river, writing a letter to the OSPCB about this on 9 September 2008. Many people and animals have developed body sores after bathing in the river, and at least two people have died, covered in sores. Meanwhile, residents of Bondhaguda and other villages close to the refinery and approach road are suffering from lung diseases. Yet, once again, in June 2009, Vedanta won a Golden Peacock award for excellence in its environmental record![41]

OSPCB reports are also explicit about haphazard disposal of Spent Pot Lining (SPL), classed as a hazardous material (at least in the US), which we have seen lying exposed outside the smelters in Korba. As for air-borne emissions, the IAI claims that reduced carbon consumption and emissions have reduced the electricity needed for smelting a ton of aluminium from 21 kilowatt hours to 13, while PFC emissions have been reduced by about 60 per cent in 1990–2000 by 63 per cent of aluminium producers, and fluoride emissions were reduced from an average 12–15 kg per ton of aluminium (up to 1955), to 2–6 kg (1955–75), and to 0.5–1 kg (since 1975).[42]

Again, these claims are impossible to verify, but we have witnessed the effects of skeletal fluoridosis on people, cattle, and plants in villages near the Angul and Hirakud smelters. This is mentioned in OSPCB reports (1995 and 2002), which confirm unacceptably high levels of fluoride in the ground water. Producing a ton of aluminium consumes an estimated 30 kilos of cryolite, and emits 2,000-3,000 cubic metres of waste gas, including hydrogen fluoride from the cryolite solution. The other main gases are carbon dioxide and monoxide, sulphur dioxide, silicon tetrafluoride, carbonyl sulfide, carbon disulfide, and hydrocarbons, including CFC-14 and

CFC-16, among the most potent GHGs, which come mainly from aluminium smelters, and are estimated to remain in the atmosphere for 10,000 years.

Villagers near Odisha's two existing smelters often protest strongly, furious at the lies they are told, when company officials try and deny the fluoride problem, and this denial prevents effective medical help. On the morning of 19 September 2008

> farmers in Nuagujatal and Gundurupada village near Hindalco [formerly Indal] aluminium smelter ... found that their paddy crops have turned from green to yellow.

Similar damage takes place every year,

> but in the year 2003, the local farmer association had revolted against the local aluminium smelter plant holding it responsible for the damage and the protest continued for nearly three months and finally, the factory was forced to provide compensation to the farmers.

In times of heavy rain, the factory sometimes released a large amount of

> noxious emission, mostly fluoride wastes, which in contact with the rain water became acid rain and damaged the crop, as alleged by Jayadurga Krishak Sangha [farmers' association] and other agricultural scientists.... Similar incident had taken place at Nalco smelter plant at Angul, Orissa in 2005 and the government had declared ex-gratia of 35 lakh to the affected farmers.[43]

In the US, Alcoa and Reynolds smelters have been heavily fined for contaminating the St Lawrence river with PCBs, which have been found in the breast milk of indigenous Mohawk Indians living downstream, and harmed beluga whales near the river mouth.[44]

There is evidence of serious fluoride pollution and brain-damage among smelters workers, and we recall that workers at Korba implied they would be in serious trouble if they revealed their real health situation. Hospitals serving company workers do not, it seems, tend to keep an accurate record of industrial diseases.[45]

Refineries spout large quantities of sulphur dioxide into the air, from heating the caustic soda solution and drying out the alumina —approximately 6,000 lbs per million tons of alumina. Dispersing this over a large area (the minimum pollution control), is the reason refinery chimneys have to be made so tall. Workers in refineries are exposed to alumina dust and boiler ash, as well as to asbestos used in the machinery.[46]

These are some of the reasons why the chairman of the OSPCB attempted to veto any more refineries and smelters in Odisha in 1996—understanding all too well how easily emission regulations are violated, and how new technology reduces fluoride and other emissions only marginally.[47] OSPCB and EIA legislation did not exist in the 1960s or 1980s when the Hirakud and Angul smelters were commissioned, but it exists now. So how come two more smelters are being built in Odisha? And how can Vedanta get away with building a smelter whose EIA shows it falls far short of international standards on pollution and sulphur dioxide controls? [48]

All in all, contrary to aluminium company propaganda, aluminium is the ungreenest of metals, and its present expansion is a model of unsustainability.

Resource curse

Calling aluminium a 'green metal' when its reality is the opposite recalls one of the classic PR exercises in greenwash: Shell's notorious campaign to hide its massive environmental and human rights abuses in Nigeria's oilfields. Nigeria is as rich in oil and gas deposits as Odisha is in mineral deposits. The scale of oil industry abuses in Nigeria and South America ought to be understood in advance if Odisha is to escape such devastation. This brings us to the subject of the resource curse—the general rule that those regions most richly endowed with natural resources have tended to be severely impoverished by extraction.

> Contrary to the widely held belief that abundant resources aid economic growth and are ... positive for political stability, most empirical evidence suggests that countries economically dependent on the export of primary commodities are at a higher risk of political instability and armed conflict.[49]

The resource curse thesis was first presented by Auty (1993), who showed the tendency for 'natural assets' to distort the economy to such a degree that they become a curse. In economies dependent on earnings from minerals, a major reason is that *'the mining sector displays marked enclave tendencies'* because it is so capital-intensive. As a result there tend to be few 'local product linkages and low revenue retention since a large fraction of the export earnings flow immediately overseas to service the foreign capital investment.'

The thesis is still occasionally contested,[50] but has been corroborated by a succession of empirical studies, including one by Jeffrey Sachs (2001), which show that an increase in natural resource exploitation correlates with a decline in economic growth. Many economists and other researchers have reinforced these findings and shed more light on the reasons for the resource curse, e.g. the tendency for mineral resource abundance to stimulate corruption in many countries, with impacts of diminishing growth as well as quality of welfare,[51] and the tendency for politicians to allow an over-extraction of natural resources for immediate gain, with negative future impacts, in countries where institutions are characterised by poor accountability.[52]

Ross (2000) highlighted a trend for governance to become less accountable and transparent, especially where there is 'a failure by the state to enforce property rights'. As we have seen, this is certainly the case in Indian projects. Even the MMSD report (2002) notes that human rights abuses are most likely to occur when a mining company 'is willing to work with repressive regimes or in countries with weak governance or rule of law.' [53] Again, the wording here distorts the reality we have followed, unfolding in many areas of India now, where mining companies influence state actors to become more authoritarian and repressive.

The resource curse reflects exploitation within as well as between countries—an exploitation built into how the mining industry works. The huge increase in the extraction of mineral and hydro-resources is an important factor in the recently spiralling growth rates in India and China, but it has been extensively demonstrated, especially for India, that the country's most mineral-rich regions show a dramatic decline in the quality of most people's lives when the industry takes over. Odisha's mining districts are its poorest, and in Koraput, where development has been oriented around Nalco's refinery, an amazing 79 per cent of the population lives below the poverty line, making it one of the poorest districts in India.[54] Among the main impacts of mining (documented in CSE 2008), are the disruption of communities and their food security, rising incidence of rape and prostitution, and of pollution-caused diseases, including industrial diseases by workers. The employment opportunities promised at the start of every project contrast sharply with what really happens. After initial construction work, where labour conditions tend to be very harsh, the industry's increasing emphasis on mechanisation keeps employment low.

Questions about the existence and reasons for the resource curse become secondary when it is understood that the nature of companies in general, and mining companies in particular, is to exploit, that what they promise is in many ways the polar opposite of what they actually do, and that the primacy of the profit motive is built into their legal definition. Even Adam Smith observed that corporate power tends towards tyranny and uncontrolled exploitation.[55]

A bottom-up or grassroots approach to understanding the resource curse starts from the experience of people whose area is invaded by companies seeking their resources, such as the villagers in Kashipur or Lanjigarh. How do their resources become their curse?

The answer lies in the details we have examined—distortions in EIAs, manipulation of Public Hearings, construction orchestrated with an influx of outsiders, a hierarchy of sub-contractors, overseen by company engineers and managers on a 'BOOT' basis (Build, Operate, Own & Transfer), in a process that involves a total takeover of villagers' land: the first resource acquired by mining companies. This includes public as well as private land, usually purchased at a minimum price, or even taken without payment. Water resources follow, channelled, again for minimum payment, to the benefit of factories.

When the real nature and behaviour of extractive companies is understood, the resource curse falls into focus. Oil companies, under the spotlight in Iraq, have long been among the worst transgressors on tribal land in Ecuador, Peru and Columbia, as well as Nigeria. Their behaviour in Nigeria has been exposed in two recent, well-researched books, which have also inspired our work.[56] Striking similarities with the aluminium companies in Odisha include:

- *Profits are divided between the company and the government to the exclusion of local benefits.* In Nigeria, the *'black hole of corruption'* and foreign bank accounts involved are notorious, making the country a centre of corruption worldwide. Shell claims that 90 per cent of profits go to the Nigerian government and that it gets only $1 profit per barrel, while it invests £20 million annually, though critics maintain Shell actually gets a far larger share. What is certain is that an appalling impoverishment and environmental degradation has taken hold throughout the oil-rich areas. The village of Oloibiri where oil was first discovered is a case study in poverty and neglect. A fund to channel 3 per cent of profits for local development is basically a façade.[57]
- *The company actually pays the army/police to carry out violent suppression of peaceful agitation against gross abuses and injustice.*[58]
- *Turning a blind eye to corruption,* e.g. an admission that Shell spent more on bribes than good works.[59]
- *Greenwash*: use of PR firms by Shell, echoed by Vedanta's CSR literature, and its donations to music, religion, art, and invitations to journalists and lawyers.[60]
- *Denial of environmental devastation,* turning truth on its head, as when Shell pretends there is no environmental devastation in Ogoniland, or that oil spills are mostly caused by sabotage, paralleled in Odisha by claims that 'Bauxite mining is actually good for the environment.'[61]
- *Environment Impact Assessments totally inadequate, or kept under wraps,* even when stated to be publicly available.[62]
- *Organisations committed to non-violence labelled violent, and a minority of violent incidents given much greater media coverage than far more numerous non-violent incidents,* with environmental activists accused of being 'eco-terrorists', 'anti-development', or even Maoists.[63]

Resource extraction is among the root causes of numerous civil wars and regional conflicts, not least in financing them. This is particularly obvious in the case of 'conflict diamonds', which highlights a risk from present diamond prospecting in Odisha, Chhattisgarh and MP. Mining is a clear factor in numerous other particularly ghastly civil wars and situations of internal repression, for example in Indonesia, Phillipines, New Guinea and Bougainville, Burma, and several African countries.

The aluminium industry is an extreme case of the resource curse, because of the scale of factories and foreign investment, leading to *enclave colonialism* in numerous countries, as we have seen. Neither bauxite mining nor aluminium production has ever made a Third World country rich, due to the externalisation of costs and the pricing riddle, which keep local prices low, while accumulating vast profits among directors, banks, metal traders and speculators far from the scene.

CHAPTER THIRTEEN

Cultural Genocide: The Real Impacts of 'Development-Induced Displacement' [1]

East India's Highland Clearances

In Bhagaban's words:

> We have sought an explanation from the government about people who have already been displaced in the name of development. How many have been properly rehabilitated? You have not provided them with jobs. You have not rehabilitated them at all. How can you again displace more people? Where will you relocate them and what jobs will you give them? You tell us first. The government has failed to answer our questions. Our fundamental question is: how can we survive if our lands are taken away from us? We are tribal farmers. We are earthworms [*matiro poko*]. Like fishes that die when taken out of water, a cultivator dies when his land is taken away from him. So we won't leave our land. We want permanent development. (Das 2005)

A *reality gap* stands between what is supposed to happen and what actually happens. Industrialisation has displaced an estimated 60 million Indian villagers within the last 60 years, more than 2 million in Odisha alone. Every year about a million more are displaced (15 million villagers worldwide). Most also lose their livelihood as cultivators of the soil. Around 75 per cent are Adivasis and Dalits.[2]

Very few have been properly compensated, let alone improved their standard of living, so for most of these people, as they often say themselves, these projects have been the opposite of development. This reality contrasts starkly with companies' rhetoric of 'generous R&R packages' [Resettlement and Rehabilitation], 'Sustainable Development' and CSR [Corporate Social Responsibility]. It is hard to keep track of the large number of mining, metal, dam and power projects, and the hundreds of villages they are currently threatening to displace in the name of 'development', 'growth', and even 'reducing poverty'.

Whatever wealth India's industrialisation generates for the business elite, it is important always to bear in mind that the people it displaces face a worse poverty than anything they knew before: *'projects meant to reduce poverty are the ones adding to the numbers of the poor.'*[3] Often even more painful than the poverty itself, is the erosion of people's sense of community and cultural identity, values, and traditions, which invariably accompanies their separation from the land which they and their ancestors cultivated over many generations.

Industrialisation has often involved a process of dispossessing people from the land in huge numbers, with extreme misery exacerbated by environmental degradation. All over Britain, before and during the industrial revolution, the Enclosures fenced off common land and turned it into private property. This process is taking place throughout India's tribal areas now. But there is nothing inevitable about this process. It stems from policy decisions to promote industrialisation, and a collective devaluing of the people and cultures being displaced.

Western Scotland suffered a cataclysm known as the Highland Clearances. After Bonnie Prince Charlie's failed revolt of 1747, when thousands of Highland clansmen were slaughtered by English soldiers at the battle of Culloden, these soldiers went on a rampage through the Highlands and Islands, burning villages and killing. The next hundred years consolidated a process of clearing crofters off the land. Lairds were encouraged to make their estates more 'productive' through sheep farming, etc., and to evict villagers who were unable to pay increased rents—just as the British encouraged Odisha's Rajas to increase their revenue during the nineteenth century.

The Scottish Highlands today are largely depopulated, full of ruined crofts evoking the vanished culture of the Clans. Intellectuals of the 'Edinburgh Enlightenment' painted a picture of these crofters as sunk in poverty and warfare, their stone houses as dirty hovels, and their lifestyle as backward and uneconomic. Using this justification, hundreds of communities were permanently erased, and thousands of people died from starvation and disease. Of those that survived, many had to become factory workers. Thousands emigrated to Britain's colonies, in America, Australia and South Africa, where they displaced the natives just as they had been displaced themselves. Many served in the army in various outreaches of the British empire, including India. The Kond areas of west Odisha that are now the scene of invasion by aluminium companies were forced under British rule by a series of Scottish highland officers: Macpherson, Campbell, MacViccar, McNeill....[4]

Scotland's Highland Clearances cleared people from the land and erased communities, but also cleared forests and farmland to make way for sheep and plantations of foreign trees for timber and paper. Another phase of clearances started in the early twentieth century when some of the world's first dams were built to generate hydropower for aluminium smelters. These reservoirs fill valleys emptied of their people. The water level is low and a sterile gap of at least 30 feet separates the water from land vegetation. Even back in 1910, when about a third of the world's aluminium was being produced in Scotland, a union leader contrasted the British aluminium company's picture of its main smelter enclave as a *'Garden of Eden'*, with the *'misery and degradation'* which workers endured.[5] Then as now, this included a high incidence of industrial diseases among smelter workers, whose true extent has never been revealed.

Dozer levelling Kinari village to make the site for Lanjigarh refinery

In Odisha, hundreds of communities have ceased to exist, and hundreds more are threatened with extinction. Local tribal and non-tribal politicians and landlords in Kashipur and Lanjigarh have sold out their communities just as the Scottish Lairds did.[6] There is no 'empire' for Odisha's displaced people to emigrate to. Factory and construction work is every bit as dangerous and degrading as it was in nineteenth century Britain, but in the present age of mechanisation, permanent jobs are much fewer.

Also, environmental degradation works alongside the decline in living standards, even more than in industrialising Britain. Around the Upper Indravati reservoir, displaced people cut down the remaining forest, because they lost their land along with their traditional forest-based livelihood system. Often, selling the timber as firewood is all that saves them from starvation.

Many aspects of this process find close parallels with what is happening in East India today. The crofters' way of life, based on small-scale cultivation, was dismissed as 'uneconomic'. Their beautiful stone and turf houses were denigrated as 'hovels', just as Adivasi houses, well-made of natural materials that remain cool in summer and warm in winter, are dismissed as 'mud huts' in corporate discourse. Before they were evicted, some crofters were offered Food For Work programmes building roads, just as in Odisha today.

In America, railways and heavy industries took off after the civil war from the 1860s, when the robber barons took the power of corporations to new limits, and consolidated vast trusts or cartels of steel, coal, oil, as well as aluminium. Many of these enterprises, as well as the gold rushes that started in 1849, involved an invasion of native territory, and brought genocide to many of the native tribes. The Yahi were a tribe of several thousand hunter-gatherers who happened to occupy the California mountain land invaded by the '49 gold rush. After occasional attacks by Indians (sources record 12 whites they killed, compared with 600 Yahi killed by whites), a group of cowboys attempted to exterminate all of them in 1864, publishing a couple of books about their exploits. A lone Yahi survivor, who surfaced in 1912, lived out his last years in a museum of ethnology.[7]

Better known are the tribes who fought back on horseback, such as the Lakota (or Sioux) and Apaches. The war which Lakota waged for the Black Hills, to protect their sacred heartland from mines, ranches and railroads, is the best-known of the Indian Wars, when Sitting Bull, Crazy Horse and other leaders won initial victories, wiping out General Custer and his men. But in every case, the whites won by sheer superiority of numbers and firepower, massacring hundreds of communities and exiling survivors to reservations. What happened to native Americans set a model for two forms of genocide: physical extermination (suffered by the Yahi and others), and cultural genocide, when appropriation of a people's land ended their traditional livelihood and destroyed their social structure.[8]

Thayer Scudder's WB reports on forced resettlement show that the 200 projects approved by the WB in 1986–93 displaced about 2,500,000 people, dams generally the largest number, followed by factories and mines.[9] According to WB and other international standards on involuntary resettlement, if a project really constitutes 'development', then *'the first rule is that all parties to the project should be better off'*:[10]

> The fundamental goal of the Bank's policy is to restore the living standards and earning capacities of displaced persons—and where possible to improve them.

This basic aim is very rarely met. Scudder found 'that only 4 out of 50 projects' could claim this, and WB studies admit that 'income restoration' remains elusive. The hard fact is that most oustees' standard of living shows a massive decline.[11]

As we saw on the Hirakud, Kolab and Indravati dams, no reliable statistics have been kept of the number of people displaced, and in every case, compensation was woefully inadequate. The statistics in Table 10 give a meagre sense of the trauma of dispossession for all the people affected, and err on the minimal side.

The human tragedies behind these statistics have been neglected both institutionally and conceptually. Projects involving displacement are still not required to make a Social Impact Assessment, and officials in charge of the process have no special training or sensitivity to mitigate the trauma. Their focus tends to be preventing 'disorder' and denying the problem. Studies of the displacement process have multiplied in recent years, but remain highly inadequate in terms of conceptualising the enormity of cultural and social structural change. Several Indian and Odisha journals have published special issues in 2006-8 devoted to the issue. One of the main models is that of Impoverishment Risks and Rehabiliation, propounded by Michael Cernea. Part of the reason for its popularity is probably that it builds rehabilitation into the model, even though his work shows that development for tribal people comes as displacement, and that real rehabilitation, restoring a pre-displacement standard of living, is extremely rare.[12]

From tribal people's perspective, all these projects should probably be called *displacement projects*—the word *development* acts as a mask, and contradicts their experience. Most of the written discourse adds insult to injury by reducing people to 'oustees' and their pain to a de-personalised analysis. Very few draw on the words and understanding of dispossessed people to understand the reality of displacement.

A recent Odisha R&R policy, announced in mid-2006 during confrontations with Kalinganagar Adivasis and anti-Posco protestors, states an intention *'to avoid displacement wherever possible.'* The Fifth Schedule of India's Constitution lays down certain principles for tribal people's protection in designated districts, where they predominate, especially the non-alienability of tribal land 'except for projects in the national interest'. This exception has proved a loophole that is invoked for every large displacement project. The Samatha Judgment re-established this principle—which state governments have tried to

	Estimated no. of villages displaced	families	persons
Hirakud Dam	285	22,144	180,000
Rengali Dam plus irrigation	287	11,725	
Upper Indravati Dam	99	5,301	40,000+
Balimela Dam	91	2,000	60,000
3 Subarnarekha Dams	75	5,214	
Upper Kolab Dam	49	3,179	14,000
Khadkei	36		
Lower Suktel Dam	32		
Ib Dam	29	3,092	
Ong Dam	29		
Lower Indravati Dam	25	1,462	
Ramial Dam	22		
Pilasalkhi Dam (near Phulbani)	17		
Ranupur Dam	16	1,634	
Talcher Coal Mines	61	1,790	
T.S.Thermal Power, Kaniha	53	1,940	
Rourkela steel plant	30 [64]	2,367	[23,000]
Ib Valley Coal Mines	18	1,353	
Nalco smelter, Angul	40	3,997	
Nalco refinery, Damanjodi	19	788	3,000

Table 10. Displacement by some of Odisha's biggest dams, mines and factories[13]

circumvent through Cabinet orders or use of Public Sector mining companies (OMC in Odisha, APMDC in Andhra), as we saw in Chapter Seven.

Laws meant to protect tribal rights and the environment, as we have seen, are often very poorly implemented. The Odisha

Scheduled Areas Transfer of Immovable Property Regulation (1956) has been used for recovering alienated tribal lands, but neglected as a means to prevent displacement. The EIA Notification Act (1994) required Environment Impact Assessments, and in 1997 made Public Hearings mandatory for getting Environmental Clearance, but both are regularly manipulated to a point of absurdity. Recently, following a suggestion from the WB's Country Environmental Analysis for India, the GoI passed a resolution barring non-local activists and NGOs from Public Hearings, on the grounds that outsiders were instigating opposition.[14] One reason seems to be to try and prevent independent witnesses from reporting what actually happens at the Hearings, since 'consent' is often manipulated, even when nearly everyone expresses opposition.

It is significant in this context that the WB and DFID refused to ratify the Extractive Industries Review (EIR, the in-depth study of mining projects worldwide commissioned by the WB), because it advocated the principle that people should give their 'Free Prior Informed Consent' (FPIC) before a decision is made to displace them (below, p. 448). This refusal by the WB and DFID ensured that the vast majority of people forced to move are victims of a policy of *involuntary displacement*. The reason for this refusal was simple: very few people would freely give their consent to be displaced. In other words, the Public Hearings are mainly for show, to allow the public to vent their feelings, but also to claim 'consent' has been given, and local people 'consulted'.

This raises the question of who is really pulling the strings? In Chapters Sixteen and Seventeen we shall see that the overall policy decisions imposed on Adivasis are often decided from London and Washington, in a hierarchy of power that is hidden from the people affected. A letter we shall examine from the DFID fundamentally misrepresents the issue of community land rights, refusing tribal people the right to veto a mining project displacing them—precisely the same mindset and remoteness from people as colonial attitudes which prevailed during East India Company times. When India's Constitution insists that tribal land in Scheduled Areas cannot be bought by non-tribals, how come this principle is flouted so flagrantly and often?

Resettlement and Rehabilitation (R&R)

Of all India's citizens, Adivasis can least afford to lose their land and community, and after years of exploitation and oppression by outsiders, they least deserve to. The Indravati reservoir was supposed to include a generous Resettlement and Rehabilitation (R&R) component. About this an Agragamee report observes:

> The WB funded this. But during the socio-economic survey of the displaced it was found out that the rates of compensation paid for the land, houses and trees are so low that they do not permit a family to reconstruct their life styles at even half the level they were used to.[15]

Orissa's 2006 R&R policy was drafted with help from the DFID and UNDP, and is claimed as 'very progressive and comprehensive', yet it falls far short of international standards, as set for example by the ILO (International Labour Organisation), which insists on the principle of land for land (compensation in land for land that is lost), while the Orissa policy limits compensation to cash and jobs. Moreover, the draconian Land Acquisition Act of 1894, with its colonial-era concept of 'eminent domain', remains the basis of appropriating land. One of the most obnoxious features of this is that tribal people who do not have land deeds (*patta*) to the land they cultivate and occupy are still classed as 'encroachers on government land'.

The more widespread reality is an *encroachment* by non-tribals and their projects onto tribal land. Often, as with the Khondalite mountains, land being encroached by mining projects and dams has the character of tribal territory or 'commons'. But because the British, when they ruled India, had no category of communally owned territory, and wished to lay claim and generate revenue from all the land they could, they classified all land that was not privately owned as government land.

The whole issue of displacement is routinely neglected. While Environment Impact Assessments are often rudimentary, their shortcomings can at least be scrutinised and questioned in the courts. Social Impact Assessments are not even required in most projects, and administration of R&R is usually relegated to poorly trained personnel, in a low-status government post, when their task requires the utmost sensitivity.[16] Officials' normal response to the inevitable complex difficulties—since almost every displaced family faces trauma and often injustice—is to deny the problem. Much energy apparently goes into distorting the truth to mask painful realities and abuses of power, accentuating the economic and cultural risks inherent in displacement.[17]

Implicit in most displacement is an enforced change of livelihood from agricultural self-sufficiency to industrial worker. Adivasis' traditional skills and knowledge are not recognised, and they are thrown immediately to the bottom of the pile in terms of jobs, through their classification as 'unskilled'. This switch involves a radical discontinuity with their culture, history and identity. This is a key problem with Cernea's model—traditional tribal social structure is far from 'simple'. It is highly sophisticated, in terms of an extremely deeply rooted balance between people and their natural environment. Displacement dislocates them into a social structure of broken relationships and fragmented space. From being in basic control of their space and time, their area is invaded, and they become virtually powerless in relation to the company hierarchy which now controls the space all around their communities.

The total contrast between a policy of improving people's standard of living and a reality of invariably lowering it exemplifies the reality gap at the centre of R&R. Between what is supposed to happen and what actually happens is a gulf—often no correlation at all. Since most projects have no Social Impact Assessment, since displaced people are not made part of the decision-making process, and there is no proper check on the success of R&R, or even proper ways to assess this, let alone any disciplinary action against officials responsible for failure, this reality gap remains almost completely outside the approved discourse on R&R.

As a state-sector company, which has tried to 'get it right', and is often cited as a positive example, it is worth looking at Nalco's displacement of tribal communities at Damanjodi. The first pages of a book written for Nalco about this shows underlying assumptions:

> The process of socio-economic development initiated soon after Independence under the successive plans, has given rise to the building

Gurbari Majhi on her fields near Lanjigarh, facing imminent displacement

of large scale irrigation projects and industrial complexes in endemic resource regions which were the traditional home of a large number of isolated groups of tribes. Although industrialisation, a necessary concomitant of development, has brought about manifold benefits for the nation as a whole, however, it resulted in large-scale deforestation not only for raw material but also for acquisition of vast pieces of land under cultivation for the establishment of factories and the needed residential complexes. The unintended consequences of this action have been not only loss of habitat for the tribes but also their means of livelihood ... who, for historical reasons, have been living for ages in these isolated environs.

The Government of Odisha, as well as NALCO, has taken the view that the homesteads lost by the tribal families were practically of no value as they were small mud huts. As no compensation could be paid for loss of such homesteads, durable houses (partly pucca) could be constructed for them at the cost of NALCO. Secondly, the concept of rehabilitation was based on the fact that it was necessary for NALCO alumina project to create a certain amount of community relationship with those who have lost all their assets in the larger

Newly finished Vedantanagar, under guard

interest of the nation, by offering them various types of employment opportunites as well as social support by way of health, medical and educational facilities.

It is well known that the tribal culture and ways of living have no future orientation. Naturally, sudden influx of money into their hands induces extravagance in them. Of course the amount of compensation paid to them for loss of their land was rather small because of third-grade land possessed by them. In order to insure against repeating mistake of this type, NALCO has taken the initiative in drawing up a plan of action. In this process, the displaced tribals themselves would be the active participants in their own rehabilitation. The action plan envisages provision of a house and some land, though much smaller than what they had lost, for cultivation, which was their way of life.

It was comprehended that the needed action programmes are to be worked out and implemented so that people who were happy peasants enjoying fruits of their labour amidst natural surroundings yesterday are not rendered homeless and unemployed today leading the life of destitutes because of their sacrifices in the national interest. (Muthayya 1984, pp. 1–8)

Among features here that are endlessly repeated in project literature, we notice:

- emphasis on the idea that tribals have to make a 'sacrifice' 'in the national interest', for the 'manifold benefits for the nation as a whole'—a concept which underlies the whole idea that it is justifiable to displace tribal people to make way for industrial development. This boils down to an assumption that it is necessary to sacrifice 'marginal' people for the sake of others' prosperity
- a fundamental arrogance, in negative stereotypes and patronising attitudes towards 'isolated groups of tribes', who 'have no future orientation'—a gross distortion, when the culture is based on cultivating land in a careful progression through the seasons. To denigrate their land as 'third grade' and their houses as 'mud huts ... practically of no value' is an outrageous distortion
- Nalco is depicted as a generous conferer of benefits, reflecting how company officials like to see themselves, but certainly not how people around Damanjodi see them! As for 'opportunities for gainful employment' this is a patronising way to describe the lowest grade of jobs in mines and factories, involving hard labour in conditions that are generally terrible in health and safety standards
- The passage attempts an impersonally abstract style, using long words to mask simple distortions. 'Experts' are called on to study the psychology as well as work habits of the displaced people. The book is full of statistics, but the displaced people have no voice. The study does not record their views on any aspect. The implication of this silence is that these people have nothing to say, or are too uneducated to say anything of value.

In reality, people in Damanjodi are often articulate about their situation and the company. What follows is from an interview with a young tribal woman, who was displaced as a child from a tribal village to Amlabadi, Nalco's main resettlement colony at Damanjodi. Her parents made sure she got a good education. When we first met her she was studying for an MA degree, and later got a teaching post in a village outside Damanjodi. Nalco would not give her a job, despite their quota for displaced persons.

I loved my village, it was very pleasant though remote. When I was a little child my parents took me to the school. Then we came here. When I was in class six, my father gave me a bicycle so that I could get to school and continue to 12th standard. Then I graduated and now I'm doing my masters in Jeypore. Even so, I have not got a job. I loved sports and participated in the district and state level too ... I tried several times, learned computers, stenography.... They promised, *"Do this and do that, we will give you a job."* Even though we have quota for LDP [Land Displaced People], we can't get jobs.

We had cattle, and I used to look after them. We had goats and sheep, a kitchen garden. It was so nice when I was little. We used to cultivate vegetables on our own. I am so much interested in it but there is no space here.

They kept us here. An asbestos roof, and everything else is earthen, only a thin layer of cement. It is unsafe to live in. The kitchen room is small. We all have extended our houses on our own. In Damanjodi people are living with hardship, some even have not enough to eat a meal. It was nice before, at least they had land, nobody was starving. Now, no land and no cattle. So no food. Unemployment and even educated unemployed are everywhere. The people of Kashipur should be informed about this, so that they can get better facilities. If their father and mother are employed, their children should get these jobs too. This was the system here, but not anymore.... You can see unemployed graduates here too. What more can I say?

Those who have not lost their land and home are not fighting for their rights, only us. Were I not qualified, I would have never expected a job in Nalco. We have lost everything ... that is why I am hoping ... but it seems impossible ... Nalco has given us a lot of problems. Nalco is death for us. (Das 2005)

The contrast between houses before and after displacement demonstrates a far-reaching difference in values and culture. Traditional tribal villages, without too much outside interference, have a high quality of life in that each man and woman is self-employed on their own land. They have clean water and a daily bath in a flowing stream—better than the most lavish bathroom! They make their own houses out of earth and wood—officially classified as mere 'mud huts', which means that people receive minimal compensation when they are destroyed. Yet they are far superior in many ways to pukka concrete houses, remaining cool in summer and warm in winter, unlike concrete buildings in resettlement colonies. They are beautifully painted with clays and well-mixed natural glazes; and have many secret spaces for cooking, storing things, and worship of gods and ancestors. Traditional houses are an expression of cultural pride, while the pukka houses that are 'gifted' to oustees as if far superior are soulless, inconvenient, and alien in culture. Since oustees rarely have any design input, these houses lack the spatial arrangement that binds people into a living community.

To bridge the reality gap, we need to address several issues of fundamental importance on the ground, which find little or no mention in most of the literature on displacement. One set of issues involves Cultural Genocide and the sacrificing of people's quality of life. Another area is that in most, if not all the project areas, various forms of intimidation and coercion appear to be standard procedure towards people unwilling to be displaced, by police and administrative authorities, as well as by a mafia network of *goondas*. This intimidation also operates around people who have been displaced from traditional communities to a resettlement colony. In a traditional tribal village, differences of status are relatively small. Once displaced from their village and land, they find themselves at the bottom of a hierarchy that is often extremely cruel and corrupt.

This corruption is conspicuous by its absence from most models of R&R, and at the heart of the fundamental discrepancies between theory and practice. In the awarding of contracts, for constructing a colony, and at every stage of a displacing project, corruption is rampant, from mining deals with politicians down to the level where workers have to pay bribes to get even the hardest labouring jobs.

Development-induced displacement

Many Adivasis get displaced two or three times. Balaram and Mukund Saonta are a pair of Kond brothers displaced first by the Kolab dam, then by HAL, presently facing threat of a third displacement by mining. They sang us a song in Kui accompanied on a one-string *dunduna,* giving an atmospheric drone and rhythm:

Should we start here?

How painful was our past
Our family scattered all over the place,
Losing everything
Thinking about it tears come to my eyes

Oh my dear brother
Don't forget this experience
Of how we had to leave our Motherland
Each time the developers came.
This is our song.... (Balaram and Mukund Saonta, in Das 2005)

Utkal, like other mining companies, claims to offer 'an exceptionally generous R&R package', that will make people's lives 'more sustainable':

> Although a certain level of social disruption is unavoidable during a limited transitional period, Utkal firmly believes that socially responsible industrial development will contribute to an improved and more sustainable standard of living.[18]

No-one claims to be 'against development'. But as Bhagaban asks, what is development? What is 'sustainable'? Shouldn't it mean improving everyone's quality of life? Or are some people to be *sacrificed* for others' profit?

The whole administration of tribal people is couched in terms of 'development', as in the Dongria Kond Development Agency (DKDA). Worldwide, countries are defined as 'developed' or 'developing'. As Esteva says (1992), when Truman popularised the term 'underdevelopement' in 1949, he defined two billion people as 'underdeveloped', and in need of 'change'.[19]

The prime meaning of development refers to an organic process of change and growth. Official usage has focused on a narrow material sense, as if development is something imposed, rather than evolving from within. As a verb, 'develop' has even shifted from the correct intransitive usage ('people develop in different ways'), to become a transitive verb ('the tribal people must be developed', 'we must develop them'), which changes its sense fundamentally. In other words, it has come to denote imposed change—a process managed by official agencies, with specific theories and techniques of change along a uniform path, rather than as something which is free, under people's choice and control. In this way, it has become a cover-word for unasked-for changes that are imposed from the outside.

What is masked by this misuse of 'development' is, essentially, power. Tribal communities' own power to decide how they wish to develop is undermined by the imposition of standardised changes by an entrenched power structure. The concept of 'sustainability' has also been badly distorted from Brundtland's definition of meeting present needs without compromising the needs of future generations. 'Sustainable mining', as promoted by the MMSD project, is a contradiction in terms. Change is a key value in modern society. In tribal society, until recent times, continuity with tradition has been a prime value, which is why these societies have sustained so long.

A strong Adivasi perspective emerges in a letter written to the Chief Minister of Madhya Pradesh, Digvijaya Singh, by someone about to be displaced by one of India's largest and most notorious dams, on the Narmada river:

> Respected Diggy Raja,
> ... You advise us every now and then to go to Gujarat, for our economic condition will improve there. There will be development. We have been, however, saying no and fighting you for the last 8 years ... You are spending a lot of money and using force to evict us ... To you who are part of the government and the towndwellers, our land seems to be just some Hills and Forests. But we are living in comfort in this land of Hills and Forests on the banks of Mother Narmada.
>
> You take us to be poor. But we're not. We live in harmony and cooperation with each other ... We get good Crops from Mother Earth. Clouds give us Water ... We produce many kinds of Grains with our own efforts, and we don't need money. We use Seeds produced by us ... The lands in Gujarat are addicted. You cannot have a crop there without hybrid seeds [i.e. synthetic fertilisers and pesticides have spoilt that land's natural fertility].
>
> You people live in separate houses in your towns. You don't bother about the joy or suffering of each other. But we live on the support of our kith and kin. We all work together ... In the spirit of *Laha* (communal labour) we construct a house in just one day ... How does such fellow feeling prevail in our villages? For we help each other. We enjoy equal standing. We've been born in our village. Our *Nara* (umbilical cord) is buried here. (Baba Mahariya 2001)

Cultural Genocide

Anthropological analysis shows what happens to a tribal community once it is displaced: basically, its social structure is destroyed. Tribal culture exists through relationships ordered in a carefully maintained system, the subject of traditional anthropological analysis. Every part of this system is torn apart by displacement:

- The *Economic System*, along with the whole tradition of cultivation is completely destroyed with people's removal from their land, and the termination of their existence as farmers.
- The *Kinship System* is fractured by displacement from villages, where social relations follow the pattern of a village's traditional layout, and spatial distance from kin in neighbouring villages. In every area where a project causes displacement, there is a split in long-standing relationships, and tension between those who accept compensation and move, and those who remain opposed.
- The *religious system* is undermined by removal of sacred village sites, as well as the mining of venerated mountains. As the Kinari woman said to us days after being moved to Vedantanagar colony to make way for the Lanjigarh refinery, after seeing bulldozers flatten her village and its central earth shrine, 'They even destroyed our gods.' Losing her land means she can never grow her own food again, so the whole *system of values* attached to the customary way people have supported themselves is undermined.
- The *material culture*, as a system in which people make most of the things they need, is destroyed as soon as the houses people built from local earth and wood are knocked down and replaced with concrete ones.
- Above all, the *power structure* is transformed. From being in control of their area and its resources, people find themselves at the bottom of an extreme hierarchy of power and authority. Traditional tribal society is remarkably egalitarian, and women have a higher status than in much of mainstream society, which they lose when new, corporate forms of domination invade their area. In many ways women have even more to lose than

men, which is why they are often at the forefront of campaigns against displacing projects.

Adivasi social values are centred on their relationship with their land and natural environment, and with each other. They take pride in being self-sufficient for most of their needs by their own labour: for food, building their own houses, etc. To call them 'poor' is correct only when the system of exploitation imposed on them by trader-moneylenders is already taking away a large part of the food they grow.

Large 'development' projects imposed on Adivasis amount to an invasion and dispossession of their land and traditional culture, which carries further the colonial, colonising process which the British began.

The term 'genocide' was first used in 1944–45, to describe Nazi treatment of Jews. What is classed as genocide now is often a sensitive political issue: while most people class Turkey's slaughter and mass displacement of its Armenian population in 1916–18, and Sudan's ongoing slaughter and mass displacement of Darfur's population as cases of genocide, this is hotly disputed by those countries' governments. However, the classic model of genocide, applied to countless tribes that were exterminated all over the continents of America and Australia, is not in dispute.

'Genocide' means killing (Latin *caedo*) a people, race or tribe (*genus*). Examining what was involved in the American tribes' genocide, it is evident that there are two levels to what was killed: the physical extermination, and the killing of a culture. Contemporary accounts record that native Americans often preferred to die rather than survive physically without their land and culture. The US policy from the late nineteenth century was to take over tribal territories and resettle surviving members in reservations, where they could no longer support themselves. A conscious policy of 'detribalising' them was pursued by forcibly taking children away from their families and putting them in schools where any attempt to maintain traditional customs or speak tribal languages was punished, 'killing the Indian in them to save the man'—an example cited by a US anthropologist who prefers the word 'culturicide'. But this term is clumsy and does not conjure the appropriate sense of death and outrage. UNESCO's San Jose Declaration (1981) defined 'Ethnocide, that is, cultural genocide' as 'a violation of international law equivalent to genocide'.[20] 'Cultural Genocide' means essentially the killing of people's culture by uprooting them from their ancestral lands.

In popular usage now, 'culture' often means just 'the pretty bits', exemplified by tribal or classical dances. But its original meaning, from Latin *cultus*, refers to '*cultivation*' of the soil as well as the traditions of a society ('*culture*'), and religion ('*cult*'). In other words, tribal people's economic and political systems are fundamental to their culture, and when dispossessed of their land, these systems are effectively destroyed. Losing their land brings the death of all they value. The sacredness of nature, respect for elders' knowledge, ritual contact with the ancestors, growing their own food on family land and making their own houses and tools, exchanging food with neighbours with an egalitarian spirit: these things are swept away by corporate values, which emphasise money and financial power. 'We're being flooded out with money' is an accurate description of how a culture is killed, that CSR 'experts' do not yet comprehend.

Actual killings at Maikanch and Kalinganagar may be relatively few (though in the Salwa Judum civil war presently raging in south Chhattisgarh, the killings are anything but few), but they symbolise a deeper, psychic death. Underlying this Cultural Genocide is the invaders' total lack of respect for tribal people's traditions and connection with the land. Mainstream culture ceased a long time ago to be rooted in the soil. As land prices shoot up, collective attachment to the land a village has worked over successive generations has no value in incomers' eyes, which focus only on profits they hope to generate. This leads to the situation B. D. Sharma defined as a 'declaration of war', in his 29th Report of the Commissioner for Scheduled Castes and Tribes:

> The spree of development in tribal areas without any consideration for the situation of the tribal people living there is in a way a declaration of war against those people.[21]

And where do displaced people go? Many displaced Adivasis and Dalits join the army of migrants to the cities as labourers, domestic servants and economic refugees. Here they live in *basti*s: a recent UN study shows that a sixth of the world's population now lives in slums.[22]

And where does India's real culture still exist? Is it in festivals of dance, music and worship, whose main patrons in Odisha now are mining companies like Tata and Vedanta? Or in the paintings of Odisha's artists, whose high prices are set by the executives of these companies presently buying their paintings? Or is it rooted in the traditions of indigenous people still practising an ancient, sustainable system of *cultus—chaso—*cultivating the earth? Gandhi's view was that India's culture exists most strongly in its villages. Odisha's tribal communities preserve a vibrant culture in the broadest, most holistic sense, from an economy still rooted in ecology to a sense of community based in shared ritual and work, and egalitarian values expressed most fully in dance—a culture where no-one accumulates too much or puts themselves too far above their fellows. These are the communities, and this is the culture, sustained over centuries, now threatened with permanent destruction.

For some, culture is a 'bad word' now, seeing the fascist travesty of 'culture' by nationalists who perpetrate atrocities in its name. What we speak of here is a more ancient, unstandardised kind of culture, still rooted in the earth.[23]

National sacrifice

When it is admitted that R&R hardly ever improves people's standard of living, the argument comes in that tribal people have to make 'sacrifices in the national interest'. This is the theme of a song taught to the children of displaced families in Vedantanagar, which they sang in front of the CEC team at Lanjigarh in mid-2005:

> This country, this earth, is our mother.
> We will sacrifice ourselves in service of it,
> and make our nation proud of us. (Das 2005)

The term 'National Sacrifice Areas' was coined by the US Academy of Sciences in 1973 for the Four Corners region of the US Midwest, which had been devastated by toxic waste 'owing to relentless corporate stripping of its coal, oil, gas and uranium reserves.'[24] Uranium mining has affected several native American reservations. As Russell Means (1982) speaks of his tribe's response:

> Right now, today, we who live on Pine Ridge Reservation are living in what White Society has designated a 'National Sacrifice Area'. What this means is that we have alot of uranium deposits here, and white culture, not us, needs this uranium as energy production material. The cheapest, most efficient way for industry to extract and deal with the processing of this uranium is to dump the waste products right here at the digging site—right here, where we live. This waste is radioactive, and will make the entire region uninhabitable for ever. This is considered by industry, and by the white society that created this industry, to be an 'acceptable price to pay' for 'energy resource development'.
>
> The same sort of thing is happening down in the land of the Navajo and Hopi, up in the land of the Northern Cheyenne and Crow, and elsewhere. Thirty per cent of the coal in the west and half of the uranium deposits in the US have been found to lie under 'Reservation Land', so there's no way this can be called a minor issue. We are resisting being turned into a 'National Sacrifice Area'. We are resisting being turned into a 'National Sacrifice People'. The costs of this industrial process are not acceptable to us. It is genocide to dig uranium here and drain the ground water.

Is sacrificing Adivasis really an acceptable cost? Is Odisha about to become a *National Sacrifice Area* to gift the world vast quantities of aluminium and steel?

In tribal villages that still remain far from industry, there is a silence at night—a peace, that vibrates softly with the song of *jhintika* (crickets). When a factory is nearby, this peace is shattered by the unceasing sounds of heavy machinery and vehicles, together with the shattering of the community's social structure, and the pollution by dust and smog.

Scotland's glens, like Odisha's reservoirs, are full of a different kind of silence—the silence of a land emptied of its people—post-industrial silence, post-people emptiness.

The Highland Clearances did not stop with the evictions. When Kinlochleven and Lochaber smelters were built in the 1900s–1920s, they were the world's largest, and the hydro-schemes to supply them with water and electricity were among the world's biggest dams. Thousands of navvies, German prisoners-of-war and conscientious objectors laboured to build these dams, smelters, and connecting roads. Patrick McGee was an Irish navvy who got a job building Kinlochleven, and wrote a famous book about the experience (1914), *Children of the Dead End*.

From the silence of tribal villages at night, to the silence of vanished villages, to another kind of silence: our own, when we fail to speak about what is really happening...

Salu Majhi

In the years we have known Kucheipadar, it has changed beyond recognition—a slow death in front of people's eyes of so much they have loved and valued.

Salu Majhi is a blind elder of Kucheipadar who sings the most beautiful songs in Kui, playing the *dunduna*. On 15–16 June 2005, police lathicharged and arrested protestors in Guguput village, so that Utkal could finally begin constructing its refinery. Fifteen Kucheipadar villagers were among those arrested. Samarendra was visiting, and had asked Salu to sing a song to end the film. Salu was asking about the missing people: 'Have they returned yet? What shall I sing?' 'Should I suggest a theme?' asks his neighbour, a woman called Salai. 'They are coming from all over and taking our people to jail, but we will not leave our ancestral land. We would rather die than leave our birth-land.' Another neighbour, Joli, lights thick *sal*-resin incense, placing it in a bowl in front of him as inspiration while he squats on the floor. Asking about one person after another who has failed to return to the village, Salu mutters, 'We're all getting swept away. What's going to happen?' and starts to strum the *dunduna*, singing softly in the Kui language, in a tune of searing beauty. (Das 2005)

> Oh my dear people of my land my country
> The time has come to leave, my friend
> Ai, ai, for our birth-land
> Where can I stand, or sit?

They are doing these things to us
So that we will leave this land
Ai no, are they really coming?
Thinking about this I cannot sleep
Nor can I live my day

> Ai, ai ...
> So many companies from so many countries are coming
> Time is running out, what do I do?
> I lose my voice
> But I can regain it too
> We won't leave our land

So many police, my friend
Taking us to jails
They come in hundreds
Better to mingle with our mother earth

> Who will speak for us?
> They are coming
> With marching legs and arms

> They are crying to buy our land
> Where will we go?
> Oh are you taking us to paradise?

Oh my children sleep
We will fight
We don't know their machines
My soul is boiling
They are flooding us with money

> They are coming to take our mountain
> And use it all up in twenty-five years
> Very clever, dear friend

Oh dear frogs and fishes of my river,
Will we be able to blink at each other anymore?
Will I be able to catch them?

> We are tired of this struggle
> The lazy people are invading

We are Kui people
Storing water in tanks won't keep us alive
Our life is in our flowing streams

CHAPTER FOURTEEN

Cost Benefit Analysis

How should balanced decisions be made about any of the bauxite/aluminium projects? In this chapter we examine ways of weighing up costs against benefits. The starting point is transparency. All over East India, too many decisions for industrial projects have been taken behind closed doors, without an open assessment of costs and benefits.

Taking the three Vedanta projects, separately or as a whole—Lanjigarh refinery, Burkhamunda smelter, Niyamgiri bauxite mine—or the Birla projects (Utkal refinery, bauxite mines planned on Bapla Mali, Kodinga Mali and Mali Parbat, and smelter in Sambalpur), or similar projects planned by Jindal, L&T with Dubal, and others, how should a proper Cost Benefit Analysis be made?

How to strike a correct balance between economic development and environmental protection, as the Supreme Court Judges put it in their Order concerning Niyamgiri dated 8 August 2008?

To start with, a basic list of costs and benefits, for the Niyamgiri mine:

Costs	Benefits
Forest on the mountain top destroyed (unique biodiversity)	Re-forestation (suspect claim of higher tree density)
Also forest on mountain side approached by mining road, etc.	
Damage to water regime from mountain (denied by mine supporters)	
Pollution of Bansadhara river (already extensive from refinery)	Company profits, Government revenue
Violation of Dongria sacred area	
Invasion of Dongria area (four Dongria villages losing land, etc. to mining road, many others affected by sound and light pollution and influx of outsiders)	Jobs + Massive foreign investment
'Flooding us out with money'	5 per cent of profits for local development
Corruption, Intimidation	

For the Lanjigarh refinery, an extreme contrast is evident between the claims of Sterlite/Vedanta in Sustainable Development reports (2006–08), and claims of local villagers and campaigners, that their life has been made unbearable by the project:

Benefits	Costs
A state-of-the-art alumina refinery	Forest and fields lost
	Numerous death of labours and on the roads
Employment: a few hundred direct jobs, and several thousand contract/construction jobs	Little employment for local people (several demonstrations on this)
CSR: new schools, medical centres, agriculture projects, SHGs	CSR development seen as a con by villagers and campaigners

'Developing a backward region' New roads	Massive pollution of Bansadhara river, of the air, of villages and fields by dust, danger from vehicles, etc.
'There was nothing here before'	Invasion of hundreds of outsiders who show no respect for tribal culture plus oppression by *goondas*
Giving the people of Kalahandi 'two square meals a day', in an area notorious for starvation deaths	Land taken from village cultivators, taking away their food security turning people into industrial labours against their will

And financially?

Benefits	Costs
Royalty from the bauxite and various taxes and various taxes	Long-term costs of deforestation, pollution and removal of bauxite
Employment	Villagers' loss of land, livelihood and culture/community
Donations from the company to various temples and festivals in Odisha to musical and dance festivals and to a long list of individuals	
As FDI, stimulating Odisha's economy: 'multiplier effects'	
Profits for company directors, shareholders and investors, including consortium of banks based in London	

Benefits

A summary from London's International Aluminium Institute, gives a mainstream view on the benefits of aluminium in general, starting from the concept of Sustainable Development:

> The World Business Council for Sustainable Development has defined it as 'ensuring a better quality of life for everyone, for now and for generations to come.' It combines economic, social and environmental concerns, (often called the triple bottom line) and offers business opportunities for companies that improve the lives of the world's population....
>
> In 1900 annual output of aluminium was one thousand tonnes. By the end of the twentieth century annual production had reached 32 million tonnes of primary aluminium and 8 million tonnes from recycled metal. This makes aluminium the second most used metal. A world without aluminium has become unimaginable. The business traveller, the tourist and the freight company are dependent on aluminium, as the commercial aviation and space industries would never have achieved 'lift off' without it.
>
> The metal makes a key contribution to fuel-efficient engines in cars and trucks as well as to high speed rail and sea travel. By reducing the vehicles' weight it cuts down on fuel consumption and emissions, without compromising the size or the safety of the vehicles. Aluminium facilitates the construction of erosion-resistant and low maintenance buildings. Around the world, most long distance overhead transmission and distribution lines are made of aluminium.
>
> Aluminium in packaging preserves food quality, reduces waste and provides convenience for the users. It can be rolled into ultra-thin foils, which are light, strong and have unique barrier and insulation qualities. It preserves food, cosmetics and pharmaceutical products by protecting them from ultra-violet light, odours and bacteria. Packaging of all types, including aluminium, saves about 30 per cent of the world's food from wastage. Less than an ounce of aluminium sprayed on a polymer forms a thin heat-reflecting sheet that can keep a newborn baby warm or save the life of someone on an exposed mountain top. Aluminium has a particular advantage for use in arctic climates, as it retains all its performance properties at low temperatures.
>
> The aluminium industry directly employs over a million people worldwide and indirectly generates four times as many jobs in downstream and service industries.[1]

The image of prosperity that the industry promotes is essentially a 'modern lifestyle' of conspicuous consumption, speed and practical benefits—a lifestyle heavily dependent on aluminium, in which per capita aluminium consumption rises from India's 0.6 kg per year to 10 or 20 kg per year (as in 'developed countries'). The IAI advertises the benefits of setting up a bauxite/aluminium industry as follows:

Net benefits to local communities, regions and countries from bauxite mining can come from:

- Investment;
- Export earnings;
- Compensation payments;
- Federal, state and municipal tax payments;
- Employment;
- Education and training;
- The development of local industries and businesses;
- The development of infrastructure;
- The provision of health and other community programmes.

Benefits which Nalco, or any other aluminium company, offers for Odisha include:

1. Profits, which the company shares with local communities.
2. Revenue for the GoI and GoO in terms of royalty, taxes, etc., in foreign currency (but what will the real percentage of aluminium companies profits invested locally be?)
3. Business and profits for other construction, engineering, transport, etc. companies. Benefits to the local, State or national economy by stimulating other industries.
4. Benefits to local population in terms of employment, medical care, new roads, 'pukka' houses and other infrastructure and 'Corporate Social Responsibility' (but promises to displaced populations have rarely been kept in practice)

In monetary terms, what does this mean?

1. Company's profits (including directors' salaries), and the profits for their shareholders and investors, especially the banks and metal trading firms.
2. Bauxite Royalty and Taxes: e.g. Nalco wrote a cheque to the

GoI for Rs 224.6 crores as its dividend for 2001–02 ('62.75 per cent of its after-tax profit')
3. Initial investment costs, aiding infrastructure: roads, medical centres, schools, etc., compensation and payments for buying land, etc.
4. Employment wages: Nalco spends Rs 290 crore per year on 7,085 staff (2005). If Vedanta at Lanjigarh employs 300 people as stated, this will provide wages of 15 crore per year at the same rate. CSR, schools, clubs, training schemes …
5. Stimulating other industries: e.g. construction by Metro Builders of Vedantanagar colony, of infrastructure by Sensex and other subcontractors …

Costs of Production

The refineries being promoted in Odisha and Andhra are geared to exploiting the mountain-top bauxite deposits. While we have been writing this book, aluminium prices were mostly rising (2002–08), thanks to demand from China and a worldwide scarcity of new deposits; but from October 2008 there has been a sharp fall in prices. Given wide variations in costs of production, Odisha's attraction shows in Nalco's cost advantage as one of the cheapest producers.

The reason Nalco's cost of production is so low lies partly in cheap costs of labour, and partly in the mineral composition of Odisha's bauxite, which is gibbsitic (tri-hydrate), and because its silica/quartz content is exceptionally low, so that the temperature needed to digest the bauxite at Damanjodi refinery is 100 degrees less than in most refineries (Tamotia 2001 and 2004).[2]

The cost of electricity generation is quite high in India, which is why Nalco sells some of its alumina to be smelted at newly built plants in Bahrain, UAE (Dubai) and Iran, and why Nalco announced plans in early 2008 for new smelters in Iran, South Africa and Indonesia. Of the global alumina market, 45 per cent is estimated to be globally traded, while 55 per cent is internally shifted within integrated companies.

As for aluminium's cost of production: the LME price in 2004 was between $1,380 and $1845 per ton, while the average Business

Operating Cost was estimated at around $1,200, breaking down roughly as follows:

Alumina 38%	$490
Electricity 29%	$300
Carbon inputs 10%	$125 (80% for calcined petcoke for anodes and cathodes, 20% for coal tar pitch as binder for anodes and cathodes)
Labour 11%	$135
Other costs 12%	$150

Table 11. Average cost of production per ton of aluminium

This calculation is done taking account of 'backward and forward linkages', meaning what is paid for raw materials (backward links), and what is paid by those who buy the alumina and aluminium (forward links).

However, analysing aluminium's cost of production like this conceals externalised costs. For example, we have seen how the costs of infrastructure developments taking place in Odisha, for which the aluminium industry is a primary beneficiary, is borne through loans from the WB (roads, coal), IFAD (Kashipur roads), Saudi Fund for Development (railway), Japanese banks (Indravati dams), etc. This is what has sunk the Odisha government so steeply into debt and diminished the funds it has available for proper maintenance of social services, from health and education to salaries and water pumps. A proper CoP calculation should include externalised costs as well as conventionally included costs.

Shivaji Pattnaik's CPM pamphlet (2003), *Stall the conspiracy of privatizing Nalco*, argues that Nalco's cheaper prices are an advantage that should stay in India. He mentions that when Naveen Patnaik was Minister for Steel and Mines in the central government in the mid-90s he masterminded a disinvestment of 13 per cent of Nalco, and draws attention to Odisha's first mined-out mountain, Gorumahisani, whose orphaned labourers and tribals give a terrible example of what private mining companies do. He speculates that

Included Costs:
> Construction of plants: the initial outlay/investment, including purchase of land
> Bauxite/Alumina
> Taxes & Royalty
> Labour of directly employed work-force
> Electricity (a mix of hydropower and coal-fired captive power plants—ccpps) (estimated as 21–30% of CoP)
> Coal, pitch, tar, caustic soda and cryolite (Sodium Aluminium Fluoride—NaAlF) refining one ton of alumina is estimated to need 75 kg of caustic soda, 48 kg of lime and 30 kg of cryolite
> Freight (transport by road, rail and sea)
> Water (for which only a bare minimum is paid)

Externalised: i. Economic and Environmental Costs:
> Cost of infrastructure construction: transport, roads, railway, etc.
> Real cost of electric power generation, water, and land acquired
> Dam construction, coal-mines, power stations
> Deforestation and destruction of mountains, drying out of streams
> Excessive use and pollution of water (including red mud, ash ponds, etc.)
> Carbon and other emissions, impacts on local rainfall, global warming ...

ii. Costs to People/Society:
> Displacement of villages and loss of their agricultural land
> Deteriorating health from contamination of water, drying-out of land
> Disruption of community life (Cultural Genocide)
> Dangers of environmental degradation for future generations

Table 12. Included and Externalised costs

Hindalco would buy up Nalco as Sterlite bought Balco for a *'sago macho doro'* ('spinach-fish price').

This comment reveals the basic fact about bauxite: it is sold far too cheaply. The primary aim of the aluminium cartel is to keep prices of bauxite as low as possible (Chapter Eleven). There is no 'free market' for bauxite, and companies' starting point of 'value creation' is acquiring a source as cheaply as possible. Only Jamaica and the IBA managed to raise the bauxite price substantially, for a short period in the early 1970s, and this feat has never been repeated.

Estimates for the Eastern Ghat bauxite deposits in Odisha and Andhra vary between 1.6 and 3 billion tons (the difference between 'recoverable resources', i.e. 'proved reserves' as against 'probable and possible reserves'), dwarfing India's other deposits. Calculating at some of the highest recent alumina and aluminium prices for bauxite, alumina and aluminium, and their ideal ratio of 4 tons of bauxite>2 tons alumina>1 ton aluminium, one could calculate all the deposits' financial value roughly as follows:

Sold as bauxite at $30 per ton: 3,000 million x $30	= $90 billion
Sold as alumina at $600 per ton: 1,500 million x $600	= $900 billion
Sold as aluminium at $3,000 per ton: 750 million x $3,000	= $ 2.25 trillion ($1,000 billion)

Table 13. Estimated value of the bauxite reserves of Odisha and Andhra Pradesh

However, this valuation represents a gross under-valuation considering the devastation which extracting and processing this ore would cause to the ecosystem and population of Odisha and Andhra. If the externality costs were properly priced, including for now just the figures given (Chapter Twelve) for producing a ton of aluminium (more than 1,300 tons of water consumed, 6–20 tons of CO_2 emitted, 'abiotic intensity' of 85 tons, etc.), these costs would come to well over $10 trillion.

The factors that go into fixing the prices of bauxite and aluminium are more complex and manipulative than can easily be understood. In fact, a mystique has grown up of making pricing policy highly secret and hard to understand—a trend that has increased hugely in recent years.

As an example, the National Resources Institute (London), which used to analyse UK prices in relation to world prices, was privatised in 1994, when its staff was cut from 375 to just 130. It lost its expertise, and began to hire consultants. In India, the Bureau of Industrial Costs and Prices (BICP), which we have seen recommended against expanding the aluminium industry due to excessive costs in 1988, no longer maintains an independent Indian perspective, but presently follows international prices as a yardstick. Meanwhile, commodity analysts who estimate price trends have become some of the world's most highly paid consultants, in line with the $19,000 price of CRU's *Analysis Report: Bauxite Mining Costs* (2007). One trend is clear: a growing disparity generally between commodity prices for primary and secondary goods. This is one of the main reasons why exploiting Odisha's bauxite is bound to be grossly exploitative. The price of CRU's information forms an essential aspect of this exploitation.

Actual Costs

There are many different ways that a Cost Benefit Analysis (CBA) can be done. A UN report in 2002 noted that for mining to be truly economic, all costs should be covered (i.e. none should be externalised).[3] But certain key costs are impossible to evaluate financially. How can actual costs to water, forest, air quality, or people's sense of community and well-being be reduced to figures? Estimates vary vastly. 'Green accounting', that calculates the Net Present Value of forests and biodiversity such as those on Niyam Dongar, despite its *caveats*, provides a formula for corporates that vastly undervalues natural forest and its biodiversity—let alone its cultural and sacred significance.

The size of mining companies' externality costs explains why CBA is not calculated more openly. What follows is a sketch of some of the main costs, to place against the benefits of bauxite mines and aluminium plants in Odisha or Andhra.

A. Environmental Costs:

1. Removal of forest cover, overburden and the bauxite itself, which means permanent removal of a non-renewable resource, breaking apart the top of a mountain, and impacting the perennial flow of its water-sources. Loss of forest lessens local rainfall as well as bio-diversity.

2. Environmental cost of producing the electrical power in terms of the coal industry and carbon emissions, since each aluminium plant has its own captive coal-fired power plant (ccpp). Coal mining is mostly done in huge open pits now, destroying forest, fields and villages. Coal-fired power stations put their effluent in highly toxic ash ponds and periodically these burst their dams and inundate land and rivers.

3. Environmental cost of producing the electricity in terms of hydropower schemes, which in India, as worldwide, supply an estimated 50 per cent or more of the aluminium plants' power. Environmental and social costs of big dams should therefore be included in the cost of setting up refineries and smelters. The cost of big dams, as we have seen, include:

   i. Forest cover and biodiversity lost
   ii. Agricultural land lost
   iii. Reservoirs' emission of gases like methane from decaying trees
   iv. Impediment to rivers' flow, drying up sections, stopping fish migration and killing off many riverine species, deadening (de-oxygenating) the quality of water;
   v. Salinisation of the soil in surrounding areas
   vi. Danger of dams breaking in times of excessive rainfall and sudden releases of water causing floods (as has happened several times), and danger of provoking earthquakes

4. Cost of taking the water: aluminium plants guzzle over 1,000 tons of water to produce one ton of aluminium, so add to depletion

of the water table, and the non-availability of water for farmers (cause of huge demonstrations at Hirakud 2006–8)

5. Costs of Pollution by smoke-stack:
   i. Carbon Dioxide: 991 kg of CO_2 emissions per ton of alumina refined, and between 6 and 20 tons of CO_2 emissions per ton of aluminium smelted
   ii. Carbon Monoxide
   iii. Sulphur Dioxide
   iv. PFCs (perfluorocarbons): 0.3 kgs of C_2F_4 (tetrafluoromethane) and 0.03 kgs of C_2F_6 (hexafluoroethane) per ton (= 2.2 tons of CO_2)
   v. Fluoride from smelters

6. Pollution in terms of solid and effluent waste:
   i. Bauxite Dust
   ii. Toxic Red Mud, which inevitably leaches into ground water and often rivers (already polluting the Bansadhara within months of Lanjigarh refinery's start-up)
   iii. Spent Pot Lining

Attempts to work out the financial cost of some of these factors include:

1. Of forest lost, the MoEF handbook of guidelines estimates that 1 hectare of forest at density 1:1 should be valued at Rs 126.74 lakhs (accruing over 50 years). So the 660 hectares of Reserved Forest on Niyam Dongar alone, assuming an average density of 50 per cent, should be valued at Rs 417 crores. 'Green accounting' attempts to fix a monetary value on forest, to facilitate policy trade-offs. M. M. Sahu's Gandhamardan booklet (written in Odia in the 1980s) gives far higher values for trees lost, and primary forest on a mountain such as Gandhamardan or Niyamgiri performs so many services and possesses so many different kinds of value, that putting a financial figure on it is banal.[4]

2. Of carbon emissions, we have seen (Chapter Twelve) that the Stern Report (2006) costs the damage from a ton of CO_2 emission at $85. Producing a ton of aluminium emits between 6 and 20 tons of

CO_2, 20 if the supply is all from coal, 6 tons if it is all from hydro.[5] Most in India is a mix, but all the plants have a captive coal-fired power station, so at slightly more than half from coal, 15 X 85 = $1,275 per ton of aluminium, this being a minimum estimate of carbon costs externalised onto a region where aluminium plants are located. This is why so many aluminium plants have been closed recently in Europe—electricity costs have gone up and the companies can no longer get the subsidies they need on the electricity and water prices; environmental legislation is being applied more effectively than before. Of all sectors of the economy, metal production has by far the highest ratio of carbon emissions to profits, because of markets' historic inability to internalise pollution costs in commodity prices (Morrison 2007). One ton of alumina requires around 250 MW electricity, so the 6 million tous per year refinery at Lanjigarh is set to consume at least 1,500 million MW a year, producing at least 60 million tons of CO_2. At $85 per ton, the total cost of carbon emissions will come to over $5 billion per year.

3. Climate Change/Global Heating: in terms of the broader picture of India's increasing CO_2 emissions, the country already produces an estimated 4.7 per cent of the world's CO_2 emissions. This may seem small compared to 24 per cent of worldwide emissions from the US, which has a fraction of the population. But present plans for coal-fired power stations and metal factories alone will increase this percentage greatly, and is bound to have a major adverse impact on rainfall and climate in India/Odisha. The fact is, plans for India's further rapid industrialisation follow the path set by the US and Europe. Improvements in technology will only marginally improve carbon emissions, and the alternative path of nuclear power is fraught with dangers as well as hidden costs.

4. Similar analysis is needed of the water consumed and polluted, pollution from the north Odisha smelters, and so on. Financial analysis has strict limits. An attempt to put monetary values on non-renewable resources, or reduce the sources of life to monetary value can only go so far. This is even clearer when we come to:

B. Social/Human Costs:

1. Displacement of villages and cultivated land, forcing people who have lived a largely self-sufficient and sustainable life to become landless labourers and struggle for jobs.
2. Destruction of communities, breaking apart tribal society's social structure, which is based on cultivating land and egalitarian relations among kin and neighbours.
3. Lowering people's standard of living because of the environmental cost, depletion of water, scarcity of agricultural land, etc. Degradation of the environment is a principal cause of poverty.[6]
4. Cost to future generations in terms of destruction of the natural environment, permanent removal of mineral resources and damage to regional fertility.
5. Cost in terms of conflict, splitting apart society into those for and against the industry, introducing a harsh competitiveness and disparities of wealth.
6. Cost in terms of corruption of values, for example the murder and rape cases reported from Lanjigarh, deterioration of older, cooperation-based values, and 'flooding us out with money', or the invasion of outsiders and corruption.
7. Cost in terms of the inevitable penetration of remote forest areas by the timber and hunting mafias, who recklessly destroy valuable forest for immediate profit, systematically exterminate the larger predators, and sometimes kill people who stand in their way.[7]
8. Industrial disease: among the people most directly affected are workers inside the factories. A lot of evidence suggests statistics of lung and other diseases are systematically concealed in many if not most aluminium plants. Interviews at Damanjodi and Korba are emphatic on this.
9. Dangers for general health in terms of aluminium leaching from packaging, pots, and water supply, building up in the human body, causing Alzheimer's disease and cancers (Chapter Twelve).
10. Proliferation of the arms industry, aluminium feeding the world's wars, in output of bombs, missiles, warplanes and construction of military bases (Chapter Ten).

So how to compute the relative value of what is lost and what is gained? A CBA is not realistic unless it takes into account the cost to the environment and tribal cultures, and, indeed, the future well-being of Odisha's population as a whole. But since no way has been evolved to calculate this in economic terms, 'non-economic' costs tend to be discounted completely. Trying to put a price on the environment has been used increasingly as a strategy by companies and courts, as well as certain NGOs.

If the bauxite on Odisha's mountains, along with the trees and bushes that cover them, are what preserves Odisha's fertility, how can the bauxite be sold off for sums as small as $17 per ton? Even if the companies gave $1,000 per ton of bauxite mined, this would still lead to a destruction of Odisha's environment, but at least the price would begin to reflect what is being destroyed.

And which scientists have studied 'objectively' the impact of mining bauxite on the surrounding environment? All the science in aluminium conferences and journals is in effect 'pseudo-science', aimed at breaking bauxite down more effectively and making a profit for the aluminium companies, not geared towards actually understanding bauxite's place in a whole eco-system. Human and environmental costs are regarded as 'externalities', not calculated as part of the equation. Yet they are far more real in their impact on human life than the profits, which mostly disappear into the bank accounts of senior executives. Even sums spent on 'tribal development' are mostly channelled into profits for contractors. Not a little is spent on bribes, as in the unexplained Rs 70 crore widely believed to have been distributed by Utkal as bribes (Chapter Five), and a similar largesse known to be operating around Lanjigarh. To be accurate, a CBA should include an estimate of the bribes being paid to grease a project's path. When we understand the fertility and future potential that is being lost and sold off, damaging the mountains forever, shouldn't the price of bauxite be as high as the price of gold? What price would justify destroying the water-holding capacity of East India's biggest mountains? And who is orchestrating this sell-off?

Whose prosperity?

A world of difference divides the aluminium executives and their investors from the village people losing their land and communities in Odisha and neighbouring states. The dominant neoliberal theory is that as the nation's growth rate rises (measured by GNP—Gross National Product), this growth reduces poverty. Conventional economists still apparently believe this 'trickle down' model, as shown by Jeffery Sachs' influential book, *The End of Poverty* (2005). To comprehend the difference between theory and reality is to confront the essence of *Homo Hierarchicus* (Chapter Nineteen).

Areas affected by the aluminium industry exemplify the Resource Curse and extreme forms of hierarchy—these are places where the poor get a lot poorer, and the rich make obscene profits.[8] Different experts give widely differing analyses of whether India's economy is helped or held back by new investments in mining. With several projects held up by protest on the ground and in the courts, the state governments and companies are lining up to offer huge sums on the principle of '5 per cent of profits' towards local 'tribal development' and 'conservation plans'. These offers are highly deceptive. The top-down vision and past experience shows that the kind of 'development' on offer is not geared to empower local people and enrich their quality of life, but consists of construction-intensive infrastructure, with medical and educational projects that are top-down and non-accountable.

At the top are the company directors, investors and shareholders. Below this, the social structure forms a steep hierarchy from 'highly skilled' to 'unskilled'—negating any appreciation of Adivasi's traditional skills, as they are uprooted and turned into an industrial labour force. In this process, most get the opposite of prosperity; construction and factory workers and miners get minimal wages and minimal compensation for industrial accidents, often having to compete for scarce jobs, such as the villagers near Panchpat Mali who have to give large bribes for priority in labouring jobs. Skilled workers at Balco faced harsh conditions in the transfer to Vedanta ownership, when at least 1,300 were forced into Voluntary Retirement Schemes (VRS), *'through various forms of coercion'* of which all but 21 were paid less than was promised, according to a study by the National Labour Institute, which shows that 'most of the protection theoretically provided to the workers at the time of handover has been wilfully violated by Anil Agarwal's UK-based company.'[9]

The classic model of bauxite mining exploitation was exemplified by Alusuisse in Sierra Leone just before the terrible civil war that erupted in 1991, and one of its probable causes. *Transfer pricing* between Switzerland and Africa meant that no profits were showing in the local subsidiary Sieromco (Sierra Leone Ore & Metal Co.), so the government had been persuaded to take a nominal fee and impose no tax. In fact, Alusuisse was making huge profits by buying bauxite from its subsidiary for $18 per ton, while other companies were charged $30. Transfer pricing is

> a process of artificially redistributing a company's costs between different stages of process in its products, and/or between the company's operations in different countries, for financial advantage. Although the process can be quite complex, and of its nature is a highly secretive procedure, in essence it is quite simple. Materials, goods, or services, are priced by a company at an untrue, low rate in a high-tax zone, in order to escape heavy duties, and the difference in value added is made up by inflating production charges at another stage in a low-tax or tax-free zone. Thus, true production costs and product value are disguised in a way that suits the company best. The larger the corporation, the more massive the tax evasion can become.[10]

It seems that in various forms, transfer pricing is endemic in the mining industry, and at the heart of how East India stands to be exploited. Through the 'global accounting system' used by Alusuisse, Iceland lost millions of dollars in the 1970s–80s:

> the government alleged that over a period of seven years Alusuisse witheld a total of $47.5 million of profit from its smelter which would otherwise have been subject to taxation. Alusuisse through its "global accounting system" decides the price to charge its operations in different countries.[11]

The accountancy firm Coopers & Lybrand found that the Straumsvik smelter (ISAL, the Icelandic subsidiary of Alussuise) was under-capitalising. 'Increased by the sea' is how Iceland's Industry

Minister described the profits that Alusuisse creamed off by transferring between its foreign enclaves.

The transfer of mining funds between different countries offers many loopholes to an astute director. The shifting of funds between interlocking companies in the Sterlite-Vedanta group offers a series of examples. The initial scam with Harshad Mehta's Damayanti group took place in April–May 1998, when Sterlite raised its share price by artificial manipulation to make a bid to buy a stake in Indal (which failed). A similar scam was apparently behind the tenfold rise of Sterlite's share price on the Bombay Stock Exchange which preceded the move to London: between 5 June and 4 December 2003, the share price rose from Rs 165 to Rs 1,610, and assets were transferred to the Mauritius-registered company Twinstar Trading, avoiding tax; which in turn transferred them to Bahamas-registered Volcan Investments; which transferred them to a company first registered in London as Angelchange Ltd, renamed as Vedanta Resources Holdings Ltd, renamed as Vedanta Resources plc.[12] Understanding the complex trading deals that created *Vedanta's Billions* is beyond our scope here. Suffice it to say, the questions surrounding Sterlite/Vedanta's rapid accumulation of capital mirror questions asked about *Mellon's Millions* about the banker behind Alcoa (O'Connor 1933).

Sunil (2004) has given a compelling analysis of the dangers in 'dollarisation', spelling out the share market scams and drawing attention to Mauritius' role as a tax-haven, aided by a 'double tax avoidance treaty'. Behind Vedanta stand an army of financial investors and metal traders, including J. P. Morgan, HSBC and other banks, who prepared an extensive report before Vedanta's 2003 London flotation, Morgan Stanley/Citigroup, who prepared a report for a 2007 flotation in the US, and many others. These come into sharper focus through the lists of investors in mining projects given in the Thomson report on mining finance.[13] This barely mentions mining projects in India, with the exception of Vedanta's 2003 Initial Public Offering—the biggest to date worldwide.

Alongside the industrial houses, the media play a key role. It is worth noting that the *Financial Times* has maintained a virtual censorship on negative news about Vedanta, distorting their Niyamgiri lease as a 'secure' investment, and never mentioning the CEC's recommendation against giving clearance for this, and the long-drawn case at the Supreme Court. This omission could be seen as a form of share price manipulation, especially when the *FT* has failed to publish well-researched letters on the issue, despite assurances to the contrary.[14]

State governments often appear desperate to get as much FDI as possible, without apparently realising that Foreign Direct Investment means foreign financial insititutions buying up India's most precious assets. As people throughout India are swept up in the craze for new 'consumer durables' and aluminium-packed foodstuffs, are the country's mountains and rivers the price?

Behind the banks are the hedge funds, private equity funds, and the *Wall of Money* they move around in a multi-trillion dollar game of split-second speculation, based on tax havens, *derivatives trading*, *dumping risk, performance-oriented financial products* and *leverage buy outs*—concepts that boil down to using debt to generate unprecedented profits. Hedge funds are known to be pouring investment into Third World infrastructure and mining projects now. Commodity speculation by hedge funds has played a major role in driving metal prices up recently, and this price rise is a major cause of mining companies' present scramble after East India's minerals.[15]

About 60 US and 30 UK hedge funds are known to have snapped up a large part of Vedanta's initial shares within hours of their flotation on the London Stock Exchange on 5 December 2003, selling them hours later, and buying again when the price went down and Vedanta unexpectedly issued another tranche of shares. About 90 per cent of hedge funds' trading decisions are estimated to be made in London and New York. For metal traders, Odisha's debts and the low price for bauxite are a likely source of unprecedented prosperity, even while mining projects uproot Adivasis and plunge them into unprecedented poverty.

Huge electricity susbidies are vital to keeping costs of production low. Rising electricity prices and tighter legislation are driving smelters out of Europe. We have seen that aluminium production has been progressively 'outsourced' to Third World countries, where costs are far cheaper.[16] Aluminium gives more profits in 'downstream' trading and manufacturing, especially for aerospace. The fact that arms companies' main customers are the world's governments is perhaps a main reason that the price of aluminium is so heavily subsidised. Certainly, rises and falls in supply and demand affect the price of aluminium far more than costs of production. While Europe, Japan, and the US have reduced their number of refineries and smelters dramatically, this is less true of the manufacturing mills which process aluminium ingot into rolled products (including foil), extrusions and protrusions (Appendix VI), and presumably into alloys for aerospace, etc.[17]

Keeping the price of bauxite low, and fostering competition between exporting countries, is similar to the manipulation of prices for other goods exported from 'developing countries', such as coffee. The 1980 price for a ton of coffee was $3,989. By 2002 this had reduced by a third to $1,234. Taking inflation into account, a ton of coffee was selling for about 13 per cent of the price it fetched 22 years before. Yet in the same period, the price paid by consumers for coffee more than doubled. In other words, the companies which control the transport and packaging get far more of the profit than the growers, and their ability to corner this profit for themselves has grown exponentially. Even 'fair trade' coffee does nothing to counteract this trend, which starts with an orchestrated over-production. Coffee growing has been promoted by western governments as 'aid' in many Third World countries, which has had the effect of making them all dependent on coffee exports, and in constant competition with each other. This is what keeps the coffee price so low, to the advantage of the companies that buy and market it—not to mention the aluminium foil producers who package it so nicely.[18]

Coffee competition, fostered to the detriment of exporting countries, illuminates the metals industry, where mining companies keep ore prices outrageously low. However, it is not made obvious that the price is low, because all the companies making aluminium act together to enforce a low price, by making bauxite-producers compete—one of the main functions of the aluminium cartel. bauxite mining itself makes no profit at all. Refining alumina and smelting aluminium only make a profit artificially, thanks to subsidies. By contrast, India's retail trade is estimated at $300 billion and rising fast, including a large section going to packaging and transport companies.[19]

In Gandhi's well-known analysis, basic prosperity consists in enough for everyone, on the principle that the world's resources, with careful management and fair distribution, are enough for everyone's need, but not for even one man's greed.

> That economics is untrue which ignores or disregards moral values. The extension of the law of non-violence in the domain of economics means nothing less than the introduction of moral values as a factor to be considered in regulating international commerce. (1924)
>
> According to me ... everyone should be able to get sufficient work to enable him to make the two ends meet. And this ideal can be universally realised only if the means of production of the elementary necessaries of life remain in the control of the masses. These should be freely available to all as God's air and water ought to be; they should not be made a vehicle of traffic for exploitation of others. Their monopolisation by any country, nation or group of persons would be unjust. The neglect of this simple principle is the cause of the destitution that we witness today not only in this unhappy land but in other parts of the world too. (1928)[20]

Gandhi fought the exploitation of India under British rule, but saw that the situation would hardly improve with Independence, if the system of dispossession and exploitation remained in place. Why have economists failed to get to grips with understanding this? Eighty years, and no real development: the means of production are as alienated from the masses as totally as they were in the time of Marx or Gandhi. 'Real Development' would see an end to the exploitation, inequality and lies.

The ramifications of Gandhi's philosophy for economics were worked out by J.C.Kumarappa, whose work *The Economics of Permanence* (1946) formed the inspiration for Schumacher's *Small is Beautiful* (1973). Kumarappa characterises the modern capitalist economy as parasitic in nature—i.e. based on exploitation, and in the long term, unsustainable. Proper agriculture consists of *'local self-sufficiency in food production'*, and village self-reliance, rather than an increasing emphasis on cash crops and transporting food. Centralised production tends to reduce workers to a condition of enslavement. Machines and factories involve a basic inequality between the enslaved labour of those who mine the ore and make it into primary metal, and those they work for. As for exports, 'When ores are sent out of the country, the heritage of the people of the land is being sold out.'[21]

Niyamgiri forest, preserved by the Dongria

Measuring prosperity in purely economic terms brings in a great distortion. For instance, displaced villagers throughout East India are drawn into a wage economy at the same time as they lose their food security and enter an economic insecurity where they can no longer grow their own food. The aluminium industry in Odisha has already shattered the well-being of thousands of Adivasis and become a merciless exploiter. The concept of 'prosperity' that is driving the industry needs proper analysis and de-masking.

The reality that mining areas suffer a massive drop in living standards and endemic poverty is well documented worldwide as well as within India, for example in Eduardo Galeano's *Open Veins of Latin America: Five Centuries of the Pillage of a Continent.*[22] As Bhagaban says (Das 2005):

> We ask one fundamental question: How can we survive if our lands are taken away from us? We are tribal farmers. We are earthworms. Like fishes that die when taken out of water, a farmer dies when his

land is taken away from him. So we won't leave our land. We want permanent development. Provide us with irrigation to our lands. Give us hospitals. Give us medicines. Give us schools and teachers. Provide us with lands and forests. The forests we want. We don't need the company. Get rid of the company.

We do not oppose development. In fact we all want development. But what we need is stable development. We won't allow our billions of years old water and land to go to ruin just to pander to the greed of some officers. We ask them not to get engaged in these destructive works. Stop this work. Give us what we want if you really mean development. We tell this to our leaders. But the government has not even agreed to talk to us. They should think that nature is not only for just one or two, or three or four generations. Nature has created us, it helps us survive.

Being rulers, how can you adopt policies that would destroy our land in the coming 30–35 years?

PART IV

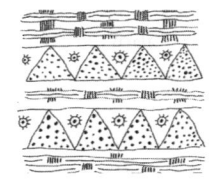

Company Rule

So what kind of development are the mining companies really promoting in Odisha? Have they brought prosperity to ordinary people? Have they eradicated poverty or made it worse? How have these companies become so powerful so fast? What is the nature of their power? How does it fit with government authority? And what is the role of foreign banks and governments?

Sometimes it looks as if the police and administration are taking orders, in effect, from the companies. Has government authority been subverted in the notorious incidents of police firing, and in the selling-off and depletion of Odisha's natural resources and dispossession of large sections of the indigenous population?

As for the mining companies, sometimes they seem to be re-creating the kind of power and exploitation of the East India Company, staging an extraction of resources on a scale unimaginable in East India Company times. One of the institutions that has given them this power, through loans and close connections with corporations and the world's 'top' governments, is the World Bank. Working closely with it, dictating the 'liberalisation' process and financial policies of India's mineral-richest states, is the DFID, Department For International Development of the British government.

What is the role of NGOs alongside the companies and donor agencies?

How to conceptualise the overall pattern of what is happening and understand the phenomenon of the company itself, in particular the mining company, and aluminium company? What is striking about companies, sociologically, is the extent of their hierarchy; the power they now exercise over and above the power of governments and elected politicians; their organisation around one principal aim of creating profit for their investors and directors; their PR machinery; and their system of values and beliefs.

Grand beginnings in the 1600s involved several major overseas trading ventures. The East India Company was among the first, and gave birth to the Government of India during the eighteenth century. Shortly before this, the South Sea Company, trying to make a profit out of Britain's National Debt, created a classic bubble that burst, alerting people to the dangers of companies, of which Adam Smith in particular gave prophetic warnings. So legislation held companies in check, until the second half of the nineteenth century, when their power was gradually unleashed in a 'second industrial revolution' based on oil, railways, electricity, and a vastly increased scale of mining and use of metals. This process culminated in the first Trusts or Cartels, formed by the robber barons. An Anti-Trust drive split up Rockefeller's Standard Oil, Carnegie steel, and Alcoa's naked attempts at an aluminium monopoly. After the Depression in the1920s, Roosevelt's New Deal put more brakes on companies, holding corporate power in check until Reagan and Thatcher let them loose in the Age of Neoliberalisation we live in now....

CHAPTER FIFTEEN

Corporate Takeover

Rapidly imposed industrialisation

India's 9 per cent growth rate (2007–08) is connected with an extensive land-grab in central India, as indigenous cultivators of the soil are dispossessed to make way for mines, dams, power plants and factories. The process has accelerated with the National Mineral Policy and Special Economic Zones, pushing the neoliberal agenda of inviting a massive influx of Foreign Direct Investment, privatisation, streamlining mining leases, and removing the 'restrictive legislation' which protected India's environment and people's rights.

Distinction between foreign and Indian companies is blurred now. Indian companies have bought up foreign ones and get large amounts of finance from abroad, while foreign companies still mostly hide their face through joint ventures with Indian companies, and investments in the mining companies that are rapidly acquiring natural resources and setting up projects.

At the same time, East India presents a shining example of people's movements aginst corporate invasion and forced displacement—

movements that are also a worldwide phenomenon. On the other side of the earth, indigenous Peruvians in the Amazon region face a similar power nexus facilitated by a 'Law of the Jungle' sell-off to oil companies. A blockade by about 30,000 trying to stop oil and gas prospectors invading their lands met severe police violence on 5–6 June 2009, with a large number of people killed. The indigenous leader Alberto Pizango's words apply to India too:

> In the 21st century, indigenous people are still being killed for standing up for our life, land, sovereignty and dignity.[1]

What is happening in East India is on a vast scale, and there are many ways of understanding it. Where did it all begin?

The first industrial revolution, that ushered in the modern age, is usually located in 18th–19th century Britain, through a proliferation of canals, steam power, coal and iron-ore mining, copper smelting and steel factories. The world's biggest copper smelters were near Swansea in Wales, and deep pit mining for tin in Cornwall and coal in Wales and the North led world production. Among the masterminds of the industrial revolution were a number of free-thinking individuals with a passion for invention, who helped to free technology from academic science. Among them were Charles Darwin's two grandfathers, Erasmus Darwin and Josiah Wedgewood, who formed the Lunar society, meeting every full moon, guided by a conviction that their inventions and factories would improve the lot of mankind, without any conception of where the process would lead.

But in Wales, and all the industrialising areas, a brutal exploitation of men, women and children took place in the mines and metal factories, especially from the 1830s. Thousands were killed in hideous work accidents and cholera epidemics, and protestors demanding only the most basic of rights—tolerable working conditions and unions—met severe repression from the iron masters and dragoons—events that set the pattern for events unfolding in India today.[2]

In the US soon after, massive land grabs and financial manipulation built unprecedented fortunes for the 'robber barons', culminating in J. P. Morgan's empire and Andrew Mellon's Alcoa-Gulf Oil interests. The hatred which these men faced for their endless scams and ruthless exploitation of workers, investors and fellow citizens was balanced by their status as American 'heroes', and their industries helped turn America into today's superpower, even while they brought genocide to native Americans. Their US model of interlocking companies, as well as the love-hate status of super-rich company heads, set the pattern for corporate India. We have seen how Birla and other Indian magnates formed ties over aluminium with American magnates such as Kaiser, and Anil Agarwal's Vedanta-Sterlite group has travelled a similar path, for example enlisting a report from J. P. Morgan to register in London.

Probably the most quickly and violently imposed industrialisation processes of all were those orchestrated by Stalin in the USSR and Mao in China. Stalin's policy involved forcibly removing people from the land, and was linked to a rapid construction of steel plants, aluminium factories and dams, partly by American engineers, financed through his secret sale of outstanding artworks to Andrew Mellon (Chapter Two). In 1932–33, at least seven million Ukranians died from starvation and related causes, due to Stalin's harsh Collectivisation programme. Another virtually unrecorded famine followed from Russia's enforced transition to neoliberal capitalism in the early 1990s, resulting in about 4 million starvation deaths in Russia alone.[3]

China followed Russia's pattern of imposing industrialisation at great speed. The 'Great Leap Forward' enforced a move from agriculture to steel production, causing a famine in which an estimated 30 million died. Numbers are disputed, but this highlights a parallel with displacement in India, where no reliable tally of affected people is kept. The policy was driven by Mao's obsession with raising steel output, liquidating anyone rash enough to try and tell him what was really happening.[4] This is part of the world's 'hidden history', neglected by Maoists and capitalists alike, but vital for comprehending present dangers of rapidly imposed industrialisation—a story that continues in China with thousands dying in coal mining accidents each year, and millions affected by the Three Gorges dams.[5]

In other countries, the process of rapidly imposed industrialisation has tended to follow these models, often orchestrated by the WB and similar agencies. Brazil offers a particularly close example for Odisha, on a vaster scale (Chapter Nine).

What is happening now in India is summarised in the Centre for Science and Environment's 2008 report, *Rich Lands, Poor People: Is Sustainable Mining Possible?* though this does not attempt to analyse the pattern of corporate takeover. Obviously, this pattern is worldwide, not confined to India. It has gathered pace since Reagan and Thatcher started to dismantle the constraints on corporate power, and our chapter title is taken from George Monbiot's *Captive State: The Corporate Takeover of Britain* (2000). It is important to remember that even the neoliberals' hero Adam Smith saw strong constraints on companies as essential to prevent them from making a 'conspiracy against the public'.[6]

The company Adam Smith particularly criticised was the East India Company, for its outrageous exploitation of India, and the way it assumed the functions of government, through gross manipulation of law and finance. So it is an irony of history that East India is precisely one of the areas of the world showing some of the strongest resistance to corporate takeovers. For the moment, foreign investment is held back, by people's movements as well as the recession. As one of India's top commodity analysts puts it: 'Time's bad for launching new steel projects' (Kunal Bose, *Business Standard*, 26 January 2009).

This resistance manifests in dozens of 'slow wars' going on in East India—similar to 'resource wars' in many parts of the world—that enter the world's media only sporadically. Since metal production fuels war through the military-industrial complex, East India's 'slow war' over land and resources is a structural counterpart to the 'War on Terror'. Mining and war feed each other, and both are driven by patterns of financial investment and metals trading orchestrated from London and other capitals. This context helps to explain the significance of the current David-Goliath power struggle going on between indigenous communities and big companies over land and resources in this part of the world.

The scramble for East India's mineral resources

Present deals to acquire mining leases in the tribal areas of East India are reminiscent of the European powers' 'scramble for Africa' in the late nineteenth century (part of that too was a scramble after minerals). Odisha possesses the largest quantities of India's chromite (98 per cent), bauxite (51 per cent), and manganese (35 per cent), coming second in coal (24 per cent) and iron-ore (17 per cent).[7]

The effect on environment and communities from existing mines is already vast, especially in north Odisha, from iron and coal mines and sponge-iron factories. Huge open-cast coal mines scar the Ib valley (Jharsaguda) and Talcher (Angul) areas (Panda 2007). Underground coal mines started in Talcher in the 1920s and went open cast in the 1960s.[8] The chromite mines of Sukinda (Jajpur) were named one of the ten most polluted spots on earth in September 2007,[9] and the quarried and mined-out hills covering large areas of Jajpur district call to mind T. S. Eliot's *Waste Land*.

Odisha has long been famous for its precious or semi-precious gemstones, which entrepreneurs have been mining and trading illegally for years. Recently, as the Rio Tinto speech indicated (Chapter Seven), diamonds have been discovered along the Mahanadi. BHP Billiton, RT and De Beers have signed deals for prospecting leases in an area covering 6,900 square kilometres in Odisha and Chhattisgarh.[10]

Rio Tinto has also been involved in iron-ore mines in Keonjhar, where we visited its venture with SAIL on the Gandhamardan range (a different Gandhamardan from the bauxite-capped mountain in west Odisha), whose flanks are devoured by explosives and diggers, while tribal labourers crush the ore below. Like much of Keonjhar, this is an area where mining has devastated elephant-forest, communities and water (Sethi 2007). As a tribal woman said, about the difficulty of fetching water in an area where it used to be abundant,

> Everything is so dry now. Our streams and waterfalls have disappeared. What have they done to them? (Das 2005)

Odisha's industrialisation started with Tata's first iron-ore mines on a densely forested 3,000-foot mountain in the north (Lala 1992), now derelict, deforested and sterile.

> Once upon a time, cows and buffaloes used to graze on these mountains, so it was called Gorumahisani (cattle buffalo hill). A dream was sown here in 1904-1905 under British rule, that "mining will bring prosperity." The geologist Pramath Nath Bose was working

for the king of Mayurbhanj. The mountain was leased without any royalty to a company called Tata. Then the company paid three and a half anna (1/4th of a penny) per ton of iron-ore to the king. That's how the first Indian private company, Tata, was born. (Das 2005)

Studies of India's coal and iron reserves in the early nineteenth century by the East India Company for its ships and railways led to the formation of the Geological Survey of India in Calcutta. Tata's dream of steel led to the founding of Tatanagar at Jamshedpur (now in Jharkhand), where steel was first produced, using Mayurbhanj iron-ore, in 1912.

Contemporary with Hirakud in the 1950s, the Rourkela steel plant was Odisha's first mega-industry, run by SAIL (Steel Authority India Ltd), a public sector company. Along with Mandira dam, it displaced at least 23,000 Adivasis from 64 villages.[11]

The first of Odisha's new steel plants, near Gopalpur, was thwarted by a strong people's movement. Tisco signed a deal with the Orissa government in August 1995, backed by foreign interest and finance from several Japanese companies, Posco, BHP, and others from Western Europe, after earlier plans for an ambitious steel plant by Biju Patnaik and Lord Swaraj Paul had fallen through.[12]

Prime Minister Narasimha Rao laid the foundation stone for Gopalpur steel plant on 30 December 1995—broken by furious villagers the next day. The factory threatened to displace about 25,000 people from 25 villages, who stood to lose a rich agricultural economy, and swiftly established a *Gana Sangram Samiti* to fight the plant. Women formed a *Nari Sena* (women's army), and came to the forefront of protests when about 6,000 armed police were sent to cow resistance in August 1996, and arrested hundreds of men. In repeated *lathi* charges, many women were injured, and two died from their wounds: D. Laxamma of Badaputti village, and S. Iramma of Laxmipur. Police invaded the area again in March 1997, and meeting strong resistance again, opened fire, injuring four severely. People set up 14 gates to prevent entry by company officials and police, erecting a pillar inscribed with the words: '*Water, land and environment belong to us and no-one else has any rights to them.*'

The movement managed to stop the plant and a dam on the Rushikulya River 120 km away, which would have displaced about

5,000 Adivasis. Yet Tisco displaced several of the Gopalpur villages, enclosing 5,000 acres with a high wall, though till now, this land has remained unused.[13]

Steel plants need chrome and manganese as well as iron. When strong pressure was being brought on the Ministry of Mines in Delhi to clear a number of crucial chromite mining leases in Sukinda, by IMFA, Jindal and other steel companies, the senior bureaucrat in charge of this issue died in suspicious circumstances on 27 September 1997, jumping or being thrown out of a window in Shastri Bhavan. The man who died was M. C. Mahapatra, Joint Secretary to the Ministry. The CBI's inquiry into his death and the pressure to grant leases has never been made public, and questions were asked on the issue in the Rajya Sabha on 6 July 1998 by Ghufran Azam to the Minsiter of Steel and Mines, who was then Naveen Patnaik. If the Sukinda chromite mines are extremely polluting, they also involve large profits (so by implication large-scale corruption), because chrome is a vital ingredient for making certain kinds of steel, and nearly all of India's chromite deposits are near Sukinda.[14] This corruption continues, surfacing in 2005 over a shady deal between Jindal Strips and Idcol (Industrial Development Corporation of Orissa Ltd.) at Tangarpadar in Dhenkanal.[15]

The Kalinganagar complex of steel plants is conveniently close to Sukinda. It was first conceived in the 1980s, and the government started negotiating for land acquisition in 1990. The first steel plant was completed by Nilachal Ispat Nigam Ltd. on 2,700 acres, starting production in 2000, and displacing 634 families, some of whom accepted small plots in Gobarghati colony, 12 km away. Several other companies, including Jindal, have also completed steel plants. But in May 2005, police lathicharged a protest against a *Bhumipuja* (propitiation of the earth) being performed by Maharashtra Seamless Steel. Footage of this event shown in *Matiro Poko* shows the Additional District Magistrate (ADM) ordering seated Adivasi protestors to disperse, after which police disarm and then attack them, while women roll on the ground screaming. One woman was crushed to death under a truck, and two children died from neglect in the villages while their parents were detained for 22 days at Kalinganagar police station.[16] Maharashtra Seamless withdrew soon after this event.

But pressure to start construction of another company's steel led to the police firing which has made Kalinganagar a major symbol of tribal resistance to imposed industrialisation—echoes of a different invasion over 2,000 years ago, when Ashoka's army massacred the Kalinga people (Chapter Three).

Memorial to the thirteen Adivasis killed at Kalinganagar

On 2 January 2006, hundreds of Adivasis from 25 villages heard that Tata was about to start construction on their land near Champakoili village, and collected in a stand-off with twelve platoons of police (about 420 policemen), who were escorting construction workers with six bulldozers in a desperate attempt to make a start. Most Adivasis are without *patta* (land-deeds), so they had received no proper compensation, and Idco (Industrial Development Corp.) had bought land for absurdly little, selling it on for ten times the amount. Just as the bulldozers were about to start levelling the ground, and a delegation of tribals had met with no response from the authorities, it seems that a stick of dynamite exploded in a group of advancing Adivasis, injuring four, and blowing the foot off one Birasingh Gop.

When others came close, more dynamite was triggered, apparently laid around the work site with a trip wire. This is when 'a mob of armed miscreants attacked the policemen standing on duty', and 'Havildar C. P. Mohanty was hacked to a brutal death.'[17]

This death triggered the police firing, which lasted for about an hour. Among those killed and seriously injured, many were innocent bystanders, including a woman of Champakoili standing by her house. The 13 Adivasis who died (one later in hospital) were from seven villages, while 38 people were seriously injured. Police took six bodies away immediately afterwards, and when these were returned, their hands (and unconfirmed reports said also their genitals) had been cut off. Some accounts immediately after the incident stated that these six were taken away wounded and killed in custody.[18]

After these killings, the Bisthapana Birodhi Jan Manch (BBJM, People's Platform Against Displacement) created a lot of publicity with its blockade on Odisha's major north-south highway, demanding the cancelling of 'false cases' and punishment of officials responsible for the firing and mutilations. The blockade was finally lifted in March 2007, under intense pressure and promises from the government, without the Adivasis agreeing to accept relocation. Since then, Tata has started construction, but progress has been slow. By the road where the blockade was, stands a sombre memorial to the thirteen martyred Adivasis in the idiom of their Ho-Munda culture, of thirteen standing stones on a platform, inscribed with distinctive symbols.

Some sections of the Orissa government and media tried to portray the Kalinganagar protestors as 'taken over by Maoists', and '90 per cent not really from Orissa.' These villagers' ancestors came from Jharkhand over 100 years ago, when the Sukinda raja had marriage relations with the Seraikela royal house, inviting tribals from there to bring Sukinda forest lands under cultivation. About 80 per cent never received *patta* (written land-deeds), and only those with *patta* are considered eligible for compensation. During the blockade, in May 2006, the Orissa government passed a new R&R policy, with special policies for Kalinganagar and Posco oustees, billed as very generous, and offering a good price for land plus cash for building new homes and job guarantees for a member of each displaced family and a promise to 'facilitate skill up-gradation of the nominated [family] member'. Implicit in this, is an intention to convert the displaced people from cultivators to industrial workers, which means classifying them as 'unskilled'.[19] As Kalinganagar Adivasis continue their opposition, they face attacks and threats from *goondas*, who shot dead Amin 'Shyam' Banara in May 2008.[20]

Posco (Pohang Steel Company of South Korea) was also drawing up plans for a contentious steel plant at this time, on the coast near Paradip port, in Jagatsingpur district. The primary aim was to get a lease for mining iron in north Odisha, but the GoO made it clear that this would only be forthcoming if it was made into steel within the state. Posco's main application is for an area of unspoilt forest on the beautiful Khandadhara mountain (Sundargarh district), which has Odisha's most spectacular waterfall, and which is also sought by the Kudramukh iron-ore company.[21]

People of the Pahari Bhuiya tribe are preparing to resist this invasion. Meanwhile, farmers in Jagatsingpur have put up a determined resistance.

Posco is seeking 1,620 hectares for its plant and port, 10 km north of Paradip, offering the biggest foreign investment in India: $12 billion for a 12 million ton steel plant. The villagers here are basically betel-vine cultivators, and the project offers Rs 6,000 per decimal of cultivated land. This land includes forest that protected the area during the cyclone of December 1999, as well as betel vine fields. Threatened with displacement are 22,000 people from 3,700 families in 11 villages (500 families according to official figures). These people have enjoyed a good standard of life, since their fields are fertile and their betel vines highly profitable. Since 2006 the villages have been surrounded, and under constant pressure. They erected barricades (as in the Gopalpur movement), and in May 2007 kidnapped Posco officials for a couple of days when these trespassed onto village land, and again on 13 October. The project received environmental clearance in August 2007, and serious violence erupted on 29 November, when pro-Posco *goondas* threw bombs at a crowd consisting largely of women, and a leading government official, Priyabrat Patnaik, made a statement on TV that 'those people have been taught a lesson.'

The Posco Pratirodh Sangram Samiti has resisted all attempts at a land survey, and when platoons were sent to enforce a survey on 12 February 2008, around 3,000 villagers faced them off. Pressure from *goonda* attacks culminated in the killing of Dula Mandal in

Khandadhara waterfall

June 2008, after a day of communal work dredging the Jatadhari river mouth, which had angered contractors who had hoped to make a lot of money doing this. Dhinkia is the village leading resistance. One of its leaders, Abhaya Sahu, of the CPI, was arrested on 12 October 2008 when ill-health forced him to leave his village and seek medical help in Bhubaneswar for acute rheumatoid arthritis. Despite this condition, he has been photographed wearing leg-irons on a hospital bed. A widespread campaign demanding his release was successful only after ten months.[22]

Similar intimidation, by *goondas* as well as police, began at a Public Hearing on 10 March 2008 for a Tata thermal power plant at Naraj, near Cuttack, that threatens to displace several villagers. This meeting initiated villagers entirely new to this kind of treatment to unprovoked beatings by police, making them determined to stand firm against displacement.[23]

Atrocities have taken place at many sponge-iron factories in north Odisha, for example police charged a crowd protesting at pollution and other abuses outside the Nepaz factory on 24 March 2006, and arrested about 100, mostly women and children, some of whom were kept behind bars for weeks. Bhushan's new steel plant, near Hirakud reservoir, is particularly notorious for its water consumption and pollution as well as its human rights record. Many workers have been killed or maimed in accidents without proper compensation, with bodies reportedly hidden in the factory grounds. Bhushan security forces opened fire on a crowd of protestors on 20 May 2006, after a spate of accident deaths (some in nearby sponge-iron factories). After about 200 worker deaths, more violence erupted on 29 December 2007, while a UNDP report catalogued the plant's bad safety record and 'hostile work environment'.[24]

Arcelor Mittal's designs on a mountain in Keonjhar were forced through with a Public Hearing on 6 November 2008. Just before, police arrested 250 tribal villagers, including 110 women, known to be strongly opposed to the mine, keeping them in Keonjhar jail for a day while the meeting took place. Another leading protestor was badly beaten up by *goondas*. The Collector reported that people from ten villages were present, and that 80 per cent supported the project and were willing to receive compensation![25]

Jharkhand has a long history of opposition to dams and mines, as well as subverted Public Hearings (Nazir 2007). Repression forcing through construction of the Koel Karo and Subarnarekha dams caused violent deaths in the 1980s, and the state has a similar number of sponge-iron factories as Odisha, and a horrific record of impoverishment and degradation from coal mines, especially at Jharia (Raja 2007), where underground fires have been burning for years, and Parej, where WB loans to improve displaced Adivasis' living standards have been a conspicuous failure.[26] Jaduguda is the site of India's main uranium mine, and one of the most dangerously polluted places in the country (Dias 2007).[27] Jharkhand was created as a new State in 2000 by splitting Bihar in fulfilment of a long-standing tribal dream. The way it was immediately taken over by non-tribal, especially mining company interests, is a history of betrayal. As in Odisha, these interests are driving a new wave of mining and metal factory projects, some on greenfield sites of outstanding cultural and natural significance, adding to already massive displacement of Adivasis and pressures on the environment.

Andhra has a long history of resistance to mining, marked by the Samatha Judgment, and opposition to moves by Jindal and the RAK to start bauxite mines and factories. Polavaram, a colossal dam planned on the Godavari, has met sustained opposition (not least for the land and villages it would flood in adjacent areas of Odisha and Chhattisgarh), as has a proposed uranium mine at Nalgonda.[28]

Chhattisgarh was created in 2000, like Jharkhand, without the same kind of movement, but with similar results of takeovers by mining companies. Older industries are represented by the Bhilai steel plant and Balco's refinery-smelter complex at Korba, with an open-cast coal mine at least a kilometre deep on the edge of town, and high-altitude bauxite mines (Agrawal 2007). Bailadila iron-ore mines started in the 1960s, with a special railway line to take the ore to Vizag for export to Japan. The ore was mined by displacing Maria Gond Adivasis and devastating their mountains and rivers. Plans for a steel plant in Bastar have repeatedly met with determined tribal opposition. However, iron/steel interests blossomed when Chhatisgarh was formed, and there are now about 70 sponge-iron factories. Jindal's huge iron/steel plant in Raigarh has gained a terrible reputation for pollution (despite receiving huge sums for carbon credits on the basis of its purported Clean Development Mechanism projects!) and has faced furious opposition from locals, after making their lives hell (Lohmann 2006, pp. 258–60).

Bastar (south Chhattisgarh) is India's tribal heartland, and new plans for steel plants still meet strong opposition there, but since mid-2005, this area has been the scene of the Salwa Judum civil war—a key theatre of the 'War on Terror' in India. Official statistics list 644 villages in Dantewada district as burnt by the Salwa Judum and just under 50,000 people as displaced to twenty registered refugee camps. The reality is probably nearer 200,000, of whom at least 20,000 have fled to neighbouring states, especially Andhra, to escape the horrors of Salwa Judum's camps and atrocities.

Salwa Judum started just as the Chhattisgarh government signed deals with Tata and Essar for new steels plants in June–July 2005, showing a suspicious nexus of interests fuelling the war. At Lohandiguda in Bastar and Dhurli in Dantewada, Adivasis have faced long sagas of police intimidation, yet continue to resist attempts to shift them.[29] The steel plant plans are predicated on more iron-ore mines in the Bailadila range and on Raoghat mountain, where opposition is strong despite being muted by the war.

The Chhattisgarh Assembly passed a draconian Security Act in 2005 that forbade independent reporting of the war. Special police trained in jungle warfare from Nagaland and Mizoram have been deployed, repeating a similar history of human rights abuses reported from North-East India. In fact, the Indian Army is directly involved in training the paramilitary forces for counterinsurgency operations in Adivasi areas of Central and East India. A Brigadier of the Indian Army, in charge of jungle warfare training for anti-naxal forces in Chhattisgarh, interviewed for a documentary shown on Channel 4 (UK), said the Naxalites had to be brought to book: 'We must come down on them like a ton of bricks.'[30] Adivasis are caught in the crossfire of what seems to be a resource war driven by mining interests.

West Bengal has witnessed particularly violent confrontations over industrial projects, involving fierce opposition at two main sites to mega-factories imposed by the CPI-M: Nandigram, 150 km south of Kolkata, where the Indonesian firm Salim Industries (notorious as a key Chinese firm that supported Suharto's infamous regime) planned a chemical complex (probably including cathodes for aluminium smelters); and Singur, where Tata's planned car factory was a joint venture with Fiat. Ironically, considering its 'pro-people' reputation, West Bengal's CPI-M government embraced the neoliberal agenda of rapid industrialisation with a special fervour. Buddhadev Bhattacharjee, Chief Minister of West Bengal, has tried to justify these projects by stating the underlying policy more openly than most:

> The people need to understand that the industrial process being initiated by the state government is irreversible and transition from agriculture to industry is an inevitable course.[31]

Singur and Nandigram projects are both sited on prime agricultural land, so well-watered that farmers could grow three crops a year. In both places, the main protestors were Dalit farmers, and in both places, the projects were successfully thrown out in 2007–08, but at a terrible cost in deaths, destroyed homes, ravaged land and divided communities. One of the most terrible deaths was that of Tapasi Malik, a young female activist at Singur, who took a leading role in organising resistance to the company, and was raped and killed on 18 December 2006.[32] At Singur, Nandigram and, more recently, among Santal protestors against Jindal, women have been prominent. There were several among the fourteen people killed in the notorious police firing at Nandigram on 14 March 2007, and many more among the wounded.

It was plans for a new Jindal steel plant SEZ that led to an unprecedented mass uprising of Santal Adivasis in West Midnapur district against police atrocities in November 2008, which quickly threw up an alternative working model of participatory democracy that functioned efficiently for nearly six months, even as all organs of state power remained effectively paralysed. This happened after police went on a rampage brutally torturing people, including many women, in Santal villages near the site of a landmine blast by Maoists that had unsuccessfully targeted the Chief Minister on his visit to the Jindal site.[33] A massive paramilitary operation was started in mid-2009 to restore the authority of the Indian State by crushing the mass uprising, and as we write, the Home Ministry is intensifying repression against the Santals' Platform Against Police Atrocities, in the name of targeting the Maoists.

The accusation by politicians and business leaders, orchestrated through the media, that the protests in Kalinganagar, Dhinkia, Nandigram or West Midnapur are organised by Maoists/Naxalites, should be understood as part of a strategy to crush all kinds of indigenous opposition based on the people's refusal to be displaced, to allow their land to be snatched away and their communities to be torn apart. Such use of the Maoist label to discredit people's movements is not warranted. Although Maoists have enlisted many oppressed peoples into their cause, most of the movements against displacement are in no way Maoist in inspiration or organisation. As Chakradhara Haiburu said (60-year-old spokesman for the Bisthapan Birodhi Jan Manch), after his friend was shot dead in May 2008, naming the gangster arrested for his murder: 'If Maoists were involved, it would be Arbind Sing (the gangster) lying dead, not Amin Banara.'[34]

Aluminium and power

In each state, whichever political party is in power makes the main deals with the mining companies, and party cadres often actively promote the companies, while parties in opposition often support local groups opposing industrial projects—Trinamool Congress in West Bengal, a section of the Congress under Bhakta Das in Odisha, along with the CPI and other Left parties, CPI again in Andhra and Chhattisgarh.

In some places, such as Kashipur, all-party committees have promoted a project (Chapter Five). In reply to criticism that Naveen Patnaik's BJD has signed mining deals with Vedanta and other companies against Odisha's interests, BJD politicians point out that many such deals were signed while the Congress was in power, for example the original Lanjigarh MoU between the OMC and Sterlite back in 1997. The BJD 'supremo' Pyari Mohan Mohapatra is one among several key individuals in the state government pushing the industrial projects. In his case, it is significant that he was a director of Nalco, a post he resigned from in 2004.

We have seen that when Brazil set up the mega-phase of its aluminium industry in the 1980s, with new dams and smelters, the state electricity company ran into huge debts even as the signed agreements forced it to sell electricity dirt cheap to the smelters, below the cost of production (Chapter Nine).

It is significant in this context that Odisha's power sector reforms were India's first.[35] Are the new electricity companies being placed in a similar position? Gridco is known to owe a massive debt to Nalco. The electricity unbundling that caused this situation is where the corporate takeover started in Odisha, although Odisha's mineral deposits are undoubtedly the top prize in the sights of foreign companies and agencies.

The privatisation of electricity was orchestrated by the DFID and WB. After this, reforms in the water, telecom, health, education and forestry sectors have followed in the same neoliberal direction. Dams are another form of privatisation, since they divert water from flowing freely through public space in rivers, and channel it to factories as well as fertiliser-intensive fields. It is definitely factories that take precedence in the present business climate. New dams tend to be explicitly private ventures.

In November 1993 the WB drew up an agreement with the Orissa government and State Electricity Board, which started by 'unbundling' the Board into three units: Gridco (Grid Corporation of Orissa), OHPC (Orissa Hydropower Corp.) and OPGC (Orissa Power Generation Corp. for thermal power). These three companies took off in 1996 through the Orissa Electricity Reform Act (1995), raising electricity prices by 67 per cent (1992–95). The WB's loans for the Upper Indravati dams had already started an involvement with Odisha's power sector. After that project ran into difficulties and the WB cancelled a loan of $156 million in December 1991, the Indian authorities persuaded it to convert these funds into assistance for starting the power sector reforms—or was this rather a case of the WB persuading the Orissa government?! The WB arranged total funding of $997 million, of which it loaned $350 million (35 per cent), while the UK government (ODA, which became DFID), and the Asian Development Bank together contributed 36 per cent.

The reforms demanded a separation of regulation from government control, so in 1996 the Orissa Electricity Regulation Commission was formed. Distribution was then further 'unbundled', as a further step to privatisation: Gridco (retained by the GoO) separated off 4 regional companies, dividing up the state. Of these, Cesco (Central Electricity Supply Co.) was bought up by BSES (Bombay Suburban Electricity Supply) in 1996. Within six months this enterprise had failed, and when a 51 per cent stake in the 4 companies was offered in 1998, BSES bought the other 3 (Nesco, Southco and Wesco), while Cesco was bought by a joint venture between Jyoti Structures and AES, a major US company, which held a 95 per cent share in this JV, as well as a 49 per cent stake in OPGC. AES was badly hit by the super cyclone of October 1999, losing new equipment. This led to a bitter dispute with the regulatory body.[36]

Money failed to move properly between the new entities. In 2000-01, Gridco owed OPGC Rs 1.8 billion, while the four distribution companies owed Gridco Rs 1.6 billion. AES, with its commanding shares of Cesco (95 per cent of 51 per cent) and OPGC (49 per cent) was thus debtor as well as creditor with Gridco. The hike in electricity prices and lack of transparency in the reform process sparked riots in Bhubaneswar in January 2001, which wrecked the Cesco/AES office.

This is a bare summary of the early stage of Odisha's power sector reforms. The full story is far more complicated than this. One aspect is the amount of money spent on consultants, most of them employed by foreign-based companies that command a high price for their services. These included ECC (US), KPMG (UK), Cameron McKenna (UK, legal), NERA (UK and US), Monenco Agra (Canada, engineering and sales), PriceWaterhouseCoopers (UK), Merz & McLean (UK), NIFES (UK), SAC (US), SRCI (US), Lovelock & Lewis (UK, evaluation). These cost a total of Rs 3 billion.[37]

The whole reform situation was reviewed by the Kanungo Committee in 2001, and Gridco offset the more than Rs 10 billion debt it owed to Nalco, particularly for drawing electricity from Nalco's captive power station, by issuing it with redeemable bonds for Rs 1.5 billion.[38] The complexity and manipulation here recalls India's Enron scandal of the Dhabol power station in Maharashtra, which enmeshed the state electricity company and loaning entities in debt: a model of how foreign companies, including those applying for an SEZ, externalise their costs.[39]

While land and minerals are being taken progressively out of the public domain and sold off into private ownership, water is also being gradually privatised through Pani Panchayats and dams.[40] A similar process is also happening with the forests through schemes like Joint Forest Management (see Savyasaachi 2008 for an example).

The social structure of collusion

Displacing tribals to make way for industry is part of a privatisation of land itself. Though receiving a new momentum from neoliberal policies, the legal apparatus was put in place during colonial times, with the Permanent Settlement (1793) and the Land Acquisition Act (1894). As an administrator in Odisha expressed the set of values which many British rulers saw as their main legacy to India:

> It is by what we have implanted in the living people, rather than what we have built upon the dead earth, that our name will survive. The permanent aspect of British Rule in India is the growth of Private Rights.
>
> By a wise limitation of our state ownership we have raised up a permanent Proprietary Body, composed of mutually hostile classes; but each of which, from the grand seigneurs down to the Resident Husbandmen, holds its lands under documents issued by British officials.[41]

This divide and rule legacy of British colonialism is bearing fruit now, in internal colonialism carried out through large-scale privatisation of resources, and takeovers of huge tracts of cultivated and forest land, by mining and construction companies, in Odisha and neighbouring states. Like colonial officials, the companies see this land as 'dead earth', and treat it as such, killing countless life-forms by ripping it open.

Collusion is of many kinds. Police firings at Maikanch and Kalinganagar show close coordination between powerful companies, politicians and security forces. Visiting Kalinganagar on 16 December

2009, Naveen Patnaik thanked the steel companies for constructing a police post near the firing site, at a cost of 66.2 lakh rupees. It has been known locally in many areas that mining companies pay the police, but rarely admitted openly like this, in a context where Haibaru and other headers of the Kalinganagar movement have been arrested and terrorised by *goondas*, and girls have been raped.

The media play a significant role by *manufacturing consent* through biased coverage (Kedar Mishra 2007). Apart from actors within India, responsibility for what is happening involves powerful individuals and institutions abroad, as we shall see.

Rather than simply blame the government or even the companies, we also need to look at our own lifestyle choices. More and more, our lives rely on a high turnover of 'consumer durables'—mobiles, Ipods, laptops, motorbikes, cars—all aluminium-rich, with a high degree of built-in-redundancy. The throw-away, conspicuous consumption habit is also particularly visible in packaging, where aluminium is in mass use. Like the Konds, drawn by the East India Company into 'new tastes and new wants' that gradually become 'necessities of life', we too let ourselves be drawn. To many of us, mobiles are indispensible now. The price is an increasing invasion of public as well as private space. Mobile towers dominate India's towns and air-waves, and we take for granted mobiles' incessant interruption of normal human interaction, even though they threaten our privacy with the technology of a surveillance society, and have an unknown impact on our brains that many say is dangerous. Aluminium is the main conductor in mobiles, and they are a symbol of the Aluminium Age.

When most insurance companies, banks, local councils in Britain and pension funds invest heavily in mining companies such as Vedanta, where does the collusion stop? The question becomes—how to free ourselves? How to support others who are trying to retain their freedom on their land, and protect our planet?

There is a need now for a fundamental critique of the industrialisation model, producing a consensus before it's too late—a revulsion against the rape of the earth and dislocation of people who live close to the earth, and a much wider understanding by people at all levels of society about the dangers which unlimited growth based on industrialisation unleash.

CHAPTER SIXTEEN

Starvation Deaths and Foreign Aid

The lawyers arguing Vedanta's case at the Supreme Court in 2007 laid great emphasis on Odisha's poverty, mentioning the prevalence of starvation deaths in Kalahandi, and praising Vedanta's offer of millions of rupees for 'tribal development', promising that the Niyamgiri-Lanjigarh project would bring the people of Kalahandi 'two square meals a day'.

But Odisha's poverty has a cause that's as simple as it is hard to unravel: gross exploitation. The evidence suggests that industrialisation makes both exploitation and poverty a lot worse, by displacing people and undermining their food security. This is the main, rarely spoken reason for the Resource Curse: rich resources bring a huge increase in the level of exploitation.

So what is the reality of Odisha's starvation deaths? Where people are still in their villages, what difficulties do they face? Does the industrial model of development ever improve their situation? And is the foreign aid from the British Governemt's DFID helping to eliminate poverty in Odisha, or is it, as many allege, making the situation worse?

Starvation and suicide

In a Pengo tribal village near the Indravati reservoir, sitting with a man about to carry a load of wood into Tentulikhunti *haat* (market) at 6 in the morning, he explained how he had to cut trees and carry the wood to sell as firewood in town to keep his family from starving. He told us how every rupee of 'aid' for Adivasis—from the government or from abroad through NGOs—fails to reach them, because it is systematically 'eaten' by a whole hierarchy of middlemen and officials.

Sitting there at dawn, with Adivasis who are cutting down their forest for survival after the Indravati reservoir drowned their forest and fields, gave us an unforgettable insight into the deeply ingrained system of exploitation that haunts tribal areas all over India. A pervasive sign of what is happening is the procession of tribal men and women walking into the towns every day to sell head- and shoulder-loads of forest wood as fuel for a few rupees.

Starvation deaths in Odisha were first highlighted by Kishen Pattnayak when he was an MP in 1967. In his book (2000), he describes how he raised the issue of drought and famine in two sessions of Parliament. Starvation deaths in Kashipur and Kalahandi were the focus of a series of petitions and articles by Kishenji and others from 1985. Since then, the media has often highlighted starvation deaths in this region. These acounts have a basis that is all too real, though often they are full of stereotypes and distortions. Facts are scarce, and there has been much debate on the authenticity of individual deaths. The media attention on starvation has also been manipulated for political ends, for example by one political faction to discredit another, to solicit aid money, and as a tool to justify industrialisation.

There is no longer any doubt that a large number of people have starved to death. In fact there is evidence that starvation is a lot more widespread than is officially acknowledged all over Odisha and neighbouring states. What is so shocking is that starvation exists side by side with the seemingly normal prosperity of richer townspeople. Traders continue to exploit Adivasis, even when these are in a constant state of hunger, which steals imperceptibly over the edge into actual starvation. In other words, people who are comfortably off live side by side with people on the edge of starvation, and barely notice or care, continuing the exploitative behaviour that causes starvation conditions, while those who are starving barely complain—because there is no point, they won't be listened to—and out of wounded dignity. It is said that 'you never see a starving person in the street', and among the main reasons for this is pride, or shame, which is also a reason that news about starvation does not spread straightforwardly. Even when starvation becomes a major political issue, it is rarely the people starving who make it so, but others, using it to further their own agenda.

Marudi (drought) and *durbikhyo* (famine) have deep roots in Odisha, going back to the terrible famine in 1866, when a third of Odisha's population is said to have died. Droughts occur periodically, but they are not the only—or main—cause of starvation conditions. Famine relief is institutionalised as a 'third harvest'—a source of profit for grain traders. A large part is 'siphoned off', and relatively little actually reaches those who live in a near-permanent state of malnutrition, even when they are actually starving. Investigating the many varied scams through which famine relief funds 'go astray' gave the journalist P. Sainath the title for his book, *Everybody Loves a Good Drought* (1996). Bob Currie has studied the Kalahandi situation in *The Politics of Hunger in India* (2000).

Kishen Pattnayak made a Writ Petition with Kapil Narayan Tiwary to the Chief Justice in Delhi in October 1985 accusing the Government of Orissa of causing and covering up starvation deaths. Another petition was made in 1987 by advocate Nagbhushan Pattnaik of the Indian People's Front (IPF), the electoral platform lauched by CPI-ML, a Naxalite group (underground till 1992) of which he was a leader. Among the allegations was that *distress sales* of paddy had taken place: a starving population was being preyed upon by a system of rice profiteering. This involved FCI (Food Corporation of India) officials who were also merchants, and had been buying paddy from farmers at below the minimum price and selling it at a profit. Also, there had been a rising trend of illegal transfers of tribal land to non-tribal owners through banned land mortgage arrangements, due to indebtedness from moneylending at illegal compound interest rates. Linked with this, bonded labour was still widely prevalent as 'distress sale of labour'.[1]

The Supreme Court appointed a single judge to investigate these allegations, P. C. Panda, who avoided meeting those critical of the Orissa government, and wrote a report exonerating it, blaming instead

> the failure of local persons to take advantage of opportunities offered in government schemes ... enough measures have been taken by the government to develop the people, specially the poor and downtrodden economically. Inspite of all efforts of the government, there is no marked development with the people, or they are misutilizing the different benefits conferred upon them and diverting those benefits in other manners and not for the purposes for which the benefits have been conferred [due to] their own laziness and reluctance to take an interest in their own self-improvement.[2]

Panda's report and conclusions were widely criticised, along with his claim that Odisha development programmes were already 'transforming Kalahandi into one of the most prosperous districts in the state.' Panda's language was suspiciously close to that of Chief Minister J. B. Patnaik's strident denials that any starvation deaths had happened, and his adverts promising prosperity for Kalahandi.[3]

As a sample of the starvation death discourse, it is worth quoting one crucial newspaper feature on it—a special English-language supplement for the Odia newspaper *Samaj*, timed to coincide with Prime Minister Rajiv Gandhi's visit to drought-affected areas of south-west Odisha on 24 September 1987. Accounts like this by journalists tend to be formulaic and stereotyped, dwelling on the helplessness and poverty of 'victims'—stereotypes reinforced by photos of starving villagers. The main article on the frontpage (p. A) reads:

> **Orissa IS THE VERY EPITOME OF INDIA'S POVERTY**
> **So said Mahatma Gandhi during his first visit to Orissa in March 1921 ...**
> **Government Report confirms Starvation Deaths**
>
> Report of Mr A. M. Dalavai, IAS, SDO, Gunupur on the basis of his first-hand study on the starvation as well as unusual deaths in Bissamcuttack area [that] occurred between 28-12-1986 to 28-3-1987.

This article lists 38 starvation deaths in villages near Bissamcuttack, with photos of people in a starving condition from the Kashipur area. Another front-page article describes measures taken by the Orissa Assembly. Inside, a report by a group of Congress(I) MLAs single out Kashipur as an area where over 400 recent starvation deaths are alleged, criticising the callousness and inadequacy of local officials, for their failure to insist that rice be sold at the proper rate—i.e. grain profiteering was rampant. An article recalls the 'Kalahandi drought and man-made famine' of 1966, tracing the history of famine in Odisha from 1866. A report by Ram Chandra Ulaka, leader of the Congress (I) MLAs, lists 504 starvation-related deaths, and calls for Lift Irrigation schemes to harness the streams in Kashipur. On the last page, an article by Radhanath Rath, editor of *Samaj*, describes the mis-spending of relief funds. This broadsheet was produced specially for Rajiv, and its arguments—supplemented no doubt by the politicians who guided his Orissa tour—were a major factor in securing the IFAD loan for Kashipur's 'development' (Chapter Five).

At the same time, Bhawani Mund and advocate A.C. Pradhan brought a case against the Orissa government in the Orissa High Court, succesfully challenging Panda's verdict.[4] District Judge Baidyanath Mishra's report in 1991 confirmed at least five cases of death by starvation, and identified illegal practices by banks and moneylenders, involving land transfers to non-tribals. The SC ordered the Orissa government to pay compensation to the families of those proved to have starved, and to take appropriate measures to prevent future starvation deaths.[5] Meanwhile J. B. Patnaik's Congress government was defeated by Biju Patnaik (Janata Dal) in Odisha's March 1990 elections, in which starvation deaths were a campaigning issue. They were also highlighted in an important article by Jagdish Pradhan (1993).

But starvation deaths continued, and were reported in the media in 1996, when another petition was heard at the Supreme Court, and the National Human Rights Commission made an investigation. Several MLAs reported cases, which the Orissa government denied. Rabi Dash submitted two affidavits, describing numerous deaths by starvation, showing how the Supreme Court's order of 1992 had not been carried out, and the Relief Code had been violated, for example by diverting Rs 54 crore from the National Calamity Relief Fund for road, water, electricity and housing projects, where contractors made a profit, instead of giving priority to ensuring food supply and medical aid.[6] 104 doctors' posts were lying vacant in Kalahandi and Nuapada, hundreds of people had died of malaria, and the area had one of the country's highest infant mortality rates. The Commission investigated over 20 homes of people who had apparently starved to death and 'witnessed human suffering and destitution of an alarming magnitude', finding evidence of corruption in the Public Distribution System (PDS), and the Food For Work programme (FFW), which stopped food reaching people on the edge of famine.[7] This corruption is still normal; labourers in FFW schemes continue to be regularly underpaid in the grain they receive for their work in road construction, etc.

As Kishen Pattnayak summarised the situation (30 June 1998): the SC in 1985 had made a good start by accepting that starvation deaths had taken place, and ordering the reconstitution of a Kalahandi District National Calamities Committee. However, this did not function effectively, because of poor methodology: the 'crop-cutting' criteria used to identify a drought dated back to colonial times, and claimed to be 'scientific', but were actually far less reliable than village people's advance-prognosis of forthcoming drought. The Committee had not understood that when people know a drought is imminent (from experiencing bad rains, and watching crops dying), many migrate to find work elsewhere, abandoning their fields. Also, starvation deaths are routinely denied on the basis of doctors' certificates which give diseases (not starvation) as the cause of death, and find the stomach not completely empty. No attempt is made to verify starvation conditions by studying the levels of malnutrition and economic condition prevailing in the deceased's neighbourhood.[8] (Similar factors apply in the case of large numbers of death from industrial diseases)

The 'KBK districts' were earmarked for special treatment in these years, and large amounts of money were set aside for development projects there, with the intention of eradicating poverty and improving people's standard of living. However, little if any of this money reached ordinary people (as Rabi Dash mentioned for relief funds) or reduced their poverty.[9]

Why not? Five of the eight districts have bauxite-aluminium plans, and we have already seen (Chapter Five) how IFAD money was diverted to prepare Kashipur's infrastructure for the industry.

So we found it shocking, as well as fascinating, to witness during hearings at the Supreme Court in 2007, how Vedanta and Orissa government lawyers mentioned Kalahandi's starvation deaths and poverty as an argument for allowing the aluminium companies to come in and develop the area. What they did not mention is that even after 20 years of 'development' in Kashipur by IFAD, URDS and the Tribal Development Corporation, people in the region still face starvation. In Kashipur and nearby areas in 2007, at least 100 people died from cholera (Saroj 2007)—a disease known to attack people weakened by malnourishment. Moreover, the Damanjodi area, held up as a model of 'development' by Nalco, suffers a higher level of poverty than anywhere in India.[10]

During these last ten years, the issue of farmers' suicides has also reached epidemic proportions, reported from Maharashtra, Karnataka, Andhra and other states as well as Odisha. Over 2,500 farmers committed suicide in three drought-affected districts of Andhra in 2002 alone. The reason for these suicides is often given as just poverty, and individual failure to make agriculture as profitable as it should be. The real reasons have to do with the modes of exploitation and moneylending. It is clear to many witnesses that these suicides are increasing. In other words, the modes of exploitation are getting more intense, and involve not so much the traditional moneylender as the companies selling seeds and other inputs. As agriculture is industrialised, the seed and biotech corporations are ruthless. GM cotton is a frequent cause of impossible debts. Farmers are tempted to go in for new cash crops, but the economics is heavily stacked against small-scale farmers—another area of corporate takeover. Cultivators get into debt, lose their fields and homes, and cannot bear the downward spiral, losing everything which made families' lives worth living.[11]

Roots of impoverishment

Denying starvation-deaths or blaming them on 'poverty', 'backwardness', or 'natural calamities', misrepresent the situation and serve to justify imposing projects that take away people's land and destroy their food security completely, leaving them even poorer and hungrier.

Starvation is an extreme manifestation of poverty. Odisha is India's poorest state by several indices. 48 per cent live below the poverty line. It is one of the most indebted States, and has one of the highest infant mortality rates, as well as high rates of under-nutrition, infectious diseases and illiteracy. DFID recently commissioned a report on the causes of poverty in Odisha. Though we were originally asked to contribute to this, the report is classified and it is typical of DFID's lack of transparency that we have not been able to see a copy.[12]

The main cause of Odisha's poverty is a system of endemic exploitation. The basic reason that there is so much exploitation in Odisha is that there is so much to exploit. Along with its neighbouring states in East India, Odisha is one of India's richest in natural resources, in terms of water and forest as well as minerals, laying it open to the classic dangers of the resource curse. The exploitation happens both at the small level of people preying on the produce from Adivasi fields and forest, and at the macro-level of companies coming to take the resources and, above all, people's land. To understand the causes of Odisha's starvation deaths, it is necessary to understand the history and social structure of this systematic exploitation, which the invasion of aluminium companies compounds.

In medieval times, Hindu Rajas exerted only a limited authority over the Konds, legitimising their power through religion, by patronising the cult of prominent tribal deities, sometimes through human sacrifice, as well as through the all-Odisha cult of Jagannath. When the British conquered west Odisha, the Rajas gradually changed their mode of legitimation. Jagannath remained important to assure their status in the eyes of Hindu Odias, but their power was now bolstered by the British, who could de-throne them on a whim, so it became more important to legitimise their power in British eyes than in the eyes of tribal subjects, especially since the British demanded large amounts of revenue or tribute, and made clear that what they respected, above all, was developing their territory in ways that increased profits from the land. This is why the exploitation of cultivators increased exponentially during British rule. In the name of maintaining law and order, stimulating 'progress' and increasing revenue, the British set up a system worse than human sacrifice—*a sacrifice of human being*—which continues till today.[13]

Throughout the nineteenth century, as their kingdoms came under British influence, Rajas forced Kond villages off their land, and brought in other groups from distant areas. This process of dispossession happened in Kalahandi, Nyagarh, and many other areas. This was also the time that the Raja of Sukinda brought in Munda and Ho tribals from the region north of Odisha, to bring the jungles under cultivation and raise his revenue.[14]

Police forces were set up during this time and Dinobandu Patnaik, the first Tehsildar of the Kondmals (Kandhamal), exercised a 'reign of terror' from the 1850s–80s. British officials rarely believed their own subordinate officers guilty of extortion, but readily accused each others'. Their records make it clear that the police regularly abused their position when they visited villages, and though the British reprimanded them when they found out, usually they did not find out. Moreover, this oppression by their juniors helped cow the population into accepting British rule, so extortion became an unacknowledged yet normal part of the actual system of law and order.

The same basic situation has prevailed ever since. The SP of Rayagada in 1999, after reading through the Preface to *The Sacrifice of Human Being*, made this point as follows: 'You have said that in the British times the police were demanding bribes and all when they visit the tribal villages, and even now the same thing is happening, and I'm afraid you are correct.' The majority of junior officers habitually demand bribes. And in a sense, it is hard to blame them. To become a police constable, or forest officer, normally involves paying at least Rs 100,000 in bribes to a hierarchy of officials. The constable's family often has to take out a loan to pay these sums, so naturally, when he starts duty, he starts to recover this sum by doing what his colleagues do, demanding bribes on a regular basis. In the case of forest officers, people found cutting wood or carrying headloads of timber into town are simply fined. Money goes into pockets and the system continues. The forest is also under pressure from the timber mafia, who move into areas of remote forests with chain saws, trucks and guns, especially where roads have opened a way in, often around areas where mining companies operate. The timber mafia colludes with paper mills and corrupt elements of the forest service.

In this system it is not just Odisha's forests and human inhabitants who suffer. Several of the apex species are facing extinction now in Odisha and other states. Many people know about the threatened extinction facing tigers. Few realise how systematically the hunting mafia has been targeting India's tigers, leopards, bears and elephants, with feelers into all the remote pockets, 'cleaning out' the animals, converting their hides and bones into hard cash.[15] Another factor comes in here. As the world outside India wakes up to the threatened extinction of these magnificent species, people in foreign countries are willing to pay a lot of money to groups trying to conserve them. One strategy is to create core areas of inviolate forest, sometimes moving villages of forest dwellers out. In this process, conflict develops between conservationists and Adivasis, along with the human rights or political activists fighting to protect them with far less funds. Wildlife and Adivasis suffer from the same system of exploitation by mafia and corrupt foresters, but their supporters get divided and turned against each other in a classic 'divide and rule', instead of uniting to confront the system.

A system of endemic exploitation

During British times, and even before, a large number of Adivasis lost their land. The dispossession accelerated from the mid-nineteenth century till now, as Bob Currie shows in *The Politics of Hunger in India* (2000). For example, in Nuapada district, 'One third of the total land owned by tribals was transferred to moneylenders and businessmen between 1891 and 1910' (Currie, p. 74). This statistic is the tip of an iceberg. The process of Adivasis losing their lands to non-tribals has been relentless throughout East India, from then till now.

Kashipur was one of five Zamindaries under the Kalahandi Raj in the nineteenth century, whose ruler Udit Prataap Deo (1853–81) invited in traders and cultivators, especially of the Kolta caste from Sambalpur, in order to raise his revenue by increasing the land's 'productivity', which involved higher rates of taxation and extortion, and more land deforested and turned to cultivation. This increased revenue was partly to pass on to his British overlords, and partly for his own aggrandisement.[16] Koltas were more efficient at making money out of land than Konds. Their exploitation and dispossession of Konds created intense resentment, and Konds killed a large number in their rebellion of 1882, which the British suppressed brutally.

The loss of tribal land has often taken place through encroachment of tribal or communal lands by higher castes, who registered their title in the official record, in contrast to traditional tribal land rights which did not depend on paperwork; and also through moneylending, in a cycle of impoverishment that used compound rates of interest and institutionalised bribes to government officials. The classic account of west Odisha's system of endemic exploitation is Gopinath Mohanty's wonderful but harrowing novel *Paraja*.[17]

'*The Konds here pay taxes, a fact which speaks volumes for their advancement ...*' as a Scottish Captain put it in 1852, approving how this made them '*more under subjection*'.[18] Revenue collection was central to the process of land alienation, and Land Settlements between 1868 and 1891 strengthened enormously the authoritarian and hierarchical structures of control by non-tribals over tribal people.[19]

Another aspect was taking away tribal rights to the forest, which under colonial rule was classified in stages as essentially government property, and which was often felled systematically, to sell as timber while increasing cultivation. Many areas where the way of life revolved around the forest, in cycles of self-sufficiency, were suddenly deforested and sucked into an exploited position in the mainstream economy. So before 1900, a pattern of dispossessing Adivasis of their land was set, that has continued ever since. 'Development-Induced Displacement' to make way for aluminium or steel is just the latest stage, on a bigger, faster scale.

The history of deforestation in south-west Odisha is linked with this process of tribal dispossession. Uncovering it in detail is all but impossible—the timber mafia keeps no records, while most people blame the tribal people. It's true that tribals are often the main fellers of trees. Yet the main culprit is not their practice of shifting cultivation, but the extreme pressures of exploitation they face. Sensitive forest officials are well aware that the timber mafia is a much bigger agent of deforestation—though, of course, it often employs Adivasis as the actual fellers. Exactly when and how the plains of Kashipur and Jeypore were so radically deforested is a mystery we cannot answer. Timber mafia and corruption played a part, but at a certain point too, Adivasis often turn their anger against the very forest that sustained them for centuries, which everyone else exploits, and which forest officials 'protect'.

Another major agent of deforestation has been the Orissa Forest Development Corporation (OFDC), which is supposed to protect the forest, but clears large areas of bamboo to supply paper mills. Adivasis have always harvested bamboo sustainably, leaving new growth and mature plants, unlike the corporations, which bulldoze 'everything in sight, on a mass scale. Young or old bamboos, whatever the size, variety or age, it's all the same to them.'[20]

Laws forbidding the alienation of tribal land (i.e. its acquisition by non-tribals) have been easily circumvented in practice.[21] Until recent times, Adivasis did not need written proof of land ownership, so thousands have lost legal title to their land with the stroke of a pen (or lack of). Lawyers too are often notorious exploiters of Adivasis, offering help, but charging unfair sums. Often their help is a sham, and they are in league with the original exploiters, who come from their own 'clean' castes, and pay better.

The other major cause of land alienation has been moneylending. It is still normal (though illegal) for the lender to ask for tribal lands as surety for a loan, and when repayment is impossible due to lethal systems of compound interest—rates of 120–380 per cent are common—Adivasis lose their land for good. Mortgaging land like this, as well as lending at compound interest and even the sale of tribal land to non-tribals, are all illegal now, but still widespread in practice. Even more pernicious practices include the *gothi* system, in which a debtor who cannot pay is reduced to the status of a *gothi* or bonded labourer—in effect, a slave. Once ownership of land passes to non-tribals, the same Adivasis may still cultivate their land, but as tenants, paying a large percentage of the produce to the new owners—this is not supposed to exceed a quarter, but half or more is standard.

Even when Adivasis continue to own the land they work, the burden of debt they live under often becomes a nightmare. This is the endlessly recurring story which Gopinath Mohanty tells with such pathos in *Paraja*—a system that keeps thousands of Adivasis on the edge of starvation. It becomes next to impossible for them to avoid the traps set out for them, since the market they sell to is controlled against them. As a result, they often migrate for months or even years, to sell their labour.[22]

Crores of rupees spent by state governments on drought relief have failed to even begin to tackle the main problems. This applies to Odisha's anti-drought project, started by India's Prime Minister Narasimha Rao in 1995, the Drought-Prone Areas Programme, the Food For Work Programme (FFW), and many others.[23] FFW contractors regularly expand their profits by paying labourers less than the minimum wage. The whole concept comes out of the colonial system: Scottish clansmen in the Highlands were offered degrading, badly-paid 'relief work' building unneeded roads as part of the process of their dispossession, during the 1830s–50s.[24]

Everyone agrees in blaming moneylenders. *Sundi*s (*mohua* distillers, who include the Sahus, and are well-known for this role) coexist as takers-over of Adivasi lands with other higher-caste Odias and Telugus. The class of *sahukar*s merges into other landowning groups.[25] In theory, the administration is supposed to protect tribals against losing their lands. In practice, the reverse is the case, since the administration, including the police force and forest service, the FCI and PDS, are dominated by the same high castes—many people collude in the system. Tribals are easily portrayed as sunk in poverty due to laziness and lack of enterprise, while the landowning, business and government service elites share a common culture with status symbols and a proud veneer of respectability. Places are 'reserved' for Dalits, fewer for Adivasis,[26] but when Dalits and Adivasis enter the administration, they have to conform to high-caste norms, otherwise they become a laughing stock and are discriminated against.

The extortion of Adivasi land, crops and labour is a basic fact in the history of central Odisha. But this endemic exploitation involves several more complex mechanisms. One of these is frequent connivance by FCI officials with mill owners and grain traders, who pay below the minimum price for cultivators' produce. Even this minimum price of rice is often too low to allow farmers a proper living. When the rains fail or come in excess, this becomes *profiteering*. This is why farmers in west Odisha protest strongly about the administration's failure to enforce the minimum price, as well as the distribution of imported rice—some of it apparently a surplus dumped on India as 'US Aid' or through hidden conditions attached to foreign loans.[27] Cultivators who grow the nation's rice are entitled to a fair price. Is the system conspiring to make small-scale farming 'uneconomic'?

The system of endemic exploitation outlined so far is not a pretty thing to face up to. Nor is it the whole story. There are plenty of good officials, traders and lawyers, as well as police and forest officials of the highest integrity, who are determined to do their duty, and make a stand whenever they can. There are excellent laws protecting cultivators' rights, which some advocates have fought long and hard to ensure are applied properly, and new legislation upholding basic rights: OSATIP, PESA, National Regional Employment Guarantee Scheme, Right to Food, Right to Information, Forest Rights Act …

On the other side, the land grab is becoming more complex, driven by a new breed of corporate exploiters, such as seed and bio-tech companies, including Monsanto. Traditional seed types are disappearing as GM seeds come in that do not reproduce but have to be bought each year. All these companies promote fertilisers and pesticides, and sell their products with tempting loans that become a nightmare when promised profits do not materialise. Hence the farmer suicides.

To comprehend the system of exploitation, it helps to analyse it in terms of a social structure of set roles, which work together:

The administration ideally implements the laws supporting Adivasi land rights. A government servant is supposed to serve the people and protect the poor, and there is an honourable tradition of officials who take on this role. But for the reasons outlined, corruption is endemic, with huge bribes from companies wishing to appropriate tribal lands for those near the top; while ordinary forest, police, revenue, and famine relief officials see themselves as having to extort bribes on a daily basis to survive and thrive.

This is the reality gap between what is supposed to happen and what actually happens. Laws are turned upside down, while the legal process and most of the lawyers are in the pockets of the rich. This came home to us talking to Adivasis from Kashipur who have been enmeshed in 'false cases' to dampen their opposition to Utkal. Every week they have to appear at Rayagada court, where a series of court officials and lawyers fleece them, so that—far from upholding the law—law courts often function as centres of corruption. Government officials retain the sense of colonial hierarchy which the British Raj established, along with the '*saheb*' role' of talking down to 'inferiors', who pass this on with interest. As Gopinath Mohanty showed, a constable or forest guard too often enters a tribal village as if he's its lord and master, to be placated by food and 'gifts'.

The merchant role exists in many individual traders and contractors, but nowadays is institutionalised in the companies and banks. A merchant of knowledge role is played out through reams written about tribals by journalists, economists, anthropologists, and highly paid consultants, whose discourse 'objectifies' them, rarely quoting their words and hardly ever conveying their perspective to understand their situation.

'At the bottom', still maintaining dignity and frankness, Odisha's villagers still work the land and grow our food, despite the pressures and stereotypes. In a sense, keeping tribal people on the edge of starvation functions as one of the ways that non-tribals 'keep them down'—a long-term daily grind of attrition. These ground-realities are the starting point to comprehend the impacts of industrial 'development'.

African models of famine

The level of starvation in the KBK districts has been compared to Ethiopia—a comparison that is used, as we have seen, to justify huge-scale development projects, even though these tend to facilitate a more systematic exploitation of these districts' resources and people. The danger of *marudi* has not disappeared. If anything, enforced industrialisation and displacement compound it. To get a proper perspective on the present situation of widespread malnutrition, and how it is manipulated, we must look a little into the worldwide history of famines.

To start with, we need to remember Odisha's Great Famine of 1866, in which a quarter or third of the population died. Mr Ravenshaw, the British Commissioner, had been assured by local contacts that there was no danger of famine, and that local zamindars and traders had ample stocks to supply the population in case of widespread crop-failure. Government unpreparedness, as well as profiteering by grain-merchants during the famine, was highlighted in the Famine Enquiry Commissions, which started in the 1860s–70s and continued till 1898. But then, as now, famines were not seen by those who endured them as simply 'natural calamities'. A popular Odia song of the time blamed '*Manchester cotton and Leicester salt*'—i.e. foreign goods undercutting local ware—just as the import of foreign grain (often under the guise of 'aid') interferes in the local economy now.[28]

The 1866 Odisha famine shook the British, and led to the first measures to combat famine in 1867, which helped reduce mortality in the Bihar famine of 1874 and the Bombay famine of 1876. The Second Famine Commission, set up in 1880, produced a series of ground-breaking Famine Codes, updated in 1898. A huge number of people nevertheless died in famines in India in 1896–97 and 1899–1901. By this time, famine had become a political issue. The Indian National Congress passed resolutions in 1896 which linked poverty and hunger to the burdens of British rule, and a series of books did the same.[29] So the Famine Codes were revised between 1901 and 1907, and applied until the Second World War in 1942, when the system broke down, and food stocks desperately needed for famine victims in Bengal were requisitioned for the war effort in the East. These *Famine Crimes* were a major cause of the Quit India Movement, leading to widespread disturbances in Odisha that involved police firings, setting the pattern for events unfolding now.

Another significant precedent was the Irish Famine of 1846–47. Here too, the local economy had been tampered with, and the population had become artificially dependent on a single crop: potatoes. It was said that 'the poor starve in the midst of plenty,' since Ireland was exporting food even as people were starving to death—a similarity with Kashipur, which exports the best of its crops. Ireland's 'relief effort' was miniscule, and in the hands of a 'free enterprise zealot' who blamed the famine on Irish laziness and endemic poverty. Malthus' doctrine of famine striking down oversized populations, combined with Adam Smith's free enterprise strictures against government interference in the grain trade, paved the way for the Irish famine and the callousness of the British government's response:

> Believing that unalterable economic forces were at work, which should on no account be interfered with, London provided very modest and belated relief and even allowed food to be exported from the island.[30]

The British government's blinkered adherence to a rigid doctrine of free trade played a major role in both the Irish famine of 1846–47 and Indian famines. But the twentieth century (not least its last quarter!) saw famines as bad as any in history, and the response was often dictated through similar 'free-trade' blinkers, blinding the public and many experts alike to actual causes.

Some of the worst famines have been simply denied. In Ukraine, Stalin used mass starvation to cow a population who (he believed) wanted to break from the USSR. At least 7–10 million people died there in 1932–33, at an average of 25,000 a day. Not for lack of grain—there too, people's harvest was taken from them by force. And the *New York Times* followed Soviet propaganda in denying reports that this was happening![31]

The Bengal famine of 1943 is widely seen as a result of British expropriation of grains 'for the war effort', who similarly denied this causality.[32] Starvation in rural India today is not presently on the massive scale of the famous famines in colonial India, or recent famines in Africa. It may be getting close however: India is listed in the orange, 'alarming' category in the WHO Global Hunger Index.[33]

The famine Mao caused with his 'great leap forward' was among the world's worst, in terms of numbers, as well as hypocrisy.[34]

Since then, a number of famines in Africa have become world news. Popular ideas seeing these as a tragic result of over-population or natural disasters are not confirmed by proper investigation. Alex de Waal's book *Famine Crimes* (1997) shows conclusively that the main causes have been war and repression by the regimes involved, while famine relief from Western aid agencies has often colluded in this repression, and Western journalists (who normally follow in the wake of these agencies and depend on them for moving around) are often complicit in the cover-up.

In Ethiopia's 1973 famine, at least 50,000 died and Haile Selassie largely ignored what was happening. When the international media publicised it, this fuelled the movement that led to Selassie's downfall (1974). Far from bettering the situation, Mengistu's regime used famine as a means of warfare, while getting Western donors to pour 'aid' into his country, as the US and USSR jostled for influence.

This is the untold story behind Ethiopia's notorious famine of 1983–85 and Band Aid, showing that even when great international publicity puts spotlights on a famine, its nature and causes are often completely distorted. At the time, this famine was popularly blamed on over-population, drought, and even backwardness in farming, because the UN and other foreign aid agencies and media colluded with the Mengistu regime in covering up the way that famine was being created by military offensives against Eritrean and Tigray rebels.[35] Very little of the foreign aid reached the northern hills where the famine was concentrated, because that population was under attack by Mengistu's army and airforce, who were bombing it, making normal cultivation impossible. Officially there was 'no war', so although the UN and aid agencies were aware that a large part of the food they brought was going straight to the soldiers, they kept quiet about it, in case Mengistu closed them down.

The scam was much worse than this, too. Mengistu's forced resettlement of the population into collectives was actually being funded by the WB in a programme that killed at least 50,000 people, and was a main cause of the disruption in agriculture causing the famine. Thus 'one of the most written-about famines is one of the least understood.'[36] The special UN agency that was set up to deal with this famine, the UN Emergency Office for Ethiopia (UNEOE), acted as 'a screening device' to give the impression of competent action, and to conceal the misallocation of food and funds, as well as throwing a blanket of confusion and haze around the war in Ethiopia and the forced resettlement of populations that was the real cause of famine. The US government even declared, after an 'enquiry', that starvation was not being used as a weapon in Ethiopia—truth distorted here in service of a cold war strategy to draw Mengistu out of Soviet and into America's sphere of influence.

Similarly in the case of Sudan's terrible famines in 1983–5 and 1988–90. Nimeiri denied what was happening until January 1985, after an estimated 250,000 had died. As head of a key 'anti-communist' state, he was allowed 8 re-schedulings of USAID, even though these loans were feeding corruption: 'Khartoum made symbolic gestures towards reform and debt repayments, but in reality the money disappeared into the vortex of corruption.'[37] Meanwhile, the civil war between north and south was sparked off in 1984 by the US company Chevron drilling for oil in the south. Both sides in this long-lasting war used starvation as a weapon.

By contrast, de Waal argues that the British in India maintained their rule in part by creating and applying the world's best famine code (until 1943). International standards have been systematically eroded since the 1970s, especially in Africa, due to the lack of a political contract between governments and people. The international aid industry has failed to deal with or even identify the real causes of Africa's famines, which lie in extreme state repression and exploitation, which is often driven by foreign economic exploitation and/or political agenda. The growing power of the aid industry actually represents a retreat from any kind of political contract or accountability. The famines in Ethiopia in 1983–5 and in Somalia in 1987 (among others) were notorious for unheeded warnings, and for manipulation by aid agencies as well as governments.[38] Among the main underlying causes of starvation is (nearly always) the weight of foreign debt, frequently compounded by highly inappropriate 'food aid', which undercuts local prices, with dire consequences for local cultivators.

It helps to know what actually happened in Ethiopia, and other countries. These African situations of 'engineered' famine read as a warning. If the KBK districts of Odisha are already being compared to Ethiopia for their near-starvation conditions, and the Odisha government has been in official denial of the existence of starvation deaths for over 20 years—or of the corruption and exploitation that cause them—this echoes the pattern of denial in Africa.

The FCI's failure to fix or uphold proper minimum prices for grains which cultivators depend on selling at a proper price, and the hoarding of grains to hike their price in times of scarcity, point the way to a serious deterioration of civil society—a corruption at several levels. As in similar or worse situations in other countries, local causes of starvation are complex, but revolve around endemic exploitation and patterns of hierarchical behaviour and extortion that are too rarely articulated or analysed, let alone confronted.

The causes of starvation-poverty in Odisha are not just local. The behaviour of *sahukars*, enmeshing Adivasis into a vicious cycle of debt and dispossession, are a reflection of activities at the top of the hierarchy by the world's biggest moneylenders. Lending money at interest is how the WB makes money, and it has systematically drawn one country after another into unrepayable debt, for reasons we shall understand better in the next chapter.

Worldwide—as the WB and UN agencies warn—there is unprecedented food insecurity, and the World Food Programme has announced it can no longer afford to feed the world's starving people. Food riots have erupted in many countries destabilised by war and corporate takeovers.[39] In some, national government has broken down completely. When one perceives clearly the history of financial control and interference, orchestrated through the WB and other institutions, one understands that widespread starvation conditions are largely a result of a systematic corruption of one governing elite after another (Ethiopia, Sudan, Congo/Zaire ...), that has alienated them from responsibility to their own people—especially from village people growing the food, who have been increasingly exploited and marginalised.

In India, the hunger and external manipulation have not reached such a crisis point yet. But the dividing-up of India, by state governments' unrepayable debts and new industrial enclaves (SEZs), invites a dangerous level of indebtedness and foreign interference in the economy and agriculture. This affects Adivasis in many ways, compounding their dispossession and exploitation. Could India's long tradition of challenging corporate power structures change this picture?

Poverty reduction programmes from London

This is the context of the British government's work in Odisha through DFID (Department For International Development), which defines its role as 'responsible for the UK government's contribution to the global campaign to eliminate poverty'. Odisha is one of four states in India receiving special focus, along with Andhra Pradesh, Tamil Nadu and Madhya Pradesh.

Of these, Odisha was the first to accept ODA/DFID grants for privatising its electricity, as well as for public sector reforms to reform governance. We have seen that privatising electricity was controversial, and raised prices. It took place immediately after India's balance of payment crisis and new economic policy (1991), in the first wave of neoliberal reforms (1992–5), presumably because Odisha's debts were already exceptionally large, offering a lever to insist on these reforms. Grants to the other three states followed Odisha's lead.[40]

Clare Short was DFID's first head when it was formed (1997), followed by Hilary Benn. The hierarchy of power is anything but transparent. Decisions are highly devolved to Delhi, where DFID coordinates closely with agencies like the WB, UNDP and IFAD, and British economic interests work directly through the Delhi office in liaison with Trade Secretaries at the High Commission.

Reducing (originally 'eliminating') poverty is given as DFID's overriding aim, defined through the Millenium Development Goals. The approach is through analysing and trying to tackle 'factors that limit growth'.

> Objective 1. Poverty reduction through accountable governance and effective use of resources.
>
> The GoO has set itself a poverty reduction target of 5 per cent during the 10th plan period. But it has acknowledged that without

> decisive action to promote accountable government and address the causes of Odisha's fiscal crisis, resources will not be freed up to reduce poverty. DFID will support GoO to free those resources and invest them effectively for poverty reduction.[41]

This is because Odisha's debt is so big that servicing it threatens to take up all the funds available, with none left for development work. DFID's assistance is through the WB's Orissa Socio-Economic Development Programme, especially for Public Sector Reform, Public Financial Management and Improved Service Delivery. One question that needs to be asked at this point is whether the Odisha government is likely to make itself more accountable and transparent, when DFID's role of influence over it is anything but?

> Objective 2. Human development to improve health and education outcomes especially for the poor.

DFID assistance on health promotes a generalised approach focusing on the poorest in an attempt to improve equal access. DFID gives funding through a National Rural Health Mission programme (2005–12), and in education, supported the District Primary Health Programmes till 2008, when the Sarva Shiksha Abhiyan took over. In effect, this promotes a creeping privatisation of health and education.

> Objective 3. Improved and sustainable rural livelihoods and economic growth opportunites for the poor.

Since 85 per cent of Odias live in rural areas, DFID promotes Forest Management Programmes, watershed development through check dams, the West Orissa Rural Livelihoods Project, and Orissa Tribal Empowerment & Livelihoods Programme, aimed at 'empowering' members of Scheduled Castes and Tribes. This concern with the most marginalised finds expression in an organisation closely linked to DFID called the Poorest Areas Civil Society (PACS) Programme, and to a DFID concern with land registration and reform.[42]

DFID literature stresses that Odisha is vulnerable to slow and sudden shocks, in the form of drought, flood and cyclones. Above all,

> Continued stagnation in Orissa's economic growth rate could threaten all development work in Orissa.

This shows DFID's basic assumption: poverty can only be reduced by increasing the growth rate (GDP).

Priority themes in all three DFID objectives include 'tackling inequality and social exclusion'. But how? All these programmes are irredeemably top-down, and therefore likely to accentuate the hierarchy imposed over Adivasis and Dalits, since they lack any analysis of the systematic exploitation that takes place, let alone how to prevent it. Moreover, the overall view is that

> Orissa's economy is highly dependent on the agricultural sector, where growth is sluggish.

The implication is clear, though unstated: too many people are still tied to the land, where traditional small-scale farmers are not generating enough profit. Odisha is rich in minerals, and has potential for massive further industrialisation. DFID never spells this out in public documents, though the fact that it helped draft Odisha's 2006 R&R policy, shows its involvement in plans to move cultivators off the land.

Obviously, this would hardly be a popular policy. It's left to the politicians to implement, and the only Chief Minister brave enough to spell out the implications was Buddhadev in West Bengal, who justified CPI-M attempts to force farmers off their land through a Marxist doctrine that sees industrialisation as a necessary stage of development: it may be hard, but millions of cultivators will have to make the transition to industrial workers, and industrialisation will involve building new, massive factories on cultivated land, to generate profits far higher than agriculture can yield. In other words, another stage of the colonial process of expropriating people's land to make it more profitable, spelt out by capitalist theoreticians from the nineteenth to the twenty-first centuries.[43]

But does the *wall of money* coming into the country actually improve people's standard of living? And does a high growth rate really reduce poverty, as neoliberal dogma asserts? Between economic theory and reality lies a gap. One aspect is a shifting definition of poverty at the WB, which has accompanied a shifting definition of India's poverty line, delinking it from, for example, minimum nutrition. This delinking has served to distort the figures: a marked increase in poverty, as measured by increasing malnutrition and many other indices, has been masked by regional variation and this shifting poverty line.[44]

Power relations and systems of exploitation play little or no part in DFID's (and other mainstream) analysis of poverty.[45] As mentioned earlier, a recent DFID study of Odisha's poverty remains confidential, and published DFID statements show little if any understanding that exploitation is a principal cause of poverty. So it is not surprising that there is also no sign of comprehension that foreign-funded development projects are a prime cause of impoverishment through the displacement/dispossession they bring about—let alone awareness of the cultural genocide this causes.

In other words, DFID couches all its programmes in terms of reducing poverty, on the theoretical assumption that growth reduces poverty. This masks the overall situation in India right now, where overall growth has massively increased poverty, through displacement, declining labour conditions and deteriorating food security.[46] David Mosse's book *Cultivating Development* (2005) analyses the gulf between DFID theory and practice in a flagship project in MP.

So as exploitation sucks the resources out of the land, the danger of famine has not gone away. Dispossession of Adivasis from their land destroys a centuries-old system of sustaining themselves through cultivation, and therefore their food security, while (as we shall see in the next chapter) the labour policy promoted by the WB's socio-economic development plan promotes unemployment among the growing class of landless labourers. Meanwhile, the water table is going down and mountains' capacity to store water is being permanently damaged by mining, while metal factories are taking and polluting ever-larger quantities of water.

> Even after all this devastation,
> We are still singing the same old song.
> Odisha is rich in natural resources,
> But it is the poorest state of India. (Das 2005)

The theory is that Odisha can only become rich if it sells off its mineral resources for a lot of money. Poverty, in this way, becomes an excuse for taking over large tracts of land to make them more productive and profitable in the short term, and if the land belongs to tribal people who get displaced and thrown into a far worse poverty—this may be tough for them at first, but it will draw them into the mainstream and 'develop them', ending their 'primitive condition'.

DFID's programmes of poverty elimination are its most visible work in Odisha. Much less transparent are the neoliberal reforms of administration, finance, electricity and water, in effect preparing Odisha for the new wave of industrialisation, laying the ground for a series of corporate takeovers by power, telecom, insurance, engineering, construction, biotech, as well as mining companies.

So underlying DFID's stated aims of promoting Sustainable Development, Good Governance, and Poverty Eradication, is a broader aim of promoting a new order based on liberalisation and privatisation, in coordination with the WB. The basic purpose seems to be imposing a Structural Adjustment Programme in all but name, following the WB-IMF imposed model already implemented in many other countries. In Odisha and other chosen states, DFID has acted as an implementing agency for this programme, while channelling direct grants of official foreign aid (rather than making loans like the WB), and also—to put it rather bluntly (which many people do in Odisha)—as a business contractor for companies.

In effect, DFID programmes privatise health and education, while Governance Reforms privatise many functions and responsibilites of the administration, leaving the government as a 'shell', reducing its role (as the New Mineral Policy spells out) to that of a 'facilitator' for companies. The way DFID masterminded Odisha's power sector reforms, 'de-bundling' the state's electricity into separate companies, shows a pattern which is now being applied to water, as well as forest and its produce. Forest Management Committees, like Pani Panchayats, inevitably get into the hands of richer landowners. Similarly with Non-Timber Forest Produce (NTFP), which many Adivasis have collected from the forest and sold as a basic part of their economy for over a century.[47]

DFID's fundamental policy of promoting privatisation is shown by the role of the Commonwealth Development Corporation (CDC), owned by DFID, whose function is 'promoting the private sector in the developing world'. Its activities are opaque, but include partners in Odisha, such as the JK Paper Mill. The CDC in turn has a subsidiary power company, Globeleq, which promotes the privatisation of electricity, in part buying up privatised electricity companies that have failed, from several US companies including AES (the company in Odisha). It props up programmes privatising electricity, despite DFID research showing these have generally decreased profitability and employment and increased debt, and is known to be increasing its presence in India (War on Want 2006).[48]

Decoding DFID power

'All DFID support is on grant terms and is separate from the UK's commercial interests.' (DFID 2005) This point is debatable. What is certain is that DFID grants work alongside WB loans, applying the same secret 'conditionalities'. In other words, the WB's programme of neoliberal reforms in Odisha is being implemented, in effect, by an arm of the British government. DFID and the WB have dictated the Odisha government's financial policy for several years—with relative ease because of Odisha's large deficit.

Undeniably, a large part of Britain's foreign aid to India goes in fees to British consultancy firms. The phrasing (above) is to counter evidence collected by War on Want, Action Aid, and many other NGOs showing that 47 per cent or more of UK's (and other countries') foreign aid has been phantom aid or tied aid, giving 'immense sums' to private sector consultants, such as the Adam Smith Institute, which received £34 million in 1999–2004, while most indices show that the policy of privatisation has increased, not decreased poverty.[49] An analysis of the main consultants advising on privatisation of power, governance, water, etc., in India include the UK firms, PriceWaterhouseCoopers, Ernst & Young, KPMG, Deloitte Touche Tohmatsu, Robert Fleming Holdings and the Adam Smith Institute. The first four of these are the 'big four' accountancy firms, based in London, which also function as management and legal advisors. Their role in India seems to be that of aid contractors. During the 1990s, estimates of technical assistance of this kind, in structural adjustment programmes, amounted to about a third of Overseas Development Assistance (ODA).[50]

India is by far the biggest recipient of UK (DFID) aid. Aid for Odisha works out at roughly a tenth of total aid for India.[51] Under DFID's predecessor, the ODA (Overseas Development Authority), it was clearer, perhaps, that a large percentage was to be spent on British companies—a special 'tranche' in the aid budget: the 'Aid-Trade Provision'. In the words of Chris Patten during the 1980s, when Mrs Thatcher wanted to cut aid spending:

> We shouldn't be coy about the extent to which to do what is right is also to do what is best for Britain. [And in the words of his Ministry:] *Most British bilateral aid has to be spent on British goods and services,* but this does not mean that we cannot provide worthwhile help to the poorest groups in developing countries. By choosing programmes well we can ensure that benefits go to them at the same time as offering real opportunities to British firms. (emphasis added)

During the 1980s, at least 80 per cent (in the case of Bangladesh 99 per cent) of UK aid was estimated to be spent on British companies.[52]

The aid industry, then, is not what it seems. Aid and development rhetoric help to camouflage the corporate exploitation of 'developing countries', which aid agencies such as DFID promote; and also to camouflage these agencies' blatant interference in independent countries' policies and legislation. Recipient governments 'stand at the end of a cascade of decisions from above. ... the multitude of aid-driven activities frustrate governments' efforts to govern.' DFID and WB officials periodically come to Odisha, and reprimand government officials for 'misappropriation of funds', but *'Donors have no incentive to look for proof of corruption when they themselves are force-feeding the beneficiaries. ...'*[53]

Odisha's first protests against DFID and WB took place in 2002, when a People's Tribunal rejected the concept of Pani Panchayats (Water User Associations) as unacceptable, seeing them as a prelude to water privatisation. After this, a Campaign Against Marketisation of Water led opposition to Odisha's Pani Panchayat Bill, on the basis that the WB and DFID were laying down the rules. In August of the same year, 75 organisations took part in a rally in Bhubaneswar, whose convenor Abani Boral said:

The DFID and WB are controlling the state's budget, health sector, power reforms and primary education.

Rabi Ray, ex-Speaker of the Lok Sabha pointed out that Rs 350 crore had been given by DFID to consultancy firms advising on the privatisation process:

> The bureaucrats and ministers have turned agents of DFID in order to further their interests.[54]

Since then, DFID has managed to stay out of the news, or to enter it, with the WB, only occasionally, in visits exhorting the Odisha government to manage its finances better, with occasional harsh words that enter the media about corruption.[55]

If the DFID gives only grants to Odisha, what is their purpose? Are they free gifts? The effect of the reforms they pay for are certainly positioning the state for penetration by foreign companies. But who does the money go to? This question was also raised by a statement made to us by a senior British academic, who has coordinated DFID work in Odisha, that 'I have signed milllions of pounds to intellectuals in Orissa'. Many questions ought to be asked about how money has been channelled to Odisha and other parts of India—who to and what for?

The Adam Smith Institute is an institution infamous in the UK for its promotion of neoliberal ideology, whose website incidentally gives a very one-sided interpretation of Adam Smith, with no mention of his deep opposition to corporations. In Bhubaneswar the Institute is strategically placed just opposite the DFID's office in Forest Row. The high salaries received by Adam Smith consultants reflect little local knowledge about the society they are changing. And, as we have seen, the same big four accountancy firms given expensive contracts by the DFID are also employed, for example, by Vedanta Resources.

DFID's links with industrialisation are hidden but very strong. We have seen that it studied the Utkal project (Barney et al. 2000), and was linked to it through the Business Partners for Development (BPD) project at the WB. Its link with Vedanta/Sterlite's Lanjigarh refinery was clear through the UK government's Trade and Investment website entry, and we heard informally but conclusively that a senior DFID official was instrumental in helping establish Vedanta Resources in London. The website mentioned Sterlite's alumina refinery at Lanjigarh as a potential opportunity for British business. When a British activist wrote to his MP about human rights abuses there, and the MP (the Hon. Keith Hill) made an enquiry from the Foreign & Commonwealth Office, Sterlite was taken off the website, without explanation. Copies of the website on 5 March 2004 and 18 October 2004 showed the same list except for the presence/absence of Sterlite, under the title *Metallurgical Process Plant Market in India*, mentioning steel and aluminium projects, with an afterword:

> Aid-funded Business was launched in Sept 1998 in order to raise greater awareness of UK firms to substantial opportunities that exist in aid-funded business. It also aims to help firms tap into such business, which emanates from the WB, the European Commission, the UN agencies and some bilateral development programmes.[56]

Apart from Sterlite, the projects listed as potential partners for British business include Tata, Bhushan, Jindal, Ispat and several other iron and steel factories, as well as Nalco, 'the largest Indian investment in the aluminium sector in recent times.' [57]

One of the companies on the list, Jindal, has half built a steel plant at Kalinganagar, at great human and environmental cost,[58] and is currently planning another, advertised as 'India's biggest steel plant', near Angul, which is to be financed through an Export Credit Guarantee (ECG) from the UK government's ECG Department (March 2008). Export Credit Agencies (ECAs) occupy a 'grey zone of official aid', as the largest source of tax-payer money to private sector companies, helping them off-load onto the public the risks of their foreign investments. ECA support far exceeds WB investment, and unlike DFID, there is no pretence that UK commercial interests are not involved.[59] Tata's Kalinganagar plant, tainted by the police killings of January 2006, also involves several components made by British engineering firms.

DFID is based at No.1 Palace Street in the heart of London, from where a large bureaucracy controls operations in over 70 countries, though with considerable power devolved to regional capitals, for example, Delhi. The nature and motives of this power being orchestrated from London show distinct parallels with the East

India Company's power over 150 years ago—especially since India is the largest recipient of UK aid!

The letter sent in 2003 from DFID's director of Policy Divison, to Professor Emil Salim, the Eminent Person overseeing the Extractives Industries Review (EIR), reveals the structure of power exercised by DFID particularly clearly (above, p. 355). She warns that there was a 'real risk' that the WB Board would reject the Report (which happened), unless certain basic changes were made:

1. The Report was 'unduly negative, and fails to acknowledge either the potential benefit the sector can bring, or the changes made in bank policy in recent years ... the British government would like to see a more balanced report emerging from the EIR with a constructive critique of current policy.'
2. It showed 'significant confusion about the right roles of government, WB and NGOs.' Responsibility for engagement with civil society and NGOs should lie with local governments, not the WB.
3. Furthermore, it is not the Bank's role to start 'formal acts of acknowledgement and contrition for the wrongs done to indigenous communities [from] centuries of European colonial expansion.' [what about responsibility for 50 years of Bank-funded disasters and cultural genocide?]
4. 'The recommendations in the report could be clearer. Much is already in Bank safeguards policy—the question is how to ensure that it is adequately carried out and monitored. Recommendations on staff and civil society monitoring processes would be welcome here.'
5. 'The issue of Prior Informed Consent' [note 'Free' has disappeared] (PIC) needs some clarification. It is not clear whether consent is a blanket requirement over the whole project or just there [sic] settlement package. *To what extent is the Bank or government prepared to veto a national development package on the basis of disagreement from an individual?* (emphasis ours)[60]

This letter is a naked expression of power. The DFID and WB not agreeing to FPIC is equivalent to validating the process going on now, throughout India, where 'consent' in Public Hearings is manipulated by heavy-handed police presence and threats, leading to *involuntary displacement*, and a life of hell for thousands.

Moreover, DFID, with the UNDP, has been instrumental in formulating the R&R policies that the governments of Odisha and India have drawn up: policies contradicting ILO [International Labour Organisation] requirements that people displaced from land should be compensated in land, and policies whose provision of compensation in cash and promises of employment virtually guarantee (as we saw in Chapter Thirteen) a downward spiral of impoverishment, exploitation and cultural genocide.[61]

We have seen that the channelling of Hirakud water for factories has been strongly contested by farmers (Chapter Four). It seems that DFID gave a $39 million grant for refurbishing the reservoir in 2003–5. Work on this project hit farmers hard, reducing the flow. When this work was over, and newspapers announced that water was about to be released, this did not happen. The head of the Sason canal (one of the 2 main systems coming out of the reservoir) remained dry. It emerged that Bhushan steel plant had started taking water from this canal, building a road to its lift-off point that obstructed the in-flow from the Ib river. Many of the farmers promised irrigation from Hirakud 50 years ago never received it, and had hoped they would after this refurbishment.

Hirakud canal system is notoriously inefficient: only 18 per cent of farmers at the canals' tail end get water, and only 35 per cent of those in the middle. The reservoir's storage capacity is decreasing rapidly due to sedimentation, and five major dams on the Mahanadi plus tributaries in Chhattisgarh. Also, most controversially, due to a six-fold increase in industrial use since 1997. Twelve major factory complexes now draw water from the reservoir. Indal's smelter has been joined by Bhushan's huge steel plant (2005), the new smelters of Vedanta and Hindalco, and another 15 factories have permission to draw water in the future. These industries have been given the incentive of paying half the water rates which farmers pay![62]

With the water they are getting already decreasing dramatically, Odisha's farmers are furious. On 26 October 2006 about 20,000 people formed a 20 kilometre human chain around the reservoir. A year later, on 6 November 2007, 30,000 farmers gathered near Talab village and stormed the reservoir site. Lathicharged by police, the farmers remained non-violent and held the area, building a 16 foot long wall above an underground intake pipe laid by Vedanta. This wall they named *Chasiro Rekha* (Farmers' Line). They prevented work on a second Hindalco intake pipe on 2 December, when Congress organised a rally of 40,000 farmers in Sambalpur. Farmers mobilised again against a second Bhushan pipe on 5 December. Meanwhile, Naveen Patnaik made a statement that not a drop of water would be diverted to industry, which he soon changed to saying no surplus water would be given, and that farmers would have priority, promising a Rs 200 crore package for renovating the Hirakud canals (part of a WB loan for Odisha's water sector).[63]

In March 2008, after a huge rally, farmers' representatives, including Ashok Pradhan and Lingaraj from Borogorh, came to meet the CM in Bhubaneswar, explained the errors in his advisers' figures, and showed how it would be impossible to meet his promises to industry as well as to the farmers. For example, the minimum flow to the reservoir was originally planned as 25 million acre feet. By 2000 the flow was down to a precarious 16 million acre feet. With the canals drying up and failing to meet the farmer's needs, how can more water be diverted for industry? The GoO's own study shows that the water requirements for Vedanta and Hindalco's new smelters alone will deprive farmers of the water they need. Both were building new water intake pipelines before getting permission (a familiar pattern set by Vedanta's refinery), and Bhushan's actions contravened regulations. Naveen admitted that he was unable to force Bhushan to comply, and also he had not understand the figures correctly, pleading 'I'm an artist!' To which the activists replied 'But it's your job to understand. You're our Chief Minister!'[64]

In fact, the CM was indeed powerless, in the sense that a policy shift in water allocation 'from the top' (i.e. 'recommended' by the WB and DFID) had recently prioritised industry above agriculture.[65]

In other words, there has been a policy shift from supporting Odisha's agriculture with minimal subsidies sustaining a minimal support price for them to sell their grain, to massive subsidies supporting the water and other infrastructure and power needs of new aluminium and steel plants, even though these threaten to deplete the state's water fast. With aluminium production needing 1,378 tons of water per ton of aluminium, it is clear that the new smelters alone spell disaster for over 300,000 farmers dependent on Hirakud's water.

Mystery of the Courts of London

Samarendra's great-grandfather, who was minister to the king of Chikiti in south Odisha, wrote a play called *The Mystery of the Courts of London*, which was performed to troops returning from Europe after the First World War. Only the title survives, evoking a history of opaque centres of power in London which exert a distant but controlling influence over millions of people's lives in India. Through DFID, Britain is still India's largest donor, and India gets more DFID grants than any other country. This foreign aid functions as a mask for foreign control. India's economic policy, and to a considerable extent its legislation too, is still controlled from London, as firmly as in the days of the East India Company and Raj, though this power is more hidden now, and operates through financial control and debt. And just as the East India Company's purpose was to generate wealth from India for its shareholders, the purpose of this control boils down to exploiting India's resources, especially in Odisha, Andhra Pradesh, MP and TN (the four primary states under DFID control), extracting them at a rate unimaginable during the days of open British rule.

London is still the centre of the mining industry too, so it is important to demystify its power structure. A power-map of central London has pride of place in *The Next Gulf: London, Washington and Oil Conflict in Nigeria* (Rowell et al. 2005), which shows the geography within London of the power centres controlling policies in Nigeria, through Shell and branches of the government. DFID's influence in India is in a category of its own, but it seems to work in a similar way in other former colonies, such as Nigeria and Kenya.

The way one particular people has been treated reveals the brutality and deceit which often characterises the power exercised from central London, and demonstrates a seamless continuity in the colonial attitudes dictating policy right up to present times, through successive governments' disgraceful attempts at *maintaining the fiction*.[66] The Chagos Islanders' experience of displacement from near-paradise on Diego Garcia to urban squalor in the slums of Mauritius and Seychelles, making way for their island to become a key US military base, involved a 'policy of concealment' by the Foreign Office. In some ways, the Chagos Islanders' experience sets an unsettling model for the Dongrias in Niyamgiri. In fact, Sir Paul Gore-Booth (father of Sir David, one of Vedanta's first directors in 2003-4), was Permanent Under-Secretary there in 1966. The memo he wrote to implement this policy of removing the Chagos Islanders by pretending they never existed stated:

> We must surely be very tough about this. The object of this exercise is to get some rocks which will remain ours. There will be no indigenous population except seagulls who have not yet got a Committee (the Status of Women Committee does not yet cover the rights of birds).[67]

An order to dispossess a whole people is thus implemented with an amused irony. The result was a life of hell, with no compensation. Many of the Chagos Islanders died of grief and poverty, suicide and prostitution. In recent years, their initial victories in the London courts have been overturned by Royal Decree and appealed by Tony Blair's government, in order to maintain the fiction. Officials questioned by journalist John Pilger denigrate attempts to uncover the truth as 'muck-raking'. As Pilger points out, Britain went to war for a population of about 2,000 Falkland Islanders. A similar population of British subjects on the Chagos Islands were sacrificed with shameful cruelty for questionable diplomatic goals.

The Courts of London which exercise a controlling influence over India's economy today are a network of power centres, each with its own hierarchy, sphere of influence and culture of traditions and etiquette. DFID's base in Palace Street, the Foreign & Commonwealth Office and Ministry of Defence are all close to the PM's residence in Downing Street and the Houses of Parliament. Other centres include the Old Bailey, Bank of England, BBC's headquarters at Bush House and other major media centres at Canary Wharf. One must not forget the Queen in Buckingham Palace, who as Britain's head of state, read out the Decree banning the Chagos Islanders' return home, drafted on Blair's orders. The International Aluminium Association at New Zealand House is near Piccadilly Circus. Hidden away in the Defence Ministry is its infamous Defence Export Sevices Organisation (DESO, in charge of arms sales), and major arms companies are based nearby, such as BAe Systems (British Aerospace).

And how accountable are the accountants? Sampson's analysis shows that the 'big four' are all old London firms, who have gradually extended their empires and income since the mid-nineteenth century. We have seen that Ernst & Young, PriceWaterhouseCoopers, KPMG and Deloitte & Touche are all prominent recipients of Britain's foreign aid via DFID grants in India. Their fee income ranged up to £2,281 million in 2002, and the pronouncements of the Institute of Chartered Accountants, in the words of a key member who resigned in December 2003 (just as Vedanta was registering in London, using two of these firms), are *almost always designed to obfuscate rather than clarify in simple terms.* [68]

World aluminium prices are set five days a week in the arcane hand gestures used by traders in the Bull Ring at the London Metal Exchange. Vedanta has raised huge finance for its aluminium projects in Odisha and Chhattisgarh since registering on London's Stock Exchange. Anil Agarwal's Mayfair house, that used to belong to the Shah of Iran, serves as headquarters for Vedanta Resources. About half the world's Hedge Funds are run from London (though registered in tax havens such as the Bahamas and Mauritius). Their commodity trading in derivatives has been a major factor driving up metal prices in recent years, building the pressure to set up aluminium projects in Odisha. Many influential NGOs are based in London, including IIED (International Institute of Environment and Development), which coordinated the MMSD report.

Anthony Sampson's *Anatomy of Britain* (1993/2004) analyses these power centres, assessing DFID's influence, through foreign aid, above that of the Foreign Office.[69]

Anil Agarwal's father wrote a book of aphorisms in Hindi in praise of cleverness, one of them about Churchill short-circuiting a donor's request for favours, which shows an Indian understanding of how the court system works.[70] Naveen Patnaik, as a highly anglicised Odia who 'knows everyone worth knowing in Britain's elite' is a very convenient figurehead to preside over DFID's liberalising of Odisha. Delhi too has its Courts, and so do Bhubaneswar and Cuttack, imposing decisions on the rest of the state in a grand hierarchy modelled, if one really traces it back, to a Roman emperor model of power.

What are the implications of Odisha being controlled financially from London? West Odisha and London seem worlds apart, but as we have seen, they are closely connected through present lines of power, as well as a long history back to the 18th–19th centuries, when the British extended their rule over Kond areas through military campaigns. Today's Collectors, SPs and DFOs are exercising power in a colonial structure inherited uncritically from British times. There is a familiarity here and a weird interlinking of patterns of power.[71]

Odisha has a wealth of natural resources and a wealth of cultures that are being invaded and desecrated as a direct result of the liberalisation programme DFID has imposed on Odisha. What is going on now is a rape of a country's natural wealth. Though orchestrated from London, the looting of Odisha's resources is being done on the ground by a *mafia raj* of corruption and exploitation. The dire working and road conditions, high pollution levels, rapid depletion of water resources and erosion of people's food security, the displacement and cultural genocide faced by hundreds of communities: all these follow from Odisha's enforced opening up to 'penetration' by foreign capital, masterminded from London through DFID, and from Washington by the institutions known as the Washington Consensus.[72]

CHAPTER SEVENTEEN

Moneylender Colonialism and Bad Economics: The World Bank Cartel

Facilitating the aluminium companies

You are a woman and we are women.... You are a literate person from a big country. You understand these things are happening to us. So please, as a woman, help us.

Unusually, a WB consultant recorded the words of some tribal women who surrounded her and spoke about coming effects from the Indravati dams, while they were still being built, in 1993. A man standing nearby chipped in.

The human society living in America must know what is going on in another human society living in India. And they are responsible, because we're all humans, living on earth. They can't escape, you know. If I starve, you also bear a responsibility.

This is an expression of *advaita vedanta*. We are in this together. Between you and me, in as much as our actions affect each other, there is no real separation.[1] Yet, individually or collectively, what responsibility have WB employees taken for all the disastrous projects they have funded?

As we have seen, the WB forms an intrinsic part of the power structure imposing aluminium projects in one country after another,[2] and plays a major role behind the scenes, promoting the industry in Odisha. It promoted the Utkal project as part of its BPD (Business Partners for Development) scheme, organising meetings in Rayagada shortly before the Maikanch killings. WB loans financed the Upper Indravati dams (whose water now flows to the Lanjigarh refinery), and presently funds major road enlargement schemes in Odisha, in line with its 1983 investment analysis of the aluminium industry.

The Bank's present policy is spelt out in a May 2007 report, *Towards Mineral-Intensive Growth in Orissa: Managing Environmental and Social Impacts*, where the starting point is a decision to free up and speed up the extraction of the state's mineral wealth. This document's ostensible purpose is to get good environmental and social practices adopted so that the externalities of mining will no longer fall on the poor, but benefit them. A previous draft (joint WB and GoO) was drawn up a year before, formulating the problem in approved MMSD/ICMM language of 'sustainable development'.[3] The opening (2007) emphasises Orissa's potential and conjures an economic imperative to increase mining:

> 1. Orissa is rich in mineral sources. It is endowed with an abundance of minerals, timber, marine resources, and a plentiful supply of water. ... About 30 per cent of its area is under forest cover, which provides for the livelihood of a large and growing tribal population. It is also one of the richest biodiversity regions in India.
> 2. In the past several years, Orissa has emerged as a dynamic and reforming state that is poised to turn around its development fortunes, using as a major driver, an investment boom in the mineral sector and downstream industries. An initial set of reforms that has arrested fiscal deficit, improved governance and accelerated economic growth [*sic*]. Building on this success, the Government of Orissa (GoO) is developing and implementing a comprehensive vision and strategy for sustaining these achievements and ensuring lasting inclusive growth.

Yet the impacts of mining-based growth on environment and society have often been ill-managed. The document is careful to say the right things about a need to protect tribal people and environment, incorporating some of the latest critical perspectives:

II. MINING AND EXTERNALITIES

2.9 Most of Orissa's mineral deposits are in forests that are inhabited by tribal populations, who are heavily dependent on forests for livelihood and have lower adaptive capacity to economic and social changes. Mineral extraction often leaves an "ecological footprint" which may adversely impact on these communities, their economic landscape and the environment.... Addressing these impacts is a prerequisite for ensuring sustainable and inclusive growth and sustaining the momentum of economic reforms.

2.10 This is especially important given the scale of the proposed new investment in heavy industries. In two pollution-intensive sectors—iron/steel and alumina—the proposed expansion involves a 35-fold increase in steel production and three-fold rise in alumina plants. An expansion of such magnitude calls for compensating policy.

As we have seen, however, there is a reality gap between fine words acknowledging the biodiversity and recommending inclusive growth, and a situation where corruption, hierarchy and exclusion are the norm. This document fails to even begin to address this gap, and therefore does nothing to bridge it.

The reality is that mining companies, and banks investing in them, are poised to become the effective owners of some of Odisha's best-forested mountains and their minerals, with a view to rapid extraction. The double standards in applying law to village people and to mining companies, means that checks on actual impacts are abysmal (Chapter Seven), even as WB conditionality clauses promote a further dilution of legislation protecting labour or land rights and the environment.

The WB rejected key conclusions of its own Extractive Industries Review (EIR) in 2004, which had shown that WB involvement in mining was having disastrous effects on the environment and society, recommending phasing it out.[4] And the WB hushed up its involvement in Utkal, which had been a flagship BPD project of tri-partite development between mining companies, an All-Party Committee (i.e. the government) and NGOs. Without Agragamee, URDS lost its legitimacy, and after the Maikanch killings, the whole project fell into disrepute and signs of WB involvement had to disappear (Chapter Five).

Looking at Odisha's foreign loans as a whole, the WB has been the main lender, and played a key role in arranging loans from other IFIs too, including IFAD in Kashipur, a Japanese loan for the Kolab dam, and a Saudi one for the Rayagada-Koraput railway. By getting Odisha so deeply in debt, the WB effectively put it in a position where the government may seem to have no choice but to open its doors to foreign companies and sell off its mineral assets. This has been the 'advice' pressed on the GoO by its foreign creditors and financial advisers. Getting Odisha into such un-repayable debt, while financing projects like Upper Indravati that would assist future mining projects, has functioned as part of an over-all plan for foreign companies to get hold of Odisha's minerals at the cheapest cost.

We have seen how it exerted a decisive, though hidden pressure on aluminium companies' behalf in several countries, especially by threatening to cut off further loans (Chapter Nine). The WB President George Woods was instrumental in arranging loans for Kaiser aluminium projects—the Rihand dam in India and Akosombo in Ghana—as well as loans to Tata and SAIL to increase steel production. In Ghana his role contributed to removing Nkrumah from power. After leaving the WB, he joined the Kaiser Foundation Board, in the kind of 'revolving door' we often take for granted now.[5]

Crusade against poverty

The WB often defines its aims in terms of getting rid of poverty by boosting economic development. Advertised as 'a crusade against poverty', in practice WB projects have often had the aspect of a *crusade against the poor*. What is certain is that for millions of villagers displaced by projects it has funded, the WB has thrown them into poverty far worse than anything they knew before.

Lords of Poverty is the title of a book by Brian Hancock exposing the aid industry's corruption (1989). At the annual IMF-WB conference, speeches reaffirm the aim of aiding the poor, while first class cuisine at 96 parties in Washington cost an estimated $10 million. Every third year the event takes place in a 'developing country', and in Seoul in 1985 the Korean government razed 128 buildings to make way for a parking lot next to the main hotel, while a 3-day summit in Bangkok in 1991 cost the Thai government over $100 million on new buildings and other preparations, bringing into sharp contrast two worlds: designer-luxury for a few thousand foreign delegates, attendant journalists and other hangers-on, against worsening poverty for several 100,000 Thais removed from sustainable village lifestyles by WB-funded dams, and 2,000 slum-dwellers removed by the army from the conference vicinity. Yet in his opening address, Lewis Preston, the WB President, outlined the bank's objective as 'poverty reduction'. *Mortgaging the Earth* (Bruce Rich 1994) also highlights this contradiction.

Catherine Caufield's *Masters of Illusion: The World Bank and the Poverty of Nations* (1998) is a comprehensive analysis. As a top economist who defected, Joseph Stiglitz's *Globalization and its Discontents* (2002) is a critique by a privileged insider. WB economics have been critiqued by Samir Amin (1997), Gray (1998), Harvey (2005), Naomi Klein (2007) and others, while books by Pilger (1998, 2002) and Palast (2003) highlight some of the most sinister aspects of the way the WB wields power. Neeraj (2001), Arvind (2002), and Chandrasekhar and Ghosh (2002) examine India's experience.

Robert McNamara was director of Ford Motors, before becoming US Defence Secretary, where he was an architect of the Vietnam war. After this, Nixon appointed him to be the fifth President of the WB (1968–1981). It was McNamara who defined the Bank's Mission as a *'crusade on poverty'*, at the same time as he pushed its expansion through an aggressive, uncritical increase in lending targets—from $953 million to $12,400 million per year—and in bank staff from 1,574 to 5,201. He generated *'unprecedented and tremendous pressure on staff'* to go ahead with loans without proper investigation of consequences, or safeguards on how the loan would be actually spent, starting a system where lending to each country was worked out in a 5-year Country Programme Paper, which was confidential even to the Executive Director representing the recipient country! Boosting industrialisation in the Third World was considered his main achievement.[6]

McNamara's policies increased poverty spectacularly, not just by numerous projects displacing people, but also through agricultural policies which favoured richer against poorer farmers, and enmeshed both into debts for fertilisers and pesticides, as part of a drive to increase production of cash crops (the policy of India's Green Revolution). The WB gave over a billion dollars in loans to India for financing fertiliser and pesticide factories, including banned substances such as DDT. A WB report entitled *Assault on Poverty* (1975) advocated lending to richer farmers able to 'produce a significant marketable surplus'. The Green Revolution increased India's food production, without spreading real benefits to India's poorer farmers.[7]

McNamara's successor Tom Clausen, as head of Bank of America, had worked closely with the WB, arranging a parallel increase in private sector loans to developing countries. But on succeeding McNamara, he announced he was not going to continue the focus on poverty. Clausen was the choice of Ronald Reagan, to oversee a drastic escalation in economic reforms imposed throughout the world, especially by the banks' Structural Adjustment Programmes (SAPs).[8]

Crusader imagery is embedded in WB language, with talk of 'missions' to poor countries, and a missionary zeal in bank officials' implementation of economic 'doctrine', as 'apostles of the new life'. Like Christian missions, *'The WB was founded in a disdain for—and even a fear of—local knowledge and opinion'*. This showed from the WB's first mission to Columbia in the early 1950s, one of whose senior members later admitted:

> We in the Bank had an extraordinary arrogance in those days ... we had money, and that made us brilliant! The worst thing about this was that the people with whom we dealt in these countries actually accepted much of what we said, or at least kept quiet because they distrusted themselves.... Who wanted to give up that kind of power? Of course, I didn't know what I was talking about half the time, but it was a wonderful feeling. (Caufield, pp. 60–61).

The bank's complex hierarchy and regulations are geared towards making a large profit from its loans. But who does it serve? Its Board of Executive directors consists of Finance Ministers, with the richest countries in control. Clearly it serves the economic interests of these countries and their companies, and especially the richest country of all, in whose capital it is based.

A history of social and environmental catastrophe

The WB and IMF were set up during the last stages of the Second World War to promote a fairer economic system between nations. Why have they so conspicuously failed to do this?

When John Maynard Keynes in Britain was hammering out the WB-IMF format in negotiations with Harry White in Washington (1944–5), Keynes

> was not very keen on international investment, holding that the indebtedness thereby created was dangerous in relation to the balance of payments of the recipient countries.[9]

Keynes tried unsuccessfully to get the WB and IMF located first in London, then in New York, away from inevitable political influence in Washington. The conference at Bretton Woods (New Hampshire) that hammered out the WB-IMF set-up came to an end on 22 July 1944, when Keynes expressed the hope that these institutions would usher in a new age of 'the Brotherhood of Man', but warned of the curse in *Sleeping Beauty*: the danger of political influence lying ahead for 'the two multilateral foundlings, 'Master Fund' and 'Miss Bank'.

Keynes' worst fears were realised. To understand how and why, we have to look at the WB's history under a succession of Presidents, whose background in banking/business and politics illustrate the *revolving doors* which form a conspicuous feature of WB social structure.

Keynes had envisaged that the directors would be impartial international civil servants. By contrast, the US Congress insisted that US Executive directors should be 'first and foremost representatives of the US government'.[10] Accountability was weakened by Meyers' battle of wills with his Board of Directors.[11] McCoy's tenure was taken up with gaining acceptability on Wall Street, and four initial

	WB Presidency	Previous Jobs	Appointed by
1. Eugene Meyers	June–December 1946	Publisher of Washington Post	Truman
2. John McCoy	1947–49	Wall Street Lawyer and Assistant Secretary of War	
3. Eugene Black	1949–62	At Chase Manhattan Bank	
4. George Woods	1962–68	Chairman of First Boston Investment Bank	
5. Robert Strange McNamara	1968–81	CEO of Ford, then US Defence Secretary	Nixon
6. Tom Clausen	1981–86	Head of Bank of America	Reagan
7. Barber Conable	1986–91	A popular Republican Congressman	Reagan
8. Lewis Preston	1991–95	Chairman of J. P. Morgan Investment Bank	
9. James Wolfensohn	1996–2005	Formed his own Investment Bank (Australian by birth)	
10. Paul Wolfowitz	2005–07	US Defence Secretary in 'War on Terror'	G. W. Bush
11. Robert Zoellick	2007		

Table 14. Presidents of the WB

loans to European countries for Reconstruction—one of which was to the Netherlands, agreed just 17 days after the start of its vicious war to try and prevent Indonesia's Independence (7 August 1947), which it helped to finance. This contravened a UN ruling, and the same year, the WB defined its relationship with the UN so that critical information would be confidential from the UN, setting a pattern of *'blanket confidentiality and secretiveness'*, which still applies to the majority of its project documents.

Under Black and Woods, WB loans were targeted on large dams, transport systems and cash crops.

> Many of these projects had very adverse environmental and social consequences, which were almost totally ignored. (Rich, p. 73)

Chile was the first country to get a development loan, for a large dam in 1948. The next year, Columbia became the first to opt for a comprehensive development plan, financed by a series of loans and controlled by a semi-independent agency. Several WB staffers involved in this first venture, including economist Albert Hirschman, were critical in later years of the extreme power thrust upon them:

> One aspect of this affair made me particularly uneasy. The task was supposedly crucial for Columbia's development, yet no Columbian was to be found who had any inkling of how to go about it. That knowledge was held only by a few foreign experts.[13]

WB 'experts' financed new railways and roads in Columbia that caused deforestation and displacement on a massive scale, while knowing nothing about the country.[14]

More than a quarter of the loans approved by Black went to finance big dams. All involved a basic lack of local knowledge. The result was corruption on a monumental scale, and a vast increase in poverty. Researchers in India and Bangladesh have shown how 50–60 per cent of WB funds for irrigation and agriculture 'illicitly disappeared into the hands of contractors, corrupt officials, and local politicians'.[15] WB-funded wells were taken over by richer farmers, and WB support for cash crops helped rich farmers displace poorer ones, sucking these towards today's epidemic of debt spirals and suicides. On top of this, nearly all projects proved uneconomic. The WB's India Agriculture Operations Division made a confidential review in 1991, which concluded that 'project performance and economic viability have been poor all along for most projects'.[16] As McNamara increased the volume of loans, many projects had extraordinarily bad effects on the environment and civil society, especially on indigenous peoples.

When General Suharto in Indonesia mounted a coup against the socialist leader Sukarno in 1967, the US administration (smarting from Vietnam) authorised the CIA to give Suharto a long list of 'subversives', while the WB oversaw Suharto's economic planning, disbursing its first loan in 1968, and making this country a 'model pupil' during Suharto's worst excesses. About 40,000 'communists' were killed immediately. Many more deaths were caused by WB funding for Suharto's Transmigration programme of 3 million settlers from central Indonesia to distant regions, subdued by force, displacing indigenous populations and devastating their fragile ecologies in a search for quick profits from timber and plantations. A WB report in 1985 showed that half the migrants themselves were still living below the poverty line.[17] In Ethiopia, we have seen how the WB funded Mengistu's 'collectivisation programme' with its brutal 'transfer of populations'.[18] Amazingly, the WB funded similar collectivisation in Ceausescu's Romania, prioritised by McNamara from 1972, with no proper studies, and falsified statistics.[19] Yet WB loans were withdrawn from Chile till Pinochet overthrew Allende's socialist government.[20]

In all these countries, surveying the WB's history is to face a whole cycle of catastrophes compounded by violent injustice, over-rapid extraction of resources and environmental damage on a scale unprecedented in human history.

In Brazil too, the WB (supposedly apolitical!) refused to lend to a left-leaning government in the early 1960s, but started record loans to the military dictatorship which overthrew this in 1964, funding the vast Grand Carajás iron-ore and Polonoroeste projects which opened up Brazil's north through Trans-Amazon Highway 364. These were the projects that started a new era of destruction for the Amazon forest, through iron and bauxite mining, aluminium factories and megadams. Anthropologist David Price, a consultant on Polonoroeste (1980), gave testimony before Congress in 1983 that WB policy had brought about a slow genocide of the Nambiquara (forcibly moved from their home in 1968) and other tribes, and that the WB had deliberately suppressed and distorted his findings. When initial loans were approved in 1980, the Board of Directors knew nothing of a series of confidential memos expressing grave doubts about the soundness of the project, and in 1984, the WB was still denying evidence that terms of loan agreements specifying protection of forest and Indians had been violated repeatedly. It also ignored a warning from the charismatic rubber-tapper Chico Mendes just before he was murdered in 1988, that Polonoroeste II was bound to compound the devastation. Only in 1990, after it had lent more than $500 million, did the WB admit that this project was responsible for devastating the Amazon rainforest and its inhabitants.[21]

The 1983 Congress hearing on Polonoroeste opened up debate about the WB's policy on the environment and indigenous people, and from 1986 the annual WB-IMF meet was shadowed for the first time by a counter-meet of NGOs and activists. Barber Conable responded by greatly increasing the Bank's 'green' staff, though the main effect was greenwash, and an even bigger gap between the Bank's fine words and horrific ground realities. 'Robert Goodland had been the Bank's sole ecologist and its environmental conscience' for years. By 1991, environmental staff numbered 140, drowning out his voice, funding new forestry projects—*drawn up with the help of timber company executives*'!—which brought eucalyptus plantations on a mass scale to India, and deforested vast areas in Guinea and other West African countries.[22]

Most disturbing to observers, the WB was not learning from its mistakes, but continued to fund projects with the same dire and senseless effects on environment and society, while taking no responsibility for the consequences of its loans.

The WB's biggest project in India was the Singrauli coal mines and power complex near Rihand dam, inaugurated by Nehru in 1962. From 1977, the WB made record loans of more than $2.6 billion to the National Thermal Power Corp. (NTPC, started 1975). By 1994 there were 12 vast open-cast coal pits at Singrauli plus five giant coal-fired power plants, with a sixth for Hindalco's Shaktinagar/Renukoot plants.

> Singrauli, the energy capital of India, stinks. It stinks of human degradation and it stinks of the negligence of the Indian government and the WB which have together created an environment described here as the lower circle of Dante's Inferno ... and 70,000 contract labourers now work in semi-slave conditions under corrupt labour contractors.[23]

The land's fertility is destroyed for miles around, groundwater polluted. Yet following the WB lead, British, German, French, Japanese and Russian IFIs made additional loans. Singrauli's displaced people (more than 20,000) started to demonstrate for proper compensation in 1987, and it emerged that 8 of the 12 super-size ccpps funded by the WB in India had no resettlement component at all. The WB drew up a rehabilitation plan, but NTPC refused to take a loan for this, and the issue had been sidelined by 1993, when the WB started a new round of loans totalling $4 billion to intensify coal mining and power plants, channelled through NTPC: advance infrastructure for the long-planned aluminium industry.

> In the new loan virtually no funds are allocated for compensating and rehabilitating.... A WB vice-president and environment director have been to Singrauli and left, Bank staff had raised expectations, and millions have been paid to foreign consultants for studies, but there have been few tangible improvements for the development refugees of Singrauli. Their desperation has only deepened.[24]

A few years later the WB was financing Sarshatali coal mines in West Bengal, as a BPD scheme (like Utkal), only to discover, yet again, that its guidelines had been seriously flouted, jeopardising thousands of villagers' livelihoods.

In Odisha, WB loans funded the NTPC's mega thermal power plant at Talcher from around 1978, along with captive coal mines. A WB consultant who saw this project before and after, described the shock she felt at the devastation of farmland, and displaced indigenous families, whose new schools and playgrounds were substandard compared with those for the invading NTPC employees.

The Subarnarekha dams caused record protests, savagely suppressed. A year after the Bank approved a $127 million loan, police opened fire on about 8,000 tribal people, killing four (30 April 1978), and in 1982, police killed a charismatic leader of this movement, Gangaram Kalundia. The inundation in 1988, when Chandil closed its gates, left tens of thousands of Adivasis homeless, forcing the WB to suspend its loan disbursements (nearly complete!), though these started again in 1990, and more mass protests took place at the Icha dam site in April 1991. The WB disbursed its main funds before withdrawing from the project again.[25]

The same happened with the Sardar Sarovar dam on the Narmada, whose catalogue of incompetence and 'gross delinquency' formed the subject of an Independent Review Commission the WB appointed: the Morse Report. The four Commissioners exposed the destructiveness of this project on every level, estimating the displaced at 240,000, and finding a pattern of distortion and cover-up of basic information within the WB, as well as by GoI agencies. This report's publication in June 1992 created a storm of protest against the WB, which published a highly misleading report 10 weeks later, *Narmada: Next Steps*, in order to continue funding till April 1993, when all the WB's special low-interest loans, totalling $250 million, had gone through! Only $30 million out of $200 million normal-rate loans had been disbursed. However, the WB soon announced record new loans for India, totalling $2.3 billion![26]

The Morse Report was followed by an internal report by the WB's vice-president Willi Wapenhans, which found that this pattern of violations of WB policy and their devastating effects was standard, emanating from a 'culture of approval' with a complete lack of proper assessment or accountability. As a result, the WB set up a semi-independent Inspection Panel to review complaints. The first case reviewed was the Arun III Hydro-electric Project in Nepal, where the adverse results were so clear that funding was cancelled after intervention by the WB President (October 1994), though appeals to this Panel since then have achieved little.[27]

The Indravati dams are less known than the Narmada dams, though no less destructive of forest and people's livelihoods. How come no-one can be held responsible and put on trial for crimes against humanity such as these?

The Bank's policy statement for 2003, *India: Sustaining Reform, Reducing Poverty*, is worth examining to understand the reality gap on poverty:

> Sustained growth is the most powerful drive of poverty reduction. But poverty reduction also requires investment in human development. Health and education are the most important assets of the poor, allowing them to both contribute to and benefit from growth through higher-paying employment. In addition, when incomes fall below certain minimum standards, the poor and vulnerable need access to effective social safety nets.[28]

This language is intentionally opaque. What exactly is human development? Are WB staffers experts? Do they consider themselves particularly highly developed as human beings? If their aim is really to reduce poverty, the employment policy they promote is bizarre: much greater flexibility in the hiring and firing of workers, and removal of restrictions on the use of contract labour (where workers have far less rights).

> Labor market restrictions on the hiring and firing of workers are identified as one of the greatest challenges of doing business in India. ... Employment in India's registered firms ... is highly protected.... These provisions make labor rationalisation very difficult.... They are obviously especially burdensome for exporters who have to compete with producers in other exporting countries ... this ["*rationalisation*"] requires enactment of labor changes by Parliament (repealing section 5B of the Industrial Disputes Act), and the political sensitivity of such changes are *[sic]* likely to make them very difficult to implement ... Amendments to the Contract Labor Act, currently being considered by GoI, would allow the use of contract labor for all activities—not just for activities of a temporary nature.[29]

Adivasi miners at Bodai Daldali, Kawardha, Chhattisgarh

So where 'the poor' are supporting themselves through labouring jobs, all the legislation that has guaranteed them security and a decent wage is to be removed. This passage makes clear that the WB and its consultants have played a key part in bringing pressure to remove this protective legislation, directly increasing poverty among workers who have to fight to get jobs at even a minimum wage. The requirement to remove or steer around these laws clearly formed an important part of the WB's loan conditionalities to India.

This explains why promises of employment in all the aluminium projects are hollow. Most workers are hired on a contract basis and have few rights. The forced redundancies in Balco factories, appalling conditions in its bauxite mines, and repeated strikes over employment terms at Lanjigarh show precisely how WB reforms have increased poverty—'poverty reduction' could not be further from the mark.

The debt trap

When Woods took over in 1962, he discovered that many countries were dangerously in debt. Half their income from exports and foreign aid was going into servicing this debt: 40 per cent in South Asia and 87 per cent in Latin America. Yet instead of cutting back on loans, he increased spending dramatically, with support from Wall Street, inventing a new kind of loan, interfering more deeply in countries' policies and legislation.[30]

India topped the list of most heavily indebted countries, followed by Ghana (reeling from the Valco agreement), Sri Lanka and Pakistan. These four were so deeply in debt

> that they are likely to encounter serious and protracted debt service difficulties unless large amounts of external assistance are available to them.

In other words, more loans to keep up interest payments on previous loans! This needed a new type of quick-disbursing loan, not tied to particular projects—*'balance of payment loans'*—expressly forbidden in the WB's original Articles of Agreement, when Keynes and others had foreseen this danger of spiralling debt. To get round this,

In the end, it wasn't necessary to create a new facility, because when we got into the business of making large loans to facilitate India's imports we simply called them "industrial import loans"... It was Woods who took the decision himself. Why can't we just make them a loan? Make a list of things they are going to import. ... As far as he was concerned, it was a project [but] it was [actually] balance of payment support; it had the same effect as a balance of payment loan.[31]

India got 11 'industrial import loans' (1964–76), totalling $1.5 billion, which deferred the balance of payment crisis, while building massive debts to finance a programme of industrialisation masterminded abroad.

From 1968, McNamara's 'frontal assault on poverty' demanded a further escalation in lending. He made it clear he was not interested in the creditworthiness or otherwise of borrowers. Instead, he put a lot of pressure on bank staff to disburse oversize loans, especially near the end of the financial year, in May–June. As a result, there was hardly any proper vetting of WB projects at all in the McNamara years.[32] The lending frenzy spread to commercial banks, while capital flight from recipient countries accelerated, along with the debts, especially in Latin America.

This is why in India, as in other Asian, African and Latin American countries, it is too easy to blame corruption on local conditions. The WB system, without proper checks on how money is spent, feeds corruption, and builds a cycle of dependency and foreign control.

Countries began to crash. Zaire first, in 1976—Mobutu's personal fortune was $4 billion, while Zaire's external debt stood at $5 billion.[33] Peru crashed the same year, and the 'stabilisation program' the WB imposed as a condition for more loans—an early version of 'Structural Adjustment', with devalued currency, drastic cut in public spending and raised taxes—caused riots in Lima.[34] In 1977 Turkey crashed, and the WB would not bail it out until a tough military regime in 1980 promised to impose what was in effect the WB's first Structural Adjustment Program (SAP). Fifteen years later, its aims still had not been met! Despite $3 billion more loans, Turkey's economic crisis was worse than ever, with $70 billion of foreign debt.[35] Mexico's infamous crash in 1982 elicited a WB bail-out of

13 new-style, quick-disbursing loans totalling $6 billion by 1991. The age of the SAPs had begun, and Mexico was the model pupil. By 1995, 88 countries had accepted SAPs.

The trouble was, they didn't work. In 1992 the *Financial Times* was calling Mexico 'the darling of the Bank's economists', yet it had not achieved the main aims of adjustment: economic growth and poverty reduction. Poverty had increased exponentially. The result exploded in the headlines on 1 January 1994: the Zapatista rebellion in Chiapas, Mexico's poorest province. Private investors, who had poured money into Mexico following the WB's lead, got scared and started pulling it out. To plaster over this crisis, the country received $50 billion more in loans.[36]

In other words, the WB's policies were a disaster: trapping the 'developing countries' in unrepayable debts that made the poor poorer, while devastating the environment.

Or were they a disaster? What if the whole point of WB strategy was precisely this?—to trap these countries into unrepayable debts so that they could be 'penetrated' by Western-style companies and their resources extracted to accumulate profits in the world's top capitals, more efficiently than ever happened under colonial governments?

Confessions of an Economic Hit Man (John Perkins 2005) reveals precisely this: Perkins' training was to entice Third World government leaders into accepting huge loans, that they could never repay, by making the most persuasive, scientific-looking forecasts of GNP growth 20–25 years into the future.

> The unspoken aspect of every one of these projects was that they were intended to create large profits for the contractors, and to make a handful of wealthy and influential families in the receiving countries very happy, while ensuring the long-term financial dependence and therefore the political loyalty of governments around the world. The larger the loan, the better. The fact that the debt burden placed on a country would deprive its poorest citizens of health, education, and other social services for decades to come was not taken into consideration. (Perkins 2005, p. 15)

When the forecasts are presented by experts from the world's top capitals (for example Japanese offers to Brazil for Tucurui), their offers of fast cash to boost growth seem all but irresistible—especially when the debt burden breaks out in a Balance of Payments crisis (BoP)—a situation of 'no choice'.

Dictating policy from abroad

India's BoP crisis came in 1990-91. After averting this in 1964 by getting the 11 industrialisation loans, India's debt burden escalated from $20.58 billion in 1980 to $83.7 billion in 1990, while the WB studied India's economy, including no doubt, its statewise spread of debt and key mineral and other assets. The Anderson Memorandum, submitted in November 1990, outlined the WB plan for India's Structural Adjustment. Chandrashekhar's government was not in a position to implement this. It started by selling 20 tons of gold for $200 million and pledging more. In May 1991, Narasimha Rao was elected PM, and his Finance Minister was a WB trainee, initiated into the latest doctrine at the EDI (Economic Development Institute), the WB's staff training college in Washington. The stage was set for India's Structural Adjustment, pushed through in the New Economic Policy (1991), and National Mineral Policy (1993).

The new Finance Minister was Manmohan Singh, and his reforms were carefully stage-managed, concealing the extent of the BoP crisis, and introducing selective reforms so that India did not lose all its financial and legal independence at one go. Anderson had recommended opening the economy to foreign investment and making it export-oriented, privatising PSUs (Public Sector Utilities), ending protection to small-scale industries and removing restrictions on big companies. In July, the rupee was devalued by 22 per cent, and Manmohan announced a Union Budget and a new Statement on Industrial Policy. Immediately, the WB sanctioned a massive injection of fast-disbursing loans, raising India's foreign exchange reserves from $975,000,000 to $5,631,000,000,000 by March 1992. ($975 million to $5,631 billion). To summarise Manmohan's reforms:

   i. The rupee's exchange rate opened to a market-determined mechanism.
   ii. Restrictions on imports removed, tariffs lowered, exports freed from all constraints.

iii. Industrial policy liberalised: controls on foreign investment for industry gradually removed, in some sectors ownership up to 100 per cent allowed. Controls on big business removed, along with subsidies for small ones.
iv. Mineral wealth and natural resources opened up to foreign companies.
v. Agricultural subsidies drastically cut, and private investment in agriculture sought, by taking measures like removing land ceiling restrictions.
vi. India's patent laws modified in compliance with WTO rules.
vii. Finance sector liberalised, removing restrictions on capital flows, allowing banks to deal in shares, etc.
viii. Privatisation at several levels, allowing foreign investors to take over assets (for example, Enron and AES bought up privatised electricity companies)
ix. Ending price controls, including controls which had prevented speculation in essential food-grains. Lowering subsidies for the poor through the PDS.
x. Trimming fiscal deficit by raising indirect taxes (paid by everyone), without raising taxes on big business or the rich, plus attempts to freeze wages.
xi. Changing labour laws by restricting labour rights, allowing companies to retrench their labour force at will (as, for example, Vedanta did at Korba).[37]

By 1994, India had changed more than twenty major laws, including the Trade Unions Act, Industrial Disputes Act, Land Ceilings Act, and Maternity Benefits Act.[38]

This exemplifies the system of moneylender colonialism: dictating a country's policies and legislation, through *'conditionalities'* that require new laws or removal of 'restrictive' ones. Conditionalities function as commands that have to be obeyed. The WB waits till a country faces a BoP crisis to insist on them. As WB vice-president Shahed Husain admitted when Turkey accepted the first SAP, the WB was making extraordinary demands: 'These loans go to the heart of the political management of an economy. We will have to approach them with humility.'[39]

Humility and great skill are certainly evident in the path Manmohan Singh has steered, from his WB-imposed reforms as Finance Minister to his present tenure as India's PM. He saved India from the kind of violent shocks experienced by most other countries during Structural Adjustment. The cost is this: India's assets lie open to plunder on a scale unimaginable before the 1990s.

Odisha has the highest debt ratio of any state in India. We can see why now: the dams and other infrastructure projects laid the ground for mining companies, at the same time as building an unrepayable debt. For the financial year 1999-2000 the Orissa government's debt repayment totalled Rs 3,068.43 crore, while its loan receipt was Rs 3,690.40 crore. These are basic facts behind Orissa's Fiscal Reforms, and the recent pressure to mobilise mining projects.[40] Hence the power sector reforms, implemented through the DFID, paving the way for deals to bring Odisha's famous mineral deposits under control of foreign companies and banks (Chapter Fifteen).

To understand what is happening in Odisha today, we need to decode a sample WB document. The IBRD and IDA's *Program Document* (PD) *for a loan ($85 million) and credit (=$40 million) to India for the Socio-economic Development Program* (28 Sept 2004), mentions the 'close cooperation with other donors, particularly the UK DFID', for ensuring that 'significant technical assistance is available to follow through on the reform measures.' This loan is for Orissa, defined (as in school textbooks) as rich in minerals but poor.

> Despite its rich endowment of mineral wealth, forests, lakes, rivers, and a long coastline, Orissa remains the poorest, and perhaps the most fiscally-stressed, of India's 14 major states, and growth performance lags [behind] the all-India average.' [41]

Orissa's population is given as 35 million, over half BPL (Below the Poverty Line), 85 per cent rural, 22 per cent tribal.

> A key reason for Orissa's relatively low growth is the poor performance of agriculture.... Over half the rural poor work as casual labourers and over one-third struggle to subsist by cultivating small plots of land. Orissa's agriculture is less diversified and less commercialised than in any other major Indian state ... attributable in part to ... regulatory constraints on private investment in marketing yards and storage facilities, which, with poor road connectivity, limits the market price realisable by farmers in the state.

The implication is, these small-scale farmers will never make large profits, so the larger farmers should be freed from constraints so that they can expand—broadly, the history of farming in Europe, in which most small farmers got pushed off the land.

Among the private enterprises the PD mentions as needing to be freed from constraints are ferro-chrome, aluminium and steel. State-level reforms are seen as the key to India's development, to facilitate Odisha 'catching up' with the more 'developed' states, in a context where its high rate of poverty 'is linked to low wages in agriculture, which are in turn linked with low land productivity'.[42] Left implied but unstated is the overall plan for developing Odisha's mineral resources in projects that produce far higher profits from the land.

> The emerging growth strategy is based on the recognition that the state has potential to grow much faster if it can better utilise and market its considerable endowment of cultural and natural resources and improve the climate for private investment. Reforms instituted by the GoI during the 1990s have contributed to enhancing Orissa's growth potential. In particular the policy of cross-subsidisation of transport costs under the old freight equalisation arrangements, annulled Orissa's attraction as a location for mineral processing industries, and since GoI terminated the freight equalisation scheme, private investor interest in Orissa has increased in such sectors as ferro-chrome, aluminium and steel....
>
> GoO understands that without improving the productivity and market-orientation of agriculture in the State, it would be impossible to achieve a visible reduction in poverty.[43]

'*GoO understands...*' is a thinly veiled command. The language echoes documents from the East India Company time. There is a close connection in ideas too—the stress on privatisation and 'free trade'. What the WB proposes is a rapid commercialisation of Odisha's natural resources, on the theory that this will reduce poverty.

Shock doctrine

An Investment Analysis for Orissa was produced in 1996 by the accountancy firm Coopers & Lybrand (paid for out of ODA funds as part of UK aid to Odisha?). This calls Odisha 'an investors' paradise', with 'an extremely investor-friendly Bureaucracy and supportive Government', spelling out 'certain shortcomings' that hamper the desired programme of industrialisation based on extracting its mineral wealth.[44] This probably formed the impetus for the Congress government in Odisha to make the Niyamgiri deal in 1997, and to push ahead with Utkal. But a certain shock to the system has to take place before a state can sell off its prime assets, which in Odisha, as in other places, is focused through an escalating crisis of unrepayable debt.

'Science is measurement.' To understand the shock doctrine we have to go back to the Chicago Economics Department during the 1950s, where the neoliberal doctrine took shape. These words, written above the Social Science Building, express the founding fathers' teaching that economic theories are 'a sacred feature of the system', rather than hypotheses open to debate. A free market follows when individuals follow their self-interest. Any restriction is a deviation. Friedrich Hayek, one of the founders, formed the Mont Pelerin Society as a club of free market economists meeting in Switzerland. Among its members was Hayek's star pupil, Milton Friedman, whose book *Capitalism and Freedom* (1962) introduced a new era of ultra-capitalism to the world.

Friedman gave a triple formula: *deregulate* (remove all regulations standing in the way of accumulation of profits), *privatise* (sell off any public assets which companies could run for profit, including the health and education systems), and *cut back* (social programmes, labour rights, etc.).

Their great enemy were the Developmentalists in the Southern Cone of Latin America, leftist economists centred at the UN Economic Commission for Latin America at Santiago (Chile), headed (1950–63) by economist Raúl Prebisch, who was busy training economists to help manage the subcontinent's economies—a symbol of hope for poor countries around the world. Wherever Prebisch-trained economists got influence, the gap between rich and poor was narrowing.

The Chicago doctrine was considered lunatic extremism until the 1970s–80s, when Thatcher and Reagan promoted its rapid diffusion.

US President Eisenhower took the first step, seeing Developmentalism as leading to Communism. His administration funded an Economics Department in Santiago's conservative Catholic University to counteract it, where Arnold Harberger (a 'seriously dedicated missionary') undertook to spread the Chicago doctrine, along with *los Chicago Boys*—Latin American students, returning from Chicago 'even more Friedmanite than Friedman himself'. The Chile Project was launched officially in 1956, using US taxpayers' funds and grants from the Ford Foundation and USAID to pay for several hundred Latin American students to study in Chicago—against certain reservations within the Ford Foundation about funding such an overtly ideological program.[45]

The CIA was created in these years, and launched a bloody campaign against 'creeping communism' by instigating the overthrow of Mossadegh in Iran (1953–4, replaced by the Shah dynasty), and Guzmán in Guatemala, for expropriating land belonging to the US United Fruit Company (1954, replaced by a military dictatorship). These events were pushed, among others, by the CIA head and Eisenhower's Secretary of State, who were brothers, Allen Dulles and John Foster Dulles.[46] The CIA, as we have seen, funded two more military coups in 1964–5: against Brazil's land-reforming President Goulart, and left-leaning Sukarno in Indonesia, with large loans dispensed to both regimes soon after the coups by the WB. Suharto's Indonesia became the WB's 'model pupil', run by the 'Berkeley Mafia'—a group of Indonesian economists, educated through another Ford Foundation grant at the University of California.[47]

Then came 11 September 1973: the overthrow of Allende in Chile in another CIA-funded military coup, in the interests of several US companies, including Anaconda and Kennecott Copper, ITT, Pepsicola and Citibank. While the tanks and soldiers were killing Allende's men in the Presidential Palace, streets and universities, the Chicago Boys printed a document called *The Brick*, prescribing Friedmanite economic reforms, which General Pinochet carried out faithfully in the weeks and months that followed, as his troops rounded up and tortured 'subversives'. About 3,200 people disappeared or were killed and 80,000 imprisoned, most of these with torture, while about 200,000 fled the country.

When Friedman and Harberger flew to Santiago in March 1975, they were warmly welcomed in a private meeting with Pinochet, who had already received WB support. In speeches and interviews, well covered in Chile's media, Friedman used a new term for what Pinochet's Chile had to do: *'Shock treatment'* ... 'the only medicine' ... 'There is no other long term solution.' Applying this properly would allow the General to take credit for an *'economic miracle'*.[48] Incredibly, Friedmanites still pretend the Chicago Boys effected an economic miracle in Chile, though the evidence shows otherwise. In 1982 the economy crashed, with massive debts, hyperinflation and 30 per cent unemployment. Pinochet dismissed the Chicago Boys, nationalised key companies, and retained Allende's nationalised copper mining company Codelco, which provided 85 per cent of Chile's export revenues, giving the lie to any idea that Chile fully implemented Friedman's privatising prescriptions. As Friedman's former student, André Gunder Frank, pointed out in an *Open Letter to Arnold Harberger and Milton Friedman*, their theory was being implemented with the twin elements of 'military force and political terror'.[49]

Friedman denied all connection with the violence. But as Orlando Letelier (Allende's former Ambassador to the US) insisted, Friedman shared responsibility for Pinochet's crimes as the 'intellectual architect and unofficial adviser for the team of economists now running the Chilean economy'. Including another crime about to happen—just 3 weeks after Letelier's article was published, assassins killed him in a car bomb as he drove through central Washinton on 21 September 1976.[50]

Chile's coup was followed by another in Uruguay, whose leaders invited a group of Chicago Boys to oversee economic reforms, and another in Argentina (1976), every bit as bloody, but more covertly so: 30,000 people disappeared, many killed in the streets, but most in custody or thrown from planes. Nixon, Kissenger and the CIA played major roles orchestrating these events, while Friedman had visited Brazil at the height of its repression in 1973. In 1976 he was awarded the Nobel prize—shortly after Letelier had publicly blamed him and been assassinated. The next year, Amnesty International was awarded the Nobel prize, for its reports on human rights abuses in Chile and Argentina—a landmark, though they made no mention of the economic 'shock treatment' going on at the same time. Friedman and the Chicago Boys are not even mentioned.[51]

In line with this, the Ford Foundation, facing strong criticism for its role training the Berkeley Mafia, started human rights work, spending $30 million in Latin America alone. It had funded the Santiago programme, and Ford Motors worked closely with the Chile and Argentina regimes, carrying fulsome advertisements celebrating Argentina's coup, supplying cars to the military and reasserting strict control over workers at factories. Its definition of human rights was narrow, disconnected from any attempt to understand the causes of repression, let alone who was responsible.[52]

Naomi Klein's *Shock Doctrine* (2007) pinpoints a connecting thread missing from most analyses. The torture and terror used to implement economic shock therapy in Latin America were linked with the doctrine of Structural Adjustment at a fundamental level of belief and practice. The model came from Electro-Convulsive Therapy (ECT), which was developed into the *Kubark* torture techniques (1963). Multi-level shock and repression were nearly always necessary to implement SAPs.

Often the WB/IMF played a key role inducing economic crisis in the first place, as shown by the history of forced lending alternating with threats to withhold loans. Economists spoke of their role as healthy 'antibodies to combat anti-economic ideas and policies' or 'the plague of inflation'; of 'depatterning' people back to health through a series of intense shocks—eliminating 'diseased elements' in society.[53] Friedman put this clearly in *Capitalism and Freedom* (1962):

> Only a crisis—actual or perceived—produces real change. When that crisis occurs, the actions that are taken depend on the ideas that are lying around. That, I believe, is our basic function: to develop alternatives to existing policies, to keep them alive and available until the politically impossible becomes politically inevitable.[54]

Whatever the crisis, the idea is to use it as an opportunity to impose rapid, irreversible change before a crisis-ridden society can slip back into 'the tyranny of the status quo'—a variation, as Klein observes, of Machiavelli's advice to inflict injuries 'all at once'. *Shock and Awe: achieving rapid dominance*, the US military doctrine formulated in 1996, is another example.

This doctrine of multi-level, sudden shock was Friedman's most enduring legacy, and makes sense of the terror spreading all over Latin America: it served as a cover as well as a means to inflict hateful economic reforms over shocked and cowed populations.

Margaret Thatcher and Ronald Reagan were among the doctrine's most ardent adherents. In 1981 Hayek encouraged Thatcher to implement the doctrine in Britain—a political impossibility she replied. Her rating was at a record low of 25 per cent. But when Argentina's generals invaded the Falklands in April 1982, they gave her a perfect opportunity. After winning this war, she turned to 'the enemy within', smashing the coal-miners' strikes, and imposing free market reforms, to start *the corporate takeover of Britain*.[55]

The next country where Friedman's shock therapy won a dramatic success was Bolivia in 1985, where Jeffrey Sachs used it on a crisis of hyperinflation caused by spiralling debts. Sachs' stabilisation plan was implemented with shocking suddenness and force, reducing inflation from 14,000 per cent to 10 per cent in 2 years. But the cost of this fell on the poor. Unemployment rose to 30 per cent, and thousands were soon living near starvation. Sachs visited the country as its adviser, stiffening resolve not to waver, but his success in reviving the economy and beating inflation was actually aided by a mass move back to growing cocaine, and a year later, the country was hit by the Volcker Shock, which reduced the price of tin by 55 per cent and caused a downsizing of the country's miners from 28,000 to 6,000.

When countries were sent spiralling into crisis in the eighties, they had nowhere else to turn but the WB and IMF. When they did, they hit a wall of orthodox Chicago Boys, trained to see their economic catastrophes not as problems to solve but as precious opportunities to leverage in order to secure a new free-market frontier. Crisis opportunism was now the guiding logic of the world's most powerful financial institutions.[56]

In 1989, the Chicago doctrine was labelled the *Washington Consensus* by John Williamson, a key adviser to the WB and IMF, defining it as 'the common core of wisdom embraced by all serious economists'.

WB loans had always come with policy 'recommendations', but from the 1980s they came with the demand for full-fledged structural adjustment. The official mandate was still crisis prevention through stabilisation. But as a senior IMF economist who designed SAPs later admitted,

> everything we did from 1983 onwards was based on our new sense of mission to have the south "privatised" or die; towards this end we ignominiously created economic bedlam in Latin America and Africa in 1983–88.[57]

Opening countries to foreign penetration by the 'free market' was not the way to end the crises. This was known by the economists imposing the policy, but—as some later admitted—this fact was obfuscated in service to the goal of privatisation.

To Poland, freed from communism in 1988–9, the IMF refused any debt relief unless it accepted a SAP. Here again, Sachs was the key adviser. China went the Friedman way of reforms in 1988,—a key cause of the massacre in Tiananmen Square on 4 June. As in Chile and Argentina, neither media nor human rights reports highlighted the fact that Deng Xiapong was facing massive protests in mid-1989 because of the Friedmanite program he was forcing through. In the 3 years that followed the Tianenmen shock, China opened its country to foreign investment and a huge boost to exports through thousands of sweatshop factories and SEZs, which in China comprise several very large areas on the coast. The Western media criticised the repression, but failed to understand it or reveal that its purpose was to force through neoliberal reforms prescribed by Western economists.[58]

In the winter of 1989, Francis Fukuyama coined his infamous phrase *'the end of history',* to mean a total lack of 'convergence between capitalism and socialism ... an unabashed victory of economic and political liberalism.'[59]

One culmination of this 'end of history' was the collapse of the Soviet Union. In July 1991, after unilaterally ending the Cold War, Gorbachev was invited to join the G7 talks in London. Instead of a hero's welcome, he faced an astonishing level of pressure to 'become a Pinochet' and impose economic shock therapy. Instead, almost immediately, Yeltsin took over, first by seeming to abort a military coup in August, when he stood on a tank and took command, and then forcing Gorbachev to resign by getting the Soviet Union disbanded. He invited Sachs to Russia to advise on the prescribed economic reforms, and Sachs recalled Yeltsin saying:

> "Gentlemen, I just want to announce that the Soviet Union has ended ..." And I said, "Gee, you know, this is once in a century. This is the most incredible thing you can imagine; this is true liberation; let's help these people." [60]

What followed was not very liberating. The G7 leaders refused to lend money till shock therapy was under way. Yeltsin delegated this job to a team of Russian 'young reformers' under Yegor Gaidar and advised by Sachs. These imposed their program just one week after Gorbachev had gone, promising just six months' pain. Instead, the pain went on and on: millions of Russians lost their life's savings, and millions of workers were not paid. A third of the population fell below the poverty line, while obscenely wealthy 'oligarchs' emerged from a mafia-ised society. By March 1993, Russians were furious. Parliament voted to take away the special powers it had granted Yeltsin to push through the reforms, and passed an anti-IMF budget. Lawrence Summers, for years a key power at the WB but now US Treasury Under-Secretary, warned that 'the momentum for Russian reform must be reinvigorated and intensified to ensure sustained multilateral support', and the IMF obliged, making an official leak to the press that a promised $1.5 billion would be withheld because it was 'unhappy with Russia's backtracking on reforms'.

This was the signal Yeltsin needed to take the 'Pinochet option'. He abolished the Constitution, and when Parliament, in Moscow's White House, voted 636-2 to impeach him, he sent troops to surround it. After two weeks of popular peaceful demonstrations supporting Parliament's stand, Yeltsin was still assured that the IMF and US leadership supported him. He doubled military salaries to ensure army loyalty, and after troops had fired into a crowd of protestors near the central TV station, killing around 100, he ordered the military to attack the very Parliament which he had saved two years before, bombarding it with tanks. About 500 people were killed, 1,000 wounded and 1,700 arrested (4 October 1993). The Western press reported it as 'Victory seen for Democracy' (*Boston Globe*), and 'Yeltsin Receives Widespread Backing for Assault' (*Washington Post*).[61]

As we have seen, Russia's 'aluminium wars' took off from this time, at the heart of the mafia-isation instigated by Gaider's privatisation process. At the same time, Yeltsin started the terrible Chechen wars (1994), diverting attention from his economic reforms and repression. About 100,000 civilians died in these wars.

A similar set of Friedmanite reforms were imposed in South Africa, just when everyone was rejoicing at liberation from apartheid in 1994. The economic reforms had been negotiated in secret as a condition for De Klerk giving up white supremacy, and left the structures of real financial power unchanged, making it impossible to fulfil the wonderful vision of an equal society contained in the ANC's original Freedom Charter.[62]

Jeffrey Sachs dismissed Yeltsin's opponents as 'former communists'. *The End of Poverty* (Sachs 2005) contains no mention of Yeltsin's repression or that in Bolivia. Another influential book, Thomas L. Friedman's *The World is Flat: A Brief History of the Twenty-First Century* (2005), extends the metaphor of the 'level playing field' to paint a fairy-tale picture of healthy competition with no mention of exploitation or the violent shocks, poverty and bloodshed which Milton Friedman's doctrine had spread around the world.

Not least in Iraq, where military 'shock and awe' was followed in September 2003 by a full neoliberal program of privatisation, imposed by the US representative running the country, in the interests of US companies, particularly those in the oil and construction business.[63]

The Washington Consensus established the 'three pillars' of Milton Friedman's extremist doctrine as the panacea for all economic ills, to be imposed rigorously by every country that sought WB loans, as soon as it reached a BoP crisis. Wolfensohn in effect renamed SAPs 'Poverty Reduction Programmes'—yet another turn in the screw of language. In the name of reducing poverty, the shock doctrine has widened the gap between rich and poor, creating a new class of super-rich, including the oligarchs in Russia, while reducing 'the poor' to unprecedented impoverishment.

Bad economics

'Make the economy scream' was Nixon's command regarding Allende's Chile. Witholding loans till certain 'conditionalities' are met, or a country implements IMF-demanded reforms, is a basic WB tactic we have seen in various situations. In a sense, the debt burden makes an economy scream whenever the screw is turned by threats to cut off further loans.

Stiglitz (2002, pp. 22–33) illustrates the IMF method by describing his own initiation in 1997 on a WB mission to Ethiopia, whose PM Meles Zenawi was trying to rebuild his country's economy after 17 years' civil war. WB loans for Mengistu's forced relocations had to be paid off, with interest. The IMF was threatening Zenawi because of early repayment of a US bank loan without IMF permission. It told him his country could not afford schools and hospitals, and ordered him to privatise Ethiopia's banks (even though 14 of Kenya's banks had crashed when it had done this recently). Foreign banks would buy into the country's core assets, so this prescription made no economic sense at all. At the IMF,

> Decisions were made on the basis of what seemed a curious blend of ideology and *bad economics*, dogma that sometimes seemed to be thinly veiling special interests. When crises hit, the IMF prescribed outmoded, inappropriate, if "standard" solutions, without considering the effects they would have on the people in the countries told to follow these policies. Rarely did I see thoughtful discussions and analyses of the consequences of alternative policies. There was a single prescription. Alternative opinions were not sought. Open, frank discussion was discouraged—there was no room for it. Ideology guided policy prescription and countries were expected to follow the IMF guidelines without debate. (2002, pp. xiii–xiv, emphasis ours)

IMF-WB economics is bad in many senses: because it encourages cash flows of 'hot money' (speculation) to enter and leave a country very fast, which is destabilising; because it operates through a rigid hierarchy, without concern for effects on people; because its SAPs have failed to reduce poverty in one country after another, yet it keeps imposing the same policies; and because the effects of its actions encourage a country to sell off its prime assets for ludicrously little return. Insistence to repay loans for Mengistu's collectivisation with interest exemplifies its refusal to take responsibility for funding crimes against humanity.

At the root of the IMF's bad economics is a rigid adherence to flawed theories, and a betrayal of its original role, which was to avoid another great depression, through collective action at the global level to correct market malfunction, especially through 'expansionary economic policies'. It was created as a public institution, paid for by taxpayers around the world, though it reports only to top finance ministries and central banks. Neoliberalism inverted the IMF programme into its polar opposite: 'Founded on the belief that markets often worked badly, it now champions market supremacy with ideological fervour.... It is clear that the IMF has failed in its mission.'

Far from the stabilising influence it was meant to exert, IMF-WB prescriptions have often made crises worse, especially for the poor, and especially through premature liberalisation, forcing 'developing countries' and ex-communist countries alike to open their economies far too fast (2002, pp. 12–15).

'Our dream is a world without poverty' is the WB's motto, inscribed in its huge entrance hall. On the opposite side of the street, the IMF entrance hall is even grander, 'graced with abundant flora', but contains no such motto. The IMF's purpose is to create global stability—an aim subverted by the shock doctrine.

What is so strange, and sinister, about this bad economics is that the trail of devastating failures (to promote stability or reduce poverty) is evident to everyone who looks, and the double standards are blatant. It seems that neoliberal doctrine operates at two levels: on the one hand a set of beliefs and prescriptions that are adhered to rigidly, but which most people know are not true; on the other, a set of actual aims—of accumulating profit and power through moneylending, and of undermining countries' economic independence, forcing them to surrender their assets to investment from foreign-based companies and banks. Judged by these aims of control and exploitation, perhaps the IMF-WB has not failed—'From the perspective of the creditors, the policies worked, and remarkably quickly' (ibid., p. 210).

Our history of aluminium economics showed that the economic independence of several countries was undermined from the start by highly exploitative terms of trade for bauxite and hydropower. The aluminium cartel, enforcing outrageous subsidies and a ludicrously cheap price for bauxite, is based on propagating bad economics, contravening US law and undermining the principles of free trade.

Double standards are especially evident in pressure to remove trade barriers. All the richer nations became strong by protecting their markets, promoting their exports while trying to prevent imports at all but the most favourable terms.

> Western countries have pushed poor countries to eliminate trade barriers, but kept up their own barriers, preventing developing countries from exporting their agricultural products and so depriving them of desperately needed export income.[64]

In India's case, economic independence was undermined in stages, as the debt burden mounted, and the new economic and mineral policies from the 1990s opened up the country's resources to foreign penetration.

Stiglitz calls shock therapy economics 'the Bolshevik approach to market reform'. The economics behind WB and IMF policies is thus bad in two senses: because it does not work as it pretends to, and because it promotes the interests of the most unscrupulous and acquisitive people in society at others' expense. The institutions are run by economists who appear completely closed to any real input from social anthropology or ecology—input badly needed to correct glaring faults in theory and policy. The number of anthropologists and ecologists employed by the WB grew in each case from just one in the 1960s–70s to around 150 in the 1990s, but this expansion has been geared to ensuring a 'Christmas tree decoration' of politically correct language—i.e. *greenwash*. The power and policy decisions are all with the runaway economists.[65]

So are those running the WB and IMF just bad economists, or are they basically financial terrorists? It does not take a degree in economics to see that the free trade they promote is anything but free. When O'Neill and Alcoa set up an aluminium cartel at the heart of the US administration, this was more than just a distortion in the market. It was a violation of the basic principles of non-interference advocated by free trade economists.

The Great Transformation (Karl Polanyi 1944), shows how the concept of freedom is subverted by economists to mean its opposite, and 'thus degenerates into a mere advocacy of free trade'. The flip side of the freedom we all seek is a bad kind of freedom: the freedom to exploit others and hoard wealth, or 'freedom to profit from public calamities secretly engineered for private advantage'—the freedom of cowboys to commit genocide and exterminate the natives—the freedom of the strong to oppress the weak: might as right. 'The good freedoms are lost, the bad ones take over.' [66]

A social structure of revolving doors

The ideology driving the IMF-WB seems full of contradictions to a non-initiate, but it is vital that key people in recipient countries adhere.

> The Bank is eager to internalise its thinking in the governments it lends to. And it does this through an amazing revolving door activity, not just in India, but in Africa and Latin America as well.[67]

To understand the WB social structure, and its connection with aluminium interests, anthropology would distinguish its formal, official structures (the etic level of how a group defines itself) from its informal, non-official structures (the emic level of how it really works). The formal structure expresses itself through a vast literature of WB-commissioned reports, stereotyped and bureaucratic in style. The informal level shows in its actions, in statements 'off the record', and in a prosopography of key actors' careers, such as WB Presidents' effortless shifts between top levels of banking, business and politics. Clausen had been head of Bank of America, and Lewis Preston at J. P. Morgan had earned the title 'the most influential behind-the scenes banker in America'.[68] None had any experience or training in understanding other cultures or environmental science, or even development issues, before taking office. And on leaving, they took up even more lucrative bank or company directorships. Revolving doors between business and politics characterise public life, and glaring conflicts of interest seem to be increasingly tolerated.[69]

The WB is located in Washington at 1818 H Street, opposite the IMF, and the Treasury Department. Its President is always a

US citizen, usually personally selected by the US President, while the IMF's Managing Director is traditionally a European. Under the President are several Vice-Presidents and key economists. Formal power rests with a Board of Governors, which consists of the Finance Minister or equivalent of each country. Of these Governors, 24 are chosen to form a Board of Executive Directors (EDs), in a system where countries which pay the largest contributions have the largest percentage of the vote. Since the US contribution is largest, at 17 per cent, the US director is at the top, with 17 per cent of the vote.[70]

The structure under this Board of Governors consists of a labyrinthine system of Networks, Families and Units. A majority of WB staffers are economists, hugely outnumbering social scientists and environmentalists. Economists hold sway in the influential Poverty Reduction and Economic Management (PREM) Network, while social anthropologists' main input is in the 'Social Development Family' within the Environmentally and Socially Sustainable (ESSD) Network. They are absent from the policy-formulating Research Department (DECRG), but present in several subordinate Vice Presidential Units (VPUs), Regional Departments and the Operations Evaluation Department (OED).[71]

The WB consists of several separate institutions: the IBRD (International Bank for Reconstruction and Development) is the original bank (1946); joined in 1956 by the EDI (Economic Development Institute), funded by the Ford and Rockefeller Foundations, as the training college for WB staffers and Finance Ministers-to-be; and the IFC (International Finance Corporation), set up to lend to private companies, forming joint ventures with them in projects—a 'separate and distinct' entity from the IBRD, though run by the same staff. This is also true for the IDA (International Development Association), added in 1960, to give 'soft' low-interest loans to the poorest countries.[72]

The IFC moves faster than the IBRD, streamlining procedure, with rudimentary or non-existent EIAs for its projects. It maintains an even stricter 'commercial confidentiality', and plays an advisory role on environmental and social impact issues to another private sector arm of the WB: MIGA (Multilateral Investment Guarantee Agency), which was added in 1988, and has established an appalling human rights record, ever since it took on the Freeport copper and gold mine in West Papua as its first client, which ranks among the world's worst mines for its environmental devastation and repression of indigenous protestors by Indonesian soldiers.[73]

Most influential of the hundreds of reports the WB commissions each year are the annual World Development Reports (WDRs), which have the status of 'voice of the experts', and represent authority. The 2008 WDR focuses on Agriculture, and 'gives the green light to the shifting of poor agricultural workers to "more efficient" sectors'—i.e. it spells out the policy of removing them from the land and turning them into an industrial labour force.[74]

IMF economists make key decisions formulating WB policy and its theoretical base. The WTO was formed out of the GATT process, and along with the General Agreement on Trade and Services (GATS) is at the heart of the liberalisation process of forcing countries to open up to foreign companies.[75] The WB is in daily touch with the US Treasury Department across the street (its largest shareholder), and WB decisions usually reflect US political or corporate interests, as we have seen in the WB's support for aluminium companies in various countries (Chapter Nine).

In terms of how the WB system actually works, Vice-Presidents, and senior, long-term employees often exert more real power than the WB President.[76] The system is extremely hierarchical, with power apparently controlled by a handful of long-termers at the top, who form decisions behind closed doors, in consultation with the IMF and Treasury Department. Even the Board of Executive Directors exercise little real power, since they cannot propose loans—only approve or reject them—and in practice they always approve them.

The Project Cycle starts with Identification, then Preparation, and then Appraisal, which is when staff 'go on Mission' to the target countries, employing highly-paid consultants to study different aspects of a project. This stage is followed by Negotiations, when Agreements are drawn up with borrowers, and the Board of EDs gives its Approval, after which, agreements are signed. In other words, the Board's role is that of a rubber stamp, subservient to decisions made higher up.[77]

After an agreement is signed, the Implementation stage begins, when the Bank is supposed to play a Supervision role, monitoring a project. This has a low status, and is usually inadequate, which is why corruption in the allocation of WB funds is so widespread, and terms in the loan agreement specifying environmental and social provisions are routinely violated. After the final loan is disbursed, a Project Completion Report is submitted to the Board. These reports 'seldom provide a full and accurate portrait' of a project. For example the final report for the WB-funded Chixoi dam in Guatemala did not even mention the huge-scale killing of indigenous protestors in 1980–82, when at least 360 people died—probably the largest number of people directly killed for any dam.[78]

The WB is sometimes disarmingly honest about the shortcomings of projects it has funded—but only after the last loan has been disbursed. It established an Operations Evaluation Department (OED) only in 1970, which aims to audit just 40 per cent of WB-funded projects. Out of nearly 4,000 projects audited in 1974–93 more than two-thirds were rated unsatisfactory! These reports

> can be brutally frank about the shortcomings of Bank operations and often contain information from which future operations would benefit. Nonetheless, they are largely ignored by the staff and the board. It seems, indeed, that few board members or staffers even read the reports.... The OED has concluded that the Bank "focuses on what is intended, not on what is actually being delivered." This means that the Bank is unlikely to learn from its past mistakes.'[79]

The WB's primary business is making money by lending to poor countries, and enforcing repayment takes priority. The fact that many projects are not really good investments for the countries concerned, or highly destructive for their environment and citizens, is considered no responsibility of the Bank. The projects also give huge contracts to construction companies, consultancy firms, etc.

Lying at the centre of the whole web of foreign aid and investment in 'developing countries', and leading the road on lending, the WB is a nexus of vested interests. Its boundaries are opaque, like those of the corporations it promotes. The system of revolving doors between government and corporations is institutionalised, because its Governors are simultaneously the Finance Ministers (or equivalent) of the world's governments, and because WB policies are closely coordinated with those of the US Treasury Department to such an extent that it tends to function in effect as an instrument of US interests. At the level of contact with government officials in developing countries, corruption is a major problem. Often,

> foreign direct investment comes only at the price of undermining the democratic process. This is particularly true for investments in mining, oil and natural resources, where foreigners have a real incentive to obtain the concessions at low prices.[80]

WB staff in Washington live in a self-contained world of great luxury, so rarely complain. Michael Irwin was an exception, publishing his resignation in *The Wall Street Journal* in 1990, where he drew attention to the WB's 'bloated and overpaid bureaucracy, wasteful practices, poor management, and unjustified arrogance', as well as some of its worldwide impacts.[81] The scandal that erupted in 2007 after Wolfowitz promoted his girlfriend, and was finally forced to resign despite full support from President Bush, shows the kind of nepotism or corruption normal in the WB.[82]

But WB staff 'are the best and the brightest', 'supremely self-confident'—even though there seems little basis for self-confidence, in as much as they are collectively responsible, whether they understand this or not, for causing death and misery on a colossal scale around the world. 'It's all a game, really. You give money to a government and you don't know where it goes', as one official admitted to Caufield.[83]

Contaminated governance

'Transparency' is an aspect of Good Governance advocated by the WB and DFID. Yet both are closed and secretive in the extreme. Despite drawing attention to 'lack of transparency' in Third World governments, it is they who set the example. Many WB reports are not even circulated internally to those who need to know. Even more so in the IMF, whose 'culture of secrecy' ensures that all key decisions are made far from public view. These institutions set a terrible example of 'disdain for local knowledge' and 'self-imposed ignorance' about the countries and peoples over whom they exercise such power.[84]

Moneylender colonialism involves a ruthless hierarchy of power, and an undermining of countries' economic sovereignty. Stiglitz highlights a rare glimpse of this hierarchy that got into the press, in the form of an un-posed photo of Michael Camdessus, Managing Director of the IMF, standing over a humiliated Indonesian President as the latter bends to the IMF will.[85] The IMF-WB system is one of 'taxation without representation'—'global governance without global government'.[86]

'They are seeing themselves more and more as a World Government. ... The Fund and the Bank have begun to see themselves as the new maharajas,' a key Indian negotiator commented, about the IMF deal in 1991 and the kinds of pressure exerted, by the WB directly, by the IMF more distantly, onto government officials.

The WB's EDI (Economic Development Institute) plays a significant part in the social structure, by 'converting' key people in key governments into orthodox adherents of the neoliberal doctrine: 'initiates', primed to apply WB policy around the world—'the EDI mafia'. Many EDI alumni become Finance Ministers, perfectly positioned to implement the Washington Consensus in their respective countries. Manmohan Singh was trained in the EDI, and automatically became India's representative on the WB Board of Governors. This is an area where boundaries are blurred and doors revolve. Do Finance Ministers act as citizens of the countries they serve, or as officials of the WB responsible to those higher up the WB-IMF hierarchy? This question also applies to India's other negotiators: Montek Singh Ahluwalia was India's Finance Secretary as well as a WB official, becoming director of the Independent Evaluation Office at the IMF from 2001, and Deputy Chairman of India's Planning Commission from 2004. His subordinate Shankar Acharya was on leave of absence from the WB at the same time as he was Chief Economic adviser to the GoI.[87]

The concept of 'Governance' casts a web of confusion over the issue of government. Now we can see why. As Harvey puts this:

a shift from government (state power on its own) to governance (a broader configuration of key elements of state and key elements in civil society) has ... been marked under neoliberalism (2005, p. 77).

The confusion is deliberate. The intention, at least by the key theorists spreading the new concept, is to cover over the dismantling of governments worldwide, by undermining traditional notions of government, at the same time as dismantling its traditional functions—reducing it to an empty shell, whose main purpose is to facilitate corporations.

The most dangerous fundamentalism

The World is Flat encapsulates the belief system driving industrialisation and the WB. 'Flat-earthism' is a fitting title for the neoliberal doctrine the WB has propagated around the world. A central concept is that freeing the market levels the playing field—a fundamental lie, as we have seen. The free market is nowhere free, and even if it was, the resulting free-for-all is fundamentally opposed to real human freedom. Black is not white, and the emperor is stark naked—his new clothes don't exist, though sometimes only a child can point this out.[88]

But it is certainly true that the earth is being flattened in many places. Kashipur, Lanjigarh, Sukinda and Kalinganagar all have hills, villages, mango groves, fields and rock formations bulldozed to make vast spaces of flat earth to build factories on. As soon as people are forced out of their villages and fields, these are erased, as we witnessed at Lanjigarh early in 2004—making sure the people cannot come back and occupy their homes or cultivate their land, ever again. Bulldozers remove the topsoil. The land's fertility is gone, generations of well-tended fields and channelled streams turned into sterile earth, good only for 'development'.

Despite its glaring inconsistencies and hypocrisy, the body of 'orthodox' neoliberal theory is often referred to as a 'doctrine'. The analogy with religion and theology is not just superficial. Analysing the key values that generate WB thinking and action is complicated by a mass of verbiage, where words are often used to mask or invert meaning. We are not dealing here with religion in a popular sense.

The theology of the Inquisition, Free Masonry, or the emperor cult in imperial Rome offer closer models. This is a body of doctrine with various levels of interpretation: the popular level gives the Free Trade ideology, subverting the concept of Freedom to offer prosperity to anyone willing to sell their soul and join the bandwagon. But understanding how to apply the doctrine and over-ride its many contradictions, is a matter for economist initiates only: this is not something meant to be easily understood.

Missionary imagery is deeply embedded in WB language. Even Keynes said 'We need to go out from here as missionaries', during the Bretton Woods meetings. As Walt Rostow put this, early WB mission staff saw theselves as

> development crusaders ... exposing previously apathetic peoples to the possibility of change. ... We were in the line that reached back ... to the missionaries in Western societies who went out to distant and often obscure places, not merely to promulgate the faith but also to teach and to heal.[89]

One aspect conjures up Christian ideas about suffering as good for the soul. IMF economists ignore the pain their policies promote. Even starvation moves them not at all, since

> market efficiency requires free markets, and eventually, efficiency leads to growth, and growth benefits all. Suffering and pain become part of the process of redemption, evidence that a country was on the right track.[90]

This goes some way to explaining the extraordinary callousness of the economists towards the suffering they cause. This is not a healthy detachment. It shows a missionary, fundamentalist arrogance, as if only they knew the truth; and the same psychopathic inability to understand another's viewpoint, values and feelings that Joel Bakan analysed in *The Corporation* (2004). It also shows a rationality gone haywire, not rooted in open, verifiable assumptions.

What we are dealing with here is nothing less than the belief system of ultra-capitalism, whether it is called neoliberalism, structural adjustmentism, Friedmanism, or flat-earthism. Monetarism was an appropriate description, but went out of fashion, perhaps because it made it too obvious that money is the main value. Adam Smith's 'hidden hand of the market' was treated with ultimate reverence by the Chicago theorists. 'Market forces' become the closest thing in human affairs to God: 'Money is not God, but by God, it's no less than God.'

Many of the people promoting flat-earthism at the WB and other institutions are nice, normal people. But as Hannah Arendt showed in *The Banality of Evil*, people who do great harm, usually, are just doing what's normal in the power structures they form part of, and don't like to question.[91] A system itself is evil in as much as it encourages people to do harm without taking responsibility for their actions.

The WB's Policy on Indigenous Peoples was formulated far too late and remains far from implemented, especially in its aim that resettlement should be avoided, and if it happens, that people's standard of living must not fall. As Thayer Scudder and many others have made clear, displaced tribal people hardly ever regain their standard of living. Free Prior Informed Consent should be a basic right allowing them to veto projects on their land. Their lifestyle is based on long-term sustainability, and needs to be seen as something of greater long-term value than the projects they resist, which destroy the land's ecology.[92] The polar opposite of flat-earthism is Konds' religion of mountains.

CHAPTER EIGHTEEN

NGOs and the Culture of Appropriation

Non-Governmental Organisations: Critiques from Left and Right

The WB sits at the apex of the aid industry. Its pattern of power and value system serve as models for organisations working at the village level too, not least in the assumption that 'development' needs foreign funds—an assumption that goes very deep on the side of givers as well as takers. Well-known donor NGOs in Western (or Northern) countries get a large proportion of their funds from private donations on the basis of their charitable status. As charities, they represent competing causes, some for the environment, and others for specific groups of people or in the Third World: disaster relief, children, human rights, alleviating poverty ...

In other words, NGOs are basically funded through charity—indeed their status as charitable trusts makes them exempt from tax. The history of NGOs funding Third World projects goes back to the Missionary Societies of the nineteenth century, retaining certain basic features, such as a focus on health and education, and an overall aim of promoting 'good works' abroad. As with missionaries, this makes NGOs a sensitive and complex subject to analyse. Some of them tread a delicate balance in the structure of power to do vital work under great pressure. At the same time, most are top-down and often extremely arrogant. Indian NGOs' foreign funding supports a lifestyle that few government officials can afford, let alone grassroots activists. So tensions exist between NGOs and government institutions on the one hand, and between NGOs and activists on the other. In writing this book there is no area the two of us (and other friends) have argued about more passionately!

NGOs play a significant role for and against the aluminium industry in India, with some supporting people's movements, but more supporting aluminium companies, by implementing their R&R or CSR components. Often people are confused about which side NGOs are really on, especially since they are 'non-political' by definition, and tend to maintain an image of neutrality. Even when NGOs are keen to support a genuine movement, this is one issue on a list of 'projects', and support sometimes proves counterproductive. Funds and publicity are often seen as distorting or diluting a movement, and NGOs' motives are often suspect, especially when there are signs that an NGO is trying to direct or take control of a movement.

Many people in NGOs are keen to correct mistakes and listen to constructive criticism, and what we write here is in this spirit. NGOs need to operate in a way that is a lot more open and egalitarian, as well as accountable to the people they wish to serve, learning and taking initiatives from them rather than imposing their own agenda, let alone agenda set by companies or foreign governments. Even an NGO's employees often do not know or are uncomfortable about how it is funded, and the identity of its trustees and real decision-makers.

There is too little awareness of how NGOs multiply to fill the vacuum left by government as it gets privatised and shrinks. Even as NGOs criticise the exploiters and the WB, their place in the overall social structure tends to be defined and controlled by corporations and governments. Often NGOs unconsciously serve a WB agenda.[1]

This means that people working in them need to exercise the utmost vigilance if they are to avoid aiding the overall *disempowerment* of the very people they claim to be trying to empower.

NGOs and other types of CSO (Civil Society Organisations) are mushrooming in India, and thousands operate in Odisha alone. Some do vital social work. Many are notoriously corrupt. As a result, they come in for criticism from both sides. This is illustrated by the case of the four NGOs deregistered in Kashipur after three Norwegians from Norsk Hydro had been kidnapped for a day near Kucheipadar (Chapter Five). Government officials who flew to Kashipur (17 November 1998) blamed these NGOs for inciting people against Utkal.

They were blamed for the Maikanch incident too, and deregistered again, after an editorial in *Sambad* (20 December 2000) called for this to be done by Orissa's Finance Minister, Ramakrishna Patnaik—the man many saw as instrumental in sending the police to Maikanch. The editorial said that from 5,817 in 1994, NGOs in Orissa had increased to 8,000 in 2000, feeding off disaster relief for the 1999 cyclone, stirring up opposition to industrialisation, trading in poverty, tarnishing Orissa's image abroad, and living a lavish lifestyle at odds with their stated aims.

These four NGOs certainly played an important role in alerting the outside world to what was going on in Kashipur. Achyut and Vidhya Das from Agragamee wrote a series of important articles from 1995.[2] Yet as we saw, in reality, these NGOs were not involved in the kidnapping or Maikanch, and tribal activists were very critical of them. Why were they under fire from both sides at the same time?

Samarendra wrote a letter on this theme, asking why NGOs were being targeted by the government and their role exaggerated in the press, when they were not really in the movement at all, to Suresh Tripathi, an SJP activist who had lived in Kashipur. Suresh's response (4 July 2001) is worth quoting:

> After the Emergency [1977] a number of foreign aid agencies succeeded in attracting many youth leaders from the *Chattra Yuba Sangharsha Vahini* [Student Youth Resistance Force], founded by Jai Prakash Narain. By 1982 CYSV had fragmented on the NGO issue.

... These groups always spoke progressively and projected themselves as radical....We need to understand NGOs and their donors. The most damaging thing about them is that they try to discourage people from engaging in politics.... Should we not engage in politics?... This question has become even more relevant now that most of our political parties have become servants of the rich and the corporations. (translated from Odia)

When CYSV was splintering, the Samata Sangathan was formed in 1980 as a non-electoral political organisation. At its second general conference in Varanasi (1982), Kishen Pattnayak wrote a pamphlet asking a series of questions: what are the basic issues concerning foreign funding? Is funding from Indian capitalists equally dangerous? How can activists support themselves with minimal funding? Should there be a complete boycott on foreign funding? Who are the foreign donors, and where do they get money from? Many, it seems, get money from foreign government funding agencies, as a tool of diplomacy. As Kishenji pointed out:

Before dispensing funds, the donors ask for a project proposal. Only after vetting this and asking for amendments, they give money, and afterwards they demand a report. In this way, the organisation and its workers become intimately linked with the donors.... With foreign funding you are always bound and under the donors' surveillance.[3]

This issue was raised back in 1956, when Gopabandhu Chaudhuri witnessed how the Bhoodan (land gift) movement was getting subverted by money. As Gopinath Mohanty described this:

Gopa Babu was thinking: if constructive work is done by obtaining funds from outside of local resources, will people be inclined to become self-reliant? Rather they will learn to be dependent on others. Further, money may become the sole consideration. Greed may overwhelm the workers and may generate indiscipline and violence. The moral foundations may crumble ... when funds flow, can the workers remain steadfast in their views and maintain their sincerity? The primary objective is to create a healthy society on the foundation of the consciousness that collective responsibility generates. Non-violence will be the hallmark of such a society and exploitation will be absent there. If funds come from outside, will this objective anymore attract the people?

Since then, 'allurement of funds' and greed 'have become more and more obvious in dominating the NGO psyche'.[4] Just like WB loans, NGOs' foreign funds often perpetuate corruption and dependency.

From the early 1980s, as foreign funding became more widespread, left-wing critics started to question this tendency, seeing collusion between NGOs and capitalist donor agencies. Prakash Karat (later the General Secretary of the CPI-M) wrote one of the early critiques (1984), singling out the Gandhi Peace Foundation (Delhi) as a foreign-funded organisation that played a key role in de-radicalising socialists in the 1960s. A similar Marxist critique came from P. G. James in Kerala (1995), who showed how NGOs such as USAID and CARE helped implement Structural Adjustment (SAPs) from the early 1980s.

This process has been clear throughout Latin America, starting with Chile under Pinochet, and Bolivia after 1985.

> The NGOs supported "soup kitchens" which allowed victimised families to survive the first wave of shock treatments administered by the neoliberal dictatorships. This period created a favourable image of NGOs even among the left.
>
> Even then, however, the limits of the NGOs were evident. While they attacked the human rights violations of local dictatorships, they rarely denounced the US and European patrons who financed and advised them. Nor was there a serious effort to link the neoliberal economic policies and human rights violations to the new turn in the imperialist system. Obviously the external sources of funding limited the sphere of criticism and human rights action.
>
> As opposition to neoliberalism grew in the 1980s, the US and European governments and the WB increased their funding of NGOs.[5]

In the Phillipines, Indonesia and Thailand, NGOs have mushroomed under neoliberal policies, replacing representative democracy with 'virtual representation' based on a charity model, that lacks accountability (Clarke 2003, Ungpakorn 2004).

The WB and dominant governments organised lavish funding for NGOs to mitigate the effects of Bolivia's shock treatment, though little of this reached the poor. Most was siphoned off to pay administrative costs and professional salaries.[6] Promoting NGOs helped to depoliticise opposition to the neoliberal programme and short-circuit people's movements, by co-opting and subverting the language of the left—'*neoliberalism from below*'. NGOs were primed to take the place of government welfare schemes, in health and education, just as the government withdrew from its responsibilities in these areas. The WB encouraged NGOs to criticise the state from the left, just as its own economists were masterminding the corporate takeover of power from the right.

As a SAP hits the poor, NGOs promote Self-Help Groups (SHGs) and 'empowerment training', that co-opts emerging leaders into a market-linked ideology, and short-circuits any critique against the overall system of exploitation, promoting private enterprise at the expense of public action:

> the NGO ideology of "private voluntaristic activity" undermines the sense of the "public": the idea that the government has an obligation to look after its citizens.... Against this notion of public responsibility, the NGOs foster the idea of private responsibility for social problems and the importance of private resources to solve these problems.[7]

So NGOs play a significant role in the power structure of 'development', alongside the mining companies, banks and WB-DFID nexus, and UN agencies. Some accept funds from aluminium companies, others take a stand confronting the corporations and pro-corporate government policies. Overall, NGOs exert a significant influence on public opinion and government policy.

In reality, non-governmental organisations are not non-governmental. They receive funds from overseas governments or work as private subcontractors for local governments. Frequently they openly collaborate with governmental agencies at home or overseas. More importantly, their programmes are not accountable to the local people but to overseas donors. In that sense NGOs undermine democracy by taking social programmes out of the hands of local people and their elected officials to create dependence on non-elected, overseas officials and their locally anointed officials.[8]

So there is a paradox in the name. If we look at NGOs as part of an overall social structure, we see many ways that they interweave with governments. Since the Business Partners for Development (BPD) project was formed in the mid-1990s, this interweaving involves a triumvirate of power: companies (including banks), governments (alongside the WB and UN agencies) and NGOs, as representatives of civil society. Yet they are not elected as such. So what is an NGO?

The Society Registration Act of 1860 (India) and Charity Commission (UK) defined a charity as a non-political organisation, to be incorporated like a company, with a limited gaurantee. So at a formal level, an NGO has a similar structure to a company, with a board of directors and trustees, secretary, accountant, annual general meeting, and usually a considerable hierarchy of status, salary and decision-making. The 1860 Act constrains NGOs' ability to talk politics. Historically they developed out of Missionary Societies, and though many work on Adivasis' behalf, few if any in Odisha are presently directed or controlled by Adivasis.

NGOs in India are constrained to mute their criticism of government policy by having to register through the Foreign Contribution Regulation Act, that allows them to receive foreign funds. Many Odisha NGOs work on health and education issues. Some promote SHGs with micro-finance, some work on land rights and environmental issues, while others work in conservation. A front-page article in the Bhubaneswar edition of *Times of India* on 28 June 2005 carried a warning:

> Flushed with the success of having inked the Posco deal—at $12 billion, India's largest FDI ever—which brought in its wake a slew of proposals for more such mineral-based clones in the state, the Naveen Patnaik government has upped the ante against organisations that have consistently placed hurdles on the road to industrialisation.
>
> The government, in a tough and far-reaching move, is drafting the blueprint of a mechanism to blacklist select non-government organisations (NGOs) that are perceived to be "anti-industry." A confidential note from the state home department has recommended debarring at least four NGOs that are involved in welfare work in tribal pockets.

Intelligence officials see NGOs as leading 'the obdurate opposition to the government's ongoing industrialisation process.'

> Mandarins now want to send a strong message to all organisations that may turn out to be an impediment in the relentless surge towards industrialisation in Naveen Patnaik's "look-ahead" dispensation.

Similarly in south Chhattisgarh, where a few NGOs have played a vital role supporting a traumatised population who lack the most basic amenities. Yet when they help people in Maoist areas, or speak out against atrocities done by both sides, NGOs are criticised as colluding with the Maoists. This is why Dr Binayak Sen was jailed, and why Himanshu Kumar's Vanvasi Chetna Ashram, near Dantewada, was destroyed by police on 17 May 2009.[9]

On the other hand, the Maikanch and Kalinganagar police killings were symptoms. The disease lies in the policies and overall construction of power that NGOs do little to question. The tendency is for NGOs to tackle the symptoms of poverty piecemeal, at a superficial level, assisting governments to shrink their responsibilities towards those marginalised by structural adjustment.[10] This is why the big NGOs in the West lobby for human rights and environment issues, but tend to avoid free and frank discussions of policy. They see themselves as spokesmen for Third World communities, and often bring the leaders of these communities to the West, but their political engagement with these communities is limited, and campaigns tend to remain on a circumscribed, non-political level, with a lack of proportional or holistic thinking. For example, Friends of the Earth criticises aluminium companies to a certain point, but not beyond. Like them, it highlights recycling, rather than emphasising the basic need to reduce *extraction* and *consumption*. In the European Aluminium Association (EAA), we were told they had a joint project with FoE (Italy) on the theme of recycling plus use of aluminium in cars, while FoE (Finland) brought a Gond woman to speak about the Niyamgiri issue at the European Social Forum at Malmo in Sweden (September 2008), who had no connection or first-hand knowledge about the movement.

As this example illustrates, environmental NGOs tend to coordinate little with social activists, creating conflict counterproductive to both sides. National Parks have become a deeply divisive issue, since they displace more tribal villages, provoking resentment against Project Tiger and conservationists, and turning forest people against the forest and wildlife they have always lived in basic harmony with.

In many ways, NGOs resemble companies, each with its own hierarchy and promotional logo. It is hard for donor NGOs to know exactly what the NGOs they fund are really doing, and foreign funding, as Gopabandhu and Kishenji warned, tends to feed local corruption and hierarchy, which is why Adivasis often distrust them. As a friend who works for Odisha NGOs confided, knowing how to cream off a certain percentage is part of the job. Yet hundreds of villages face extreme government neglect, making them increasingly dependent on NGO support.

Stronger critiques have been made on NGOs in Africa and Latin America than India, by James Petras and others, highlighting their role in the neoliberal order—the human face of modern imperialism.[11] Among the NGOs strongest in its critique of corporations (including Vedanta) and DFID's role in promoting them, is War On Want.[12]

'Centres of foreign government'

In a remote village just below Niyam Dongar, Dongria men once described local NGOs to us as 'centres of foreign government'. Gradually, we perceived an astute accuracy in this formulation, which applies at several levels.

At one level, as Kishenji warned in 1982, foreign governments make use of the NGOs they fund to apply certain policies, or even to undermine the authority of government representatives. With a privatisation of social services, former powers or duties of government are increasingly delegated to NGOs, just as Christian Missions were used in colonial times to 'civilise the natives' through schools and hospitals. NGOs are at the centre of the privatisation drive, taking away the government's social service role, by getting 'foreign aid to eliminate poverty'. Many see NGO-funded schools and health centres as the thin end of the wedge of the privatising process. This also applies to Pani Panchayats and Community Forest Management Committees, promoted by DFID. Nearly always, these end up being controlled by richer farmers, who use them to increase their hold over scarce resources.

NGOs are perceived as colluding with foreign governments, who supply around 40 per cent of the funds of many big NGOs. This makes these NGOs uncritical of, for example, the UK government on key issues such as privatisation of health, education and water, or industrial growth. NGOs also tend to promote foreign culture and values, through hierarchies whose top part is outside India. Accountability is to donor NGOs more than to local people. Donated funds create local elites who are pretty much 'indoctrinated' (through intensive training programmes) with mainstream ideas and techniques of 'development'. There is a ladder in NGOs as in companies and governments, and as one rises up, involvement in government processes often increases along with salary. NGO directors contribute in various ways to formulating government policies that reflect a donor-dominated approach from Northern/Western countries.

We saw in Chapter Five how Action Aid supported an Agragamee programme for Indravati oustees, whose plight should have been the government's responsibility. This led to what Agragamee members described as a bitter experience. Agragamee's director sat on a committee together with local administrators overseeing a process that ended up in desperate impoverishment.

NGOs generally claim to be 'non-political' (like the WB!), and their charitable status demands a non-political stance, yet on the one hand the whole space they operate in is defined by politics and policy decisions, and on the other, foreign NGOs' ways of operating have the effect of *shrinking the political space* in which activists operate, by carrying on a dialogue with foreign governments and politicians which usually excludes ordinary people; writing reports which too rarely get back to affected communities; and by funding health and educational tasks that used to be seen as the responsibility of the government.

Even though NGOs' non-political stance shrinks the political space, NGOs frequently operate using political connections, though usually not openly. An example that shocked many activists is the way that Ekta Parishad (not technically an NGO but similar in its hierarchical structures and foreign funding) forged an alliance with the Congress Party in 1992 at Damoh in MP, distributing pamphlets to a crowd of 10,000, urging them to support the CM Digvijay Singh, and vote Congress in the forthcoming election (against grassroots candidates).

Ekta Parishad uses all the right slogans, such as *Jal, Jungle, Jami* (Water, Forest, Land), but tends to 'take over' people's movements, sweeping them into centralised, stereotyped campaigns. In October 2007 it organised a mass rally and march into Delhi that drew at least 20,000 village people from 11 States, 70 per cent Adivasi. Its leaflets said:

> Ekta Parishad is not a trade union, a political party or an NGO; It is a mass organisation based on Gandhian principles.

This is questionable. It receives huge funds from foreign NGOs, and indirectly, from foreign government sources, though also,

> In every Ekta Parishad village people are planning to collect at least 3,000 rupees to support their representatives coming to walk in Janadesh.

A prime aim is 'to make positive changes in people's lives through building awareness and mass action, whilst also working to influence policies, legislation and programmes of the government.' What worries activists is the hierarchical organisation, with a cult of its 'Gandhian' leader, Rajgopal, and standardised, green-white colour scheme and logo, like a mega-NGO. EP brought thousands of Adivasis to the Mumbai World Social Forum in 2004, where their events were stage-managed spectacles rather than 'bottom-up', spontaneous events. The organisation enjoys wide credibility in the West, but has a history of subverting or depoliticising movements, steering them towards a centralised agenda where their specific goals get diluted. On land issues, the leaflet articulates 3 main demands:

> Establish a "National Land Authority" to provide a clear statement of land utilisation in India, identify the lands available for redistribution and regularise holdings of poor and marginal peasantry.
> Establish "Fast Track Courts" to settle past and present conflicts and disputes related to land.
> Establish a "Single Windows System" so that land issues can be resolved easily and freely without wasting time, money and energy.

These aims are fine, except that they do not mention the key issue (affecting many on the march) of displacement by industry, and do not follow Adivasi activists' prime message of 'No More Displacement'. Talk of 'fast-tracking' and a 'single window system' bears an uncanny resemblance to the language of the new Mineral

Policy, whose aim is fast-tracking clearance for mining leases. In other words, consciously or not, it looks as if the whole exercise was coordinated with corporate interests. And what kind of awareness is the organisation building if it is not talking openly about mining companies, displacement and neoliberal policies?

NGOs centred in London or Delhi habitually draw on contact with MPs, briefing them on situations, calling on them to make a statement. Which is often exactly what is needed—except that it does not happen democratically and openly, through a political process involving grassroots activists. Influence on a Prime Minister is much sought after—even though PMs are often less involved in tough policy decisions than people generally believe. In the early 1990s, Survival International commissioned famous artists to paint pictures on the theme of 'paradise', inviting Mrs Thatcher as chief guest. Felix was present when she made a speech arguing passionately for the preservation of tribal cultures—surreal to listen to, when one knew this was in direct contradiction to the monetarist policies she was pursuing around the world. As she walked around, admiring the paintings and being briefed about critical situations (including the Narmada dams), it was apparent she was impervious, and would not act.

Mining companies were starting to engage closely with NGOs in the 1990s, employing them mainly to improve their image and internalise politically correct language, or to manage CSR components. About 3,000 NGOs have consultative status at the UN, and a number have written strong critiques of extractive industries. Others participated in Tony Blair's Extractive Industries Transparency Initiative.[13]

Two faces

As mining companies open a dialogue with NGOs, there is a tendency for both sides to shift their ground. Companies learn how to take criticism, though they often use this to perfect their greenwash more than really changing their actions, while NGOs get tempted by serious money in return for legitimising the greenwash.

The role of NGOs is full of ambiguity. One face is set towards a welfare role of serving the poor, the other towards pleasing donors. Odisha's NGOs often write all the politically correct words, advertising their work to solicit funds, even though this contrasts starkly with patronising, top-down behaviour to the people they are meant to be serving. The discourse oriented to funders appears servile. Language tends to function as a series of magic formulae to attract funds.

NGOs' place in the overall social structure is often a comfortable niche in the middle of a great hierarchy, and their behaviour perpetuates this hierarchy, from foreign donors they depend on to villagers who depend on them. Many tribal activists feel extremely distrustful of NGOs for these reasons, seeing them as compromised. To summarise:

- NGOs cultivate a humble image in some contexts, but come across as arrogant in others.
- They use clichés of ignorance, backwardness and illiteracy to describe tribals, and in their educational and medical projects they rarely even recognise that a tribal system of knowledge exists, let alone make it a basic part of their plan to learn from them.
- Their workers are not usually allowed to mix too closely with villagers, and to drink or dance with them.
- They are seen as two-faced, saying all the right things to foreign donors, while talking down to Adivasis and making decisions on their behalf instead of following tribal decisions and ways of deciding and doing things. This is why they are often seen as not supporting tribal leaders and movements, so much as trying to control or even divide them.

Talk Left, Walk Right, the title of Patrick Bond's study of betrayal in South Africa's transition from Apartheid (2004), sums this up. NGOs tend to act as unwitting collaborators, 'servile to the West but arrogant to their people,' as Birendra Nayak puts it, with authoritarian personality traits.[14] Nayak quotes Chomsky on the cultural imperialism which NGOs frequently exemplify. Yet Chomsky himself has been curiously unwilling to criticise NGOs, agreeing with an activist from Odisha that NGOs frequently play a significant role in depoliticising and mentally incapacitating people who need to organise proper resistance, but arguing that many NGOs are combating the neoliberal processes.[15] Petras agrees that a small minority of NGOs offer genuine solidarity to genuine movements. The key for him, as for most grassroots activists in India, is that these refuse funds from corporate or government sources.[16] Most NGOs 'create a political world where the appearance of solidarity and social action cloaks a conservative conformity with the international and national structure of power.' What is also confusing is that many people who start and head NGOs were formerly grassroots or Trade Union leaders,

> attracted by the hope—or the illusion—that [NGOs] might give them access to levers of power which would allow them to do some good. But in any case, the offer is tempting: higher pay (occasionally in hard currency), prestige and recognition by overseas donors, overseas conferences and networks, office staff, and relative security from repression. In contrast, the socio-political movements offer few material benefits but greater respect and independence and, more importantly, the freedom to challenge the political and economic system.[17]

The 'NO ENTRY WITHOUT PARMITION' sign at Kucheipadar singled out NGOs as well as administrators, politicians and police. Many activists blamed NGOs for colluding with the companies and government in dividing them.[18]

Part of the NGO arrogance comes down to a matter of style: their approach is often bureaucratic, their style of dress is respectably modern—well-ironed white shirts preferred, loincloths and bare feet rare, in contrast to villagers' normal dress code. They tend to travel to villages by motorbike or car, rather than walking or cycling, and their high education is visible in everything they do. Too few show any real interest in learning from tribal people about their own system of knowledge, or make an effort to adopt tribal culture in matters of etiquette or lifestyle. The material culture they make use of is distinctively modern, and their bureaucracy privileges writing against oral tradition. NGO buildings are mostly four-square, brick and concrete, *pukka* structures, in preference to indigenous *kuchha* (earth and wood) ones, even though the latter are cooler in summer and cheaper to build. All these symbols are signs of conformity, asserting high status in the overall hierarchy.

Because you are schooled
You think yourself as wise
And think of others as zero[19]

Birendra Nayak quotes an article by Bunker Roy called 'Scum in the Voluntary Sector', where Roy pours scorn on NGOs at a WB meeting for ingratiating themselves,

> with minds like babus, selfish to the core and so careful to say the right thing.... They live entirely off foreign money with no independent source and that is why it is so important to be hypocrites and grovel in front of the WB president.... They are accountable to no-one.... The WB successfully divided the groups while the president was here. Those inside had to send their bio-data to be allowed in—no self-respecting voluntary worker would have agreed to this humiliation. But do we have any self-respect left? Many of those inside, when it suited them, have been outspoken champions against big dams and the policies of the WB. What on earth were they doing sitting inside when they should have been showing solidarity with one voice against the WB? Its hidden agendas, bread and butter issues, maintaining life styles, wanting foreign money, wanting to be on the right side of everyone and be invited as consultant.

This passage is revealing, as Nayak says, because Bunker Roy himself 'unleashed NGO culture' in India during the 1980s, when he was a consultant to the Planning Commission, promoting a policy of privatising education.[20] Bunker Roy is also interesting from the aluminium perspective, because he was the first person in India to accept Alcan's Sustainability Award, in 2006, which other activists perceived as selling out—receiving funds and bogus credentials from a company promoting non-sustainability around the world.[21]

Dancing with donors: How funding determines 'knowledge'

Funding is a crucial issue in the NGO debate, and attempts by activists to determine the trustworthiness of a particular NGO often focus on who has funded it, and how open it is about this.

One aspect of the funding issue is that fighting over funds keeps many NGOs in a relationship of competition with each other, when their overall work would be more constructive if they cooperated more freely. Another is that the richer NGOs, especially those financed by mining companies, often make conspicuous donations to villages, which undermine their self-reliance and promote dependency and a poverty mentality. Vedanta's strategy in Lanjigarh is to make larger and larger donations, to show their 'good works' to the outside world, and win over villagers.

Another problem is, as Kishenji warned, and many critics have pointed out, that NGOs tend to say what donors want to hear, otherwise they are seen as 'blockers' who 'cause problems', and do not get contracts again, just like WB consultants.[22] And what donors want to hear—or do *not* want to hear—is often a decisive factor in the direction and style of NGO discourse, constraining it within acceptable, predictable limits, which is why NGO critiques (of the WB, government policies, corporations ...) so often fall short of the fundamental statements that are needed.

Of course, NGOs are extremely varied. While a few small ones refuse all corporate and government funds and maintain a genuine independence, most compromise at some level, and a large number accept and even seek corporate finance. Some of the biggest, most powerful NGOs are almost completely corporate-controlled. This applies to NGOs that are actually set up by companies (Bingos—Business NGOs), such as TERI in Delhi, which began as Tata Energy & Resources Institute, and became The Energy and Resources Institute. In organisations like this, it is obvious how funding determines knowledge. For example, TERI publishes books promoting bio-fuels and carbon-trading, and its head is the same R. K. Pachauri who heads the IPCC, which, as we saw in Chapter Twelve, has promoted these two concepts as policies, when it is increasingly obvious that they do nothing to prevent global heating, and compound the problem.[23]

A similar example is the well-known one of oil companies promoting climate change denial.[24] In these examples, funding determines knowledge to the utmost extent. We have seen similar criticism of the Ford Foundation funding human rights work that keeps a narrow focus by not linking abuses with neoliberal policies (Chapter Seventeen). The Ford Foundation also funds a great deal of mining-related research in India, including the Centre for Science and Environment, whose 2008 report is excellent for its overview, yet all but silent on the question of the neoliberal mining policy changes that have promoted this, uncritically following certain aspects of the MMSD/ICMM perspective. In fact the whole MMSD iniative itself was instigated by two exceptionally powerful NGOs, the International Institute for Environment and Development in London, and the World Business Council for Sustainable Development, lobbying the World Economic Forum at Davos.[25]

The WWF began life as the World Wildlife Fund, funded like the Nobel prize out of arms deals (Chapter Ten). Large donations were made to this organisation by Alcoa, one of whose directors, Kathryn Fuller, became a director of WWF, which apparently prevented the organisation from joining the campaign against Iceland's dams and smelters.[26]

Save the Children has a long-term tie-up with Norsk Hydro, whose employees donate funds to this charity on a regular basis.[27]

We have seen that certain NGOs play a far from independent role in the convoluted story of mining companies' applications for Environmental Clearance. For example, the Wildlife Institute of India in Dehra Dun wrote an excellent report on Niyamgiri warning of an environmental disaster, until it was leaned on by the MoEF and Orissa government, when it had to write an addendum, while the other Institute that submitted a report to the Supreme Court (2006), the Central Mine Planning & Design Institute, is a subsidiary of Coal India Ltd, so hardly an independent body. Similarly, Tata AIG (American International Group), who wrote Sterlite's EIA, is not a neutral organisation, and (from their report, mentioned in Chapter Six) clearly lacks competence in the area of environmental protection.

There are thus various levels at which funding determines knowledge. The aluminium industry funds a lot of scientific research, and many different aspects of 'scientific knowledge' about aluminium seem to be more or less determined by this, due to a lack of independent funding for research on topics such as bauxite's place in an ecosystem (since aluminium companies are only interested in extracting it). The scientific research that casts doubt on well-attested links between aluminium consumption and Alzheimers Disease for example, is largely aluminium company-funded.[28]

In the Vedanta case at the Supreme Court, a crucial role was played by 'green accounting' studies of the Net Present Value of forests (Gundimenda et al. 2005, 2006) by the NGO Green Indian States Trust (GIST), funded by Deutsche Bank and Centurian Bank of Punjab. Compensatory afforestation schemes were facilitated by a Report from an Expert Committee of the Institute of Economic Growth under its director Kanchan Chopra, commissioned by the Supreme Court in 2005.[29] Deutsche Bank is an investor in Vedanta Resources, and no doubt many other mining projects in India that are certain to clear a lot of forests and fields. The studies it has funded make it easy for compensatory packages to be worked out, that sound generous, but grossly underestimate the real environmental and social costs, in relation to profits being generated for the banks.

Alcoa, following the path set by Alcan's sustainability award, has offered research fellowhips on sustainability issues, advertised in Odisha (where, as we have seen, it is known to have had secret talks with the government about bauxite mining).[30]

BHP Billiton has been more forward still, sponsoring medical work in Odisha, as well as a hydro-scheme with Gram Vikas in Karlapat. Oxfam-Australia's joint effort with BHP, organising a series of workshops with NGOs in Orissa in 2002–4 on the theme of a Corporate Community Leadership Program seriously embarrassed and angered several of the NGOs involved when information about BHP's alumina plans in the state emerged during the last workshop.[31]

Dancing with Donors is how Marcus Colchester, from the Forest Peoples' Network, sums up the tendency of NGOs to collude with their corporate funders.[32]

The Sigrid Rausing Trust is an example of a different kind of donor agency, using the Tetra Pak fortune created by Sigrid's grandfather Ruben and father Hans, to fund some of the best, most independent-thinking NGOs, that are searching solutions to the world's most intractable environmental, financial and human rights problems (£60 million of donations by 2006). The Tetra Pak business was moved from Sweden to Switzerland, with Trusts registered in the Cayman Islands (notorious as a tax haven). Sigrid is an anthropologist, focusing on the former USSR and human rights.[33]

A frequent criticism which activists make of NGOs is that they tend to appropriate and hoard information, not returning to communities reports based on information these gave freely, and marketing this information. Time and again, communities say they gave information to NGO people, who collected this as 'data' from the 'field', and never returned its final form to their informants. Or when the publications and photos do go back, their language and mode of presentation often appear bureaucratic and alien, reflecting the dehumanising framework of mining companies, WB, or government modes of thinking rather than that of the people who shared their lives for a while.[34]

This brings up the key question, since trans-cultural communication is at issue here, of what constitutes knowledge? Corporations lay great emphasis on accurate data, and we have seen the high price for which CRU and Roskill sell commercial data about bauxite and alumina (Chapter Eleven). Yet the basic fact of Niyamgiri's supreme environmental and cultural value, which caused over 3 years' 'delay' of Vedanta's mining project, did not figure in J. P. Morgan's multi-million dollar report, on whose basis Vedanta was listed in London.

Older traditions about knowledge, such as the *vedanta* tradition, see it as something that cannot be commodified, and has to be exchanged freely. Attempts to restrict and commodify knowledge poison it, along with the atmosphere between people, amounting to a perversion of the truth.

Donor NGOs receive funds from bigger donors, including secretive trusts and government agencies, and the parameters of the knowledge they give are often set by these richer agencies. With environmental and other science, evidence suggests that scientists who show the flaws in a corporate-funded consensus are often cruelly discriminated against and marginalised.[35]

The knowledge about situations which NGOs give out in their publications is often over-simplified—an artificial construct, stereotyping people's situations and putting them into a formula, rather than reflecting the actual knowledge of people in communities. How much do NGOs really follow a lead from communities and serve their needs? How much do NGOs 'turn movements into projects' through a bureaucracy and hierarchy in the corporate mould?

Tri-sector power: Business Partners for Development

A prime reason that the Kashipur NGOs were mistrusted by activists was that Agragamee had taken part in the IFAD project (1988–93), which paved the way for Utkal's Bingo, URDS (Utkal Rural Development Society), a front for the company. Agragamee left because IFAD's local implementer, the Orissa Tribal Development Project (OTDP), was uncompromisingly top-down and did not listen to feedback from villagers or the NGO. But Agragamee also took Action Aid funding from 1993 for a project overseeing resettlement for the Indravati reservoir. Both these partnerships compromised it in the eyes of many activists (Chapter Five).

URDS was the 'civil society' component of the Utkal project, which was taken by the WB for a while as a flagship of its BPD scheme. Business Partners for Development was 'a project-based initiative created by the WB in 1998 and funded in part by the DFID.' It 'aimed to study, support and promote strategic examples of tri-sector partnering.' The BPD website defined these as 'the private sector, civil society and government working together to put communities at the centre of development, and deliver real and sustainable benefits for all'. At a time when the population is rising fast, FDI is nearly 5 times the amount of official ODA, and 'partnerships with the private sector are therefore coming to be seen by many as an important strategy for poverty reduction.'[36]

The trouble was that URDS was in no way representative of civil society. Most of its directors were from Utkal. Its social work was seen as bogus, providing PR for the company. Agragamee was closer to civil society, but still distrusted by a large segment. The PSSP was a genuine 'bottom-up' Civil Society Organisation, but it was implacably opposed to Utkal. It is interesting that when URDS was set up in 1997, it used CSR to mean 'Community Social Responsibility', and also 'Combined Social Responsibility', translated from *Milito Samajik Dayitvo*. Similarly, from 'Business Partners for Development', BPD has more recently become 'Building Partners for Development'.

The original BPD initiative during the 1990s was divided into four Clusters:

- Natural Resources, focusing on extractive industries: mining, oil and gas projects
- Water and sanitation private participation (i.e., water privatisation schemes)
- Global Partnership for Youth Development: education, health and economic opportunities
- Global Road Safety Partnership

Of these, the extractive industries cluster was clearly the most important. A dozen projects were chosen worldwide. Every single one was beset by major problems.[37] As we have seen, Utkal was silently withdrawn from the BPD list and website after the Maikanch killings (December 2000), shortly after a series of WB meetings in Odisha.

But the model of public-private partnerships (PPP) has endured. It received a major boost at the Johannesberg summit (2002), when Tony Blair was criticised for travelling and coordinating closely with the heads of large companies such as Shell and Rio Tinto, before announcing his Extractive Industries Transparency Initiative. Government and Industry were now extremely cosy, 'revolving doors' were revolving, and NGOs were being brought into these partnerships in large numbers. The tendency was always there—NGOs played a role back in the 1980s implementing SAPs, as we have seen. But the new age of corporate power invites NGOs or CSOs to be more active partners. In countless cases, company promises of benefits to communities routinely invert the truth, and NGOs who accept these partnerships are seen as sold-out collaborators by a large section of civil society. NGO staff are no more elected by local people and accountable to them than company officials, and whatever welfare they bring is not on a basis of public decisions, but 'given' in the idiom of charity, and imposed regardless of public opinion.

Some NGOs work hand-in-glove with mining companies to implement their R&R or CSR components, while others maintain an independent stance. The MoEF report on Odisha's bauxite mountains, presented at the Supreme Court on 5 October 2007, and the Honourable Judges' questions and comments, made clear that large-scale compensatory spending has official sanction as the way forward for implementing these highly contentious projects.

This spending involves public-private partnerships, in which NGOs/CSOs implement projects for Tribal Development, Compensatory Afforestation and Wildlife Management. Vedanta has been in negotiation with a company called Access Development Services, with a view to forming a partnership for the Lanjigarh-Niyamgiri area—an offshoot of CARE specialising in microcredit.[38]

Introducing *NGO Futures Beyond Aid,* a special feature in the *Third World Quarterly,* Alan Fowler argues that Non-Governmental Development Organisations (NGDOs) need to consciously locate themselves in a *Fourth Position,* linked to Civil Society, Markets, and the State, but independent, and based in ethics and human rights. As an ideal this is fine, but the articles here hardly get to grips with the situations on the ground, of huge temptations and pressures on NGOs to toe a corporate line, coming from companies rather than the abstraction of 'markets'.[39]

SHGs (Self Help Groups) represent an important aspect of public-private partnerships, where NGOs or companies connect communities with markets through microcredit, with a 90 per cent repayment rate. Jeffrey Sachs mentions Grameen Bank and BRAC (Bangladesh Rural Advancement Committee) for the benefits they bring to Bangladeshi women (2005, p.13). Vedanta's 2007 Sustainable Development Report mentions 550 SHGs in partnerships with NGOs across Vedanta-Sterlite operations, highlighting VAL's Lanjigarh SHG called *Budhima Mahila Samiti,* whose president Sulochana has increased her earnings from 600 to 1,000 rupees per month, making 'Niyamgiri phenyl' (eucalyptus scented toilet cleaner), and winning an award presented by the Chief Minister for best SHG in June 2006.[40]

But the subject of SHGs is not so simple. In India, as in Bangladesh, the *empowerment* these groups bestow tends to wear off after the initial loan money has been spent, and the 90 per cent repayment rate actually represents a draconian enforcement of repayment comparable to the WB's own record. When repayment pressures start, SHG interest rates average 3 times normal bank rates (around 18 per cent). Anu Mohammed, an activist from Bangladesh, writes that various studies in this country show that only about 5 per cent of SHG women improve their position, compared to 45 per cent whose position deteriorates, and about 50 per cent who manage to maintain their position, usually through taking other loans to keep up repayments.[41] Activists in India report a similar situation. From a grassroots perspective, microcredit is the ultimate depoliticiser, since it enmeshes communities into the market through individual debts to the banks.

Which may be why the WB is so interested and has promoted the Bangladesh model so widely—it gained even more kudos when Grameen's founder, Mohammed Yunus, was awarded the Nobel prize in 2007. The WB organised a microcredit summit back in 1997, inviting Grameen Bank along with USAID and UNDP, to promote the model widely. Citibank was the sponsor, joined for the second summit a few years later by Monsanto. WB recommendations were to

> Integrate NGOs with commercial finance markets by: a) developing an appropriate regulatory framework for the financial operations of the NGO sector; (b) encouraging large NGOs to establish themselves as banks; (c) encouraging "wholesaling" of credit to established NGOs; and (d) using smaller NGOs as brokers to mobilise self-help savings groups.[42]

The Dongria Konds, deep in their Niyamgiri villages, are being targeted for microcredit as we write, by the DKDA (Dongria Kond Development Agency). SHGs landed over 6,000 people in serious debt in Kandhamal district, after 238 SHGs gave loans for buying vehicles, which were mostly taken over by non-tribals as maintenance costs escalated. Samarendra drew Naveen Patnaik's attention to a study he wrote about this situation when the CM visited Phulbani in April 2001.[43]

The product of a typical company-NGO partnership is a study commissioned by Tata on the DPs and PAPs (Displaced Persons and Project Affected Persons) at its Kalinganagar steel plant site. This was put together by people from three organisations: the Harsha Trust, Xavier Institute of Management in Bhubaneswar, and the District Action Group, Jajpur (three, five, and thirteen persons respectively). The study starts by thanking 'the DPs and PAPs who bore the brunt of some irate and hostile communities and came forward and shared their views with us.' In other words, most of the Kalinganagar people would have nothing to do with this study—hardly surprising, since it was undertaken just four months after thirteen people of these villages had been killed by police in the 2 January 2006 firing incident.

> As an unfortunate coincidence, the victims were found to be evenly distributed in each of the villages [so that] in many occasions it was impossible to break the barrier and gain entry into some hamlets. ... It was repeatedly emphasised to them that this survey has been initiated only to strengthen the cause of the affected people. Sometimes it worked, paving way for future deliberations.[44]

This study is characterised by a dehumanising discourse about villagers who were standing up to Tata and the full power of the state, maintaining a major road blockade. The kind of 'knowledge' in the study is geared towards facilitating Tata's aims.

> The very fact that the displaced persons have spelt-out their options and preferences for their relocation, resettlement and rehabilitation indicates that they are willing to accept the project. It also indicates that they are mentally preparing themselves to get displaced to give way for the project.[45]

This shows how displacement is made to seem 'voluntary' and 'inevitable' when it is not. The writers admit their data covers only 50-60 per cent of the villagers, and one village out of 21 could not be covered at all, while 7 others could not be visited. This creates some confusion, as the survey presents population figures for twenty villages, so whether these are estimates of the total or represent about half the total is not made clear. Above all, people's words are never quoted.

The study is at least clear about the administration's lack of proper communication with the villagers, and some data are highly significant. The Kalinganagar special package does not include rehabilitation for PAPs. Around 80 per cent of both categories do not possess a BPL card (i.e., do not get benefits due to people classed as 'Below the Poverty Line'). 72 per cent of DPs are classed as living on encroached government lands, and 48.12 per cent 'admitted that they are cultivating on encroached lands.' Only 59 DP families had *patta*. However the last land survey was done in 1927. Its records are 'obsolete and improper', showing how mistaken it is to class those without *patta* as encroachers. A major source of resentment is the huge difference in prices paid as compensation to certain families whose lands were acquired in 1992–93 (at Rs 37,000 per acre), and prices paid by Tata to Idco, which were nearly ten times as much (Rs 335,000 per acre).[46] The study says it is important to make displaced people 'feel and realise that they are partners of the project and not outsiders', but there is no insight in this report that might help Tata to understand the values or skills of the people resisting them so strongly.[47]

The missionary mode

Historically, NGOs developed out of the Missionary Societies sent to India and other countries, and like missionaries during colonial times, NGOs both work alongside governments, and at times take on a key role in criticising them.[48] Their value system still owes a lot to missionary models, and many have a strong Christian identity. Others, in reaction, promote an almost fascist Hindu identity, funded by the RSS or other Hindutva organisations.[49] Political parties often have their own NGOs, as companies do too (e.g. URDS).

Leaving aside the contentious subject of religious conversion, the colonial power structure defined the missionary sphere of activities as a role centred around education, medicine and welfare work or 'social uplift for the poor'. This role has been increasingly taken over by NGOs, and is still with us, implicit in WB schemes of using NGOs to take over the role of caring for poor people, and as agents of change, tying them into markets though means like SHGs.

The aim of 'converting people' is implicit in the NGO role, as an inheritance from the missionary role. We saw that neoliberal economics has many features of a religious doctrine, while WB officials have often consciously embraced a missionary role. But basically, the religion being spread by a multitude of 'development' organisations is capitalism. If traditional tribal values of respect for nature are being fast eroded, this is because of a relentless promotion of capitalist values, ever since Russell set up markets for 'introducing new wants.' (Chapter Three).

NGOs play a significant part in eroding the power of the state, as critics from the left as well as right have pointed out, and maybe this is why they rarely mention 'capitalism'. This means that even when their criticism of government oppression is most justified, their position in the overall power structure makes them useful to the right-wing elements promoting a corporate takeover of power.

If NGOs inherit a missionary role in caring for the poor through health and education, their formal structure resembles that of corporations, and through 'tri-sector partnerships' they are often placed in positions of power over village people or 'Displaced Persons'—undemocratic power, in that those exercising it are not elected or accountable in the way that government officials are as public servants. In the Kalinganagar report we saw a sample of an extremely widespread NGO discourse, constructing a false and alien 'knowledge' about tribal people geared towards controlling and dispossessing them.

NGO discourse is very varied. Big NGOs sell their work as a 'brand' just like corporations do, each with its individual style of logo, photography, vocabulary and personalities. Some play a role of complete subservience to corporate interests (such as the Kalinganagar report), while others are free-spirited and independent in their critique of human rights abuses or environmental destruction.

Most NGOs define their sphere of activity in a way that diverts attention from the wider power structure—especially (as we saw in Chapter Seventeen) from the neoliberal agenda. It is partly this market competition that pits human rights NGOs against conservationist NGOs—a division that has had a deeply destructive, 'divide and rule' effect in India, where both sides are fighting the same power structure of an assault by mining companies and the timber mafia on India's last surviving forests.

Questioning the culture of appropriation

There is also a terrifying uniformity in NGO discourse. Partly this stems from the way they have to sell and promote their work in competition with each other, which involves a 'dumbing down' and superficialisation of knowledge about situations. To take an example from an NGO that promotes the cause of tribal people, and has played a vital role highlighting the assault on the Dongria, Survival International writes about each tribal situation through a certain formula, that reduces each tribe's situation to more or less the same story, removing the complexity. This tendency is clear in the literature of most large NGOs—Action Aid, Concern, Christian Aid, Oxfam, Greenpeace, Friends of the Earth, Amnesty International, FIAN… Each does invaluable work, but their literature is so repetitive that it sometimes becomes unreadable, telling the same basic story, ironing out complex local details, with too little questioning of the overall power structure and neoliberal ideology.

Action Aid has also been one of the most pro-active in the campaign to save Niyamgiri's tribal people from corporate clutches.[50] Yet like Agragamee, it often comes in for severe criticism from activists who see it as top-down and divisive. It is a complex organisation, that has shifted its headquarters from London to South Africa, with an elaborate bureaucracy between its various centres, distinguishing Action Aid UK, Action Aid International, Action Aid Asia, Action Aid India, etc. It funded Agragamee over the disastrous Indravati resettlement plan (1992–2002). An observer at Vedanta's AGMs since 2006, it has revealed how DFID pays foreign aid money to corrupt consultancy firms (Action Aid 2006), but refrains from a wider critique, and receives some funds from DFID itself. In some campaigners' eyes, it is suspiciously close to DFID policies, and some sections of it appear to take a radical stance, potentially undermined by other sections, following agenda set further up the hierarchy.

Action Aid Asia received a donation of Rs 41 lakh from Sterlite Foundation in 2003, with which it supported *Ashraya Adhikar Abhijan* in Delhi, a shelter for homeless children that was doing good work, was seen as becoming co-opted, i.e., more hierarchical and less democratic, at this time. In 2004, Action Aid India signed a MoU with ICICI (a major investor in Vedanta) and other banks.[51]

Amnesty International campaigns on human right abuses in every country, through it keeps a narrow focus (as we saw in its groundbreaking reports on Chile and Argentina), and falls short of opposing greenfield mines. Its report *Dont mine us out of existence* (February 2010) lays bare the violations at Lanjigarh and Niyamgiri.

Oxfam was a pioneer back in the 1940s–50s, starting out by delivering vitally needed relief during the Greek civil war. Now it is one of biggest NGOs, with a huge bureaucracy, in frequent dialogue with government people, in the UK and India. Its US branch has produced an important critique of mining (Ross 2001), but its Australia branch did joint workshops with BHP Billiton in Odisha and Andhra, seen by several NGOs as paving this company's entry to these states (Loza and Price 2004). FIAN is a German NGO based in Heidelberg that focuses on people's rights to food and work in India, supporting people's movements in principle without getting closely involved. This is also true for Norad and Norwatch (Chapter Four).

Greenpeace supported the Lanjigarh movement for a while through Ekta Parishad, but has otherwise shown little interest in the aluminium issue, and a policy director in London started a meeting with Felix with the words 'We're no angels, but we're not the worst …' Greenpeace commissioned a report which outlined the devastating environmental impacts which Tata's Dhamra port would have, which created a storm of protest from the Odisha government.

Gram Vikas is an Indian NGO that accepted a large grant from BHP Billiton for mini-hydropower development work in the Karlapat area of Kalahandi, and is thus one of the NGOs seen as having 'sold out' to the aluminium companies.

NGOs' role in fighting the corporate takeover is important, especially if they can disseminate in-depth information (rather than the dumbed-down information they so often offer), but they cannot be real catalysts for change, and need to recognise the authenticity of grassroots movements and leaders, and support their initiatives as a priority over the dynamic of their own projects.

NGOs work through funding, without a political mandate. As 'charities' they inherit a top-down model of 'benefiting' people, and exist as a counterpart to the business interests of big corporations—corrective yet frequently ineffective or merely palliative, and often actually following corporate interests.

For example, the DFID, funding Action Aid as well as Ekta Parishad, defines them as 'stakeholders', when they have no mandate from the people. As the New Economic Policy was coming into effect, Action Aid India (AAI) formed a Corporate Partnership unit in 1993, which became 'Partners in Change' (PIC) in 1995, with funding from the Ford Foundation (NB above, pp. 477-79), DFID and Novib. The DFID report on Utkal etc. (Barney et al 2000) was also financed by PIC. Forming PIC laid the ground for AAI MoUs with Sterlite, ICICI and other corporate houses: business partnerships that raise questions about AAI's involvement in the movement to save Niyamgiri. A more blatant example is the US NGO International Watch Society, registered in Delhi to facilitate R&R for villages to be displaced by Posco.[52]

The trouble is, NGOs give hope, and collect funds based on the hope they offer. Often this hope is an illusion. Business partnerships are often seen as essential to save the environment, yet the extent of greenwash by corporate 'self-regulation' or CSR, offers little ground for real hope. People donate to NGOs because they have an active conscience and genuinely wish to help deserving causes.

NGO business partnerships form part of the power structure negating communities' political space to exert effective resistance when corporations and/or governments try to take away people's land or basic rights.

So the NGO role needs examining in relation to people's movements and the role of grassroots activists, who work 'bottom-up', with far less funds. NGOs' custom of sponsoring selected 'leaders' often turns divisive, undermining leaders' power when they are perceived as 'taken over' by NGOs.

The more NGOs are able to transform the missionary role they have inherited and get free of business partnership interests, the more positive is the role they can play. Many NGOS do work that has to be done, and no other institution is doing. But their position in the overall social structure of modern life is compromised, and to be effective catalysts of the real change we all hope for, NGOs will have to swim a lot harder against mainstream currents.

CHAPTER NINETEEN

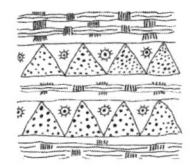

Homo Hierarchicus: Company Man

History of the Company

If views about aluminium companies are polarised, this is also true of companies generally, and mining companies in particular, but aluminium companies are an extreme case because of the scale of their energy consumption and impacts on the environment and human well-being. A company presents one face through the self-image promoted through brochures and PR. A different face shows in behaviour towards people who stand in a company's way, or receive the full impact of its pollution, such as Adivasi and Dalit villagers in Kashipur, Lanjigarh and many other places.

To get at the truth about a company, there are bare statistics of profits and operations, information in the public domain about mergers and acquisitions, and stories about what really goes on behind the scenes and what the critics say: stories about tax evasion and bribes that get into the media or get talked about locally or by whistleblowers of various kinds, and court cases against the companies that shed light on their behaviour. Most of the history of industrial displacement and the campaigns of police intimidation that force tribal people off their land is kept out of the news and the history books. So the real history of how the steel plants and aluminium companies set up shop tends to be airbrushed out of public awareness.

What an anthropologist can offer is an overview of mining companies' customary behaviour, their system of values and beliefs and the pattern of their relationships.

The hierarchical nature of companies is striking, from a Board of Directors at the top, down through many ranks, including an officer class of engineers, accountants, etc., to the factory workers and miners, and beneath these, the people dispossessed from their land and excluded from stable employment.

Dumont analysed Indian society in terms of *Homo Hierarchicus*—'Hierarchical Man'.[1] Yet Indian hierarchy as it exists today is actually a marriage of Western and Indian forms: British colonial hierarchy plus traditional caste hierarchy. 'Caste' is the European concept used to translate *jati*, meaning 'race' or 'species', 'caste' or 'tribe'. It connotes difference, rather than hierarchy. However extreme caste hierarchy is, the idea of it has also been exaggerated through foreign perceptions, and hardened by contact with the hierarchy of administrative and financial power which British rule established in India.

Far from disappearing at Independence, this was preserved, both at the formal level of a power pyramid of ranks, and in a way of abasing oneself towards 'superiors' that blends Indian and colonial forms: '*Saheb*', '*Maharaj*'.... The model of hierarchy was set in the customary way an East India Company officer signed a report to his superior: 'I have the Honor to be, Sir, Your most Obedient Servant.' British rule in India started out as Company rule, and the forms which that Company created were based on domination over the native population, and exploitation.[2]

So *contra* Dumont: if Western society formulated the ideal of equality, this has indigenous parallels in India, especially evident in tribal societies, but at many other levels too. And in the West it always coexisted with a mainstream tendency towards hierarchy. The history of modern 'democracy' may have lessened the hierarchy for a while. Abolishing slavery, the rise of trade unions, and modern democracy based on votes for everyone, all reinforced the egalitarian tendency. But since the collapse of the 'Communist Block', the opposite hierarchical tendency has been much in evidence.

This modern form of hierarchy is found above all in the Company or Corporation—an extreme manifestation of Hierarchical Man. As Chomsky puts this,

> maybe the most totalitarian institution in human history … is a corporation: it's a centrally managed institution in which authority is structured strictly from top to bottom, control is in the hands of owners and investors, if you're inside the organisation you take orders from above and transmit them down, if you're outside it there are only extremely weak popular controls, which indeed are fast eroding.[3]

Now is an age *When companies rule the world*, when we witness a *corporate takeover of Britain*, and of national government in most nation-states, who use nationalism and other polarising '-isms' to hide this.[4]

In India this history is charged by the way colonial rule was imposed by one Company in particular. The Government of India was a creation of the East India Company. So when foreign companies, or Indian companies formed on the foreign model, behave as if they *are* the government, or at least control it, this has a strong and particular resonance in India.

What is a company? Since big companies such as Rio Tinto and Vedanta sit near the centre of modern power, shifting its forms in a way that affects us all, it will be helpful to look at how the concept and institution evolved. Two recent books that approach this very differently are Micklethwaite and Wooldridge 2003, *The Company: a Short History of a Revolutionary Idea*, which gives the company viewpoint, and Joel Bakan 2004, *The Corporation: the Pathological Pursuit of Profit and Power*, which gives a fundamental critique. Anthony Sampson's books on oil companies, arms companies, banks and the *Anatomy of Britain* (1975–2004) give much useful background material. Mathew Josephson's *Robber Barons* (1934/1963) gives essential insights into the formation of modern corporations in late nineteenth century America. Martin Lynch 2002 gives an overall view of the world's biggest mining companies in their own terms.

Adivasis' understanding of the kind of power they face offers another perspective of great accuracy. Opposing '*Company Hawa*' they confront a power that permeates government and police, and spreads an extreme change in values and behaviour, through manipulating peoples' fears and desires. They experience companies' actual behaviour and full impact in the raw, and thus perceive them as a whole, unsoftened by 'PR offensives' carried out in towns and cities far distant from the *commodity frontier*.

To get an accurate overview of the social structure of corporations, it is important to understand their origins. The first companies, in the modern sense of a chartered joint-stock company, were mostly formed for the purpose of exploiting distant lands. The Muscovy Company was technically the world's first, set up in 1555 for British trade with Russia. It became the model for the Hudson Bay Company for Canada (1570), and the East India Company, incorporated in 1600, which fought off competition from rival Dutch, French and Danish East India Companies.

Before this, the company's history goes back to the twelfth and thirteenth centuries, to the Italian *compagnia* and the English *guild*. The north European guilds (from Saxon *gilden*, to pay) had some characteristics of cartels, others of trade unions, regulating the prices and taxes of a particular product, and forming the concept of 'corporate persons'. Among these was one corporation which still exists.

> The Corporation of London, which dates back to the twelfth century, still owns a quarter of the land in the city of London, as well as three private schools, four markets, and Hampstead Heath.[5]

The Italians gave the world the name, *compagnia* (from Latin *cum* plus *pane* meaning 'with bread': those who broke bread and ate together). As this word implies, companies incorporated their own egalitarian model of *partnership*, beginning as family firms and operating on the principle of joint liability: all partners were jointly liable to the value of their worldly goods. Venetian and Florentine partnerships financed foreign trading ventures. The history of these Italian companies

> is closely intertwined with the banchi, named after the banco, or bench, behind which Italian money lenders used to sit.

But moneylending was against Christian principles.

> And in many cities bankers were forbidden, with prostitutes, from receiving communion.

This is why many early moneylenders were Jews, whose religion did not forbid usury. But the *grossi banchi* (big banks) were Christian, financing kings and their wars. When Edward III of England defaulted in 1339 on the loans he had taken from Italian banks to finance his wars, he brought down Florence's two biggest Banks. The Medici Bank grew up in their wake, financing the Pope.

> To get around the papal ban on Christians receiving interest, bankers like the Medici were often paid in foreign currency (with hidden premiums) or with licences or with goods, thus sucking them into other businesses.

The chartered joint-stock company was a formation of the late sixteenth century to cash in on the 'New World' opened up by voyages to India and Indonesia to the East, and America to the West.

Multinationals' ancestor: The East India Company

In September 1599, 80 British merchants met at the Founders Hall in London, and elected fifteen directors, to petition Queen Elizabeth I to set up a Company for trading with the East Indies. On 31 December 1600, the Queen granted this petition to what was now a group of 218 men—'the Governor and Company of Merchants trading to the East Indies'—with a 15-year monopoly, under James Lancaster, who set sail two months later, returning in 1603 with 500 tons of pepper, and a factory in Java.[6]

France's East India Company, founded in 1664, was the first to engage in Indian politics, establishing control over the Nizam of Hyderabad through intrigue, murder and war, with a view to displacing the English from Madras. The English took this model much further against the Nawab of Bengal. The battles of the English and French Companies in India started out through supporting rival factions of local states, and ended up after Plassey (1757), with the English usurping those states' power, and especially their collection of taxes and judicial powers.

The exploitation culminated in the Bengal famine of 1769–70, and its counterpart in the financial scandal known as the 'Bengal bubble'. Major political trials followed, of Clive and his successor, Warren Hastings. An 18-month Parliamentary Inquiry acquitted Clive but damaged his reputation beyond repair. His gruesome suicide (1774) caused Dr Johnson to comment that Clive had

> acquired his fortune by such crimes that the consciousness of them impelled him to cut his own throat.[7]

Warren Hastings was impeached by the Irish philosopher and MP, Edmund Burke, who pin-pointed the basic problem of the Company's imperfect accountability:

> To whom then would I make the East India Company accountable? Why, to Parliament, to be sure.

Hastings too was eventually acquitted (1795). The oppressiveness of East India Company trade had spread far by then. It was three East India Company ships which American colonists boarded in 1774, throwing their cargo of tea from India into the sea, as a protest against excessive taxation, that sparked America's War of Independence—the 'Boston tea party'.

A Parliamentary Inquiry was held into corrupt deals between the Court and East India House after England's Glorious Revolution (1688). One of this Inquiry's leading members, John Pollexfen, made the telling comment that *'Companies have bodies, but they have no souls; if no souls, no consciences.'*

Modern multinationals replicate many features of the power evolved by the East India Company—*The Corporation that Changed the World* (Robins 2006). It is salutary to remember that one of the harshest critics of the East India Company and companies in general was Adam Smith:

> In *The Wealth of Nations* (1776), Adam Smith uses the East India Company as a case study to show how monopoly capitalism undermines both Liberty and Justice, and how the management of shareholder-controlled corporations invariably ends in "negligence, profusion and malversation." Yet nothing of Smith's skepticism of corporations, his criticism of their pursuit of monopoly and of their faulty system of governance, enters the speeches of today's free-market advocates.[8]

Adam Smith 'was obsessed with the East India Company's abuses in Bengal', and warned of the fearsome power which joint stock companies would wield if the restrictions curtailing their power were ever relaxed. How is it that corporate ideology reveres Adam Smith, when no-one was more critical of the unaccountable, despotic form of power which corporations embodied than he?

The East India Company was one of the world's first and biggest companies. It set up the Government of India in stages, through extending its trade prerogatives, through battles won by Clive and his successors against Indian rulers who opposed them, and through manipulations of finance and law that were breathtaking in their audacity and immorality. Hastings' successor, Cornwallis, formalised the East India Company's judicial and revenue system, and the first 'civil servants' were employees of the 'Honorable Company'.

The East India Company's early conquests were all in East India, so although the company's name originally referred to the East Indies, the region exploited by East India Company employees corresponds to the area presently threatened by the aluminium industry, especially the remote, forested mountainous area once known as the 'northern Sircars', ceded by Hyderabad to the French and taken by the British in the 1760s.

Odisha proper was conquered in 1803, and the Konds were forced under British rule through the Ghumsur and Chokra Bissoi wars in 1835–36 and 1845–47, when British officers led sepoys all over central and south Orissa, fighting and burning the villages of those who resisted, and performing public hangings of leaders.[9] By conquering Bengal, the East India Company acquired an extensive tax system, as well as Bihar's fields of opium poppies. Pressing this opium onto China to pay for goods there caused the infamous Opium Wars in the 1840s. The East India Company was the world's biggest, best-organised drugs dealer.

In 1857, when Company *sipahis* rebelled and fought a war to drive the British out of India and establish Independence, British reprisal was savage, but those controlling the system of government recognised that the situation of ruling India through a commercial company was anomalous. The East India Company was dissolved, and India came under direct rule subject to the British Crown and Parliament.

Yet even after 1947, the structure of India's administration retains elements of the original Company, as in the title 'Collector' of a district's top official, after his Company function of collecting tribute.

Most notorious of the early companies was the South Sea Company, founded in London in 1711 with a monopoly of trade with Latin America, including the exclusive right to supply slaves from Africa. In 1720 this company expanded to take over Britain's entire national debt. The shares it sold led to a frenzy of speculation that finally burst after a few weeks. The 'South Sea Bubble' caused financial disaster and gave companies a bad name for years to come, showing the dangers of speculation and company power. It was excitement about East India Company loot from India after Clive's victory at Plassey (1757) which caused the Bengal Bubble.[10]

Suspicions aroused by these bubbles and Parliamentary Inquiries acted as a brake on company power for a while, especially since the Bubble Act of 1720 made Parliamentary approval necessary for setting up a new company.

Legacy of the Robber Barons

When these checks on company power and size were removed during the nineteenth century, the company came into a new kind of ascendancy on a pattern laid out by a number of self-made millionaires in the US. The Robber Barons' pattern of legal, financial and political manipulation, 'robbing the public' to create personal fortunes for feudal-type business dynasties, is still with us today, in India as much as the West.

The Bubble Act was repealed in 1825, and new companies were incorporated for building every new stretch of Britain's railways. Laws from 1844–62, culminating in the Companies Act of that year, 'set the joint stock company free', with the principle of *limited liability*, which meant a removal of personal responsibility for company actions. The Act also allowed companies to own shares in each other.

In the US, companies took off on a grander scale, starting with the Bank of North America (1781). After the American civil war, the Barons developed a larger, more aggressive model that drove the pace of America's industrialisation.

The historic character of the age of the Robber Barons is marked by its drive towards concentration, towards monopoly in large-scale industries and banking, consummated in such centralised trusts as Vanderbilt's in railways, Rockefeller's in oil, Carnegie's in steel, and Morgan's banking consortium. The constructive labors, however, were accompanied by great waste of natural resources, and also by widespread political corruption at areas of contact between big business and representative government.[11]

Railways led America's industrialisation as well as its stock market.

From the end of the Civil War till the 1890s, Wall Street existed almost entirely to finance the railroads ... as in Britain, it was railways that spawned an investor culture.[12]

Making and implementing the law was frequently subordinated to accommodating the big men's wishes, in return for their money (Chapter Seven). The Tariff Act (1864) provided 'a sheltering wall of subsidies'. Then, as now, double standards existed between 'free trade' ideology and huge subsidies in practice.

These men's contemporaries saw the principle of 'deception' or 'superior cunning' as the chief element of their success. The slogan that captured this was 'Hide the profits and say nothing'. J. P. Morgan's system of investment banking aimed

to capture the differential between the price he arranged to pay for capital and the price which he could induce a broad public of savers and investors to pay him for it when he distributed it piecemeal.[13]

This method of profit culminated in the last great railway war in 1901, a 'battle of giants', where Morgan's and Hill's fight with Rockefeller and Harriman for control of a particular line sent the world's stock markets into a dangerous spin on 6 May. Meeting and making up publicly a few days later, to deceive their 'common enemy, the public', the antagonists disclaimed all responsibility and dismissed the stock crisis as 'an Indian dance'. This attitude towards the public is summarised in a dictum of Vanderbilt the younger (Billy), justifying raising rail fares in 1879: 'The public be damned! I'm working for my stockholders.'

Rockefeller set up his Standard Oil Company in 1870, using devious tactics to defeat and take over rival companies. By the 1880s, his company's wealth and power exceeded that of the state governments. When Ohio's Supreme Court declared Standard Oil illegal, the business was reconstituted in New Jersey in 1899.[14] When Rockefeller's and Morgan's empires united in 1901, a new order of power was born. President Theodore Roosevelt (1901–09) made a show of confronting them with anti-Trust cases, and the 'Square Deal' (1902). But the Robber Barons were the biggest contributors to his re-election campaign in 1904.[15]

The tactics honed in the US for setting up vast copper, coal, steel, nickel and aluminium works and the Trusts or Cartels which 'consolidated' them, established enduring models for company behaviour: of ruthless aggression towards rivals, and indifference towards the suffering they caused. There is a profound ambivalence towards Robber Barons, whether in nineteenth-century America or India today. Their scale of success, power and wealth make them symbols of national pride, yet their ruthlessness and corrupt manipulation of politics, law and finance is known and felt.

Nowhere was this ruthlessness more evident than in their genocidal impact on native American peoples, which set the mould for interactions with indigenous people worldwide. Soldiers and cowboys carried out countless unprovoked massacres of Indian communities to support miners and settlers taking over their land—a paradigm which the Maikanch and Kalinganagar killings repeat. Repression of workers is a parallel theme, from the Merthyr riots in Wales (UK) in 1831, when dragoons opened fire on mine workers objecting to starvation conditions, to massacres of striking workers at Carnegie's Homestead steelworks in Chicago in 1892, and at Rockefeller's Ludlow coalfield in Colorado in 1914.[16]

When the iron, steel and coal interests of Carnegie and Rockefeller were bought up by their rival Robber Baron, Morgan, in 1901, this merger amalgamated 112 corporations, and gave birth to a new kind of conglomeration, where banking, metal production, oil, transport, electricity, insurance, paper, timber, food and newspapers were all managed by an integrated team of directors. The steel interests alone united nearly 800 mines and factories into the US

Steel Corporation. In 1902 Carnegie branched out into the latest alloy for arms, forming the International Nickel Company (Inco), to create a monopoly on nickel steel plate, whose effectiveness for armour plating had recently been proved in two crucial naval battles during the Spanish-American War (1898).

Anti-Trust legislation put a check on Alcoa in 1912, but only slightly: its monopoly was never really challenged, and Mellon helped consolidate its international acquisitions (making discrete early use of the telephone) while he was US Treasury Secretary. When President J. D. Roosevelt (Theodore's nephew) inaugurated his New Deal against Morgan's entrenched banking interests, Mellon faced protracted legal investigation. He was acquitted but (like Clive and Warren Hastings 150 years before) remained guilty in popular perception.

Roosevelt came under intense criticism from corporate interests, even while President-elect. After an assassination attempt in Miami on 15 February 1933, Morgan was called to give evidence. Roosevelt's New Deal was attacked as 'class hatred preached from the White House' by Hoover, his Republican rival. Compelling evidence of a plot to remove Roosevelt and install a fascist system on the model of Mussolini and Hitler, exposed by General Butler in November 1934, was ridiculed by newspapers controlled by Morgan.[17] As we saw, peace was made between Mellon and Roosevelt through Mellon's donation of his art collection to a new National Gallery of Washington, where the Hermitage paintings he had bought secretly from Stalin to finance steel and aluminium plants assumed pride of place,[18] and Roosevelt became a leading patron of the aluminium industry and its supply for the arms industry (Chapter Ten).

Post-war, we saw how similar patterns of intense exploitation were imposed in one country after another as the aluminium industry expanded. The oil industry showed a similar consolidation of wealth and power, despite the break-up of Standard Oil.[19] When former colonies started to become independent, companies held on to vital economic assets, forming industrial enclaves that undermined these countries' economic independence from the start.

The Robber Baron pattern of corporate power and exploitation is *why the rich nations get richer and the poor nations get poorer.*[20] The election of Thatcher and Reagan started to remove all constraints on corporations that the New Deal had put in place, leading to an even deeper penetration of countries' natural resources, driven by a *'creditors' cartel*' of the leading banks, controlling prices in favour of the richer countries and their corporations, not to mention speculation in metals trading.[21] This is the background to the present situation where mining companies seem poised to start extracting all East India's remaining mineral deposits from the mountains, starting with two of the best forested: Niyamgiri and Khandadhara.

'Democratic elections' sometimes seem to make little difference to policy, because the power and influence of corporations behind the scenes is overwhelming. Newly-elected governments promise change, but any attempt to limit the power of the oil, arms or aluminium companies meets entrenched financial interests, committed to an expansion that exceeds the carrying capacity of our earth and climate.[22]

Social Structure

Alcoa under Mellon and Davis established the structure we have examined of subsidiary aluminium companies (Demba, Alcan, etc.), plus bauxite mines, dams, power companies and railways, intertwined closely with cement and construction companies, banks, accountancy firms, credit rating agencies, PR firms, arms companies and vested government interests.

The pattern of subsidiary aluminium companies involves *enclave colonialism* on foreign soil—prototypes of the SEZs being promoted in India today. The history of aluminium enclaves, from bauxite-mining enclaves in Guyana, Jamaica, Sierra Leone or Guinea, to refinery or smelter enclaves in Australia, Iceland, Ghana or Brazil shows how these subsidiaries are 'kept poor' to avail of benefits like lower taxes, and because the profits from aluminium are not made at the level of these factories at all, but far away in the world's trading capitals. From Demba, Valco, Jamalco and QAL to VAL and UAIL, aluminium enclaves are designed to suck a region's wealth, protected by long-term, secret, and highly exploitative deals.

This geographical hierarchy between the cities where top aluminium companies are centred and the remote regions exploited, is replicated in the social hierarchy, from company directors, who receive enormous salaries and wield enormous power and influence, to Adivasi bauxite miners in Chhattisgarh. In terms of how power is concentrated at the top, company hierarchy has much in common with army structures of command.

> The corporations developed elaborate hierarchies and tiers of management in quasi-military style.[23]

The model imposed on industrialising areas of India is basically an import from Western countries, growing out of and extending the colonial attitude towards indigenous peoples: 'legislation has never yet enabled an inferior to stand before a superior race.'[24] Decolonised governments have usually allowed mining companies to behave as oppressively as any colonial government. Most of the finance comes from abroad, and we have seen how this exploits the Odisha government's extreme indebtedness—financial crisis repeatedly masked by a succession of further loans, which in effect mortgage the state's resources, and direct policy towards expanding the mines and metal factories.

Many of the Robber Barons formed dynasties, and the point of the feudal analogy is that 'Baron' was a hereditary status. We have seen this dynasty model with the Mellon and Davies families in Alcoa and Alcan; with Kaiser; and in India with the Tatas, Birlas, J & K Singhania and many others. Hereditary wealth and status like this is reminiscent of royal families rather than modern democracy. How has modern society, largely rejecting feudal lines of royal succession, taken the company model of family power so easily for granted?

Competing and consorting

On the surface, companies compete with each other. Yet the pattern of vicious competition between companies is a kind of jousting match that the baronial class engages in for financial gain, but also as a game, like the 'Indian dance' enacted by Morgan and Rockefeller against their 'common enemy, the public'.

The history of mining companies is marked by continuous attempts at cartels, as a counter-force to the competition, with a view to keeping prices for a particular metal advantageous for all the companies, buying ores for as little as possible, and keeping industrial, electrical, transport and labour costs as low as possible. For example, most of Odisha's new roads, rail-lines and ports are not being paid for by the companies that need them, but funded by a foreign 'wall of money'.

Swansea's Associated Copper Smelters established the cartel model for mining companies in the eighteenth and nineteenth centuries, coordinating to keep ore prices as low as possible, imposing a system of ruthless exploitation on Welsh and Cornish miners. When Thatcher closed the coal mines in the 1980s, this was because cheaper coal could be bought from East Europe and South America. This repeated a pattern from 150 years before, when British copper mines closed because cheaper copper was available from Chile, facilitated in an industrialising military dictatorship from the 1830s, where 'trade was considered the engine of growth, and mining was considered the engine of trade'. But the British copper companies were active in Chile throughout the nineteenth century, transporting the ore halfway across the world to Swansea, and it was their interests that led to the formation of the London Metal Exchange in 1876.[25]

Since the Second World War, Alcoa divided the American market with rivals. In India, Indal is taken over by Hindalco, Sterlite acquires Balco. But in fact the companies are not discrete entities: they join their 'rivals' in a vast jigsaw of consortia abroad, and in lobbying governments for subsidies and concessions.

So companies' famed tendency to compete is secondary to their tendency to consort, and while some companies relate to each other more or less as equals (for example aluminium companies with oil and construction companies, car and arms manufacturers), others relate hierarchically, as we observe with local subsidiaries set up to harvest the basic commodities of bauxite or hydropower. The parent companies' profits from complex trading deals in the world's capitals depend on cartel coordination to enforce prices to get the basic product dirt cheap. There is undoubtedly rampant competition between different mining companies and their directors to acquire mining leases for the bauxite on Odisha's and Andhra's mountains. But they act together to dismantle India's 'restrictive legislation', and executives move from one company to another with increasing ease.

PR, CSR and the manufacturing of consent

To make up for their repeated robberies of the public, America's Robber Barons set a precedent of conspicuous 'philanthropy', endowing hospitals, schools, universities, making donations for the poor or a church, gifting an art collection....

This is a model of 'conspicuous charity' for the people—as a recompense for undermining their hard-won rights? This pattern goes further back too, to the medieval age, when feudal Barons expanded their territory through brute force, making up for their oppression by building churches and cathedrals, and 'houses for the poor', as if to wipe away their sins—a baronial pyramid of power, using largesse as a status symbol and a mask.

As the neoliberal system spreads, the government's responsibility for social welfare is replaced by a privatised model of 'charity welfare'—CSR.

Corporate Social Responsibility is essentially a PR exercise. Public Relations manipulates the psychology of desire. The 'father' of PR was Edward Bernays, nephew of Sigmund Freud, who applied his uncle's insights to advertising and political campaigning. This was carried on by Freud's great-grandson Matthew Freud, a PR consultant who helped bring New Labour to power in 1990s Britain. Applied to company propaganda and political campaigns, PR *manufactures consent* through a *social construction of reality*, playing on people's desires for a better life and security, using multi-media to create a reassuring, yet basically illusory and misleading sense of intended outcomes as 'normal' and 'right'.[26]

The power of PR firms was revealed in a BBC documentary about the use Georgian and Russian sides made of London/Brussels-based PR firms in their bitter war in 2008, to 'sell' their version of the other's atrocities.[27]

Vedanta employs two London-based PR firms, Finsbury ('one of the leading financial, regulatory and political agencies in the world'), which counts Shell and Rio Tinto among its clients, and CO3 which serves ICMM, the lobby group for mining companies that formalised the MMSD process, with its dangerous principle of self-regulation.[28] CO3 was started in 2002 by Tim Purcell from Finsbury, and specialises in 'CSR-related matters'. Since April 2008, it has handled Vedanta's communication with the public and shareholders, and helped produce its Sustainable Development reports.

CSR is defined by the European Commission as a concept that is supposed to integrate social and environmental concerns into a company's business operations and relations with stakeholders, on a voluntary basis. What this latter phrase means in effect is that a company is free to set its own goal posts, and report what it likes. As Claire Fauset says, in a study of CSR for the NGO Corporate Watch:

> CSR was, is and always will be about avoiding regulation, covering up the damage corporations cause to society and the environment and maintaining public cooperation with the corporate-dominated system.[29]

The environment consultancy firm SustainAbility defines CSR as 'the triple bottom line' of managing a company's social, environmental and economic impacts. The WBSCD (World Business Council on Sustainable Development) defines it as commitment to contribute to economic development, improving the quality of life of employees, local communities and society at large. But what defines the quality of people's lives? For companies, in Fauset's analysis, CSR investment means:

- *Reputation Management*
- *Risk Management*—'a euphemism for imposing risk on others, without their knowledge or consent'[30]
- *'Stealing the NGOs' Thunder'* by funding corporate front groups
- Keeping up an appearance of *employee satisfaction*
- *Investor Relations* and access to capital
- *Competitiveness and Market Positioning*—'investing in CSR now means that a company can position itself as the market leader in its field'
- *Operational Efficiency*

- *Maintaining the Licence to Operate*

The type of activities companies undertake in an attempt to be seen as socially responsible include:

- *Corporate Philanthropy*, such as donations to charities [Vedanta sponsorship of music-dance events, patronage of famous painters, major religious festivals and lawyer conferences in Odisha]
- *Cause-related Marketing*, for example partnership between a company and a charity
- *Sponsoring Awards*, for example the Reebok Human Rights Award, Nestlé's Social Commitment Prize and Alcan Prize for Sustainability are high profile examples
- *Stakeholder Engagement* is another key strategy, though 'decisions on which groups of people count as stakeholders and the mechanisms through which they are engaged are entirely at the discretion of the company.'
- *Community Investment* involves sponsoring schools, playgrounds, health centres, etc.
- *Eco-Efficiency* is one of the terms the BCSD coined prior to the Rio Summit in 1992 to circumvent regulation and promote the idea of self-regulation—a profitable and misleading concept for those promoting carbon trading and similar scams.
- *Drawing up Corporate Codes of Conduct.* These are explicit statements of a company's 'values' and standards. Codes vary in quality and content and cover some or all of the following issues:
treatment of workers
community impact
environmental impact
human rights commitments
health and safety
transparency

Some codes are monitored by external verifiers, especially the 'big four' accounting firms. This has led to the criticism that monitors will place the aims of the company, and not the environment or society, at the forefront when carrying out their assessment. Junia Yimprasert of the Thai Labour Campaign accuses these monitoring consultancies of 'turn[ing] workers' lives into business opportunities.'[31]

For example, Vedanta's Sustainability Report (Annual Report 2007, p. 49) is 'verified' by a top accountancy company, PriceWaterhouseCoopers (Mumbai branch), which states that

(a) The Vedanta senior management is committed to sustainable development based on our limited review of its HSE [Health, Safety & Environment] performance.

(b) Vedanta has attempted to report its sustainable development performance as per requirements of Global Reporting Initiative (GRI) 2006 Guidelines (G3) which demonstrates its management's focus on transparency, clarity and purpose.

(c) During our review we have not noticed any misrepresentation of HSE information that we reviewed, and the information presented on HSE parameters reviewed by us appears to be a fair and balanced representation.

The large number of construction and road deaths in and around the refinery are barely mentioned in Vedanta's reports to its shareholders (though many have been reported in the press), presumably because the responsibility for these deaths is lost, or 'outsourced', in the complex web of sub-contractors working at Lanjigarh. For example, the trucks carrying bauxite and alumina that have caused most deaths may be servicing Vedanta, but officially, the drivers and owners are responsible for that, as subcontractors, so it's 'nothing to do with the company'.[32]

'Community Investment' is a key Vedanta strategy. The tendency of company officials is to equate building things with 'development'. Vedanta's PR job on Lanjigarh and other sites is laid out at length in its annual Sustainable Development Reports, and in a local publication, *Darpan: The Mirror of VAL, CSR Newsletter of Vedanta Alumina Ltd*,[33] which gives Vedanta's CSR Philosophy:

Our Purpose: Harnessing natural resources in harmony with nature to enhance economic well-being and quality of life.

Our Social Mission: To work with communities in and around our plants to contribute to their sustainable development.

Our Role: Proactive Enabler and Partners in Development.

An article on 'Vedanta Nagar (Rehab Colony): A Model Village', tells the story of 106 familes from five villages, each given a *pukka* house, with a toilet, as well as *pukka* roads, dispensary, school, child care centre, playground, crematorium, market complex with 10 shops [not actually functioning as of April 2008], 2 temples [to Dharni and Thakurani, with big Vedanta logos by their doors], 'community hall with entertainment facilities like TV/VCD player, sound system… retaining walls and sitting platforms, you name it.' The article mentions that eight SHGs involve 92 members in productive activities. Vedanta directors, as we saw at Vedanta Resources' AGM in London in August 2007, when questioned about the 'development' their company has brought to Lanjigarh, read out a list of material benefits like this from the SD report.

The article concludes that 'Vedanta's participatory effort has resulted in improving the living standards of the people'. This is not what most people in the colony say, when they speak candidly, away from the ears of their corporate minders. People we speak with see their life there as wretched, and bitterly regret selling their land to Vedanta, experiencing a poverty far worse than anything they faced before, compounded by terrible ailments brought on by pollution (Chapter Twelve). Basically, what the company discourse conceals is that they have taken away these people's freedom, dignity and whole identity, which was based on a high degree of self-sufficiency and self-reliance as cultivators of their own land.

> Vedanta has also built a 20 bedded hospital [not functioning as of 2008]. The police barrack under construction in Lanjigarh is also done by VAL. The street lights in the area is also a gift of VAL to the local mass … Vedanta has also constructed 10 km long road connecting Dahikhal to Lanjigarh.

This road was the scene of Sukru Majhi's death in March 2005, soon after it was completed. It appropriated land from many villagers, for example at Asurpara, who remain angry. The fact that the refinery has already badly polluted the Bansadhara river, poisoning people and cattle, failing to comply with OSPCB orders, and operating above or outside the law on numerous fronts, is simply denied: words and photos are used to construct a 'reality' opposite of the truth.

Finsbury was acquired in 2001 by a firm called WPP (Wire & Plastic Products), which also acquired Fitch (one of the three biggest credit rating agencies) in 2004. WPP has a close link with Oleg Deripaska: its chairman, Philip Lader, is also a director of Rusal—an ex-US ambassador to the UK, and a former Deputy Chief of Staff of the White House. WPP boasts $6.1 billion profits (2008), $31.7 billion capitalisation, and 131,000 employees.[34] This shows the kind of business and political links that have aided Vedanta, spanning 'top of the top' contacts in the US, UK and Russia.

Fauset describes how CSR and the GRI/ISO system came about as follows. The OECD unfurled the first official Guidelines for MNCs in 1976. This led to the formation of UNCTAD (UN Conference on Trade and Development), out of the ruins of plans for a system of proper regulation of companies, which was ambushed by the new WBCSD (Moody 2007, pp. 156–8). 'De-railing the Rio Earth Summit' established the companies' principle of *self-regulation*, which should properly be called 'token regulation'.

The history of Shell's PR disaster in 1995, when Saro-Wiwa was killed by the Nigerian regime (Chapter Twelve), and Shell spent £20 million trying to turn that around with a PR offensive to 'buy credibility', forms an important chapter in CSR history. It made Shell one of the first companies to write special CSR reports. 77 of the world's top 100 companies were doing this by 2006. In 1995 Shell hired the PR firm Fishburn Hedges, and soon produced its 'business principles outlining its core values of 'honesty, integrity and respect for people ... focused on "the magic keys—openness and dialogue".' The CSR element in Shell's 1998 Report was endorsed by SustainAbility, which had previously been critical. '*Tell Shell*' was at the heart of the PR campaign selling an image of Shell as a company that listened to its stakeholders and encouraged their active involvement.

The International Organisation for Standardisation was set up in London to give accreditation to 'international standards' for industrial sites, starting the ISO 14001 series in 1996. Many of the large aluminium and steel plants we have mentioned have this accreditation (including the Lanjigarh refinery from 2009). ISO relies on the principle of self-regulation—the Global Reporting Initiative

(GRI), Sustainability Reporting Guidelines (1997), and the UN Global Compact (1999), designed by Secretary-General Kofi Annan's office with input from the ICC to ensure a 'business friendly' approach. It had nine principles on human rights, labour rights and environmental sustainability, with a tenth on corruption added soon after. The trouble is—it has no monitoring or enforcement mechanism whatsoever. After the Enron scam was exposed, the US and UK set up a system of nominal regulation. But even the UK's Operating Financial Review (OFR) left the content of reporting—such as what information to include or exclude—entirely to a company's discretion! From the idea of a regulated agreement, the World Summit on Sustainable Development (WSSD) in 2002 crowned the CSR principle with the vague concept of 'international best practice', witnessing the formation of 280 high profile business-government partnerships.

As for the case against Corporate Social Responsibility—what is the definition of 'responsibility' it rests on? It 'should' mean that companies, or the people running them, can be held responsible and liable for their actions. But defining corporations as having 'limited liability' tends to prevent individual directors from being held properly accountable. This leads to the extraordinary linguistic contortion that companies' 'responsibility' refers to 'actions taken by companies which go beyond legal requirements', leaving the concept 'self-defined and not socially defined'. Milton Friedman was franker than most, when he stated that because a company is the property of its shareholders, *CSR can only be insincere*.[35]

A decision favouring the wider social good is only correct if the outcome is also the most profitable. The wider social good can only be incidental to the aim of making a profit. This is an expression of the neoliberal belief that the greater common good is brought about by placing self-interest above the interests of others, or of society.

Alcoa, Shell, Coca-Cola, British American Tobacco and Toyota are a few of the companies that have invested most in CSR, where the contrast to public perceptions and revelations is particularly strong—for example the smelter and dams which Alcoa is constructing in Iceland, marked by enormous environmental destruction and considerable repression of protestors. As Fauset and others summarise the impact of CSR:

- Voluntary codes of conduct don't work
- Socially Responsible Investment (SRI) is not enough
- Corporations gain more from CSR than society does
- CSR is a strategy for avoiding regulation, based on expensive PR campaigns lobbying against regulation

It is of interest to note that the DFID defends CSR and the self-regulation principle, and

> dismissed the idea of an international legally binding framework for MNCs saying that it would *"divert attention away from encouraging corporate social responsibility and towards legal processes."* As this quotation shows, without any evidence for its effectiveness, the government is choosing CSR over making corporate exploitation and abuse illegal.[36]

As Fauset argues, what a truly socially responsible company would need to do is basically:

Address Climate Change
Not sell products known to be intrinsically harmful
Stop deceiving the public through PR campaigns
Internalise costs
Pay taxes in full
Stop all lobbying against public interest
Democratise the workplace
Reduce consumption
Limit growth

This is a reasonable list of what aluminium companies need to do if they are intending real Sustainable Development in Odisha, Andhra or anywhere else.

Manufacturing a green illusion

A golden peacock awarded to VAL for best environmental management was put on hold when 20 protestors took the stage in a meeting on 11 June 2009 in Palampur, Himachal Pradesh. This award was made, as in previous years, by the World Environmental Foundation (WEF), registered in India and Britain (1998/2000), this time with three ex-Chief Justices of India on the jury. WEF is a creation of Madhav Mehra, along with Institute of Directors, India, and the World Council for Corporate Governance (2002), which Lord Swaraj Paul chaired for a while, placing it on record later that 'There were too many things going on between some of the directors.' Mehra's call for 'transparency, accountability, integrity, equity and responsibility' highlights a need for these qualities in his own corporate network, as an article in *The Observer* observed.[37] 'Combating Climate Change through Market Driven Strategies' was the title of a WEF/Mehra conference in Himachal Pradesh in June 2007.

Learning about Vedanta's misdeeds at Lanjigarh, the Tibetan PM-in-exile, who was Chief Guest, left the function—Himachal's CM had already been briefed and turned down the invitation. 'Stop Greenwashing Corporate Crimes' and 'Stop Selling Climate Change' read the banners brought in by protestors, whom the *Tribune* (12 June 2009) labelled 'hardcore environmentalists'. What's the difference between hardcore and softcore environmentalism one wonders? If the truth is hardcore, what is softcore?

Tetra Pak is a company that cultivates an exemplary green image, even though we have seen that the plastic-aluminium fused packaging it promotes is bad for the environment, since it is extremely energy-intensive to de-fuse and therefore usually landfill-dumped, and probably bad for consumers too. The company is careful to say all the right things though: 'Tetra Pak welcomes the new IPPR/Green Alliance Report "Zero Waste UK"'. The EU claims to recycle 30 per cent of its tetra-cartons, and Germany 65 per cent, but Tetra Pak emphasises 'a full life cycle approach', by reducing the quantity of materials used in the first place—since its layers of aluminium and plastic are extremely thin—rather than the Report's end-of-cycle emphasis, that is, landfill dumping.[38]

The micro-thin layers of aluminium in tetra cartons are more than offset by the relentless expansion of Tetra Pak factories. In India the brand is promoted for milk as well as juices. When Tetra Pak wanted duties cut on aluminium, it hired Dilip Cherian, a lobbyist based in Delhi who charges clients $100,000 a year, who launched a grassroots-seeming campaign getting farmers' co-ops to lobby MPs to cut duty on aluminium to subsidise Tetra Pak cartons.[39]

PR is even less regulated in India than in the West. Even James Wolfensohn (former WB president) admits that 'the earlier efforts of lobbying in the developing countries was really writing checks to the parliamentarians and officials.' Cherian heads one of India's top PR firms, Perfect Relations, and is ex-President of FICCI.[40] Perfect Relations was in charge of Congress' 2004 election campaign, and is employed by Posco, with an office in Forest Park, Bhubaneswar, next to DFID, Adam Smith Institute, and Continental Resources (the US company, with an MoU on Gandhamardan).

Often it is hard to see what is really going on, when claims of 'social benefits' are the opposite of companies' actual behaviour. Joel Bakan (2004) shows that profit 'for their shareholders' is the supreme value for companies, enshrined in law through the case *Dodge v. Ford* (1916), which established that Ford had no right to keep its prices low as a service to customers, since directors have no right to put wider social interests before shareholders' profits. In the view of Friedman's pupil Peter Drucker, a key business guru, CSR should never get in the way of profit, and is only useful for selling an image, intrinsically insincere.

Manufacturing consent is particularly hard for mining and oil companies, because the processes of extraction are so damaging, to people and environment. This is why key corporations (Shell, Rio Tinto, ICMM, Vedanta and others) pay so much for the services of experienced PR firms. PR is closely linked to the role of credit rating agencies (as we saw through the Finsbury-WPP connection). These august institutions (Moody's, Standard and Poor's, Fitch, Egan-Jones, and Crisil in India) came under strong, and well-justified criticism during the credit crunch (October-November 2008), for recommending, for example, the Iceland banks, and not foreseeing the collapse of numerous banks and companies, due to their high levels of toxic debt.

Another aspect concerns manipulation in the media (Chomsky and Hermann 1988). This has been evident in Posco inviting journalists to South Korea, Vedanta inviting groups to Lanjigarh, and so on. The pattern of media doing PR for mining companies in Odisha is spelt out by Kedar Mishra (2007). But India has its fair share of independent journalists. Praful Bidwai (2008) draws attention to the way Indian policymakers are 'falling back on pseudo-science' to justify policies of rapid industrial expansion and rapid increase in GHG emissions—an Indian sequel to the denial of human-caused global-heating in the US and UK. The Civil Society Coalition on Climate Change published a pamphlet attacking the IPCC and the idea of capping GHG emissions, as 'counterproductive' and 'harming the poor'! This was inaugurated by Montek Singh Ahluwalia, Deputy Chairman of India's Planning Commission, on 2 April 2008.[41]

The corporate conceptual structure of beliefs and values

Vedanta's core ideology is presented in an article in *Darpan* by S. K. Pattnaik, VAL's Head of Human Resources:

> We have a vision for this land of Orissa ... we dream to see Kalahandi as a socio-economically developed region of Orissa, and as a torchbearer of green and eco-friendly industrialisation in Orissa and India.
> We at Vedanta Alumina Ltd. aim to be a "Living Organisation" in sync and harmony with our surrounding communities, society and environment. We see ripples of growth and industrialisation around our first efforts, which will envelop the entire people of this land and raise the standard of living through more opportunities, better productivity and greater aspirations.
> To realise this dream, our CSR Team presses on relentlessly and selflessly understanding the challenges and aspirations of our neighbours, and envisioning them of development through a path of self-discipline, diligence, activity and productiveness.
> The invaluable efforts of our CSR Team are indeed praiseworthy and show us that we are capable and have greater heights to achieve. As a family, all the members of Vedanta Alumina Ltd. join hands to hearts to march towards our goal. Success is a journey and we're looking forward to your cooperation for a well developed, thriving, and a model Kalahandi and Orissa.[42]

The verbal hints depicting VAL's relentless expansion onto tribal people's land in terms of 'improving' them, reveal a modern missionary/charity theme. In many ways, this passage is a clear statement of fascism.

An article called 'Infrastructure Development by Vedanta: Seeing is Believing', attacks people who criticise the company.

None who cries hoarse over the Vedanta Alumina project in Kalahandi seems to have ever attempted to find out from the project site in Lanjigarh if people who are said to have been affected are unhappy. Or, if the company discharges its social and developmental obligations in true spirit. Nobody has seen it on the site, yet everybody seems to be believing, though in a contrary fashion. After having a tour on all these photographs of the peripheral areas of Vedanta site at Lanjigarh, one can easily realise how off-the-mark the politicians and media personnel had been describing the projects as some kind of bane. In fact, it is just the opposite. People here, are happy. The company has achieved in just over a year's period what the state administration could not over the last four decades. Vedanta Alumina Ltd. (VAL) is one among those few corporates who are working in the sector of infrastructure and trying their best to avail almost each and every facility to the people of the peripheral villages. If one will visit the peripheral area of the plant, he will find that the area is not the same as it used to be three years back.

Bodai Daldali

This is an understatement. Before the villages' removal early in 2004, people here had never experienced the heavy pollution of air, water, earth and sound that define their daily reality now. They had never witnessed destruction like the leveling of villages, fields, trees and rock formations that started then. Nor had they experienced the corruption of values all around them now: the briberisation; the accident deaths; the sexual exploitation, or the turning upside down of truth regarding Vedanta's environmental 'achievements': *the real face of Vedanta*. Local people have articulated these violations on countless occasions.[43]

The dig at the administration—four decades and no proper development—evokes the neoliberal power structure, in which basic services are to be bestowed by companies as *largesse*, no longer built into the duties of government and rights of the people. Many administrators have facilitated this takeover.

And however respectable company officials may be in their private life, their service to their company forces them into the *'pathological pursuit of profit and power'* (Bakan 2004). The psychology of companies is similar to that of psychopaths in that they have no concern or sense of responsibility for the effects of their actions on other people or the natural environment, they use charm and guile to persuade and manipulate people, they exaggerate and relate superficially to mask their company's dangerous, exploitative intentions. Dangers to human life (of employees, customers, locals) are counted as 'externalities'.

Company ideology builds on the belief that people who are 'civilised' and 'stronger' need to impose their will over 'backward', 'weaker' people—for the latter's benefit; and if the stronger make a good profit, this is seen as a just reward for their hard work and cleverness. This fascist ideology is a variant of 'social evolutionism'— the idea that society evolves through set stages from 'primitive' to 'modern industrial', popularised by Herbert Spencer, who coined the phrase 'survival of the fittest'. Andrew Mellon's father grew up on Spencer's writings and often referred to them.[44]

This is the set of beliefs that also inspired the British empire in India—a mindset completely closed to hearing what people from indigenous communities say, or learning from them—a set of beliefs that leads to extraordinarily ruthless behaviour, often masked by an elaborate self-justification and even a show of religious charity (whether

Christian or Hindu). Whatever ideology may be used, profit is the overriding goal, to which everything else is 'sacrificed'.

The link between low-church Christian belief and the ideology that drives capitalism has been studied by Marx, Weber (*The Protestant Ethic and the Spirit of Capitalism* 1904), R.H.Tawney (*Religion and the Rise of Capitalism* 1922) and others. The Calvinistic, Puritan doctrines of pre-determined salvation and hard work as a sign of being saved gave birth to the ideology of accumulating profit through thrift and productive work, as if this was an outward sign of spiritual merit. Defoe in England and Benjamin Franklin in America were among those who secularised and spread this doctrine: 'Time is money' (Franklin), and the way to wealth as to salvation lies in 'industry and frugality'.[45]

Companies such as IMFA and Vedanta, like Birla, build big, marble temples and donate large sums to older ones. Some of India's mining chiefs are pious Hindus, abstemious and vegetarian. Lakshmi, like the Robber Barons' version of God, is invoked to help with accumulation of personal fortunes, without any sense of contradiction between religious piety and ruthlessness to fellow humans.

Russia's aluminium barons epitomise the mafiaisation at the heart of aluminium economics. Deripaska's fortune has fallen since the Recession, and he was shown with Putin making him pay workers, allegedly after a Kremlin bail-out; yet Rusal plans an expansion of its Guinea refinery, even after a police firing on Rusal workers and a military coup (October and December 2008), despite African governments' allegations that Rusal has paid little or nothing for their assets.[46]

Environmental concerns, and the interests of people displaced by projects come right at the bottom of this scale of values. The low value set on human life shows rawest when people are killed to enforce the will of company men: at Merthyr (Wales) 1831; striking copper miners shot at Rio Tinto in Spain, 1888; the Chixoy dam killings (Guatemala) 1980–82; Indonesian repression around Freeport mine, the war on Bougainville around Rio Tinto's mine, in Nigeria and Peru for oil[47], and in Guinea for bauxite.

The Maikanch and Kalinganagr killings also follow a distinct colonial pattern of police firings in India, from Dyer at Amritsar (13

April 1919) to Odisha during the Quit India Movement (1942), to a long list of repression against 'environmental activism of the poor' in India since Independence.[48]

The system of values and beliefs fuelling industrialisation are a variant of the doctrine of 'social evolutionism'.

The subtitle of Charles Darwin's *Origin of Species* (1859) was unfortunate, in that it was quickly misused as PR for capitalism, by Herbert Spencer and others:

> 'The Origin of Species by means of Natural Selection, or The Preservation of Favoured Races in the Struggle for Life'

Darwin's subject was how races or species of animal, bird, fish, insect and plant evolved. Implicitly, this questioned literal interpretations of the Bible, where God is said to have created all species as fixed creations. Darwin's theory of how change occurs in natural species was misapplied to society by Herbert Spencer and others as the doctrine of social evolutionism, where it formed a justification for dispossessing 'primitive races', and fuelled the 'march of industrialisation'. Darwin himself, while fiercely criticising the racist theory that justified the slave trade (the idea that certain human races were inferior by nature), was unable to escape the view of tribal people as inferior by culture, representing a 'savage stage', and needing to be civilised. Nor could Marx escape this view—few could at that time—and the Engels/Marx classification of 'stages of evolution' in society from 'primitive communism' to feudalism, capitalism, and advanced communism, is one of the most influential variants of social evolutionism.

The aluminium companies' propaganda of benefiting people by 'giving them the fruits of development' appears to be a direct extension of this belief system. A cultural aspect emerges in an article 'What They See, What They Say …', about a visit to Lanjigarh refinery of two influential Odias, geologist G. B. Mishra and artist Dinanath Pathi.

> "A remarkably satisfying and informative visit." They were particularly impressed with efficient project management, care and concern for the environment, rehabilitation of the displaced and the protection of native tribal lifestyle and culture.

Among other things, the visiting artists like Dr Pathi conducted a painting and essay competition among the children. They were impressed by the way Vedanta has, "protected and promoted the traditional and ethnic tribal culture and the way Vedanta has become an integral part of the younger generation psyche as evident from their paintings and essays."[49]

Why do essays and paintings have to compete? Are these children learning to think for themselves and rely on their own judgment, or to compete with each other in producing work that will please their teacher/boss? And when Vedanta produces a glossy diary, *Kalahandi—a Way of Life*, using photographs of Dongria, are they marketing a lifestyle they are poised to pollute and destroy?

In India, *naukri* (service) is an enduring value. But service in a company, driven by the pursuit of profit to the exclusion of other values, can lead to a kind of slave empire run by unelected executives and bankers. Uprooting tribal communities contravenes the Fifth Schedule of India's Constitution, as well as Adivasis' deep-seated sense of law. Adam Smith would turn in his grave to see how the corporate pattern of ruthless exploitation is still being imposed in India, using his name. Those selected to serve the people are serving, all too often, other interests entirely. How to recover a sense of serving rooted in accountability, and service to others?

PART V.

Movements for Life

To what extent are the movements against mining projects separate and local, and to what extent do they form a single movement? To what extent are they 'indigenous'? What different streams can be identified as inspiring them?

Adivasi movements against exploitation and dispossession have a long history. There were many during colonial times, and they formed a significant strand in India's freedom struggle, especially during the Quit India Movement in Odisha, when they were suppressed with brutal police firings that prefigure events at Maikanch and Kalinganagar.

Current movements have a complex lineage back to Marx, Lenin, Gandhi, Ambedkar, Lohia, Kishen Pattnayak and many others. The farmers' movement in west Odisha, demanding a fair price for rice and proper allocation of water resources for agriculture, has highlighted the iniquities of Hirakud and other reservoirs, which give excessive water to aluminium and steel factories.

Simultaneously, the Naxalite or Maoist movement, given the Salwa Judum counterinsurgency mobilisation against that movement, turns outrage at injustice towards a vicious cycle of violence.

The Kashipur, Niyamgiri, Kalinganagar, anti-Posco and many other movements against the invasion of cultivators' land by mining companies are among the most significant acts of resistance to corporate power going on worldwide today. Central to these movements is the question, *What is Development?* and an insistence that displacement is not development.

These movements are sustained by a sense of justice, and of balance with nature, that mainstream culture has largely lost sight of. How can the ruling classes' respect and compassion be awakened for other people, with different values? Why is denial of environmental destruction so widespread? How to listen to our conscience, at the same time as expanding a consciousness of these situations? And what have we learnt now from aluminium? How to take stock? What policies are called for? Where do we go from here?

CHAPTER TWENTY

Andolan

Gandhamardan's ghost-town

As Rayadhar Lohar said in his deathbed interview:
Andolan ete sohojo kotha nuhe ...
(Movement is not such an easy thing.)

The ghost-town colony that Balco built near Paikmal, for 2,000 workers who never came, has been taken over by beautiful trees now. Flats, just like in Delhi—standard design, spacious, 'civilised' blocks, three stories high—a model township that never was. The setting is spectacular—against the backdrop of Gandhamardan mountain range, with fertile fields all around, and trees flowering in every corner.

But never used, and now unusable, abandoned, with a couple of lonely guards, from homes in Chhattisgarh. For those who believe in the industrialisation model of development, a terrible waste. For the construction companies and contractors who built the flats, a job they earned from anyway. For Adivasis, Dalits, activists and devotees of the nearby pilgrim temples of Narsingh Nath and Hari

Shankar, the ghost-town is a monument to victory against vested interests and violence that would have destroyed Gandhamardan's magnificent blend of nature and culture.

Balco's ghost-colony at Paikmal, below Gandhamardan

The alliance was broad, from local Adivasis and Dalits to Hindu priests and pilgrims, protecting the temples and mountains as a sacred legacy, in conjunction with the Hindu Mazdoor Kisan Parishad (under the VHP umbrella), political campaigners and intellectuals from Odisha's towns, students from Sambalpur University, activists from the Chattra Yuba Sangharsha Vahini, and supporters from further afield, such as Sunderlal Bahuguna from the Himalayas, and allies in the administration, including the MoEF, who refused to give Environmental Clearance—a turning of the tide, and a sign that the tide could turn further.

It takes a lot of mental strength and clarity to stand up against the companies' sustained propaganda of dire threats and lavish promises designed to undermine the people's determination, including frequent use of violence and 'false cases'. As Bhagaban wrote in a letter to Samarendra (27 September 2003), regarding the strategy to be used to counter the World Mining Congress, then about to meet in Delhi (November 2003):

Gandhamardan

Company ebe nua nua sukhama sukhama upaya panchuchi tiari koruchi (The companies keep devising new, subtler methods and strategies, spreading propaganda and trying to trap people in false cases, to get them entangled in the court).

What often makes it tough to stand firm is the role of politicians and their parties on the one hand, and NGOs on the other, who offer support, but withdraw or get co-opted when the pressure builds. This happened to the Gopalpur movement where people had united *stronger than steel* against Tata's plans for a steel plant, but were betrayed by politicians in 1998–9, and three villages, consisting of about 1,000 families, were forcibly evicted to a rehab colony about 14 km away.

After the Maikanch killings in December 2000, politicians of several parties blamed NGOs for instigating resistance, partly as a way of belittling the movement and even denying its existence. Many officials could not accept it at face value, and thought

"*This kind of resistance by illiterate tribals is not possible, someone else must be behind this.*" All of us live in an atomised society. Middle class townspeople find it hard to recognise that these tribals can get together and fight like this. (Saroj 2008)

The Kashipur movement against Utkal Alumina remained a symbol of resistance for about twelve years. But just as the Narmada Bachao Andolan failed to save the Narmada river, Vedanta and Utkal Alumina's projects now often appear unstoppable. Though resistance continues, several villages have already been displaced, and many others have seen a total change in their physical and social environment. The movements have been divided, with many people getting jobs out of dire necessity. So was people's sacrifice wasted? It is worthwhile comparing the Gandhamardan and Kashipur movements.

The derelict concrete structures in Gandhamardan's ghost-town represent structures of power that were here, for once, defeated, but remain in place in dozens of other places.

After pro-Posco *goondas* had thrown bombs at protesting villagers, the comment on TV by Odisha's ex-Industry Secretary, Priyabrat Patnaik, '*this will teach them a lesson,*' was one of those moments when the veil lifts enough for us to clearly see the collusion between

Gandhamardan	Kashipur
Opposition parties support the movement	No such support
Middle-class religious sentiments	Not relevant
Support from a multitude of "outsiders"	More restricted outside support
Media support	Largely hostile media
No NGOs involved or documentaries	Many NGOs and documentaries, apoliticising the movement
Mass base of small pamphlets	
Heavy policing and jailing	Even heavier policing, tying activists up in hundreds of 'false cases'

Table 15. Comparing the Gandhamardan and Kashipur movements

an influential clique in the administration and the *goondas* on the ground. Priyabrat is also President of the Bhubaneswar Club, an elite organisation in the capital that acts as a social centre for corporate interests and top bureaucrats, that has applied for a mining lease on Khandadhara. In analysing the power system, caste affiliation is often relevant. Patnaik is one of the main titles of the Karana (scribe) caste, who were clerks or bureaucrats in the traditional royal hierarchy, with a high status only just below that of Brahmins, and often a lot of power. Certain royal families still wield power behind the scenes, especially on mining issues, such as the Singh Deos of Kalahandi and Bolangir. On the social structure of the *goondas,* some of the biggest bosses faced charges in Naveen Patnaik's early years, such as the feared Hyder and Tito gangs (based in Bolangir and Kendrapara respectively) who terrorised Keonjhar's mining areas with numerous contract killings. Among contractors, Mahima Mishra and his Orissa Stevedores Ltd have a key contract for Lanjigarh's trucks and transport, as well as construction at Gopalpur port, geared for Vedanta, while Piyush Mohanty's Metro Builders have built colonies at Lanjigarh, UAIL and Kalinganagar.

The sheer number of industrial projects coming up in the scramble for East India's resources is often overwhelming. Some, as at Gandhamardan, build their colonies first, to move oustees and start construction of a key structure, seeking to build up a momentum to thwart local opposition, as with Vedanta's Lanjigarh and Burkhamunda projects, and Tata's project at Kalinganagar.

The intense opposition to displacement projects makes it hard enough for Indian companies, such as Tata and Hindalco, but even harder for foreign ones. This is well understood by village people, such as the farmers in West Bengal, who during 2008 saw the defeat of Salim Industries and Tata's Nano car factory, after over two years of intensely painful campaigning and violent division.

Posco's village opponents have gained public support from Korean and US steel-workers (March 2008), and on 1 April, just after Posco cancelled its *bhumi-puja* and announced further delays, several thousand people held a rally, reclaiming villages that had been pro-Posco for a while, burning all their Posco papers together. They came ready to die that day, and a heavy police presence was withdrawn from the area soon after. *Goondas* killed Dula in June, after a day's work alongside hundreds of others, dredging the Jatadhari river mouth. Villagers had alerted the authorities to the importance of this task to avert floods, but after huge delays, and government talk of a 20 crore contract for the job, the villagers had decided to do it themselves, which angered businessmen who had hoped to get this contract. After finishing the dredging on 30 June, they held a memorial for Dula attended by 3,000 villagers and supporters.

But Posco's main interest is in the iron deposits in north Odisha, including the deeply forested Khandadhara mountain in Sundargarh, whose 600 million tons of iron-ore is worth $108 billion (at 2007 prices of $180 per ton).[1] This is why Mittal played a different tactic, suddenly forcing through a Public Hearing for iron mines in Keonjhar in November 2008 by getting police to arrest 250 villagers.

Grassroots resistance

A Kond woman sits on her verandah shelling beans, in the village of Putsil, close to Deo Mali, Odisha's highest mountain, where both Ashapura and Bhushan have been angling for clearance (above, Chapter Fifteen). She wears a large nose ornament half-covering her mouth. She is asked 'tell us about how you stopped the MLA, Jayram Pangi?'

> On 8 March 2008 we were going to Boro Manjili. On the same day the MLA was passing by car. We stopped him and asked him—
> "Where are you going?"
> "Who are you to stop me like this?" he asked, but we said
> "No, you must tell us where you're going," and finally he said
> "No, I'm going because of the mining. Don't worry—I'll make sure you Putsil people get work, and others of this area, and I'll feed you in my own house" ['*posibi*'—I'll nurture/domesticate].
> "Why have you sold our mountain to the company?"
> "What company?"
> "We know that some Tata or Birla company has taken this."
> Finally he said "OK, as long as I'm MLA I won't allow any mining."
> That same day we went to Boro Manjili. All the women came together, *gherao*ed the tehsil office, and submitted a memorandum against mining the mountain.

A month after this event, the villages around Deo Mali organised a meeting at Upara Kanti, the village after Putsil (13 April 2008). Prafulla Samantara, one of Odisha's best-known activists, who writes articles in the press and is a frequent spokesman for people's movements on television, was invited to this meeting. He is pro-active in going wherever he is called, inspiring people and giving them a basic knowledge about their situation. As he said at Upara Kanti:

> About a year and a half ago someone told me that Ashapura is coming to Deo Mali after its bauxite, and I came here. You people of this area had already passed a gram sabha resolution against Ashapura, and have now passed another against Bhushan, and had given memoranda to the government that this earth, this water, this jungle, this mountain is yours and not for sale. ... When I came back to Putsil a year ago I found that after you had objected to the proposed mining, the Tehsildar wrote a strong letter to the higher authorities explaining that people here are objecting to Ashapura's plan, supporting your view that there should be no mining. And within a week that Tehsildar was transferred to Machkhund!

Whoever speaks for the people, for you, is not tolerated. The Collector and higher authorities do not allow such officers to remain with the people in these areas. Since the companies have no use for such people, they are transferred and officers who favour the companies are brought in....

After this I came and had a camp and discussed how to save your land, water, forest, mountain. I wrote articles in the press: "If you kill Deo Mali, Koraput too will die." [*Deo Maliku marile, Koraput bi moribo*] If you mine these mountains, the water here will dry up and become toxic [*pani visakht hei jibo*]. In the last 50–60 years we have destroyed a lot of our country's forest and water resources by letting in various companies. But you people have been here for a thousand years....

Last year I went around the mountain where Nalco is mining [Panchpat Mali] and found streams have dried up—no more water, in a place where they'd done watershed development! If the bauxite in these mountains is removed, all the streams will dry up. The government is lying when they say *"We'll open the mountains and there'll be lots of water."* Today's the Odia new year ... It's supposed to be the hottest day of the year, but it's cool and pleasant here, as we're in the midst of nature, forest, greenery, water.... Let's pledge to stand up against those who've come to obliterate all this [*dhwonso koriba*], and convey this to those ruling us [*sason koruchanti*]. They have become the brokers [*dalal*] for the companies. They're selling our forest, mountains, water ... going to Bhubaneswar and amassing wealth by selling our assets.... The Collector and Tehsildar exist for the company [*compani pai collector achanti, compani pai tehsildar achanti*]. What development will there be? Demand an account. [*Ki vikas hebo? Hisab mango*]

After a handful of men spoke, women got up one after another, and spoke with passion, most in Kui, but one in Odia:

> When the government comes, we get afraid and give away our property.... We have to protect our area from being destroyed.... We won't give our mountain, Deo Mali.... Our cattle, buffalo, sheep and goats would die ... We won't let them have our precious fields.... Like this, our sons and daughters [*puo jhio*] will sustain. ... We won't sustain as construction or mine workers.... We grow our own *mandia and bhato* [millet and rice]. If that's finished, how could we buy it? Some of us may die and some will live, but we

have to fight to save our mountain.... The government will come, but they're not our father and mother. This land doesn't belong to them.... If we're all united we'll be able to save our mountain.... Even if the Collector or MLA or MP comes, don't be afraid. They can't feed us. We made them MP and they're meant to serve us. When the government comes we'll tell them, "If you want to kill us, just kill us, but we all Adivasis and Harijans won't let you mine our mountain." We mustn't let them divide us. That'd make it easy for them, to sell Deo Mali like they've sold Mali Parbat [to Hindalco, that is, Birla]. We sustain ourselves with our digging sticks. If we lose our land where will we go?

Upara Kanti is one of seven villages that have already been served notice about mining projects up on Deo Mali: Ashapura has applied for a staggering 5,000 hectares [about 70 times the size of the Niyam Dongar lease!], and Bhushan 2,000. These speeches took place three days before we transcribed these words.[2]

Spirited resistance is going on throughout East India. When people see that their livelihoods and whole culture are at stake, they are determined to resist, and look on promises of a better life by accepting displacement and R&R as lies. The Posco and Kalinganagar movements have galvanised countless people. Though many middle-class, urban Odias still believe in the promises of industrialisation, or are seduced by the symbols of modernity sweeping the state, or by prospects of fast money, village people are organising to resist the juggernaut. The movements to stop mining companies from invading and taking over large tracts of Odisha should be understood as a vital expression of civil society against forced dispossession. They remain basically non-violent, despite the extensive violence they face from police and company thugs. While the majority of those active in the movement are Adivasis, because they have the most to lose, and the very roots of their culture and way of life are threatened, large numbers of Dalits and other non-tribals are with them. It is instructive to witness how this broad coalition has been misrepresented by government and company propaganda in the media, which at times even implies that the activists are Naxalites.

One of the harshest effects on society whenever a mining company enters an indigenous area is to split the community into those for and those against the enterprise. This tendency is also evident in the movements, where the role of NGOs is a particularly divisive issue, especially the question of NGOs' funding from foreign governments and institutions with corporate links, dividing people who are essentially on the same side. Saroj, an activist with the Kashipur movement over many years, explains how people from foreign NGOs like the Stromme Foundation and Norwatch first came to Kucheipadar in 1995, asking loaded questions such as 'What compensation would satisfy you to leave your land?' and how NGOs would try to dissuade people from demonstrating with their weapons: 'You can't fight the company directly—find other ways. Don't go with weapons to the rallies.' Like most activists, he looks at both NGOs and political parties with suspicion for the ways in which they try to take control of a movement, often dividing or subverting it.

> NGOs try to mould people into their own image…. In 1997 this came to a head when they fell out at a strategy meeting with the PSSP…. NGOs used to call tribal leaders to come and meet them, trying to control their direction, and brought a competitive spirit to the movement…. Have they got the people's mandate?… They co-opt the leaders and destroy the democratic set-up. Outsiders compete to be friends of the Adivasis…. The media is driven by outside intellectuals, and is mostly owned by the political parties. NGOs often brief the media, but even when they support the movement, they don't bring the people's voice, or else they brief their chosen representatives on what to say and how to say it, trying to control the movement. (Saroj 1999)
>
> The political parties and NGOs created a sense of dependency by inviting people to meetings, feeding and trucking them. This is difficult to organise for movement people, who can't afford to treat journalists to mutton and biriyani as the political parties and NGOs do, so the journalists don't publish our statements. (Saroj 2000)

Yet one strength of these movements is actually their diversity: the very fact that people from different classes and walks of life and interests have come together and taken great risks to defend Odisha's tribal culture and environment is a great strength. Dividing the activists is a classic tactic of corporate power, reinforced by stern warnings from the Odisha government that opposition to its programme of rapid industrialisation will not be tolerated.

As in the days of India's freedom struggle, the 'enemy' exploiting India's resources and oppressing the people is still funded from abroad, but this is not as directly visible as it was when the British ruled India. And behind the foreign companies and financial institutions is a foreign system of relating and valuing, which comes down to a single aim: maximising profit. The company, as we have seen, exists purely to make a profit. Effects of its actions on people are considered irrelevant. It represents a totally hierarchical, unaccountable form of power, with no long-term safeguards. To oppose mining companies effectively needs a coming together of different classes and ideologies. Being on guard against forces trying to control or co-opt the movement has to be balanced by an openness to different approaches.

It is also true that the multitude of movements in Odisha, let alone in neighbouring states or the whole of India, are little coordinated. People rarely organise till their own area is invaded, and by then it is often too late, since interlocking deals and loans for a project may already be in place. However, as the resistance to Posco shows, these movements can still be effective, because they come from people deeply rooted in the earth, who know what is at stake, coming from lines of ancestors who always sustained themselves by growing their own food. These are people who never forget (as many dwellers in cities and towns do) that water, forest, mountains, fields and soil are sources of life.

Odisha's freedom struggles

The history of Odisha's freedom struggle is still fresh in the minds of many rural Odias—a basic part of their collective memory and identity. Adivasis and non-tribals were equally involved in opposing various forms of gross exploitation under British rule, though the true stories of freedom fighters are often obscured by myth and ideology, and close parallels between those struggles against British rule and today's against imposed 'development' are ignored in official discourse.

Kond resistance to British rule was strong from the start, with Chokra Bissoi's rebellion in the 1840s, or rather, his war against invasion, since he never accepted the Government of India that the

Project supporters	Movement supporters
Mining company officials	People in villages displaced or affected
Construction company officials	Most Adivasis and other villagers
Many business people in towns	Social activists
Most engineers and geologists	Environmentalists and some geologists
Mainstream economists	Alternative economists
Political parties in power	Political parties in opposition
Some NGOs	Some NGOs
Dominant clique in the administration	Many administrators
Everyone who believes in the ideology of "development"	Gandhians, and everyone who questions the development ideology

Table 16. Polarisation into project and movement supporters

British imposed. The Kalahandi uprising in the 1880s opposed a huge increase in exploitation and dispossession. The police firings in 1942 were a suppression of similar grievances: for awakening people's consciousness of injustice and their own power, Laxman Nayak was executed.

'Sir, by favour of the Government, I am a Raja,' wrote one Odia Raja to a British official, exonerating himself of charges that he had aided Chokra Bissoi.[3] Before the British, kings had to legitimise their rule equally in the eyes of their tribal subjects, who would get rid of any Raja who went against their interests and wishes, and in Hindu eyes, through Jagannath's temple next to the palace. Under British rule, Jagannath's importance was reaffirmed, but Rajas' need for legitimation towards tribal subjects was replaced by pressure to legitimise their rule in British eyes through modernisation and by increasing the profit from their lands in terms of revenue, as well as the aggrandisement of their palaces and English-style education for their children. As British arms and better roads brought their tribal subjects more firmly under control, Rajas gradually ceased to be dependent on Adivasi approval. Several even expelled Konds and replaced them with non-tribal cultivators (the cause of the Kalahandi rebellion).

The Raja role, in the degenerate form it acquired under British *hukm*, is still with us. Neither administrators nor elected politicians tend to behave as the public servants they are meant to be, but more as Rajas holding court. People's enemies and the forms of exploitation are more complex and pervasive than ever.

In today's freedom struggles, what are the different streams which resistors draw from? Throughout this book we have analysed the various mainstream roles. What are the alternative roles and traditions?

1. Since India's freedom struggle and before, indigenous tribal movements for justice have a strong tradition in Odisha and neighbouring states. The Gandhamardan movement and other movements in the 1980s have drawn inspiration from tribal and Dalit identity, as well as the identity of cultivators in general, including traditions such as that of Ambedkar, standing for the rights of the downtrodden.

2. Gandhi is interpreted in many ways. The Quit India Movement in 1942, to 'Do or Die', inspired sustained demonstrations in Odisha. As India gained Independence, and Gandhi witnessed the same patterns of injustice persisting in villages, with Indians exploiting Indians, he moved closer to the socialist tradition and took a strong stand against Western models of industrialisation, arguing against Nehru that India would not achieve economic independence like this. His faith in India's village culture is alive in the present movements. Ram Manohar Lohia represented the tradition from an atheist perpective after Gandhi had gone, with an incisive critique in Parliament of Nehru's programme of industrialisation. Kishen Pattnayak, Lingaraj, Lingaraj Azad, Manmohan Choudhary, Rabi Ray and many others represent this tradition of non-violent but sustained resistance into modern times, and extend it to a fundamental critique of mining-based industrialisation as a path to prosperity. This critique is made

strongly by the Samajvadi Jan Parishad (SJP), and in statements by Kishen Pattnayak.
3. Various nationalistic traditions play a role in opposing foreign-funded exploitation. One strand is represented by BJP leaders such as Jual Oram in north Odisha, whose Bhuiya Adivasi culture is an ancient strand in Indian culture, under threat from companies that want to mine Khandadhara. Mining companies represent a Western materialism fundamentally opposed to the more holistic vision of India's spiritual traditions. Nevertheless, Indian nationalist sentiments are often aroused on behalf of industry, especially when names such as 'Utkal' and 'Vedanta' conjure pride in a glorious past—without awareness of mining companies' corrosive impact on authentic Indian traditions.
4. We have examined the NGO role in terms of a 'soft critique' and protest (as in 'Protestant') that comes basically out of Christian and missionary traditions, and its marriage with indigenous Indian forms.
5. The many sects of Marxism represent another strong current, with deep roots in India. The Naxalites/Maoists in India follow the tradition of communist struggles for social justice and redistribution of wealth, and of armed struggle, from Lenin to Sendero Luminoso (Peru). Nepal's Maoist insurgents, who laid down their guns and got elected to form Nepal's government early in 2008, remained at the helm for nearly a year. The CPI-ML—a formerly underground party that has been contesting elections for Assembly and Parliamentary seats for nearly two decades now—and, at times, even the CPI and CPI-M, have taken a strong stand against mineral exploitation.

The idea that mining companies bring real development was given the lie by the cholera epidemic that swept Kashipur in mid-2007, after twenty years of IFAD loans and URDS-funded programmes. The PSSP first drew attention to the situation with a *chokka jam* on 22 August, after 93 people had already died. It took a while after this before the administration and media woke up to what was happening. A principal reason for the epidemic was that people have lost their food security. As in the 1960s, there is extensive corruption in the

PDS system of ensuring food for people below the poverty line, and food for work programmes are not coordinated with the times when people are busy or free in the cultivation cycle. As for doctors, the Kashipur region needs at least twelve for its five health centres, but has only two—a ratio of about 1:100,000. SHGs manifestly failed to play any positive role in giving loans for healthcare (Saroj 2008).

In other words, the conditions of exploitation and impoverishment have changed only superficially, and the freedom struggle is still with us. The invasion of Kalinga is still happening, more than 2,000 years on, and if we don't stop it, who will?

Left, Right ... The role of ideology

At the other extreme to the endemic exploitation are the Naxalites: revolutionaries in the Maoist mould, who have been expanding their territory and influence throughout rural, especially tribal, areas of East India. Sometimes as tyrannical and arbitrary as the system they oppose, they nevertheless seem to offer justice, and especially the redistribution of wealth that is so sorely needed. The spread of their operations in the poorest areas of rural Odisha and neighbouring states points to the increasing failure of the government to check the rot of corruption and injustice. Rural India is becoming like what rural Nepal was a few years back—a battleground of violent warfare between Maoists and the counterinsurgency forces. Can India follow Nepal's path and open up talks between the Maoists and the mainstream?

Maoists often replicate government-style hierarchies and use of 'terror', and are sometimes as insensitive to tribal traditions as the mainstream. One needs to remember that the CPI(Maoist) may be underground, but it is a political party with similar hierarchy to other parties.[4] This party system of communist organisation relates to the shadow side of communist history. Few of the 'communist' countries established real socialism; Cuba is an outstanding example of one that succeeded. Many of the countries that were called communist were ruled by the most violent elites, who took power by killing off moderates: from Stalin and Mao, to East European dictators. It is significant that the WB did business with two of the worst—Ceausescu in Romania and Mengistu in Ethiopia—effectively funding their transfer of populations. Some of the communist struggles that failed were also excessively violent, such as Pol Pot in Cambodia and Sendero Luminoso in Peru. These are histories that should not be denied or forgotten.

As a critic of capitalism, Marx is excellent, and as an ideal, communism has a lot to offer. But if we follow his tradition, we need to keep the same openness he had, to observe clearly what is happening around us. Marx, like nearly everyone else in the nineteenth century, could not escape a belief in 'social evolutionism' (Chapter Nineteen). Tribal societies have strong communistic features, but the facts of recent human history do not fit into any simplistic 'stages of development' scheme. This is easier to see now than it was in Marx's time, especially because few people understood then the massive assault on the environment involved in industrialisation.

The common ground between SJP socialists and Marxists includes a belief in equality and an end to exploitation, and their persistent effort and risk to make this a better and fairer world. But, unlike the Marxists, who argue that the violence inherent in class-divided society cannot be transcended without 'revolutionary violence' to smash the institutions and mechanisms of class rule, the SJP socialists firmly believe that violence—'revolutionary' or otherwise—only breeds more violence. The number of revolutions in the name of Marx and communism that have paved the way for regimes as corrupt, ruthless and exploitative as the ones they did away with, show this all too well. Stalin exemplifies this, liquidating opponents and imposing mass-scale industrialisation, carried out with covert help from Andrew Mellon's purchase of Russian art treasures and American engineers building the factories.

Russell Means, from the American Indian Movement, saw Marxism as ultimately 'the same old song' as capitalism, in its tendency to *desacralise* nature, alienating people from it and treating it as purely material and inanimate: 'there to be exploited and utilized.' He questions the concept of revolution too.

> Newton for example, revolutionised Physics and the so-called "Natural Sciences" by reducing the physical universe to a linear mathematical equation. Descartes did the same thing with Culture, John Locke

did it with Politics, and Adam Smith did it with Economics. Each one of these "thinkers" took a piece of the spirituality of human existence, and converted it into a code, an abstraction. They picked up where Christianity ended. They secularised Christian religion, as the "scholars" like to say, and in doing so they made Europe more able and ready to act as an expansionist culture. Each of these intellectual "revolutions" served to abstract the European mentality even further—to remove the wonderful complexity and spirituality from the Universe, and to replace it with a logical sequence: One, two, three—Answer!

This is what has come to be termed "efficiency" in the European mind. Whatever is mechanical is perfect. Whatever seems to work at the moment [and gives a financial profit] "proves" the mechanical model to be the right one, and is considered "correct", even when it is clearly untrue. This is why "truth" changes so fast in the European mind. The answers which result from such a process are only stop-gaps—only temporary. They must be continually discarded in favour of new stop-gaps which support the mechanical models.... Hegel finished the process of "secularizing theology"—and that is put in his own terms: he secularised the religious thinking through which Europe understood the Universe. Then Marx put Hegel's philosophy in terms of "Materialism", which is to say that Marx de-spiritualised Hegel's work altogether. Again this is in Marx's own terms.... Europeans may see this as revolutionary, but American Indians see it as simply more of that same old European conflict between *Being* and *Gaining*. (1982)

Above all, Marxists do not seem to have come to terms with the problem of power: how to stop the most ruthless and cruel people from taking power by force in order to reassert the system of exploitation?

We have seen how China imposed neoliberal economics through the Tiananmen Square massacre and SEZs, and became ultra-capitalist in all but name, and how the CPI-M follows the same seamless transition in West Bengal, with neoliberal labour laws, similar violence, even imitating China by forbidding Tibetan demonstrations (mid-April 2008).

The tragedy of the Salwa Judum war is that Adivasis are pressed into fighting each other for non-tribal ideologies: the interests of right-wing politicians, bureaucrats and mining companies on one side, and Maoist ideology on the other. Neither seems to care about the Adivasi culture being obliterated as a result, or the suffering of about 200,000 refugees, caught in the middle of a proxy war.[5] The level of official denial is extraordinary.

> No air raids on Maoists: Centre
> Union Home Secretary V. K. Duggal in Bhubaneswar, Orissa commented on the record number of Naxalites "neutralised" and commended Salwa Judum as a "People's Movement": "Initially we had some reservations but we found that it is a people's movement. People have shown courage to stop recruitment by Maoists. It has served its purpose. The rule of law has to prevail. There is no other option left in a civil society. We want the misguided youths to come back to the mainstream development process. They should take advantage of the multiple growth opportunities instead of staying in jungles."
> (*Times of India*, 29 December 2006, frontpage)

What is the rule of law? The unpunished transgressions of law by corporates, feudalistic rural elites and the bureaucracy are precisely what bolster the Naxalites' appeal among the people who suffer the consequences. Therefore, to claim that the Salwa Judum is a genuine people's movement is an abuse of language and truth. 'It has served its purpose,' sums it up.

Nari Sena: Sustaining life through activism

People made great sacrifices to win the Gandhamardan movement. As Rayadhar said, the success of a movement often depends especially on the women:

> Do you fear death? Look at the girls here and their mothers ... Do you have such brave girls in Kashipur? The day you find them, you will be successful in saving your mountain.

Women in the Gopalpur movement formed a *Nari Sena,* and in every movement, women are in the forefront. Carrying the life of future generations in their wombs makes caring for their descendants' future a concrete reality, more than for men.

Also, displacement lowers women's quality of life even more than men's. From growing their own food and selling it directly, having full control over when, where and how they work, they suddenly lose all of that, becoming more dependent on their menfolk, or having to work as labourers in horrible conditions themselves, while their fathers, husbands and sons drink more, as despair takes over. All the slums of displaced people and mining workers are full of domestic violence, as well as prostitution. The SHG model of 'women's empowerment' is often, basically, a lie. Loans empower women at first, but when repayment demands build up, SHGs enmesh women and their families in debt and often impoverish them further, sapping their freedom and incapacitating their ability to take a leading place in activism. Some women pay a terrible price for their courage, as we saw in the murder of Tapasi Malik in Singur, and other women killed in Gopalpur, Nandigram and Kalinganagar.

So it is wrong to see these movements as simply 'against' various projects—let alone as 'anti-development'. On the contrary, these movements are about sustaining life, by protecting mountains, streams, rivers, forest, fields. They are motivated by cultivators' rootedness to the soil and bond with the life-force of the mountains, which give their names to movements: Niyamgiri or Mali Parbat Surakhya Samiti. These movements *are* development.

They also uphold a particular kind of lifestyle, that accords closely with Gandhi's ideal of the self-sufficient village community, outlined in *Hind Swaraj* (1909), and with modern environmental awareness. Activists in East India deserve to be seen as the grassroots cutting edge of worldwide movements against the 'death culture' of unbridled corporate growth.

International activists are motivated by similar sentiments when they demonstrate against secretive WTO and G8 meets, the Iraq war, and the aluminium companies in Europe. Saving Iceland is an organisation campaigning against Alcoa and its huge dams. In July 2006 a police officer drove his vehicle straight at Saving Iceland's founder, Pall Olafur Sigurdson, when he went up from a group of activists to negotiate. Ola was lucky to survive—and a case was still (26 April 2008) brought by the police against him for damaging the police car![6]

Tribal and non-tribal small-scale farmers form the heart of these movements in India, supported by activists from many walks of life. We all share this earth, and our grandchildren face a common danger as climate change and water scarcity become prevalent and more widely perceived. The west Odisha farmers' movement has focused attention in Odisha on the metal factories' threat to the growing of food.

NGOs play an important part in communicating with the media and middle classes when they support these movements, though as 'public-private partnerships' co-opt an increasing number of NGOs into corporate interests, it is hardly surprising if most activists remain suspicious of most NGOs.

Often, the lack of media attention these movements get is frustrating. For example, *The Guardian* (UK) has published several highly distorted articles on the theme of 'Maoist guerrillas and tribal rebels threaten India's industrial boom' (2 August 2006), which echoes corporate propaganda portraying resistance against forced industrialisation as Maoist-inspired. While an article in *The Independent* (3 December 2007) describes the dangers posed by Posco for Olive Ridley turtles without mentioning the anti-Posco movement—currently (2006–09) among India's most significant people's movements.[7]

These movements obviously gain strength from all-India as well as foreign recognition. The non-violent fight to preserve sustainable lifestyles is part of a larger movement to sustain human life on earth, calling a limit to industrial growth.

Another stage in this prognosis opened on 20 November 2009, when police opened fire from the roof of Narayanpatna police station on tribal people who had come to protest at atrocities by armed CRPF forces in surrounding villages as they combed the area for Maoists. These people belonged to the Chasi Mulia Adivasi Sangha (Cultivation Labourers Adivasi Society), which had recently taken back about 1,000 acres of land illegally acquired by moneylenders of the *Sundi* and other castes. In this firing, a leader of the CMAS was killled, K. Singana, along with Andrew Nachika, and several people were badly hurt. Civil society leaders protested this 'was a well-plotted murder, it wasn't self-defence,' judging from the number of bullets that hit Singana. After this incident, 2-4,000 police combed the area, arresting at least 80 CMAS members and terrorising villagers under the pretext of searching for Maoists, who have supported CMAS, although Prafulla Samantara and CPI-ML leaders pointed out that CMAS is 'a democratic organisation and existed much before the Maoists'. Apart from the land issue, CMAS has also taken a stand against mining plans by Hindalco, Ashapura, etc., targeting Kodinga Mali, Mali Parbat and Deo Mali.[8]

One of the first people to question the received wisdom that Odisha had to exploit its minerals in order to get rid of its poverty, was the veteran Gandhian politician, and our mentor in this work, Kishen Pattnayak, who articulated this with clarity:

> Odisha has enormous mineral reserves. This is considered to be the biggest asset to increase the prosperity of Odisha. This is really a myth. Mining areas of Odisha have never been known for being rich or developed. Now the condition is becoming much worse.
>
> A few national/multi-national companies and their contractors and those ministers and officials helping these companies in an unlawful, unethical manner become the owners of huge property. Odisha as a state is not going to get any benefit from this.
>
> Overall the state and the people will suffer the loss, only a small class of rich people will be created. Rich will become richer, poor poorer. Mining is a curse to the indigenous people and the environment.[9]

CHAPTER TWENTY-ONE

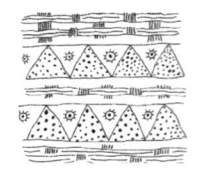

Sense of Sacredness

Dhatu: Mineral wealth in a living earth

Two very different kinds of religion: tribal cults viewing mountains as gods, and neoliberalism effectively replacing the idea of God with *'the hidden hand of the market'*.[1]

Mountains as a religion might be looked on by 'civilised people' as the ultimate in superstition. Yet the idea balances the spiritual with the material, and contains an intrinsic intelligence. The land's fertility comes from the mountains, which store rain water and release it gradually, mixed with mineral nutrients. Treating mountains as gods is common sense, a prescription for long-term sustainability. The Dongria preserving primary forest on the Niyamgiri summits in the name of Niyam Raja and Sora Penu is a prime example.

By contrast, the neoliberal doctrine is full of glaring contradictions, as many economists and others have shown clearly. Freeing market forces makes the rich richer and guarantees power to the most unscrupulous, reducing sustainable cultivators of the soil to a desperate impoverishment at the edge of starvation, their food security gone, their culture killed. Sacrificing long-term sustainability for short-term financial gain comes from a belief system full of holes. As a religion, 'money is God' threatens us all with destruction.

Adivasi religion is based in a sense of sacredness in nature. Kond 'deities', such as Dharni penu, Sora penu, Loha penu (spirits of earth, mountain and iron) could just as well be called 'elements' of life, or 'elementals'.

Dhatu (minerals) represent the hidden forces latent in nature. Tribal people sometimes describe mining a mountain in terms of a bear attacking a human and eating the brain. Most indigenous people hold minerals as sacred. In the native American view, which has a longer history of articulation to the non-tribal world, rocks and mountains are the earth's skeleton, and minerals are her brain cells.[2] This tradition sees the earth as our grandmother. Thanking and honouring the earth is at the heart of native American spirituality.

The Kogi in Columbia have a similar view, seeing great danger in the present time, emanating from mainstream cultures' disrespect for the earth.[3]

Tribal people often say that many substances buried in the earth need to remain there if the earth is to stay healthy, and that extracting these substances on the massive scale now being done all over the world dessicates and impoverishes the earth in a way that is insane. Many, like the Kogi, understand that the earth is sick from overexploitation and pollution, and try, when possible, to teach this to their 'younger brothers' in mainstream society.

Tribal knowledge about the soil and plants comes from a continuum of experience, in distinction to mainstream forms of knowledge, compartmentalised into different specialised disciplines, which tend to lose a sense of the functioning whole. To native Americans, rocks and minerals speak and teach people. Gems embody 'the highest form of aluminium' and its connection with colour. But, in native American understanding, rock goes crazy when it is out of balance—as we see in the destabilised 'heavy metals' in mineral waste such as red mud.

The soil's chemistry becomes deficient in the right balance of aluminium wherever fertilisers pour nitrates and phosphates into the soil, drying it out. Initial yields may be high, but the water consumption is exorbitant. All over India, dam water is channelled to fertiliser-intensive fields. But the water levels are falling, and there is a danger that the fertilisers are causing long-term damage to the soil over huge areas of India, and other countries, as Rachel Carson warned in *Silent Spring* (1962). The PR campaign launched against this book was funded by the fertiliser and pesticide companies.[4]

The science advocated by Rudolf Steiner looks at the relationship between mineral elements in terms of balance between different forces.[5] Correct balance is essential to the health of the soil, and in our bodies too. Before the aluminium age, the aluminium content of our bodies was miniscule, yet played a role in the overall balance. Processed food is notoriously deficient in this balance—whatever the nutrient information on the package—while foil's leaching of tiny but significant quantities of pure aluminium (i.e., destabilised from the molecular bonding with oxygen and other elements always found in nature) has built a dangerous residue in all our bodies (Chapter Twelve). Organic vegetables are increasingly appreciated for their full range of nutrients—for those who can still afford to buy them—just as corporate packaged food and fertiliser-fed vegetables are taking over from organic, living food over much of India.

As we have seen, bauxite is a very special mineral, formed over millions of years at the top of mountains, where it performs the essential function of conserving monsoon water and releasing it slowly throughout the year. If removing it creates certain kinds of imbalance, the splitting of aluminium molecules achieved in smelters creates another, ushering in a whole new age of material benefits, at the cost of unleashing new dimensions of material instability into the world. Aluminium has strong powers for death as well as life.

It is a 'new' metal, discovered just 200 years ago, and a 'hidden metal', in that it never occurs in nature in its pure form, but always in molecular bindings with other elements. This ability to blend with other elements is an essential ingredient of the chemistry of aluminium, from its role in the soil, holding moisture and transmitting it to the roots of plants, to its importance in colouring the world of form, visible in the 'noble rust' hues of gem-stones. This blendability finds expression in the ease with which industry applies it to a vast range of alloys.

The age of aluminium has brought us many wonders. From high speed travel in the aluminium birds and other 'magic carpets' of the modern world, to use as a conductor of electricity in cables, mobiles, computers; its thousands of applications in the satellite and arms industries, from nano-particle jet fuel (already seriously polluting outer space) to its applications in the technology of nuclear missiles, where the split of aluminium from oxygen forms part of the technology of bombs. If we blow ourselves up in nuclear explosions, and terminate as a species, aluminium is at the heart of how we shall do this.

As a key 'strategic metal', aluminium production fuels the arms industry and the world's wars. In many ways, modern society is a warrior society gone haywire and in denial. TVs pour out a constant diet of violent fighting as 'entertainment', while out of view, our soldiers at the borders (as well as other security forces inside) commit acts of terror we have no sense of, which are officially denied, and for which the other side is always blamed ... 'Where have all the young men gone?... Gone for soldiers every one ... When will they ever learn?' US arms companies such as Lockheed Martin and Boeing, for whose output a steady supply of large quantities of aluminium is essential, played a blatant role lobbying for the Iraq war, and have made huge profits from it, as have other construction, military contract and oil companies, such as Halliburton, Carlyle, Bechtel and Fluor.[6]

Increasingly, aluminium wraps our food and drinks in a cool embrace, leaching in tiny but steady quantities into our bones and brains. What is the ease it has given us? By removing it in huge quantities from its hiding place in the earth, where its proper balance preserves moisture and ensures the nourishment of plants, what have we done? Have we even begun to understand?

Dharma and the laws of nature

The concept of *dharma* links a sense of moral law with the idea of 'laws of nature' in science. A similar sense of neutrality obtains: the law of *karma* operates as totally and impersonally in our own lives as laws of nature define the behaviour of particles of matter. The Kond elder's comment about selling off their sacred mountain

(Chapter Seven) is a succinct summary of vedantic philosophy: '*Taro Koroma, Amoro Dhoroma*'—'His the *Karma* (action, sin), ours the *Dharma* (Law, truth, right)'.

The concept of *dharma* re-connects consciousness with conscience—being aware and doing what is right are inextricably linked. The concept of *satyagraha* (action based in truth) is relevant here. Whether we refer to God and divine law, or simply follow the logic of correct behaviour makes little difference now. When we face the dangers of climate change and pollution, and *the problem of power* which humans have so far failed to solve, we are all faced with the same basic challenges.

These days, religion is one of the most potent sources of conflict and division between people. Which is crazy when you think about it. If God exists He must be at His wits end with us! If there is any truth in religion, surely its real purpose is the quest for a deeper meaning in life, and the ability to live in harmony with people who are different (the 'good Samaritan') by discovering the springs of *karuna* (compassion) in our heart. In all religions there is a wealth of truth. But also, in their present forms, a multitude of limitations and distortions—a degeneration of spirituality into empty rituals and dogma, precisely what Jesus and the Buddha rejected.

Seeing his father's huge but empty sacrifices to the gods, the *Upanishad* hero Nachiketa says, 'Offer me too'. All over Odisha, in the last few years, public funds from politicians and private donations have knocked down old temples and erected big, grandiose structures in their place. Mining companies' huge concrete and marble temples, with pretty gardens near their factories, exemplify the very tendency that Nachiketa questioned—a show of piety to make up for the sin of corruption and the lives sacrificed for profit.

We have tended to make religion into a rigid system of rules and exclusive sects, letting these define and divide us—the polarising, dualistic tendency so widespread now—instead of using it to bring us together.

This applies also to atheists and communists. One does not have to believe in God to value life on earth. Jainism and Buddhism were often atheistic too. We all come into being through love and have a heart that we can open or close. Can we rediscover the truth of our religion or ideology in our hearts? Chief Joseph of the Nez Percé tribe (in the north-west US), after his people had been conquered and forced onto a reservation, rejected schools and churches on the grounds that '*They teach us to argue about God. We do not wish to learn that.*' [7]

In all religions and philosophies there is at least a residual sense of sacredness in nature, as well as a sense of natural or divine law which pervades the universe, which Hinduism and Buddhism call *dharma* and *karma*—the laws of cause and effect. *Karma* is the fruits of one's action. Its essence is that what you put out comes back to you—'there is no escape', as villagers in the Indravati region tried to explain to a WB consultant (above, Chapter Twelve).

The Vedic religion was close to Adivasi belief as well as practice in this regard, including a sense of sacredness of fire, water, air and earth, and the sacredness of many specific animals and other life-forms. Elephants, tigers, bears and monkeys are still considered sacred to Ganesh, Durga, Jambudveep and Hanuman. But in the way these animals are being hounded out of existence in Odisha and neighbouring states, killed for tusks, teeth, bones or hide, trapped for sale to 'reclamation centres' (bear cubs) or as pets (monkeys), where is this sacredness now?

Vedanta is the body of sacred knowledge in the *Veda*s which culminates in the *Upanishads*. As formulated by Shankaracharya around the eighth century AD, *Advaita Vedanta* formulates the philopshy of non-dualism: that, at the level of ultimate reality, there is no separation between *Atman* and *Brahman* (the soul and the One, i.e., God). What separates us is basically a delusory sense of separation, which the true practitioner works to overcome. The essence is a willingness to renounce an identification with the world of *maya*—illusory form, including material wealth. This is similar to Jesus' injunction to a rich man: 'Give up your wealth and follow me'. What is asked for is not renunciation in the sense of 'withdrawal from the world', but withdrawal from identification with the world, which means renouncing an identification with or lust for wealth and power.[8]

Recent scholarship has shown that modern reinterpretations of *Vedanta*, known as *Neo-Vedanta*, have seriously distorted its essence.

The reason is a Western influence, stemming from an inability of Western scholars to comprehend that *Vedanta*'s philosophical depth matched that of their own tradition. The reason for this seems to be that Western philosophy started with similar questions of ontology that Indian philosophy never departed from—basic questions such as 'why are we here?' embodied in the command written above the entrance to Delphi (*Gnowthi sown*, '*Know thyself*')—but retreated later into questions of epistemology (logic of meaning). As part of this shift, Western philosophy separated early on from religion: the Presocratic philosophers did this around 600 BC, while modern philosophers such as Hegel, Hume and Kant did this in Europe in the eighteenth and nineteenth centuries. As a result, Western philosophers who met Indian philosophy in the nineteenth and early twentieth centuries, were embarrassed by its fusion of ethics with ontology and epistemology, and therefore did not take it seriously.[9]

To defend it, many Indian philosophers tried to make it 'respectable' by emphasing features that seemed in line with Western philosophy, such as rationality, and downplaying others, such as seeing the material world as illusory and renouncing attachment to it. So in the process of trying to defend it, a dominant strand in modern Indian philosophy seriously distorted *Vedanta* and Westernised it—turning it into a matter of Indian pride consistent with a society that was taking on Western values of rationality and materialism, and the idea of progress and development, along with the whole enterprise of industrialisation.

This history is shown in an outstanding work on Indian philosophy, *Neo-Vedanta and Modernity*, by Bithika Mukerji (1983/2008). In the modern era, from the nineteenth century, *Vedanta* no longer had to defend itself against its original rivals such as Buddhism and dualism, but only against one adversary: the superiority claimed by Western culture and philosophy. As a result, it was reformulated in a way that made it appear consistent with Western ideas about progress and development, and the aim of rapid industrialisation as a means for India to 'catch up with' and maybe even overtake the West.[10]

The trouble is, the essence of *Vedanta* is a refusal to identify with the world of form and matter and its goals of wealth and power. Nachiketa succeeds in his quest by rejecting his father's lavish gifts (donations, sacrifice). The Indian scholars who popularised *Neo-Vedanta*, however, completely subverted the original message, albeit without meaning to do so. This includes, for example, the former President of India, S. Radhakrishnan, whose philosophical lectures and writings had a huge influence in the West as well as in India, where they still have pride of place in the system of higher education and the centre in Mussourie that trains India's top bureaucrats.

In effect, these scholars reversed *Vedanta*'s original message of non-attachment to activity or material wealth into an encouragement for Western-style development—an implicit acceptance of the 'progress-oriented ethos of the West'.[11] Along with this came a popular view of technology as 'value neutral', which is highly misleading:

> It is vain delusion to believe that technology is an instrument which human beings can use as they choose. It is an affirmation about Being and as such penetrates every aspect of a civilisation when it becomes the way of that civilisation.[12]

This being so, it is an extreme irony for a mining company to take the name *Vedanta*, especially one that is doing such exceptional violence to nature, for the sake of creating wealth. Polluting the elements represents a fundamental denial of the principles of *Vedanta*. The name itself should remind the people controlling this company that the forest on a sacred mountain should be left inviolate, that between their souls and the souls of the Adivasis they harm there is no separation, and that the harm they do to others, they do also to themselves.

Corruption of belief: Greed as God

Mining is an extreme expression of materialism. Nothing disrespects the land and denies its fertility and sacredness like ripping the tops or sides off mountains to mine them. In considering mountains primarily as 'mineral deposits', and relegating their water-storing and life-giving aspect to a secondary status, the modern, Westernised ideology is an expression of 'Greed is God'. The damage done to the earth in the name of profit is something that can only arise from an extreme sense of separation from the earth. By contrast, both

Dongria triangles on a shrine

tribal religion and environmentalism focus on a holistic awareness of cause and effect.

One of the paradigms of greed was laid by the conquistadors and their lust for gold, who filled a chamber with gold as ransom for the Inca, then killed him anyway, with a show of Christian piety. Some of the churches in Latin America demonstrate this materialism in their lavish decoration with silver and gold plate, bought with the blood of thousands of Indians who died in silver and gold mines. In Central and South America, Spanish conquistadors imposed a system of unspeakable cruelty over the indigenous people, whose lifestyle and reverence for nature they did all they could to destroy. Eduardo Galeano summarises this history in *Open Veins of Latin America: Five Centuries of the Pillage of a Continent* (1971).

When the gold standard was dropped, metals remained the basis of capital, but in a more hidden way, through investment and trade in mining and metals, and their use in aerospace, the world's most profitable and powerful industry. In other words, metals are the source of modern wealth and power in the most devious and devastating ways. From gold and silver to aluminium and uranium, our currencies are still based on metals, and the system is more exploitative and costly than ever before in terms of the sacrifice of human life and nature.

Tribal religion sacrifices chickens, goats and buffalos to the deities, just as the ancient Vedic religion did. The Hinduism of the *Bhagavad Gita* has a subtler sense of sacrifice, recognising 'lower forms' such as blood sacrifice, but seeing one's work and how one lives and dies as a truer form. Modern values often invert the sense of sacrifice altogether, sacrificing things of great and permanent value, such as the health of a mountain and villagers' quality of life, for something transient—immediate profit.[13]

The accumulation of wealth in modern society contrasts strongly with the ethic of many tribal societies, where traditionally, to possess was seen as an aberration, and giving away one's wealth to others was to claim the highest status, in a radically different sense from Robber Baron 'philanthropy'. The *give-away* of native American cultures contains a sense of letting go of one's wealth and attachment to one's most prized possessions, remaining with nothing. This is similar to the ideal of traditional India, where an individual moves beyond the life of a householder to renounce wealth and social status. The Robber Barons gave only their 'surplus' to 'good causes' or 'the nation'—for example, Mellon's art works, bought with profits from aluminium and oil, becoming the National Museum in Washington:

there is a clear intention to make capital out of this gift, exactly like Nachiketa's father's lavish sacrifices, or modern industrialists, starting with Birla, constructing lavish marble temples.

Religion was already deeply corrupted in the Middle Ages, when Christians killed each other in hundreds as heretics or witches, and waged crusades against Muslims, while Muslims massacred Hindus and Buddhists, and Hindu Rajas fought endlessly among themselves, worshipping *Violent Gods,* using the anti-war Mahabharata in an inversion of its original *ahimsa* intention.[14]

What we witness now is a more extreme corruption still, and one that applies to believers and non-believers alike. As strands in all the main religions degenerate into fundamentalism, we suggest that the world's most dangerous fundamentalism is the theory of economics that has dictated the financial policy imposed in almost every country since the 1970s–80s—neoliberal flat-earthism (Chapter Seventeen)—which is 'bad economics', both because it does the opposite of what it pretends to do (i.e., it increases poverty instead of eradicating it), and because it increases untruth, injustice, instability and terror in the world.

Neoliberalism represents materialism in its extreme form, as a doctrine closed to questioning by anyone outside a narrow elite of 'in' economists, and as an ideology that increases the power and material gain by politicians and businessmen applying the theory. It is interesting in this respect, how easily neoliberal policies are being embraced by Marxists, in India as well as China. Though Marx challenged capitalism, he took its materialist orientation even further.

Economic fundamentalism often fits cosily with religious belief. The Robber Barons in the US, and their counterparts in Europe, etc., were mostly deeply religious church-goers. In *The Protestant Ethic and the Spirit of Capitalism,* Max Weber explains how the Calvinistic and Lutheran doctrines fitted with the most extreme and ruthless forms of 19th–20th century capitalism, through the idea that creating wealth and saving money was a sign of a saved soul. As we saw (Chapter Nineteen), these 'captains of industry' established a pattern of 'pathological pursuit of profit' to the exclusion of other aims. 'Greed is good' became a popular slogan during the 1980s.

'The hidden hand of the market' effectively takes on the role of God in neoliberal doctrine. Making profit the ultimate good, neoliberal capitalism brings about a final debasement: 'Greed is God'.[15]

In India, we have seen how the bribe giving and taking culture of mining deals is based on the idea that 'money is no less than God' (Chapter 7). The Hindu form of corporate power is just as dangerous, ruthless and blind to its real effects on people and nature as the Protestant form—a celebration of wealth while causing mass poverty and not caring. The neoliberal ideology finds as comfortable a coexistence in Hinduism as in Chistianity, with worship of Lakshmi for individual or family gain, purifying one's sins in the Ganga and building lavish temples, or even a Vedanta University to perpetuate one's philanthropy and name.

'*Companies have bodies, but they have no souls; if no souls, no consciences.*'[16]

Both atheists and believers show double standards, making material wealth a prime value, with a show of 'good works' to give people 'development'. Communist ideology often loses sight of the value Marx placed on human life and on equality, to follow the the ultra-capitalist priorities of neoliberalism.

If flat-earth neoliberalism represents today's dominant fundamentalism, another aspect of this is a widespread cynicism, at the core of modern modes of belief. Everyone pays lip service to some 'good' belief or other, as a good Hindu, Christian, Communist, scientist or economist. Yet there is a widespread tendency for these beliefs to give way before the might-is-right, greed-is-god ethic. This contradiction leads to an erosion of belief itself, till it becomes an artificial structure, to which one attempts to attach one's identity, instead of something based in one's own experience.

The mining industry spreads this cynicism through greenwash and lies. As nature and matter are desacralised, people pursue a distorted, ungrounded spirituality, looking for the spiritual in false words and meaningless expenditures of wealth, like Nachiketa's father, while splitting off from their roots in physicality and nature.

Marx recognised the evils of capitalism. But he took on its central doctrine of materialism, compounding the break with nature.

Materialism is what frees the profit motive to destroy us. It completes a process of despiritising or desacralising nature and matter. In Russell Means' words (1982):

> *"Science will find a way." "Industrialisation is fine and necessary"*... Science has become the new European religion for both Capitalists and Marxists....
>
> Distilled to its basic terms, European Faith, including the new faith in Science, equals the belief that Man is God.... American Indians know this to be totally absurd.... Humans are the weakest of all creatures.... able to survive only through the exercise of rationality.... But rationality is a curse, since it can cause humans to forget the natural order of things, in ways other creatures do not.... We pray our thanks to the Deer, our Relations, for allowing us their flesh to eat. Europeans simply take the flesh for granted and consider the deer inferior....
>
> All European tradition, Marxism included, has conspired to defy the Natural Order of Things. Mother Earth has been abused. The powers have been abused. And this cannot go on for ever....
>
> Mother Earth will retaliate. The powers will retaliate, and the abusers will be eliminated. Things come full circle, back to where they started: that's revolution. And that's the prophesy of my people, of the Hopi people, and of other Correct Peoples.... It's only a matter of time before what Europeans call *"a major catastrophe of global proportions"* will occur. It's the role of American Indian Peoples, of all Natural Beings, to survive. A part of our survival is to resist—resist not to overthrow a government or take political power, but because it's natural to resist extermination, to survive. We don't want power over white institutions. We want white institutions to disappear.... When I use the term "European" I'm not referring to a skin colour or a particular genetic structure. What I'm referring to is a Mindset, a World View that is a product of the development of European culture.... the Death Culture.

First peoples: Safeguarding the earth

In India, there is no dividing line between Adivasi religion and Hinduism. In Dharni penu, the Konds use a Sanskrit word for their earth deity. They take part in the *Jagannath Yatra* and *Shiv Ratri* festivals, but have no use for Brahmin priests as intermediaries. Their own *Jani, Dissari, Beju* and *Bejuni* seek guidance from dreams and trance.

Tribal religion is at one with their economy, based on cultivating the soil with skills that go back hundreds of years, long before the age of fertilisers, which in Adivasi eyes dry out the soil and 'addict' it. Their pride in the fields they make through hard labour on steep hill-sides is at the heart of Adivasi culture—something which outsiders rarely comprehend. The policy of displacing them and turning them into an industrial labour force destroys this culture, without even acknowledging that it exists. Yet Adivasis are literally India's First People, and their cultures are certainly among India's oldest. Moreover, they are still rooted in the soil. Where else does India's culture exist? In its famous musical, literary, textile traditions or cuisine? These became marketed and lost most of their connection with the soil a long time ago. Adivasis have sustained their culture in the original sense of *cultus*, cultivating the soil with a cult of the earth.

This sense of sacredness in nature goes along with an outstanding sense of community. Tribal villages are models of real democracy, in its original sense of *demo-kratia* (people power), unmediated by political ideology and rival parties. Decisions are to be reached through open discussion and consensus, sitting on the ground. Adivasi society is radically egalitarian in the equal importance it gives to male and female, elder and younger, and rich and poor. Respect for elders and male prominence is balanced by an essential equality. Status often depends on the number of sons, as well as a person's altruism, doing what's right on behalf of the whole community. The norm in tribal culture is for those with more food to share with those who have less.

This is not a romantic view. Tribal society has its shadow side, and has often been corrupted, not least by the hierarchical tendency emphasised by the British rulers when they bolstered the status of headmen. But the sense of community in non-tribal as well as tribal villages now struggling to maintain their existence in the face of corporate takeover comes very close to Gandhi's ideal of village India, largely self-sufficient and non-dependent on outsiders for food or other necessities of life.

Unlike Gandhi's ideal, however, Adivasis are not vegetarian. They hunt and kill animals to eat. They drink and swing their axes in anger. Many have been drawn to the Naxalite path. Yet the movements we describe in this book are remarkably non-violent, partly from the sense that this is more effective—since violence is invariably met by much greater violence from the security forces—and partly from the example of Gandhi and countless other activists in the tradition of *ahimsa*.

We will have to start a process of learning from tribal people if we are to survive as a species—a process of relearning or reintegrating what many of us lost many generations ago, which comes down to a sense of real community and rootedness in the soil. The starting point is that we have to comprehend the ways in which tribal people are more highly developed than mainstream society, because they have developed and maintained the principle of real, i.e. long-term, sustainability by limiting consumption and individual wealth.

Dongria

When a tribal elder asks, 'We're all saints here—where are the saints in your society?', he is referring to a control on greed, the principles of sharing and living simply, close to the earth, minimising one's wants—an ideal that has been strong in all the main religions, and used to be very strong in India. At present the globalising economy appears to be weakening it. Relearning the art of minimal needs is becoming essential for human survival now. Adivasis are our best teachers.

Many tourists, flying to India from other countries in the aluminium birds, take a 'tribal tour' from Puri, photographing Adivasis dancing for money. Many Indians travel the other way in the aluminium birds, seeking their fortune in foreign lands. But India's real culture exists in the villages, preserving a material culture and values going back thousands of years—things one cannot take a picture of, patronise or possess. The attempt to do so damages the product.

This is something one can only be open to, or not. The mainstream tendency is still to despise tribal culture, seeing it as something old-fashioned, to be swept away, and preserved only in museums and dance programmes.

Bathing in a clean stream is not only quintessential to the quality of life Adivasis lose when industry invades, but also to the joys we could all relearn. Sustainability means freely flowing water, not dams.

When Adivasis are displaced from their land and turned into industrial labourers, or their sacred mountains are mined, 'company man' cannot comprehend the enormity of what is lost, or people's outrage at this wanton destruction. Cultural genocide is accompanied by a permanent destruction of the environment and its life-giving fertility. Those taking the key decisions to allow mining throughout tribal territories do not yet realise what is at stake. Or is it that they no longer care about the future of this earth?

Niyam Raja, the presiding deity of Niyamgiri, epitomises Adivasis' sense of a Law implicit in creation—*Dharma*. In standing up for their rights and refusing to be displaced, they are protecting not just themselves, and not only their offspring and future generations. They are protecting the earth for all of us, and preserving our natural environment at a time when it is mightily challenged by global heating and other man-made horrors. They are standing up to protect our future as a species.

But Adivasis' viewpoint is still rarely taken seriously. Recognising the power in nature and the sacredness of mountains, streams and other natural features is central to tribal values. Adivasi religion does not build temples on its most sacred spots. *Gudi*s (shrines), in remote parts of the forest, are simple structures. For any sacrifice, a *mandala* is made of fresh leaves and grains. Most big festivals mark the sowing of seeds or collecting of first fruits. Processes of taking from nature and growing crops are based in a sense of sacredness that contrasts starkly with the proliferation of fertilisers, pesticides, biotechnology and biofuels, and with nearly every feature of modern farming, culminating in unrepayable debts and farmers' suicides.

America's tribal peoples are often more outspoken, from their history of facing waves of genocide. Their message is passed on in works such as those of Eric Fromm (*To Have or to Be?* 1976), Murray Bookchin (*Ecology of Freedom* 1982), Jerry Mander (*In the Absence of the Sacred* 1992) and many others. In the words of Russell Means, again:

> Being is a spiritual proposition. Gaining is a material act. Traditionally, American Indians have always attempted to be the best people they could. Part of that spiritual process was, and is, to give away wealth—to discard wealth, in order not to gain. *Material gain is an indicator of false status among Traditional People*, while it is "proof that the system works" to Europeans....
>
> But let's look at a major implication of this. It's not merely an intellectual debate. *The European materialist tradition of de-spiritualizing the Universe is very similar to the mental process that goes into dehumanizing another person.* And who seems most expert at dehumanizing other people, and why? Soldiers.... learn to do this to the enemy before going.... into combat. Nazi SS guards did it to concentration camp inmates. Cops do it. Corporation leaders do it to the workers they send into the uranium mines and steel mills. Politicians do it to everyone in sight. And what the process has in common for each group doing the dehumanizing is that it makes it "alright" to kill and otherwise destroy other people....
>
> In terms of the de-spiritualization of the Universe, the mental process works so that it becomes 'virtuous' to destroy the planet.

Terms like "progress" and "development" are used as cover-words here, the way "victory" and "freedom" are used to justify butchery and the de-humanization process. For example, a Real Estate Agent may refer to "developing" a parcel of ground by opening a gravel quarry. "Development" here means total permanent destruction, with the earth itself removed. But the European logic has "gained" a few tons of gravel, with which some more land can be "developed" through the construction of road beds. Ultimately the whole Universe is open, in the European view, to this kind of insanity.

Most important here perhaps is that Europeans feel no sense of loss in this. After all, their philosophers have de-spiritualized reality, so there is no satisfaction for them to be gained in simply observing the wonder of a mountain, or a lake, or a people, in Being. No, satisfaction is measured in terms of gaining material, so the mountain becomes gravel [or aluminium], and the lake [or river] becomes coolant for a factory, and the people are rounded up for "processing" through the indoctrination-mills Europeans like to call "schools".

But each new piece of that "progress" ups the ante out in the real world. Take fuel for the industrial machine as an example. Little more than two centuries ago, nearly everyone used wood—a replenishable, natural item—as fuel for the very human needs of cooking and staying warm. Along came the Industrial Revolution, and coal became the dominant fuel. As production became the social imperative for Europe, pollution began to become a problem in the cities, and the earth was ripped open to provide coal.... Later, oil became the major fuel.... Pollution increased dramatically, and nobody yet knows what the environmental cost of pumping all that oil out of the ground will really be in the long run. Now there's an energy crisis, and uranium is becoming the dominant fuel.... (1982, emphasis ours)

Like the growing of food, the issue of mining and metals is not peripheral to any of our lives, whether the mines and metals factories are on our doorstep or far away in remote areas, where people seen as 'marginal' by the mainstream are being *sacrificed* to 'benefit' the rest of us. The people being dispossessed are precisely those humans who are still living most sustainably. Displacing them is a modern version of human sacrifice, and it is a process that leads inevitably to our own destruction too. Unless we can find a way to control the companies and their out-of-order doctrine of quick profit, we sacrifice our collective future too.

Naveen Patnaik clearly believes that the mining projects he has promoted will bring prosperity to Odisha. So it is worth quoting words he wrote introducing a beautiful book published before he became Chief Minister, on India's tradition of using plants for healing—a tradition still very strong among the Dongria and many other tribes. He starts by saying that Ayurveda is

> based on knowledge and an awareness that man is interdependent with all other forms of life. Spirit is described as the intelligence of life, matter as its energy. Both are manifestations of the principle of Brahman, the one-ness of life.... The man who recognises how he is linked with universal life is a man who possesses a sound soul because he is not isolated from his own energies, nor from the energies of nature. But as the highest form of life, man also becomes its guardian, recognising his very survival depends on seeing that the fragile balance of nature, and living organisms, is not disturbed.
>
> In Ayurvedic terms, this means that man must prevent wanton destruction. What he takes he must replace, to preserve the equilibrium of nature. If he cuts down a tree for his own use, he must plant another. He must ensure the purity of water. He must not poison the air. He must not poison the soil. Ayurveda, some four thousand years ago, was already propagating the arguments which inform the ecological debate of our own time.... If a man wilfully disturbed the balance of living things he inevitably damaged himself.... The destruction of forests and the pollution of water was banned by imperial edicts carved on rock.... which continue to astonish the contemporary mind with their extraordinary and compassionate vision.[17]

One could hardly make a clearer statement of the philosophy of Ayurveda and *Vedanta:* the harm one does to others or to nature, one does to one's own soul. Cutting off from an awareness of our interdependence with nature is very dangerous, because it leads people to destroy and pollute the sources of life, accelerating our own destruction. The highest mission of man is to be a guardian of nature.

Respecting and guarding nature is what Adivasi culture is all about. True, when the system of exploitation gets on top of tribal people, they too can turn against nature and destroy it. Top-down forestry regulations have been counterproductive, eroding a balance between tribal culture and the forest that sustained for centuries. The tribal areas between India's kingdoms preserved areas of outstanding forest and wildlife better than Europe, where a pattern of domination of nature and conquering/converting tribal peoples was the norm since the time of Roman conquest. The reason that India's balance is threatened now is that the European pattern of exploitation has entered Indian culture through the power of the company.

Yet, against all odds, tribal cultures survive. Adivasis keep alive a culture and values based on safeguarding nature, knowing that they face extinction if they lose their land. The non-alienability of tribal land is guaranteed by India's Constitution because without their land, their culture dies, and so does India's environment. In Dandu Sikoka's words, '*We need the Mountain and the Mountain needs us.*'

Developing wisdom

How to draw conclusions from the material in this book? What should be done about the aluminium industry?

What we are not saying is that it should all stop at once. What we are saying is that to allow more growth of the industry into unspoilt areas of Odisha, Andhra Pradesh, Chhattisgarh, Iceland, Jamaica, Trinidad, Vietnam, Indonesia or anywhere else is an assault against the communities who live there as well as against the fabric of life itself. The age is past when we can perpetuate this mode of unconscious human sacrifice any longer. More people are becoming more and more aware that this pattern is also a sacrifice of future generations. To nurture the lives of future generations as yet unborn and undreamt of, we need to preserve the minerals in the mountains, for the fertility they promote as well as for future mineral needs.

Aluminium's ability to be recycled without loss in quality needs to be actualised much more widely, while strict controls need to be in place against more 'greenfield' bauxite mines, refineries or smelters. The aim should now be to lower aluminium consumption in India and every country.

If 'Sustainable Development' is the correct way forward, the original meaning of *sustainability* has to be asserted over the gross misuse of the concept by MMSD and the corporate lobby groups. Sustainable development, in Brundtland's words, means satisfying the needs of the present without sacrificing the needs of future generations. To plan responsibly, we should be thinking in terms of a thousand years or more, and in terms of preserving nature without polluting it.

Climate change scientists advise that if we fail to make a 90 per cent cut in emissions within the next ten years, runaway global heating will almost certainly destroy us, or our children.[18] The inability to agree on decisive cuts at Copenhagen (December 2009) shows manipulation by the corporations and their lobby groups, flooding us all out with money. It also shows a lack of shared understanding that we are all in this together: rich countries have to accept drastic cuts, and 'developing countries' have to cut back radically on new industrial projects, which are basically serving financial interests in London and other top capitals. An elite in India is getting a slice, thousands of people are getting work in the first burst of activity, but thousands have lost their well-being altogether, and the influx of money will not be able to lead to a sustainable income, since it is based on *permanent extraction* of non-renewable resources.

We hope this book has shown how the new mining and metal factories in East India are being driven by a nexus of interlocking deals: deals in London, at the London Metal Exchange etc., over future contracts for supply and demand, deals with central and state govenments over MoUs and subsidies in electricity, water, transport, coal etc. Deals with the banks investing in mining companies: a spider's web of deals for loans, in a state that is already (one of) the most indebted in India.

At the Lanjigarh refinery, numerous companies are involved. Larsen & Toubro is presently (2010) building 88 new precipitation tanks, each 36 metres high and 12 metres in diameter, as well as major construction works. It employs a workforce of about 3,000 workers. The dust pollution they endure causes severe respiratory problems, with hundreds of lorries and other vehicles operating in and coming to the factory. Workers' health is not properly maintained, despite lip-service to 'best practice' rules. The dust in the refinery is a major problem, and required water-sprinkling 'makes it better for barely ten minutes.' Mecon Ltd is a major engineering firm, with contracts for Ashapura, Jindal and Vanasree group in Odisha (that is, their plans for mining Mali Parbat and other mountains and making nearby refineries), for Nalco and Jindal (S.Kota refinery) plans in Andhra, for Aditya Birla and Jindal plants in Jharkhand, for Birla copper and Sterlite zinc projects, and Zoom aluminium group in Oman.[19]

The Bansadhara river is badly polluted. The Bheden river near the Burkhamunda smelter in Jharsaguda river is polluted with fluoride, and if all the fish have died in the vicinity of five villages after the smelter has been running for a year, what is the long-term damage to the environment? Where will thousands of people go, whose families have drunk and bathed here for centuries?[20] Will they stay to slowly die, or join the numberless thousands of displaced, moving to slums and insecure work in cities?

New tarmac roads have been built during 2006–9 into the heart of Niyamgiri, overseen by the Dongria Kondh Development Agency, and funded by the PM's fund for new roads. Timber mafia have used these roads to bring lakhs-worth of timber out, deforesting the mountains, while an elite of local Dongrias and Dalits have been given motorbikes, mobiles and smart clothes to close the area to people seen to be against working the company's interests.

The events of November–December 2009 in the Narayanpatna area of Koraput district, south Odisha, show a descent into war by the state, in the name of defeating Maoists. In effect this is a 'resource war' instigated by the landowning classes (from whom Adivasis of the CMAS had taken back their alienated lands), in collusion with *goondas* pushing the interests of mining companies, trying to force access to the bauxite deposits covering Kodinga Mali, Mali Parbat and Deo Mali (Odisha's highest mountain). Behind the *goondas,* our evidence shows clearly that foreign financial interests are driving this violence. Maoists are the excuse. It seems that their support for the CMAS gave the forces representing these financial interests an excuse to start a programme of severe repression.[21]

Real development has to work at every level, not just material increase. Material growth leads to corruption and negates real development, unless there is also ethical growth, which involves a widespread growth of awareness and self-restraint; and a growth in people's fundamental rights, through the community and cooperative organisations, and through laws that are implemented equally for everyone—a return to the Rights of Man, but expanded to include the rights of women, children and future generations. This means that the rights of other species in nature must also be preserved and protected.

The recession that started in October 2008 showed the insanity of the old order of unbridled capitalism. If a new order of sustainable development is to arise from the ashes, we need to impose strict limits on growth and the exploitation of minerals. Moreover, there has to be a ceiling on private property, so that the wealth of company directors does not grow at the expense of other people's misery.

The mainstream models of economic growth, which we have analysed as the world's most dangerous fundamentalism, need to be shown up for the fallacy they are. As we write, the insane bubble built on derivatives-trading is bursting and many metal prices have fallen dramatically, slowing down some of the projects we write about. Industrialisation, as Gandhi saw it, should mean a return to small-scale local industries, which would not only improve the lives of workers and consumers alike, but also narrow the gap between working and consuming. Complementing millions of indigenous cultivators, Odisha, along with the whole of East India, has been for centuries the centre of countless manufacturing traditions, including weaving and indigenous metal-work: crafts that are dying off fast in the face of corporate competition, and deserve a strong revival. There is no lack of alternatives on our earth. *Bikalpaheen nahi hai duniya.*[22]

Notes

Chapter 1

1. www.alcoa.com, consulted 2005 and since.
2. Kishen Pattnayak, in an unpublished piece on mining he wrote shortly before his death in 2004. He expressed similar views in his article 'Visions of development...' (2004).
3. Indian *Power Sector Reforms* Prayas and C. S. Venkata Ratnam 2003.
4. Nalco is the only remaining public sector aluminium company. Its near-privatisation in 2002–3 was modelled on Sterlite's takeover of Balco in 2001, at a price estimated at only a tenth or less of its actual value (Bidwai 2001).
5. Nehru to Gandhi, 9 October 1945, from 'Selected Letters' in *The Selected Works of Mahatma Gandhi*, vol. V, pp. 122–25.
6. G. D. Birla, *Towards Swadeshi: Wide-ranging Correspondence with Gandhiji*, ed. V. B. Kulkarni, Bombay: Bharatiya Vidya Bhavan, 1980, p. 118, and Karunakar Supkar 2007, pp. 28–32. Birla's appeal to Orissa's High Court was on 30 October 1953. Also see *Mystery of Birla House* (Burman 1950), in which a senior Tax Commissioner, focused on tax evasion by Birla's Orient Paper Mill.

Chapter 2

1. This and the following quotations are from *The Secrets of Metals* (Pelikan 1973, pp. 151–53).
2. The formula for the calcium type of feldspar is $CaO\ Al_2O_3\ SiO_2$. Aluminium is reckoned to form 8 per cent of the earth's crust, the third commonest element after oxygen (50 per cent) and silicon (25 per cent). Commoner than iron (4 per cent), and other minerals, all less than 1 per cent, including copper (0.01 per cent), zinc (0.004 per cent), lead (0.002 per cent), tin (0.001 per cent), uranium (0.0004 per cent), silver (0.00001 per cent), and gold (0.000001). See also Hauschka (1966/1983, pp. 132–35).
3. This is the view from scientists in the tradition of Rudolf Steiner. Pelikan (1973), Cloos (1977) and Hauschka (1966/1983) follow the tradition of Goethe's scientific work, via Rudolf Steiner, as do Tompkins and Bird

(1998), and J. P. S. Uberoi (1984) in *The Other Mind of Europe: Goethe as a Scientist*. This Goethian or Steiner-inspired tradition of science is fundamental for a holistic understanding of how matter combines with spirit. This tradition has many links with Ayurveda and other branches of ancient Indian science.

4. Hauschka (1966/1983, p. 118), Tompkins and Bird (1998 pp. xiv–xxiii and *passim*), Paul Hepperly at www.NewFarm.org/columns/research_paul/2005/aug05/ghana2_/prints.html, on how aluminium ions are put into harmful solution by chemical fertilisers. *Silent Spring* (Rachel Carson 1962) is the best-known critique of the pesticide-fertiliser industry.

5. Tompkins and Bird give references to the links between chemical fertilisers and the arms industry (1998, pp. xiv–xxiii), as well as the seminal works which have studied humus and the living soil, including Sir Albert Howard's *Agricultural Testament* and *Soil and Health* (inaugurating the movement for organic farming from years of research that learnt from traditional Indian methods), Lady Eve Balfour's *The Living Soil* (and founding of the *Soil Association*), and J. S. Joffe's *Pedology* (1936, revised as *The ABC of Soils* 1949, Tompkins and Bird, p. 118 ff). Prof. P. K. Senapati of Sambalpur University has revived this need for a Pedology (from the Greek, *to pedon*: the earth) to study the 'pedosphere' as a whole and on an equal basis to scientific study of the 'biosphere' and the 'atmosphere'. Particularly urgent in areas such as Odisha, which are poised to implement huge industries whose devastating long-term effects on the soil and geology have not been properly studied.

6. *Mapoon—Book Three* (Roberts and McLean 1976, p. 84) quotes articles by botanists on the evolution of flowering plants on Cape York, as an indication of bauxite's link with areas of the world's best forests.

7. Alum and Alunite are classed as sulphates of aluminium, mixed with sodium and potassium: $Al_2(SO_4)_3 + 6NaOH$, and $Al(SO_4)_2 + 12H_2O$.

8. *Elements of Chemical Philosophy* (Davy 1812) reviewed in *Quarterly Review* no. 15, September 1812, pp. 65–85.

9. Deville published his book *De l'Aluminium* in 1859. Alfred Rangod, who named the company Pechiney, took over the Salindres factory from Merle in 1877.

10. G. D. Smith (1988, pp. 21–22 and 39) on the Cowles-Pittsburgh controversy. As Holloway 1988 summarises this (p. 16): 'In an out-of-court settlement (1893), Pittsburgh Reduction paid Cowles $1.4 million to stop producing aluminium.'

11. G. D. Smith, (p. 34) gives a price list showing the dramatic fall in price from $545 for a pound (1852), $113 (1855), $34 (1856), $11–12 (1862–86), $8 (1887–88), $4+ (1888–89), $1–2 (1890–91), 86 cents (1892) to 36 cents (1897).

12. Alcan, *Aluminium and the Sea* (no date), printed by Alcan Aerospace, Transportation and Industry.

13. G. D. Smith (1988, pp. 86–87 and 127).
14. On the first cartels, see Chapter Eleven. Shorter summaries are in Holloway (1988) and Lynch (2002, p. 284), who highlights the 1901 cartel and the French cartel, L'Aluminium Français, which the three French firms formed in 1911.
15. British Aluminium Company [BAC] (1955, pp. 39–41), and Andrew Perchard 2008, 'Sculpting the "Garden of Eden": Patronage, Community and the British Aluminium Company in the Scottish Highlands, 1895–1982', paper presented to a seminar on bauxite in Paris 1982, part of a forthcoming book, *Aluminiumville: Metal, the British Government and the Scottish Highlands*.
16. Roberts and McLean (1976, pp. 86–89) on the process of laterisation. Only in Greece is bauxite mined underground.
17. *Times of India*, 30 December 2006, p. 3.
18. Polychlorinated biphenyls, mentioned by Greer and Bruno (1996, p. 175), in a chapter devoted to Alcoa's pollution who also mention the Fluoro-Carbons, which Dean Abrahamson of Minnesota University has researched on.
19. Graham (1982, p. 19); BAC (1955, p. 18 ff); Fox (1932, pp. 192–93).
20. The Mellon and art side of the story is told in Cannadine's biography of Mellon (2006, pp. 410–27). On the Volkhov smelter near Leningrad, built with Alcoa help from 1931, and dismantled ahead of the Nazi advance, see Lynch (2002, pp. 295 and 301). The Bogoslovsk smelter produced its first aluminium on 14 May 1932. Novohuznetsk was the first smelter in Siberia (started 1943–45). Among the first refineries was Tikhvin/Boxitogorsk (dismantled and taken to Siberia in 1938).
21. Aluminium has 60 per cent the conductivity of copper, yet is lighter and corrodes less (Nwoke 1987, p. 138).
22. G. D. Smith (1988). Graham (1982) and Holloway (1988 p. 23 and *passim*) on how Alcoa manipulated the world cartel.
23. Barham and Bunker (1995, pp. 57–58).
24. Graham (pp. 68 and 176).
25. Peter Colley, 'Political Economy of Mining' in Evans, Goodman and Lansbury 2002, p. 21.
26. Gitlitz (1993); Martinez-Alier (2002, p. 63).

Chapter 3

1. 'The Challenge of India's Iron Wealth', by Shilpa Kannan, Business reporter, *BBC News India Business Report*.
2. Nayak and Kujur (2007).

3. R. Thapar 1961, pp. 255–57. The first and second passages are from the 13th Rock Edict, the third is in the Odisha inscriptions.
4. Walter Fernandes (1992, 1997, 2006, p. 110).
5. This is extensively documented in A. Eschmann, H. Kulke and G. C. Tripathi (eds.), *The Cult of Jagannath and the Regional Tradition of Orissa*, Delhi: Manohar 1978.
6. Kui is officially the north-eastern form of the language spoken in Kandhamal district, and Kubi or Kuwi the form spoken towards the south. In fact, there is a vast range of dialects that merge into each other.
7. For example, *Feudatory States of Orissa* (Cobden-Ramsay 1910).
8. Gopinath Mohanty's autobiography (2000), *Sroto Swati*, Part III, p. 324.
9. *The East Coast Bauxite Deposits of India* (Rao and Raman 1979) raised India's estimated bauxite deposits from 350 million tons in 1971 to 2,000 million tons in 1977. Compare Weipa's estimated 1,200 million tons (the largest single deposit). India's deposits now stand at 2,300–3,000 million tons accouring for instance, to Patricia A. Plunkert, American Aluminum Industry: A Period in Transition. US Geological Survey, 2004.
10. KBK refers to Koraput, Bolangir and Kalahandi, the three old districts that have since been divided into eight: from former Koraput have come Rayagada, Nowrangpur and Malkangiri; from Bolangir, Sonepur; and, from Kalahandi, Nuaparna.
11. The purity of Odisha's bauxite consists in its high alumina and low silica content, with an average of less than 4 per cent silica, less than 2 per cent titanium, 8–28 per cent iron, and 42–56 per cent alumina, similar to the 52 per cent average near Les Baux.
12. Sasu-Bohu is also called Anmala Mali and merges with Indragiri.
13. *Sal* (*Shorea Robusta*) is one of India's main forest and timber trees. *Amla* is an important plant with bitter berries, used in medicines and hair oil.
14. Kautilya's *Arthashastra*, ed. R. P. Kangle, Bombay: Bombay University Press, 1963, book 2, sections 26 ('Misappropriation of revenue by officers and its recovery') and 30 ('Starting of mines and factories').
15. Padel (2000 [1995], pp. 240–41, 261–63).
16. Russell (1836) and Elphinstone (1841), cited in Padel 2000 (1995), p. 179.
17. The MMSD Report, *Breaking New Ground* was published in 2002. In November 2005, the MMSD negotiated with the IUCN for access to certain protected areas. *Rich Lands, Poor People: Is "Sustainable" Mining Possible?* (Centre for Science and Environment 2008) catalogues the non-sustainable nature of mining in India, which degrades the environment and displaces millions of Adivasis.
18. Evans, Goodman and Lansbury (2002).

19. A Kond song from a village on the shores of the Indravati reservoir near Padepadar, taught to us by Nimai Majhi. This features in *Matiro Poko, Company Loko*.

Chapter 4

1. Gitlitz (1993), McCully (1996).
2. Prebble (1963).
3. Richard Cowen, 'Geology, History and People', chapter 14 (Cartels and the aluminium industry), www.geology.ucdavis.edu/~cowen/~GEL115/1 15CH14aluminium.html.
4. Gitlitz (1993, p. 29), quotes the following statistics from the US Bureau of Mines and other sources: over 6 per cent of worldwide hydropower is used for aluminium plants; 61 out of 84 smelters in the top ten aluminium-producing countries (excluding China, data lacking) use hydropower (1990); 93 out of 152 smelters in 31 out of 40 countries worldwide use hydropower; 18 per cent of world electricity demand is met by hydropower (p. 4); in India, 34 per cent of aluminium production uses hydropower (p. 30), probably an underestimate.
5. Ritthoff et al. (2002).
6. Gitlitz (1993 p. 19) follows the US Bureau of Mines in estimating electricity as the second highest cost (21 per cent) in smelting aluminium after material inputs of alumina, coal, coke, soda and lime (31 per cent), which should properly be considered separate components. Other studies put the electricity cost as nearer 30 per cent of total costs.
7. Gitlitz (1993, chapters 7 and 11).
8. Officially, 33.6 per cent of power goes to industry according to the Planning Commission of India, 1999, (Rangachari et al. 2000, p. 147).
9. Rangachari et al (2000), gives 1998 figures: 21,891 MW hydropower out of a total of 89,000 MW generated in India, i.e. approx. 25 per cent. This dropped from around 50 per cent in 1963.
10. The difference between living and dead water is brought out in Theodor Schwarz, *Sensitive Chaos: The Creation of Flowing Forms in Water and Air* (translated 1966), Rudolf Steiner Press, 1996, and the film, *What the Bleep Do We Know* (2004), by William Arntz and Betsy Chasse, which shows the extraordinary difference in crystals of water.
11. *World Aluminium Newsletter*, June 2006, London: IAI, p. 6.
12. Fernandes (2006, p. 109).
13. World Commission on Dams, and independent assessment by Lokayan, etc., 1999–2001, pdf.wri.org/wcd_back.pdf, http://www.wcdassessment.org.
14. Some of this history is referred to in an article *'Sarkar Javaab Diantu'* ('Government, explain') in *Dharitri* newspaper by B. Krishna Dhalo, 23 October 2007.

15. No proper study was made of the Hirakud displaced until Viegas 1992. Odisha's last British Governor, Sir Harthrun Lewis, laid the stone in 1946. Of 285 villages displaced, 249 were in Sambalpur district and 36 in Raigarh. Their estimated population was 22,144 families, i.e. 110,000–180,000 people. Of these only 11 per cent (or 4,744 families) were resettled in 'colonies' about 50 km away; the rest were left to fend for themselves. Rangachari et al. (2000) gives 80,000 as the number of displaced. Compensation for land was given in cash. Tribal landowners who lacked written ownership documents were often excluded. The low sums, and the demeaning and corrupt way the cash was given, were notorious. The cash was quickly spent. The dam is claimed to be the world's longest at 5 km, supplemented by earthen dykes on either side (another 21 km). The agricultural land submerged (nearly 120,000 acres) was famous for its rice. Prime forest (another 50,000 acres or so) was also lost.
16. Paschim Orissa Krushak Sangathan Samanbaya Samiti, in *New Indian Express*, Bhubaneswar, 27 September 2007.
17. Articles in *New Indian Express*, Bhubaneswar: 'No Hirakud water for industries', 8 November 2007, front page; 'Industries eye other dams too', 26 November 2007, front page ('Currently 13 industries are drawing water from Hirakud and another 20 are in agreement with the government to do the same'); 'Naveen's water woes overflowing', 27 November 2007, p. 3; 'Farmers reject Naveen largesse', 28 November 2008, p. 6; 'Industries default on water cess', 28 December 2007, p. 6. Also POKSSS 2008.
18. Articles in *Economic and Political Weekly*: Rajagopalam et al. (1981) Subrahmanyan (1982).
19. Muthayya (1984) says the refinery displaced 15 villages fully (610 families = 2,368 people), and partially displaced four more (178 families = 736 people).
20. CSE (2008). Vijay and the Bahinipati family are our source for the number of work deaths, etc.
21. Initially it was estimated that 6,400 families would be affected in 147 villages, but government estimates kept changing, and displacement took place in several phases between 1984 and 1990 as the water level rose, so that 'there is no consistency in the data available from different sources. Government data is also not consistent' (survey by Bipin Jojo 2002). The final official estimate was that 53 villages were displaced, 26 of them fully, i.e. 3,180 families (c.14,000 people). No information is available on another 57 villages, and some estimates put the figures much higher at 13,095 families from 149 villages (= over 50,000 people). S. C. Mohanty 2006 estimates 3,067 famiies as fully displaced, from 50 villages fully submerged.
22. Mohanty et al. (2004, p. 33), in an article by Golak Bihari Nath. Samarendra visited this man's family in 2005, shortly before he was due for release.

23. Rangachari et al. (2000) lists just over 4,000 oustees, but there may have been many more.
24. Newspaper reports: *Indian Express* and *Asian Age*, 1–11 January 2001.
25. It seems that the effluent treatment was by Mitsui. Norad gave Rs 40 crore for Odisha's environment, in a five-year plan from 1992–97, including Rs 1.2 crore to DAG (District Action Group, an alliance of 21 NGOs in Angul District), which highlighted the pollution. This funding reportedly dried up after a senior Norwegian government official held secret talks with the GoO.
26. This SC Monitoring Committee report is item 34 in Environment Protection Group Orissa's website (freewebs.com/epgOrissa). A fertiliser factory upstream at Talcher is another source of pollution for these rivers. A number of films have been made about the pollution of the Nandira river by these plants.
27. Sterlite and Tata were the only other bidders from India. Other foreign bidders included Pechiney, Alcoa, and Glencore. The Central Government Cabinet Committee on Disinvestment (under Arun Shourie) planned to divest nearly 30 per cent of the government's equity in the project, giving a controlling stake to a 'strategic partner'. See V. Sridhar (2003). GoI, *Ministry of Mines: Annual Report 2002–3* (pp. 45, 47), describes the policy after mentioning disaffection by workers: 'The government has taken a decision to further disinvest 30 per cent equity of Nalco through a public offer (in the mix of domestic market 10 per cent and through ADR 20 per cent) and sale of 29.15 per cent equity to a strategic partner bringing the government equity down to 26 per cent after reserving up to 2 per cent of the equity for Nalco employees.' On the attempt to disinvest 20 per cent under Naveen Patnaik in the 1990s, see 'Nalco exposes political parties' *Financial Express*, 3 July 2006, at http://www.financialexpress.com/news/nalco-issue-exposes-political-parties/162140/0.
28. GoI, *Ministry of Mines: Annual Report 2002–3*, pp. 43–44 has a photo of this giant cheque. Nalco's report for 2000–01 shows export sales increasing from 37.69 per cent (1998–99) to 45.50 per cent (1999–2000) and 51.25 per cent (2000–01), while sales within India went down from 52.13 per cent to 42.68 per cent.
29. Muthayya (1984, p. 2). It would be next to impossible to work out how much of Nalco's profits went to Pechiney, as the standard practice is to hide this through technology transfer and transfer pricing (see Chapter Eleven).
30. Quoting Jyotirmoy Khora, from P. Sainath (1986, pp. 88–97). 'Encroaching' is a particularly misused term, as our late guide Kumuda Chandra Mullick always stressed. Whereas richer landowners and 'developers' are constantly encroaching or appropriating land that has been worked for generations by Adivasis, the term is twisted around and applied to Adivasis who do not hold the written document of land title

(*patta*), which law requires, but which they have never been given, since traditionally, customary recognition of their land rights was enough. *The Nowhere People* is the title of the book on displacement (edited by Silby Thakaran), in which Jojo's article on the Upper Kolab is published.
31. *New Indian Express*, Bhubaneswar edition, 20 January 2007, p. 7, and 21 December 2007, front page: 'Boeing outsources work to HAL'.
32. On the Hasdeo Bango villages: PIL lodged in Raipur High Court by Herambo Prasad (Deshbandhu 180304). The Amarkantak and Phutka Pahar deposits are situated on mountains 40 km west and 32 km north of Korba. Both were surveyed by the Geological Survey of India. An article by A. K. Nandi in *BAUXMET 1998: Proceedings of Interactive Meet on Bauxite, 6–7 March* (p. 85 ff) is entitled 'Mine leasing policies ... problems to start mining operations: case history of BALCO'.
33. *Onlooker*, 1–15 July 1986: 'Adivasis up in Arms to Save Nature'—one of the first articles highlighting the Gandhamardan movement. See also Meena Menon in *The Hindu Survey of the Environment* (2001), p. 148, and BALCO 1983.
34. *Dams, Rivers and People*, (January 2005, p. 9–10), giving the HC order as WP (C) No. 13232 of 2004. The villages named are Pardhiapali, Dunguripali and Koindapali of Loisingha Block. The interviews mentioned, from later in 2005, feature in *Matiro Poko*.
35. *State of Orissa's Environment: A Citizens' Report*, 1994, Bhubaneswar: Manoj Pradhan and Council of Professional Social Workers, Chapter 5 on Water. Arundhati' Roys *Costing the Earth* and Patrick McCully's *Silenced Rivers* highlight the problems of dams, but reveal little about the foreign construction companies involved in building India's dams, whose profits from dams are among the biggest.
36. *State of Orissa's Environment*, p. 144–45.
37. Caufield (1998, p. 227), quoting her own interview with a WB consultant, which we return to at the start of Chapter Seventeen, on the WB.
38. In denying promised electricity to villages, the Indravati dam resembles Ghana's notorious Akosombo (Chapter Nine), and hydro-dams in many other countries.
39. Agragamee Plan and Budget, (2000, p. 29). Agragamee started work in Kashipur in 1987. When we visited the NGO's Padepadar centre in December 2002, it employed 16 full-time workers, and an Animator in each village, paid Rs 1,000 a month.

Chapter 5

1. This special English-language issue of the paper for Rajiv's visit, with its open attack on government corruption, has been pretty much suppressed since. Kishenji's Writ Petition no. 12847 of 1985 is highlighted in Rabi Dash (1998, pp. 1–9).

2. The ITDA was created in the 1950s, modelled on Elwin's 'philosophy for NEFA' (North-East Frontier Agency) as a basis for administration of India's tribal areas. The OTDP was set up by IFAD in Rayagada/Kashipur to try and liaise with villagers. Both ITDA and OTDP were under the same Project Director, delegating authority to a Project Management Unit (PMU) in Kashipur. It was intended to employ between 64 and 138 staff, but housing had to be constructed to attract staff, delaying the project considerably. Eighty-five staff houses were constructed by 1993, by which time 132 were employed, with the conspicuous absence of a Project Accountant—a glaring omission, given later charges of gross misappropriation of funds in the project!
3. Among the OTDP's main activities were (according to the project's mid-term report, 1993):
(i) HRD (Human Resource Development), whose 'software component' involved 'improving awareness among villagers of environmental, economic and social problems, and stimulating their demand for the development services', plus identifying planning and training needs; and whose 'hardware' component involved a 'Model Village Scheme', to fund investments for 'educational facilities, commercial services and market improvements', etc. By 1993 this work was initiated in only seven out of the 24 projected villages, and 'HRD expenditure [was] substantially behind appraisal projections'.
(ii) NRD (Natural Resource Development), included 'vegetative bunding' (carried out by 1993 on 2,700 hectares, mostly on *dongar* lands as part of agro- and community-forestry programmes, though with a high mortality rate of plants, and minimal participation of 'beneficiaries') and 'construction of gully control structures', though 'diversion drains' could not be made due to tribals' unwillingness to part with any land, so 400 km of stone bunds and contour trenches were made instead; getting tribal *dongar* lands registered in their names (which met bureaucratic delays); and, most significantly, road construction, along with drainage and bridges, of which the Tikiri–Dongarsil stretch was opened to traffic by 1993.
4. The IFAD loan of $12.2 million was a little less than 55 crore rupees at the exchange rate of 1$ = Rs 45. The WFP loan was, therefore, about seven crores.
5. Among IFAD's 'achievements' listed in the end report were 130 km of roads constructed or upgraded, 'which now provide a vital lifeline for transport and communications in an area where access to remote villages/tribal areas previously was very treacherous'—a highly significant description. Also constructed were ten bridges, five community centres and three health centres, with the confessed drawbacks of a lack of participation by tribals, except as wage labourers. The project also claimed to have acquired *patta* rights for 6,837 families (wife and husband) in 236

villages, though without being able to address the issue of community rights over forest and other communally used land, as had been hoped. The project also 'had a reasonable impact not only in increasing the resource productivity of the area, but also in transforming the ecosystem of the area and living conditions of the people [introducing] the replacement of traditional and low-yield varieties of seeds by high-yield hybrid varieties' (IFAD 1998)—a frank but dangerous admission. Finally, the project constructed '221 water harvesting structures for irrigation' and '5,320 gully control structures', and brought 3,111 hectares under 'vegetative cultivation' and 5,595 under 'green manuring'—of limited use, it was admitted, since a supply and marketing system was not set up to continue after 1997. The most visible signs of planting are the conspicuous plantations of eucalyptus and acacia, presumably done in coordination with JK to feed their paper factory. The HRD component was judged a failure due to Agragamee's pullout. The 'power struggle' that arose between Agragamee and the PMU was due to Agragamee's perception that tribals were not being properly consulted, while the PMU thought Agragamee was steering them towards an incompatible political agenda. The OTDP had a succession of twelve managers within nine years. Only two were judged good, and the general approach was admitted to be much too 'top-down'. OTDP auditing was admitted to have been 'weak', with several key concerns (especially misappropriation of funds) barely addressed.

IFAD's final assessment of this project found many problems. Among these was the Orissa government transferring tribal lands to the alumina project without consulting local panchayats. The HRD claimed to have set up 278 non-formal education centres and 42 grain banks, and trained 250 teachers and 76 community leaders. But the end assessment admits that: 'The participation of tribals in the HRD programme was low … The quality of training imparted under the project was questionable … [and] did not cover many important areas, such as environmental concerns, social reforms, exploitation in trading, money lending and women's rights … The project did not realise the prime importance … of the HRD component to the entire project process.' One result was that construction works, including roads and irrigation, were already starting to deteriorate less than a year after the end of the project. A Water Users' Society (WUS), aimed at 'foster[ing] participatory management and maintenance of the irrigation assets' was boycotted. WUSs are part of a scheme being introduced in phases all over Odisha to privatise water, and make farmers pay for their irrigation, which always used to be essentially free.

6. Barney et al. (2000, p. 39). IFAD was essentially hijacked in the early 1990s by the donor nations' agenda (Sogge 2002, p. 68 and Hancock 1989, p. 51), since when it has been far more top-down. As we write,

IFAD is planning more projects in Kandhamal, Gajapati, Rayagada and other districts of Odisha.
7. Blurb advertising the opening of this rail line, 1995.
8. Studies on rural populations and the environment in remote areas through which railways have been built in northern England and Canada in the nineteenth century, and in Columbia in the 1950s as one of the first big projects financed by the WB, show that the impact is enormous, including deforestation, social disruption, sexual exploitation, and proliferation of sexually transmitted diseases. Top WB officials realised privately that the Columbian project had produced a highly negative impact in terms of deforestation; see Caufield (1998) and Chapter Seventeen.
9. L&T was reportedly backed by either Alusuisse or the world's biggest aluminium company, Alcoa, which merged with Alusuisse in 2000.
10. It would be interesting to know how the title PSSP was arrived at. PSSP translates as 'Natural Resources Defence Council', the name of an organisation in Washington DC that has worked with big corporations and often played a suspect role (e.g. Greg Pallast 2002, pp. 201–2).
11. Compensation details and lists of villages vary considerably. According to a company magazine, *Utkal Jyoti*, 2,183 families or 2,196 land-losers were due for compensation, of which '144 persons have not received compensation due to … non-appearance before land acquisition officer' (Jan–March 2001). A government document, 'Land Acquisition at a Glance' (2001), confirms the appointment of a Special Land Acquisition Officer from January 2001 with powers as the Collector, '2186 persons were affected [losing land] in 24 villages … All the land losers have taken their compensation amount leaving 99 persons of Kucheipadar village … who are anti-project persons. An amount of Rs 22,07,825 being compensation amount for 76 persons (Anti-project personnels) who have shown their unwillingness to receive their compensation … has been deposited … in the district treasury, Rayagada.' By 2001 UAIL had given Rs 6.78 crores in compensation. The report notes that the company had not yet started work due to the enquiry into the police firing, 'caused by conflict between pro- and anti-project people', and also that L&T had applied for land acquisition in three villages (Puhundi, Phulajuba and Podapadi). DFID's Swansea report (Barney et al. 2000, p. 38) says that an original list of 136 fully displaced families in three villages—35 in Ramibeda (all tribal), 58 in Koral and 43 in Dumundi (all SC)—was later changed to 147. Another 1,462 families were listed as 'PAPs' (Project Affected Persons) in twelve villages. Confusion abounds in these lists: these figures basically count a whole family as one 'PAP'. Utkal proclaims its R&R offer as extremely generous—a baseless statement, to say the least. It is apparently based on Orissa's R&R policy for the irrigation and water sector (i.e. it is modelled on displacement by dams, whose pathetic record is notorious), but does not take account, for

instance, of International Labour Organisation (ILO) Conventions 107 and 169, which India has signed, stipulating that compensation should be in 'land for land' (rather than simply in cash): i.e. land of the same quality as of that being taken, should be offered in compensation. Also, as Kashipur's villagers are now well aware, far more people would lose their lands and become displaced than those in these lists.

12. Barney et al. (2000), pp. 43 and 46). More information in *Utkal Jyoti* and UAIL's *CSR*. Lunheim wrote a report for Utkal/Norsk, 'Suggested ethical principles of UAIL concerning environmental and social issues' (28 June 1995), which speaks of 'spiritual mapping' and the possible impact on Bapla Mali's sacred caves. There were several other expensive Norwegian and Indian studies carried out on Utkal's behalf at this time: Alf Morten Jerve and Kai Greg, *International Standards and Social Impacts of the Proposed Utkal Alumina Project,* Christian Michelson Institute, February 1998; Bharat Agro-Industries Foundation Development Research Foundation, *Potential Land-base of Activities for the People Affected by the Utkal Alumina Project,* 1997; Rajesh Patnaik, *Anthropological Investigation of UAIL's Project Site for Identifying Significant Religious and Ritual Sites,* 1997. Also associated was a *Social and Environmental Impact Assessment* by the NGO, Integrated Development through Environmental Awareness (IDEA), sponsored by the Norwegian government aid agency, Norad.

These references are from a History diploma thesis from Oslo University by Kjetil Lenes (2007), 'Norsk Hydro's attempts to participate in bauxite and alumina production in India 1993–2002', which also mentions Paul N. Gooderham and Odd Nordhang, *Cross-boundary Challenge: Norsk Hydro's Utkal Venture in Orissa* (2003, International Marketing: Ethics and Social Responsibility in MNCs). An internal Norsk memo described the company's ambition as 'that of a minority partner, securing a low cost source of alumina …' (20 May 1997). By late 1998, a travel report memo mentioned that among Utkal staff 'the disillusionment and lack of competence is obvious' (23 November 1998).

13. The BPD was formed in 1998 with four 'clusters' (Chapter Eighteen), of which natural resources was the most important and involved the DFID as well as the US NGO, CARE. However, all the projects in this cluster proved problematic. After Utkal was withdrawn, a Brazil-Bolivia pipeline was substituted, and this too was withdrawn after major protests in 2003. By this time only two projects were approved by the accountancy firm PriceWaterhouseCoopers, and the WB had to withdraw from one of these, the Sarshatali coal mine in West Bengal, when it emerged that WB guidelines had not been followed (Moody 2005, pp. 86–88).

14. On Tata in Odisha, see e.g. Barney et al. 2000, p. 40. A private communication from Ratan Tata (cited in Kjetil Lenes' thesis) to Odd Henrik Robberstad of Norsk, dated 26 November 1998: 'The Tata executives looking after the Utkal project have indicated that they have

serious concerns with the complexity of the joint venture agreement arising from different interests that our respective companies have in this project. They have indicated this may make completion of a mutually acceptable JV Agreement difficult. Tatas understand that proceeding with Utkal is important for your company. We would therefore not like our different priorities to stand in the way of the implementation of Utkal.'

15. *The Great Samatha versus AP Government Judgment*, SC 1997, 3297 AIR, printed by Kutumbakam Vasudhaiv. See also Vagholkar et al, *Undermining India*, Kalpavriksh, 2003. Hindalco, Grasim Cement and Birla Periclase are three of the companies in the Aditya Birla group. Aditya is the grandson of Gandhi's friend, G. D. Birla (see Chapter Seven). Attempts to bypass the Samatha Judgment in Andhra are based on making joint ventures with the APMDC (a state company) and shifting Jindal's site out of Scheduled Areas.

16. A four-page typed letter to the National Human Rights Commission (NHRC) in Delhi, dated 30 January 1998, by P. Samantara; and a two-page typed letter from the NHRC to the Chief Secretary, Government of Orissa, dated 20 February 1998.

17. A three-page handwritten letter by Lingaraj and Samantara to Guru Mohanty (advocate in Cuttack and Secretary of PUCL, a human rights group), dated 31 March 1998; one-page typed letters to the director General of Orissa Police, dated 31 March 1998 and 1 April 1998, by Sudhir Pattnaik (Secretary of Sanhati NGO Alliance) and Guru Mohanty; two-page letter from Samantara and Lingaraj to Rayagada SP, 1 April 1998.

18. Internal memo, cited from Lenes' History thesis.

19. Richard Mahapatra 1999. The note composed by villagers, which the Norsk officials signed, reads: '1. The people are not interested in the plant. They want to continue agriculture. 2. The whole Kashipur Block and project area are against the project. 3. They want the project site shifted. 4. Otta and Mahapatra have file of unjustified court cases against the people. Many people are arrested. Cases must be withdrawn. Suspension of Government servants without cause must be lifted. No police charges must be made against men, women and children. Payment has been done [i.e. compensation paid] by threatening.'

20. Barney et al. 2000, p. 41, Richard Mahapatra 1999, Goodland 2007. The theme of why these NGOs were targeted is picked up in Chapter Eighteen.

21. This plan shows Kodinga Mali, an alumina refinery, and a township and rehabilitation colony north of it, just south-east of Purhaparhi village (4 km south of Tikiri), and an ash pond and red mud pond north-west and west of the Mali respectively. The refinery is superimposed over Kansariguda village. Was this plan drawn up shortly before Hindalco took over Indal? Was it perhaps a major factor in the merger of these companies?

22. FIR, Kashipur Police Station, submitted by Binod Naik, dated 15 December 2000. Bhaskar Rao was the BJD party president for Rayagada district.
23. Utkal was one of the last projects to be listed as a 'Business Partners for Development' (BPD) scheme, and the first to be withdrawn. It was withdrawn without explanation, obviously because the deaths made it too sensitive, counterproductive to the effect the WB wanted to achieve.
24. Affidavit to Mishra's inquiry, from Bijay Kumar Otta, signed Cuttack, 20 June 2001.
25. P. K. Mishra went on a study tour in the USA from 2 to 16 March 2002, with seven other senior judges and District Magistrates. Among the main institutions they attended were the Environmental Protection Agency and National Environmental Trust (Washington), and the National Resources Defence Council (Oregon).
26. A study by the Centre for Science and Environment (CSE) that apparently had access to the secret EIA testifies to this (www.freewebs.com/epgOrissa/UTKAL). Alcan't In India (www.alcantinindia.org) campaigned for Alcan to withdraw from Kashipur, which was accomplished in 2007.
27. Girard (2005, p. 24), Barney et al. (2000, p. 41), *Utkal Jyoti* 2001; Goodland (2007). Many of the published accounts of percentages and dates differ.
28. Several newspaper articles appeared. See Samajvadi Jan Parishad: Kashipur update 16 December 2004 at aflatoon4.tripod.com/id8.html (consulted January 2009). On the Guguput and other attacks, see PUDR report of May 2005, and report of the Indian Peoples Tribunal team, *Panel assessing Orissa mining impacts,* October 2006. The team was headed by S. N. Bhargava, retired Chief Justice of Sikkim High Court.
29. www.freewebs.com/epgOrissa carries a letter addressed to the OSPCB, dated 14 October 2006.
30. Jayram has continued to support the villagers. 'Aditya Aluminium Company opposed by villagers of Biriguda, Laxmipur' (www.dailypioneer.com, 5 December 2007) mentions the Kansariguda refinery's designs on 66.02 acres of forest land and 1.77 acres of non-forest land.
31. Mali Parbat and Kodinga Mali: www.freewebs.com/epgOrissa updates for November–December 2005 (Express News Service, 19 December), and letters from *Maliparbat Surakhya Samiti,* dated 31August 2005 and 27 September 2006. See also K. Sudhakar Patnaik, 'Project at Mali Parbat: How Environment Friendly?' (12 April 2008) at http://www.merinews.com/catFull.jsp?articleID=132320.
32. http://www.thehindubusinessline.com/2005/09/23/stories/-2005092302890200.htm.
33. *Times of India,* Bhubaneswar edition, 19 October 2007, p. 3, and www.imfa.co.in.
34. *Statesman,* 28 March 2007 (www.freewebs.com/epgOrissa). *The Hindu,* 3 March 2008, describes an MoU signing as imminent between Nalco and the AP government, and mentions the company's 'expansion drive' to

Indonesia and South Africa. *The Economic Times*, 4 June 2008, mentions Iran too. These plans, also described to us by a senior Nalco executive, involve a fully integrated industry in Indonesia (bauxite mine, refinery and smelter), and smelters in Iran and South Africa.

35. BHP first announced its plans for a bauxite mine in Kalahandi in March 2006, severely embarrassing NGOs, such as WIDA, that were in the midst of joint programmes with the company, which immediately opposed these plans (more fully described in Chapter Eighteen). See 'Orissa Wildlife Society under pressure to redraw Karlapat elephant sanctuary' (www.freewebs.com/epgOrissa, update, November–December 2005).

36. 'Orissa finds another bauxite reserve, explores new mines', *Financial Express*, 13 July 2008, describing the deposit as 8 million tons on the Ushabali plateau.

37. www.dnaindia.com, 28 November 2006.

38. Rio Tinto's plans were announced in PTI on 15 October 2008, outlining a plan to mine bauxite and build a 1.4 million tons refinery, a 250,000 ton smelter, and a captive coal-fired power plant (ccpp), either in Odisha or Andhra, investing Rs 9,000 crore in a project that includes a Joint Venture with Coal India to supply coal for the ccpp.

39. 'Trouble brews over "holy" hill as Vedanta applies for lease', 17 June 2008, http://www.business-standard.com/india/storypage.php?autono=326336.

40. MoEF 2007. The MoEF document claims to list the mountains in Kalahandi and Koraput districts, though its inclusion of several from Rayagada district imply that the old, undivided Koraput is referred to. The four major mountains left out of its list are Bapla Mali, Sasu-Bohu Mali, Ghusri Mali and Deo Mali (Odisha's highest mountain). The three Malis where clearance has been applied for are Niyam Dongar, Mali Parbat and Kodinga Mali.

41. Minutes of meetings of the AP government with CM, 22 April 2005, outline Nalco's plans to mine bauxite and set up a refinery and smelter in AP, and with the Mining, Forest and Revenue Ministers, 2 July 2005, outline Jindal's plans with the APMDC.

42. 'Naveen's affair with Jindal Strips: Government stripped layer by layer by Orissa High Court', 17 December 2004, http://Orissamatters.com/2004/12/17/stripped-layer-by-layer.

43. 'Bauxite mines in Andhra Pradesh draw tribal ire', *Down to Earth*, 15 March 2008 (www.downtoearth.org.in).

44. 'Helicopter survey on bauxite mining area triggers fresh controversy', *The Hindu*, 5 March 2008, and *Down to Earth*, 15 March 2008.

45. 11 June 2008, http://www.pressreleasepoint.com/we-humans-are-depriving-ourselves-and-subjecting-other-life-forms-their-pleasant-environment-have-fr.

46. Articles in *The Hindu*: 14 March 2008, 22 June 2008, 6 September 2008, 19 September 2008, 21 September 2008, 26 September 08, 6

October 2008 ('Hearing boycott puts PCB in a fix'), 7 October 2008, 10 October 2008 ('EIA report on Jerrela mines faulty') and 17 October 08 ('Bauxite mining in AP opposed'). The latter piece lists the population of the eight Odisha villages as 1,470 Adivasis and 83 Dalits. See also *Deccan Chronicle*, 25 October 2008; www.deccan.com, 22 September 2008 ('Mining minefield'); economictimes.indiatimes.com, 7 October 2008 ('UAE company's Rs 9,000 crore plan in Andhra runs into rough weather'); Press Trust of India, 25 March 2007, and Orissa Diary News, 30 March 2007, in www.freewebs.com/epgOrissa; and *The Hindu*, 5 June 2007, on opposition to Jindal and the ruling Congress party at S. Kota, and *The Hindu*, 26 December 2007, on BJP support to the protestors.

Chapter 6

1. Letter from the Collector, Kalahandi, no. 205 (400), giving application for land acquisition by Sterlite Industries (India) Ltd (SIIL).
2. Samantara (2006, p. 16).
3. Bithika Mukerji 1983/2008, on the philosophy of Vedanta and its distortion to accommodate twentieth-century materialism.
4. This point is established in the report on Vedanta by the Council on Ethics, Norwegian Government Pension Fund (May 2007), among many other sources. On Malco, see Nostromo Research, (pp. 9–10, 14 and 22–24), and Indian Peoples Tribunal Report on environment and human rights violations by Chemplast Industries and Malco at Mettur, Tamil Nadu, July 2004.
5. Nostromo Research (2005), Sridhar (2003).
6. 'Police Arrest 3 Balco officials over Chimney Disaster' by Arpan Mukherjee, *Wall Street Journal* 17 November 2009 (www.mines and communities.org/article.php?=9665) The tenth chapter of J. P. Morgan's report on Vedanta Resources is a Technical report by SRK Consulting (Steffen Robertson and Kirsten UK Ltd.), of which Part B concerns aluminium (pp. 313–45). Among many other details, this mentions two more bauxite mines under exploration, at Jamirapat (Surguja) and Pandrapat (Jashpur).
7. Nostromo Research (2005, p. 5). See also 'Land grab mud on BALCO', *The Telegraph*, Calcutta, 18 June 2005; NewIndPress, 24 June 2005; Indo-Asian News Service (IANS), 13 July 2005; IANS, 25 July 2005.
8. On HZL in Rajasthan: Nostromo Research (2005, p. 11), and Arun Kumar Singh, *The Privatisation of Rivers in India* (Vikas Adhyayan Kendra, Delhi, 2004, and www.struggleindia.com, 8 April 2004).
9. Nostromo Research (2005, pp. 3–4, 17–19).
10. Bidwai (2001), Nostromo Research (2005).

11. *The Independent*, 4 December 2003, on the unfair dismissal of Rajat Bhatia. The Mt Lyell mine in Tasmania has caused a large amount of pollution through acid drainage, etc. Sterlite's subsidiary Copper Mines of Tasmania Pty Ltd. (CMT) is indemnified by a special CMT (Agreement) Act passed by the State of Tasmania in 1999.
12. Much has been written about Sterlite/Vedanta's operations in Armenia and Zambia, especially on the minesandcommunities.com website and in the *Financial Times*. Many of these are collected in Rohit Poddar's book *Vedanta's Billions* (2006). A condensed summary is available in WoW 2008, where chapter 3 gives details of Vedanta's violations of the environment and human rights in India, Zambia and Armenia.
13. These quotations are from interviews in *Matiro Poko*. Our photo of Gurbari on page 358 was taken shortly before she was forced to leave.
14. PUCL report, 16 May 2003, see www.indymedia.org:8080. NBS. Das' Odia articles, February and May 2003.
15. *Vedanta Resources plc: Listing Particulars*, sponsored by J. P. Morgan, December 2003.
16. www.indiaresource.org/news/2004/1055.html.
17. 'Vedanta shares hammered after warning to investors', *Daily Telegraph*, 27 January 2004.
18. Worley Parsons has a long relationship with Worsley refinery (Australia) and Bechtel. www.worleyparsons.com/GlobalPresence/ANZ/News/Pages/WorsleyAluminaEfficiencyGrowthExpansionProjects.
19. http://www.minesandcommunities.org/article.php?a=33. PUDR report, May 2005, http://kashipursolidarity.tripod.com/id18.html. S. Das May 2003.
20. 18 December 2007, http://www.indianexpress.com/news/With-soaring-profits-&-exports,-Balco-sends-a-rejoinder-to-all-those-who-opposed-its-sale/251924/. Production statistics in Appendix I.
21. 'Land grab mud on Balco' in *The Telegraph*, 18 June 2005; NewIndpress, 24 June 2005; IANS, 13 July 2005 and 25 July 2005; and Nostromo Research (2005, p. 12).
22. www.freewebs.com/epgOrissa updates for November–December 2005 and March 2007. The smelter case brought by Prafulla at the Appellate Court is listed as Appeal no. 4 of 2007, and Mark Chernaik' Evaluation of the smelter's EIA is dated October 2005. When the company questioned Prafulla's standing in this case, his right was upheld by the Delhi High Court in May 2009, which ordered Vedanta to pay Rs 50,000 as costs.
23. *Business India*, 13 March 2005.
24. 'Sunil Mittal, Anil Agarwal in Forbes philanthropy list', *Economic Times*, 5 March 2009.

25. On Jindal Strips case, see 'Naveen's affair with Jindal Strips: Government stripped layer by layer by Orissa High Court', 17 December 2004, http://Orissamatters.com/2004/12/17/stripped-layer-by-layer.
26. Report submitted in March 2005, summarised in CEC, 21 September 2005, pp. 32–38 and 62–65.
27. CEC, 21 September 2005, signed M. K. Jiwrajka (Member Secretary), p. 86.
28. CEC, September 2005, p. 16 and pp. 38–41. Sterlite (2002, pp. 1–3) gives this area as 1073.4 hectares, 56 per cent in Kalahandi.
29. CEC, September 2005, pp. 51, 60–62, 82–83 and 86.
30. Ibid., pp. 8 and 81.
31. Ibid., pp. 5–6.
32. Ibid., p. 9.
33. Ibid., pp. 13–14, and Chapter Twelve.
34. Ibid., p. 58.
35. Ibid., pp. 73–78, quoting the GoO affidavit of 16 February 2005: 'The 58.94 ha. of forest land [28.94 ha. "suitable for village forest" and 30 ha. of reserve forest] is an integral part of the Vedanta Alumina Project. This land is required for development of Alumina Refinery complex over 26.12 ha. and construction of service corridor, conveyor belt and approach road over 32.82 ha'.
36. WII report, July 2006, is available at freewebs.com/epgOrissa.
37. Nostromo Research 2005, p. 12; *The Telegraph* (Kolkata), 18 June 2005; IANS, 13 June and 25 July 2005.
38. P. C. Rauta, OSPCB Regional Officer, and Chudamani Seth, Additional District Magistrate, Kalahandi: Proceedings of the Public Hearing of M/S Vedanta Aluminium Ltd. for its expansion of alumina refinery from 1.0mtpa to 6.0mtpa ... village Belamba, signed by Madhu Malhotra, Deputy Program director, Asia-Pacific Region. Faults in the expansion plan are outlined in an Open Letter by Amnesty International to the Orissa government, 24 April 2009, www.amnesty.org/en/library/info/ASA20/004/2009/en. 'Vedanta flouts rules in Orissa, central government wants to know why', 27 November 2009, at http://www.indiaenews.com/business/20091127/234229.htm; 'Vedanta flouted Centre's 'norms', *Hindustan Times* 28 November 2009, at http://www.hindustantimes.com/india-news/newdelhi/Vedanta-flouted-Centre-s-norms/Article1-480906.aspx; 'No 'in-principle' nod projects: MoEF', *New Indian Express* 29 November 2009.
39. From Vedanta's website, sparring with Survival International: 'Vedanta rejects claim that new mine will damage tribe's way of life' (May 2008); 'We have changed', on Dongria health camps (March 2009); 'NGOs misguiding Dongria Kondhs in Orissa', on visit to Panchpat Mali (3 April 2009) (http://www.pressreleasepoint.com/dongria-kondh-tribe-appreciates-vedanta039s-efforts). A Survival International website carries 'Behind the

lies', exposing Vedanta's PR offensive, at www.survival-international.org/behindthelies/vedanta. On villagers thwarting Vedanta attempts to take vehicles up the mountain from January 2009, see Action Aid International-India (www.minesandcommunities.org/article.php?a=9008).

40. Akshaya (2007); NDTV Profit; and 'Balco resorting to contract labour', Press Trust of India, 5 December 2007.
41. For example, Das (June 2000); Mohammed (December 2006) and Saroj (January 2008).
42. Reports come in every week on biofuel list-serves about the destructive effects of jatropha in India and other 'developing countries', taking over common land, increasing hunger by replacing foodcrops, poisoning children, etc. For example, 'Miracle plant's monstrous potential', 14 July 2008 (www.eurekastreet.com.au/article.aspx?aeid=7908).
43. Opposition MLAs in Orissa Assembly demanding CBI probe into Vedanta's donations to political parties, especially BJD, *The Hindu*, 7 July 2007, (www.hindu.com/2007/07/07/stories/2007070757150300.htm).
44. The *FT* announced plans for 'Vedanta University' in July 2006. The plan has faced strong opposition ever since, e.g. 'Court stays land acquisition for Vedanta university' (http://indiaedunews.net/Orissa/Court_stays_land_acquisition_for_Vedanta_University_4328/). 'Government signs MoU for fourth port', *New Indian Express*, 23 December 2008, p. 3, introduces Astranga, in addition to three other ports being built or upgraded for exporting Odisha's ores and metals: Gopalpur, Dhamra and Kirtania. '*Vedanta tanka nei marpeet*' (Blows over taking Vedanta money), *Dharitri*, 24 December 2008, about one Ramchandra Pradhan of Gopalpur village (in Posco area), accepting Rs 65 lakh for communally owned land, to the fury of fellow-villagers.
45. *Sambad*, 14 January 2007, back page. More on WEF in Chapter Nineteen.
46. *Live Mint*, 31 December 2007, http://www.livemint.com/2007/12/31235248/Govt-rejects-Balco-expansion-p.html.
47. 'MALCO to stop illegal mining in Kolli Hills', 21 December 2008 (http://www.minesandcommunities.org//article.php?a=3876).
48. EPG, 21 April 2008.
49. ISO 14001 for an Environment Management System, 18001 for health and safety, 9001 for quality management (http://www.indiaprwire.com/pressrelease/mining-metals/2009012818790.htm).
50. www.hindu.com/2007/04/25/stories/2007042505011800.htm; Reuters, 22 May 2009, http://mandgoa.blogspot.com/2009/04/mining-companies-threatens-advalpal.html.
51. http://steelguru. com/news/ index/2008/ 03/13/MzkxMTk per cent 3D/Vedanta_ announces_ aluminum_ smelter_in_WB.html, http://www.metalbulletin.com/Article/1903590/Soaring-aluminium.html, www.thaindian.com/newsportal/india-news/desperate-villagers-in-Orissa-stage-anti-mining-protest_10083246.html.

52. 'Troubles mount for Vedanta: OECD accepts Survival complaint as Chairman faces fraud enquiry', SI press release, 30 March 2009 (http://www.survival-international.org/news/3804); 'Lanjigarh to London' and other features at actionaidindia.org, actionaidusa.org, etc.; Action Aid International 2007; WoW 2008.
53. http://www.topnews.in/rahul-gandhi-visit-tribal-pockets-madhya-pradesh-chhattisgarh-237540, www.survival-international.org/news/3305.
54. For example, in *Tehelka* weekly magazine: 'Last Stand of Niyam Raja' by Anjali Lal Gupta, 25 May 2008; 'New Era in Lanjigarh' by Bibhuti Pati, 21 June 2008, which gives the company gloss; and letters in the next week's issue, critiquing this article (www.tehelka.com/story_main38.asp?filename=cr190408thelast.asp*).
55. A demonstration against Vedanta's planned mine, led by Bhakta Das in Bhubaneswar, reported in *The Hindu*, 8 May 2008.
56. 'Former Nalco chief jailed for three years in graft case', *Times of India*, 27 February 2009.
57. 'Company increases effluent outlets instead of plugging them', *Down to Earth*, 9 August 2009, on OSPCB reports in April and July; *Dharitri* 4 December 2009, reporting an initiative of Gobardhan Sharma of Kherual.
58. Article in *Aromv* (Agenda for Reinforcement of Ordinary Men's Voices) Odia daily newspaper (Bhubaneswar), 5 December 2009.

Chapter 7

1. For example, Bidwai (2001), Rohit Poddar's banned book *Vedanta's Billions* (2005 and 2006), the Norway Government Ethics Committee report on Vedanta (2007), the War on Want report on UK companies violating human rights (2008), and numerous articles listed on the Mines and Communities website. On a contempt of court case brought against senior advocated Prashant Bhushan for drawing attention to Kapadia's conflict of interest in the case, since he had shares in Sterlite, see *Outlook* 9 December 2009, at http://outlookindia.com/article.aspx?263230.
2. Alastair Fraser and John Lungu, March 2006, *For Whom the Windfalls: Winners and Losers in the Privatization of Zambia's Copper Mines* (Civil Society Trade Network of Zambia and Catholic Centre for Justice Development and Peace); Action for South Africa (ACTSA), Christian Aid, SCIAF (Scotland's Aid Agency), October 2007, *Undermining Development: Copper Mining in Zambia* (on EPG website); Moody 2007, 'The Base Alchemist' (p. 85 and note 5); WoW 2008; Council on Ethics 2007. Kafue river supplies water to at least 75,000 people. It was found to have 1,000 times the permitted levels of copper, 10,000 times of cobalt, and 77,000 times of manganese.

3. Moody (2007, p. 97); John Helmer, 'Armenia may start prosecution of Vedanta-controlled Zod mine', *Mineweb* 28 February 2007; Ernst & Young, *Supplement to Business Standard*, December 2008, with an article about Agarwal, 'Such a Long Journey', where he describes himself as 'a man from the street'.
4. Bidwai (2001); Moody (2007, p. 87 and note 13), among many other sources. A full version of the SEBI indictment is given in Poddar's *Vedanta's Billions* (2006).
5. Moody (2007, p. 100). A summary of violations in 1994–95 was prepared by Nityanand Jayaraman (October 2005) for the Corporate Accountability desk of Chennai-based Other Media.
6. *Impact of Privatisation of Labour: A Study of BALCO Disinvestment*, by V. V. Giri National Labour Institute, affiliated to the Ministry of Labour (Moody 2007, p. 85).
7. Bauxite mining at Bodai Daldali in Kawardha compounds the violation of the Samatha Judgment and the Fifth Schedule, because it started after Sterlite took over, and infringes a specific order of the MP government forbidding mining in this district except by a PSU (notification no. 2918/2875/12 of 16 June 1969). M.P. Chandra Shekhar Dubey raised these issues in Parliament, and attested that Sterlite illegally mortgaged the Mainpat and Bodai Daldali mines to get a loan for infrastructure from Leasing and Financial Services Company Ltd., in October 2004 (N. Agrawal 2007, pp. 110–13). Bidwai 2001 states: 'The [Balco] deal is economically irrational, politically deplorable, legally unsustainable and environmentally unsound ... it violates a fundamental rights verdict of the Supreme Court in the landmark Samatha case, which vests ownership of Adivasi land in tribal people.'
8. Agrawal (2007, pp. 103–04).
9. Balaji Metal and Mineral Company was known to have absconded with unpaid wages of Rs 1,80,00,000 it owed to labourers, yet the Chhattisgarh Mineral Development Corporation (CMDC) tried to contract this company for another job, until a strike foiled this plan (Agrawal 2007, pp. 107–08).
10. Agrawal (2007, p. 113). Refining Chhattisgarh bauxite outside Chhattisgarh infringes state laws. We have witnessed the terrible health and safety conditions at Bodai Daldali and Mainpat several times in 2004–06. Anil Agrawal himself has assured us several times at London AGMs that these would improve, but as far as we know, they have not.
11. Nostromo Research (2005); Moody (2007, pp. 91–92).
12. Intervention Application (IA) on Writ Petition 2002 of 1995. The MoEF report and a counter-report presented with S. Nayak's petition are available on the EPG website. The objections registered on 5 October 2007 focused on the fact that the MoEF report does not provide a real picture of bauxite mining's impact on forest or tribes, and seems

to have been prepared with the sole purpose of justifying mining: the report's contention that the plateau tops have almost no vegetation is completely false; compensatory afforestation cannot replace original forest; the statement that dense forests have been created by Nalco is untrue; wildlife management plans will not be able to deal with the damage due to mining, and elephants regularly visit the Niyamgiri plateau, which has extensive wildlife, including rare species; Alcoa's Jarrahdale bauxite mine in west Australia—cited as an example of good reclamation—is not attested by any independent witness; and the claim that Nalco's Damanjodi operations have had a positive impact on tribals is false, as shown, for example, by an all-India record of 79 per cent of Koraput district living below the poverty line (CSE 2008).

13. The article in the *New Indian Express* (22 February 2008) is revealing: 'In the light of repeated acrimonious exchanges between the Central Empowered Committee (CEC)—a court-appointed panel to look into forest cases—and the Ministry of Environment, the Supreme Court on Thursday directed inclusion of Director General (Forests) as one of the members of CEC. In the past one year, there have been several showdowns between CEC and the ministry. The most acrimonious was over the inclusion of names of non-official members in the Forest Advisory Committee (FAC), the government panel that approves diversion of forest land for developmental projects ... The inclusion of P. R. Mohanty, the present DG (Forests), as a member of CEC, is being seen as a step that would bridge the rift between the two. Mohanty also heads the FAC ... CEC would now have seven members instead of five, directed Justice Arijit Pasayat . . . Valmik Thapar and N. K. Joshi, former DG (Forests), will no longer be CEC members. The court has included three new members besides Mohanty. They include A. R. Chaddha, an official of Ministry of Health; S. K. Patnaik, former Chief Wildlife Warden, Orissa; and M. M. Muthut, former member of FAC. The Ministry of Environment and Forests (MoEF) filed an affidavit in September last year seeking the termination of CEC ... This was countered by the amicus curiae [Harish Salve] who said if any specific instance of the CEC overstepping its authority could be pointed out, he would agree to suitable changes and safeguards. The Thursday order puts to rest the uncertainity over the existence of CEC for some time to come.'
14. *The Hindu*, 11 March 2007.
15. 'Sensitise masses on environmental laws', *New Indian Express*, Bhubaneswar, 20 December 2007, p. 3.
16. Indian Peoples Tribunal report (October 2006, team led by Justice Bhargava), and accounts of these false cases and bribes by the villagers concerned.
17. Nazir (2007, p. 165), gives details of highly flawed PHs in Jharkhand, involving coercion and various illegalities: by Indal for bauxite mining

(24 June 2004); three for coal mining (2004–06); Tata for iron ore mining (25 September 2004); Uranium Corp of India Ltd. for uranium mining (25 February 2005); Hindalco for bauxite mining at Orsapat (26 March 2006); and NTPC for a power plant (5 January 2007).

18. CSE 2008, pp. 138–40, quoting M. N. Mitra, 'Red alert' in *Down To Earth*, 31 October 2006, pp. 27–28, and *Daily Chhattisgarh*, 9 September 2006.
19. Padmaparna Ghosh, 'MOEF approved project on plagiarized report: are the government's green clearances a farce?' (30 December 2007), www.livemint.org. Appeal to NEAA under NEAA Act 1997 by Ritwick Dutta, Rahul Choudhary and Priyabrata Satpathy (29 December 2006). See also, Aruna Murthy and Himansu Sekhar Patra, 'EIA Process in India and the Drawbacks', September 2005, item 35 on EPG website.
20. *New Indian Express*, 25 December 2007.
21. 'We feel extremely sorry for wasting your precious time in this matter as we had been grossly confused about Maliparbat Mining activities … This kind of confusion would not have taken place had the officials of Hindalco interacted with the concerned villagers at the right time. Now they are regularly in touch with all the villagers and they have cleared all doubts to their satisfaction regarding Environment and Pollution hazards …' This letter to the Koraput Collector and Orissa Governor is signed by the MSS President and Advisor, and contradicts a letter opposing the project, dated 31 August 2005, which bears the signatures or thumb prints of over 300 villagers.
22. *Samaj*, 6 November 2008.
23. *London Calling*, 24 June 2006; mineweb.co.za, 20 April 2007.
24. On 20 January 2007, a brake was announced on SEZs at Sonia Gandhi's insistence. In January 2008, the Goa administration scrapped 15 SEZs, with the commerce ministry at first saying this was impossible, but then conceding.
25. Sanjay Parikh, 'Development of Environmental Law: a critical appraisal', at a National Consultation on Judicial Trends in Environment Law held at Nehru Museum, Teen Murti House, New Delhi, on 23 and 24 February 2008. This paper points out that the 42nd amendment to India's Constitution was based on the Stockholm Declaration of the UN Conference on Human Environment (1972) and the Brundtland report, while Article 21 of the Constitution included the right to environment under the right to life.
26. IA no. 2134 of 2007 on Writ Petition no. 202 of 1995, of petitioner T. N. Godavaraman Thirumulpad (petitioner) *versus* Union of India and others (respondents), in the matter of Sterlite Industries (applicant).
27. Paragraphs 0.2.4–5 and 7.2.0–4.
28. 'NGO wants hearing on Jindal unit postponed,' *Hindu Business Line*, 1 June 2007.

29. *The Hindu*, 23 December 2007, 'The hills are on fire as massive project goes through "on the nod"'; and Samatha's letter to the MoEF, 23 December 2007, on www.minesandcommunities.com.
30. 'Mineral industry up in arms against Dang panel report', *Financial Express*, 27 September 2005. Abstract at http://www.mckinsey.com/locations/india/mckinseyonidia/pdf/Turning_Minerals_Mining_Potential. pdf. West Bengal's CM also commissioned McKinsey for the prototype of the industrialisation plan that has been so strongly opposed at Singur, Nandigram etc.
31. 'Mining Policy: Protecting environment and people or investment?' CPI-ML website, July 2007, www.cpiml.org/liberation/year_2007/July/mining_policy, which gives the statistics of forest loss above.
32. Chapter 1, sections 36 and 62. These refer to the early, December 2006 draft of the NMP.
33. Ibid. Chapter 3.4–7.
34. Ibid. Chapter 3.8–18.
35. Ibid. Chapter 3.19–46.
36. Ibid. Chapters 4–8.
37. http://www.riotinto.com/documents/Media-Speeches/GRE-India_270606. pdf (consulted 2008).
38. Moody (2007, pp. 16–19 and 156–60).
39. IUCN, *Mining and Indigenous Peoples*, p. 25.
40. *Sunday Express*, 16 November 2003.
41. Josephson (1962, pp. 15, 352, 354).
42. Korten (1995, p. 58).
43. Josephson (1962, p. 43).
44. *Statesman*, Bhubaneswar, 23 May 2006.
45. For example, Raja Acharya, who was arrested for this murder, had a close connection with senior IAS officer Priyabrat Patnaik, who, Raja said, had offered him a contract to work for Posco (*Kalinga Times*, 5 May 2008).
46. On these two killings, see 'Tata steel bullets' (Samadrusti TV) on youtube. com, and *The Statesman*, 26 June 2008.
47. Cullinan (2002, p. 30).
48. Ibid., p. 38.
49. *Hindustan Times*, 9 May 09; Balakrishnan's comments on 24 May 2009 at epaper.expressbuzz.com/NE/NE/2009/05/24/ArticleHtmls/24_05_2009_009_007.shtml?Mode=1.
50. *Niyamgiri, the Mountain of Law* is the title of a documentary film made for Samadrusti TV (Surya Dash 2008).

Chapter 8

1. $1.2million to the Political and Public Awareness Fund in 2004, $1.3million to the Political and Public Awareness Trust in 2005, etc (Vedanta Reports 2004–06).
2. An 'emic' account is actors' culture-specific understanding of their own behaviour. An 'etic' account is a 'culturally neutral' understanding of behaviour by a neutral observer.
3. We were shown this list at the Nagpur office. The IBM Yearbook for 2003 records 173 registered mines run by 73 producers.
4. http://www.gsi.gov.in/hist.htm, and L. L. Fermor on the GSI's first 25 years, at http://www.portal.gsi.gov.in/portal/page?_pageid=127,529293&_dad=portal&_schema=PORTAL (accessed November 2008).
5. Parliament of India: Rajya Sabha nos. 66 and 80 (March and December 2002). The UNDP gave Rs 17 crore and the GoI, 19 crore. Among JNARDDC's first functions was an international meeting on bauxite (Bauxmet) in 1998, and its projects include evaluating the Kuturu Mali deposit for L&T, and Kodinga Mali for Hindalco.
6. For example, a JNARDDC contract for Nalco examined how to de-ironise bauxite more effectively (known as the Romelt process or benefication), and Nalco signed an agreement in March 2001 with two Russian companies on extracting iron from Red Mud, the Moscow Institute of Steel and Alloys, and Russian and Romelt SAIL Ltd.
7. GoI, *Ministry of Mines: Annual Report 2002–3*, p. 53.
8. Information from a geologist in central Orissa, and www.fugroairborne.com
9. www.ibef.org. For example, Priyabrat Patnaik is Managing director of IDCOL and Tamotia is on the Board of IPICOL (2008).
10. Quotations from Alok Sheel (2001, p. 3), and 'About me' at www.aloksheel.com/abt_me.htm (browsed 2008, also available, December 2008, at eac.gov.in, the website for the Economic Advisory Council to the PM, for which he was Secretary from September 2007 to October 2008, since when he has been Joint Secretary to the Department of Economic Affairs, GoI).
11. INCAL 2003, pp. 699 ff and 737 ff: 'Project financing and risk management'. Under 'Debt Financing Sources—Offshore', they write: 'Export Credit Agencies (ECAs) have played a very important part in almost all project financing in India and are expected to do so in case of large Indian projects with significant capital goods import ... Multilateral Agencies could enhance the potential acceptability/credibility of the Project, but tend to have a long lead-time, be more restrictive in environmental issues and documentation, but less restrictive in usage of funds.'
12. Words of the Chairman of the House of Commons Environmental Audit, from Minutes of Evidence (www.publications.parliament.uk/pa/

cm199899/cmselect/cmenvaud/326/9062406.htm), asking a Dr Iddon about the proposed Levy, who replies that at the time he was 'doing some work for DETR on economic instruments to promote the demands for secondary materials, so I happened to be talking quite frequently to ALFED, and whenever I phoned them towards 30 May they were keen that I should get off the phone as quickly as possible, because this is what they were working on [i.e. a lobby of MPs to prevent a major emissions levy being imposed on aluminium production]. I suppose that perhaps the real question is to what extent has the decision already been made when it might have been left more open to consultation prior to being made....' Thanking Iddon, the Chairman says, 'and we hope we have not damaged your chances of getting any government contracts in this area.'

13. *The Independent*, 26 October 2008; 'Mandelson met oligarch earlier than he admitted', *The Guardian*, 24 October. As EU Trade Commissioner, Mandelson cut aluminium import duties twice, for which Deripaska's Rusal was a main beneficiary. See also on these scandals: *The Guardian* 21, 23 and 27 October 2008; *Washington Post*, 25 January 2008 and http://www.latimes.com/news/nationworld/world/la-na-vaticanscam11-2008sep11,0,5421278.story.

14. The Aluminium Manufacturing Co.'s factory at Dum-Dum near Calcutta (1922) and Wolverhampton Works Co.'s factory in Bombay (1931); BAC (1955, p. 60).

15. The cement company Lafarge moved from Britain to India in 1920 when Indian laterite surpassed Portland clay in alumina quality (Fox 1932 pp. xv, pp. 122–27, 204–11 and 243). The first mining area was at Kapadvanj, east of Ahmedabad.

16. *J.K.: The Architects of the J.K. Organisation*, a company brochure. The Rayagada DFO told us that the timber mafia area supplied this factory, and tests on its paper confirmed this.

17. From Indal's brochure: *Small is Big*. Indal's assets include: bauxite mines at Lohardaga (Jharkhand), Durgmanwadi and Chandgad (Maharashtra). The Alupuram plant also manufactures aluminium 'extrusions' and there is a sheet rolling mill at Belur (West Bengal). At Taloja (Maharashtra), Indal made India's first aluminium scrap recycling centre, and there is a foil factory nearby at Kalwa.

18. Heiner (1991, p. 305).

19. Madhu Kudaisya (2003, pp. 334–35); Gita Piramal (1996). According to Kudaisya, the Rihand dam was originally conceived for irrigation and water supply, and many were angry when this took second place to supplying the aluminium smelter. C. B. Gupta (a Congress leader in UP, and later its CM) was apparently behind this. The smelter had a capacity at first to produce 20,000 tons per year, for which it needed 48,000 kW. When this capacity was first doubled and then tripled

through expansion, the Renusagar Power Plant was built, after the UP government asked Hindalco to build its own captive power station. The agreement for 1.99 *paise* per unit for 25 years had an option to be raised by just 10 per cent after ten years.
20. BAC (1955, p. 62).
21. Kulke and Rothermund (2004, pp. 289 and 317).
22. Roger Moody (1992, pp. 581–85).
23. On the Alcan–Pechiney merger, see Girard (2005). Novelis in 2007 includes refineries/smelters in Brazil, and rolling factories in a number of countries (www.novelis.com, 2007). When Alcan made its 'hostile takeover' of Pechiney for $4.5 billion in 2004, Novelis was created as a spin-off company of Pechiney and Alcan. With 38 plants in twelve countries and based in Atlanta, it is the world's largest rolled products aluminium company. Hindalco bought Novelis in February 2007 for $5.9 billion (which included $2.4 billion debt), with loans from UBC, ABN AMRO and Bank of America, just two weeks after Tata bought up Corus (British Steel).
24. On Norsk Hydro: www.hydro.com (2006); Greer and Bruno (1996, pp. 120–29) on fertilisers.
25. www.larsenandtoubro.com, www.Intecc.com. ECC, the Engineering Construction and Contracts division of L&T, is India's biggest construction company (*The Hindu Business Line*, 23 September 2005: 'L&T, Dubal to set up Rs.1500-cr refinery').
26. In April 2002, Sterlite Opportunities and Ventures Ltd. (SOVL) bought a 26 per cent share (soon 46 per cent) and management control of Hindustan Zinc Ltd. (HZL), which had started in 1966. It had three lead and zinc mines in Rajasthan, two smelters in Rajasthan (one zinc and lead, one just zinc), one zinc smelter at Vizag in Andhra, and Tundoo lead smelter in Jharkhand. In 2003–04, Sterlite's share of India's zinc business rose from 62 per cent to 75 per cent. Vedanta in 2006 controlled 42 per cent of India's copper, with a refinery at Silvassa (Gujarat), and the infamous refinery and smelter at Tuticorin, supplied from its mines in Australia and Zambia. Vedanta increased its copper capacity from 180,000 tons per year to 300,000 in 2005. We were personally assured at the Vedanta AGM on 29 July 2004 that this would not lead to a recurrence of groundwater pollution—a promise that does not appear to have been kept (GoI, *Ministry of Mines Report 2002–3*, pp. 50 and 58, Vedanta Resources plc: *Annual Report 2004*, and information on the mines and communities website).
27. Toxic Bob was named after a gold mine at Summitville in Colorado (1985–92), which was closed after a colossal toxic waste spill through badly contained metal pilings. Bob fled to Canada, until Clinton 'pardoned' him in 2000, and he agreed to pay $27 million for the clean-up (a fraction of the real cost). He caused another appalling spill at Omai gold mine

in Guyana, managed via a Canadian company, Golden Star Resources. The Omai holding dam collapsed in 1995, spilling 3.2 billion tons of cyanide and heavy metals into Guyana's main river, the Essequibo. Bob had just left the company and paid nothing towards a clean-up of the mining industry's biggest ever cyanide spill.

28. Fraser and Lungu 2007; WoW 2008; Jean-Christophe Servant, 'Rivers of Acid: Mined out in Zambia', *Le Monde Diplomatique* (English edition), 9 May 2009, at *mondediplo.com/2009/05/09zambia*.
29. *India Times*, 28 February 2009, 'Police slap case against Vedanta', and *TNN*, 17 March 2009.
30. Gelder 2004, for the Dutch organisation, Profundo. Monte Paschi (Italy) and Franklin Mutual Advisers (US) were other leading investors. In December 2003 Vedanta raised assets of $825 million, which increased to nearly $3,000 million by March 2004.
31. A list of UK investors, put together by Profundo in June 2008 included Wolverhampton and Middlesborough Councils and Teeside Pension Fund.
32. Press Trust of India, 6 November 2008, http://profit.ndtv.com/2008/11/06184150/Vedanta-may-cut-India-investme.html.
33. *Business Standard*, 20 May 2009; *Times of India*, 2 March 2009.
34. Letter to Vedanta shareholders, key articles on Asarco negotiations on minesandcommunities.org, *Wall Street Journal*, 15 March 2009; Reuters, 7 May 2009.

Chapter 9

1. See Appendix II. Sources include *US Geological Survey* 2006; Patricia A. Plunkert, *Bauxite and Alumina* (2004); and Wikipedia. Estimates vary in different sources and we make no claim for full accuracy in the tables we have compiled. Nor have we entered properly into the complex distinction between 'resources' and 'resource base', or estimated *versus* verified reserves. Since 2005, Vietnam's reserves have been estimated at up to 8 billion tons, perhaps exceeding India's.
2. Graham (1982, pp. 9, 20–23 and 93–101), is our main source in this section (also for quotations), supplemented by Cheddi Jagan, *The West on Trial: the Fight for Guyana's Freedom* (1975); Marcus Colchester (1997); Curtis (2003 ch. 17).
3. Curtis 2003 (ch. 16) on the Malaysian war.
4. Roberts and McLean (1976, p. 54), on the threat to the Akawaio Indians.
5. Colchester (1997, pp. 33–34 and 75–77).
6. The inevitable victory of mining companies in an endless tussle with governments for profits is the theme of Nwoke 1987—a victory that

ignores the interests of local people, who get ousted from their land, which gets lost in this tussle.
7. Joseph B. Treaster, 'Surinam war is devastating a bush society', *The New York Times*, 18 June 1987: an extensive report that revealed to the outside world the atrocities against Mapoons.
8. On Suriname: Colchester (1995 and 1997), and an in-depth study of the Bakhuis mining project by Robert Goodland, 14 April 2006 (www.caribbeannetnews.com).
9. Denis O'Hearn (1994).
10. Girvan's book *Foreign Capital and Economic Underdevelopment in Jamaica* (1971) is the seminal work on bauxite exploitation. Samarendra spent time with him during 2008, when Girvan invited him to the Pre-Conference on Bauxite History in Paris in September 2008. Girvan presented a paper there with Lou Anne Barclay: 'Transnational Restructuring and the Jamaican Bauxite Industry: The Swinging Pendulum of Bargaining Power'. Girvan and Barclay's book *Institutional Efficiency and FDI-facilitated Development: The Case of the Aluminium Industry in Selected CARICOM Countries* is forthcoming. See also Graham (1982, p. 259).
11. Blum (2003, p. 263). On Jamaica's hike of royalty see Bonnie Campbell (1995, p. 199); Holloway, (1988, p. 73) which expresses it misleadingly as a six-fold increase from $2 to $12); and Jamaica Information Service (jis@jis.gov.jm), 14 March 2006.
12. Zadie Neufville, 'Environment–Jamaica: Bauxite mining blamed for deforestation', Inter Press Service, Kingston, 6 April 2001.
13. Jamaican Bauxite Environmental Organisation at www.jbeo.com, and Switkes (2005, p. 11).
14. John Maxwell (18 February 2007), 'Is Bauxite Worth More than People?' (jankunnu@gmail.com, 2007); Oli Munion, 'Corporate Crimes in the Carribean: How Jamaica and Iceland Face a Common Enemy,' in *Voices of the Wilderness*, Saving Iceland (www.savingiceland.org), summer 2008.
15. Holloway (1989, pp. 50–51), Switkes (2005, pp. 7 and 10).
16. Bradley Cross, 'White Metal: Capital, and the Land, Under Multinational Aluminium Corporations in Guyana, Jamaica [and eventually Australia] in the 20th Century', paper presented at a Pre-Conference on the Global Economic History of Bauxite, Paris, 22–23 September 2008, hosted by the Institute for the History of Aluminium in Paris.
17. Mats Lundahl (1992), *Politics or Markets? Essays on Haitian Underdevelopment*, Routledge, pp. 102–04; and Hu Gentles, *Haiti Adieu*, in Jamaican Bauxite Institute Journal, vol. 2, no. 2, Kingston, Jamaica, summer 1983, pp. 191–98, which outlines the 60-year agreement signed with Reynolds in 1943–44, which fixed the price of a ton of Haitian bauxite at 1.2% of the price of a pound of aluminium ingot: just 30 cents per ton!

18. Bond (2006), and 'No aluminium smelter for Coega?' (January 2008) at http://theantidote.wordpress.com/2008/01/18/no-aluminium-smelter-for-coega/.
19. Gitlitz (1993, ch. 8), Forest Peoples Programme (2000, p. 12).
20. Gitlitz (1993, ch. 9), Switkes (2005), www.the-scientist/yr2000/oct/research_001002.html; and Lapointe 1994.
21. alcantinindia.org, 2005–07.
22. Andrew Perchard, 'Sculpting the "Garden of Eden": Patronage, Community and the British Aluminium Company in the Scottish Highlands, 1895–1982', paper for the Bauxite History Pre-Conference in Paris, September 2008, part of a forthcoming book about the aluminium industry in Scotland (Perchard [forthcoming]). Our paper (Padel and Das, December 2008) explores parallels between Scotland and Odisha.
23. Above, Chapter Seven. Rio Tinto has carried out explorations for iron ore in Keonjhar, and for diamonds along the Mahanadi, referred to in Guy Elliot's revealing speech quoted in Chapter Seven. See also Girard (2005), Goodland (2007).
24. On Kaiser's dams: Heiner (1991, pp. 50–68) and McCully (1996, pp. 17–18, 33–34 and 117).
25. On Kaiser Aluminium: Heiner (1991, pp. 263–307).
26. Graham (1982, pp. 21–22 and 117–88). The complex twists and turns of these negotiations for Ghana's dam and smelter take up a large part of Graham's book.
27. Gitlitz (1993 ch. 5).
28. Graham (1982, pp. 182–84 and 215–16). The crucial meeting between President Johnson, Edgar Kaiser and the CIA was in 1964.
29. In this delusion Nkrumah was supported by several prominent Western diplomats and financiers, like Sir Robert Jackson, head of a commission set up by the British government in 1953, and his wife Barbara Ward, who was an influential advisor to several heads of the WB. McCully (1996, pp. 265–66), Caufield (1996, pp. 179–83) and Gitlitz (1993 ch. 4) are our main sources in this section.
30. *Statesman*, Accra (Ghana) 21 June 2008; Switkes (2005); and Agbemabiese and Byrne (2005), who give a recent, compelling interpretation of the Volta project in terms of neo-colonial knowledge systems.
31. This and the following quotation are from Graham (1982, pp. 101–10).
32. BBC report, 10 October 2008 at http://news.bbc.co.uk/1/hi/world/africa/7663573.stm.
33. The film is by Stephen Hewitt. Peter Robbins has shared the results of his study with us, and written about the transfer pricing (1998). WB Report no. 26141-SL 25 July 2005: 'Tapping the Mineral Wealth for Human Progress—A Break with the Past' (www-wds.worldbank.org).
34. Peter Griffiths (2003).

35. Roberts and McLean (1976, pp. 9–13, 22, 29, 56–57 and 73).
36. On the Gladstone, Bluff and Bell Bay plants: Roberts and McLean (1976, pp. 12–15 and 94–101); and a 1977 publication by Peter Lush and Ron Currie: *The Amazing Adventures of NZ's no.1 Power Junky: The True Story of Comalco in NZ*, which explains the complex and crazy political manipulation behind the deals.
37. Moody (1992, pp. 230–40). David Broadbent is the reporter on *Melbourne Age*, and Paul Wilson the sociologist.
38. Hansard Committee on Mapoon land issue (2000) at www.capeyorkturtlerescue.com.
39. On Aurukun, Roberts and McLean (1976, pp. 35–50) and Moody (1992). After Comalco got a lease for 750 square miles of Aurukun land, another consortium consisting of an American land and ranch company called Tipperary, Billiton and Pechiney (40 per cent-40 per cent-20 per cent) bought a second lease for 800 square miles in 1968.
40. IUCN with ICMM, *Integrating Mining and Biodiversity Conservation: Case Studies from Around the World*, pp. 20–21, on Alcoa's rehabilitation of Jarrah forest, www.oecd.org/dataoecd/16/16/34982001.pdf.
41. Switkes (2005, pp. 7 and 12); *Guardian*, 7 August 2007, on Brockovitch.
42. John Hemming's *Red Gold: The Conquest of the Brazilian Indians* (1978) gives the fullest history. Numerous campaigns by Survival International and others tell the more recent stories.
43. Roberts and McClean (1976).
44. McCully (1998, pp. 104 and 160).
45. Gitlitz (1993) Switkes (2005); Barham, Bunker and O'Hearn (1995); Bunker and Ciccantell (2005).
46. Bunker et al. (2005, p. 67 ff).
47. Billiton was originally a Dutch company that mined tin in Dutch Indonesia. In 1963–73 it acquired 720,000 acres in Mato Grosso/Rodonia, including parts of what had been the Aripuana Indian Park—territory of the Cintas Largas, who by 1973 were a fraction of their number before 1963. The massacres included attacks by helicopter and on the ground. Roberts and McClean 1976 summarise the evidence (pp. 48–49 and 58–59).
48. We summarise the Nigerian situation in Chapter Twelve as an example of the *resource curse*. See Okonta and Douglas (2003), Rowell et al. (2005).
49. BHP was founded in 1885. The merger with Billiton created the world's biggest mining company. On Ok Tedi's sins see Moody (1992, pp. 144–47) and Kirsch (2006), among many other sources. BHP Billiton was one of the three leading mining companies that oversaw the Minerals and Metals for Sustainable Development (MMSD) Review.

50. Chapters Five to Seven. Loza and Price (2004) document a BHP Billiton initiative with NGOs in Odisha, where the company has been a potential partner in the Posco steel project and an investor in Kalahandi bauxite.
51. Data on Brazil's plants is based on www.wikipedia.com 2008; www.alcortechnology.com, April 2007; www.ame.com (2004), with UNCTAD 1995.
52. Martinez-Alier (2002, p. 63); Gitlitz (1993 ch. 11).
53. Switkes (2005), www.elaw.org (December 2004).
54. Gitlitz (1993 ch. 6).
55. Switkes (2005), on Mozambique and Bakun dam, on which see: 'The Dam that Wouldn't Die', *Asia Sentinel*, 15 August 2007 at http://www.asiasentinel.com/index.php?Itemid=178&id=637&option=com_content&task=view (May 2009).
56. See www.savingiceland.org (2006–08 entries), and R. Muradian in *Journal of Ecological Economics* (2001). Susan De Muth's article in *The Guardian* (29 November 2003) was one of the first pieces to highlight the danger of the campaign and the dangers for Iceland.
57. Miriam Rose, 'The Icelandic energy dilemma and how to help: a masterplan to exploit Europe's greatest wilderness', in *Voices of the Wilderness*, Saving Iceland (www.savingiceland.org), summer 2008. Rose was a British environmental scientist living in Iceland, who was threatened with deportation in September 2007, cancelled after a public outcry.
58. The anti-corruption group Greco, cited in Susan De Muth's article (note 56 above). See also Jon Henley, 'Saga of Survival', in *The Guardian* (7 November 2008).
59. Statements on Greenland and Trinidad made for this book at our request, November 2009. See also on Trinidad: Wayne Kublal-Singh 2009, Burton Sankeralli 2009, and 'TRINIDAD: Anti-Smelter Camp may be a Permanent Fixture', 31 October 2008 (Peter Richards at http://ipsnews.net/news.asp?idnews=35314)
60. 'Century announces it is stopping new investment in Helguvik,' 23 October 2008 at http://savingiceland.puscii.nl/?p=3360&language=en.
61. John C. Wu on Vietnam, in US Department of the Interior for US Geological Survey, June 2007 at the http://minerals.usgs.gov/minerals/pubs/country/2005/vmmyb05.pdf, and *vietnamnews.vnagency.com.vn/showarticle.php?num=01IND080406*.
62. Sergei Blagov in *Asia Times*, 24 May 2006, at www.atimes.com/atimes/Southeast_Asia/HE24Ae01.html, *and 27 October 2008 at* www.tradefinancemagazine.com/default.asp?page=2&PubID=187&ISS=25020&SID=713569&ReturnPag.
63. *International Herald Tribune*, 15 January 2008. See also 'Vietnam, bauxite and China,' *The Economist* 23 April 2009. On swiftly unfolding plans

to mine newly-surveyed bauxite deposits in Laos and Cambodia, as well as Vietnam, see Lazarus 2009.

Chapter 10

1. Mark Thomas, in *CAAT News*, Issue 197, August–September 2006, p. 11.
2. This and following quotes are from Sampson (1977, pp. 35–37).
3. C. S. Fox (1932, p. 197); G. D. Smith (1988, pp. 86–87 and 127); BAC (1955, pp. 47, 57 and 60).
4. Sampson (1977, pp. 66–89). Helmut C. Engelbrecht and C. Hanighen were the authors of *The Merchants of Death* (1934). A. J. P. Taylor's book, *War by Timetable: How the First World War Began* (ch. 9), showed how the arms build-up was a major cause of the Great War.
5. Smith (1988, pp. 142–44 and 154).
6. www.wordiq.com (2005). Modern napalm bombs apparently use aluminium only in the casing.
7. G. D. Smith, (pp. 193–214) (1988).
8. Sampson (1977, pp. 99–100) Smith (1988, p. 150 ff); Graham (1982, p. 55); and Alan Greenspan, *The Age of Turbulence: Adventures in a New World* (2007), Penguin, p. 43. Greenspan is mentioned by S. Das (2001) as one of the twenty 'dirtiest' world business and political leaders responsible for the present turbulence.
9. www.allwoodwings.com.
10. *The Guardian*, 21 May 1981; Graham (1982, p. 250), gives no reference for this figure.
11. globalsec.org, alcoa.com (Aerospace: History).
12. www.ilr.ing.tu-bs, azonano.com.
13. discoverychannel.co.uk/newscientist/week02/article04.shtml.
14. 2mag.org, nucleararchive.org.
15. *Weekly Guardian*, 15–21 April 2005, p. 6.
16. Sampson (1977, pp. 180, 231, 271–72, 279, 281–83, 286–88, 295, 301 and 317). A continual update on arms companies is available online at sipri.org (Stockholm International Peace Research Institute).
17. *CAAT News*, Issue 196, June/July 2006.
18. *Guardian Weekly*, 19–25 January 2007, p. 9.
19. 'CAAT infiltration: UK Information Commissioner proves BAe link', *CAAT Report* 31/07/05: 'Campaign Against Arms Trade (CAAT) today (29 July) publishes material from the UK Information Commissioner which substantively links its former Campaigns Coordinator, Martin Hogbin, to a private investigator, Evelyn Le Chene. Le Chene was employed by British Aerospace (now BAe Systems) to collect confidential about CAAT, according to evidence revealed by a Sunday Times investigation … A

Timesonline article reported that, starting in 1995, British Aerospace ... paid a company directed by one Evelyn Le Chene to infiltrate CAAT...'

20. *New Indian Express*, Bhubaneswar, 30 January 2007, p. 9.
21. Smith (1991, pp. 284 and 288); and *The Telegraph* (Calcutta), 2 March 2001, on Balco's deal supplying lightweight aluminium alloys for India's Agni and Prithvi nuclear missiles.
22. Girard, July 2005.
23. *Indian Express* (21 June 2006); *New Indian Express* (30 September 2007, p. 13) on Mittal being invited by the BAe board; IRIS news (23 November 2007); and most of the Indian newspapers on 8 February 2007, with photos of Ratan Tata sitting in the cockpit of an F-16, about to co-pilot it (in.rediff.com/money/2007/feb/08tata). On Naresh Chandra, see *The Hindu*, 11 September 2009, and www.defence.pk/forums/india-defence/34061-bae-pitches-strong-footpritnts-india.
24. Sharon Weinberger, 'Scary things come in small packages', *Washington Post* (28 March 2004).
25. Nathan Hodge in the *Financial Times* (30 June 2005), 'Pentagon studies China's influence on the price of weapons metals'.
26. Rod Dreher in *New York Post*, quoted in Christopher Ruddy (19 February 2001), newsmax.com.
27. *Forbes Magazine*, 7 September 1998. Marc Rich bought up Jamalco, sending Jamaican bauxite to his Vialco refinery at St. Croix in the Virgin Islands—both eventually bought up by Alcoa. In 1988 he bought Kaiser's Ravenswood smelter and locked out its unionised workers, who organised a picket of his home at Zug in Switzerland. See Wysham 2001 and Craig Copels' book about Marc Rich (1985/2001).
28. 'London Calling' entries in minesandcommunities.com for 8 July 2003 and 9 July 2004 collate sources on Russia's aluminium wars.
29. *FT*, 12 April 2000.
30. 'London Calling', mines and communities.org, 8 July 2003, 3 June 2004, 9 and 21 July 2004; John Helmer at Mineweb, 28 September 2004; and www.sual.com (2006). The IBRD, US Export–Import Bank, etc., have been supporting sales of foreign equipment to Russia, though the murders of journalists investigating this web of corruption have continued.
31. On Yukos: *The Independent*, 14 September 2006.
32. *The Times*, 30 August 2006: 'Glencore to join in RusAl–Sual merger'.
33. Klebnikov grew up in the US and worked for Forbes. His *Conversation with a Barbarian: Interviews with a Chechen Field Commander on Banditry and Islam* (2003) focuses on his 15-hour interview with a Chechen crime lord, politician and guerrilla commander, Khozh-Ahmed Noukhaev.

Chapter 11

1. Current reports as we write include:
   Roskill's *Economics of Aluminium*, 2003 (287 pp., 120 tables, 60 figures), $3,600;
   Roskill's *Economics of Bauxite and Alumina*, 2005 (366 pp., 211 tables, 72 figures), $4,200 (7th edition, February 2008, $5,000);
   CRU's *Analysis Report: Alumina Refinery Costs* (2007), £9,950 [$19,000];
   CRU's *Analysis Report: Bauxite Mining Costs* (2007), £9,950.
2. Morrison (2007), selling for £795.
3. *Business Standard*, 12 November 2008. LME prices for aluminium dropped from $3,200 per ton on 2 July 2008 to 1,871 per ton on 14 November 2008.
4. Articles on the UK scandal in *The Guardian*, 23 and 27 October 2008; and Deripaska's links with Rick Davis and John McCain in *Washington Post*, 25 January 2008, and 12 June 2008 at onlinejournal.com/artman/publish/article_3364.
5. Sam Jones in *FT* (18/19 October 2008), 'When junk was gold', on Moody's questioning before a Senate Sub-committee, and Stephen Crawley in *New York Times* (8 October 2008) on how Greenspan encouraged derivatives-trading as Federal Reserve Chairman (1987–2006).
6. Moody (2005, pp. 23–26).
7. Testimony (22 October 2008), at www.standardandpoors.com.
8. Allen L. Roland, 13 October 2008, 'Unspoken cause of financial collapse in derivative trading', opednews.com and http://blogs.salon.com/0002255/2008/09/16.html. See also Nick Hildyard's 'Wall of Money' analysis at http://www.thecornerhouse.org.uk/pdf/briefing/39wallmoney.pdf.
9. Prem Sikka in *The Guardian* (7 October 2008), 'The auditors have failed'.
10. Articles in *New Indian Express*, Bhubaneswar. On the CM's initial rebuff, see the newspaper of 6 December 2007. They met the PM on the 19th. By the 18th, focus had shifted to containing the Naxalites through a major road-building project in west Odisha (18 December 2007: 'Orissa will submit "roadmap" to tackle Naxals'), and bigger funds to fight the rebels. 'Earmark 5 per cent profit for growth, Naveen tells PSUs' (21 December 2007, p. 1), mentions PSUs—Nalco and the OMC—as well as private companies working in Scheduled Areas, singling out Vedanta's joint venture with the OMC. A few days later, while welcoming a huge planned expansion of the Rourkela steel plant, Naveen reiterated his request for PSUs to spend 5 per cent of their profits on local development. He described how 'reputed players from all segments are evincing keen interest in Greenfield projects', and how he had urged the PM to increase

royalty, so that the state receives a proper share of profits (5 January 2008, p. 1). Offering 5 per cent of profits for local development is also the NMP's interpretation of the Samatha Judgment, and the MoEF's answer to Niyamgiri mining impacts in its crucial, yet flawed report, presented at the SC on 5 October 2007.

11. Tamotia (2001, 2004). The pathological nature of corporations is a principal theme in Noel Bakan's book and film *The Corporation* (2004).
12. Stefan Giljum, Christian Lutz and Ariane Jungnitz, 'Quantifying indirect material flows of traded products with a multi-regional environmental input-output model', presented at the Liepzig conference of the European Society of Ecological Economics, June 2007. Also Hartmann (1998).
13. Mark Chernaik, *Evaluation of the EIA for the proposed aluminium smelter (2,50,000 TPA) near Jharsuguda*, October 2005.
14. Gitlitz (1993, p. 19).
15. Ibid., p. 41.
16. Ibid., p. 113.
17. Ken Stanford, p. 92 in *The Ringsider: Metals 2005*. London: LME.
18. The cost per kWH was just Canadian$0.007 as late as 1987. It got land for C$1.60 per acre that was assessed soon after at C$633, and paid 5 per cent of the going rate for water. Gitlitz (1993, pp. 67–69).
19. Ibid., pp. 90–91.
20. Eurometaux/European Association of Metals, 'The Green Paper for Sustainable, Competitive and Secure Energy' (Brussels, July 2006): 'Urgent measures are required for functioning electricity markets. Eurometaux proposes a set of solutions'.
21. The aluminium price in Norway varies between $0.0055 to $0.025 per kilowatt hour, averaging about one cent ($0.01) [1993 prices]. This compares with residential and commercial prices of over 6 cents, and is lower than other subsidised industries, including mining, manufacturing and paper ($0.022–0.024), though the chemical industry, steel and ferro-alloys, is only slightly closer ($0.018). Gitlitz (1993, pp. 58–60).
22. Jones (1977), and information from Andrew Perchard's forthcoming book on Scotland's aluminium industry.
23. Josephson (1963).
24. Brown et al, *Worldwide Investment Analysis: The Case of Aluminium*, WB Staff Working Paper No. 603, which compares production costs in different countries, as well as, for example., distance from bauxite mines to ports.
25. India's bauxite royalty has increased as follows:
    1949   5 per cent of sale value at pit's mouth
    1963   Rs 2/- per ton for chemical grade, Rs 1/- for metal grade
    1968   Rs 2.50
    1975   Rs 4/-

1981	Rs 8/-
1987	Rs 10/-
1992	Rs 34/-
1997	Rs 41/-
2001	0.35 per cent of LME aluminium price chargeable on aluminium content in ore
2004	a) 0.4 per cent for bauxite refined to metal-grade alumina in India
	b) 20 per cent of sale price for other uses and for export, i.e. approximately Rs 68/- per ton.

Ministry of Mines, royalty rate sheet, EPG website (with thanks to Patrik Oskarsson). The cost of labour for raising bauxite (which averages a third of the mining cost) varied in the mid-80s from $0.70 in Brazil to $6.70 in Greece (which has one of the few underground bauxite mines). In alumina refining, labour costs vary from $4.30 per ton (Brazil) to $61 (Germany) and total operating costs from $51.20 (Brazil) to $266.80 (Germany). Bunker and Ciccantell in Barham, Bunker and O'Hearn (1995, pp. 43 and 46).

26. A BJD pamphlet dated December 2006: 'Transparent Government Stable Government'.
27. www.thehindubusinessline.com/2006/09/23/stories.
28. freewebs.com/epgOrissa, summarising Nalco reports.
29. Attached to the letter is a calculation of Nalco's finances. The company started production in 1987 with loans of 980 million euro-dollars and 1050 million francs, entirely repaid by 1998, making Nalco a 'zero-debt company'. Its net profit was 522 crore in 2002–03, and the 15-year total by March 2003 was 4848.04 crore, with about 50 per cent of sales revenue generated through exports. To the central government, Nalco paid a 40 per cent dividend amounting to 257 crore in 2001–02 (63 per cent of company profit after tax), in addition to about 250 crore in sales tax and other duties each year. It employs 6,600 people directly, of whom 2,200 are SC or ST, and more than 25 per cent are from the 1,750 people registered as displaced by Nalco, with another 25,000 contract workers employed in the plant areas. Tax and Royalty to the GoO amounts to 2,000 crores up to March 2003, with 17 crore spent on 'peripheral developmen'. Nalco sells surplus electricity from its coal-fired power plants to the Odisha grid, which the GoO sells on at a profit, generating about 100 crore per year, earning 1550 crores to date. Nalco has planted 6 million trees. Panchpat Mali is sufficient to meet the company's bauxite requirements for the next 100 years. The average cost is just $17 of bauxite per ton of alumina (38 per cent lower than Alcoa, the next cheapest producer), and alumina is produced at $100 per ton (against the global average of $140), while the Angul smelter gets electricity from its captive plant at 65 per cent lower than the local rate.

The future promises a doubling of gross sales to profits of 1200 crores per year. The loss, if a private company took over, would be a massive drop in government revenues, and Odisha's bauxite reserves would be rapidly sold off to foreign-based companies.

30. *Sunday Times of India*, Bhubaneswar, 23 September 2007, p. 4: 'Rupee gain triggers loss for Nalco'. *Business Standard*, 5 December 2008, 'Nalco slips into crisis', mentions as a main reason the price of coal, which Nalco was having to import from countries like Indonesia at Rs 9,500 per ton, as against Indian coal at Rs 800 per ton.
31. Sunil is an SJP activist in Madhya Pradesh. His essay in Hindi (2004) is the clearest analysis of the dangers and scams that follow from tying India's economy to the dollar.
32. *FT*, 5 November 2003, p. 5, Special Report on Aluminium, by Khozen Merchant and Kunal Bose.
33. *FT*, 3 November 2004, p. 4, by Kunal Bose.
34. March/April 2005, pp. 20–22.
35. Ian Boyne, 'Jamaica Bauxite Institute playing critical role' (14 March 2006), on www.jis.gov.jm.
36. *The Ringsider: Metals 2005*. London: LME.
37. For example, *Mining Journal* (8 August 2003), London, pp. 89 and 96.
38. Appendix V for full list of aluminium prices.
39. 'China: Voracious demand fuels prices', *FT*, 5 November 2003, aluminium supplement.
40. Morrison (2007).
41. *Prospectus* (18 June 2007) for sale on 22nd of 130,440 American Depositary Shares.
42. Richard Cowen 1999, *Geology, History and People* (ch. 14), Cartels and the aluminium industry, 'Cartels and various Metal Cans of Worms', at www.geology.ucdavis.edu/~cowen/~GEL115/115CH14aluminium.html. On cartels generally, Robert Liefmann, *Cartels, Concerns and Trusts*, in German 1932 (translated and with introduction by D. H. Macgregor, Ontario: Botoche Books, 1921).
43. The Ford-McCumber hike. William Hoffman 1974, *Paul Mellon: Portrait of an Oil Baron*. Alcoa's 'biography' (Smith 1988) is explicit about Alcoa/Alcan participation in pre-First World War cartels, but brings no mention of involvement in the 1920s–30s cartels.
44. The 1931 cartel gave Alcan 28.5 per cent of the market, Pechiney 21 per cent (PCAC now merged with SEMF), VAW 20 per cent, AIAG 15.5 per cent, and BAC 15 per cent. Other companies in Italy (including Montecatini that started Malco soon after), Norway, Germany, Austria and Spain were subsidiary members.
45. Holloway (1988, p. 70); and Girvan (1971).
46. Holloway (1988, p. 72), a quote from *Forbes magazine* 1979.
47. Chapter Seven; Moody (2007, p. 36); and Chapter Sixteen.

48. Stiglitz (2002, pp. 173–74). Quotations and material in the following paragraphs are from the section of *Globalization and its Discontents* focusing on the aluminium cartel (pp. 171–79).
49. Girard (2005, p. 21), on Alcan's influence through Alfed.

Chapter 12

1. EAA, *Aluminium Packaging: Tomorrow's Packaging Today* [n.d.], pp. 2–32.
2. Kalam and Rajan (1998), IBM (2002).
3. On Tata's joint-venture with Fiat in Singur, and the saga of events there, see, for example, *New York Times* (2 September 2008).
4. Key phrase from Thorstein Veblen, *Theory of the Leisure Class*, 1899.
5. Recycled figures from www.aluminium-international.org (consulted 2008).
6. For example, Richard Robbins 2003, and Mary Douglas and Baron Isherwood 1978, *The World of Goods: Towards an Anthropology of Consumption*.
7. Inge Røpke, PhD thesis (published 2006), *Consumption and Environment: Ecological Economics Perspectives*, Department of Environment, Technology and Social Studies, University of Roskilde, Denmark; and www.storyofstuff.com
8. NB oil company funded lobbying that promoted 'scepticism' about global heating, summarised, for example, in Monbiot 2006.
9. C. R. Harrington, 'The aetiology of Alzheimer's disease: Routes into a common tau pathway,' in Exley (2001, pp. 97–132).
10. Priest and O'Donnell (1998).
11. ITV news special report (UK), 11 September 2008; Michael Moore (2001, p. 123).
12. IAI, *Aluminium Applications and Society: Automotive, Paper 1*, May 2000. See also IAI *Sustainability Report* [n.d.], pp. 19–20, and *Aluminium for Future Generations: Sustainability Update 2005*; EAA, *Aluminium Packaging* [n.d.]; *Do Not Hamper the Recycling of Aluminium!* (1999). Where is the recycling done? The IAI implies, in the UK, but in fact, the only recycling centres in the UK are apparently for exporting it. In India the only recycling plant we know of is Indal/Hindalco's at Taloja, 45 km from Mumbai, started in 1971.
13. A serious mould contamination of Tetra Pak into milk in cartons in Russia was traced to a material called Tetra Fino Aseptic, produced at a Tetra Pak factory in India (12 December 2005 at www.cee-foodindustry.com/news/printNewsBis.asp?id=64488). The Press Release Distribution Service, PRLog, reports (2 September 2008) that Tetra Pak recycling in the UK increased from 5 per cent in mid-2007 to 85 per cent in 2008! (http://www.prlog.org/10112749-uk-energy-saving-pleased-that-tetra-pak-

recycling-facilities-are-on-the-increase.html). This illustrates the naivity and PR distortion surrounding recycling. The article blithely reports that a majority of councils now separate Tetra Pak cartons and send them for recycling abroad. The Tetra Pak website also makes claims that seem misleading about recycling. Some of the paper/cardboard content of Tetra Paks is probably recycled, and it seems some of the aluminium content may be 'down-cycled' into pencils, but from what we have discovered, it seems that separating the aluminium content for reuse is too energy-intensive to be viable. A piece dated 10 October 2008 mentions a new plant being built in India in addition to the first one near Pune, which had started functioning in 1997.

14. *Guardian*, 9 June 2004, 'Family Fortunes'. See www.tetrapakrecycling.co.uk for the company's claims to aim at a 30 per cent recycling rate, where the argument stresses voluntary recycling measures, and implies that recycling is of subsidiary importance to reducing materials and energy efficiency.
15. Gitlitz (1993, pp. 24–25).
16. Ibid., pp. 26–27.
17. Roberts (1976, p. 102).
18. The EAA told us that the 'al for future generations' campaign was done in conjunction with FoE Italy.
19. CRI and IRN, Press Release, 17 May 2006, www.container-recycling.org and www.irn.org.
20. 'The "Hidden" trade of metals in the United States', Jeremiah Johnson and T. E. Graedel in *Journal of Industrial Ecology*, vol. 12, no. 5/6, 2008. Sanat Mohanty, 'The economics of externalities', www.thesouthasian.org/archives/2005/economics_of_externalities.html.
21. 'Most … environmental costs have not been factored into the price of aluminium. According to a recent study by the Tellus Institute, whose research focuses on energy, solid waste and other environmental issues, "The externality costs vary from several hundred dollars per ton (for paper, glass and steel) to $2,000 for [virgin] aluminium and from $600 to $1,000-plus for several types of plastic"' (Gitlitz 1993, p. 138).
22. Ritthoff et al (2002, p. 49). These figures compare with other materials as follows (ton per ton):

	abiotic intensity	water consumption	air intensity
primary aluminium	**85.38**	**1,378.6**	**9.78**
recycled al	**3.45**	**60.9**	**0.37**
primary steel	6.97	44.6	1.3
primary copper	500260	2	
heating oil	1.5	11.4	0.03

On the Wuppertal website, the figures are given slightly differently (with areas where calculated):

Alumina	7.43	58.6	0.45	(Germany)
primary aluminium	37	1,047.7	10.87	(Europe)
basic oxygen steel	9.32	81.9	0.772	(World)
stainless steel	17.94	240.3	3.382	(Europe)
(17 per cent Cr 12 per cent Ni)				
ferrochrome low	21.58	504.9	5.075	(World)
carbon (60 per cent Cr)				

from 'Material intensity of materials, fuels, transport services', Wuppertal website, www.wupperinst.org (2007).

23. This is their factor 4 or factor 10 theme, meaning we should reduce consumption by a quarter or a tenth.
24. For example, in their publication *Earth Politics* (German, 1989, and in English translation, 1997).
25. Friedrich Hinterberger, Stefan Giljum and Mark Hammer's 2003 article for *Encyclopaedia of Ecological Economics*, 'Material Flow Accounting and Analysis (MFA)', Sustainable Europe Research Institute, Vienna [friedrich.hinterberger@seri.at]; Stefan Giljum, Christian Lutz and Ariane Jungnitz 2007, 'Quantifying indirect material flows of traded products with a multi-regional environmental input-output analysis: a methodological concept paper' presented at the conference on Environmental Economics at Liepzig in June 2007; Haberl et al. in *EPW* 2006: 'Ecological embeddedness of the economy…'
26. Nicholas Stern, Review on the Economics of Climate Change, 30 October 2006, UK government. A previous report by the Department for the Environment of the UK government estimated $56–223 per ton of CO_2 (Andrew Simms in Ann Pettifor 2003, p. 66). Richard Cowen estimates that producing a ton of aluminium gives off emissions of 5.6 tons of CO_2 if the smelter is hydropowered from a dam; and 20.6 tons if it is powered by a captive coal-fired power station (www.geology.ucdavis.edu/~cowen/~GEL115/115CH14aluminium.html). Most of India's smelters apparently use a combination of electricity from dams and from their own coal-fired power stations. For a critique of Stern see Spash (2007).
27. Lohmann (2006, pp. 255–61), and several articles exposing carbon trading and 'the great CDM scam' in Soumitra Ghosh and Subrat Sahu (2008). UN Framework Convention on climate Change, 19 October 200, http://cdm.unfec.int/E8/035/ebo35rep.pdf.
28. Ibid., p. 255, quoting Soumitra Ghosh.
29. Ibid., pp. 39–63, describing how economists Ronald Coase and Milton Friedman persuaded the US Presidency and WB-WTO-UN bureaucracy to open up pollution credits to the free market as a major source of profit. See also on the flip-side of the IPCC, David Wasdell, *Beyond the Tipping Point and Analysis of the Political Oppression of the IPCC Text* (www.meridian.org.uk), and Bidwai 2008. See also Walter Fernands, 'Climate Justice in the Northeast', 5 December 2009 (at www.assamtribune.com/scripts/details.asp?id=dec0609/edit2).

30. Among a growing literature on the dangers of biofuels, see, for example, Mark Lynas, 'Frankenstein Fuels', in *New Statesman* (7 August 2006).
31. EAA Press Release, 19 July 2006; IAI, *Aluminium Applications and Society: Automotive, Paper 1*, May 2000. See also IAI website, which gives the following statistics: 100 kg of aluminium saves 10 grams of emissions per km; the EU 2008 target of reducing emissions to 140 g of CO_2 per km cannot be met, but aluminium allows an EU directive for 85 per cent materials recycling to be met. There is a 5–10 per cent fuel savings per 10 per cent weight reduction. Each ton of replacement aluminium saves about 20 tons of CO_2 (13.9 tons if the aluminium is all primary, 26.7 tons if it is 95 per cent recycled), and each kg of aluminium saves 3–7 litres for every 100,000 km driven, so a car with 100 kg of aluminium saves 3–7 litres every 1,000 km. But see following note.
32. Thea Picton, 'Aluminium: green metal?' in *Mining Monitor*, October 1998. Alex Mathias, 'Greening Aluminium,' in The Carbon Challenge magazine October 2003, brings evidence from the Massachusetts Institute of Technology that disproves claims by the IAI etc, which do not take either Al production externalities or built-in redundancy in cars sufficiently into account.
33. IAI, *Third Bauxite Mine Rehabilitation Survey*, June 2004. This gives glowing accounts of Alcoa's mines, as well as Alcan in Arnhemland and Comalco on Weipa, also mentioning Jamalco (Jamaica) and Nalco on Panchpat Mali.
34. Ibid., p. 25.
35. http://www.icmm.com/page/889/restoring-a-forest-after-bauxite-mining.
36. Roberts et al. (1976), and Chapter Nine.
37. Letters from OSPCB to Vedanta and government authorities dated 23 November 2007, 9 September 2008, and 12 January 2009 list the violations and the company's non-compliance with orders. Residue from the red mud lake was seeping continuously into the Bansadhara, the lake's lining was leaking, and the slurry mix was too alkaline. A subsequent site visit on 29–30 January 2008 revealed non-compliance with these orders: the slurry was still too alkaline, the red mud lake lining was eroded and still leaking, and a storm water drain within the refinery compound, near the railway crossing, was diverting polluted waste slurry to the clean water pond, from where it was discharging into the Bansadhara.
38. Proceedings of the International Conference on Bauxite Tailings at Kingston, Jamaica, 1986, published by the Jamaican Bauxite Institute, pp. 81–83. T. A. Venugopalan is the Hindalco official.
39. Personal communication by senior Orissa government geologist, Dr. Anil Pal.
40. www.redmud.org, consulted on 15 November 2008, under 'Red Mud, Industrial Uses'. Sea dumping seems to have been a general practice until recently, and took place in Greece's sensitive Gulf of Corinth. The

main researchers profiled on this website include five from India, four from Greece and one from China. One of the Indian scientists, Harish K. Chandwani had helped set up Korba and the JNARRDC.

41. Ashutosh Mishra in *Down to Earth* (17 November 2008), 'Extracting a cost: Vedanta's refinery pollutes river, sickens people in Orissa', http://www.downtoearth.org.in/full6.asp?foldername=20081130&filename=news&sec_id=4&sid=1#.
42. OSPCB reports to the Central Pollution Control Board in Delhi, during 1995 and 2002. IAI, *Sustainability Report* [n.d.]. On smelter pollution see also, in the context of plans for a plan in Greenland, http://www.aluminium.gl/content/us/about_the_project/environment.
43. Chapter Four. Article by Sankar Pani, 14 October 2008 on merinews.com. Santosh Telenga, the farmer quoted in Chapter Four, interviewed for *Matiro Poko*, showing the damage to his plants, lost all his plants even before this incident.
44. Greer and Bruno (1996, p. 173).
45. On a tour around Muri refinery we saw large areas of asbestos which workers are exposed to.
46. On workers: 'Most can't stand the conditions. The heat's way over 100 on the potlines' (Roberts et al 1976, pp. 93–94).
47. R. C. Das (1996).
48. Mark Chernaik 2005: assessment of Vedanta's Burkhamunda smelter EIA.
49. Billon (2001, p. 562–63), with references to Ross (1999) and Collier (2000), *Economic Causes of Civil Conflict and their Implications for Policy*, Washington, DC: WB.
50. Rosser (2006) summarises critiques of the resource curse thesis. Kuntala Lahiri-Dutt ('"May God Give Us Chaos, So That We Can Plunder": A critique of "resource curse" and conflict theories', in *Development*, 2006, 49(3), pp. 14–21, www.sidint.org/development) shows the importance of the non-formal or illegal mining sector in providing jobs for workers, but does not contest the central issue that exploiting abundant mineral resource has a tendency to lower people's standard of living, and to feed conflicts.
51. Erwin H. Bulte, Richard Damania and Robert Deacon, 'Resource abundance, poverty and development', 2003, Paper 21–04, University of California, Santa Barbara, richard.damania@adelaide.edu.au. Sachs' explanation (2001) is that 'Resource-abundant countries tended to be high-price economies and, perhaps as a consequence, these countries tended to miss-out on export-led growth.'
52. James A. Robinson, Ragnor Torvik and Thierry Verdier, 'Political foundations of the resource curse', 9 May 2005, paper prepared for the conference to celebrate Pranab Bardhan's tenure as editor of the *Journal of Development Economics*.

53. MMSD (2002), pp. 174, 188, quoted by Ballard and Banks (2003, p. 296).
54. CSE 2008, pp. 15–19, 42–61, 66–108 and 234.
55. Bakan (2004) and Chapter Nineteen.
56. Okonta and Douglas (2003), Rowell, Marriott and Stockman (2005).
57. Okonta and Douglas (2003, pp. 96 and 108).
58. Well-corroborated accounts show that, among other similar, systematic payments in 1993–99, Shell paid the most notorious officer, Paul Okuntino, who led massacres of numerous Ogoni villages, and that Chevron also instigated massacres and provided transport, Ibid., pp. 145–51, 153–54 and 180.
59. Ibid., p. 182.
60. Shell has spent billions on PR, a story summarised in Okonta and Douglas (ch. 7), 'A game for spin doctors'.
61. *Business Standard Today*, 23 Jan 2008. Okonta and Douglas contrast Shell's propaganda with the reality investigated by one researcher who found a devastating oil spill in a remote area still with no clean-up twelve months after (p. 188).
62. Okonta and Douglas, (pp. 185–86).
63. Ibid., p. 166.

Chapter 13

1. This is the title of our essay published in the Council for Social Development's *Social Development Report 2008: Development and Displacement*, pp. 103–15, ed. H. M. Mathur.
2. Fernandes (2006, pp. 110–11).
3. Mathur (ed.) 2006, p. 2.
4. John Prebble 1969 [1963], *The Highland Clearances*, Penguin; Padel 2000 [1995].
5. Andrew Perchard, forthcoming.
6. Saroj (2008).
7. Theodora Kroeber, *Ishi: In Two Worlds—A Biography of the Last Wild Indian in North America*, 1961.
8. Dee Brown 1975 (1970).
9. Caufield (1998, p. 262), quoting Scudder in WB 1994, pp. 2–7.
10. David Pearce quoted by Cernea in Mathur (ed.) 2006, p. 22 (previous quote), and WB 1994, p. vi.
11. WB OED Report no.17538, cited in Mathur (ed.) 2006, pp. 61–62; Scudder in Caufield (1998, p. 234).
12. Cernea, April and December 2006, and a statement of his model published by the WB (2000); Mathur 2006 and 2008; and our articles 2007–08: each of us with articles in *Social Change* (2006 or 2008), Cernea and Mathur with articles in *Adivasi* (2006), etc.

13. After Pandey (1998), who lists these as the largest displacements, out of a much longer list, and gives a total of over 1,500 villages displaced in Odisha, i.e. over 100,000 families. Pandey's figures for villages displaced seem to merge those partially displaced (which lost a large part of their land, but remained on the ground) with fully displaced villages. The figures for *people* displaced are from estimates elsewhere in our book.
14. Announced in the Indian press in *Times of India*, 12 April 2007, p. 12.
15. *Agragamee Plan and Budget for 2000*, p. 29.
16. Mathur (ed.) 2006, pp. 48 and 69–70.
17. Cernea (2006, pp. 26–28).
18. *Utkal Jyoti*, January–March 2001, section 6 on CSR.
19. See also Esteva (1985), *Development: Metaphor, Myth, Threat*, in 'Seeds of Change', vol. iii, Washington.
20. Fenelon (1998); and Savyasaachi (2008, p. 287), on UNESCO.
21. B. D. Sharma (1990).
22. Article in *The Guardian*, 4 Oct 2003, p. 17: 'Every third person will be a slum dweller within 30 years, UN agency warns'.
23. Archana Prasad's argument (2003) that 'tribal culture' is an artificial construct by romantic anthropologists, flies in the face of extensive evidence about the egalitarian outlook inherent in 'organic societies' (e.g. in Bookchin 1982) and serves to legitimise the process of dispossession. Works on Hindu nationalism (Shubh Mathur 2008, Chatterji 2009) rightly stress misuse of 'culture', as well as the co-opting of tribal militants. This is a very different, manipulated concept of culture, delinked from a system of cultivating the soil.
24. Four Corners is where Utah, Colorado, Arizona and New Mexico meet. See Moody (2007, p. 127).

Chapter 14

1. IAI, *The Aluminium Industry's Sustainable Development Report* (n.d.).
2. The average temperature reached by a refinery is 1200 degrees centigrade, and by a smelter 800, though a smelter needs to maintain this continuously (Barham and Bunker 1995, pp. 44 and 47, mention 960–70 and 1300 degrees centigrade, i.e. 1760–80 and 2400 degrees fahrenheit). Nalco produces bauxite for Rs 150–200 per ton, compared with Balco/Hindalco figure of Rs 500–600. The overall picture has been that Nalco is producing alumina for much less than its rivals, Hindalco and Balco, as much as Rs 1,000 less per ton of alumina.
3. UN Environment Programme, WB Mining Department, International Finance Corporation and MMSD, *Finance, Mining and Sustainability 2001–02* (www.mineralresourcesforum.org), p. 10. This document forms

part of the MMSD process, and reflecting the mining company interests in charge, it does not adequately address this question of inconsistencies in the CBA.
4. Gundimeda et al. (2005 and 2006). M. M. Sahu's booklet on Gandhamardan was written during the movement (1987), showing the impossibly high value of Gandhamardan's forest, spelling out many reasons why conventional estimates are much too low.
5. Cowen's estimate, referred to in Note 26 of Chapter Twelve. A recent report by the Department for the Environment of the UK government gave the higher estimate of $56–223 per ton of CO_2 (Andrew Simms in Ann Pettifor 2003, p. 66).
6. FoE's evidence to the International Audit Committee on International Trade and the WTO (www.foe.co.uk), June 2006.
7. Ruth Padel (2005) shows how the tiger mafia works and gives numerous examples of corruption in the forest department. Das (2006) reveals the forced displacement of Adivasis by 'save the tiger' projects.
8. *Rich Lands, Poor People: Is Sustainable Mining Possible?* CSE's 6th *State of India's Environment Report*, December 2007. Out of India's 50 most mined districts, 60 per cent are in the most seriously impoverished category, including Koraput, where 79 per cent of the people live below the poverty line, and Keonjhar (63 per cent).
9. Akshaya Mukul, 'Balco staff "coerced" into VRS', *Times of India*, 25 January 2007; Vedanta Update (minesandcommunities.com), 25 January 2007.
10. Moody (1992, pp. 43 and 56), citing another example, concerning Alusuisse marking down the price of alumina exported from Gove (Australia) to Iceland, where its price showed higher (Ibid., p. 56).
11. Greg Crough, 'The pricing of alumina exports from Australia: a case study of the Gove project', *Jamaican Institute of Bauxite Journal*, vol. 3, no. 2, December 1985. Crough is citing a statement made by Iceland's Minister for Industry and Energy, Hjorleifur Guttormsson. His comparison of the export price for Gove alumina with the import price paid by Alusuisse's ISAL smelter in Iceland (figures from Coopers and Lybrand), shows a massive differential each year, as an example of how a company makes huge hidden profits through transfer pricing. These figures show a loss to the ISAL smelter of $60 million during 1970–83, in which period Alusuisse estimated its total loss at $107 million.
12. Poddar, *Vedanta's Billions*, 2nd edition, 2006 (presently banned in India by order of Aurangabad High Court), pp. 4, 150 and 152, on a single instance where SEBI fined SIIL for preferential allotment of shares to Twinstar Holding on 31 January 2000. In the Vedanta Resources annual report for 2004, VAL's holding company is given as SIIL, while in the 2005 report it is given as Twinstar, without any comment on how this transfer took place. 'In the 1st quarter of 2003, Sterlite's sales rose 14

per cent. Its export turnover grew threefold (by 201 per cent) while its domestic turnover fell by nearly a quarter. Its tax provision tumbled by 84 per cent, to a large extent because the increase in exports enabled the company to benefit from tax breaks on export profits' (from Poddar's letter to Chidambaram dated 31 July 2006, p. 3 of Poddar 2006). Poddar's letter dated 25 January 2006 to UK Listing Authority, Financial Services Authority, on Volcan's involvement (2006, p. 64). 'Uproar in Rajya Sabha over book reference' refers to opposition members demanding Chidambaram's resignation, holding up copies of Poddar's book (*The Hindu*, 23 October 2007 at thehindu@web1.hinduonnet.com).
13. Morrison (2007).
14. We were among a group of signatories to a letter about Vedanta and the *FT*'s coverage, which journalist Rebecca Bream of the *FT* assured us would be published, but was not.
15. With thanks to Nick Hildyard, Roger Moody, Kavaljit Singh and other friends for what we understand of these topics.
16. 'Market sentiment improves', James Salter, in LME, *The Ringsider: Metals 2005*, pp. 47–56. He observes that aluminium prices were being boosted by 'the expected power-related closure of smelting capacity in Europe ... Indeed, in mid-June 2005, there were a series of announcements suggesting that more than 1 million tours per year of European smelting capacity is under threat of closure due to high power prices.'
17. Ken Stanford, 'A global transformation', in LME, *The Ringsider: Metals 2005*, p. 91, on Alcoa's profits: 'The greatest revenue was generated not by primary production (25 per cent) but from downstream operations, of which fabricated products accounted for 49 per cent, transport 26 per cent and consumer and packaging 25 per cent.'
18. Peter Robbins (2003, ch. 1). Robbins was instrumental in setting up Traidcraft's fair trade coffee.
19. *People's Voice*, vol. 29, issue 16, August 16–31, Delhi, p. 3.
20. Gandhi in *Young India*, 26 December 1924, p. 421, and 15 November 1928, p. 381. From N. K. Bose 1957 (enlarged edition), *Selections from Gandhi*, pp. 38–39.
21. James Abraham et al. (ed.) 1993, *Appropriate Technology Lineage: Gandhi–Kumarappa–Schumacher*, p. 61.
22. Published in India at Delhi: Three Essays Collective, 2008. On India, e.g. CSE 2008.

Chapter 15

1. BBC report, 6 June 2009, and https://nacla.org/node/5879.
2. Desmond King-Hele (1999). Among Alexander Cordell's novels, based on detailed research on the mining and metals industry in nineteenth-

century Wales, are *Rape of the Fair Country* (1959), *Song of the Earth* (1969), *The Fire People* (1972).

3. *Encyclopaedia of World History*, London: Reader's Digest, 1996, p. 670; Utsa Patnaik (2007, pp. 120–21) on the starvation deaths in Russia in the 1990s.

4. *Encyclopaedia of World History*, p. 267. The figure of 30 million is strongly contested, for example by Utsa Patnaik (2007, pp. 117–19), but the famine was undoubtedly one of the world's worst, exacerbated by a plague of locusts that devoured crops after the 'great sparrow campaign' had killed off the bird population, and the local officials' false statistics of crop yields, which meant that hardly any food was left for the peasants, even as ignorance of steel technology meant that most of the 'steel' produced was useless. The crazed cruelty with which the policy was imposed is evoked in Jung Chang, *Wild Swans: Three Daughters of China* (1991), New York.

5. On recent coal mine deaths in China, see www.minesandcommunities.org.

6. On Adam Smith see Chapter Nineteen.

7. CSE (2008, pp. 4–6), whose figures place 41 per cent of India's iron ore in Karnataka, 19 per cent in Chhattisgarh, 14 per cent in Jharkhand, and 7 per cent in Andhra. Jharkhand has 29 per cent of India's coal, Chhattisgarh has 16 per cent and West Bengal 11 per cent. In manganese, Karnataka follows Odisha with 29 per cent. Rajasthan has 90 per cent of the country's lead and zinc reserves (much of this now under Vedanta's control). Coopers and Lybrand (*Prospects for Industrial Development of Orissa*, 1996) give slightly different figures for Odisha, especially for iron ore:-

Mineral	*Reserves (in mt)*	*per cent of India's reserves*	*Rank in India*
Chromite	183	98.4	1
Bauxite	1,626	69.7	1
Manganese ore	49	31.8	1
Graphite	1.5	32.6	1
Dolomite	563	12.2	1
Quartzite	-		-1
Pyrophylite	-		-2
Fireclay	88	12.5	2
Quartz	15	1.9	4
Coal	44,304	23.8	4
Iron ore	3,120	26	5

8. CSE (2008, pp. 240, 244, 256–57).

9. By the Blacksmith Institute (US). *Independent* (London), 16 September 2007 and www.blacksmithinstitute.org.

10   On De Beers and its 80 per cent control of the diamond trade, keeping prices high by enforcing scarcity, see e.g. www.minesandcommunities.org and http://www.un.org/peace/africa/Diamond.html.
11. Sarini (2006);, Nayak and Kunjur (2007, p. 25).
12. Vandana Shiva and Afsar Jaffri (1998, p. 4).
13. Ibid. This summarises the early years of the movement, but was criticised (Birendra Nayak 2000) for plagiarising without due acknowledgement an English-language bulletin, *Voices of Gopalpur*, which Birendra Nayak edited from 1996 and published from Berhampur with Prafulla Samantara.
14. 'Rajya Sabha, Unstarred Question No. 2256 to be answered on the 6th July 1998, Sukhinda Chrome-ore mines to private companies.' Ghufran Azam drew the minister's attention to the news item in *The Statesman* dated 16 April 1998 entitled 'Pressure to clear Sukhinda lease', asking whether the private sector companies proposing to take over chrome mines had been pressing the government on the issue, and if so, whether the government was considering cancelling this lease of the mines. To this Naveen Patnaik replied that with Tisco [Tata] reducing its area, '*over 50 per cent of the balance area of 855,476 hectares*' had become available for lease to four parties: Indian Metal and Ferro Alloys (IMFA) with Indian Charge Chrome Ltd., Ispat Alloys, Ferro Alloys Corp. Ltd. (FACOR), and Jindal Strips.
15. *Indian Express*, 19 and 20 November 2004.
16. Nayak and Kujur (2007, pp. 9 and 15).
17. From an Appeal for financial support for the havildar's family, written by a senior government official the day after the incident (Ibid., p. 1).
18. On different versions of what really happened at Kalinganagar, see Nayak and Kujur (2007), among other sources, and Sahu (2007) on the aftermath.
19. *Adivasi*, vol. 46, no. 2, December 2006, special issue on development, displacement and rehabilitation, gives the GoO R&R policies as an annexure. On the Harsha Trust et al survey of Kalinganagar oustees for Tata, see Chapter Nineteen.
20. 'Tata Steel Bullets' on youtube.com, posted by Samadrusti TV, May 2008.
21. Posco has also applied to mine iron ore on Malingtoli (Sundargarh) and Thakurani (Keonjhar).
22. For example, 'Medha Patkar demands Abhay Sahu's release', *The Hindu*, 31 May 2009. Statesman, 26 June 2008; CSE 2008, pp. 257–59; *stoposco. wordpress.com/2008/10/13/anti-posco-agitation-leader-arrested-on-12th-october*; 'Anti-Posco leader illegally chained to hospital bed', http://www.youtube.com/watch? v=px3d52vTEuM. On Abhay's release on 21.8.09 see *www.youtuve.com/watch?v=x8jjKG1WqVY.*
23. 'Tata Muscle Power' on youtube.com, posted by Samadrusti.
24. *Sambad*, 11 April 2006, naming four factories where workers had recently been killed (fuller account from freewebs/epgOrissa.org). 'Bhushan workers

go on a rampage', *Sunday Express*, 30 December 2007, p. 1 (Bhubaneswar), and 'Bhushan outrage was inevitable', *New Indian Express*, 31 December 2007, p. 5, mentioning the UNDP R&R survey report submitted to the Revenue Department, which specifies 200 killed and 500 critically injured in the factory within three years, and mentions the allegations that some people killed in the plant were buried on the spot.
25. *Samaj*, Bhubaneswar, 6 November 2008.
26. CSE (2008, pp. 172–77).
27. Ibid., pp. 183–89.
28. Ibid., pp. 116–19.
29. PUDR, April 2006, among several detailed reports on this war by human rights groups; M. N. Mitra, 'Red alert', *Down to Earth*, 31 October 2006, pp. 27–28. CSE (2008, pp. 137–40); and Putul (2007) on the steel plants.
30. October 2006, *www.channel4.com/news/microsites/U/unreportedworld/india.html*. The Afterword to the second edition of Nandini Sundar's book on the history of Bastar (2007) contains a good summary of the civil war. Also see Padel, September 2007 (longer version, 'How to heal a civil war?' at http://www.mail-archive.com/chhattisgarh-net@yahoogroups.com/msg00153). See also: Campaign for Peace and Justice in Chhattisgarh 2007 and Javed Iqbal November 2009.
31. 'Buddha goes soft on SEZ', *Indian Express* (Bhubaneswar), 12 February 2007, p. 1.
32. *Times of India*, 7 December 2007, at timesofindia.indiatimes.com/India/Tapasi_Malik_case_Charges_framed_CPM_leader/rssarticleshow/2604946.cms. The CPI-M view is given in an article by B. Prasant, 'Who killed Tapasi Malik at Singur?' in *People's Democracy* (weekly organ of CPI-M), vol. 31, no. 18, 6 May 2007.
33. http://sanhati.com/front-page/1083/ (as on 17 November 2008).
34. 'Tata Steel Bullets' on youtube.com, May 2008.
35. PRAYAS and C. S. Venkata Ratnam 2003.
36. Ibid., p. 44.
37. Ibid., pp. 50, 58.
38. Ibid., p. 60.
39. On the Dhabol scandal, see S. Kumar (2001) and Purkayastha and Prashad (2002).
40. A tribunal against the Pani Panchayats, which were understood as a first step to privatising water, was held at Soochna Bhavan in Bhubaneswar on 27 February 2002 by the Campaign Against Marketisation of Water.
41. W. W. Hunter, *The Annals of Rural Bengal*, vol. II, London: Smith, Elder and Co., pp. 201, 277, quoted in Padel 2000 (1995), p. 80.
42. *Times of India*, Bhubaneswar, p.2, 'Naveen pays first official visit to post-firing 'nagar'. NB Dash 2009, 'A heinous assault'.

Chapter 16

1. Kishenji's petition is mentioned in Dash (1998, pp. 1–9); and Currie (2000, pp. 176–82). Writ Petition nos. 12847 of 1985 and 1081 of 1987.
2. Quoted in Currie (2000, p. 180).
3. Currie, p. 182, quoting Panda's Report, p. 351.
4. Dash (1998, pp. 10–27).
5. Final hearing, 25 January 1992, and Judgment, 12 February 1992.
6. Affidavits to NHRC dated 15 February 1998 and 2 April 1998.
7. Dash, pp. 28–67.
8. Ibid., pp. 68–71.
9. C. P. K. Misra, in Ibid., pp. 78–81.
10. CSE (2008, pp. 15–19, 42–61, 66–108, 234).
11. Utsa Patnaik's *Republic of Hunger* (2007) gives a good analysis, and the Andhra figures, p. 101.
12. DFID, June 2005, gives the following statistics for those below the poverty line: 63.3 per cent of tribal people and 40.5 per cent of dalits; 87.1 per cent of south Odisha and 49.8 per cent of north Odisha.
13. Padel 2000 (1995) (ch. 2–5).
14. Cobden-Ramsey (1910) on the process of expelling Konds from Nayagarh and other Odia kingdoms as they came under British rule; Nayak and Kujur (2007) on the Sukinda Raja.
15. Ruth Padel (2005).
16. The East India Company took over Kalahandi from the Maratha dynasty based at Nagpur in 1853.
17. Mohanty (1945. English translation, 1987).
18. MacViccar in 1852, quoted in Padel 2000 (1995), p. 132.
19. Currie (2000) describes the system of revenue collection in detail.
20. A senior IAS officer, speaking about Malkangiri district (just south-west of Rayagada), where Koya adivasis, who had always cared for the wild bamboo, are now employed by the OFDC destroying their own forests, quoted in Sainath (1996, p. 100). Visiting the JK Paper Mill in Rayagada district and testing their paper, we found it was a mixture of bamboo and other forest trees with eucalyptus. Also see Madhu Ramnath (2004).
21. These laws started with the Central Province Land Alienation Act of 1917. Among others are the Orissa Debt Bondage Abolition Regulation of 1948 (as recommended by the Thakkur Committee, outlawing the *gothi* system); the Orissa Scheduled Areas Transfer of Immovable Property (OSATIP) Regulation of 1956, which prevents tribal land being alienated from tribal ownership without permission of the Sub-Divisional Officer; and Acts of 1953 and 1955 on behalf of tenants, who should not have to pay as rent more than a quarter of what they produce.
22. Sainath (1996, p. 197 ff).
23. Sainath (1996, p. 317 ff).

24. Prebble (1963).
25. Kampo and other Telugu cultivator and trader castes, and high-caste Odias such as Brahmins (some of whom were granted what had been tribal lands several centuries ago), Karanas (scribes, especially the Patnaiks), Paiks/Khandaits/Kshatriyas (warriors), Gauros (cowherds), etc. One could trace the history of south-west Odisha and other tribal areas in terms of waves of immigration of non-tribals, starting with Brahmins and Kshatriyas centuries ago, and accelerating from the 1950s with high-caste people, highly motivated to acquire land, from the Cuttack and Berhampur regions of coastal Odisha, as well as Telugus from Andhra.
26. The late K. C. Mullick, deeply respected President of the Kui Samaj in Phulbani, made many appeals for Adivasi reservation.
27. Campaigners in Odisha's rice price movement complain that records concerning the import of rice and other grains from the US and other countries are not open to public scrutiny. Large amounts are said to be shipped into Odisha through Paradip, undercutting indigenous rice production.
28. On the Orissa Famine of 1866, see e.g. J. K. Samal 1995, *Economic History of Orissa 1866–1912*.
29. Despite the bias of Governor-General Lytton (1876–80) against famine relief on the grounds that India had reached its population limit, and famine relief would tax the industrious to keep the lazy alive. See G. Lambert, *India: The Horror-sticken Empire* (1898); R. Dutt, *Famine in India* (1900); Dadabhai Naoroji, *Poverty and Un-British Rule in India* (1901).
30. Pilger (1998, p. 361 ff). Also see Alex de Waal (1997, pp. 12–13).
31. Waal (1997, p. 21).
32. *Weekly Guardian*, 8–14 May 2003, an article about outrage in Ukraine at the Pulitzer prize being awarded to the journalist Walter Duranty, who as Moscow correspondent for the *NY Times* in 1933 denied reports by the British journalist/writer Malcolm Muggeridge, who first exposed this famine, and revealed how it was engineered by Stalin.
33. Klaus Grebmer, Heidi Fritschel, Bella Nestorova, Tolulope Olofinbiyi, Rajul Pandya-Lorch and Yisehac Yohannes: *The challenge of hunger: The 2008 Global Hunger Index,* International Food Policy Research Institute 2008. This lists India among 33 countries in the 'alarming' categories, with 20–30% living on the edge of starvation.
34. Chapter Fifteen note 4.
35. Waal (1997, ch. 6).
36. Waal (1997, p. 132), shows how the UNEOE consistently lied to conceal the role of war and to pretend that the most needy were being fed, and how this, rather than the egalitarian relief indigenously organised by the 'insurgents', became the model for subsequent famine relief. A decisive victory in 1988 by the EPLF (Eritrean People's Liberation Front), which

37. led to the secession of Eritrea from Ethiopia, was actually reported in *The Times* as 'Stepped-up guerilla raids threaten food delivery'!!
37. Waal (1997, p. 89, ch. 5 on Sudan).
38. On the aid agencies' response to the Ethiopia famine, see also Hancock 1989 (ch. 1).
39. *The Guardian Weekly*, 29 February–6 March 2008, p. 1; and Pilger (1998 and 2002) on starvation in the sanctions period in Iraq, when lack of essential medicines and the means for water purification, etc., resulted in the deaths of about a million Iraqis, from hunger as well as basic, curable diseases. Since the US occupation, the food insecurity has often been chronic, and cholera has returned in force. Similar food insecurity affects people in Afghanistan as well.
40. Grants listed (1999–2004) include: AP Power Sector Reforms (1999–2004), MP Public Sector and Power Sector Reforms (2001–04), TN Water (2000), Orissa Public Enterprise and Regulatory Reform (1999 and 2003). See WoW press release, 'UK "aid for privatization" scandal hits India', 7 December 2004 (www.waronwant.org).
41. DFID (2005).
42. Centre for Communication and Development Studies, for Ekta Parishad, with support from PACS, *Towards a People's Land Policy*, 2007; and DFID, 'Better livelihoods for poor people: the role of land reform', consultation document, November 2002, which argues for land reform and strengthening land rights.
43. The fact that the Singur and Nandigram land is exceptionally fertile, giving three crops a year, and that people will lose their food security along with their identity as farmers, is discounted against the promises of corporate investment.
44. This lack of correlation between theory and reality is highlighted in Alternative Survey Group (2007, pp. xiii–xiv, 5, 8–9, 15–23 and 47–52); and analysed by David Mosse (2007)—a critical examination of DFID's key theory on poverty and how to reduce it.
45. Mosse (2007).
46. Mosse (2007, p. 13).
47. Friends who have worked closely with DFID and UN agencies in Odisha have explained to us in meticulous detail how these programmes end up doing the opposite of what they are supposed to do, promoting exploitation and misappropriation of villagers' land, forest, non-timber forest produce, water, etc.
48. WoW (2006, pp. 2 and 5–7). In India the CDC's first stake was a 25 per cent ownership of the Kondapalli gas-fired power station in AP, where opposition to electricity privatisation and price hikes caused three deaths and thousands of arrests in 2000. See also www.cdcgroup.com. On the JK Paper Mill, when a friend with knowledge of such factories questioned it with the DFID's senior environmental officer, he described

this factory as 'our attested partner' and refused to hear anything against it. Are there links between Vedanta and the CDC?
49. WoW (2004), Action Aid (2006), *Guardian Weekly*, 8–14 October 2004 (reviewing the WoW report).
50. Sogge (2002, p. 82). WoW press release, 7 December 2004, mentioned above, lists the DFID consultancy contracts in India to these and other firms, for programmes in the four focus states.
51. DFID State Plan for Orissa (2005) gives the following figures:-

Expenditure in Orissa:		*Planned Expenditure in India:*	
2001–02	£22m	2005–06	£280m
2002–03	£49m	2006–07	£285m
2003–04	£12m	2007–08	£300m
2004–05	£20.48m		

52. Hancock (1989, pp. 156–60).
53. Sogge (2002, pp. 76, 88 and 90), the latter from an article by B. Cooksey (1999) presented at the Ninth International Anti-Corruption Conference, Durban, South Africa (www.transparency.de/iacc).
54. 'Protest against World Bank, DFID', *Times of India*, 10 June 2002.
55. For example, 'Vigilance probe to find out tainted minister', *Sunday Express* (Bhubaneswar), 20 January 2008, pp. 1 and 3, concerning a scam uncovered by the WB in which a firm admitted paying a Rs 500,000/- bribe to the GoO Health Minister—the latest in a long line of such scams. The next day, 'WB smells scam in AIDS project too', *New Indian Express*, 21 January 2008, p. 1.
56. www.trade.uktradeinvest.gov.uk/metals/india2/opportunities/opportunities.shtml, and letter of Chris Mullin to Keith Hill, 24 August 2004.
57. The list includes (with the Sterlite entry removed by October 2004):
    * SAIL technical upgradation, Rs 80 billion
    * SAIL, Rs 60 billion, 'includes 30 billion for Bhilai long rail production'
    * SAIL, Rs 20 billion for development of Chiria mines and its subsidiary IISCO
    * SAIL, new colour-coating facility for steel pipes with state of art technology
    * TATA steel chrome plant in South Africa due to start production in 2005 (Rs 25 billion)
    * JINDAL stainless steel plant at Duburi, Jajpur D [Kalinganagar] with a 500MW ccpp
    * JVSL, increasing rolling mill capacity
    * Ispat Industries' move into long products
    * Bhushan steel and strips, with a Sumitomo agreement for manufacturing automotive strips
    * 'expanding Khopoli plant (Maharashtra) capacity'

- * SPS Group (Kolkata) Orissa sponge iron plant
- * Nalco Rs 400 billion investment to increase alumina/aluminium capacity
- * STERLITE, 1.4mtpy greenfield alumina complex at Lanjigarh by SIIL under BALCO banner
58. The late Rajendra Sarangi described to us the large number of workers' deaths in constructing this plant, the danger it poses to local resources as it expands, and the opposition of the Kalinganagar Adivasis it has displaced.
59. Jindal Export Credit Guarantee, see Sogge (2002, pp. 75–76).
60. Sharon White to Professor Emil Salim, 20 October 2003; Moody (2007, p. 36).
61. Mathur (2008), Padel and Das (2008).
62. 'Tail Enders and other deprived in the canal water distribution', a report for the Planning Commission in 2003. 'Ground swell: Orissa farmers make it clear that water from the Hirakud dam is for irrigation, not industry', *Down to Earth*, 31 December 2007, pp. 22–30.
63. POKSSS 2008.
64. Conversations with Lingaraj.
65. Conversations with Rajendra Sarangi, who devoted years to understanding Odisha's water system, and died shortly after this, and with Ashok Pradhan. As they pointed out, there is a sinister shift in the *National Water Policy* (Delhi: Ministry of Water Resources, GoI, April 2002, no. 5), in which 'agro- and non-agro-industries' are placed at no. 2 among the specified Water Allocation Priorities—drinking water, irrigation, hydropower, ecology, agro- and non-agro-industries, etc.
66. Pilger (2006, pp. 37–90 ,) (ch. 1, 'Stealing a Nation'). 'Maintaining the Fiction' (p. 51) is the title of a memo written in 1968 by Anthony Ivall Aust, who was then a 26-year-old legal advisor to the Foreign and Commonwealth Office, and spelt out for future governments how to evade responsibility for the Chagos Islanders' removal by maintaining they were only a 'floating population', not indigenous. The Creole population actually goes back to the eighteenth century when the French brought slaves from Africa to work on plantations, and to the 1840s, when the British brought indentured labourers from India. Wilson's Foreign Secretary Michael Stewart wrote a secret memo to Wilson dated 25 July 1968: 'By any stretch of the English language there was an indigenous population and the Foreign Office knew it' (p. 65). One of the American officials responsible for the crime against the Chagossians and its cover-up, used a simpler expression: '*CYA* ...[meaning] *Cover your arse*' (p. 71).
67. Ibid., pp. 61–62.
68. Sampson (2004, p. 326).
69. Ibid., p. 139.
70. Agarwal (2005).

656 | Notes

71. Padel 2000 (1995).
72. The term 'Washington Consensus' was coined by economist John Williamson in 1989 (Sogge 2002, p. 23).

Chapter 17

1. Caufield (1998, pp. 226–27).
2. In Chapter Nine we saw the WB helping to orchestrate the aluminium industry in Ghana, overseeing the Volta dam agreement and getting rid of Nkrumah, along with the CIA and MI6 (1957–66); in Guinea, forcing Halco and the government to share their Sarengedi bauxite venture with five other major aluminium companies in 1963; and exerting pressure to privatise the bauxite mines (1999) in Guyana, forcing repayment to Alcan (1971), etc.
3. Srivastav, Sanjay et al. June 2006, *Environmental and Social Challenges of Mineral-based Growth in Orissa: Building Partnership for Sustainable Development*, WB with GoO.
4. Moody (2005, pp. 75–76 and 86–87).
5. Caufield (1998, p. 86).
6. Rich (1994, pp. 85–87), Caufield (1998, p. 125).
7. Caufield (1998, pp. 106–16, esp. pp. 107 and 112).
8. Ibid., p. 144.
9. Sir Roy Harrod, quoted in Rich (1994, p. 50).
10. Rich (1994, pp. 64–65).
11. Ibid., pp. 66–67.
12. Ibid., pp. 69–72.
13. Ibid., p. 74, quoted from Hirschman's article, 'A dissenter's confession: the Strategy of Economic Development revisited', in Meier and Seers (1984).
14. Caufield (1998, pp. 58–61 and 85–86).
15. Ibid., p. 89, quoting Robert Wade, 'The system of administrative and political corruption: canal irrigation in South India', *Journal of Development Studies*, April 1982, p. 317.
16. Ibid., p. 98, quoting the WB's *India Irrigation Sector Review*, 27 June 1991, pp. 9–10.
17. Ibid., pp. 26–34, 99, 127–30, 167; Pilger (1998, Rich 1994, pp. 34–38).
18. Ethiopia: Waal (1997), Caufield (1998, pp. 206–07).
19. Caufield (1998, pp. 211–12).
20. Ibid., p. 203.
21. Rich (1994, pp. 113–15 and 167–68); Gitlitz (1993, pp. 103–04); Caufield (1998, pp. 172–77 and 186–87). For Japan's Import-Export Bank funding Alumar, and other Japanese loans, see Barham et al. (1995), Bunker et al. (2005).

22. Rich (1994, pp. 111–79); Caufield (1998, pp. 180–88).
23. S. Anklesaria Aiyar quoted in Rich (1994, pp. 38 and 40).
24. Rich (1994, pp. 42–43).
25. Ibid., pp. 43–46.
26. Ibid., pp. 150–52 and 249–54; Caufield (1998, pp. 5–29); Morse (1992).
27. Dana L. Clark, *A Citizen's Guide to the World Bank Inspection Panel*.
28. WB 2003, p. vi.
29. Ibid., p. 56.
30. Caufield (1998, pp. 89–93).
31. Ibid., p. 94, quoting an interview in the WB's archive with Irving Friedman in June 1986.
32. Ibid., pp. 98–105.
33. Zaire: Ibid., pp. 132–35.
34. Peru: Ibid., pp. 135–36.
35. Turkey: Ibid., pp. 146–49.
36. Mexico: Ibid., pp. 138–42 and 151–57; and Rich (1994, pp. 78 and 109), on the net negative transfers behind the 1982 crash.
37. Neeraj (2001, pp. 21–25).
38. Caufield (1998, p. 145), citing PIRG 1994, p. 60.
39. Ibid., p. 145, citing Ann Crittenden, 'World Bank, in Shift, Lending for Trade Debts', *New York Times*, 26 May 1980.
40. *Fiscal and Governance Reforms* (2001), Finance Department, GoO, which says that 46 per cent of Orissa's GDSP was going into paying off interest.
41. IBRD and IDA 2004, p. 1, giving $40 million IDA and $85 million IBRD 'payable in 20 years' for a multi-pronged approach following Orissa's fiscal crisis of 1999, and a substantial track record of reform:
    i. economic growth-enabling reforms covering agriculture and land administration, private enterprise, and restructuring of public enterprises;
    ii. fiscal reforms to improve the revenue system, saving on unproductive exports and enhancing the effectiveness of public spending;
    iii. strengthening governance including financial accountability, public procurement, service delivery and government organisation;
    iv. investments in poverty monitoring and human investment, including health and education;
    v. adoption and implementation of industrial policy resolution of 2001, public enterprise reform programme, closing ten unproductive units, and initiation of privatisation of many more.
42. Ibid., pp. 3 and 5.
43. Ibid., p. 9.
44. Investment report on Orissa (1996) by Coopers and Lybrand Pvt. Ltd. (which later became PriceWaterhouseCoopers) with Lovelock and Lewes Services Pvt. Ltd., London.

45. Klein (2007, pp. 55–62).
46. Ibid., pp. 58–59.
47. Ibid., pp. 66–69; Pilger (1998), Caufield (1998, pp. 200 and 210).
48. Ibid., pp. 75–81.
49. Ibid., pp. 83–87 and 105, citing Frank's *Economic Genocide in Chile: Monetarist Theory versus Humanity*, Nottingham: Spokesman Books, 1976.
50. Klein (2007, pp. 98–99), quoting Letelier's 'The Chicago Boys', in *The Nation*, 28 August 1976. Friedman denied supporting Pinochet's methods, and justified acting as his economic adviser (Klein 2007, p. 117).
51. Klein (2007, pp. 117–20), citing Amnesty's *Report on an AI Mission to Argentina, 6–15 November 1976*.
52. Klein (2007, pp. 107–09 and 121–28).
53. Ibid., pp. 111–14.
54. Quoted in ibid., p. 6.
55. Ibid., pp. 137–40; Monbiot (2000), Milne (2004).
56. Klein (2007, p. 162).
57. David Budhoo, quoted in ibid., p. 164.
58. Ibid., pp. 171–93.
59. Fukuyama introduced the concept in a speech called 'Are we approaching the end of history' at a revival meeting at the Chicago School of Economics. It appeared three years later in his book, *The End of History and the Last Man* (1992). See Klein (2007, pp. 182–83).
60. Ibid., p. 221.
61. Ibid., pp. 221–37.
62. Ibid., pp. 194–217.
63. Harvey (2005, p. 6), Klein (2007, pp. 308–82).
64. Stiglitz (2002, p. 6), Gray (1998), Harvey (2005).
65. David Mosse 2007 and 2009.
66. Quoted in Harvey (2005), pp. 36–37.
67. Caufield (1998, p. 196), quoting interview with Deepak Nayyar (3 April 1993), who was in charge of negotiations for India's IMF loans during the BoP crisis in 1991.
68. Ibid., p. 257.
69. Klein (2007).
70. Caufield (1998, p. 235). The five countries contributing the most financially to the WB have their ED on this Board.
71. Mosse (2009).
72. Caufield (1998, pp. 66–67). IDA and IBRD offer loans at different rates of interest and from different sources—IDA 'credits' are from country contributions, IBRD loans from the bond market. In 1995 there were 63 IDA countries and 62 IBRD ones, with 15 blend countries eligible for loans from both sources, including India.
73. Caufield (1998, pp. 284–85), Moody (2005).

74. *Frontier* (Kolkata), vol. 40, no. 38, 6–12 April 2008, p. 11.
75. K. Singh (2005, p. 77), Stiglitz (2002, p. 7). Negotiations on the Eight Uruguay Round of GATT (General Agreement on Trade and Tariffs) led to an agreement signed by Clinton for the US on 31 December 1994, inaugurating the WTO on 1 January1995. Over 100 nations had signed by July.
76. Caufield (1998, p. 179).
77. Ibid., pp. 216–41.
78. Ibid., pp. 207–08, 242–52. For revelations about the WB-fed corruption and manipulation in Sierra Leone that led to ten years of civil war (alongside Alusuisse's exploitation of its bauxite), see Griffiths (2003).
79. Ibid., pp. 254–55.
80. Stiglitz (2002, pp. 71–72).
81. Ibid., pp. 188–91, quoting 'Why I've had it with the World Bank', *The Wall Street Journal*, 30 March 1990.
82. 'Wolfowitz resigns after scandal over girlfriend's pay-rise', 18 May 2007, at http://www.timesonline.co.uk/tol/news/world/us_and_americas/article1805960.ece.
83. Caufield (1998, pp. 225 and 231–32).
84. Ibid., pp. 225 and 231–32; and Stiglitz (2002, pp. 34 and 51–52).
85. Stiglitz (2002, pp. 40–41).
86. Ibid., pp. 20–21.
87. Caufield (1998, pp. 195–96), quoting her interview with Nayyar (mentioned above).
88. In Hans Anderson's famous story, the emperor commissions the best tailors to make his new clothes. The clothes these tailors make don't exist, but they tell the emperor and his courtiers that only the most intelligent people can see their fabulous subtlety of design and colour. So everyone pretends to admire them, and so do the emperor's subjects when he walks in procession, until a child points out that the emperor is naked.
89. Keynes, quoted in Rich (1994, pp. 74 and 219).
90. Stiglitz (2002, p. 36).
91. Hannah Arendt, *Eichmann in Jerusalem: A Report on the Banality of Evil* (1963).
92. Fergus MacKay, *Indigenous Peoples' Right to Free, Prior and Informed Consent and the World Bank's Extractive Industries Review*, Forest Peoples Programme, UK, final draft, June 2004; Marcus Colchester (2003); and WB (2003). On Thayer Scudder's 20 years as WB consultant on forced displacement, and his reports and evidence, see Rich (1994, pp. 156–59).

Chapter 18

1. Petras (1997), Nayak (1997), Petras and Veltmeyer (2001), Kamat (2003).
2. Vidhya Das' articles in *EPW* (1995–2003), Achyut and Vidhya Das, 'Chronicle of a struggle: the Kashipur anti-mining movement', *Ecologist Asia*, vol. 12, no. 2 ('Mining: digging our own graves?'). The other three NGOs were WIDA, Ankuran and Laxman Nayak Society for Rural Development.
3. This pamphlet, translated here from Hindi, was written for the crucial second conference of Samata Sangathan activists, after which several prominent members left the organisation to found NGOs.
4. Quoted in Nayak, October 2000.
5. Petras (1997, p. 11).
6. Ibid., p. 19.
7. Ibid., p. 14.
8. Ibid., p. 13.
9. For example, en.wikipedia.org/wiki/Binayak_Sen; http://www.indianexpress.com/news/binayak-sen-release-committee-condemns-demol/464758/.
10. Hegde (2005).
11. Petras (1997 and 2001).
12. WoW 2004 and 2006.
13. Andy Howard, *Mining a changing landscape*, http://stockmarketnasdaq.com/blogs/list-direct-stock-purchase-companies/52256/.
14. Nayak (1997, p. 50).
15. Correspondence between Radhanath Pradhan in Bhawanipatna (22 March and 1 July 1996) and Noam Chomsky (22 April and 25 July 1996).
16. Petras (1997, p. 18).
17. Ibid., p. 16.
18. Saroj (1999 and 2000).
19. A tribal song from Keonjhar, played on the flute in *Matiro Poko*, to the accompaniment of an iron-ore train thundering past.
20. Nayak (1997, pp. 54–55).
21. Agragamee and other Odisha NGOs periodically send staff to Bunker Roy's training centre in Rajasthan, the Barefoot College, Tilonia. On Bunker Roy's acceptance of Alcan's $1 million Sustainability Award, see www.glinet.org/inspiredetail.asp?id=1519&CatID=316—39k and http://www.hindu.com/2006/12/01/stories/2006120101260500.htm. The award is managed by the Prince of Wales' International Business Leaders' Forum.
22. Mosse (2009).
23. For example, Lohmann (2006).
24. 'The denial industry', chapter 2 of Monbiot's *Heat* (2006).
25. Danielson (2006, pp. 10–13).

26. Severin Carrell, 'WWF in row over threat to rare birds', *The Independent on Sunday*, 16 February 2003, contrasted with an interview with Kathryn Fuller on the 'grist' website where she is questioned about conflict of interest between Alcoa and WWF over Iceland (http://www.grist.org/cgi-bin/printthis.pl?uri+/comments/interactivist/2004/11/01/fuller/in).
27. The link between Save the Children and Norsk Hydro is attested in *Primary Smelters of the World* published by Aluminium Verlag (2008).
28. On skewed funding for scientific research on bauxite and Alzheimers, above Chapters Three and Twelve, and Priest and O'Donnell 1998 *versus* Exley 2001.
29. Report Of The Expert Committee on Net Present Value, constituted by Institute of Economic Growth, Delhi, as mandated by the Supreme Court of India vide judgment dated 26 September 2005 in IA no. 826 in IA no. 566 of 2000 in Writ Petition (Civil) 202 of 1995.
30. 'Dozens of academic and practitioner fellows are currently conducting breakthrough research all over the world as part of Alcoa Foundation's Conservation'. See www.alcoa.com/global/en/community/info_page/CS_Fellowship_Program.asp.
31. Loza and Price (2004, in note 15).
32. Marcus Colchester, Tejaswini Apte, Michel Laforge, Alois Mandondo and Neema Pathak, *Bridging the Gap: Communities, Forests and International Networks—Synthesis Report of the Project 'Learning Lessons from International Community Forestry Networks'*, CIFOR Occasional Paper no. 41, Bogor, 2003, p. 18.
33. Nick Davis, 'How the richest man in Britain avoids tax', *The Guardian*, 22 April 2002; Wikipedia—Sigrid Rausing (June 2009); Sigrid Rausing, 'Closing Guantanamo won't be enough', *New Statesman*, 15 January 2009.
34. A theme in Petras (2001).
35. Copious examples regarding climate change in Monbiot (2006), Flannery (2007), Pearce (2007).
36. Tri-sector Partnerships, from www.bpdweb.org, 2000, 'developments', pp. 34–36 (consulted 2007).
37. See for example Moody (2005).
38. http://wordpress.com/tag/access-development-services/ (November 2008).
39. Alan Fowler, 'NGO futures: beyond aid—NGDO values and the fourth position', 2000.
40. *Vedanta Report 2007*, p. 41.
41. Anu Mohammed, *Monga, Microcredit, and the Nobel Prize*, December 2006, www.countercurrents.org/gl-muhammad041206.htm.
42. 'Tri-sector Partnerships', from www.bpdweb.org, 2000.
43. Samarendra Das, 7 November 2000.
44. Harsha (2006, pp. 9–10).

45. Ibid., p. iv.
46. Ibid., pp. 18–19.
47. Ibid., p. 47.
48. This theme is expanded from chapter 6 of *The Sacrifice of Human Being* (Padel 1995/ 2010), which analyses the roots of the missionary role as it was imposed over nineteenth-century Odisha.
49. Chatterji (2009), S. Mathur (2008).
50. For example, Action Aid International 2007 and websites.
51. *The Hindu* 10 February 2003, *The Hindu Business Live* 30 September 2003, *Financial Express* 22 may 2004.
52. *The Hindu Business Line* 20 May 2006.

Chapter 19

1. Dumont (1980), 1st English translation 1970 of French original 1966), a book with great influence on Indian sociology and anthropology.
2. Padel 2000 (1995), p. 163.
3. Chomsky (2002, p. 193).
4. Korten (1995), Monbiot (2000).
5. Quotations from Micklethwaite and Wooldridge (2003, pp. 18–24).
6. Ibid., p. 30.
7. This and following quotations are taken from Nick Robins, September–October 2006, and are also found in his book (2006).
8. Robins (2004.
9. Padel 2000 (1995).
10. Mentioned by Nick Robins (2006) in his book and *FT* article.
11. Josephson (1962, pp. viii–ix).
12. Micklethwaite and Wooldridge (2003, p. 65).
13. Quotations here from Josephson (1962, pp. 52, 130–31, 180, 187, 279, 292 and 440–43).
14. Lynch (2002, p. 184).
15. Josephson (1962, p. 450).
16. Ibid., pp. 368–71; Lynch (2002, p. 161).
17. The plot was apparently organised by key associates of J. P. Morgan (Thomas Lamont, John William Davis and others) through the American Liberty League. General Butler, who exposed it, was a military hero and wrote one of the first books exposing the military-industrial complex, *War is a racket* (1935). See http://www.nowtryus.com/article:Smedley_Darlington_Butler, and L. Wolfe, 'Franklin Delano Roosevelt vs. the Banks: Morgan's fascist plot and how it was defeated', at http://www.wlym.com/articles/wolfe_fdr.doc. Also http://coat.ncf.ca/our_magazine/links/53/davis.html.
18. Cannadine (2006, pp. 414–27), and Chapter Two.

19. Sampson (1975).
20. Subtitle of Sampson (1989): *The Midas Touch*.
21. Sampson (1982, 1993, pp. 107–21), Payer (1991, p. 91).
22. Hartmann (1998), Flannery (2007), Pearce (2007).
23. Sampson (1989, p. 47).
24. Quoted in Padel 2000 (1995), p. 275.
25. Lynch (2002, pp. 94 and 111).
26. Adam Curtis' BBC documentary *Century of the Self* (2002, en.wikipedia.org/wiki/The_Century_of_the_Self); Berger and Luckmann 1971 (1966); Chomsky and Herman (1988).
27. A BBC radio documentary analysed the role of PR firms in the war: www.bbc.co.uk/worldservice/documentaries/2008/10/081029_caucases_doc.shtml, www.finsbury.com.
28. www.co3.coop.
29. Fauset (2006).
30. Hildyard (2008).
31. 'More than ten years on, more pressure is needed', in Asia Monitor Resource Centre, *A Critical Guide to Corporate Codes of Conduct: Voices from the South*, 2004, p. 93, quoted by Fauset (2006, p. 3).
32. Apart from numerous articles in the local press, a piece in *Tehelka* highlights the acute food shortage faced by Adivasis who sold their land to Vedanta, and the case of a non-tribal worker named Hrudyanand Patra, whose leg was severely damaged when the ground gave way and he fell into a caustic soda pit on 19 May 2007—one of many such accidents. Anjali Lala Gupta, 'The Last Stand of Niyam Raja', *Tehelka*, 19 April 2008, pp. 44–45.
33. First two editions: July 2006 and January 2007. The SD report takes up 40 pages in the *2007 Annual Report*, and is published separately from 2008.
34. www.wpp.com (2008).
35. Fauset (2006).
36. *DFID and CSR: An Issues Paper*, DFID 09/03, p. 9, cited by Fauset 2006, p. 19.
37. Cowe (2003), 'The contradictions of Madhav Mehra', http://www.wef.org.uk/madhavmehra/aboutme.htm (2008–09). Council on Ethics 2007, and 2009 documentary, 'Sham Public Hearing: The Real Face of Vedanta' from dash.suryashankar@gmail.com. 'Activists protest Golden Peacock award by WEF to Vedanta Alumina in Himachal' at http://himachal.us/2009/06/12/activist-protest-golden-peacock-award-by-wef-to-vedanta-alumina-in-himachal/13576/news/rsood, and http://www.indopia.in/India-usa-uk-news/print-595574.html; 12 June articles: 'Protest mars climate change meet', *Himachal Times,* 'Hardcore environmentalists disrupt function', *Tribune*, and 'Plea to protect environment'; 13 June: 'Sensex crosses 6000 mark: a salute to every Indian' at http://www.wcfcg.

net/sensex.htm, where photos show Mehra meeting Manmohan Singh in 2003 with Ola Ullstein (ex-PM of Sweden), and Matthew Barrett of Barclays group at the Seventh Conference on Corporate Governance, London, May 2006. A similar award by WEF to Satyam was withdrawn just before Satyam's fraudulent accounts were exposed in January 2009 in a scam affecting all India.
38. www.tetrapakrecycling.co.uk/09.10htm, consulted 19 November 2006.
39. www.indiaresource.org/news/2006/1059.html.
40. www.perfectrelations.com, and 'Posco PR to win hearts', *The Times of India*, 4 May 2007, Bhubaneswar.
41. www.csccc.info, Bidwai 2008. The CSCCC, established in February 2007, has 40-odd member-organisations, which function as corporate lobbyists, and include Institute for Free Enterprise, Institute for Market Economics, Hayek Institute, Free Market Foundation, Minimal Government Thinkers, and Liberty Institute (Delhi).
42. *Darpan*, VAL's CSR newsletter, July 2006.
43. For example, in the Belamba Public Hearing in April 2009, and in demonstrations many for example at Muniguda on 5 October 209, shownat http://www.youtube.com/watch?v+Dm81BHv614, and other demonstratiout shown in Surya Shakar Dash's documentary: *The Real Face of Vedanta*, 2009.
44. Cannadine 2006, p. 72.
45. Padel 2000 (1995), p. 151, on Defoe's 'Robinson Crusoe' influence.
46. Abayomi Azikiwe, 'What's behind the military coup in Guinea-Conakry?' Pan-African News Wire/Workers' World, 11 January 2009; Chernoh Alpha M. Bah, 'Guniea: An example of the failure of neocolonialism', April–July 2006 at http://uhurunews.com/story?resource_name=guinea-failure-neocolonial; John Helmer, 'How Oleg Deripaska does business and settles debts' from Dances with Bears, at http://johnhelmer.net; 'Vladimiar Putin takes Oleg Deripaska to task', *The Independent*, 4 June 2009.
47. Alexander Cordell, *The Fire People* (1972) presents the Merthyr events in novel form; Martinez-Alier (2002, pp. 60 and 64), Josephson (1962, pp. 368–72) on killings of workers in America; McCully (2005, pp. 82–84); and World Rainforest Movement, January 2001, on Chixoy (http://www.wrm.org.uy/bulletin/42/Guatemala.html), in the context of a civil war in which approximately 72,000 civilians were killed in 1980–84, an estimated 93 per cent by the police and paramilitary forces; Moody (1992 and 2007); Okonta et al. (2003), Rowell et al. (2005); Chapter Twelve, on Nigeria, and Chapter Eighteen, on Peru.
48. Police firings took place in Koraput district on 21 August 1942, when Laxman Naik's demonstration at Mathili police station ended in ten to twelve deaths and 53 arrests, including that of the injured Laxman, and his eventual execution by hanging. On the 24th in Papadahandi, police

firing on a crowd of about 5,000 killed 19 and injured about 100, while 92 were arrested. In early September, a similar pattern of police killings and arrests took place in Dhenkanal and Talcher: on the 7th, a crowd was machine-gunned from the air as well as by ground forces. Further violence took place in Balasore district towards the end of September, culminating in a shooting at Iram/Melanapada on the 28th that killed 26 and injured 46. See Biswamoy Pati (1993, pp. 167–87).
49. On the back cover of *Darpan,* January 2007.

Chapter 20

1. Manshi Asher, 'State of Siege', *Tehelka,* 19 April 2008, p. 46.
2. On 13 April 2008. Translated from the Odia in footage by Surya Shankar Das. *The Times of India* (as well as *The Hindu* and *Dharitri*) carried an article about the event on 16 April 2008: 'Tribals up in arms against mining activities in Deomali range', by Satyanarayan Pattnaik: 'More than 1,000 people, who recently gathered at Upper Kanti village in Simliguda Block under the banner of Sibukodi [Sijukodi] Dharitri Surakhya Parishad and Lok Shakti Abhijan (Orissa) vowed not to give even an inch of their land for mining by private firms.'
3. Padel 2000 (1995), p. 170.
4. Rabindra Ray, (1988).
5. Reports by PUDR (April 2006) and other organisations; Padel in *Tehelka,* 22 September 2007.
6. Saving Iceland, 21 April 2008.
7. www.guardian.co.uk/business/2006/aug/02/india.internationalnews, article by Randeep Ramesh, and http://www.independent.co.uk/environment/nature/sea-turtles-face-threat-from-indian-ports-plan-761355.html.
8. *New Indian Express* articles from 25 November 2009 to 10 December 2009, including: 'Tribal outfit allege police excesses' (26.11), 'Cops intensify combing, CMAS leaders flee' (1 December), 'CMAS fear in Narayanpatna: Farmers leave crops to rot' (5 December), and *Times of India* (26 November, p.12), 'Civil groups slams state for atrocities' [*sic*] p. 12, which quotes Prafulla Samantara and CPI-ML leaders.
9. From a piece about mining Kishen Pattnayak wrote in English, unfinished at his death.

Chapter 21

1. Above, chapters Three and Seventeen.
2. This summary follows Kenneth Meadows in *The Medicine Way* (1990), p. 119 ff.

3. Alan Ereira, *The Heart of the World* (1990).
4. classwebs.spea.indiana.edu/bakerr/v600/rachel_carson_and_silent_spring.htm.
5. Pelikan (1973).
6. Klein (2007, pp. 316–22).
7. Dee Brown 1975 (1970).
8. Mukerji 2008 (1983) gives the example of Vidyaranya, the scholar who wrote important commentaries on the *Upanishads*, etc., after a brilliant career as the minister who virtually established the Vijayanagar kingdom in South India in 1336, which is a perfect expression of *vedanta*'s principle of renouncing the material world of power and wealth (Part II, p. 5).
9. Ibid., p. 131.
10. Ibid., pp. 78 and 83.
11. Ibid., pp. 78, 139, 146 and 156.
12. George Grant's foreword to Mukerji 2008 (1983), p. iv.
13. Padel 200 (1995), pp. 2–6.
14. Rajmohan Gandhi (199), Shubh Mathur (2008), Chatterji (2009).'
15. Cullinan (2002), Bakan (2004).
16. Above p.530, John Pollexfen, quoted in Robins (2006).
17. Naveen Patnaik (1993).
18. E.g. Monbiot (2006), Wasdell (2006–8).
19. Information from workers, and http://www.meconlimited.co.in/non_ferrous.aspx.
20. Chapter 12 and *Down to Earth*, 9 August 2009; Dharitri 4 December 2009.
21. Chapter 20 and references in note 9.
22. 'The world is not lacking in alternatives', the title of Kishen Pattnayak's Hindi masterpiece, *Bikalpaheen Nahi Hai Duniya* (2000).

Glossary

Dramatis Personae

One of the hard things about our story is the names of its many characters, especially of companies and other organisations that are often known by their acronyms—every bit as confusing at first as the characters in the *Mahabharata* or a Russian novel, using different names at different times and contexts.

AA: Aluminum Association, based in Washington DC, started in 1933
AAC: Alliance Aluminium Compagnie, the last 'official' aluminium cartel, started in 1931 as a company registered in Switzerland
AAI: Aluminium Association of India, Bangalore
ADB: Asian Development Bank
ADM: Additional District Magistrate
Adivasis: 'Aborigines', the indigenous or tribal people of India, also known as Scheduled Tribes
AES: a US electricity company
AGM: Annual General Meeting
Agragamee: an NGO based in Kashipur
Ahimsa: non-violence
AIAG: Aluminium Industrie Aktien Gesellschaft (Switzerland), which became Alusuisse
AIG: American International Group, an insurance company, with Indian subsidiary Tata-AIG
Alcan: Aluminium Company of Canada, a subsidiary of Alcoa till 1950, joined UAIL in Kashipur in 1997, left shortly before being merged with Rio Tinto in 2007
Alcoa: Aluminum Company of America, one of the world's oldest and biggest aluminium companies
Alfed: Aluminium Federation, based in Birmingham, UK, started 1933
Alumina: Al_2O_3, a white powder, the end product of an alumina refinery
AP: Andhra Pradesh, the state south of Odisha
APMDC: AP Mining Development Corporation (equivalent to OMC in Odisha)

Glossary

APPCB: Andhra Pradesh Pollution Control Board

Arthashastra: An ancient text on economics and politics ascribed to Kautilya in the fourth century BC

Ayurveda: the ancient, holistic system of Indian medicine

BAC: British Aluminium Corporation, taken over first by Reynolds (1959), then Alcan

BAe or BAe Systems: British Aerospace, the UK's biggest aerospace/arms company

Balco: Bharat Aluminium Company, bought up (51%) by Sterlite in 2001

BCSD: Business Council for Sustainable Development, which merged to form the WBCSD

Beju, Bejuni: Kond shaman, shamaness

BHP: Originally Broken Hill Proprietary Company (an Australian tin company), which merged with Billiton (Netherlands) in 2001–02

Bhumi: Earth, Ground

BICP: Bureau of Industrial Costs and Prices, Delhi

Birla: G. D. Birla was Gandhi's friend who started one of India's biggest business conglomerates based on a family dynasty. Aditya Birla, owner of Hindalco, etc., is G. D.'s grandson

BJD: Biju Janata Dal. Political party named after Biju Patnaik, father of Naveen, the present CM, who heads the Government of Odisha

BJP: Bharatiya Janata Party (Indian People's Party), was ruling Odisha in alliance with BJD until the latter chose to contest the 2009 elections on its own and won a sound victory in Odisha

BPD: The Business Partners for Development / Natural Resources Cluster (BPD / NRC) is a three-year programme of work, created by the World Bank Group, the British Department for International Development (DFID), CARE International, two of the world's largest mining companies and two out of the four largest oil and gas companies. It is one of four such 'clusters' initiated by the World Bank Group to explore how business, governments and civil society can work more closely together.

BPL: Below the Poverty Line. A BPL person is one who makes his/her ends meet on less than what the government officially acknowledges as the minimum income without which human beings cannot even survive. Just how much that minimum should be and the actual number of BPL people—have been the subject of frequent contentious debates. Many would assert that more than half the Indian population ekes out a BPL existence—including at least two-thirds of the people in Odisha.

CAAT: Campaign Against the Arms Trade, based in London
CARE: An American NGO active in Odisha, in close contact with the US government
CBA: Cost Benefit Analysis
CBI: Central Bureau of Investigation, one of India's intelligence agencies
ccpp: captive coal-fired power plant, possessed by most aluminium plants
CDC: Commonwealth Development Corporation, effectively a subsidiary of the DFID
CDM: Clean Development Mechanism, a carbon emissions trading unit
CEC: Central Empowered Committee, advisory body to the Supreme Court on forests
CEO: Chief Executive Officer of a company
Cesco: Central Electricity Supply Co., one of several companies set up when Odisha's electricity system was privatised in the 1990s
CFCs: Chloro-fluoro carbons, a potent form of GHGs
Chokka jam: 'wheel jam', i.e. blockade
CM: Chief Minister, the elected political leader of an Indian state government, e.g. that of Odisha
CMAS: Chasi Mulia Adivasi Sangha (Farming Labourers Adivasi Union), active in parts of Koraput district, suppressed as 'Maoist' in 2009–2010
CMPDI: Central Mining Planning and Design Institute, Ranchi
Collector: administrator in charge of a district, also called District Magistrate (DM)
Comalco: Commonwealth Aluminium Co.
Congress (I): the main faction of the Congress party, named after Indira Gandhi, who was assassinated by her bodyguards
Corus: British Steel merged with Dutch steel producer Koninklijke Hoogovens to form Corus Group in 1999. British Steel formed two-third of the merged group
CPI: Communist Party of India
CPI-M: Communist Party of India, Marxist: the party in power since 1977 in West Bengal
CPI-ML: Communist Party of India, Marxist-Leninist
CRA: Conzinc Riotinto Associates, an Australian registered subsidiary of Rio Tinto
CRAs: Credit Rating Agencies, e.g. Crisil (India), Standard & Poor's (US)

Glossary

CRPF: Central Reserve Police Force
CSD: Council for Social Development, a Delhi-based NGO
CSO: Civil Society Organisation, a more inclusive category than NGO
CSR: Corporate Social Responsibility
Dalits: 'the Suppressed'—the politically correct name for 'untouchables', also known as Harijans or Scheduled Castes
Darpan: mirror
De Beers: Diamond mining and trading company, subsidiary to Anglo-American, controls the diamond cartel
Demba: Demerara Bauxite Co., Alcan's subsidiary in Guyana
DESO: Defence Export Sevices Organisation, the arms sales department of the UK government
DFID: (commonly pronounced 'difid') Department For International Development of the British government, formed out of ODA in 1996
DFO: Divisional Forest Officer
Dharni (penu): Earth (deity), the Kond Earth goddess
Dissari: Hindu or tribal diviner
EAA: European Aluminium Association, Brussels
ECT: electro-convulsive shock therapy
EDI: Economic Development Institute, World Bank training college in Washington DC
EIA: Environmental Impact Assessment
EIC: East India Company
EIR: Extractive Industries Review, a study commissioned by the World Bank but not endorsed, due to its promotion of the concept of FPIC, etc.
EITI: Extractive Industries Transparency Initiative, set up by Blair at Johannesberg in 2002
EPW: *Economic and Political Weekly*, a reputed Indian journal
FAC: Forest Advisory Committee, for the Supreme Court in Delhi
FCI: Food Corporation of India
FDI: Foreign Direct Investment, meaning finance into a country from private sources (companies, banks, etc.)
FF: Ford Foundation
FIAN: a German NGO
FICCI: Federation of Indian Chambers of Commerce and Industry
FoE: Friends of the Earth, an NGO
FPIC: Free Prior Informed Consent—principle formulated in the EIR demanding that people threatened with displacemenmt should be

properly consulted
FRA: Forest Rights Act
FT: *Financial Times*, UK
GAMI: Guiyang Aluminium and Magnesium (Research and Development) Institute, from China, which has helped build Vedanta's refinery and smelter
GDP: Gross Domestic Product
Gherao: literally 'surround', describes a popular form of demonstration
GHGs: greenhouse gases
GIST: Green Indian States Trust, an organisation based in Chennai that propagates 'Green Accounting' that places a financial ('Net Present Value') on India's forests, etc. (Gundimeda 2005 and 2006)
GM: genetically modified crops
GNP: Gross National Product
GoI: Government of India
GoO: Government of Orissa, or Odisha, since November 2009
Goons or *goonda*s: thugs or gangsters, often employed on behalf of mining companies
GRI: Global Reporting Initiative (part of MMSD system)
GSDP: Gross State Domestic Product
GSI: Geological Survey of India
HAL: Hindustan Aeronautics Ltd., India's biggest manufacturer of military aircraft, with a factory at Sunabeda, near Damanjodi in Koraput district
Halco: Harvey Aluminium Co., managing a consortium in Guinea
Harijans: Dalits, people of Scheduled Castes, 'untouchables'
Hawa: wind, air (figuratively, which way the wind blows)
HC: High Court
HFCs: hydro-fluoro carbons
HFs: hedge funds
Hindalco: Hindustan Aluminium Co., set up through a partnership between Birla and Kaiser in 1958–59, one of India's three biggest aluminium companies
Hindutva: Hindu nationalism or fundamentalism
HSBC: Hong Kong and Shanghai Banking Corporation
Hukm: rule, authority
Hydro: Norsk Hydro, more recently Hydro Aluminium. Norway's biggest company, part of UAIL from 1993 till backing out in 2000
IAI: International Aluminium Association, London
IBA: International Bauxite Association, set up by bauxite-producing countries under Jamaican leadership in 1974

IBM: Indian Bureau of Mines, Nagpur
IBRD: International Bank for Reconstruction & Development, an arm of the World Bank
ICC: International Chamber of Commerce
ICMM: International Council on Mining and Minerals, took over MMSD mandate as a mining industry lobby group from 2002
ICOLD: International Commission on Large Dams
IDCO: Industrial Development Corporation of Orissa
IFAD: International Fund for Agricultural Development of the UN
IFC: International Finance Corporation of the World Bank, which funds private companies
IFIs: International Financial Institutions, such as the World Bank, HSBC, etc.
IIED: International Institute for Environment and Development, London
ILO: International Labour Organisation
IMF: International Monetary Fund
IMFA: Indian Metal and Ferro Alloys, company owned by the Panda family of Odisha
INCAL: Series of international conferences on aluminium organised by the AAI
Indal: Indian Aluminium Co., one of India's oldest surviving aluminium companies, set up by Alcan in 1938–43, bought by Hindalco in 2000
IPCC: Inter-governmental Panel on Climate Change
IPICOL: Industrial Promotion and Investment Corporation of Orissa Ltd.
IPO: Initial Public Offering
ISO: International Organisation for Standardisation. ISO is the univeral short form of its name, from the Greek *isos* meaning *equal*
ITDA: Integrated Tribal Development Agency, an all-India organisation set up on a model outlined by Verrier Elwin in 1957
ITT: a US telecom company involved in instigating Allende's overthrow
Jani: Kond priest
JBI: Jamaican Bauxite Institute, Kingston
Jhodia, Jhoria: One of the main tribes of the Kashipur region of Odisha
JK Corp: Group of companies run set up by Juggilal and Kamlapat Singhania in the 1920s that ran India's first aluminium plant at Asansol and has a paper factory near Rayagada
JNARDDC: Jawaharlal Nehru Aluminium Research Development and

Design Centre, Nagpur, built with a loan from the UNDP during the 1990s

Kaiser Aluminium: One of the companies founded by Henry J. Kaiser, and one of the four biggest US aluminium companies till the late 1990s

KBK: Koraput, Bolangir, Kalahandi districts, refers to a region of west Odisha, with special policies for poverty alleviation as well as industrialisation. These three districts have been subdivided, so Rayagada, Nowrangpur, Malkangiri, Baragarh and Nuapada districts are also included now as KBK districts

Konds, Khonds, Kondhos, Kandhas, Kuwinga, Kuinga: Odisha's largest tribe

Kubark: a secret CIA interrogation manual based on ECT techniques, etc.

Kui, Kuwi, Kubi: the Kond language

kWh: kilowatt hours of electricity

Lathi: wooden stave carried by police used for hitting people

L&T: Larsen and Toubro

LME: London Metals Exchange, founded 1877

Malco: Madras Aluminium Co., taken over by Sterlite in 1996

Matti: earth, soil

MECL: Mining Exploration Corporation Ltd., a private company based in Nagpur

MIGA: Multilateral Investment Guarantee Agency of the World Bank

MIPS: Material Input Per Service unit (formulated at Wuppertal Institute)

MLA: Member of the Legislative Assembly of a state government (e.g. Odisha), elected to sit in the Assembly in the state capital (e.g. Bhubaneswar)

MMCs: Metals Matrix Composites, fusions of plastic and aluminium

MNC: Multi-National Corporation, a company based in more than one country, also known as TNCs (Trans-National Corporations)

MoEF: Ministry of Environment and Forests

MoU: Memorandum of Understanding

MP: Member of Parliament, elected or nominated to sit in the Lok Sabha, Delhi; also refers to Madhya Pradesh, a state in Central India

MMSD: Mining and Minerals for Sustainable Development, a study of the mining industry by the IIED, etc., funded by leading mining companies

MW: mega watts of electricity

Nalco: National Aluminium Co., set up in 1980, based in Odisha

NAPM: National Alliance of Peoples' Movements
Naxalites/Maoists: revolutionary fighters with a Marxist-Leninist (ML) or Maoist orientation, now mostly associated with the CPI (Maoist), an underground communist party formed by the merger of CPI-ML(People's War) and the Maoist Communist Centre (MCC) on 21 September 2004
NGO: Non-Governmental Organisation, such as Action Aid or Oxfam
NEAA: National Environment Appellate Authority, a court in Delhi
NFFPFW: National Forum of Forest Peoples and Forest Workers
NHRC: National Human Rights Commission
NMP: National Mineral Policy, one in 1993, another with drafts 2006–08
Norad: a Norwegian NGO
Norsk Hydro: see Hydro
NPV: Net Present Value, the financial value placed on India's forests, fields, etc. by the 'Green Accounting' method propagated by GIST, Deutsche Bank, etc.
NRDC: Natural Resources Defence Council, Washington
NTPC: National Thermal Power Corporation
ODA: Overseas Development Administration, i.e. a country's foreign aid quota; also Overseas Development Authority (UK), DFID's predecessor
OECD: Organisation for Economic Co-operation & Development, club of rich, industrialised nations
OIC: Officer in Command of a police station
OMC: Orissa Mining Corporation
Odia: The predominant people of Odisha, and Odisha's state language
OPEC: Cartel of oil producing countries
OSPCB: Orissa State Pollution Control Board
OTDP: Orissa Tribal Development Project, an Agency set up by IFAD in Kashipur
Pani: water
Patta: land deed
PCBs: PolyChlorinated Biphenyls, a principal effluent of aluminium smelters
PDS: Public Distribution System, through which the government is supposed to distribute essential commodities to India's rural poor
Pechiney: Aluminium company of France and the world's first aluminium company, dating back to 1859
Pengo or Pengo Paraja: one of the tribes in the Kashipur region
PESA: Panchayat (Extension to Scheduled Areas) Act, passed in December 1996
PFC: Perfluorocarbons

PH: Public Hearing
Posco: Pohang Steel Company of South Korea
PR: public relations
PSSP: Prakrutika Sampada Surakshya Parishad (Natural Resources Defence Council), mass organisation of villagers in Kashipur opposing the UAIL
PSU: Public Sector Undertaking, i.e. a public sector company
PUCL: People's Union for Civil Liberties
QAL: Queensland Alumina Ltd., Australia
RAK: Ras Al Khaimah aluminium company from the UAE (also referred to as Anrak or RIMMI (Ras Al Khaimah Mining and Metal Investments)
Red mud: the toxic waste from a refinery, 1–2 tons for every ton of alumina produced
RF: Reserved Forest
R&R: Resettlement and Rehabilitation
RTZ, RT: Rio Tinto Zinc (more recently, just Rio Tinto), one of the UK's mining companies, named after the river in Spain where it started out in the nineteenth century
SAIL: Steel Authority of India Ltd., a PSU
Salwa Judum: 'Purification Hunt', a State-sponsored armed militia supported by politicians and police in Dantewada district, Chhattisgarh, responsible for hundreds of human rights abuses in the government's war against Maoists/Naxalites
Samatha: Hyderabad-based NGO, which won a landmark case against the AP government in the Supreme Court in 1996 reaffirming the non-alienability of tribal land-rights against mining companies' land acquisitions, based on Schedule V of India's Constitution
SAP: Structural Adjustment Program
SC: India's Supreme Court in Delhi
SCMCHM: Supreme Court Monitoring Committee on Hazardous Materials
SCs, STs: Scheduled Castes (Dalits), Scheduled Tribes (Adivasis)
SEBI: Securities Exchange Board of India
SEZ: Special Economic Zone. India passed the SEZ Act in 2005 to promote several hundred export-oriented industrial enclaves, modelled on a small number of much larger SEZs, which have been central to China's post-Mao economic expansion
SHGs: Self-Help Groups promoted for microcredit loans, especially for women
SIIL: Sterlite Industries (India) Ltd.

SP: Superintendent of Police
SPCB: State Pollution Control Boards in each state (e.g. OSPCB, APPCB)
SPL: Spent Pot Lining from an aluminium smelter
SRK: a UK-based consultancy firm that wrote part of J. P. Morgan's Vedanta report in 2003
Sterlite: Conglomerate of companies under Anil Agarwal, subsidiary now to Vedanta
Tata: Conglomerate of companies headed by Ratan Tata, great-grandson of J. R. D. Tata, who started iron mining and steel production in north Odisha and Tatanagar in the 1900s
Tehsil: a sub-division of a district
Tehsildar: administrators in charge of a Tehsil
Tisco: Tata Iron and Steel Co.
ton: used here in the sense of 'tonne', to mean 1000 metric kilos
UAE: United Arab Emirates
UAIL, Utkal: Utkal Alumina International Ltd., consortium set up in 1991–93 to mine Bapla Mali's bauxite and refine it into alumina in Kashipur. Also see Utkal
UNCTAD: United Nations Conference on Trade And Development
UNDP: UN Development Programme
UNEP: UN Environment Programme
Union Carbide: the US chemical company infamous for the Bhopal disaster, later bought up by Dow Chemicals
UP: Uttar Pradesh, a state in north India
URDS: Utkal Rural Development Society, an NGO set up by UAIL in Kashipur
Utkal: Utkal was an ancient name for the coastal area of north-east Odisha. Also see UAIL
Valco: Volta Aluminium Company, Ghana
VAL: Vedanta Alumina Ltd., Vedanta Aluminium Ltd.
VAW: Vereinigte Aluminium Werke, Germany's main aluminium company, started in 1915
Vedanta: the ancient body of knowledge based on the Vedas and Upanishads
Vedanta: company formed by Sterlite/Anil Agarwal in London as Vedanta Resources plc, with VAL as an Indian subsidiary
WB: World Bank
WBCSD: World Business Council for Sustainable Development, formed in 1997
WEF: World Environmental Foundation, of Madhav Mehra

WDRs: influential annual World Development Reports from the WB
WHO: World Health Organisation
WIDA: Weaker sections Integrated Development Agency
WII: Wildlife Institute of India, Dehradun
WoW: War on Want, a London-based NGO critical of certain UK companies and DFID
WTO: World Trade Organisation
WWF: originally the World Wildlife Fund, now the World Wide Fund for Nature

Appendices

Million tons per year is abbreviated to mtpy

APPENDIX I. BAUXITE AND ALUMINIUM PLANTS IN INDIA

A. Bauxite Mines	Tons mined in 2003-4	Deposits (2002 estimate in tons)
Odisha	4,934,155 (nearly 5 million)	1,733,000,000 (1.73 billion)
Andhra Pradesh	0	612,760,000 (613 million)
Gujarat	1,864,387 (1.8 million)	2,030,000 (2 million)
Jharkhand	1,518,096 (1.5 million)	117,350,000 (117 million)
Maharashtra	1,167,720 (1.17 m)	124,780,000 (125 million)
Chhattisgarh	887,359 (0.9 m)	198,220,000 (198 million)
Tamil Nadu	278,040	26,000,000
Madhya Pradesh	190,937	131,490,000
Goa	70,369	64,280,000
Karnataka	29,403	45,890,000
Kerala	16,070	14,230,000
Uttar Pradesh		18,910,000
Bihar		4,110,000
Jammu & Kashmir		2,030,000

INDIA TOTALS:
   10,956,536 tons mined 2003-4   3,075,710,000 (3 billion+ total reserves)
   12.7 million tons 2006, 13 mt 2007

In Odisha
Panchpat Mali (Nalco)
Sundargarh District, north Orissa (for steel mills?)
Planned in near future: Bapla Mali (Utkal)
                Niyamgiri (Vedanta/OMC)
                Kuturu and Siji Mali (L & T with Dubal)
In other States
Jharkhand: Lohardaga (Indal, Hindalco), and others
Chhattisgarh: Bodai-Daldali & Mainpat (Balco/Vedanta), Samripat (Hindalco)
MP, Maharashtra, Karnataka (Hindalco, Indal)
Tamil Nadu (Malco/Vedanta) on Shevaroyan, Kolli and Yercaud ranges
Gujarat (Gujarat MDC): 190 small mines in Junagar and Jamnagar Districts
AP planned: Anantagiri (Jindal) etc

B. Refineries	Alumina production	Associated Dams/Reservoirs
In Odisha		
Damanjodi (Nalco)	1,475,000 tons (2006-7), of which 773,573 tons was exported (1,600t 2007-8)	Upper Kolab, a tributary of Godaveri
Lanjigarh (Vedanta, started production Sept 07)	302,000 (2007-8), 1mtpy initial aim, raised to 6m in 2008	Upper Indravati, a tributary of Godaveri
Kashipur (Utkal, construction started 2006)	1,500,000 tpy aim	Upper Indravati
Planned:	Hindalco near Kansariguda (Kashipur)	
	L & T/Dubal near Kalyan Singpur	
	IMFA at Therubali 1,000,000 tpy aim	

In other States:

Alumina production	Associated Dams/Reservoirs
Muri (Indal/Hindalco), Jharkhand: 120,000t	Subarnarekha
Belgaum (Karnataka): 390,000 (2008)	
Renukut (Hindalco), UP: 489,000 (2008)	Rihand, a tributary of Son
Korba (Balco/Vedanta), Chhattisgarh: 205,000	Hasdeo Bango, on a tributary of Mahanadi
Mettur (Malco/Vedanta), Tamil Nadu 100,000	Mettur, on Kaveri
Planned: Jindal, AP	Polavaram mega-dam (planned)
Nalco, AP 4,200,000 tpy aim	Polavaram

INDIA TOTAL ALUMINA PRODUCTION 2004: 2,240.000 tons, 2008: 3,317,000

C. Smelters	Aluminium production	Associated Dams/Reservoirs
In Odisha		
Angul (Nalco)	2002-3 244,708 tons	Rengali on Brahmani
	2003-4 298,207	
	2004-5 338,483	
	2005-6 ?	
	2006-7 358,740 (of which 92,678 tons were exported)	
Hirakud (Indal/Hindalco)	2002-3 37,102	Hirakud (Orissa/Chattisgarh)
	2003-4 60,877	

	2004-5 65,620	
Jharsaguda (Vedanta, construction started late 2006)		Revamped Hirakud
	500,000 tpy aim	
Planned: Sambalpur (Hindalco)	500,000 tpy aim	Revamped Hirakud
Choudwar (IMFA)	25,000 tpy aim	
	(2006 plan)	

In other States:

Renukut (Hindalco), UP		Rihand (UP/Chhattisgarh)
	2002-3 266,837	
	2003-4 323,184	
	2004-5 343,448	
	2005-6 360,000	
Korba (Balco/Vedanta), Chhattisgarh		Hasdeo Bango
	2002-3 95,490	
	2003-4 97,088	
	2004-5 100,272	
	2005-6 ?	
(old & new plants)	2006-7 345,000	
Mettur (Malco/Vedanta), Tamil Nadu		Mettur/Kaveri
	2002-3 30,900	
	2003-4 32,226	
	2004-5 35,649	
	2005-6 ?	
	2006-7 40,000	
Alupuram (Indal, *now closed*), Kerala		
	2002-3 14,131	
	2003-4 4,528	

Belgaum S (Indal, *now closed*), Karnataka

Planned: Jindal near Vizag, AP Polavaram (*planned*) on Godaveri
　　　　 Nalco   "   "   "   1,000,000tpy aim (2005 plan)
　　　　 GMDC, Gujarat
INDIA TOTAL smelted per year:
　　　　 2000   649,000 tons
　　　　 2008 1,170,000 tons

APPENDIX II. WORLD BAUXITE PRODUCTION
(We have used a wide variety of sources, which often differ, to compile these lists)

Size of Bauxite Deposits (in million tons)			Tons mined per year (in mt)				
	'Reserve Base'	'Reserves'		1979	2000	2005	2007
1. Guinea	8,600	7,400	1. Australia	30.4	53.8	58	64
2. Australia	7,900	5,800	2. China		9	17	32
3. Brazil	4,900	1,900	3. Brazil		13.8	18	24
4. India	3,011	770	4. Guinea	13.5	15.7	16	14
Jamaica	2,500	2,000	5.= India		7.5	14	13
China	2,300	700	Jamaica	12.7	11.1	14	14
Guyana	900	700	7. USSR*/Russia	7.2*	4.2	6	6
Suriname	600	580	8. Venezuela		4.4	5.5	5.5
Greece	650	600	9. Kazakhstan		3.7	4.6	4.9
Kazakhstan	450	360	10. Suriname	5.3	3.6	4	5
Venezuela	350		11. Greece	3.2	1.9	2.2	2.4
Russia	200		12. Guyana	3.7	2.4	1.5	1.4
+ Vietnam	2,500 - 8,000mt estimates		Yugoslavia*	3.3*		2004	
Indonesia	1,760mt		Serbia & Montenegro		0.63	0.6	
Cameroon	1,200mt		Bosnia		0.075	0.125	
			Hungary	3.3	1	0.647	
			Indonesia		1.15	1.33	
			Ghana		0.5	0.49	
			France	2.2	0	0	
			Iran		0.4	0.5	
			Turkey		0.46	0.36	
			Malaysia		0.123	0.006 (6,000 t)	
			Mozambique		0.008	0.007	
			Pakistan		0.009	n.a.	

115mt mined 1993, 178mt 2006, 190mt 2007

Total estimated world reserves vary from: 25 billion tons (with reserve base of 32bt)
To 55bt or 75bt (Indian Planning Commission figures c.2000)

APPENDIX III. WORLD ALUMINA PRODUCTION

Alumina refined per year (in mt):	2000	2004		
A. by country				
1. Australia	15.68	16.7		
2. China	4.3	6.1		
3. USA	4.8	5.3		
4. Brazil	3.7	5.1		
5. Jamaica	3.6	4		
6. Russia	2.85	3.27		
7. India	2.28	2.26		
8. Suriname	1.8	2		
9. Venezuela	1.75	1.9		
10. Ukraine	1.36	1.56		
11. Kazakhstan	1.2	1.47		
12. Canada	1	1.17		
13.= Ireland	1.2	1.1		
Spain	1.2	1.1		
Alumina refined per year (in thousand tons)		2000	2002	2004
15. Germany		652	720	800
16. Greece		667	750	750
17. Guinea		541	670	740
18. Italy		950	500	500
19. Romania		471	361	350
20. Japan		369	333	340
21.= Azerbaijan		63	91	300
Hungary		357	294	300
23. Serbia & Montenegro		186	237	250
24. Iran			102	200
25. Turkey		155	152	170
26. Slovakia		110	112	130
27. France		200	150	100
28. Bosnia		50	50	50
29. Slovenia		70	30	30
30. UK		80	74	0

B. by company (in thousand tons)	2000
1. **Alcoa**, USA	14,000
2. **Alcan**, Canada	4,500
3. **Chalco**, China	4,200
4. **BHP Billiton**, Australia & UK	4,100
5. **Glencore**, UK [?]	2,900
6. **Kaiser**, USA	2,800

7. **Rusal**, Russia		2,000
8. **Pechiney**, France		1,800
9. **CVG**, Venezuala		1,800
10. **Rio Tinto Zinc**, UK		1,700
11. **Rusal**, Russia		1,600
12. **Nalco**, India		1,575

C. Ten biggest refineries in 2000 (with output in thousand tons)

1. QAL, Australia	3,650	6. Bauxillum, Venezuala	2,000
2. Pinjarra, "	3,100	7. Kwinana, Australia	1,800
3. Worseley "	3,000	8. Gove, "	1,780
4. Pt Comfort "	2,250	9. Paranam, Suriname	1,650
5. Wagerup "	2,200	10. Nalco, India	1,575

APPENDIX IV. WORLD ALUMINIUM PRODUCTION

Aluminium tpy smelted in 2000

1. US	3,647,000		
2. Russia	3,258,000		
3. China	2,820,000		
4. Canada	2,374,000		
5. Australia	1,762,000		
6. Brazil	1,277,000		
7. Norway	1,025,000		
8. South Africa	690,000 tons		
9. India	649,000 tons		
10. Germany	644,000 tons		

in 2008

1. China	5.9mt
2. Russia	4
3. US	3.2
4. Canada	3.1
5. Australia	1.54
6. Norway	1.36
7. Brazil	1.27
8. India	1.17
9. Bahrain	872,000
10. UAE	861,000
11. Iceland	761,000

B. by company

1. **Alcoa**, US	3,580
2. **Rusal**, Russia	2,449
3. **Alcan**, Canada	2,212
4. **BHP Billiton**, Australia & UK	962
5. **Pechiney**, France	843
6. **Norsk Hydro**, Norway	763
7. **Rio Tinto Zinc**, UK	754
8. **Chalco**, China	692
9. **Dubal**, Dubai	535
10. **Glencore**, UK	519

World Total Primary Aluminium Production per year

2008   34-37mt

APPENDIX V. WORLD METAL PRICES (in US$ per metric ton)

[falling prices in *italics*, rising prices in **bold**]

	Steel	Aluminium	Copper	Lead	Nickel	Tin	Zinc
1960	125	500	677	198	1631	2196	247
1962	125	*435*	*644*	*154*	**1762**	**2471**	*185*
1964	**131**	**493**	**968**	**278**	*1742*	**3408**	**324**
1968	**135**	*457*	**1241**	*240*	**2075**	*3126*	**262**
1969	**145**	**581**	**1466**	**289**	**2363**	**3428**	**287**
1970	**154**	*540*	*1413*	**304**	**2846**	**3673**	**295**
1971	**174**	*435*	*1076*	*252*	**2932**	*3501*	**312**
1972	*157*	*432*	*1071*	**305**	**3080**	**3770**	**376**
1973	**185**	**663**	**1805**	**439**	**3373**	**4828**	**883**
1974	**238**	**944**	**2067**	**590**	**3825**	**8201**	**1226**
1975	**252**	*690*	*1244*	*408*	**4570**	*6870*	*739*
1976	*250*	**862**	**1406**	**451**	**4974**	**7582**	*710*
1977	**280**	**991**	*1300*	**620**	**5203**	**10,762**	*583*
1978	**309**	**1045**	**1379**	**670**	*4610*	**12,908**	**597**
1979	309	**1632**	**2025**	**1202**	**5986**	**15,498**	**741**
1980	**357**	**1755**	**2165**	*895*	**6517**	**16,775**	**759**
1981	**374**	*1250*	*1734*	*721*	*5883*	*15,159*	**851**
1982	**380**	*978*	*1476*	*543*	*4753*	*12,826*	*742*
1983	**446**	**1471**	**1595**	*425*	*4674*	**12,988**	*759*
1984	**487**	*1231*	*1373*	**444**	**4742**	*12,273*	**904**
1985	**531**	*1039*	**1412**	*385*	**4828**	*11,539*	*774*
1986	531	**1144**	*1367*	**409**	*3861*	*6161*	*760*
1987	*377*	**1592**	**1858**	**596**	**5125**	**6690**	**799**
1988	**380**	**2582**	**2584**	**656**	**14,252**	**7052**	**1268**
1989	**432**	*1920*	**2810**	**667**	*12,960*	**8534**	**1657**
1990	**450**	*1649*	*2659*	**823**	*8966*	*6085*	*1515*
1991	**454**	*1280*	*2333*	*555*	*8105*	*5595*	*1109*
1992	*385*	*1270*	*2310*	*547*	*7015*	**6109**	**1256**
1993	**407**	*1133*	*1889*	*405*	*5231*	*5100*	*961*
1994		**1678**					
1995		**1724**					
1996		*1506*					
1997		**1567** (Oct. over **1600**)					
1998		*1291*					
1999		**1471** (April under *1200*)					
2000							
2001		**1600** (April c.**1600**)					
2002		1600 (April c.1600)					

2003	1300 (April *1380*, Sept. *1280*)					
2004	**1845** (Feb. **1460**, March *1380*, April **1845**)					
2005	1688 (10th March **2015**, 1st July *1688*)					
2006 av.	**2591**	6,666	1,281	23,228	8,748	3,245
Jan.	2285	4,433	1,059	13,480	6,600	1,917
May	**3240** (peak)					
end June	2596	7,431	992	21,250	8,080	3,261
Dec	**2800**	6,330	1,685	33,385	11,800	4,251
2007 av	2450					
2008 July	**3200**					
Dec	1586					

APPENDIX VI. AL-FACTORIES OF THE WORLD (2005-8)

CAPACITY (in thousand tons)

Europe	Bauxite mines	Refineries	Smelters	Mills	(Rolling Mills)
UK		closed	3 (366)	29	7
Ireland	closed	1 (1900)	0	1	
Netherland		0	2 (313)	10	6
Belgium				10	3
France	closed	4 (1144)	2 (394)	20	5
Spain		1 (1530)	3 (399)	56	8
Portugal				9	
Italy	closed	1 (1100)	2 (194)	66	12
Greece	2.4mt	1 (830)	1 (165)	16	2
Former Yugoslavia					
Serbia				3	1
Montenegro	54,000t	closed? (280)	1 (120)	1	1
Croatia			closed?	1	
Bosnia	1.66mt	1 (600)	1 (130)	1	
Macedonia				1	
Slovenia			1 (117)	?	2?
Austria				5	2
Switzerland		closed	closed	4	3
Germany		2 (950/678)	5 (679)	43	17
Denmark				2	
Norway		0	7 (1364)	5	3
Sweden		0	1 (102)		
Iceland		0	3 (761)		
Greenland			planned		
Hungary	55,000t	3 (375)	closed	1+	4
Romania		2 (740/1100) 1 (215)		1	1
Poland			1 (60)	5	2
Czech.				1	1
Slovakia		1 (180)	1 (158)	3	
Bulgaria				3	1
Ukraine		2 (1691)	1 (113)	4	1
Russia	6.6mt [19.79]	5/8 (3280/6504)	12 (4060)	10+	15
Finland				4	
Africa					
Egypt		1 (240)			4
Algeria					1
Morocco					1
Guinea	17.68/14mt	1 (755)			

Sierra Leone	1.12mt				
Ivory Coast					1
Ghana	560.000t	0	1 (200)		3
Nigeria			1 (193)		1
Cameroon			1 (100)		
South Africa			2 (855)		
Mozambique			1 (530)		1
Tanzania					1
Kenya					2

Australasia

Australia	58/64mt	7 (19,450/21.232)	6 (1930/1545)		2
New Zealand			1 (350)		

Asia

Turkey	48,000t	1 (200)	1 (65)	51	9
Tadjikistan			1 (520)		
Azerbaijan	1.87mt	1 (400, closed 1997)	1 (60)		
Kazakhstan	4.8mt	1 (1540)			
Iran	44,000t	1 (280)	2 (240)		
Bahrain			1 (872)		
UAE (Dubai)			1 (861) + 1 (700)		1
Oman			1 (330)		
Qatar			1 under construction		
Israel					1
Jordan					1
Saudia Arabia			1 under construction		1
Afghanistan					
Pakistan			0		7?
India	14mt	6 (3317)+1	5 (1170) +1		29
China	32mt 19/23 (6100/19363)	34 (3000/5887)			105
Taiwan					8
Indonesia	1.6mt	0	1 (225)		
Phillipines					4
Thailand					9
Malaysia					4
Laos					
Vietnam	30,000	2 (0)			
Bangladesh					2
Burma					1
Sri Lanka					1
South Korea		1 (200, now closed?)			29
North Korea					1
Japan	no	3 (850/0)	1 (18)		10

America

Canada	no	3 (1600)	11 (2400/3114)	4
USA	closed	5 (6000)	17 (6350/3226)	64
Jamaica	17mt	4 (4100/4400)	0	
Trinidad			planned	
Mexico			closed	5
Costa Rica				1
Panama				1
Columbia				6
Guyana	1.4mt	0		
Suriname	5.6mt	1 (2200)	closed 1999	
Venezuela	8.5mt	1 (200/2000)	2 (646)	4
Brazil	21mt	5 (8000)	7 (1678/1274)	12
Argentina			1 (272)	4
Chile				2
Peru				1
Ecuador				1

Sources include http://en.wikipedia.org for 2008 refinery & smelter figures. Where 2 figures are given this may show a marked progression 2005-8 or discrepancy

APPENDIX VII. ALUMINIUM CONSUMPTION BY COUNTRY

For the year 2000 (Source: UNCTAD):

Consumption in million tons: Share of world consumption

'Developed Market Economy Countries':

Europe:		1993	2000	
European Union (15 countries)		4	5.2	20.7%
Norway			0.2	0.8%
Switzerland			0.2	0.8%
US			4.9	20%
Canada		0.5	0.66	2.6%
Australia		0.34	0.41	1.7%
Japan		2.2	3.1	12.2%
South Africa		0.09	0.14	0.5%
	Total	12.4	14.8	67.2% (in 1993) to 58.8% (in 2000)

'Developing Countries'

The rest of Africa		0.14	0.18	0.7%

Asia:				
Turkey		0.13	0.23	0.9%
Iran		0.17	0.29	0.7 to 1.2%
Bahrain		0.47	0.73	0.7 to 2.4%
China		1.3	1.8	7.5 to 7.2%
S.Korea		0.6	1.4	3.2 to 5.9%
Taiwan		0.3	0.56	1.7 to 2.3%
India		0.475	0.729	2.7 to 2.9%
Indonesia		0.096	0.3	0.5 to 1.2%
Thailand		0.15	0.28	0.8 to 1.1%
Malaysia		0.075	0.157	0.4 to 0.6%
Singapore		0.027	0.072	0.2 to 0.3%
Hong Kong		0.46	0.55	0.3 to 0.2%
The rest of Asia		0.17	0.22	0.9%
	Total	3.6	6.9	19 to 27%

Europe:				
Former USSR		1.18	1.98	6.4 to 7.9%
Hungary		0.14	0.1	0.8% to 0.4%
Poland		0.068	0.035	0.4% to 0.1%
Former Czechoslovakia		0.6	2%	
Other countries in east Europe		0.6	2%	
	Total	1.5	2.24	8.1 to 8.8%

Total for 'Developing Countries'	4.5	8.1	24.7 to 32.3%

APPENDIX VIII. ALUMINIUM FACTORIES OF NORTH AMERICA

Smelters in USA (2009)	output in thousand tons	
Alcoa, Tennessee	210 tpy	Alcoa
Badin, N.Carolina	60	Alcoa
Evansville/Warwick, Indiana	300	Alcoa
Massena, New York (2 plants)	255 (together)	Alcoa
Rockdale, Texas	267	Alcoa
Wenatchee, Washington	184	Alcoa
Frederick, Maryland	195	Eastalco (Alcoa)
Bellingham/Ferndale, Washington	300	Intalco (Alcoa 61%)
Mt Holly/Goose Creek, Pennsylvania	225	Alcoa 50%, Century 50%
Ravenswood, West Virginia	170	Century
Hawesville, Kentucky	244	Century
Columbia Falls, Montana	180	Glencore
Hannibal, Missouri	267	Ormet
New Madrid, Missouri	253	Noranda
Goldendale, Oregon (closed)	178	Columbia Gorge aluminium
Sebree, Kentucky	196	Rio Tinto Alcan

Refineries	output in thousand tons	
Pt Comfort, Texas	2,330	Alcoa
Corpus Christi, Texas	1,610	Sherwin
Gramercy, Lousiana	1,215	Rusal
Baton Rouge, Louisiana	0	......
Burnside, Louisiana	0.5	Ormet

Smelters & Refinery in Canada (2009)	
Alma (1)	Rio Tinto Alcan
Beauharnois RTA	
Arvida/Jonquiere + Vaudreuil refinery, Saguenay (2)	RTA
Grande Baie, Saguenay (3)	RTA
Laterrière, Saguenay (3)	RTA
Kitimat, British Columbia	RTA
Shawinigan (4)	RTA
Sept Îles	RTA 90%, Hydro 10%
Becancour (5)	Alcoa 75%, RTA 25%
Baie Comeau	Alcoa
Deschambault, Saskatchewan	Alcoa

Bibliography

Action Aid International 2006. *Real Aid: Making Technical Assistance Work.* http://www.actionaidusa.org/news/publications/intl_policy/
_____ July 2007. *Vedanta Cares? Busting the myths about Vedanta's Operations in Lanjigarh, India* (on EPG website).
Adams, Patricia and Lawrence Solomon 1991 [1985]. *In the name of Progress: The Underside of Foreign Aid.* London: Earthscan.
Agbemabiese, Lawrence and John Byrne 2005. 'Commodification of Ghana's Volta River: an Example of Ellul's Autonomy of Technique,' in *Bulletin of Science, Technology and Society* vol.25 no.1, Feb 2005 pp.17–25.
Agrawal, Neeraj 2007. 'How Green was my Mountain?' in Kalshian ed. pp.103–113.
Akshaya, Mukul 25 Jan 2007. 'Balco staff 'coerced' into VRS', *Times of India.*
Alcan Booth 1973. *The Military Uses of Aluminium.* Birmingham: Alcan Booth Sheet Ltd. (ed G.W.Budd)
Altenpohl, Dietrich. G. 1998. *Aluminum: Technology, Applications, and Environment.* Washington: Aluminum Association inc. Revised and expanded English version.
Alternative Survey Group September 2007. *Alternative Economic Survey, India 2006–2007. Pampering Corporates, Pauperizing Masses.* Delhi: Daanish Books.
Amin, Samir 1997 [1988]. *Capitalism in the Age of Globalization: The Management of Contemporary Society.* London: Zed [Delhi: Madhyam].
Anderson, Dewey 1951. *Aluminum for Defence and Prosperity.* Washington: US Public Affairs Institute.
Anyadike, Nnami 1997. *Aluminium: The Challenges Ahead.* London: FT.
Arvind 2002. *Globalisation: An Attack on India's Sovereignty.* Delhi: New Vistas.
Auty, Richard M. 1993. *Sustaining Development in Mineral Economies: The Resource-Curse Thesis.* London: Routledge.
_____ and Mikesell, R.F. 1998. *Sustaining Development in Mineral Economies.* Oxford: Clarendon.

Bahuguna, Sunderlal 1986. 'A voice from Gandhamardan,' in *The Sunday Statesman* 27.4.1986.
Bakan, Joel 2004. *The Corporation: the Pathological Pursuit of Profit.* London: Constable.
BALCO: Foundation Stone Laying Ceremony: Gandhamardan Bauxite Project 2nd May 1983, Paikmal. [4 page blurb]
Ballard, Chris and Glenn Banks 2003. 'Resource Wars: the Anthropology of Mining,' *Annual Review of Anthropology* 32, pp. 287–313.
Bandhyopadhyay, D. 1999. 'Where Assertion is Insurrection,' *EPW* 13 March.
_____ 2004. 'Rayagada Story Retold: Destitutes of Development,' *EPW* 31 Jan.
Bardossy, G.Y. 1979. *Paleoenvironments of Laterites and Lateritic Bauxites – Effect of Global Tectonism on Bauxite Formation*, in Venkatesh and Ramam 1979.
Barham, Bradford, Stephen G. Bunker and Denis O'Hearn eds. 1995. *States, Firms and Raw Materials: The World Economy and the Ecology of Aluminum.* Madison: University of Wisconsin Press.
Barney, I., A.B.Ota, B.Pandey and R.Puranik 2000. *In Focus: Engaging Stakeholders. Lessons from Three Eastern India Business Case Studies.* Swansea: Centre for Development Studies and London: Resource Centre for the Social Dimensions of Business Practice. (available at International Business Leaders Forum website: www.iblf.org)
BAUXMET 1998: Proceedings of Interactive Meet on Bauxite, 6–7 March. Nagpur: JNARDDC, Nandi, A.K. et. al. eds.
Berger, Peter L. and Thomas Luckmann 1971 [1966]. *The Social Construction of Reality: A Treatise in the Sociology of Knowledge.* Penguin.
BHP Billiton Plc 2005. *A Global Perspective: Annual Report 2005.* BHP Billiton, Melbourne and London.
Bidwai, Praful 2001. 'Balco's privatization,' in *Alternative Economic Survey 2000–2001. 2nd Generation Reforms: Delusions of Development.* By Alternative Survey Group. Delhi: Rainbow Publishers, Azadi Bachao Andolan and Lokayan.
_____ 2008. 'Falling back on pseudo-science? Indian policy-makers are clutching at straws to duck their responsibility to reduce the country's greenhouse gas emissions,' in *Frontline*, 9 May 2008 pp. 96–8.
Billon, Philippe Le 2001: 'The Political Ecology of War: Natural Resources and Armed Conflicts,' *Pergamin, Political Geography* 20 pp. 561–584 (www.politicalgeography.com).
Black, Maggie 2002. *The No-Nonsense Guide to International Development.* Oxford and London: New Internationalist and Verso.

Blum, William 2003. *Killing Hope: US Militarism and CIA Interventions since World War Two*. London: Zed.

Bond, Patrick 2004. *Talk Left, Walk Right: South Africa's Frustrated Global Reforms*. Scottsville, South Africa: Univ of KwaZulu-Natal Press.

_____ Sept/Oct 2006. 'South Africa Embraces Corporate Welfare: Mega Deal Subsidies over Services for the Poor,' in *MultiNational Monitor* vol.27 no 5.

Bookchin, Murray 1982. *The Ecology of Freedom*. California: Cheshire Books.

British Aluminium Co. [BAC] 1955. *The History of the BAC Ltd 1894–1955*. London: BAC.

Brown, Dee 1975 [1970]. *Bury my Heart at Wounded Knee*. London: Pan.

Brown, Martin, Alfredo Dammert, Alexander Meeraus, Ardy Stoutjesijk 1983. *Worldwide Investment Analysis: The Case of Aluminium*. Washington DC: WB, Staff Working Paper no.603.

Bunker, Stephen and Paul S. Ciccantell 2005, *Globalization and the Race forResources*. Baltimore: John Hopkins UP.

Bureau of Industrial Costs and Prices, Dec.1988. *Energy Audit of Aluminium Industry*. Delhi: GoI.

Burman, Debyajoti 1950. *Mystery of Birla House*. Calcutta: Jugabari Sahitya Chakra.

Burrows, Gideon 2002. *The No-Nonsense Guide to the Arms Trade*. Oxford and London: New Internationalist and Verso.

Campaign Against Marketisation Of Water 2002. *Public Hearing on Water, held at Bhubaneswar, Orissa, on Feb.27, 2002: JURY'S REPORT*. Bhubaneswar: 2510(J), Kedragouri Area, Rabi Talkies Square, Bhubaneswar, Orissa 751002.

Campaign for Peace and Justice in Chhattisgarh August 2007. *Salwa Judum: Civil War in Chhattisgarh*. Delhi: www.cpjc.wordpress.com

Campbell, Bonnie K. 1995. 'The impact of the restructuring of the aluminium industry in the 1980s on productive activities in Guinea,' in Barham et al. pp. 179–214.

Cannadine, D. 2006. *Mellon: an American Life*. London: Allen Lane.

Carson, Rachel [1962]. *Silent Spring*. Goa: Other India Press.

Caufield, Catherine 1998 [1996]. *The World Bank and the Poverty of Nations*. London: Pan.

Central Empowered Committee 21 Sept. 2005. *Report in IA no.1324 regarding the alumina plant being set up by M/S Vedanta Alumina Ltd at Lanjigarh in Kalahandi District, Orissa*. Delhi: GoI.

Central Mine Planning and Design Institute August 2006. *Interim Report on the Hydrogeological Investigations, Lanjigarh Bauxite Mines, submitted to M/s OMC Ltd, Bhubaneswar.* Ranchi: CMDPI (a subsidiary of coal India Ltd).

Centre for Science and Environment 2008. *Rich Lands, Poor People: Is 'Sustainable' Mining Possible?* Delhi: CSE.

Cernea, Michael M. 2000. 'Impoverishment Risks and Reconstruction: a Model for Population Displacement and Resettlement,' chapter 1 in Cernea and McDowell eds. 2000.

_____ March 2006. 'Re-examining 'Displacement': A Redefinition of Concepts in Development and Conservation Policies', in *Social Change* vol.36 no.1, pp. 8–35.

_____ Dec.2006. 'The International Dimension of Tribal Displacement: Findings on Resettlement and Impoverishment in S. Africa,' in *Adivasi*, vol.46, no.2.

_____ and Chris McDowell eds. 2000. *Risks and Reconstruction: Experiences of Resettlers and Refugees.* Washington DC: WB.

Chakraborti, A.M. and S.N.Tutu 1971. 'Aluminium Industry (A study from the Financial Analyst's View Point),' in *Company News and Notes 1971*, vol.1 pp. 9–18.

Chandrashekhar, C.P. and Jayati Ghosh 2002. *The Market that Failed: A Decade of Neoliberal Reforms in India.* Delhi: LeftWord.

Chatterji, Angana P. 2009. *Violent Gods: Hindu Nationalism in India's Present. Narratives from Orissa.* Gurgaon: Three Essays Collective.

Chaudhuri, N.P. 2001. *Story of Geological Survey of India 1851–2001.* Kolkata: GSI.

Chernaik, Mark Oct 2005. *Evaluation of the EIA for the Proposed Aluminium Smelter (250,000TPA) near Jharsaguda, Orissa.* Prepared for Appeal no.4 of 2007, Prafulla Samantara versus MoEF, before the National Environmental Appellate Authority, New Delhi, by the Environmental Law Alliance Worldwide (US).

Chomsky, Noam 1999. *Profit over People: Neoliberalism and Global Order.* NY: Seven Stories Press [Delhi: Madhyam].

_____ and Edward S.Herman 1988. *Manufacturing Consent.* NY: Pantheon.

_____ 2003 [2002]. *Understanding Power.* Penguin.

Choudhuri, Manmohan 1989. *Exploring Gandhi.* Delhi: Gandhi Peace Foundation.

Clarke, Gerald 2003. *The Politics of NGOs in South East Asia: Participation and Protest in The Phillipines.* London: Routledge.

Cloos, Walter 1977. *Living Earth: The Organic Origin of Rocks and Minerals.* Cornwall, UK: Lanthorne Press. [original in German, 1925]

Cobden-Ramsay, L.E.B. 1910. *Feudatory States of Orissa,* Bengal Secretariat Book Depot, no.21 of the Bengal District Gazeteers. Calcutta: GoI.

Colchester, Marcus 1995. *Forest Politics in Suriname.* Utrecht: International Books with the World Rainforest Movement (WRM).

_____ 1997. *Guyana: Fragile Frontier.* London: Latin American Bureau with the WRM.

_____ ed. 2003. *Indigenous Peoples, Extractive Industries and the World Bank.* Phillipines: Tebtebba Foundation with the Forest Peoples Programme, UK.

Coopers & Lybrand April 1996. *Prospects for Industrial Development of ORISSA.* London: Coopers & Lybrand.

Copetas, A. Craig 2001. *Metal Men: How Marc Rich defrauded the country, evaded the Law, and became the World's Most Sought-After Corporate Criminal* [1st ed 1985, subtitled *Marc Rich and the 10-billion-dollar Scam.*] Harper Collins Canada.

Council on Ethics, Norwegian Govt Pension Fund May 2007. *Report on Vedanta Resources plc.* Oslo: Ministry of Finance (on EPG website).

Council for Social Development 1999. *Report on the Visit of a Team of the CSD to Rayagada and Bhubaneswar on 11–18 Jan., 1999.* Delhi: CSD (53 Lodi Estate, Delhi 1100003).

_____ 2008. *India: Social Development Report 2008. Development and Displacement.* Delhi: OUP.

Cowe, Roger 11 May 2003. 'The contradictions of Madhav Mehra', *The Observer.* UK.

Cullinan, Cormac 2002. *Wild Law: A Manifesto for Earth Justice.* Totnes: Green Books, with the Gaia Foundation, www.thegaiafoundation.org

Currie, Bob 2000. *The Politics of Hunger: A Study of Democracy, Governance and Kalahandi's poverty.* London: Macmillan.

Curtis, Mark 2003. *Web of Deceit: Britain's Real Role in the World.* London: Vintage. Danielson, Luke 2006. *Architecture for Change: an account of the MMSD project, History.* Berlin: Global Public Policy Institute.

Darwin, Charles [1881]. *The formation of vegetable mould through the action of worms with observation on their habits.* McLean, Virginia: IndyPublish.com.

Das, R.C., Chairman. March 1996. *Recommendation for environmentally sound growth of aluminium industry in Orissa.* Bhubaneswar: OSPCB.

Das, Samarendra 2004. 'Bulldozed out of their own land.' *Tehelka,* 21.2.2004. Delhi.

Das, Veena 1995. *Critical Events: An Anthropological Perspective on Contemporary India.* Delhi: OUP.
Das, Vidhya 3 June 1995. 'Development or Destruction? New Mining Projects in Orissa,' *EPW.*
_____ 14 March 1998. 'Human Rights, Inhuman Wrongs: Plight of Tribals in Orissa,' *EPW.*
_____ 14 July 2001. 'Mining Bauxite, Maiming People,' *EPW.*
_____ 4 Jan 2003. 'Kashipur: Politics of Underdevelopment,' *EPW.*
_____ 18 Oct 2003. 'Democratic Governance in Tribal Regions: a Distant Dream,' *EPW.*
Dash, Rabi 1998. *Judgements on the Poverty and Starvation Deaths in Kalahandi.* Cuttack: M/6 Samabaya Prakashan.
Dept of Environment, GoI 1986: Official Letter 11.6.86 refusing clearance for Gandhamardan project. Delhi: GoI.
DFID June 2005. *Partnership for development – DFID's country plan in India. State plan for Orissa 2004–2008.* Delhi: British High Commission. June 2005 version.
Dias, Xavier 2007. 'Never say DAE,' in Kalshian ed. pp. 140–150.
Directorate General of Technical Development, Ministry of Industry 1987. *Aluminium Industry in India: a review.* Delhi: GoI.
Dreze, Jean, Meera Samson and Satyajit Singh 1997. *The Dam and the Nation: Displacement and Resettlement in the Narmada Valley.* Delhi: OUP.
Economic and Political Weekly, Delhi 1967. 'Expensive Aluminium,' p. 2041–2 (25 Nov).
_____ 1971. 'Aluminium Costs. Whose Responsibility?' p. 1294.
_____ 1972. 'Aluminium indisustry. Who Needs Cheap Power?' p. 1101 (3 June).
_____ 1977. 'Aluminium. Hasty Imports?' pp. 71–2 (22 Jan).
_____ 1977. 'Aluminium. Short and Long of it,' pp. 1163–4 (23 July).
_____ 1978. 'Aluminium. At a price,' p. 1714 (14 Oct).
_____ 1980. 'Aluminium. Widening gap', p. 137.
Economy, Elizabeth C. 2007. 'The Great Leap Backward', *Foreign Affairs,* September-October.
Ellwood, Wayne 2002. *The No-Nonsense Guide to Globalization.* Oxford and London: New Internationalist and Verso.
Esteva, Gustavo 1992. 'Development,' in *The Development Dictionary: A Guide to Knowledge as Power,* ed Wolfgand Sachs pp. 7–25. London: Zed.
Exley, Christopher ed. 2001. *Aluminium and Alzheimer's Disease: the Science that Describes the Link.* Amsterdam: Elsevier.

Evans, G., James Goodman, and Nina Lansbury 2002. *Moving Mountains: Communities Confront Mining and Globalization.* London: Zed.

Fauset, Claire 2006. *What's Wrong with Corporate Social Responsibility? Corporate Watch CSR Report 2006* Oxford: Corporate Watch.

Fenelon, James 1998. *Culturicide, Resistance and Survival of the Lakota (Sioux Nation).* NY: Garland.

Fernandes, Walter April 2006. 'Liberalization and Development-induced Displacement,' in Mathur ed. 2006.

_____ Dec. 2006. 'Development-Induced Displacement: Impact on Tribals,' in *Adivasi* vol.46 no.2.

_____ 5 Dec. 2009. 'Climate Justice in the Northeast,' in *Assam Tribune.* Guahati.

_____ and S.A.Raj 1992. *Development, Displacement and Rehabilitation in the Tribal Areas of Orissa.* Delhi: Indian Social Institute.

_____ and M.Asif 1997. *Development-induced Displacement in Orissa 1951–1995: a database on its extent and nature.* Delhi: Indian Social Institute.

Flannery, Tim 2007 [2005]. *The Weather Makers: Our Changing Climate and What it Means for Life on Earth.* London: Penguin.

Forest Peoples Programme, Phillipine Indigenous Peoples Links and World Rainforest Movement 2000. *Undermining the Forests: the Need to Control Transnational Mining Companies: a Canadian study.* FPP, UK.

Foucault, Michel 1982. 'Why study power? The question of the subject,' in Dreyfus and Rabinow, *Michel Foucault: Beyond Structuralism and Hermeneutics.* Brighton: Harvester Press.

Fowler, Alan August 2000. 'NGO futures: beyond aid: NGDO values and the fourth position,' in *Third World Quarterly*, UK, vol.21 no.4, August 2000.

Fox, C.S. 1923. *Bauxite and Aluminous Occurences of India.* Calcutta: GSI Memoirs vol.xlix.

_____ 1932. *Bauxite and Aluminous Laterite: a Treatise Discussing in Detail...* London: Technical Press. (1st edition *Bauxite*, 1927)

Fraser, Alistair and John Lungu Jan 2007. 'For Who the Windfalls? Winners and Losers in the Privatisation of Zambia's Copper Mines.' Lusaka: Civil Society Trade Network of Zambia.

Gandhamardan Surakshya Yuva Parishad: Letter on the Nagchaudhuri Report, 6th May 1987, Paikmal.

Gandhi, Rajmohan 1999. *Revenge and Reconciliation: Understanding South Asian History.* Delhi: Penguin.

Gelder, Jan Willem van Dec. 2004. *The financing of Vedanta Resources:*

a research paper prepared for *Landelijke India Werkgroep*. Castricum, Netherlands: Profundo.

Ghosh, Soumitra and Subrat Kumar Sahu eds. July–September 2008. *Mausam: Talking Climate In Public Space*. Issue vol.1 no.1 (mausam.in@gmail.com).

Girard, Richard July 2005. *Corporate profile. Can Alcan Claim to be the Best? Its Corporate and Social Responsibility In Question*. Canada: Polaris Institute.

Girvan, Norman 1971. *Foreign Capital and Economic Underdevelopment in Jamaica*. Kingston: Institute of Social and Economic Resources, Univ of Jamaica.

――― 1976. *Corporate Imperialism: Transnational Corporations and Economic Nationalism in the Third World*. London: Monthly Review Press.

Gitlitz, Jennifer S. 1993. *The relationship between primary aluminium production and the damming of world rivers*. Berkeley: International Rivers Network, Working Paper 2.

Godoy, Ricardo 1985. 'Mining: Anthropological Perspectives,' in *Ann. Rev. Anth*. 14 pp. 199–217.

Gokhale, K.V.G.K. and T.C. Rao 1983. *Ore Deposits of India: their Distribution and Processing*. Delhi: Affiliated East-West Press. (3rd ed.)

Goodland, Robert Dec. 2005 *Suriname: Environmental and Social Reconnaissance. The Bakhuys Bauxite Mining Project*. Report prepared for Association of Indigenous Village Leaders and North-South Institute, RbtGoodland@aol.com

――― March 2007. *Utkal Bauxite and Alumina Project: Human Rights and Environmental Impacts*. (http://www.business-humanrights.org/Documents/Goodland-Utkal-Mar-2007.pdf)

Govt of India, Planning Commission, Sept. 2001. *Report of the Working Group on Mineral Exploration and Development*. Delhi.

Govt of Orissa, Finance Dept. 2001: *Fiscal and Governance Reforms*. Bhubaneswar.

Graham, Ronald 1982. *The Aluminium Industry and the Third World*. London: Zed.

Gray, John 1998. *False Dawn: The Delusions of Global Capitalism*. London: Granta.

Greer, Jed and Kenny Bruno 1996. *Greenwash: The Reality behind Corporate Enviromentalism*. Penang, Malaysia: Third World Network.

Griffiths, Peter 2003. *The Economist's Tale: a Consultant Encounters Hunger and The World Bank*. London: Zed.

Gundimeda, H.S. Sanyal, R. Sinha and P. Sukhdev 2005. *Green Accounting for Indian States Projects, Monograph 1. The Value of Timber, Carbon, Fuelwood, and Non-Timber Forest Products in India's Forests.* Delhi: TERI Press for Green Indian States Trust (GIST). Sponsored by Centurion Bank of Punjab, GIST, and Deutsche Bank.

——— 2006. *Green Accounting... Monograph 4. The Value of Biodiversity in India's Forests.* Delhi: TERI for GIST.

Haberl, Helmut, F. Krausmann and S. Gingrich 2006. 'Ecological Embeddedness of the Economy: A Sociological Perspective on Humanity's Economic Activities 1700–2000,' in *EPW* 25 Nov. pp. 4896–4904.

Hager, Nick 2006. *Hollow Men: A Study in the Politics of Deception.* Nelson, NZ: Craig Potton.

Hancock, Graham 1989. *Lords of Poverty: the Power, Prestige, and Corruption of the International Aid Business.* NY: Atlantic Monthly Press [and UK: Macmillan].

Harsha Trust, Xavier Institute of Managament and District Action Group (Jajpur) Nov. 2006. *Empirical study on people affected and displaced due to Tata Steel in Kalinganagar, Orissa.* Bhubaneswar: Harsha.

Hartmann, Thom 1998. *The Last Hours of Ancient Sunlight.* London: Hodder & Stoughton.

Harvey, David 2005. *A Brief History of Neoliberalism* USA: OUP.

Hauschka, Rudolf 1983 [1966]. *The Nature of Substance.* London: Rudolf Steiner Press.

Heiner, Albert P. 1991. *Henry J. Kaiser: Western Colossus.* San Francisco: Halo.

Hildyard, Nick [2008]. 'A (Crumbling) Wall of Money: Financial Bricolage, Derivatives and Power'. UK: The Corner House (available at http://www.thecornerhouse.org.uk/pdf/briefing/39wallmoney.pdf).

Hinmon, Ashly 2007. 'Forgeries in Steel: We Also Make Poverty,' in Kalshian ed. pp. 124–139.

Holloway, S.K. 1988. *The Aluminium Multinationals and the Bauxite Cartel.* NY: St. Martin's Press.

Hughes, Lotte 2003. *The No-Nonsense Guide to Indigenous Peoples.* Oxford and London: New Internationalist and Verso.

Human Rights Forum, Dec.2006. *Death, Displacement and Deprivation. The War in Dantewara: a Report.* Hyderabad.

IAI (International Aluminium Institute, London): June 2004. *Third Bauxite Mine Rehabilitation Survey.*

——— 2005. *Sustainability Update. Aluminium for Future Generations.*

——— n.d. *The Aluminium Industry's Sustainable Development Report* (obtained 2006).

IBM 1994. *Bauxite: a market survey*. Nagpur: IBM, Mineral Economics Division.
IBM *Yearbook, 2002*. Nagpur.
IBM *Yearbook, 2003*. Nagpur.
Ibon South Asia Jan.2008. 'SEZs in India: the Real Story,' in *IBON Facts and Figures, S.Asia edition*. (ibonsouthasia@ibon.org)
IBRD and IDA [WB] 28 Sept. 2004. *Program Document* (PD) *for a loan and credit to India for Socio-economic Development Program.* WB Report no 26550-IN, Poverty Reduction and Economic Management, S.Asia region.
IFAD: India—*Tribal Development Project* [OTDP] 1993. *Mid-term Review cum Supervision Mission: Aide Memoire*—P.Maleki, (UNDP/OPS), R.Reader (Financial Analyst)), A.Siddiqui (Agriculturalist), A.Alam (Civil Engineer). [in India 15 April–3 May 1993]
——— 1998. *Completion Evaluation Executive summary* (9–21 Nov). (browsed from www.ifad.org/evaluation/public html, in 2005)
INCAL 1998: Proceedings of the International Conference on Aluminium. Bangalore: Aluminium Association of India, Sastry, D.H. et.al. eds. (3 volumes)
INCAL 2003, vols.1–3, eds S.Subramanian and D.H.Sastry.
INDAL: Facts, 2001–02. [booklet]
INDAL: Small is big. [n.d. brochure]
INDAL at a glance. [n.d. booklet]
Indian People's Tribunal on Environment and Human Rights Oct. 2006. *Kashipur: An Enquiry into Mining and Human Rights Violations in Kashipur, Orissa.* Mumbai: IPT (*www.iptindia.org/pdf/Kashipur.pdf*). Written and ed. by Shravant Reddy, Tribunal led by S.N.Bhargava (retd.), Former Chief Justice, Sikkim High Court.
Iqbal, Javed 2009. 'Operation tribal hunt?' *The New Indian Express* 15 November p. 1.
James, P.G. 1995. *Non-Governmental Voluntary Organisations.* Kollam, Kerala: Mass Lines Publications.
Jena, Mihir, Padmini Pathi, Jagganath Dash, Kamala Patnaik, Klaus Seeland 2002. *Forest Tribes of Orissa. Vol.1 The Dongaria Kondh.* Delhi: DK Printworld.
JK company: *The architects of JK Organisation* [company brochure, n.d.].
JNARDDC Profile: In the service of Aluminium Industry. Nagpur: JNARDDC.
JNARDDC Newsletter Jan–March 2003 (vol.4 no.1), Nagpur.
Jojo, Bipin K. 2002. 'Political economy of large dam projects: a case

study of Upper Kolab Project in Koraput District, Orissa,' in Thakaran ed. 2002.

Jones, Colin 1977. *The £200,000 Job: A Study of Government. Intervention in Aluminium Smelting ... The Way the Money Goes.* London: Centre for Policy Studies.

Josephson, Matthew 1962 [1934]. *The Robber Barons: the Great American Capitalists 1861–1901.* London: Eyre & Spottiswoode.

Kabra, Kamal Nayan 1989. 'Make/Buy decisions and the uses of Domestic Resource Cost estimates,' *International Journal of Development Planning Literature* vol.4, no.2 pp. 73–90.

――― 1992. *Financial Sector Scam: Fruits of Liberalisation.* Delhi: Sehyog Prakashan, 7/1 Pant Nagar, Jangpura, Delhi 110014.

Kalam, A.P.J. and Y.S. Rajan 1998. *India 2020: a Vision for the New Millenium.* Penguin.

Kale, D.C. 8 July 1972. 'Dithering in Aluminium,' *EPW*.

Kalshian, Rakesh ed. 2007. *Caterpillar and the Mahua Flower: Tremors in India's Mining Fields.* Delhi: Panos.

Kamat, Sangeeta 2003. 'NGOs and New Democracy: The False Saviours of International Development,' in *Harvard International Review, vol.25 no.1, Development & Modernization.*

Karat, Prakash 1984. 'Action Groups/Voluntary Organisations: a Factor in Imperialist Strategy,' in *The Marxist*, April–June 1984 pp. 19–54.

Karnataka Vimochana Ranga, Kudremukh National Park Virodhi Okkuta, Manasa, People's Democratic Forum, and People's Union for Civil Liberties—Karnataka, July 2003. *The Struggle against Bauxite Mining in Orissa: Report of a Citizens' Visit to Orissa, Oct.–Dec. 2002.* Bangalore: PUCL-K, 233 6th Main, 4th Block, Jayanagar, Bangalore 560056.

Khatua, Sanjay and William Stanley June 2006. *Ecological Debt: a case study from Orissa* (item 31 on www.freewebs.com/epgorissa).

Kirsch, Stuart 2006. *Reverse Anthropology: Indigenous Analysis of Social and Environmental Relations in New Guinea.* California: Stanford UP.

Klebnikov, Paul 2000. *Godfather of the Kremlin: The Decline of Russia in the Age of Gangster Capitalism.* Orlando (US): Harcourt.

Klein, Naomi 2002. *Fences and Windows: Dispatches from the Frontline of the Globalization Debate.* Vintage Canada and Delhi: LeftWord Books.

――― 2007. *The Shock Doctrine: the Rise of Disaster Capitalism.* NY: Metropolitan.

Kochanek, Stanley A. 1974. *Business and Politics in India.* Berkeley: Univ. of California Press.

Korten, David C. 1995. *When Corporations Rule the World*. London: Earthscan.
Kublal-Singh, Wayne 2009. *Ital Revolution*. Trinidad and Tobago: Just World Publications.
Kudaisya, Medha M. 2003. *The Life and Times of G.D. Birla*. Delhi: OUP.
Kulke, Hermann and Dietmar Rothermund 2004 [1986]. *A History of India*. Routledge.
Kumar, Arun 2002 [1999]. *The Black Economy in India*. Delhi, London: Penguin.
Kumar, Surinder 2001. 'The Enron Trap,' in *Alternative Economic Survey 2000–2001. 2nd Generation Reforms: Delusions of Development*. By Alternative Survey Group. Delhi: Rainbow Publishers, Azadi Bachao Andolan and Lokayan.
Lala, R.M. 1992 [1981]. *The Creation of Wealth: The Tatas from the 19th to the 21st Century*. Delhi: Penguin.
Laniak-Herdeck, Margaret, and Gita Piramal 1985. *India's Industrialists*. Boulder: Lynne Rienner.
Lapointe, Paul-André 1994. 'Quebec: Aluminium Valley or Aluminium Republic?' in Barham, Bunker and O'Hearn eds. pp. 215–29.
Lazarus, Kate M. 2009. *In Search of Aluminium: China's role in the Mekong River*. Cambodia: Heinrich Böll Stiftung, with WWF Denmark and IISD Canada.
Liedloff, Jean 1986 [1975]. *The Continuum Concept*. London: Penguin.
Lohmann, Larry 2006. *Carbon Trading: a Critical Conversation on Climate Change, privatisation and power*. Uppsala, Sweden: Dag Hammarskjöld Centre. (www.dhf.uu.se and www.thecornerhouse.org.uk)
Loza, Jehan and John Price 9 Nov 2004. *The CCLP* [Corporate Community Leadership Program]: *'Fighting Goliath' or 'Trusting your Reflection', an Evaluation Final Report*. Social Compass for Oxfam Community Aid Abroad Australia.
Lynch, Martin 2002. *Mining in World History*. London: Reaktion Books.
Macdonald, Kate May 2009. *The reality of rights: Barriers to accessing remedies when business operates beyond borders*. London: The London School of Economics and Political Science (www.corporate-responsibility.org).
McCully, Patrick 1998. *Silenced Rivers: The Ecology and Politics of Large Dams*. Hyderabad: Orient Longman. [London: Zed, 1996]
McLaughlin, Corinne and Gordon Davidson 1994. *Spiritual Politics: Changing the World from the Inside Out*. Scotland: Findhorn Press.
Magnasson, Andri Snaer 2008. *Dreamland: A Self-Help Manual for a*

Frightened Nation. London: Citizen's Press.
Mahapatra, Richard 1999. 'Confrontation Mine', in *Down To Earth*, Delhi 15 April.
Mahariya, Baba 2001. 'Development: at Whose Cost? An Adivasi on Dislocation and Displacement,' in K.C. Yadav ed. *Beyond the Mud Walls: Indian Social Realities*. Delhi: Hope India.
Mander, Jerry 1991. *In the Absence of the Sacred: The Failure of Technology and the Survival of the Indian Nations*. San Francisco: Sierra Club.
Marr, Carolyn 1993. *Digging Deep: The Hidden Costs of Mining in Indonesia*. London: Down to Earth and Minewatch.
Martinez-Alier, Joan 2002. *The Environmentalism of the Poor: A Study of Ecological Conflicts and Valuation*. Cheltenham: Edward Elgar.
Mathur, H.M. March 2006. 'Resettling People Displaced by Development Projects: Some Critical Management Issues,' in *Social Change* vol.36 no.1, pp. 36–86.
_____ Sept 2006. 'Globalization, Resettlement, and Impoverishment Risks: Large Corporations and Tribal People in Orissa, India', Paper presented at IAPS/Bibalex Conference on Environment, Health and Sustainable Development: 'Involuntary Resettlement, Social Sustainability and Environmental Risks', Alexandria, Egypt, 14–15 September.
_____ Dec 2006. 'Development Projects and Displacement of Tribal Peoples,' in *Adivasi*, vol.46, no.2. Bhubaneswar.
_____ Dec 2008.'A New Deal for Displaced People: Orissa's Involuntary Resettlement Policy', *Social Change* vol.38 no.4, pp. 553–75.
_____ ed. March 2006. *Social Change, Special Resettlement Issue*. Delhi: Council for Social Development.
Mathur, Shubh 2008. *The Everyday Life of Hindu Nationalism: An Ethnographic Account*. Gurgaon: Three Essays Collective.
MBD 2004: International Seminar on Mineral Business Development, Nagpur.
Means, Russell 1982. 'On a New Consciousness of the American Indian Movement,' *Lokayan Bulletin* no 7, Delhi [a partial transcript of a speech given at Pine ridge reservation, South Dakota, July 1980].
Meek, R. L. 1976. *Social Science and the Ignoble Savage*. Cambridge: CUP.
Menon, Meena 1999. 'People are Starving,' in *The Hindu* 5 Dec.
_____ 2001. 'Kashipur: Bullets for Bauxite,' in *The Hindu Survey of the Environment*. The Hindu newspaper group.
Micklethwaite, John and Adrian Wooldridge 2003. *The Company: A Short History of a Revolutionary Idea*. London: Weidenfeld and Nicolson.

Midgley, Dominic and Chris Hutchins 2005. *Abramovich: The Billionaire from Nowhere.* London: HarperCollins (updated edition).
Mishra, C.R. August 1986. 'Gallium Project,' in *NALCO: Parichaya* [magazine]. Bhubaneswar: NALCO.
Mishra, Kedar 2007. 'Fifth Columnists?' in Kalshian ed. pp. 192–205.
MMSD (Mining, Minerals and Sustainable Development) 2002. *Breaking New Ground.* London: Earthscan. (www.iisd.org/mmsd)
MoEF 2007. *Note on Bauxite mining in Orissa: Report on Flora, Fauna and impact on tribal population.* Delhi: presented at the SC on 5th October 2007 by the Attorney General (on epg website, with a counter-report in petition by Siddharth Nayak).
Mohammed, Anu Dec. 2006. *Monga, Microcredit, and the Nobel Prize,* Dacca, at www.countercurrents.org
Mohanty, B.K. ed. 2003. *History of Mining in Orissa.* Bhubaneswar: OMC.
Mohanty, S.C. 2006. 'Involuntary Displacement and Rehabilitation of Project Affected Persons in Upper Kolab Project, Koraput,' in *Adivasi,* vol.46, no.2.
Monbiot, George 2000. *Captive State: The Corporate Takeover of Britain.* London: Macmillan/Pan.
―――― 2006. *Heat: How to Stop the Planet Burning.* London: Allen Lane.
Moody, Roger 1992. *The Gulliver File: Mines, Land and People—a Global Battleground.* London: Minewatch.
―――― 2005. *The Risks we Run: Mining, Communities and Political Risk Insurance.* Utrecht: International Books.
―――― 2007. *Rocks and Hard Places: The Globalization of Mining.* London: Zed.
―――― 2007. 'The Base Alchemist', in Kalshian ed. pp. 83–102.
―――― ed. 1988. *The Indigenous Voice,* 2 vols. London: Zed.
Moore, Michael 2001. *Stupid White Men.* London: Penguin.
Morrison, Rod ed. 2007. *Financing Global Mining: The Complete Picture.* London: Thomson Financial Group (published by Project Finance International in association with International Financing Review and Acquisitions Monthly).
Morse, Bradford and Thomas Berger 1992. *Sardar Sarovar: The Independent Review.* Ottawa: Resource Futures International.
Mosse, David 2005. *Cultivating Development: An Ethnography of Aid Policy and Practice.* London: Pluto.
―――― 2007. *Power and the Durability of Poverty: A critical examination of the links between Culture, Marginality and Chronic Poverty.* CPRC

Working Paper no.7, Dec 2007, pp. 1–57 (ISBN 978-1-906433-06-2, available at www.chronicpoverty.org).
_____ 2009. 'Social Analysis as Corporate Product: NonEconomists/Anthropologists at the World Bank in Washington DC,' in D.Mosse ed. *Travelling Rationalities: The Anthropology of Expert Knowledge and Professionals in International Development.* Oxford: Berghahn.
Mukerji, Bithika 2008. *Neo-Vedanta and Modernity.* Varanasi: Ashutosh Prakashan Sansthan. [1983]
Muthayya, B.C. et al. 1984. *Rehabilitation of Displaced Villages: A Study in Nalco Complex, Damanjodi, Koraput District, Orissa.* Hyderabad: National Institute of Rural Development.
Nagarik Mancha 2005. *Industrial Pollution in Durgapur.* Kolkata: Naba Dutta.
Nagchaudhuri, B.D. 1987. *Report of High Level Committee on environmental and ecological aspects of the Gandhamardan Bauxite Project, Orissa.* GoI: Dept of Mines.
NALCO: 20th Annual Report 2000–2001.
Nandy, Ashish 2007 [2003]. *The Romance of the State and the State of Dissent.* Delhi: OUP.
Nayak, Birendra Sept. 1997. 'Cultural Imperialism and Voluntary Organisations,' in *Janshakti*, pp. 40–56.
_____ 2000. "Saviours' and Feet of Clay,' *EPW* pp. 851–2 (4 March).
Nayak, Ramesh C. and Joseph M.Kujur 2007. *State Aggression and Tribal Resistance: A Case of the Police Firing at Kalinga Nagar.* Delhi: Indian Social Institute.
Naydler, Jeremy ed. 1996. *Goethe on Science.* Edinburgh: Floris Books.
Nazir, Umesh 2007. 'Full Monty, Please!' in Kalshian ed. pp. 165–177, translated by Rahul Rajesh.
Neeraj 2001. *Globalisation or Recolonisation?* Pune: Alaka Joshi.
Norwatch: *Future in Our Hands* Feb.1996. 'Protests from Indian indigenous people: Civil disobedience against Hydro's bauxite project.' Norway: *Future in Our Hands* (*FIVH*).
_____ Oct. 1997. 'Norsk-Hydro's controversial bauxite project in India: Stoltenberg fails to answer protest letter from 5,000 affected people.' Norway: *FIVH*.
Nostromo Research 2005. *Ravages through India: Vedanta Resources plc Alternative Report*, London and the India Resource Center, Delhi. (www.minesandcommunities.org)
_____ [May 2008]. *From Money to Metals: The Good Campaigners' Guide to Questionable Funders*, http://www.minesandcommunities.org//article.php?a=8536

'Notes from Nowhere' ed. 2003. *we are everywhere: the irresistable rise of global anticapitalism.* London and NY: Verso.

Nwoke, Chibuzo 1987. *Third World Minerals and Global Pricing: A New Theory.* London: Zed.

O'Connor, Harvey 1933. *Mellon's Millions.* New York: John Day co.

O'Hearn, Denis 1994. 'Producing Imperialism Anew: The United States, the United Kingdom, and Jamaican Bauxite,' in Barham, Bunker and O'Hearn eds. pp. 147–78.

Okonta, Ike and Oronto Douglas 2003. *Where Vultures Feast: Shell, Human Rights, and Oil in the Niger Delta.* NY: Sierra Club Books.

ORISSA STATE DEVELOPMENT REPORT 2001. Bhubaneswar: Nabakrishna Centre for Development Studies and ICSSR with GoO, sponsored by Planning Commission.

Padel, Felix 2000. *The Sacrifice of Human Being: British Rule and the Konds of Orissa.* Delhi: OUP. [1995 and published in a new, expanded edition in Jan 2010 as *Sacrificing People: Invasions of a Tribal Landscape.* Delhi Orient BlackSwan]

⎯⎯⎯ 1998. 'Forest Knowledge: Tribal people, their Environment and the Structure of Power,' in *Nature and the Orient: The environmental history of South and Southeast Asia,* ed. Richard H. Grove, Vinita Damodaran and Satpal Sangwan. Delhi: OUP.

⎯⎯⎯ 2006. 'Environmental and Social Impacts of Mining Industries: a Case Study of Sterlite-Vedanta in Orissa,' in *Community Forestry.* Bhubaneswar: Regional Centre for Development Cooperation (RCDC, web: www.banajata.org).

⎯⎯⎯ 22 Sept 2007 'A Cry Against the Hidden War: Bastar's Civil War,' *Tehelka* (http://www.tehelka.com/story_main34.asp?filename=cr220907A_CRY.asp)

⎯⎯⎯ Feb. 2008. 'Mining as a Fuel for War,' in *The Broken Rifle* issue no.77 p.1 (http://www.wri-irg.org/node/3576).

⎯⎯⎯ and Samarendra Das 2004. 'Exodus part two: Lanjigarh,' in *Tehelka* 13/3/2004 p. 22. Delhi.

⎯⎯⎯ 2006. 'Double Death: Aluminium's Links with Genocide,' *Social Scientist* no.394–5, pp. 55–81. Delhi.

⎯⎯⎯ 2007. 'Agya, what do you mean by development?' in Kalshian ed. pp. 24–46.

⎯⎯⎯ Oct–Nov. 2007. 'Arrested development: the bitter barter,' in *Teragreen* vol.4 issue 4, pp. 15–18 and 46–8. Delhi: TERI (www.teriin.org)

⎯⎯⎯ 2008. 'Cultural Genocide: the Real Impact of Development-Induced Displacement,' in H.M.Mathur ed. *India: Social Development Report*

2008. *Development and Displacement*, pp. 103–115. Delhi: OUP for Council for Social Development.
_____ Dec. 2008. 'Orissa's highland clearances: The reality gap in R & R,' in *Social Change* vol.38 no.4, pp. 576–608.
Padel, Ruth 2005. *Tigers in Red Weather*. London: Little, Brown.
Palast, Greg 2003 [2002]. *The Best Democracy Money can Buy: An Investigative Reporter Exposes the Truth about Globalization, Corporate Cons, and High Finance Fraudsters*. London: Robinson.
Panda, Hrushikesh 1986. 'Threat to Ecosystem: Case of Gandhamardan Hills,' in *Mainstream*, 17 May 1986 p.9. Delhi.
Panda, Ranjan K. 2007. 'Under a Black Sky,' in Kalshian ed. pp. 114–123.
Pandey, Balaji 1998. *Depriving the Underprivelaged for Development*. Bhubaneswar: Institute for Socio-Economic Development.
Pani, Shankar 2008. 'Toxic gas from smelter plant damages crop in Hirakud,' 14.10.08 in www.merinews.com
Parry, Johnathon 2007. 'The Sacrifices of Modernity in a Soviet-built Steel Town in Central India,' chapter 13 in Frances Pine and Joao De Pina-Cabral eds. *On the Margins of Religion*. Oxford: Berghahn.
Pastor, Ginés Haro and Georgina Donati 2008. *Green Gold: The Amazon fight to keep oil underground*. London: IDUN and New Internationalist.
Pati, Biswamoy 1993. *Resisting Domination: Peasants, Tribals and the National Movement in Orissa 1920–1950*. Delhi: Manohar.
Patkar, Medha ed. Jan. 2004. *River Linking: a Millenium Folly?* NAPM, Haji Habab Building, A Wing, Naigaon Crossroad, Dadar (E), Mumbai 400014.
Patnaik, Ali Kishore 2001. 'Profits over People,' *Frontline* 19th Jan.
Patnaik, Naveen 1993. *The Garden of Life: An Introduction to the Healing Plants of India*. NY: Doubleday.
Patnaik, Utsa 2007. *The Republic of Hunger and Other Essays*. Gurgaon: Three essays collective.
Patterson, Samuel H. 1967. *Bauxite Reserves and Potential Aluminium Resources of the World*. Washington: US Dept of the Interior.
Pattnayak, Kishen. 28 Sept 1985. 'Non-Party Groups and their Dependence on Foreign Money,' *EPW* vol.XX no.39 pp. 1665–6.
_____ 2004. 'Visions of development: the inevitable need for alternatives,' in *Futures* 36 pp. 671–8 (www.elsevier.com/locate/futures).
Payer, Cheryl 1991. *Lent and lost: Foreign Credit and 3rd World Development*. London: Zed.
Pearce, Fred 2007 [2006]. *The Last Generation: How Nature Will Take Her Revenge for Climate Change*. London: Transworld.

Pelikan, Wilhelm 1973. *The Secrets of Metals*. NY: Anthroposophic Press. [1952]

People's Tribunal on Nandigram Dec.2007. *Nandigram: What Really Happenned?* Delhi: Daanish Books.

People's Union of Civil Liberties (PUCL) 16 May 2003. A Fact-finding Report on physical attack on the villagers agitating against their displacement due to the proposed Sterlite Alumina Project in Lanjigarh Block of Kalahandi district. Bhubaneswar: PUCL, Rayagada and Bhubaneswar units, www.indymedia.org:8080

People's Union of Democratic Rights (PUDR) 1986. 'Report on Gandhamardan Mines,' in *Mainstream* 8 Nov. pp. 30–34.

_____ May 2005. *Investigation into the Impact on People due to the Alumina Projects in South Orissa*. Bhubaneswar.

_____ April 2006. *Where the State makes War on its Own People*. www.pudr.org/pages/salwa.judum.pdf

Perchard, Andrew 2010. *Aluminiumville: Metal, the British Government and the Scottish Highlands*. Lancaster: Carnegie Publishing. [forthcoming]

Perkins, John 2005. *Confessions of an Economic Hitman: The Shocking Inside Story of how America REALLY took over the World*. London: Ebury.

Petras, James Dec.1997. 'Imperialism and NGOs in Latin America,' *Monthly Review* pp. 10–27.

_____ and Henry Veltmeyer 2001. *Globalization Unmasked: Imperialism in the 21ˢᵗ Century*. London: Zed [and Delhi: Madhyam].

Pettifor, Ann ed. 2003. *The Real World Economic Outlook: The Legacy of Globalization—Debt and Deflation*. London: Palgrave Macmillan.

Pilger, John 1998. *Hidden Agendas*. London: Vintage.

_____ 2002. *The New Rulers of the World*. London: Verso.

_____ 2006. *Freedom Next Time*. London: Transworld.

Piramal, Gita 1996. *Business Maharajas*. Delhi: Viking.

Pradhan, Jagdish 1993. 'Drought in Kalahandi: The Real Story,' *EPW* pp. 1084–8 (29 May).

Pradhan, Satapathy Feb. 2006. *Police firing at Kalinganagar: A Report by People's Union for Civil Liberties*. Delhi: PUCL.

Prasad, Archana 2003. *Against Ecological Romanticism: Verrier Elwin and the Making of Anti-Modern Tribal Identity*. Delhi: Three Essays Collective.

Prayas and C.S.Venkata Ratnam 2003. *Indian Power Sector Reforms: Issues and Challenges for Electricity Employees*. Delhi: Public Service International.

Prebble, John 1967. *Culloden*. London: Penguin. [1961]

_____1969. *The Highland Clearances.* London: Penguin. [1963]
Priest, N.D. and T.V. O'Donnell 1998. *Health in the Aluminium Industry: Managing Health Issues in the Aluminium Industry.* London: Middlesex U.P.
Purkayastha, Prabir and Vijay Prashad 2002. *Enron Blowout: Corporate Capitalism and Theft of the Global Commons.* Delhi: LeftWord.
Putul, Alok Prakash 2007. 'No Man's Land,' in Kalshian ed. pp. 47–64.
Radford, Tim 2003. 'The future's blue,' in *The Guardian: Life* p.9, 31/7/03.
Rajagopalam, S., Srinivasan, K., Vyasalu, V. 1981 'The Orissa aluminium complex. Points towards a debate.' *EPW*, Dec. 5, p. 2005–14.
Raja, Amit 2007. 'Nero's Children,' in Kalshian ed. pp. 151–164.
Ramnath, Madhu 2004. *Crossing Boundaries: Adivasi Women and Forest Produce—a story from Central Bastar, Chhattisgarh, India.* Coonoor Printing Press shakun2000@eth.net, www.bothends.org)
Rangachari R., Nirmal Sengupta, Ramaswamy R. Iyer, Pranab Banerji and Shekhar Singh: Nov.2000. *Large Dams: India's Experience. Country case study.* Cape Town: World Commission on Dams.
Rao, M.G. and P.K. Raman October 1979. *East Coast Bauxite Deposits of India. Report by the Geological Survey of India.* Calcutta: GSI.
Ray, Rabindra 1988. *The Naxalites and their Ideology.* Delhi: OUP.
Rich, Bruce 1994. *Mortgaging the Earth: the World Bank, Environmental Impoverishment and the Crisis of Development.* London: Earthscan.
Ritthoff, Michael, Holger Rohn and Christa Liedtke 2002. *Calculating MIPS: Resource Productivity of Products and Services.* Wuppertal spezial 27e. Germany: Wuppertal Institute for Climate, Environment and Energy.
Rivero, Oswaldo de 2001. *The Myth of Development: Non-Viable Economies of the 21st Century.* London: Zed.
Robbins, Peter 1982. *Guide to Non-Ferrous Metals and their Markets.* London: Kogan Page. [1979]
_____ March 1998. 'Pulp Fiction – today many major mining operations are unprofitable – yet companies continue to extract minerals and metals in ever-increasing quantities. Ex-metals dealer Peter Robbins tells the inside story,' in *New Internationalist.* London.
_____ 2003. *Stolen Fruit: The Tropical Commodities Disaster.* London: Zed.
Robbins, Richard H. 2003. 'Anthropology, Global Studies, and Public Policy: a Proposal regarding the Proper Use of Things,' paper presented at a meeting of the Society for Applied Anthropology at Portland, Oregon, March 2003 (www.faculty.plattsburgh.edu/richard.robbins/

Anthropology_Policy.htm).

Roberts, J. and D.McLean 1976. *Mapoon—Book Three: The Cape York mining Companies and the Native Peoples*. Victoria: International Development Action.

Robins, Nick 2004. 'The World's First Multinational,' *New Statesman* 14 Dec. 2004 (www. newstatesman.org).

_____ 2006. *The Corporation that Changed the World: How the East India Company Shaped the Modern Multinational*. London: Pluto.

_____ Sept 30–October 1 2006. 'Capital Gains,' *Financial Times Magazine*. London.

Røpke, Inge 2006. *Consumption and environment – ecological economics perspectives*. PhD thesis published by Dept of Manufacturing Engineering and Management, Technical Univ. of Denmark.

Ross, Michael Jan.1999. 'The political Economy of the Resource Curse,' in *World Politics* no.51.

_____ 2001. *Extractive Sectors and the Poor: An Oxfam America Report*. Washington DC: Oxfam America.

Rosser, Andrew 2006. *The Political Economy of the Resource Curse: a Literature Survey*. Susse: Institute of Development Studies. IDS working paper 268.

Rowell, Andy, James Marriott and Lorne Stockman 2005. *The Next Gulf: London, Washington and Oil Conflict in Nigeria*. London: Constable.

Roy, Arundhati 1999. *The Cost of Living*. London: Flamingo.

_____ 2001. *The Algebra of Infinite Justice*. Penguin.

Sachs, Jeffery D. 2005. *The End of Poverty*. Penguin.

_____ and Andrew M. Walker 1997. 'Sources of Slow Growth in African Economies,' *Journal of African Economies* 6 (3), 335–376.

_____ 2001. 'Natural Resources and Economic Development: the Curse of Natural Resources,' Elsevier: *European Economic Review*, 45, pp. 827–38 (www.elsevier.com/locate/ecochase).

Sahu, Bighneswar 2007. 'Defying the Juggernaut,' in Kalshian ed. pp. 178–191.

Sainath, P. 1996. *Everybody Likes a Good Drought: Stories from India's Poorest Districts*. Delhi, London: Penguin.

Samantara , Prafulla July 2006. *Niyamgiri: Waiting for Justice*. Berhampur: Lok Shakti Abhiyan (Orissa unit).

Sampson, Anthony 1975. *The Seven Sisters: The Great Oil Companies and the World they Made*. NY: Viking.

_____ 1977. *The Arms Bazaar: The companies, the Dealers, the Bribes, from Vickers to Lockheed*. London: Hodder & Stoughton.

_____ 1982. *The Moneylenders: Bankers and a World in Turmoil.* NY:Viking.

_____ 1989. *The Midas Touch: Why the Rich Nations get Richer and the Poor stay Poor.* Penguin.

_____ 1993. *The Essential Anatomy of Britain: Democracy in Crisis.* London and NY: Harvest.

_____ 2004. *Who Runs this Place? The Anatomy of Britain in the 21st Century.* London: John Murray.

Sankeralli, Burton 2009. *The rag file: writings of the aluminium smelter wars.* Trinidad and Tobago: Just World Publications.

Sarangi, Deba Ranjan 2002. 'Surviving Against the Odds: Case of Kashipur,' *EPW* (3 Aug).

_____ 2003. 'State, NGOs and Tribals,' *EPW* (4 Jan).

_____ 2004. 'Mining 'Development' and MNCs,' *EPW* (24 April).

Sarangi, D.R., Rabishankar Pradhan and Saroj Mohanty 2005. 'State Repression in Kashipur,' *EPW* (26 March).

Sarini 2006. *Adivasis of Rourkela. Looking back on 50 years of Indo-German Economic Co-operation. Documents–Interpretations–International Law.* Bhubaneswar: Sarini and Adivasi-Koordination.

Savyasaachi 2008. 'Deforestation, Nature and Conservation: An Indigenous Discourse,' in *Contemporary Perspectives* vol.2 no.2 July–Dec, pp. 279–313.

SEBI 2001: *Sterlite Industries (India) Ltd v. Securities and Exchange Board of India* Appeal no.20/2001, decided on Oct.22 2001 before the Securities Tribunal, Mumbai.

Sethi, Aman 2007. 'Road to Perdition,' in Kalshian ed. pp. 65–82.

Sethi, Harsh 23 Feb.1985. 'The Immoral 'Other': Debate between Party and Non-Party Groups,' *EPW* vol.XX no.8 pp. 378–80.

_____ 18 Oct.2003. 'Doing without Aid?' *EPW* pp. 4421–3.

Sharma, B.D. 1990. *29th Report of the Commissioner for Scheduled Castes and Scheduled Tribes* for 1987–89. Delhi: GOI.

_____ 2001. *Tribal Affairs in India: The Crucial Transition.* Delhi: Sahyog Pustak Kuteer.

Sheel, Alok 2001. *Strategy Paper on Aluminium Tariffs for India.* Delhi: Rajiv Gandhi Institute for Contemporary Studies, Working Paper no.23.

Shiva, Vandana 2000. *Stolen Harvest: The Hijacking of the Global Food Supply.* London: Zed.

_____ and Afasar H. Jafri 1998. *Stronger than Steel: People's Movement against Globalisation and the Gopalpur Steel Plant.* Delhi: Research Foundation for Science, Technology and Ecology.

Shreedhar, Ramamurthi 2004. 'Mining and MNCs,' *EPW* (19 June), pp. 2538–9 (letter).
Simms, Andrew 2005. *Ecological Debt: The Health of the Planet and the Wealth of Nations*. London: Pluto.
Singh, Kavaljit Aug.1997. 'Órissa: from 'Backward' to 'Investors' Paradise'?' Delhi: *PIRG Update*.
───── 2005. *Questioning Globalization*. Delhi: Madhyam.
Skidelsky, Robert 2000. *John Maynard Keynes: Fighting for Britain 1937–46*. London: Macmillan. [3rd volume of biography]
Smith, G.D. 1988. *From Monopoly to Competition: The Transformations of Alcoa, 1888–1986*. Cambridge: CUP.
Sogge, David 2002. *Give and Take: What's the Matter with Foreign Aid?* Bangalore: Books for Change.
South Eastern Railway 1995. *Koraput-Rayagada Rail Link: Heralding a new Era for Orissa*.
Spash, Clive 2007. 'The economics of climate change impacts à la Stern:. Novel and nuanced or rhetorically restricted?' *Ecological Economics*, p. 706–713. (www.science direct.com)
Sridhar, S. *Globalization of Indian Aluminium Industry: financing aspects*, in *INCAL 1998*.
Sridhar, V. 2003. 'Nalco—a Story of Resistance,' in *Frontline* weekly magazine, 17.1.2003.
Srinivasan, Kannan, Vinod Vyasulu and S. Rajagopalan 1981. 'The Orissa Aluminium complex: points towards a debate,' *EPW* (5 Dec), pp. 2005–14.
Stern, Nicholas Oct 2006. *Review on the Economics of Climate Change*. London: HM Govt of UK.
Sterlite Industries (India) Ltd 2002. *Revised Executive Summary of Rapid EIA (Environmental Impact Assessment) for Lanjigarh Bauxite Mining Project, Kalahandi*. Mumbai: Tata AIG Risk Management Services.
Stiglitz, Joseph 2002. *Globalization and its Discontents*. London: Penguin.
Subramanian, S. and Sastry, D.H. eds. 2003. *INCAL 2003: Proceedings*, 23–25 April, in Delhi. Bangalore: Aluminium Association of India. (2 volumes)
Subrahmanyam, K.V. 1982. 'Orissa Aluminium Complex,' *EPW* 30 Jan.
Sundar, Nandini 2007. *Subalterns and Sovereigns: An Anthropological History of Bastar 1854–2006*. Delhi: OUP. (2nd edition)
Switkes, Glen August 2005. *Foiling the aluminium industry: a toolkit for*

communities, activists, consumers and workers. Berkeley: International Rivers Network.

Tamotia, S.K. 2001. 'Distinct cost advantage,' in *THE HINDU Survey of Indian Industry*, pp. 183–5.

―――― 2004. 'Role of Indian aluminium industry in the Fast growing Asian region,' paper at 2nd International Conference ALCASTEK, Mumbai, 20–23 January.

Tcha, M. and G.Takashina 2002. 'Is world Metal Consumption in Disarray,' in *Resources Policy* 28 pp. 61–74. Pergamum. (www.elsevier.com)

Tebtebba and Forest Peoples Programme 2003. *Extracting Promises: Indigenous Peoples, Extractive Industries and the World Bank.* Phillipines and UK.

Thakaran, Siby ed. 2002. *The Nowhere People: Responses to Internally Displaced Persons.* Bangalore: Books for Change.

Thapar, Romila 1961. *Asoka and the Decline of the Mauryas.* OUP.

Thukral, Enakshi Ganguly ed. 1992. *Big Dams, Displaced People: Rivers of sorrow, Rivers of Change.* Delhi: Sage.

Tompkins, Peter and Christopher Bird 1998. *Secrets Of the Soil: New Solutions for Restoring our Planet.* Alaska: Earthpulse Press. [Revised edition]

UAIL: *CSR: Corporate Social Responsibility.* [no publication place or date—a 14 page bulletin detailing 'R & R package', 'environmental package' etc, with colour photos on each page]

Uberoi, J.P.S. 1984. *The Other Mind of Europe: Goethe as a Scientist.* Delhi: OUP.

―――― 2002. *The European Modernity: Science, Truth and Method.* Delhi: OUP.

UNCTAD 8 Feb. 1995. *Environmental aspects of bauxite, alumina and aluminium production in Brazil.* (www.unctad.org/en/docs/pocomd49.en.pdf)

Ungpakorn, Ji Diles 2004. 'NGOs: Enemies or Allies,' in *International Socialism.* London.

US Geological Survey Jan.2006. *Mineral Commodity Summaries. (tin.er.usgs.gov/ metadata/mineplant.faq.html)*

UTKAL JYOTI: Utkal Alumina International Ltd. A DREAM PROJECT THAT GIVES MORE THAN IT TAKES, Jan–Mar 2001 quarterly news bulletin, vol.2 no.1.

UTKAL JYOTI, April–June 2001, vol.2 issue 2.

Vagholikar, Neeraj and K.A.Moghe with Ritwick Dutta 2003. *Undermining*

India: Impacts of mining on Ecologically Sensitive Areas. Delhi: Kalpavriksh.

VAL July 2006 and Jan. 2007. *Darpan: The Mirror of VAL, CSR Newsletter of Vedanta Alumina Ltd.* Bhubaneswar: VAL.

Vasudevan, N. 1999. *Collaborative Research Project: A resource-oriented overview of the material flow of metallic raw materials—Aluminium: Indian primary aluminium industry.* Forscungszentrum, Germany: Programmgruppe Systemforschung und Technologische Entwicklung.

Vedanta Resources plc: *AGM* brochure, London 29 July 2004. London: Vedanta.

_____ 2005. *Delivery and Growth: Annual Report 2005.*

_____ 2006. *Creating Value: Annual Report 2006.*

_____ 2007. *World Class Resources + Accelerating Growth = Delivering Value: Annual Report 2007.*

_____ 2008. *Enduring Value through Values: Annual Report 2008.*

_____ 2008. *Sustainable Development Report.*

Venkatesh, V. and P.K.Ramam eds. 1979. *Proceedings of the International Seminar on Lateritisation Processes, Trivandrum, India, 11–14 December 1979.* Delhi: India Book House Publishing Co. and Oxford.

Viegas, Philip 1992. 'The Hirakud Dam Oustees: Thirty Years After,' in Thukral 1992.

Waal, Alex de 1997. *Famine Crimes: Politics and the Disaster Relief Industry in Africa.* London: African Rights, Oxford: James Currey, and Indiana U.P.

Wagh, A. and P.Desai 1987. *Bauxite Tailings.* Kingston: Jamaican Bauxite Institute.

Walker, T.L. 1902. 'The Geology of Kalahandi State, Central Provinces,' *Memoirs of The Geological Survey of India*, vol.XXXIII part III pp. 1–22. Calcutta: GSI.

War On Want 2004. *Profiting from Poverty: Privatisation Consultants, DFID and Public Services.* London, www.waronwant.org/profiting

_____ Sept. 2006. *Globeleq: The Alternative Report.* London: WOW, by Joe Zacune.

_____ 2008. *Fanning the Flames: The role of British mining companies in conflict and the violations of human rights.* London, www.waronwant.org

Wasdell, David 2006–8. *Beyond the Tipping Point*, at www.meridian.org.uk

Wongar, B. 1980 [1978]. *The Track to Bralgu.* London: Pan.

Woodward, David 2001. *The Next Crisis? Direct and Equity Investment.* London: Zed.

World Bank 8 April 1994. *Resettlement and Development.* Washington: WB, Environment Dept.

_____ Development Policy Review 14 July 2003. *India – Sustaining reform, reducing poverty.* Washington, Report No. 25797-IN.

_____ May 2007. *India. Towards Mineral-Intensive Growth in Orissa: Managing Environmental and Social Impacts, Report no. 39878—IN.* Washington: WB.

Wysham, Daphne 2001. *Behind the shining: Aluminium's dark side.* Washington: IPS/SEEN/TNI. (on epgorissa website)

Publications in Odia and Hindi

Agarwal, Dwarkaprasad 2005. *Batabrukshya ke Chhayon mein* [in the shade of a banyan tree]. Mumbai: Sterlite Foundation. (in Hindi)

BJD [Biju Janata Dal Dec. 2004. *Swachha Sarkar Dakhya Sarkar.* Bhubaneswar: Biju Janata Dal.

Das, Bibekananda Jan.2001. *Kucheipadar ru Maikanch.* Bhubaneswar: CEDS communications, Jan.2001 N-1 A/32 IRC Village, Bhubaneswar 12.

Das, Samarendra 27 June 2000. '*Kondhomaloro Ribini mananko kahani*' [story of people like Ribini of Kandhamal'], in *Dainik Asha*, Berhampur.

_____ 28 Aug. 2000. '*Kondhomalo maanachitro jeonthi trutipurono sethi kagajoro bagho goroje*' [where the blureprint of K is a paper tiger roaring but full of loopholes], in *Dainik Asha.*

_____ 7 Nov. 2000. '*Dalalanko kobjare Kondhomaloro gramyoporibohono Byobostha*' [Into the clutches of the brokers: Kondhomal's village transport system], in *Dainik Asha.*

_____ 2001. *Salonki Salore.* [Salonki, St Lawrence (rivers)] Phulbani: Indumati.

_____ 1–15 Feb 2003. *Niyamgiri surakhya bahinoro ahban: Orissaku bauxite companyro lolupu drustiru bonchau* [Call of the troop for saving Niyamgiri: protect Odisha's Bauxite from the companies' greedy eyes]. Phulbani: *Tumo Amo Protikriya* p. 5.

_____ 1–15 May 2003. *Lanjigarhre Hinsa: Rashtra Adivasinku surakhya deunahi kahinki?* [Violence in Lanjigarh: Why hasn't the State protected Adivasis?] Phulbani: *Adarsh Orissa.*

Gandhamardan Surakhya Yuba Parishad October 1987. *Gandhamardanara Sandesh.* By Madan Mohan Sahu. Padampur: Misra Printing Press.

Gandhamardan Surakhya Yuba Parishad August 1992. *Gandhamardan*

Sandesh. Editorial Board: Pradeep Purohit, Jaisingh Nanda, Anup Kumar Sahu. Atabira village: Patra Printing Press.

Lingaraj 1995. '*Kashipur re Andolanara swaro: bikashara chaka na binasharo bulldozer?*' [The wheels of development or the destruction of the bulldozer?], in *Pragativadi,* Bhubaneswar:

────── 1997. '*Kashipur Ancholore Andolonoro sworo*' [The movement's voice in the Kashipur area], in *Odiya o Odisha Sameekshya* [Odia and Odisha Review] *96, Swashinottara Odishare Jono Andolon* [Post-independence people's movements in Orissa], eds. Prodyumno Bala, Birendra Nayak, Debi Prasad Dash, pp. 76–81. Bhubaneswar: Bikolpo Sandhani Manch.

Mahapatra, Ajit 2005. 'Review of Orissa's precious minerals,' in *Samaj* [Odia medium daily] 3 May.

Mahanti, Gopinath, 2000. *Sroto Swati.* Cuttack: Vidyapuri. [his autobiography in 3 parts]

Mohanty, Manoranjan and Bijay Kumar Bohidar 1993. *Odisha daridra kahinki?* [Why is Orissa Poor?] Cuttack: Orissa Bookstore.

──────, Bhupen Mohapatra and Nirakar Beura eds. 2004. *Khani, Jangal o Janata.* [Mines, Jungle and People] Bhubaneswar: Ghabesana Chakra.

Padel, Felix and Samarendra Das 2004. *Aluminium Shilporo Arthniti o Rajniti.*[The political economy of the aluminium industry] Borogorh: Bikolpo Prakashan.

Paschim Orissa Krishak Sangathan Samanbaya Samiti Feb. 2008. *Chashiro Rekha.* [*Farmers' Line*]. Sambalpur: POKSSS.

Patra, Gononath, Prafulla Samantara and Lingaraj 1998. *Kashipur re aluminium Prokolpo: Jana andolonoro padodhwoni: nibedono* [an appeal on behalf of the Kashipur movement], pamphlet.

Pattnaik, Shivaji n.d. [2003]. *Nalco Gharoikarana chakranta byartha kara.* ['Stall the conspiracy of privatizing Nalco'] Bhubaneswar: Pragati Prakashani.

Pattnayak, Kishen 2000. *Bikalpaheen nahi hai duniya* [There is no lack of alternatives]. Delhi: Rajkamal (in Hindi).

Saroj 1999. '*Kashipur bhitamati andolan: procholit bikash prokriyaku prashna*' [Kashipur's indigenous movement: questioning the ongoing process of development], in *Anwesha: Bikolpo udyamoro prerna* [Quest: inspiration for alternative initiatives] nos.3–4 pp. 87–112.

────── Dec. 2000. '*Kashipur bhitamati andolan....*' Part 2, *Anwesha,* year 3 nos.2–3 pp. 117–230

────── Jan. 2008. '*Kashipur hahakar o udasin sarkaro*' [Kashipur's desperation and apathy], in *Bikolpo Bichar*, July–Dec.2007 pp. 91–100. Boroghoro.

Sunil 2004. *Bideshi mudra ka phulta gubara: Asaliyat, khatre, ghotale.* [The foreign exchange bubble: Reality, dangers, scams]. Varanasi: SJP.

Supkar, Karunakar 2007. *Itihasoro Porihaso* [Ironies of History]. Sambalpur: Sukh-Dukh Publications.

Films

Das, Amarendra and Samarendra 2005. *Wira Pdika* or *Matiro Poko Company Loko* [Earth Worm, Company Man, in Kui/Odia with English subtitles], available from sdasorisa@hotmail.co.uk

―――― 2006. *Ladat Jaare* [The Struggle...], sdasorisa andrediffmail.com.

Dash, Surya Shankar 2008. *Niyamgiri, Mountain of Law* (in Odia with Engliash subtitles). Bhubaneswar: Samadrusti, available from dash.suryashankar@gmail.com.

―――― 2009. *The Real Face of Vedanta.* (in Odia with English subtitles). Bhubaneswar: Samadrusti.

―――― 2009. *Nolia Sahi*, a fishing village. Bhubaneswar: Samadrusti.

―――― 2009. A heinous assault. Bhubaneswar: Samadrusti.

―――― 2009. The human zoo. Bhubaneswar: Samadrusti. [All of these are available in *Madhyantara* video magazine, see youtube.com/samadrusti]

Sahu, Subrat 2009. *DAMaged!* [about the Upper Indravati reservoir], available from subrat69@gmail.com

Sarangi, Debaranjan 2010. *The Conflict—Whose Loss Whose Gain?* (in Odia with English subtitles.) Available from debasar11@yahoo.co.in

Websites

Action Aid – actionaid.org and actionaidindia.org

Centre for Science and Environment, Delhi—www.cseindia.org/misc/press-note.htm, www.cseindia.org/programme/nrml/Resources_october07.htm

Environment Protection Group Orissa—www.freewebs.com/epgorissa

Mines and Communities—minesandcommunities.org

Mines, Minerals and People—www.mmpindia.org

Saving Iceland—www.savingiceland.org

Survival International—*www.survival-international.org/*

Index

AAI & INCAL 214, 300, 320, 625, 667, 672
ABN Amro 223, 307, 320, 627
Aborigines 16, 30, 246–51
Abramovitch, Roman 290
Accountancy firms 172, 180, 210, 224–5, 295, 321, 389, 416, 444–6, 453, 475
Action Aid 99, 175, 444, 505, 522–4, 620, 693, 719
Adam Smith 398, 402, 435, 444–6, 494–5, 530–1, 554, 648
Adivasis xvii–xxvii, 1, 3, 7, 12, 18–19, 24, 29, 54–71, 72, 78, 92–9, 101 ff., 121, 143, 168, 172, 179, 181, 207–8, 218, 238, 287, 297, 325, 349–72, 406–12, 428–33, 468, 502, 506, 525, 528, 554, 555–66, 579, 583 ff., 590–600, 607, 616, 621–2, 667, 711
Aerial surveys 213
AES (US) 416, 443, 473, 667
Afghanistan 274, 278, 653
Africa xxv, 30, 33, 39, 46, 52, 233, 238 ff., 303, 347, 389, 402, 433–8, 465, 470, 481, 487, 504, 532, 552, 648, 655, 691
Agragamee 99, 105, 112, 118–19, 123, 355, 458, 498, 505, 515, 522, 608, 610, 645, 660, 667

Aid xiv, 59–60, 97, 419–20, 434, 436–8, 444–8, 451, 477, 490, 496 ff., 504, 515, 517, 653, 691, 701
Aircraft 38, 45–47, 52, 239–40, 270 ff. (esp. 274), 284, 313, 322–4, 376, 581, 593, 615, 631
Alcan 35, 46–51, 77–9, 88, 103, 115, 129–30, 177, 216–20, 230–53, 277–9, 285, 288, 299, 307, 312 ff., 321, 330, 510, 513, 537, 541, 603, 627, 630, 638, 642, 656, 660, 667, 683, 685, 693, 700
Alcoa 4, 16, 35–8, 45–51, 72, 133, 229–39, 243–6, 252, 256–63, 270 ff., 284, 288, 303, 310–21, 338, 342, 400, 486, 512–3, 535–8, 545, 575, 603, 611, 622, 634, 637–8, 642, 647, 660–1, 667, 683, 714
Alfed 216, 315, 320, 626, 638, 667
Alum 33, 34, 602
Alumina (Aluminium oxide) xiv, 3, 9, 21, 32–6, 41–44, 48, 51–2, 72, 82, 88, 101–3 ff., 156–67, 199, 221, 226 ff., 242–4, 260, 270, 288, 293 ff., 303–9, 342–3, 378–81, 457, 513–14, 542, 612, 628, 635, 637, 640, 645, 667, 683–4

Alusuisse 38, 50–1, 262, 311, 314, 389–90, 611, 646, 659, 667
Alzheimer's disease xxi, 325–8, 386, 513, 639, 661
Amazon rainforest 15, 30, 67, 251–5, 464–5
America, see US
American Indians, see Native Americans
Amnesty International 175, 478–9, 522, 618, 657
Anderson, Dewey xxi, 265, 274–8, 294, 298–9, 314, 320, 691
Andhra Pradesh xviii, 8, 9, 15, 59–62, 64, 81, 89, 116, 132, 134–7, 178, 187, 191–3, 212, 244, 262, 302, 338, 354, 378 ff., 411–14, 425, 439, 523, 538, 546, 597–9, 613, 615–16, 627, 648, 651, 653, 679–80
Anglesey smelter 40, 43, 86, 247, 300
Angul (Anugul) xxiv, 9, 56, 74, 85–8, 108, 134, 185–6, 210, 228, 304, 341–2, 354, 447, 637, 680
Anthropology xxii, 14, 17–24, 66–7, 108, 114, 116, 155, 177, 209, 297, 311, 325, 365–6, 433, 464, 484, 487, 513, 526, 612, 639, 645, 662
APMDC 134–7, 191–3, 668
Argentina 478, 480–1, 522, 657, 690
Armenia 52, 142, 147, 180, 222, 366, 617, 621
Arms industry xx–xxii, 6, 17, 19, 23, 24, 27, 36, 43, 45–48, 53, 79, 89, 210, 215–6, 239–40, 244, 265–94, 308–9, 313, 320–1, 329, 334, 386, 391–2, 453, 535, 581, 602, 633–4, 712
Arrests, see Jail
Arthashastra 65, 199–202, 668
Ashapura 64, 137, 188, 563–5, 577, 598
Ashponds/flyash 80, 85–6, 143, 169
Asia Development Bank 416
Auditing, see accountancy firms
Australia xiv, 4, 16, 31, 48–50, 59–60, 66, 142, 147, 152, 154, 166, 180, 213, 220–2, 226 ff., 234, 240–2, 246–51, 255, 303, 315–16, 338–40, 350, 366, 513, 523, 536, 617, 622, 627, 631, 642, 682–5, 689, 691
Austria 638, 641, 646, 688
Auto, see Cars
Azerbaijan 282, 682, 688

BAC 38–40, 46, 50, 217–9, 240, 244, 270, 288, 300, 311, 314, 350 603, 626–7, 630, 638, 668
Bahamas 147, 159, 221–3, 390, 453
Bahrain 223, 228–9, 305, 378, 684, 689, 691
Baiga tribe 145
Balco 87, 89–95, 110, 120, 133, 142–5, 156–7, 169–74, 181, 211, 215, 221–3, 245, 273, 284–5, 304, 319, 338–40, 381, 388, 411, 469, 538, 557, 601, 608, 616–17, 621, 634, 645–6, 655, 668, 679–81

Bangladesh 445, 463, 517–18
Banks xiv, xxiii, 11, 21, 111, 148, 153–4, 172–5, 189–90, 199, 213, 215–19, 222–3, 256–8, 262, 286, 288, 293 ff., 307, 347, 375–9, 391, 433, 462, 470, 484, 487, 501, 513, 517–18, 528–9, 533, 548, 598
Bansadhara river 9, 60–1, 64, 104, 160, 175, 180, 217, 334, 339–41, 374–5, 543, 599, 642
Bapla Mali 56, 60–63, 71, 103–138, 373, 612, 615, 679
Barclays Bank 152, 223, 307, 320, 663
Barney, Ian 106–7, 111, 124–5, 446, 610–14, 694
Basic Elements 290
Bastar 412, 650
Bauxite xiii, xviii, xxiii, 1, 4–7, 29, 31–5, 39–53, 57–64, 71, 72, 77, 79, 81–2, 86–95, 97, 101 ff. (esp. 116, 133–8), 143–5, 156–74 passim, 177–92 passim, 199, 211–19, 226 ff., esp. 235–6, 240, 244–55, 260, 262–3, 269–73, 284–6, 291, 293 ff., 301–21 passim, 330, 334, 338–9, 346–7, 373–92 passim, 403, 411, 425, 468–9, 486, 512–16, 536, 542, 563, 580, 597, 602, 604, 615, 616, 621–3, 625–6, 628–32, 635–8, 642, 645, 656, 659, 661, 679–82, 694, 700, 701
Bechtel 239, 256, 291, 581, 617
Bengal 529–32 (see also West Bengal)
Berezovsky, Boris 290–2
Bhagaban Majhi 8, 10, 109, 113–15, 121–5, 208, 559–60
BHP Billiton 8, 50–1, 64, 132–3, 136–7, 152, 156, 233–4, 250–56, 262–3, 305, 307, 321, 403–4, 513, 523, 615, 631, 668, 683, 685
Bhuiya tribe 408, 570
Bhushan 80, 137, 410, 447–50, 563–5, 654
BICP 214, 294, 382, 668
Bihar 145, 411, 531, 679
Billiton, see BHP Billiton
Biodiversity xxvi, 30, 92, 107, 135, 166, 171, 190, 194, 236, 338, 383, 456, 631
'Biofuels' 171, 335–6, 511, 594, 619
Birla 26–7, 48–9, 103, 116, 131, 136, 180, 218–9, 401, 537, 552, 563, 599, 601, 613, 668, 695, 704
Bissamcuttack 68, 104–5, 422–3
BJD party 10, 105, 121, 302, 414–15, 614, 619, 637, 668, 717
BJP party 87, 121, 145, 319, 570, 616, 668
Blair, Tony 201, 284, 452, 507, 516
Bodai Daldali, see Kawardha
Boeing 89, 240, 274, 282–5, 581, 608
Bolivia 134, 480, 483, 500, 612
Bombs 1, 23, 27, 31, 38, 45–7, 210, 231, 240, 270–3, 274, 278–81, 285–6, 581, 633–4
Borra caves 64, 116, 134, 192
BPD 115, 125, 446, 456–8, 466, 501, 515–20, 612, 614, 668
Brazil 18, 50, 52–3, 59, 73–4, 220, 226 ff., 251–5, 298–300,

305, 315–16, 329, 401, 415, 464–5, 471, 477–8, 536, 612, 627, 631, 637, 682–5, 690
Bribes, see Corruption
Britain (UK) xxv, 15, 17, 20, 26, 36, 38–40, 45–53, 79, 115, 134, 147, 153, 170, 175, 180, 198, 216, 221–4, 229 ff., 242, 257, 261, 268 ff., esp. 282, 288, 295, 303, 311, 349–51, 400, 418, 439–54, 480, 527–9, 544–5, 616, 620, 625–6, 628, 635, 639, 641, 653, 655, 683–5, 688, 697
British Aerospace (BAe) 284–5, 453, 633–4, 668
British Aluminium Corporation, see BAC
British colonialism xxiii–xxiv, 19, 47–8, 65–8, 78, 94, 225, 229–34, 240 ff., 273, 349–50, 355–6, 393, 417, 426–37, 526, 567–9, 591, 651
Brockovitch, Erin 250, 631
Brussels 216, 299, 539
Buddhism 6, 57, 582–4
Burkhamunda smelter, Jharsaguda 9, 157–8, 171, 176, 185, 297, 302, 373, 562, 599, 636, 680
Burma/Myanmar 221–2, 347
Bush, George W. 50–1, 318, 491

Cambodia 572, 632
Canada 36–7, 74, 147, 220–2, 229–38, 255–6, 271, 299, 312, 528, 627–8, 683, 685, 690, 691, 700
Capitalism xxvi, 14, 25, 263, 322–5, 393, 401, 476–9, 520–1, 530, 553, 587, 590, 600, 700
Carbon emissions xxi, 12, 41–44, 73, 252, 299, 329, 331, 334, 383–5, 641–2, 646
Carbon trading 335–6, 511, 541, 641
Carpet bombing, see 'daisycutter' bombs
Cars xx–xxi, 38, 45, 52, 202, 210–11, 214–5, 308–9, 320, 322–4, 330, 336–7, 376, 413, 509, 562, 641–2
Cartels xx–xxiii, 23, 44, 47, 50, 210, 230, 288, 292, 302, 310–21, 455–95 (esp. 486 ff.), 534–6, 538, 603, 605, 638
Cash compensation 84, 86, 98–9, 111, 120, 128, 139, 148–50, 153–4, 342, 356, 378, 407, 611–13
Caufield, Catherine 14, 19, 71, 459 ff., 491, 608, 611, 630, 644, 656–9, 695
Caustic soda 35, 41, 338–9, 342
Cazanove 222, 320
CBA (Cost Benefit Analysis) 75, 84, 197, 262, 332, 373–95, 645–7
CDM 335, 411, 641, 669
CEC 135, 159–66, 182–5, 390–1, 618, 622, 669, 695
Cement 33, 169, 215, 240, 361–2, 626
Chagos Islanders/Diego Garcia 451–3, 655
Chasi Mulia Adivasi Sangha (CMAS) 576–7, 599, 665, 669
Chhattisgarh 8, 9, 15, 24, 41, 89, 143–4, 156–8, 171, 181–2, 187–8, 195, 203, 211, 218,

302, 325, 335, 338–42, 347, 367, 403, 411–14, 449–53, 503, 597, 616, 621, 648, 650, 679–81
Chile 74, 234–5, 255, 463–4, 468, 476–81, 484, 500, 512, 538, 657, 690
China 39, 51, 54, 74, 133, 154–7, 175, 189, 198, 215, 221–3, 226–9 250, 261, 263, 298–9, 305–8, 344, 401, 481, 531, 573, 588, 632, 634, 638, 642, 648, 681–4, 689, 691
Cholera 103, 425, 570, 653
Chomsky, Noam 15, 27, 508–9, 527, 660
Christianity 14, 19, 23–4, 58, 249, 460, 494, 497, 502, 504, 520, 539, 552–3, 570, 573, 583, 586–9
Chromite/chrome xxviii, 54, 134, 159, 203, 403–5, 475, 648–9
CIA 53, 231, 234–5, 239–45, 318–19, 463, 477 ff., 630, 656, 695
Citigroup/–bank 222, 307, 309, 477, 518
'Clean Development Mechanism', see CDM
Climate change xix–xxii, 15, 95, 149, 216, 235, 259, 331–7, 383–5, 511, 546–9, 594, 598, 639, 641, 664, 699
CMAS, see Chasi Mulia Adivasi Sangha
CMPDI 165, 182, 512, 669, 694
Coal xviii, 15, 21, 22, 44, 52, 54, 73, 78–9, 85, 137, 143, 157–8, 161, 203, 211–3, 303, 333, 354, 369, 378–85, 401–4, 411, 465–6, 480, 512, 534, 538, 595, 615, 623, 637–8, 641, 648
Columbia 345, 460, 463, 579, 611, 689
Commodity analysts 293, 382, 402, 634–50
Conditionalities 23, 188, 469, 473–5
Congo 438, 470, 657
Congress party 91, 105, 121, 153, 175–6, 414, 423, 434, 450, 476, 505, 548, 616, 626
Consumption xix–xxi, 49, 205, 214–5, 228, 277, 279–80, 294, 320, 322–8, 331, 418, 503, 546, 639, 641
Continental Resources 93, 548
Contractors 209
Copper 145–6, 175, 221–3, 282, 308, 400, 477–8, 489, 534, 538, 552, 603, 620, 627, 640
'Corporate imperialism' 319–21, 443–54,
Corporations 13–17, 193–204, 209, 397–401, 417–18, 443–54, 461, 490, 494, 499, 501–3, 507–11, 517, 521–4, 525–54, 589, 594, 597–8, 611, 636
Corruption 5, 11, 12, 69, 82, 102, 105–7, 111, 118, 125, 159, 186–204 *passim* esp. 203–4, 209, 248, 258, 265, 269 ff., 282–4, 289–92, 318–19, 332, 344–6, 362, 374, 386–8, 405, 423–5, 427, 431–3, 437, 445–6, 454, 458 ff. (esp. 463, 491), 504, 525, 534, 545, 551, 571, 582, 599,

609–10, 622, 634, 654, 659, 663–4
Corus 285, 627,
Cost Benefit Analysis, see CBA
Cost of Production 378–87, 415
Courts 76, 82, 94, 116, 125–6, 133, 153, 159–67, 174, 181–206, 256 261, 306, 356, 423–5, 452, 525, 534, 560
CPI 410, 414, 570, 669
CPI–M 135, 379, 412–14, 441, 500, 570, 573, 650, 669
CPI–ML 194, 570, 624, 669
Credit rating agencies 214, 257, 295, 320, 548, 635, 670
CSR 21, 114, 168–70, 196, 216, 297, 346, 349, 357, 374 ff., 497, 507, 515–16, 524, 539–46, 612, 645, 663, 670
Cuba 571
Cultural genocide 76, 103, 248–50, 331, 348–72 (esp. 365–8), 448–54, 593, 645

'Daisycutter' bombs 278
Dalits xxii–xxiii, 55, 83, 90, 112, 119, 126, 208, 297, 349, 367, 413, 439–40, 525, 557–8, 565, 569, 599, 616, 651
Damanjodi xxiv, 41, 56, 60–1, 74, 82–5, 88, 108–111, 127, 193, 210, 285, 302, 340, 354–62, 378, 425, 622, 680
Dams xv, xix, 1, 6, 8–9, 17, 22, 23, 26, 36–40, 42, 44, 47, 53, 72–100, 210–11, 217–8, 232–3, 237, 238–43, 247, 252–60, 265, 269, 271, 277–8, 295, 298–300, 321, 331–3, 350–1, 364, 370, 383, 401, 411, 415, 455 ff. (esp. 466–7, 490), 507, 575, 605, 608, 630, 632, 641, 680–1, 700, 719
Dantewara 412, 503
Darwin, Charles 29, 66, 553, 697
Das, R.C. 113, 185–6, 294, 697
Davy, Humphrey 5, 34, 602
Debt xix, xxvi,10, 19, 171, 197, 216, 219, 262, 265, 273–4, 283–4, 289, 295, 300–1, 334, 379, 391, 398, 415, 421, 425–31, 438–40, 458–95 (esp. 461, 463, 469–74, 480, 484–6), 532, 548, 575, 594, 598, 625, 627, 651, 657
Denmark 35, 220, 259, 528, 639, 688
Deo Mali 60–64, 89, 137, 562–5, 577, 599, 615, 665
Deripaska, Oleg xxv, 216, 290, 295, 544, 552, 626, 635, 664
Derivatives/futures trading xxv, 295, 600, 635
Deutsche Bank 173, 189–90, 223, 307, 320, 513
'Development' xviii ff, xxvii, 8–14, 17–18, 25, 53, 59–60, 78, 101 ff., 134, 205, 215, 296, 348 ff., 363–4, 393–7, 425, 433, 493–4, 501, 520, 542–3, 549–54, 553, 556–8, 572, 575, 584, 592, 595, 597–600, 645, 656, 698
DFID 20, 23, 80, 87, 93, 106, 114–15, 125, 153, 158, 305, 320–1, 356, 398, 415–16, 419, 426, 439–54, 474, 491, 501, 504, 515, 522–3, 546, 611–12, 651, 653–4, 663, 670, 698, 716

Dharma 6, 55–8, 581–3, 593
Diamonds 198, 221, 238, 245, 346, 403, 630, 648
Diego Garcia, see Chagos Islanders
Displacement xiv–xv, xix, 1, 12–17, 21, 24, 70–100, 130–1, 138–40, 143, 148–55, 158, 182, 196, 204, 208, 218, 233, 237, 238, 241–3, 248–9, 252, 256, 278, 316, 332–5, 348–72, 386 ff., 397–9 ff., 406–17, 429, 442, 448–9, 458 ff., 493–6, 506, 518–21, 555–6, 562, 591, 593, 595, 599, 606, 611, 644–6
Doikhal 61, 104, 158, 166, 302
Dongria Konds xiii–xiv, xxvi, 64, 70, 140–76, 184, 187, 190, 193, 306, 363, 374, 452, 504, 518, 522, 554, 578–600 *passim*, 618, 702
Dongria triangle motif 141, 586
Dubai, Dubal 63, 132, 136, 221–3, 228, 307, 321, 373, 378, 627, 679–80, 689
Duralumin 1, 38, 46, 270

EAA 216, 299, 320, 322–4, 330, 337 ff., 503, 639–41
Earth/soil xvii–xxvii, 3–4, 18, 28–31, 34, 67–70, 83, 103, 114, 205, 235, 255, 269, 310, 326, 364–8, 371, 417–18, 493, 578–600 *passim* (esp.579, 585, 590–5), 602, 670
Earthworms xxiii, 3, 29–31, 109, 348
East India Company xix, xxv, 19–23, 65–8, 355, 397–8, 402, 418, 447–8, 451–4, 475, 526–32, 651, 712
'Eco–efficiency' 333–4, 341, 541
Ecological economics 297–8, 325, 332–4, 368, 641
Ecuador 15, 345,
Egypt 74, 241, 688
EIAs 75, 112, 129, 135, 140, 158, 162, 170, 187–9, 194–5, 214, 256, 333, 343–6, 355, 512, 614, 616, 617, 623, 636, 700
EIR 196, 316, 356, 448, 457, 670
EITI 201
Ekta Parishad 505–7, 523, 653
Electricity xix–xx, xxiii, 1, 6, 22, 30, 34, 39, 42–4, 47, 48–9, 64, 72–100 *passim* (esp.84, 99), 133, 143, 156–8, 177, 213–4, 218, 233, 238, 241–3, 247, 252–6, 265, 277, 282, 291, 298 ff., 310, 322–4, 331, 378 ff. esp 383, 391), 414–17, 439, 443–4, 605, 636–7, 641
Elephants 132, 140, 158, 160–66, 403, 428, 583, 615, 622
Employment, see jobs
'Enclave colonialism' 233, 236, 237–8, 242–4, 247, 266, 300, 344–7, 536
'Encroachers'/encroachment 89, 163, 356, 429, 519–20, 607
'Energy efficiency' 216
Enron 146, 180–1, 295, 417, 473, 545
Environmental Impact Assessments, see EIAs
Ernst & Young 180, 224, 444, 453

Essar steel 187, 412
Ethiopia 186, 432, 436–8, 464, 484, 572, 652, 656
Eucalyptus 81, 171, 217, 246, 336, 465, 610, 651
Exchange rates xx, 305, 309, 716
Exploitation xxvi, 5, 11, 16, 28, 116, 191, 205, 210, 219, 225, 231, 247, 294, 297, 302, 343–7, 366, 393, 419–39, 442, 485–6, 499, 526, 530, 536, 554–5, 567–9, 587, 597, 653
Externalities (externalised costs) 294 ff., 332–6, 379–87, 417, 456, 640, 642
Extractive Industries Review, see EIR

Falkland Islands 452, 480
Famine, see starvation
FDI 10–11, 301, 374–7, 391, 399–408, 491, 502, 515, 670
Fertilisers 30–31, 98, 107, 220, 243, 364, 415, 432, 460, 579–80, 591, 593–4, 602, 607, 627
Fifth Schedule of India's Constitution 111, 116–17, 131, 179–81, 191–7, 353–5, 554, 613, 621
Finland 503
First Dynasty Mines 147, 221–2
First World War 38, 45–7, 217, 229, 265–74 *passim,* 279, 312, 451, 633, 638
Floods 78, 85–6, 97, 158, 217, 383
'Flooding us out with money' 148, 168, 297, 367, 372, 374, 386

Fluoride, fluorine 12, 32, 35, 43, 79, 86–7, 158, 169, 176, 185–6, 341–2, 384, 599
Fluoridosis 43, 79, 86–7, 341
Fly–ash, see ashponds
Ford Foundation 477–9, 511–12, 524
Forest xvii, 31, 32, 41, 54–5, 64, 68–70, 78, 89–98, 101–8 *passim,* 121, 133–5, 140, 148, 158–67, 184–91, 194–7, 202, 205, 208, 235–6, 250–1, 261, 332 ff., 350–1, 364, 374 ff. esp. 383–6, 417, 420, 428–30, 440, 443, 465, 503, 513, 585, 596–7, 618, 622, 624, 645–6, 651
Fox, Cyril 8, 32, 33, 58, 74, 626, 699
France 34–6, 38, 46–7, 50, 88, 219–20, 223, 226, 245–6, 263, 270 ff., (esp. 282–3), 311 ff., 465, 528 ff., 681–3, 688
'Free Prior Informed Consent' (FPIC) 196, 355, 448–9, 671
Free trade 435, 486–95, 530
Friedland, Bob ('Toxic Bob') 147, 221, 289, 627
Friedman, Milton 476–83, 494, 545, 548, 641, 658
Friedman, Thomas 483, 493
Fugro 213

Galikonda 61–2, 64, 134, 137
Gallium 33, 42, 281, 285
GAMI 154, 156, 222, 671
Gandhamardan 56, 59–62, 77, 89–95, 128, 132–3, 143, 175, 233, 384, 403, 557–62, 569, 574, 608, 645–6, 694, 717

Gandhi, M.K./Gandhians xxv, 25–28, 69, 77, 90, 103, 142, 219, 324–5, 368, 393, 422, 500, 506, 555, 569, 575, 591–2, 600, 601, 613, 647
Gauros 63
Geological Survey of India (GSI) 32, 43, 59, 211, 403, 625, 671, 696
Genocide 5, 24, 55, 65–6, 252–5, 352, 366–72, 487, 534
Germany 35, 38, 45–7, 49, 51, 214, 220–3, 229, 269–73, 282, 311–13, 333, 366, 370, 465, 523, 547, 637–8, 683, 685, 688
Ghana 16, 46, 48–50, 73, 238–44, 247, 298–300, 315, 319, 458, 469, 536, 608, 630, 656, 682, 689
GHGs xix–xxii, 75, 216, 220, 297, 331, 334–42, 549, 598, 671, 694
Gilbertson, Brian 152, 155–6, 222, 255, 291, 305
Girvan, Norman 234–6, 316, 319, 629, 638, 700
Glencore 51, 222, 257, 289–91, 307, 682, 685
Gold 5, 34, 147, 180, 221–2, 352, 472, 586–7, 627–8
Gond tribes 145, 411–12, 503
Goondas 112, 115, 118, 125, 132, 151, 181, 204, 362, 375, 408–10, 418, 560–2, 599, 624, 671
Gopalpur 115, 404–5, 560–1, 574–5, 619
Graham, Ronald 6, 16–17, 23, 217, 275, 279, 628, 630, 633

Gram Vikas 64, 156, 523
Greece 41, 220, 227, 301, 603, 637, 642, 681–2, 688
'Greenfield' 51, 153, 182, 186, 199, 334, 336, 411, 512, 597, 635
Greenhouse Gas emissions, see GHGs
Greenland 32, 52, 228, 259–62, 632, 643, 688
Greenspan, Alan 274, 633, 635
'Greenwash' xx, 83, 169–71, 189–90, 259, 319, 323, 329–43, 486, 507, 524, 589, 642, 700
GRI 169, 196, 202, 224, 320, 337, 544, 671
Guatemala 490, 542
Guinea 16, 49, 59, 226–7, 234, 244–5, 315 ff., 465, 536, 552, 656, 664, 682–3, 688
Gujarat 146, 211, 217, 220, 303, 323, 364, 626–7, 679–81
Guyana 16, 31, 33, 46, 49, 227–34, 245, 254, 260, 302, 313 ff., 536, 627–8, 656, 682, 690, 697

Hafnium 285
Haiti 48–9, 66, 236, 629
HAL 88–9, 285, 362, 608, 671
Halco 244, 315, 671
Hayek, F. 476–70, 664
Health & Safety 144, 169–70, 182, 216, 335, 341, 360, 541–2, 619, 621
Hedging/hedge funds 307–9, 336, 391, 453
Himachal Pradesh 546–7, 663
Hindalco 26, 48–52, 64, 74, 80, 87, 103, 110, 115–16, 120, 129–31, 136, 142, 144–5,

211, 217–20, 228, 238–9, 243, 253, 298–305, 321, 332, 335, 338–9, 342, 381, 449–50, 465, 538, 562, 577, 613, 623, 625–7, 639, 642, 645, 671, 679
Hinduism, Hindus 6, 55–8, 65–8, 89–90, 95, 140–2, 174, 375, 426, 520, 551–2, 557–8, 568, 582 ff. (esp. 587–90), 596
Hirakud dam & smelter xxiv, 9, 26–7, 74, 77–80, 83, 97–8, 111, 131, 158, 185, 211, 333–5, 341–2, 352–3, 384, 404, 410, 449–51, 555, 606, 655, 680, 716
Ho, see Munda
Hoda Committee 193–5, 198, 320,
HSBC 175, 216, 223, 307, 320, 671
Hungary 46, 89, 143, 226, 288, 682–3, 688
Hydro, see Norsk Hydro
HZL 145

IAI 76, 216, 315, 320, 328–9, 337–41, 377, 453, 639, 641–3, 645, 671
IBA 53, 232–5, 310, 315–16, 672
IBM 211–3, 672
Iceland 39, 52, 72, 74, 178, 215, 228–9, 256–62, 295, 300, 389–90, 536, 545, 548, 575, 597, 629, 632, 646, 660–1, 665, 685, 688, 719
ICICI 175, 222, 522–4
ICMM & MMSD 69, 196–7, 200–202, 225, 320, 344, 453, 456, 512, 540, 597, 604, 631–2, 643, 645, 672, 673
IDCO, IDCOL 213, 405–6, 520, 625, 672
IFAD 105–8, 117, 321, 379, 423–5, 439, 458, 515, 570, 609–11, 672, 702
IMF 232, 245, 318–19, 443, 458, 461 ff., 479–94, 672
IMFA 88, 132, 136, 405, 552, 614, 672
INCAL, see AAI
Indal 77–9, 103 ff., 109, 115, 118, 120, 124, 126, 130, 145, 172, 211, 215, 217–20, 234, 294–6, 303, 321, 390, 538, 613, 623, 626, 639, 672
Indonesia 51–3, 74, 132, 152, 221, 227, 255, 282–3, 300, 347, 378, 529 412–13, 462–4, 478, 492, 500, 552, 597, 615, 631, 638, 682, 689, 691
Indravati 9, 39, 60–1, 71, 74, 95–100, 104, 108–111, 118, 138, 162, 214, 253, 323, 351–6, 379, 420, 455–8, 467, 505, 522, 583, 605, 608, 680, 719
Industrial disease 144, 251, 266, 342–3, 345, 350, 424, 542, 598, 643
Industrialisation xix ff., xxvii, 11, 17–18, 25–6, 76, 79, 95, 106–8, 112, 126, 132, 137, 171, 186, 219, 234, 243, 260, 267, 299, 335, 349–52, 357–60, 397–418 (esp. 413), 441, 460, 470–2 ff. Esp. 476, 502, 505, 532–7, 549–51,

553, 572, 576, 584, 590, 600, 624
Insider trading 146, 159, 390
Internal colonialism 49, 366, 417, 526 ff., 664
International Rivers Network 17, 73, 330–1
Investment 475 (see also FDI)
IPCC xix, 335, 511, 549, 641, 672
Iraq 269, 273–4, 278–9, 345, 483, 653
Iran xiii, 51, 132, 142, 226–7, 269, 282, 378, 453, 615, 681–2, 689, 691
Ireland 289, 370, 435, 530, 683, 688
Iron xviii, 33, 38, 39, 42, 44, 54, 107, 134, 137, 175, 188, 193, 197, 238, 286, 335, 403–12, 562, 603, 648, 654
Italy 46, 142, 223, 244, 283, 289, 312, 503, 528–9, 628, 638, 640, 683, 688
ISO awards 169, 175, 544, 672
Israel 283
Ivanhoe 222

Jail 96, 117–19, 129–30, 146, 176, 231, 291, 371, 410–11, 561, 613, 616
Jainism 6, 582
Jairam Ramesh 167, 176
Jamaica 47–9, 53, 60, 226–9, 234–6, 242, 260, 289, 306, 315–19, 339, 536, 597, 629, 634, 638, 642, 683, 690
Jambubati Bijira 90–1
Japan 27, 49, 53, 85, 97, 223, 252–5, 269, 272–3, 282, 307, 313–5, 329, 379, 392, 404, 411, 458, 465, 471, 656, 683, 689, 691
Jardine Fleming 143
Jatropha 169–71, 336, 619
Jerrela 61–2, 64, 135–7, 616
Jharkhand 8, 9, 15, 77, 187, 195, 211, 407, 411, 599, 623, 626–7, 648, 679–81
Jharsaguda smelter, see Burkhamunda
Jhoria tribe xxii, 103, 123–8
Jindal 64, 77, 134–7, 142, 159, 191–2, 302, 321, 335, 373, 405, 411–13, 447, 598–9, 613–16, 624, 649, 654–5, 679
JK/JKpur 104, 217, 444, 537, 610, 626, 653, 672
JNARDDC 213, 306, 625, 673
Jobs 10–11, 81–2, 88, 111, 154, 170–1, 277–8, 282–3, 294, 345, 348–51, 356–7, 360–1, 374–80, 388–9, 407–8, 468–9, 473
Journalists 19–20, 50, 123–9, 346, 418, 420–3, 433, 436, 548, 576, 614, 634, 652
J.P.Morgan 142–4, 151–2, 222, 307–10, 320, 400–1, 462, 487, 514, 533–7 616–17, 662
Judiciary 125–206 *passim*, 312–14, 421–3

Kaiser 48–51, 216–20, 234, 238–48, 272–7, 284, 288, 314–16, 401, 458, 537, 630, 634, 673, 683, 701
Kalahanadi 56–8, 61–2, 96, 98, 103–4, 132, 136, 139–76, 182–4, 190, 375, 420 ff., 523,

549–50, 554, 561, 568–9, 615, 616 ff., 632, 651, 716
Kalam, Abdul 53, 215, 284, 639, 703
Kalinga 54–5, 406, 571
Kalinganagar 12, 55–6, 134, 137, 204, 353, 367, 405–8, 414, 417–18, 447, 493, 503, 518–21, 552, 556, 562, 565, 575, 649–50, 655, 699
Kalyan Singpur 104, 221
Kandhamal 56, 59, 61–2, 133, 137, 408–9, 518, 611, 615, 717
Karlapat/Khandual Mali 7, 8, 9, 56, 58, 60–4, 104, 132, 136, 140, 156, 160, 513, 523, 615
Karnataka 195, 212, 217, 408, 425, 648, 679–81
Kashipur xviii–xxiv, 3, 9, 10, 12, 41, 60, 101–139, 186, 207–9, 216, 221, 268, 345, 350 ff., 420 ff., 435, 458, 493, 498, 515, 525, 556, 560–1, 566, 570–1, 574, 608–14, 660, 702, 717–18
Kawardha bauxite mines 9, 41, 144–5, 158, 166, 170, 182, 302, 468, 550, 621
Kazakhstan 221, 227, 288, 681–2, 689
KBK districts 59–60, 424–5, 432, 604, 673
Kennedy, President 241, 281
Kenya 451, 484
Kerala 76, 212, 217, 500, 679–81
Khandadhara 54, 203, 536, 562, 570
Khondalite xviii, 8, 33, 54, 57–9, 208, 356

Kishen Pattnayak 13, 28, 127, 155, 420–4, 499, 504, 511, 555, 569–70, 577, 600, 601, 608, 650, 665–6, 718
Kissinger 234, 478
Kodinga Mali 61–2, 64, 103–4, 110, 120, 136, 373, 577, 599, 613–15, 625
Kolab river & dam 60–1, 74, 83–4, 88, 96–7, 100, 353–4, 362–3, 458, 608, 680, 702
Konds xiii, xviii, xxii, xxvi, 4, 57–8, 64, 67–9, 81, 90, 113, 128, 148 ff., 153–4, 183–5, 325, 350–72, 418, 426–9, 495, 531, 562–9, 581–2, 590–1, 605, 651, 673
Korba xxiv, 8, 9, 41–3, 89–90, 93, 143, 152–8, 166, 169–71, 223–4, 228, 302, 336, 339–41, 342, 411, 608, 616, 642, 680
Korva tribe 143
Korean war 233, 240, 273–8
KPMG 172, 224, 416, 444, 453
Kuturu Mali 61–3, 104, 110, 112, 132, 136, 143–4, 625, 679

Land–fill 328–31, 547
Laos 279, 632, 689
Lanjigarh xviii, xxiv, xxvi, 5, 9, 10, 41, 56, 74, 100, 101, 104, 110, 129, 139–76, 185–90, 209–11, 221–4, 268, 302–3, 305–6, 334, 336–9, 345, 350 ff. (esp. 358–9, 365, 368), 373 ff., 447, 456, 469, 493, 511, 517–18, 525, 542–3, 548–54, 561–2, 598, 620, 654–5, 680, 717

Larsen & Toubro 63, 103, 110, 112, 120, 132, 136, 186, 220–1, 321, 373, 598, 611, 625, 627, 679–80
Lawyers 126, 161 ff., 179 ff., 296, 316, 336, 419–25, 430–3, 622
Laxman Nayak 117, 119, 664
League of Nations 271
Liechtenstein 315
Lingaraj 118, 296, 450, 569, 613, 655, 717–18
Lingaraj Azad 151, 569
Lithium 43, 285, 329
Loans 19, 96, 105–7, 177, 200, 218, 232, 241–3, 257, 295, 300, 309, 319, 379, 411, 415–16, 427, 437, 450, 456 ff. (esp. 459, 462–74, 483–4), 517–18, 598, 609–11, 637
Lobbying xix–xxiii, 76, 214, 216, 271, 276, 299, 311–21, 325, 330, 334– 43, 546–8
Lockheed(–Martin) 282–5, 581
Lohandiguda 412
Lohardaga bauxite mines 9, 77, 79, 626, 679
Lohia, Ram Manohar 74, 218, 555, 569
London 16, 20, 25, 35, 40, 50, 76, 142–56 *passim*, 175, 198, 201, 214, 222–5, 288–91, 305 ff. (esp. 314), 321, 328, 355, 375–6, 382, 390–1, 444–54, 481, 507, 514, 522, 528, 532, 539 ff., 598, 621, 657, 663
London Metal Exchange 52, 306–9, 316, 378, 453, 538, 598, 635–8, 647, 673

Macquarie bank 222
Madhya Pradesh (MP) 143–4, 217, 364, 439–51, 505, 621, 638, 653, 679
Mafia xxv, 64, 176, 288–92, 318–19, 362, 428–30, 454, 477–9, 482–3, 492, 521, 552, 599
Maharashtra 146, 188, 211–13, 417, 425, 626, 654, 679
Maikanch xxii, xxvi,12, 28, 61, 85, 104–5, 121–30, 137, 340, 367, 456–8, 498, 503, 552, 560, 717
Mainpat bauxite mines 9, 93, 143, 158, 170–1, 181–2, 302, 338, 621, 679
Malaya, Malaysia 231, 256, 632, 682, 689
Malco 74, 142–7, 169–70, 174, 211, 218, 221, 244, 285, 616, 619, 638, 673, 679–81
Mali Parbat 61–4, 131–2, 136, 188, 373, 575–7, 598, 614–15, 623
Manganese xviii, 54, 108, 132, 403–5, 620, 648
Mangta Majhi 119, 121
Manley, Michael 232–6, 315
Maoists/Naxalites xiv, xxv–xxvi, 24, 153, 175, 401, 407, 412–14, 421, 503, 556, 570–6, 592, 599, 635, 674
Marc Rich ('Aluminium Finger') 51, 288–9, 319, 634, 697
Market(s) 68, 199, 258, 310 ff., 320, 322–5, 335, 474–5, 481–95, 501, 517–18, 521, 578 ff. (esp. 589)
Maroons 233, 236
Marwaris 217–9
Marx, Karl/Marxism 16, 66, 393,

441, 500, 553, 555, 570–3, 588–90
Material flow analysis 297, 640–1
Mauritius 147, 159, 221, 390, 452–3
Maytas 223–5
McKinsey 624
McNamara 281, 283, 458–62, 470
MECL 64, 213, 673
Media, see Journalists, TV
Mehta, Harshad 146
Mellon, Andrew 35, 45, 47, 216, 237, 242, 271, 312–14, 318–20, 400, 535–7, 551, 572, 587, 603, 638, 695
Metal(s) xix–xxii,18, 30, 33–5, 42–4, 146, 332, 579 ff., 601
Metals trading 22, 49, 51, 210, 306–9, 347, 377, 391, 453, 711
Mexico 470–1, 657, 690
Military–industrial complex 274–6, 283, 287
Mills bombs (hand grenades) 270, 286–7
Mitsubishi 97, 253–6
Mittal 15, 52, 159, 188, 285, 410, 562, 634
MMSD, see ICMM
Mobiles 286
MoEF 92, 112, 133–7, 160–67, 174, 183–8, 193–4, 512, 516, 558, 615, 621–4, 635, 673
Mohanty, Gopinath 22, 57, 429–33, 499
Mongolia 221
Moody, Roger 14, 544, 620, 624, 627, 631, 645–7, 655–6, 664
Morgan Stanley 153, 307, 309

MoUs 134–7, 187, 192, 263, 402–14, 522–4, 619, 673
Movements xviii, xxii, xxv–xxvii, 25–28, 89–95, 96, 101, 108, 115 ff., 137, 399–414, 434, 497 ff., 505, 514, 524, 555–577, 592, 649
Mozambique 228, 255–6, 632, 681, 688
Munda and Ho tribes 407, 427
Muri refinery 9, 77, 79, 211, 217, 339, 643

Nagavali river 9, 60–1, 64, 104, 132, 162–5, 221
Nalco xxvi, 23, 41, 42, 51, 59–60, 64, 74, 81–9, 93, 107–8, 127, 132–7, 145, 172, 186, 210–11, 219–20, 245, 285, 294 ff., 301–5, 321, 334, 340–2, 345, 354–62, 377–81, 415–16, 425, 447, 564, 599, 601, 607, 615, 620, 622, 625, 635, 637–8, 642, 645, 654, 674, 679–81, 684, 718
Nandigram 137, 300, 412–14, 575, 624, 653
Napalm 272–3, 287
Narayanan, K.R. 28, 124
National Environment Appellate Authority 158, 188, 674
Native Americans 15, 22, 24, 66–7, 232, 237–8, 251–5, 342, 352, 366–9, 400–1, 464, 534, 572–3, 579, 583, 586–7, 590, 593–4, 644, 665–6
Naveen Patnaik 12, 80, 87–88, 121, 152, 157, 170, 174, 296, 305, 379, 405, 414, 418, 450, 454, 502, 518, 561, 596,

606–7, 615, 635, 649–50, 666, 709
Naxalites, see Maoists
Nayak, Birendra 508, 510
Nehru, Jawaharlal 25–6, 74, 77, 219, 465, 569
Neoliberalism 23, 258, 296, 335, 397–402, 413–18, 439–95, 500–1, 507, 512, 521, 545, 578 ff. (esp. 588–9)
Nepal 283, 570–1
'Net Present Value' of forests, see NPV
Netherlands 147, 152, 213, 233, 249, 282, 462, 528, 631, 688
Newspapers, see Journalists
New Economic Policy 1991 189, 200, 439, 472, 523
New National Mineral Policy, see NMP
New Guinea 14, 347, 552
New Zealand 74, 228, 247–50, 631, 689
NGOs xiv, 19, 64, 99–100, 106, 113–4, 119–20, 124, 153, 156, 175, 196–7, 201, 257, 261, 282, 284, 330, 355, 387, 398, 420, 444, 448, 451, 458, 465, 496–524, 540, 560–1, 566–70, 576, 608, 613, 615, 624, 632, 659–62, 699
NGO funding 64, 499–500, 503–9, 510–15, 522–4, 612
Nigeria 14–15, 255, 291, 343–6, 451, 544, 552, 631, 643–4, 689
Niyamgiri/Niyam Dongar xxiv, xxvi, 7, 9, 56, 60–2, 64, 68, 70, 104, 110, 132, 136, 139–76, 182–7, 190, 203, 206, 211, 214, 223, 296–7, 305–6, 338, 373 ff., 382–4, 452, 476, 503, 512, 514, 517–18, 522–4, 536, 556, 575, 599, 615, 622, 624, 635, 679, 713, 717
Niyam Raja xiii, 64, 68, 140, 179, 206, 578, 593, 620, 663
Nkrumah 240 ff., 458, 630, 656
NMP 1993 189, 200, 472, 674
NMP 2008 180, 186, 190–200, 238, 320, 399, 443, 506–7, 624, 635, 674
Nobel, Alfred 36, 269, 478, 518
Norad 87, 612
Norsk Hydro 47, 51, 103 ff., 109, 114, 118–19, 124, 130, 220, 250, 260, 307, 312, 330, 498, 512, 612–13, 627, 661, 671, 684
North–East India 412
Northrop(–Grumann) 216, 283–5
Norway 47, 87, 109, 119, 124, 167, 185, 220, 229, 245, 260, 299, 312, 341, 498, 523, 607, 612, 616, 620, 636, 638, 685, 688, 691
Novelis 220, 238, 252–3, 332, 627
NPV 189–90, 338, 382–4, 513, 661, 671, 674
Nuclear industry & missiles 23, 47, 215, 263, 276–81, 284–5, 299–300, 318, 333, 581, 633–4

Odisha xi, xvi, xxii–xxviii, 5–15, 19, 23–8, 32, 39–42, 51–224, 294–306, 325, 332–47, 350 ff., 369–72 ff., 397 ff.,

736 | Index

403–11, 414–35, 438–531,
533–600, 664–5, 679–81,
697, 719
OECD 175, 257, 544, 620,
650–6, 674
Oil industry xix, 6, 14–15, 33,
44, 45, 52, 211, 258, 260,
285–6, 289–91, 300, 310,
313–15, 334–7, 345–6, 398–
400, 437, 451, 483, 533–5,
552, 595, 634, 639–40,
643–4, 709
OMC 59, 126, 136, 159–67,
185, 191, 199, 354, 414, 635,
674
O'Neill, Paul 50–51, 317–18,
486
Orissa, see Odisha
Orissa Assembly xxviii, 12, 27,
78, 117, 153, 619
Orissa Mining Corporation, see
OMC
OSPCB 113, 131, 151, 167, 175,
185–7, 294, 339–43, 543,
618, 620, 642–3, 674
Oxfam 513, 522–3

Packaging xx–xxi, 48–9, 202,
210–11, 309, 320, 322–6,
329, 376, 392, 580–1, 639,
647
Pakistan 218, 268, 469
Panchpat Mali xxiv, xxvi, 56,
58–62, 81–3, 89, 134–6, 168,
210, 219, 294, 302–5, 564,
618, 637, 642
Paradip 54, 56, 408, 652
Paraja tribe 22, 429, 431
Pechiney 34, 38, 47, 50–1, 88,

172, 177, 219–20, 238, 244,
247, 305, 307, 311–5, 602,
607, 627, 631, 638, 674,
684–5
Pengo tribe 63, 103, 420
Pentagon 281–2, 634
Perfect Relations 214, 547–8
Peru 345, 400, 470, 552, 570–2,
657, 664, 690
PESA 116–17, 135, 432, 674
Phillipines 500
Pinochet, General 234, 477–8,
481, 500, 658
Planning Commission 191–4,
198, 219, 296, 320, 510, 549
Poland 481, 688, 691
Police xiv, 8, 78, 80, 82, 91, 94,
96, 112 ff., 117, 129 ff., 135,
140, 144 ff., 151–6, 181, 197,
257–8, 346, 371, 397–400,
405–10, 417–18, 427, 432,
449–50, 509, 525, 561–2,
575–7, 594, 613, 628, 665
Police firings xxii, 12, 28, 85,
122–8, 367, 397, 400, 404,
406–8, 413, 434, 466, 555,
568, 576, 644, 664
Political parties 10, 19, 121–8,
134, 209, 295–6, 300,
420–23, 499, 539, 560, 566,
570–1
'Polluter pays' 189–91
Ports 8, 21, 44, 173, 197, 233,
244, 256, 301, 333, 408, 523,
538, 561, 619, 665
Posco 54, 137, 204, 214, 353,
404, 407–10, 502, 524, 548,
556, 560–2, 565–7, 576, 619,
624, 632, 649, 664, 675

Index | 737

Poverty xx, 8, 10–11, 18, 21, 60, 83–4, 103, 105, 174, 190, 240, 266, 345, 349, 366, 386 ff., 422 ff., 439–52, 458 ff. (esp. 467–9, 475, 482–4), 496, 503, 505, 588, 622, 643, 646, 651–3, 657, 698

Power xxii, xxvii, 19, 21–3, 49–52, 444–96, 501–2, 520–4, 561, 590–1, 666

PR 76, 168, 214, 249, 253, 295–7, 322–25, 336, 343–6, 525–54 (esp. 539–40, 542, 544), 580, 619, 639, 644, 663–4, 675

PriceWaterhouseCoopers 170, 416, 444, 453, 542, 612, 657

Pricing 16, 22, 36, 44, 50, 53, 81, 96, 143, 223, 230, 235, 255, 258, 277–8, 294, 301–321, 332, 347, 381–2, 392, 416, 432, 438–9, 491, 602, 634–8, 646–8, 652, 686–7

'Primitive' 17, 65–70, 140, 350–2

Privatisation 23, 87–88, 100, 143–5, 202, 215, 221, 232, 245, 289–90, 304–5, 319, 379, 382, 415–17, 443–54, 473–6, 481–3, 504, 510, 539, 601, 616, 620, 653, 716, 718

Prostitution 345, 611

PSSP 110 ff., 611, 675

Public Hearings 75, 131, 135, 151, 157, 167, 187–90, 193, 197, 345, 355, 410–11, 449, 562, 618, 623, 663–4

PUCL 151, 613, 617

Puri 56–7, 173–4, 296, 593

Quebec xxv, 220, 230, 237–8, 299

Queensland xxv, 147, 246–50, 675, 683

R&R, see Resettlement

Radioactivity 171, 339–41

Railways 8–9, 44, 79, 85, 93, 104, 107–110, 166, 197, 203, 233, 244, 265, 300–2, 322–3, 333, 352, 379, 411, 458, 463, 532–3, 538, 611

Rajasthan 145, 170, 212, 217, 224, 616, 627, 648, 660

Rajat Bhatia 147, 180

Rajiv Gandhi 105, 283, 422–3, 608

RAK 64, 135–7, 321, 411, 675

Ratnagiri bauxite mines 188

Rayadhar Lohar 91, 557, 574

Recycling xx, 210, 308, 328–331, 336–7, 376, 639–42

Red mud xv, 5, 36, 41–2, 79, 82, 118, 143, 149, 156, 160, 169–71, 175, 185, 235, 245, 334, 338–41, 384, 625, 642, 675

'Rehabilitation' of bauxite mines 337–8

Rengali dam 9, 74, 84–5, 354

Renukoot, see Rihand

Resettlement 84–5, 100, 111, 129, 160, 196, 348–72, 407–8, 436–7, 441, 465 ff., 495, 497, 516, 524, 560, 611

Resource curse xxv, 343–7, 388, 419, 426, 643, 691, 712

Resource wars 402

'Revolving doors' xxiii, 209–10, 214, 461–2, 487–93, 516

Reynolds 47–51, 231–6, 240, 275–7, 288, 300, 314, 342,

629
Rihand dam xxiv, 9, 49, 74, 218, 239, 243, 339, 458, 465, 626–7, 680
Rio Tinto/RTZ 50–1, 130, 133, 198–9, 201, 246–50, 256, 300, 305, 307, 320, 403, 516, 527, 539, 552, 615, 624, 630, 675, 684
Rio Tinto Alcan 236–8, 250, 253
Road accidents/deaths 154–6, 302, 374, 463, 542, 551
Road building 105–8, 112, 117, 155, 176, 197, 211, 244, 301, 333, 375–9, 428, 463–5, 538, 542–3, 599, 609–10, 618, 635
Robber barons 15, 159–60, 203–4, 300, 310, 352, 398, 527, 532–5, 539, 552, 587
Rocket fuel 52
Romania 464, 572, 682, 688
Royal Bank of Scotland 288
Royalty 87, 126, 161, 197, 231, 247, 296, 301–4, 377–80, 403, 629, 635–7
Rumsfeld, Donald 285
Rusal 50–1, 143, 216, 220, 236, 245, 263, 290–1, 544, 552, 626, 634, 683–4
Russell Means 22, 67, 369, 572–3, 590, 593–4
Russia xxv, 33, 45, 50–1, 89, 226–9, 244, 256, 263, 269, 280, 288–95, 298, 305, 313–19, 329, 465, 482–3, 528, 539, 544, 552, 572, 625, 634, 639, 647, 682–5, 688

S. Kota 61, 134–5, 193, 616

Sachs, Jeffrey 258, 344, 388, 480–3, 517
Sacrifice 11–12, 84, 98, 155, 199, 359–60, 427, 452, 560, 579–82, 587, 595, 597
Salu Majhi 103, 370–2
Salwa Judum 367, 412, 556, 573–4, 675
Samajvadi Jan Parishad 151, 614, 638
Samantara, Prafulla 117–18, 160, 563–4, 577, 613, 616, 617, 665, 712
Samatha (& Judgement) 116–17, 131, 134–5, 145, 181, 190–97, 354, 411, 613, 621, 624, 635, 675
Santal tribe 413
Sasu–Bohu Mali 60–63, 104, 110, 120, 132–3, 136, 604, 615
Saudi Arabia 52, 107, 172, 282–4, 300, 379, 458, 689
Scotland 38–40, 50, 52, 72, 216, 238–42, 270, 300, 303, 349–52, 369–70, 429–31, 603, 620, 630, 636, 710
SEBI 146, 180, 621, 646, 675, 713
Second World War 31, 39, 46–9, 79, 217–9, 228 ff., 265 ff., 313–4, 434
'Security of tenure' 198–200, 305
Sesa Goa 175, 189, 224
SEZs 157, 180, 189, 197, 300, 399, 413, 417, 439, 481, 536, 573, 623, 650, 675
Sheel, Alok 215
Shell 255, 343–6, 451, 516, 539, 544, 644

SHGs 170–1, 501–2, 517–18, 520, 571, 575, 661, 675
Siberia 188, 291, 299, 603
Sierra Leone 221, 245–6, 316, 389, 536, 659, 689
Siji Mali 61–3, 103, 110, 112, 132, 136, 144
Silica 42, 44, 52, 303, 604
Singapore 143, 307, 691
Singur 137, 323, 337, 413, 575, 624, 639, 650, 653
Smith, Adam, see Adam Smith
Social evolutionism 65–6
Somalia 437
South Africa 51, 132, 152, 228–9, 237, 255, 285, 350, 378, 483, 508, 516, 522, 615, 620, 629–30, 654, 685, 689, 691
South Korea 54, 403, 459, 548, 562, 689, 691
Soviet Union 45, 50, 74, 143, 226–9, 241–3, 276, 283, 288 ff., 401, 435–7, 481–3, 513, 603, 682, 691
Spain 312, 552, 638, 688
Spent pot lining (SPL) 43, 87, 157–8, 262, 334, 341, 384
Sri Lanka 469
SRK Consulting 222
Stalin 45, 243, 401, 435, 535, 571, 652
Starvation 82, 96, 98, 103–5, 182, 243, 375, 401, 419–39, 455, 494, 530, 647, 650–1, 698
Steel 15, 21, 25, 36, 38, 45, 52, 54–5, 73, 115, 134, 137, 156, 193 197, 202, 204, 240, 285–6, 308, 310, 321, 332, 337, 398–414, 447, 457–8, 475, 526, 533, 555, 560–2, 636, 640, 654
Sterlite, see Vedanta
Stiglitz, Josef xxiii, 14, 50, 310, 317–20, 459, 484–6, 492, 638, 658–9
Stockpiling 274, 277–9, 308
'Structural Adjustment' 245, 443, 460, 470–4, 479–84, 500, 516
Sual 50, 256, 291, 634
Sub-contracting 171, 224, 345, 542
Subsidies xxiii, 17, 73, 133, 157, 197, 214, 218, 238, 241–3, 247, 253, 265, 268–9, 277, 294, 298–301, 320, 333, 450–1, 473–5, 547
Sudan 366, 437, 533
Suicides 425, 432, 452, 463, 594
Sukru Majhi 155
Suk(h)inda 56, 403–7, 427, 493, 649, 651
Suktel river, dam 9, 60–1, 77, 93–4, 133, 354
Sumitomo 250
Surinam(e) 31, 46–9, 74, 233–4, 239, 254, 260, 313, 316, 319, 629, 681–3, 690, 697, 700
Survival International 175, 507, 522, 618–20, 631, 719
'Sustainable' xxxi, 1, 6, 16, 68–9, 167–70, 174, 186, 191, 196, 201, 224, 297, 337, 349, 363–4, 376, 456, 540, 646, 660
Sweden 174, 269, 283, 289, 329,

503, 513, 688
Switzerland 38, 46, 50–1, 245, 262, 282–4, 289, 311–13, 389, 476, 513, 634, 688, 691

Tadjikistan 228, 688
Tamil Nadu xxiv, 74, 142–6, 174, 181, 212, 439, 451, 616, 653, 679–81
Tamotia, S.K. 172, 176, 215, 296, 378, 620, 625, 636, 715
Tata 15, 26, 52, 103, 109, 114–15, 130, 142, 187–8, 204, 217, 219, 285, 323, 337, 368, 403–13, 447, 458, 511, 518–20, 523, 537, 560–3, 612–13, 623–4, 627, 634, 639, 649–50, 654, 667, 676
Tata AIG 214, 512, 667
Tax havens 147, 159, 221–3, 309, 390
TetraPak xx, 52, 202, 214, 323–6, 329, 513, 547, 639
Thailand 459, 500, 541–2, 689
Thatcher, Margaret 15, 53, 398, 402, 445, 476, 480, 507, 535, 538
Tigers 428, 503, 583, 646, 709
Titanium 33, 42, 246, 285
Transfer pricing 262, 307–9, 389–90, 630
Tribal societies xvii, xx–xxvii, 5, 17–19, 28, 49, 55, 65–70, 106–8, 128, 191–2, 196, 205, 251–2, 297, 348–60, 367, 411, 455–7, 507–8, 554, 572, 591–600, 645
Trinidad 52, 228, 260–2, 597, 632, 704
Tung, Mao Tse 401, 436

Turkey 33, 76, 366, 470, 473, 657, 683, 689, 691
Tuticorin 146, 166, 181, 224, 627
TV 24, 86, 132, 287, 408, 412, 482, 561–3, 581, 639
Twinstar 147, 221, 390, 646

UAE 64, 135–7, 221, 228–9, 305, 616, 676, 684, 689
Ukraine 288, 435, 652, 682, 688
UNDP 59, 213, 356, 410, 439, 449, 518, 649, 676
UP, see Uttar Pradesh
Uranium 42, 318, 333, 369, 411, 587, 594–595, 623
URDS 114–15, 118
Uruguay 478, 658
US xiv, xxv, xxvii, 15, 17, 22, 23, 24, 27, 35–9, 44, 45–53, 65, 74, 88, 133, 158, 172, 175, 203–4, 216–20, 226 ff., 239 ff., 263, 268 ff., 288–92, 295, 298–300, 307–21, 328–32, 350–3, 368–9, 391–2, 400, 436–7, 455–95 (esp. 461–2, 483, 487–91), 500, 524, 529–30, 532–6, 544–5, 652, 572, 587, 612, 614, 627–8, 640–1, 645, 652–3, 655–9, 662, 683, 685, 690–2
USSR, see Soviet Union
Utkal project xxvi, 8, 9, 26, 41, 51, 63, 102–139 (esp. 109, 129–30), 186, 207–8, 216, 220, 238, 294, 363, 370, 373 ff., 433, 446, 456–8, 466, 476, 498, 515–16, 560, 570, 611–14, 645, 676, 679
Uttar Pradesh 74, 211–12, 217–8,

Index | 741

243, 339, 626–7, 679–80
Valco 242–4, 247, 298, 469, 676
Vedanta xiii, 141–2, 174, 455, 514, 583–4, 596, 616, 666, 676, 707
Vedanta/Sterlite xiii–xiv, xxvi, 5, 41, 51–2, 63–4, 74, 80, 93, 110, 129, 133, 136, 139–76, 179–93, 196, 207–11, 214–5, 221–5, 228, 250, 255, 284–5, 291, 294 ff., 300–310, 319, 321, 338–41, 346, 368, 373 ff., 401, 414, 418–19, 425, 446–53, 473, 504, 511, 513, 517–18, 522–4, 527, 539, 541–54, 560–1, 570, 585, 615, 616–23, 625, 627–8, 635, 642, 646, 654–5, 661, 663–4, 676, 716
'Vedanta University' 173–4, 589, 599, 619
Venezuela 53, 74, 226–7, 255–6, 681–3, 690
Vietnam xiv, 23, 221, 227, 231, 240, 247, 262–3, 273, 278, 597, 628, 632, 681, 689
Vishakhapatnam (Vizag) port & district xxiv, 8–9, 61–2, 77, 85, 107, 134–7, 145, 193, 411, 627
Volcan Investments 147, 221–3, 390, 647

Wales 15, 40, 43, 86, 125, 247, 400, 538, 552, 647, 664
Walker, T.L. 58
'War on Terror' 24, 53, 286–7, 402, 412
Washington DC 454–95 (esp. 461, 472, 478, 480, 483, 487–8), 611, 614, 655–9
Water xv, xvii, xxiii, 1, 4, 12, 23, 26–7, 29–30, 31, 32, 38, 41–2, 53, 54–5, 58–60, 68, 72–100 *passim,* 118, 135, 138), 143, 148, 161–7, 175–7, 180–2, 185, 190, 205, 208, 237, 243, 252, 286, 297, 299–300, 325–8, 332–9, 350–1, 361, 372, 374 ff., 383–5, 403, 417, 443–51, 504, 516, 555, 593, 595–6, 599, 605–6, 610, 636, 640, 650, 655, 695
West Bengal 9, 15, 137, 143, 175, 217, 300, 323, 412–14, 434–5, 441, 466, 562, 573, 612, 619, 624, 626
West Midnapore 413–14
West Papua 489
Wildlife Institute of India 164–6, 182, 512
Women 90–1, 94, 96, 109, 112, 122–9, 132, 170–1, 365–6, 404–13, 418, 455, 517–18, 562–5, 574–5, 650
Woods, George 218, 241–2, 458, 469
Work accidents/deaths 83, 97–8, 107, 171, 256, 374, 388, 400, 410, 542, 649, 655, 663
World Bank xxiii, 14, 19, 20, 21, 23, 49, 53, 70–1, 74, 76, 88, 95–100, 115, 125, 188, 191, 196, 200, 218, 232 ff., 239–46, 256, 289–91, 301–2, 315, 318–21, 352–6, 379, 397–401, 411, 415, 436–97, 500–2, 505, 510–11, 514–18, 520, 571–2, 583, 585, 608,

611–14, 630, 636, 641, 644, 654, 656–9, 716–7
Worley MMC 154, 222, 617
WTO 191–3, 473, 575, 641, 646, 677
Wuppertal Institute 73, 297, 333–4, 640–1
WWF 282, 512, 677

Xtrata 51, 291
Yeltsin 289–90
Yugoslavia 46, 226, 288, 312, 316, 681–2, 688
Zaire, see Congo
Zambia 142, 147, 180, 222, 617, 620620, 627–8
Zinc 145, 170, 221, 308–9, 648